THE **INSECT ARTIST**

Published in 2024 by Timber Press, Inc., a subsidiary of Workman
Publishing Co., Inc., a subsidiary of Hachette Book Group, Inc.
1290 Avenue of the Americas
New York, New York 10104
timberpress.com

Printed in China on responsibly sourced paper

Text and cover design by Vincent James

The publisher is not responsible for websites (or their content)
that are not owned by the publisher.

The Hachette Speakers Bureau provides a wide range of
authors for speaking events. To find out more, go to hachette-
speakersbureau.com or email HachetteSpeakers@hbgusa.com.

ISBN 978-1-60469-796-4

Catalog records for this book are available from the Library of
Congress and the British Library.

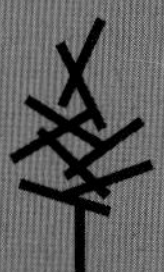

THE INSECT ARTIST

How to Observe, Draw, and Paint Butterflies, Bees, and More

ZEBITH S. THALDEN

Timber Press
Portland, Oregon

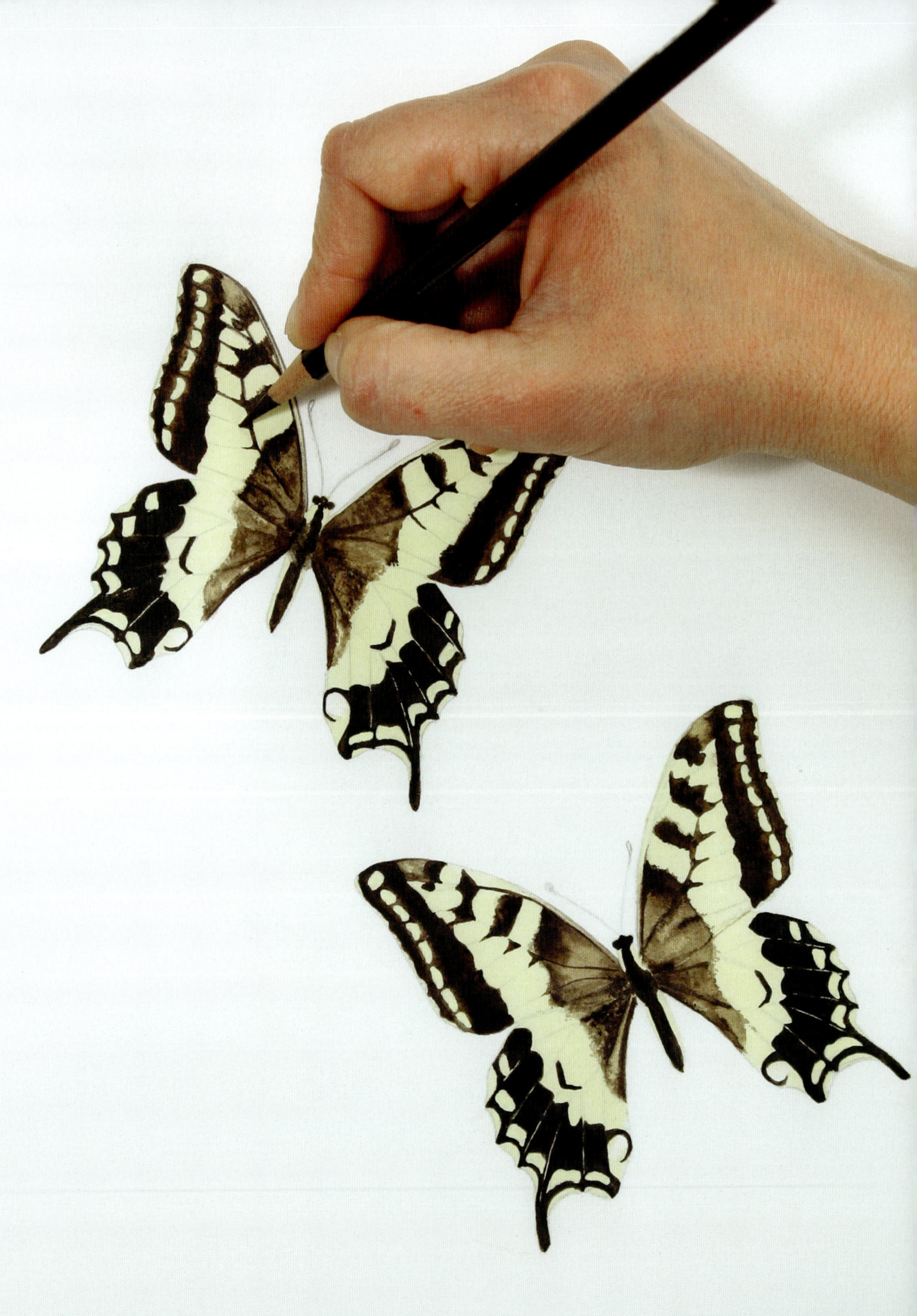

CONTENTS

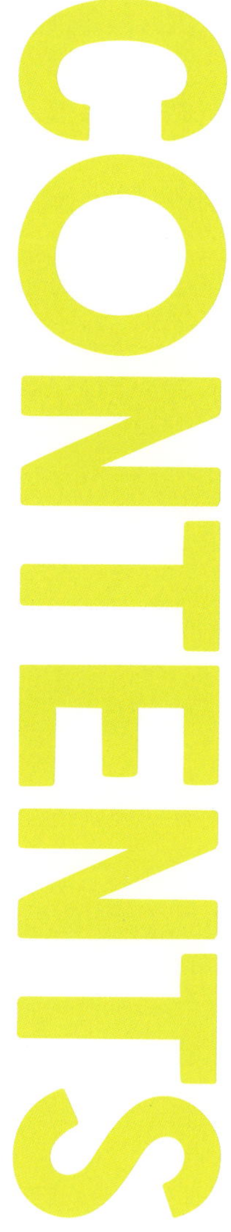

This book is written in honor of every being that has taught, supported, or believed in me throughout my lifetime. It is dedicated to my students. It is a plea and an offering of gratitude for ecological conservation.

● ACKNOWLEDGMENTS

I must begin by thanking Timber Press. Their amazing group of editors, designers, marketers, publicists, and achievers made the creation process enjoyable and the success of this book possible. This includes a heap of gratitude for Tom Fischer. In addition to inviting me to author this book, he provided unwavering kindness and support throughout the years that I spent writing and illustrating. I want to thank Jeff Gustin, Judy Alleruzzo, and William D. McClenathan from the *Garden Time* television show for initially sharing my artwork with the publisher and for their continued cordiality. From the moment that I started writing until the book was complete, I have had consistent and deep gratitude for Teresa Vanderkin. She devoted an unbelievable amount of time and expertise to proofreading. Her careful eye and thoughtful suggestions skillfully elevated the text, chapter after chapter, while her kindness touched my heart.

I thank the institutions and organizations that have invited, and continue to invite, me to speak, teach, and create artwork. It was through these offerings that I met Robert Chiavarini, Carolyn Lehl, Linda Magnuson, Carol Orange, JoAnn Pari-Mueller, and Jennifer White, who generously offered their creative energy and thoughtful feedback on the initial chapters. I would also like to thank the entomology experts who devoted their spare time to checking facts and images of species for accuracy. In addition, the detailed photographs are the result of the generous advice I received from various individuals on proper camera settings. To each of you, I offer my sincere gratitude.

On a personal note, I thank my mother for providing endless support and offering great wisdom, and for her willingness to help with just about anything that was needed. I am also grateful for the in-depth conversations that I had with my father, his ongoing interest in this work, and his willingness to share his thoughts and experiences. A huge thank-you to all of my dear friends and loved ones who listened to years of updates and continually offered their compassion, encouragement, and excitement. Over and above, I want to thank my students for their dedication, enthusiasm, and patience . . . I am delighted to say that this book is now available!

Most important, to those who find this book in their hands, who say yes to their own creative practice or encourage it in another, you give this book life. To you, I offer my deepest appreciation. Thank you.

INTRODUCTION

This book is an invitation to embark on a creative journey. Regardless of your skill level or how long it has been since you last created artwork, you can have a practice that has ease, efficiency, and advancement and that results in beautiful pieces showcasing realistic subjects. It is my absolute pleasure to share with you the unique insects featured in this book. As you create your own works of art, may you experience the wonder of the natural world and join me in honoring these extraordinary creatures.

As a child, I was mesmerized by insects. As they engaged in their activities, I watched with amazement and observed their fascinating exoskeletons, compound eyes, and delicate wings. Now, thanks to my career as an artist, I get to study the incredible characteristics, habitats, challenges, and roles that these and many other creatures have in the ecosystem. The more I research and discover, the more awe-inspiring I find these insects to be.

Insects make up the largest and most diverse group of animals in the world. What is even more amazing is that new insect species are discovered every year! Besides contributing to biological diversity, insects perform many important functions in ecosystems, including pollination, decomposition, and soil aeration. Many serve as a food source for other animals and some provide readily used by-products such as wax and silk. They are also appreciated for their bright colors, bold patterns, mesmerizing movements, and distinctive behaviors. Unfortunately, an increasing number of insect populations worldwide are considered endangered or threatened. Habitat loss and fragmentation, pesticides, introduced species and pathogens, climate change, light and air pollution, and negative attitudes toward insects by humans contribute to their decline. While this book is focused primarily on advancing your creative abilities, it also provides an opportunity to learn about insects and connect to nature through direct experience. Creating artwork that honors insects can increase their visibility and encourage others to view these organisms as autonomous creatures deserving of respectful consideration and a habitat where they can thrive.

Insect art has a long history. Since ancient times, artists have depicted insects as a primary subject or an embellishment, whether for their symbolic significance, as a means to worship or honor specific creatures, or to enhance stories, botanical texts, or figurative works. In the field of science, insect illustrations became a key tool in documenting and explaining biological discoveries. The insect art that you create is part of and contributes to this rich heritage.

How to Use This Book

Through both experimentation and the evolution of my practice, I arrived at the process described in this book, one that relies on the specific strengths of three mediums. First, you use drawing pencils to clearly outline the design on the page. Then you use diluted acrylic paint to stain the paper and create blocks of bold color, blended areas, complex patterns, and precise lines. This paint layer enhances the volume of the illustration's subject and creates depth in the finished piece. Finally, you use colored pencils to add line weight, texture, highlights, and shadows as you further define color and forms.

The content is presented like a home-study course. In-depth instructions describe each stage of the project and guide you toward making decisions about your own artwork. At each step, you improve your skills, learn new techniques, build confidence, and evolve as a creator. Most steps include accompanying illustrations that present a view into the thoughts, choices, and results I made in my studio when using the same reference images and supplies. Photographs of each insect subject (available in a reference section at the back of the book) help you discern the anatomy and coloration of that species.

The projects are assembled in three levels: Foundation Skill Building, Composition and Environments, and Advanced Techniques. Each chapter builds on the previous one, and fundamental themes outlined in earlier chapters are replaced by a focus on new techniques or creative processes. Each project has at least three parts: drawing, painting, and layering with colored pencil, with a design stage as well as a preparation section added as you progress through the book. Whether your artwork style tends to be loose or tight, a well-rounded artistic foundation ultimately provides tools you can use for any subject or style you choose in the future.

Learning new skills is not always easy and might change the speed and style in which you're accustomed to working. While the difficult stages will likely require dedication and perseverance, they can significantly advance your abilities. Give yourself time and permission to explore, experiment, and make mistakes. Be patient. Simply start where you are, enjoy the process, and celebrate every accomplishment. All that you need to do is keep going and continue to say yes to your creativity. This is what it means to be an artist.

Nature Breaks

Between the illustration projects are interludes that I call Nature Breaks. These creative outdoor excursions and skill-building exercises offer you the opportunity to fine-tune your learning and work from live, three-dimensional subjects that are possibly in motion. The informal Nature Breaks guide you to create sketches in a single session. You simply come prepared with sketchbook and supplies, find a suitable location, get as comfortable as you can, and see what is there. I encourage you to consider expanding your focus beyond insects to include an array of flora and fauna in your sketchbook.

The Nature Breaks advance to match skill progression in the book. Level I offers exercises that encourage exploration and often invite you outdoors. Level II activities focus on specific techniques that appear in upcoming projects so you have a chance to explore and prepare in advance. The prompts in Level III provide options for creative exploration so that your sketchbook continues to be an inspiring, educational, and goal-achieving part of your practice.

Nature Breaks can always be repeated on a different day or in a new environment. Since different seasons and weather can bring out different creatures, exploring nature on a midwinter or rainy day can be just as (or more) gratifying as exploring on a sunny day in early summer. You might even choose to set up a regular daily, weekly, or monthly sketchbook practice. Also, feel free to work ahead on Nature Breaks positioned later in the book. Just be sure to either review your notes or practice again before doing the project that immediately follows.

My hope is that both the projects and the Nature Breaks take you to enjoyable places, lead you to wonderful discoveries, advance your creative skills, and result in both sketches and finished illustrations that make you proud of your evolution as an art maker.

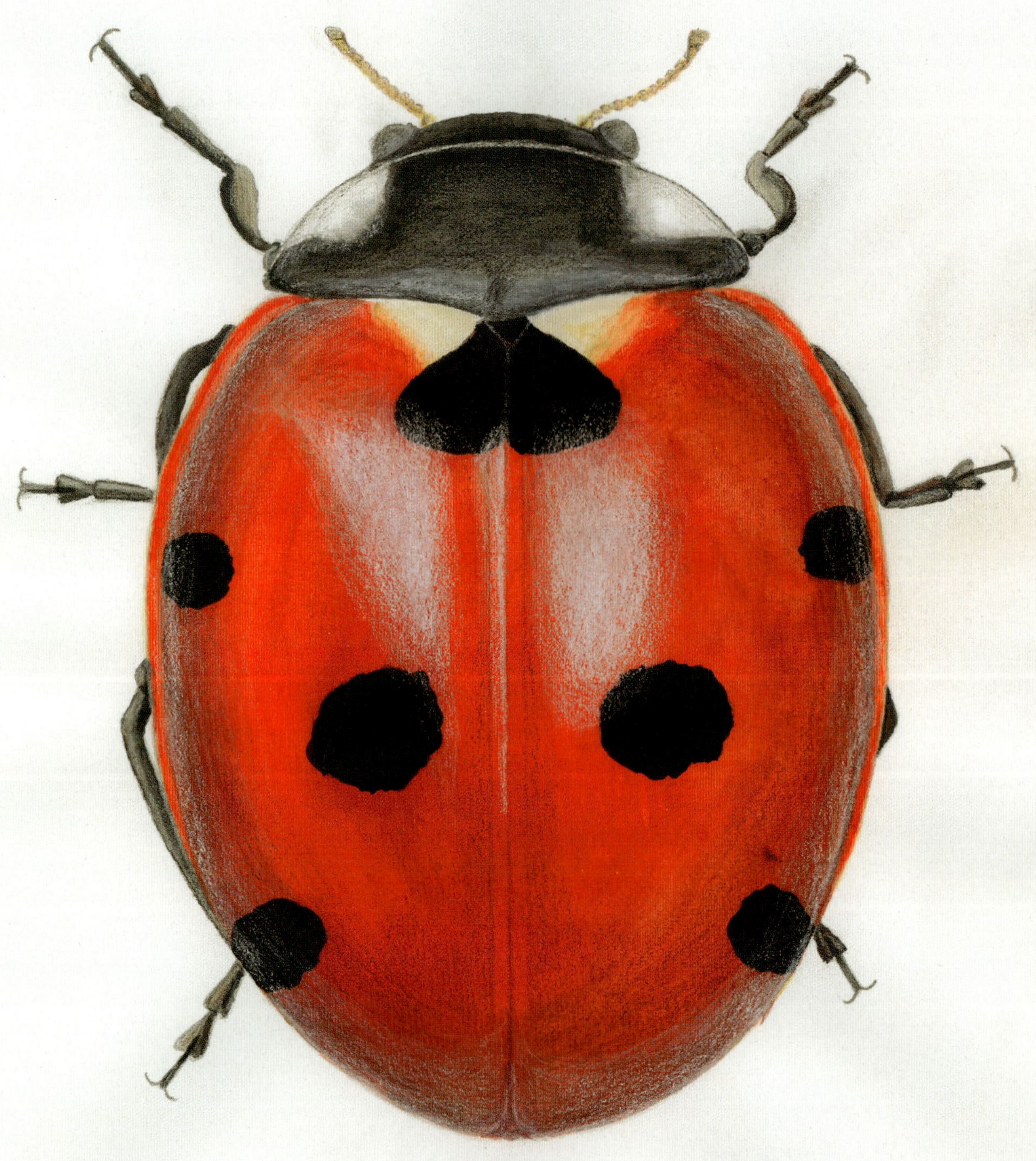

R. Chiavarini

"Each day, when sitting down to work on this beetle illustration, I was intrigued by its astounding and rich detail that went previously unnoticed. The closer I looked, I found yet another deeper layer of astounding diversity and macroscopic beauty. Such an underappreciated part of nature . . . what a beautiful world we live in."

—Robert Chiavarini, Creative Participant

PREPARATION

THE COURAGE TO BE CREATIVE

When we talk about how to be an artist, the focus is primarily on the techniques or materials used. Rarely do we discuss how it *feels* to create art. On one hand, it can seem magical to add layers of line or color and watch a composition emerge. It can be transformative, educational, fun, and filled with growth. On the other hand, making art takes discipline and can be challenging or even daunting at times. As an artist, it is important that you acknowledge your creative experience so that you set up a framework for expressive freedom and self-encouragement going forward.

Recognizing the Six Stages of the Creative Process

In its simplest form, a piece of art begins, gradually builds layer by layer, and eventually arrives at completion. Through working with students and from my own practice, I have come to recognize six distinct stages that can have a significant emotional impact during the creative process. I refer to these stages as the *blank page*, the *uncomfortable stage*, *maturation/creative flow*, *attachment*, *done*, and *beyond*. Your awareness of both the emotional and technical stages of your process can help you maintain an objective outlook on your experience and the artwork itself while it is being created.

The *blank page* stage (or a new sketchbook) is full of potential and excitement. At the same time, many people feel substantial pressure to create greatness, so they freeze up or have difficulty putting a quick mark on the page. But here's the thing to remember: you can immediately turn a blank page into a working drawing—and skirt the push for perfection—by simply making a quick gesture on the page. One mark, and you are on your way.

The *uncomfortable stage* is when a composition is solidifying but has an awkward appearance or is challenging to work on. This stage can bring up fears about the outcome and even halt productivity altogether, when it is actually an important building block in a piece's development. If you find yourself experiencing this stage, acknowledge it, be patient, and persevere. The more you work through this stage, the easier it is to distinguish between the experience of building up a piece and the recognition that issues such as technique or materials in the illustration need to be addressed or that taking a break may be beneficial.

Toward the middle of creating an illustration, you may experience a period of deep engagement, when the artwork progresses steadily and easily. It's almost as if your role as the artist shifts from being that of the maker who creates the artwork to that of a cocreator who allows the artwork to unfold. This is the *maturation/creative flow phase*. The more comfortable you are with techniques and materials, the more this creative flow can expand. In this stage, I often feel meditative or ecstatic. Many hours can pass without my knowing. I consider this phase a great gift.

Although the *attachment stage* can happen at any time, it often occurs after a session of flow. It is when your admiration for a work in progress leads to hesitation and fear that any additional marks may detract from the work. Just as with the earlier uncomfortable stage, this phase can be a roadblock. Yes, it's important to appreciate the work as it progresses, and it's a valid concern that what you like about the piece may change, but it is not yet time to critique your work. If you find yourself in the attachment phase, take a moment to admire the piece, then return to the creative flow mindset of the objective maker, and continue working so the piece can develop fully. That said, if you are preparing to add something that you are not confident about, you don't have to sacrifice your work to take that risk. Instead, test techniques or colors on a scrap piece of paper or with a Nature Break, so you can gain more confidence when applying them. Then take a deep breath and leap.

Because drawing and painting are creative endeavors, knowing when a piece reaches the *done stage* is subjective and can be difficult to identify. Sometimes you add one detail to a piece and it feels complete: you have a knowing or sensation that it is done. Other times, the urge to add more and more continues. In my practice, I look for the moment when the tweaking starts to detract from the piece instead of add to it, as if my work has reached a peak and is about to head down the other side. This is how I recognize the beginning of the *beyond stage* and know that it is time to stop working. If I were to continue, I would overwork the piece and watch the fresh vitality of the artwork become either muted or too busy. Another artist might choose to continue to work and even bring their artwork into a new sense of aliveness again and again. Each person's creative practice is different and personal.

Take time to experience your preferences, emotional stages, internal commentary, and desires, as well as the fears of your inner artist. Notice how the more you practice, the more refined, intentional, beneficial, and personalized your creative process becomes.

Conquering Insecurity

Fears and inhibiting beliefs can arise at any stage of art making, from the conception of a project to the moment you view it as a finished piece. Sometimes this inner critic offers unexpected insights, but most often the negative feelings or statements repeat themselves over and over. Fear and doubt can make creating art unpleasant or, worse yet, they may stifle artistic expression entirely. This just prolongs the hardship.

It's understandable that a seemingly complex project or technique may feel daunting. Acknowledge and consider what your fears and doubts are trying to communicate, but don't let them hold you back from continued exploration, growth, and learning. Instead, pace yourself. Work through each phase of the six-stage process and focus on one step at a time. Keep your self-talk positive, especially when you need to counteract negativity. Acknowledging every step forward, even if it seems minor, helps you recognize your progress.

Should you continue to struggle or become frustrated, pause. Reassess your process rather than force yourself to continue. Maybe you need to practice a particular technique, resolve a question through experimentation, or review previous assignments before you continue. You might transform your fear into a goal for yourself, so that it becomes a motivation to expand your practice.

In the creative arena, a temporary limitation is not a failure; it is merely a baseline on which to build. It's okay if you have fears about making art. You are not alone. It takes courage to create, and you're doing it.

Dealing with "Mistakes"

Making mistakes can be frustrating and discouraging and feel like a major setback. But seeing and correcting errors can advance your practice and teach you how to avoid unwanted results in the future. The key is to view mistake-making as a natural part of success. Support yourself from the moment you realize something is off until you have completed addressing the issue. Acknowledge that it is not easy, then persist.

Keep in mind that our capabilities ebb and flow—from hour to hour and day to day. Pay attention to your creative rhythm so you know how long to work in one sitting, when to take breaks, and what time of day or days of the week are most productive for you. Even attending to simple, fundamental needs such as food, water, and rest can significantly improve your abilities and experience.

Critiquing Your Work

As you work your way through this book, consider including a personal critique of a single project, or of a series of pieces, in your regular practice. Keep in mind that constructive criticism is useful, yes, but be careful not to label your work as "good" or "bad." Consider, instead, that every piece contributes to and documents your creative evolution. Be ready to learn what your artwork has to teach you.

Having guidelines to follow can help you create a positive outlook, keep your comments constructive, and set empowering goals for yourself. You might use the framework of the Final Artwork

Review activity on page 307: rejoice in your achievements, honor your challenges, assess your practice, look forward, and document your lessons and goals.

Or you might examine your overall practice. What fuels your creativity? What choices create ease, get you through or return you to difficult stages, help you excel, or hold you back? Are there any shifts you can make in thoughts, environment, or practice that will better support your art making? With answers in hand, revisit your goals. Make them challenging yet realistic and achievable, so that you deepen your skills and feel encouraged to strive forward. Perhaps you select one or two goals to work on at a time. And consider documenting what you learn in your sketchbook. If your notes are informative and concise, you can refer to them to stay focused, appreciate your progress, and even inspire future work.

Sharing Artwork

People are fascinated, curious, and inspired by connecting with artists. Friends, family, and even strangers may ask to see your artwork. Letting your practice be seen can help you celebrate your achievements, grow beyond your current capabilities, encourage others, or gain a different perspective. But because art making is a personal experience, it can be difficult or even painful to hear negative comments, even if the words were not intended to be disparaging.

Here's a point to keep in mind: the way you present your work often shapes how others perceive it as well as the conversation that unfolds. You can set the stage by asking questions or letting the viewer know what you want from them. For instance, a request to celebrate a specific accomplishment would bring a different response than asking for suggestions regarding improvement. You might share your inspiration, talk about triumphs and struggles, or point to a few

sections so that others see the work from your artist's point of view. Be careful not to speak in a negative way about your own abilities or the artwork itself. These judgments not only bring attention to aspects of your practice or illustration you do not like, they also shift the perspective of the viewer. Both you and your artwork deserve more considerate attention.

When you reveal your piece, consider giving viewers a moment to visually explore the work, perhaps in silence, so they can examine the piece on its own and allow a response to emerge. Sometimes a response is immediate; other times comments emerge more slowly and may evolve as the viewer continues to observe and familiarize themselves with the work. When people do comment, listen deeply to what is said about your work and ask questions to help you see through their eyes. If you are given a compliment, hear it, believe it, and appreciate it. If you are offered criticism, even if it is difficult to receive, take time to consider whether the information can improve your creative practice. Ultimately, you are the authority of your own creative expression.

Don't feel obligated to share your work. In my own practice, there have been times and particular pieces for which privacy has been essential to my creative well-being. Do whatever feels most beneficial to you. If you prefer to keep your practice private, it may help to have an artist's statement ready. That way, when people ask for a glimpse of the ideas behind your work, you can navigate the interaction with ease.

Viewing Others' Artwork

Viewing another artist's work is a wonderful means of learning new ways of working, finding inspiration, and sharing knowledge. It's also too easy to compare another person's artwork to your own! If "better than" or "less than" judgments arise, remember that every artist is unique and on their own path of advancement, exploration, and challenge. View their work as a journey, and honor their own triumphs as well as their struggles. Most important, notice their choices, their expressive style, and the specific techniques they use. Tell them what you appreciate about their work, and ask questions to learn more about their practice and deepen your own studio experience.

Supporting Your Practice

Carve time out of your schedule to create art. When you work, honor your time by avoiding distractions and interruptions. And help those around you understand what you need so you are able to focus on your work.

You might seek support for your art practice by reading more books, connecting with other artists, taking workshops, receiving individual instruction, or exploring new ways to learn, stay engaged, and feel encouraged.

If you work better with others, you might form an art club or invite someone to progress through the assignments in this book along with you. Working together, having a schedule, and being accountable to others can be a wonderful way to make great leaps forward on your creative journey. It might become an opportunity to acknowledge milestones, discuss challenges, and celebrate individuality.

Whether you work independently or include others, create a practice that is most supportive of you and your engagement with the incredible world of art creation.

TOOLS AND MATERIALS

Making art begins with vision, observation, and technique, but we can't draw or paint without first gathering the right tools and materials on which to build our creative practice. This chapter describes the key supplies you will need and offers suggestions for their use and care. You'll find a complete materials list of the essential tools and supplies, items that I encourage you to acquire, plus optional extras.

Some of the lists may seem extensive. That's because having an array of colors and supplies on hand gives you the range to create a more refined result, allowing you to color match to a greater degree and making it easier to create beautiful artwork. But if you don't have or can't acquire the exact supplies suggested, don't let that hold you back from creating art or learning the content provided in this book. Maybe you want or need to work with another brand, add more supplies, omit certain items, or choose a similar item because of personal preference, finances, or availability. As you follow project instructions, simply be aware of the adjustments you have made so that you do not confuse media choices with technique.

Let's begin with an overview of the basic materials.

GROUND OR SUBSTRATE. Artists refer to the surface used for artwork as the "ground," and the choice of ground greatly affects the outcome. While a variety of substrates are available, I prefer to use watercolor paper for these projects because it handles a wide range of paint consistencies, allows for detailed colored pencil marks, needs a small storage space, and can be trimmed to any size. There are many different types of paper finishes, ingredients, and weights from which to choose. Any high-quality watercolor paper will work well. I prefer a surface that is very smooth, so I typically use a pad of hot-press 140-pound paper. If you purchase individual sheets, be sure to check for the placement of a watermark by holding the paper up to a light; you'll want to avoid this area when you measure and cut your page for the projects. If the watermark appears to be backward, you are looking at the back side of the paper. You might want to mark this side with a pencil on each sheet. The assignments in this book are designed for an 11-by-14-inch composition, not including the ¼-inch border. When you create your illustrations, feel free to work larger or smaller—in whatever size you would like—although you may need to adjust brush sizes to reflect those changed dimensions.

DRAWING PENCILS. Artist pencils are organized by lead grade, which is represented by a number and/or a letter. *H* represents "hardness," *B* stands for "blackness," and *F* means "fine point." In this book, the goal is to select a pencil that will leave a mark light enough to erase completely so you can make changes yet dark enough to see through a layer of diluted paint. The line made by an HB pencil falls toward the center of the spectrum, and so HB pencils are recommended for the projects.

COLORED PENCILS. Every brand of colored pencil will offer a different result on your page. You'll find a huge range in price, quality, application, and color stability. Feel free to experiment with various high-quality wax- or oil-based pencils to find the style and brand that works best for you. Prismacolor Premier soft-core pencils can be a good choice when first developing a creative practice and are suggested for the projects in this book. They come in a variety of rich colors and neutral tones, have a smooth application, and blend together well. Plus they are sold individually and in sets at most art supply stores. Note, however, that some of the colors, particularly the bright blues and greens, are light sensitive and can appear faded or altered over time. More stable colored pencils are available, but they are typically sold in large sets and are significantly more expensive.

The lead of colored pencils can be brittle, so keep your pressure light when the tip is sharp. Avoid dropping the pencils onto a hard surface so that the core does not break. If you would like to work with a different brand of colored pencil, test it first to be sure it will work on top of acrylic-stained paper.

COLORLESS BLENDER PENCIL. This can be a nice addition to your toolbox once your skills advance. Blender pencils do not contain pigment and will appear transparent when applied. You can use this utensil on top of wax-based colored pencils to blend colors, to create smooth transitions from pencil to blank paper, and to draw sharp lines. Be forewarned that a blender pencil can slightly darken and lower the saturation or color intensity of an illustration.

Test the colorless blender on scrap paper to see if it will create the result you desire. First, apply the pencil colors thickly enough to create a layer of wax. Then apply the blender using directional strokes, small circular movements, or a scrubbing motion to create various results. In your experiments, you might test the blender on top of a gradient, stripes, or dashes made from colors that are similar or drastically different. You can also apply it directly to the page, then use a colored pencil with a sharp tip on top of the transparent waxy base. Although this tool can be a helpful convenience, it is important to first develop the foundation skills

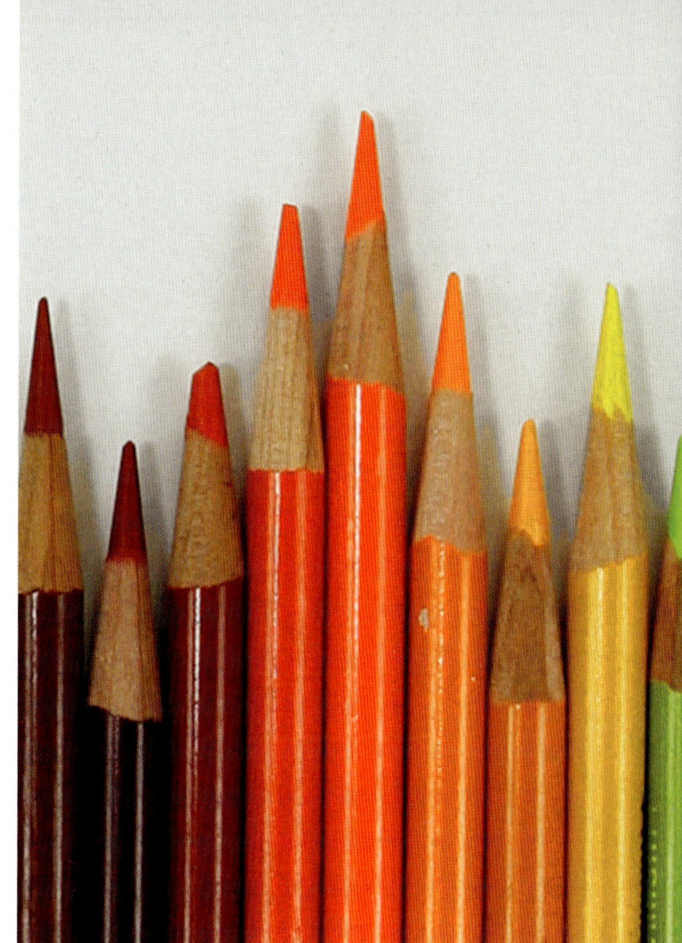

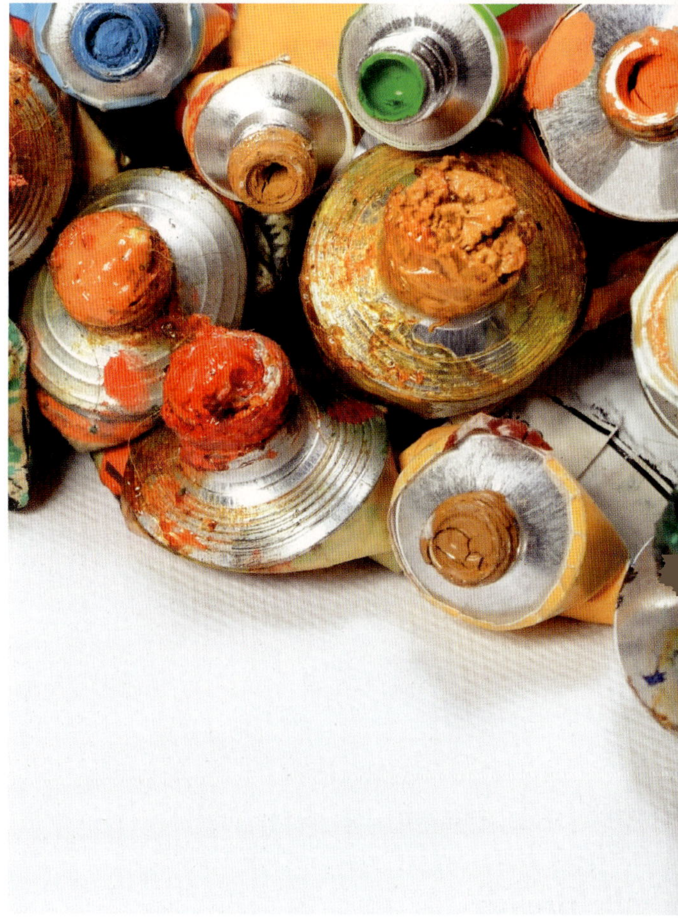

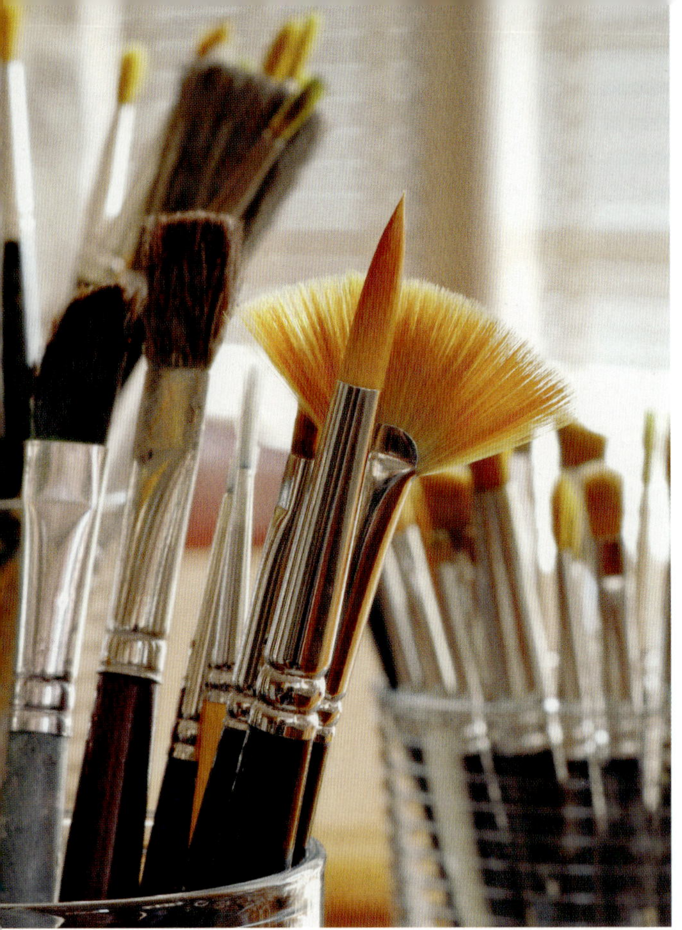

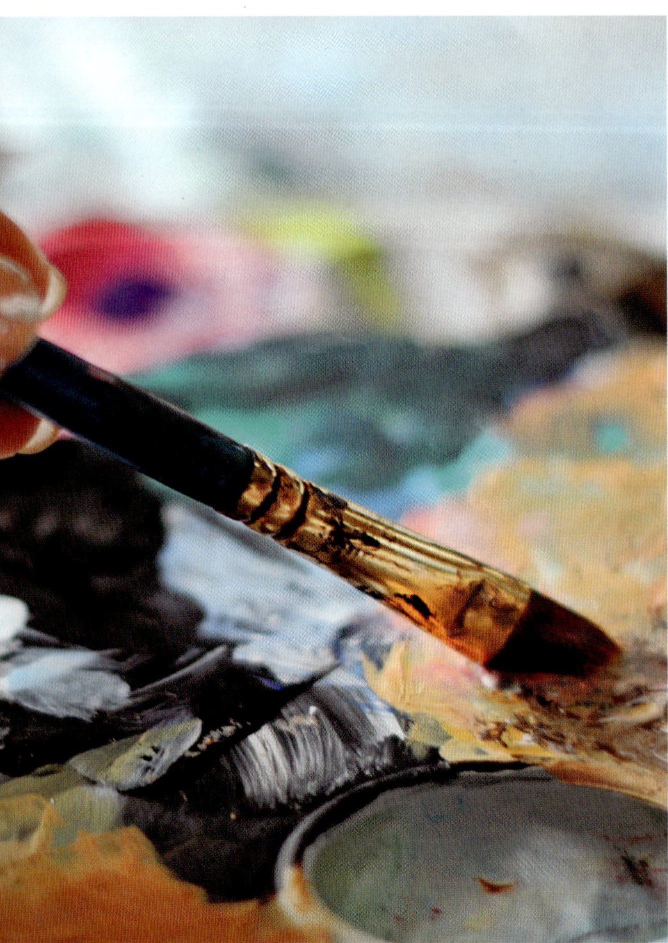

that help you accomplish a similar effect. For this reason, the colorless blender is mentioned only in the advanced section.

PAINT. Each project was created using acrylic paint. There are no toxic solvents needed for cleanup as there are with oil paint. With acrylic paint, you can paint in layers without disturbing previous work, which is not possible in watercolor. Although special attention needs to be made to keep acrylics from drying out on the palette, I think the benefits are worth it. In the projects, instead of applying paint thickly, you will be instructed to dilute it so that you create color simply by staining the paper. This makes it possible to apply a layer of colored pencil on top of the paint. Plus you'll be able to achieve a range in appearance from opaque to translucent.

PAINTBRUSHES. There are many different paintbrush brands, sizes, and bristles. Some are made of natural hair; others have synthetic filaments. Since sizes are not consistent from one company to another, I included bristle dimensions, as well as standard number sizes, in the materials list.

When you purchase new brushes, be sure to hold them before buying: consider the comfort of the brush in your hand, the rigidity of the bristles, and the length of the handle. Whichever brushes you choose, select ones designed for watercolor or acrylic paint. Over the years, I have collected and still use many different brands, though I prefer synthetic bristle paintbrushes because of their durability, the way they hold liquid and smoothly glide over the page, and how I can use them to create details.

PALETTE. There are myriad options when choosing a paint palette. When working with acrylic paint, be sure to select a palette that can be used with water and is designed for materials that may permanently adhere when completely dry. After many years of searching for an ideal palette, I am thrilled that plastic peelable artist palettes are available. These palettes allow you to wipe off wet paint and either peel or scrape dried paint so you always have a clean, neutral-colored mixing surface. There are also stay-wet palettes that include an airtight storage container to keep paints fresh, tempered glass palettes, and disposable sheets. Or you can create a homemade palette from items that you already have available.

ARTIST TAPE. Before using wet media (paint) on your illustration, attach the paper securely to a drawing board by using artist tape around the perimeter. The tape holds the paper down so you have a flat surface to paint on. If you leave the tape in place while the paint dries, the illustration will become completely flat and be easier to view and frame. And because paint won't seep under artist tape, your illustration will have a clean border. Unlike other adhesive tape, artist tape can be carefully removed days or even weeks later without tearing the surface or leaving a residue.

ACRYLIC RETARDER. This additive slows paint drying time, which is always a concern when using acrylic paints. If my studio is dry, paint on my palette can become unusable in just a few minutes if left unattended. On humid days, drying time will be longer. Either way, if I plan to work on something for a while, I add water and one or two drops of acrylic retarder to the paint mixture to extend its workability. The time gained will vary based on how much acrylic retarder you use. If you add too much, however, it can create a sticky film on your page or make your paints translucent and less stable.

MASKING FLUID. (aka liquid frisket). This liquid is waterproof as soon as it dries and can be used as a paint resist in areas with intricate details that you would rather paint over than paint around. Once the paint has dried, you remove the masking fluid to reveal the protected paper underneath.

Some cautionary words about masking fluid. First, it will block (mask) paint *any place* it touches.

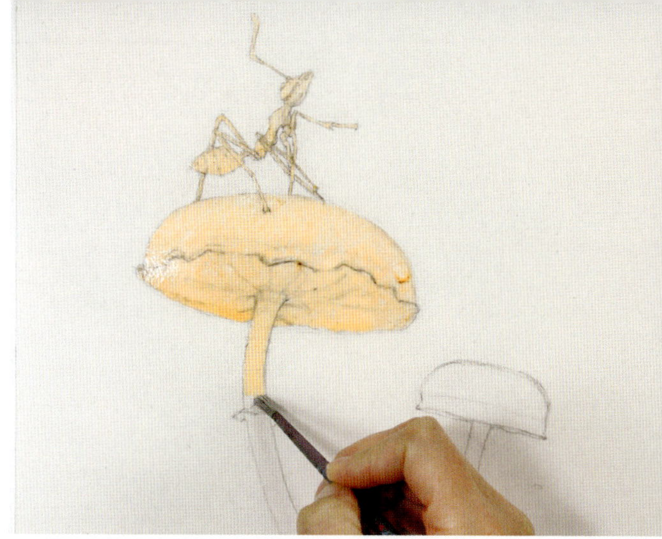

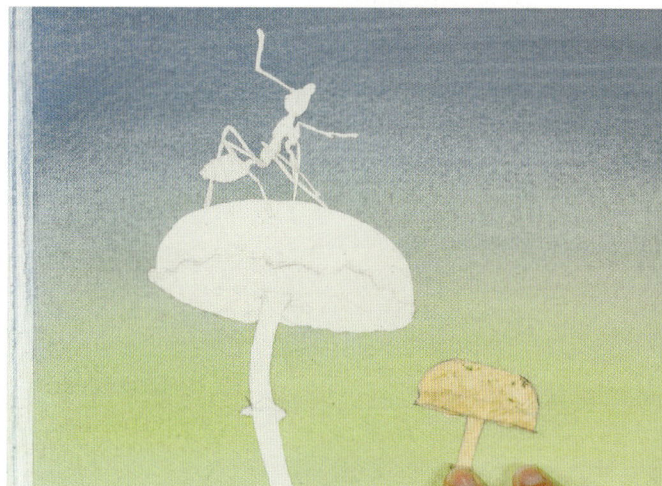

If you make a mistake when applying it to your illustration, you must wait for the fluid to dry before you can rub it away and start again. Second, removing it can pull off a bit of paper fiber. Therefore, you may want to copy anatomical details onto a sheet of tracing paper so that you can replace any lines that are difficult to see after the mask has been removed. Third, it's important to apply the mask in a well-ventilated space and remove it from the paper within twenty-four hours. Finally, if the masking fluid dries on paintbrush bristles, it can ruin them. It's best to use a color shaper with a pointed tip. This tool looks like a paintbrush but has a solid silicone tip that makes it easy to remove masking fluid after it has dried. Alternately, you can use a small designated brush, which should be rinsed intermittently and immediately after finishing the application.

DRAWING SUPPLIES

ESSENTIAL

- [ ] F artist tape: 1 inch wide
- [ ] artist pencil: HB hardness
- [ ] colored pencils (see next section)
- [ ] drawing board: Masonite, Gator Board, or other durable yet light-weight work surface that can be angled and to which artist tape will adhere
- [ ] eraser: Maped Epure or similar white vinyl eraser
- [ ] paper: ideally 140-pound hot-press watercolor paper (pad or loose sheets)
- [ ] pencil sharpener: ideally with a waste catch
- [ ] ruler: ideally metal
- [ ] sketchbook: any size, preferably made with recycled paper

ENCOURAGED

- [ ] tracing paper: roll or book, any size

EXTRA

- [ ] drafting brush
- [ ] fixative (to protect your completed illustration)
- [ ] grid ruler, transparent
- [ ] precision tip eraser, pen-style

PAINTING SUPPLIES

ESSENTIAL

- [ ] acrylic paints (see below)
- [ ] artist tape: 1 inch wide
- [ ] brushes (see below)
- [ ] paint palette (consider a plastic peelable artist palette)
- [ ] paper towels or clean rags
- [ ] scrap paper
- [ ] water container

ENCOURAGED

- [ ] acrylic retarder (to slow paint drying)
- [ ] masking fluid (liquid frisket), white
- [ ] plastic wrap or palette cover (to keep paints workable)

EXTRA

- [ ] pliers (for opening older paint tubes)
- [ ] fine-mist water sprayer
- [ ] X-Acto knife

ACRYLIC PAINTS

ESSENTIAL

- [ ] burnt sienna
- [ ] burnt umber
- [ ] cadmium red
- [ ] cadmium yellow
- [ ] cobalt blue
- [ ] Mars black
- [ ] permanent green light
- [ ] titanium white
- [ ] ultramarine blue

ENCOURAGED

- [ ] Naples yellow
- [ ] phthalo yellow green
- [ ] yellow oxide or ocher

EXTRA

- [ ] cerulean blue
- [ ] cobalt teal
- [ ] dioxazine purple
- [ ] interference blue (fine)
- [ ] Titian buff

BRUSHES

ESSENTIAL

- [ ] artist paintbrushes (ranging in size from extremely small to large)

ENCOURAGED

- [ ] round: size 000 (³⁄₁₆-inch long)
- [ ] round: size 0 (¼-inch long)
- [ ] round: size 1 (³⁄₈-inch long)
- [ ] round: size 2 (⁷⁄₁₆-inch long)
- [ ] round: size 3 (½-inch long)
- [ ] round: size 4 (⅝-inch long)
- [ ] filbert: size 12 (1⅛ inches long) or larger, for backgrounds

EXTRA

- [ ] color shaper with tapered tip (for applying masking fluid)
- [ ] small round brush (inexpensive or worn, for the sole purpose of applying masking fluid)

COLORED PENCILS

ESSENTIAL

- [ ] high-quality wax- or oil-based pencils in a range of colors and neutrals

ENCOURAGED

Prismacolor Premier soft-core pencils in the following colors:

- [ ] 10% French gray
- [ ] 30% French gray
- [ ] 50% French gray
- [ ] 70% French gray
- [ ] apple green
- [ ] black
- [ ] burnt ocher
- [ ] canary yellow
- [ ] Caribbean Sea
- [ ] cerulean blue
- [ ] chartreuse
- [ ] chocolate
- [ ] cream
- [ ] crimson lake
- [ ] dark umber
- [ ] electric blue
- [ ] goldenrod
- [ ] green ocher
- [ ] imperial violet
- [ ] indigo blue
- [ ] jasmine
- [ ] light umber
- [ ] lime peel
- [ ] mineral orange
- [ ] moss green
- [ ] orange
- [ ] pale vermillion
- [ ] Prussian green
- [ ] rosy beige
- [ ] scarlet lake
- [ ] seashell pink
- [ ] sepia
- [ ] sienna brown
- [ ] sunburst yellow
- [ ] terra-cotta
- [ ] violet
- [ ] white
- [ ] yellowed orange

EXTRA

- [ ] black raspberry pencil
- [ ] colorless blender pencil

TECHNIQUES, CONCEPTS, AND PROCESSES

This chapter introduces you to various foundation techniques, concepts, and processes you will meet in the projects and includes options for you to play with as your artwork becomes more advanced. I recommend revisiting this chapter occasionally to further integrate the information and absorb new bits that you can apply to your expanding practice.

Setting Up for Success

WARM-UPS. Before you begin a project or Nature Break, warm up by making a few quick gesture drawings in your sketchbook. Each gesture might take as little as thirty seconds or up to five minutes to create. The idea is to quickly capture the essence of a subject and transition the mind and body toward creative expression.

SKETCHBOOK. Keep this at hand for warming up, working on Nature Breaks, designing compositions, and exploring other short projects. (The illustration projects in this book are typically created on watercolor paper in multiple sessions.) I recommend that you draw on only one side of each sketchbook spread, so that your artwork is protected by the opposite page; otherwise, another work on the facing page could rub off onto your finished piece. If you fill the sketchbook from the front of the book to the end, you'll see your work's progress over time.

TWO- OR THREE-DIMENSIONAL REFERENCES. Keen observation is by far the most important skill in this style of art making. The benefits of using photographs as reference is that abundant images are readily available and, because the images are two-dimensional, the insect shapes will be relatively easy to translate to your page. For some projects, I've included multiple photos of the subject to help you understand each shape's form so that you can more accurately depict volume as well as life essence in your artwork.

If you reference the actual three-dimensional subject, you have the luxury to investigate the structure, texture, and coloration from all sides. This provides a wealth of anatomical information that helps bring a lifelike quality to your art. Your challenge will be to translate these spatial forms onto a two-dimensional page.

Many artists draw from collected specimens. Harvesting insects can keep invasive populations at bay, but it may devastate species that are dwindling. If you want to purchase a specimen, work with a company or individual who collects with environmental impact in mind so that insect populations are not depleted and symbiotic plants or animals don't suffer from their absence. Ask about a supplier's policies; ecologically centered companies are usually happy to tell you about their collection approach.

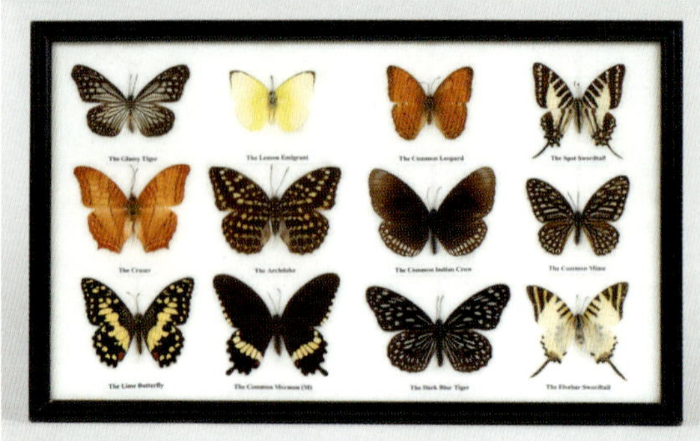

COLORED PENCIL CHART. It's helpful to create a visual guide of your pencil collection to glance at as you work. Your chart might include the name stamped on each pencil, a gradient that illustrates each pencil's value range from light to dark, and even some examples of color layering. I refer to my chart when mixing paint to determine which colors I do not have in pencil, to create an identical color match of paint and pencil, or to visualize harmonious color layers.

COLORED PENCIL SWATCHES. Pencil colors sometimes combine in unexpected ways. As you can see in the photo, lighter-colored pencil pigments do not always show up well on top of darker ones, so you may need to apply the light color first. In addition, some darker-colored pencils, such as indigo blue and black raspberry, become unexpectedly vibrant when combined with a lighter color. For that reason, I often make color swatches for my projects, especially when there are many colors with a similar value (see examples on page 267). Being aware of pencil combinations encourages you to widen the color range of your supplies and to plan combinations to avoid unwanted results.

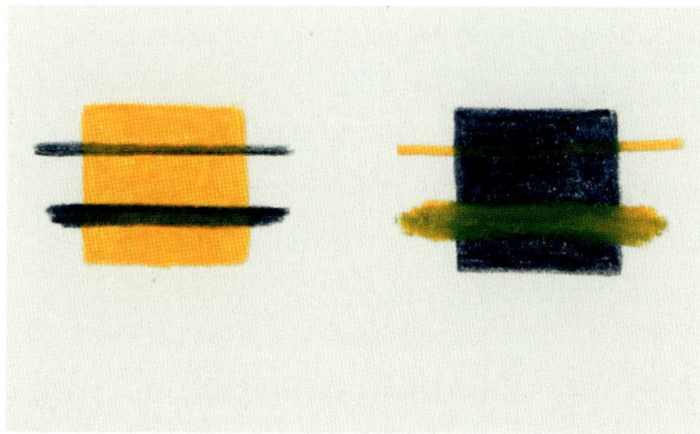

WORKFLOW TIME. How much time should you allow for the projects? It's the nature of art creation that some stages take much longer than anticipated, while others are completed with speed and ease. Sometimes a process can be completed in one step; other processes span several sessions. If creating art is new to you, plan on spending two or three hours at a time working. When you reach a new part of an assignment, I encourage you to read ahead *before* you start working. Get an idea of the workflow. Decide if you want to practice a new technique before using it in your piece. Pay attention to how you feel physically and mentally during your work sessions, and take breaks when needed. Ultimately, you'll develop a schedule that is ideal for your body and your art.

PHYSICAL COMFORT. When you draw, your body position, movement, and overall comfort level can affect the way you hold a pencil or brush, the type of line you create, your ability to focus, your overall energy level, and how you feel both during and after a work session. Make sure you have all you need to keep your body comfortable, hydrated, and fueled. Also, take time to recuperate and reenergize so that your practice can be rewarding and sustainable.

Measuring and Drawing

PENCIL TIP. Your colored pencil lead offers a range of line shapes. A sharp tip can carve precise lines or, when held upright, fill in the tooth (indentations) of the paper. A dull or blunt tip can blur edges or scrub and blend colors. Using the side of the pencil lead creates visual texture. Play with the sharpness of the tip, the angle of the pencil, and the pressure applied to accomplish the results you desire.

BACK-AND-FORTH TECHNIQUE. Whenever you work from a reference, whether two- or three-dimensional, develop the rhythmic habit of looking at the same exact spot on the reference every few seconds while you draw. This back-and-forth motion from reference to illustration will help you visualize and refine anatomical outlines in each illustration.

Of course, if you are referencing a living insect, you may not get a chance to observe it for long. When my subject is on the move, I give it full autonomy and simply work quickly to get information on the page. Instead of looking back and forth from subject to paper every few seconds, I hold my gaze on the insect and try to imprint the forms in my memory. Then I move to the page and draw a gesture from memory, including as much information as I've observed. If the subject is still present, I continue to add details and refinement to my drawing. Sometimes these speedy gestural drawings capture a sense of motion that enlivens your drawing in a way that is not possible using a still subject.

THUMB-AND-PENCIL MEASUREMENT METHOD. This technique helps you draw the subject on your page with proportions that match the reference image. Simply choose a single anatomical feature to serve as the unit of measure and use your thumbnail to place this measurement on the end of

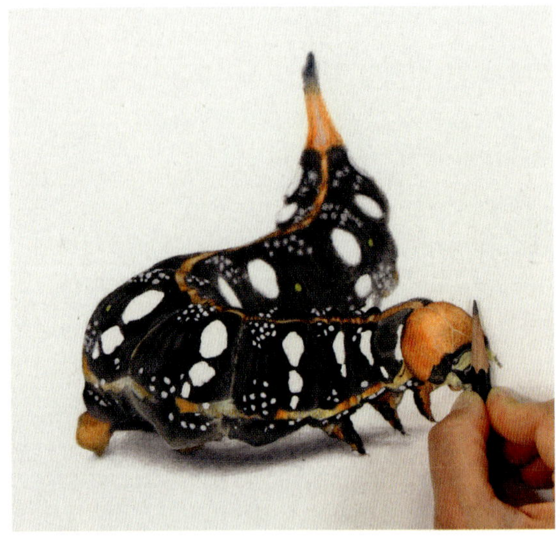

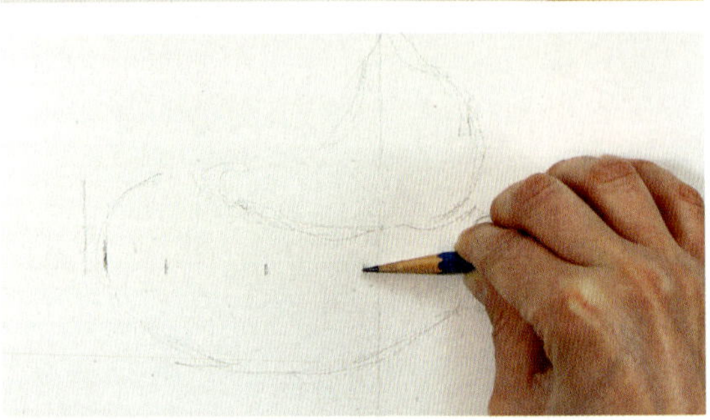

proportions of the subject will be accurate. Measuring from a vertical midline and a horizontal axis line requires minimal erasing and can help you build the foundation skill of envisioning proportional forms in future gestures. Therefore, using a grid and simply replicating patterns in each square is reserved for extremely complex compositions. There are also diagonal structural lines you can create by using the side of your pencil to pull appropriate angles from the reference image to your drawing. You'll learn more about these lines in individual projects.

OUTLINE QUALITY. As you draw your insect outline, strive for a single, smooth, clear line. Refine the line as you go, and erase any marks that could be confused with the actual form.

your pencil. Then use this distance to both measure different forms in the reference image and to mark the increments on your page. If your drawing's scale is different from the reference image, adjust to the size of the unit of measure on your gesture drawing when you move to your paper. If you are viewing a three-dimensional subject, hold the pencil vertically with your arm extended directly in front of your dominant eye. Close your other eye and keep your arm either fully extended or at an unchanging distance to measure the length and width of forms. With practice, this measurement technique speeds up your process and results in accurate anatomical forms and patterns without repeatedly erasing and redoing sections.

STRUCTURAL LINES. Grid lines or axes provide you with an immediate framework for quickly pinpointing specific locations using the thumb-and-pencil method. This can allow you to focus solely on refining your gesture knowing that the

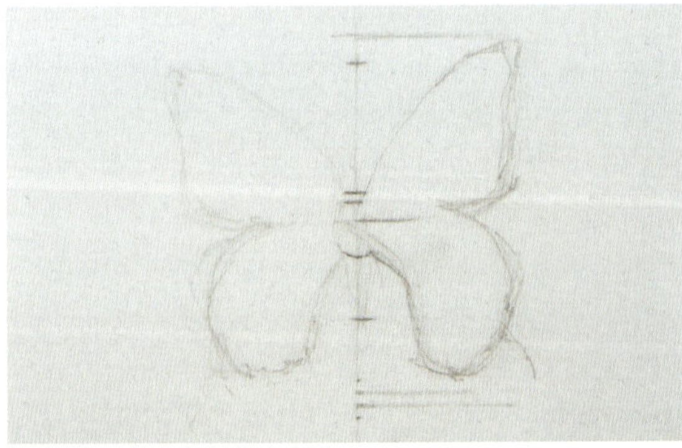

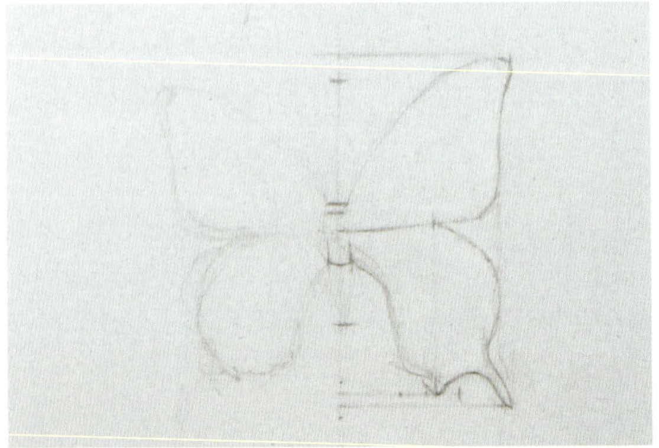

LINE WEIGHT. The weight, or value and thickness, of colored pencil marks has a profound effect on your artwork. Use an even line, especially around a perimeter, and the form will

appear flat. Vary the line and you suggest dimensionality. Random line variation won't work, however; you need a consistent theme or purpose. You might use line weight to distinguish between areas that are closest to and farthest from a light source, to differentiate least and greatest mass, to emphasize repeated shapes on undulating forms, or to indicate distance within the composition. Be aware that if your theme is not clear or the transitions too frequent, your outline can seem like a dashed line, which will flatten the image and add visual confusion instead of conveying dimensionality. Differences in line weight can be subtle, but they add finesse to your sketches or illustrations.

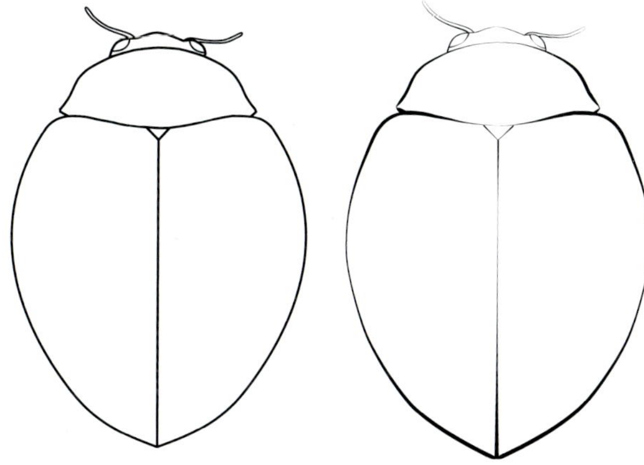

HAND POSITION. Holding your pencil similar to the way you write words—with the side of your hand firmly planted on the page—lets you make precise marks but limits your ability to create curves or graceful lines. If instead you lift your palm slightly, your arm has greater mobility. It's important to keep a physical connection to the page so you maintain control: even the tip of a pinky finger will do the trick. Play with your hand position, grip on the pencil, and range of motion. What results occur? Create a spectrum of options you can implement when you draw. New hand positions may seem awkward at first, but in time they will likely feel right.

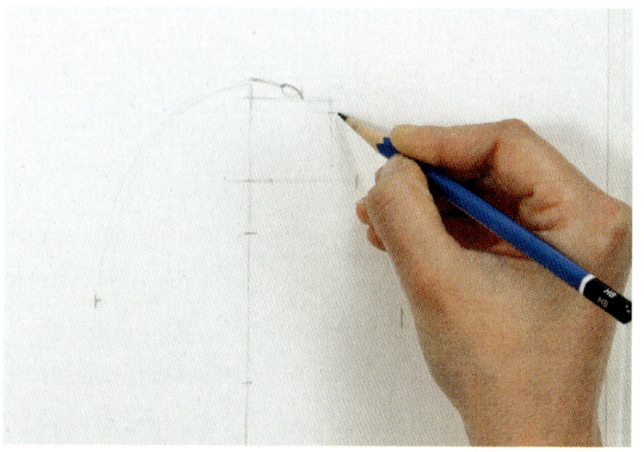

PREVENTING SMUDGES. It's all too easy to smudge pencil marks. That's why I recommend working from the upper corner farthest from your dominant hand, toward the opposite corner at the bottom of the page. This technique keeps the active work area above the place where your hand comes into contact with the page. When your drawing is finished, you can always use an eraser to lightly remove any haze that has developed on the illustration. During the colored pencil layering stage, place a piece of tracing paper between you and the artwork. The trace remains stationary and provides a resting barrier for your hand, yet it keeps the composition visible.

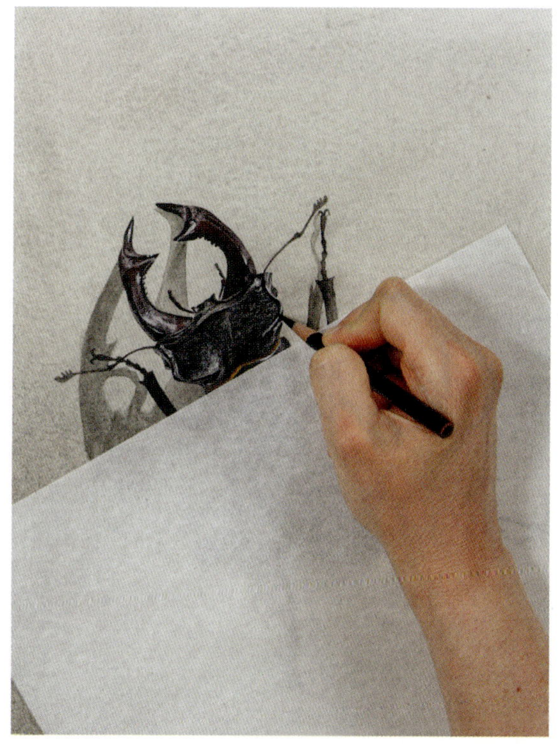

Painting Basics

PAINTBRUSH USE AND STORAGE.

Take good care of your brushes, and they will remain usable for decades. Let acrylic paint dry on the bristles, however, and your brushes may be ruined in mere minutes. For that reason, get into the practice of rinsing your brushes after every use. When using an especially small brush, like a size 000, plan to rinse it periodically while you are working.

If paint collects in the uppermost portion of the bristles, clean the brushes against the side of a water container or wash them by hand at the sink, taking care to retain the shape of their tips when you are finished. Never scrub brushes against the bottom of a container: that can permanently damage the bristles. Avoid letting your brushes soak in your rinse water container; water can quickly swell a wooden handle, distort the shape of bristles, and rust the metal ferrule that holds the brush together. Lay the cleaned brushes flat to dry.

I store dry paintbrushes vertically in a container, with bristles pointed upward, so that they maintain their shape and are readily accessible. That said, I have a couple of paintbrushes that I use only for mixing paint—I don't worry much about keeping the shape of their bristles because my focus is strictly on creating color.

PAINT ON THE PALETTE.
When I am ready to paint, I place my colors within reach. I like to keep most of my palette clear for mixing, so I align the colors along the palette edge, guesstimating how much of each I will need. (The amount will depend on the size of the area being covered and the dimensions of the composition.) Since acrylic paint dries so quickly, I include only the ones I am about to use. My diluted mixtures are typically 1 to 2 inches in diameter.

BACKGROUNDS.
When you begin to create complex compositions, you'll paint the background first, then put in the elements that support the subject, and finally provide the focal point. This enables you to reference the colors in the environment to determine the appropriate hue, value, and intensity of the subject. And it helps you recognize the amount of detail needed to create the intended level of emphasis. Though you may use small brushes to add details to both the background and the subject, keep in mind that the majority of refinement will be completed in the colored pencil stage.

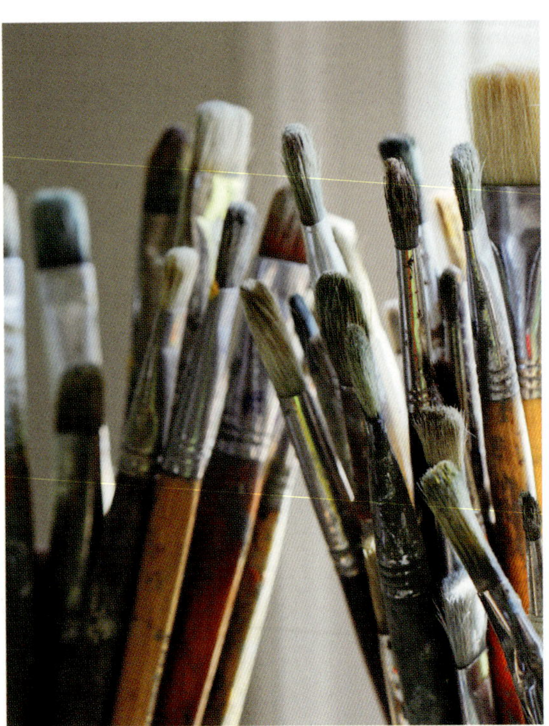

Working with Color

LOWERING SATURATION (INTENSITY).

If you combine the three primary colors (red, yellow, and blue), the result is a dark, neutral color. Therefore, if you want to lower the saturation of a color, all you have to do is add its complement: the color directly across from it on the color wheel. This is true for paint as well as colored pencil, though you will have more control with paint.

Another way to lower saturation is to add black or white to the color, which will simultaneously shift the value and the intensity. Alternatively, you can dilute the pigment to the point where the white of the page shows through, which lowers the intensity without altering the color of the paint. This translucency effect works only on paper; if you use another ground, such as canvas, the thinned pigments can flake when they dry.

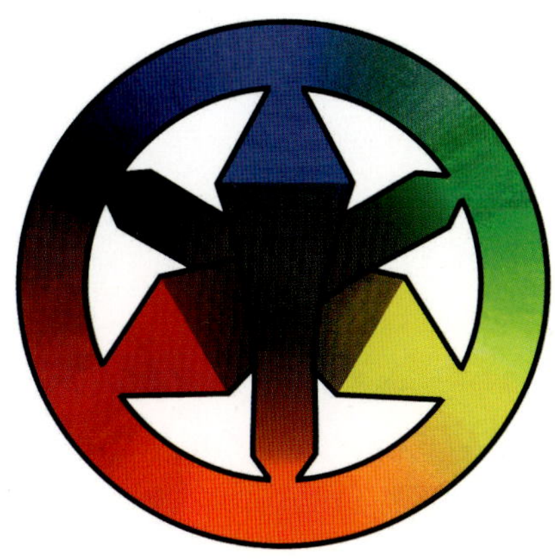

MIXING COLOR VIA INHERENT VALUE.

Each color has an inherent value, or an intrinsic degree of lightness or darkness. For this reason, I suggest you begin your paint mixtures using colors that have an inherently lighter value so that you avoid mixing more paint than you need. Yellow is very light; violet is extremely dark; red and green have a similar value. As you can imagine, adding a small amount of violet can dramatically change a mid-value mixture of paint, whereas it would take a substantial amount of yellow to have the same influence.

USING PURE BLACK.

Insects often have a section that looks completely black. If you were to paint that area with your darkest color, however, you'd find it impossible to add shadows, and the illustration could end up looking flat. I typically paint these sections dark gray instead. Not only does the deep gray appear black on the page, but it allows you to use actual black to enhance the form, which results in a more dimensional appearance.

Addressing Mistakes

ACCEPTING ERRORS.

In every project, give yourself the time to work through unplanned surprises. The moment you realize something is off, pause and consider the issue. Often the fix is something as simple as remeasuring, redrawing a pencil line, practicing a technique, or making sure the colors are correct.

RESPONDING QUICKLY.

When working with paint, speed is key to addressing spills and splatters (see next page). In my own practice, I've learned the hard way that ignoring significant discrepancies can create more problems down the line. The amount of time spent compensating far outweighs dealing with the problem at the start. Familiarize yourself with correction techniques so you can jump into action when the time comes to use one on your actual work.

EMBRACING OUTCOME.

There may be times when you try to fix something and instead make it worse. Maybe you'll need to redo the piece entirely. But other times, the result of your efforts is what you intended to achieve or, better yet, enhances the design.

FINDING THE FIX-IT FULCRUM.

That said, not every mistake needs to be addressed! Sometimes a piece has a life of its own. Look at the drawing from a few feet away. Will the mistake affect the drawing negatively? If the error won't alter your process, doesn't significantly distract you when you look at the piece, or will not affect the finished work, you might allow these alterations to add character to your art and then move on. As an artist, you have to find your own fix-it fulcrum so that the product of your work has integrity, your practice has a pleasant flow, and you feel good about the work you create.

REMOVING WET PAINT. The moment wet paint contacts paper, the paint color begins to stain the page. Use a clean paper towel or moist paintbrush to soak up highly diluted pigment. If the paint is opaque, however, immediately apply a small puddle of water to the spot, then carefully use a small brush to lift the pigment off the page. Follow by gently blotting with a clean paper towel to soak up the excess. Work quickly so that the pigment does not spread and stain a larger area. Do this technique only once in an area, and avoid scrubbing the paper so that you keep its fibers intact.

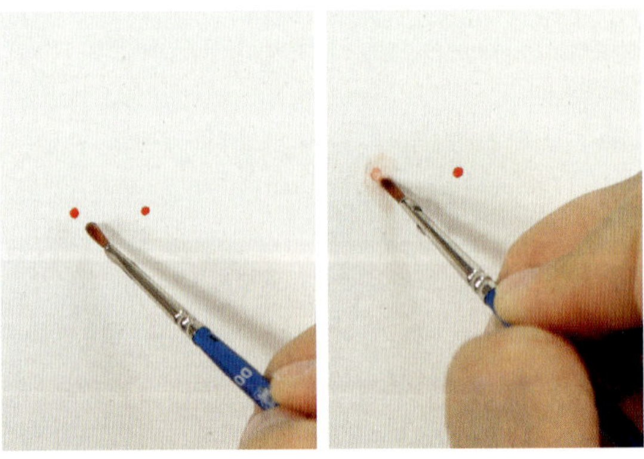

FIXING DRY PAINT. For a dry speck smaller than the head of a pin, use the side of a utility knife blade on the dry paper to scrape off the top paper fibers to remove the stain. This is especially useful when the background of your composition is white because the value, hue, and texture of white paint and colored pencil are always slightly different than the paper, and they will just stand out afterward.

If a color can cover the mistake, either create a paint mixture or use a colored pencil on top to reestablish continuity. If you apply more paint color to compensate, make sure the dried color will match the surroundings. If you use colored pencil, consider the hue and value of the mistake and select pencil colors that will effectively hide the error. You might find it necessary to stay within the boundaries of the error to hide it, or you might blend the repair into areas on either side.

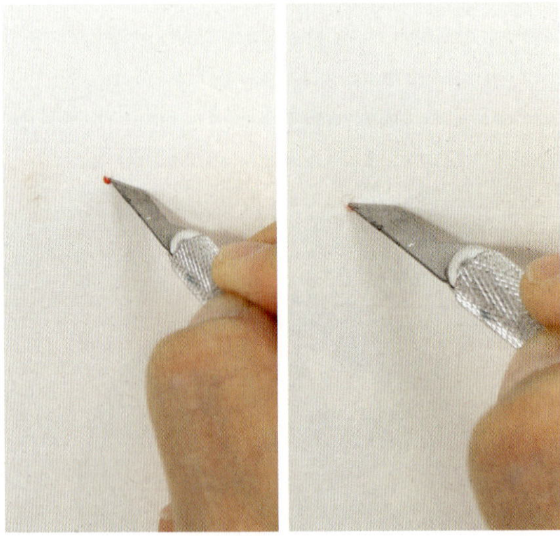

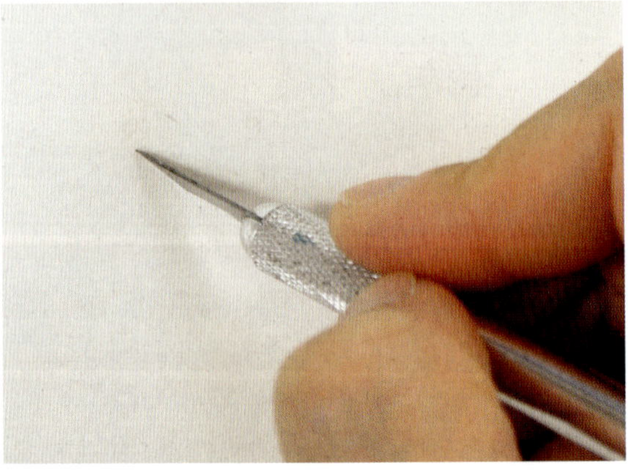

ADDRESSING A LARGE SPILL. Use creative problem-solving as a way to reorganize, integrate, or add to the piece to make the mistake look intentional. After I first notice a large permanent error, I often take a break from the work and return when my mind is fresh and ready to think of inventive possibilities. As a worst-case scenario, you may want to redo the illustration, knowing that it should take less time to re-create because you're already familiar with the process. You might create a transfer sheet to duplicate the design by copying your lines onto *both* sides of the tracing paper (to avoid making a mirror image), then flipping back to the original side to trace onto your new page.

Compositional Skills

SHAPE. Insect forms are complex, especially when you are observing to the level that is needed to create detailed drawings. When you work on your illustrations, look for a variation of simple geometric shapes to visualize the subject three-dimensionally and locate the portion that would catch the light as well as the areas that would be darkest or cast a shadow. When you begin to think in this way, a more complicated structure, like the mandible of the stag beetle, can be easier to discern.

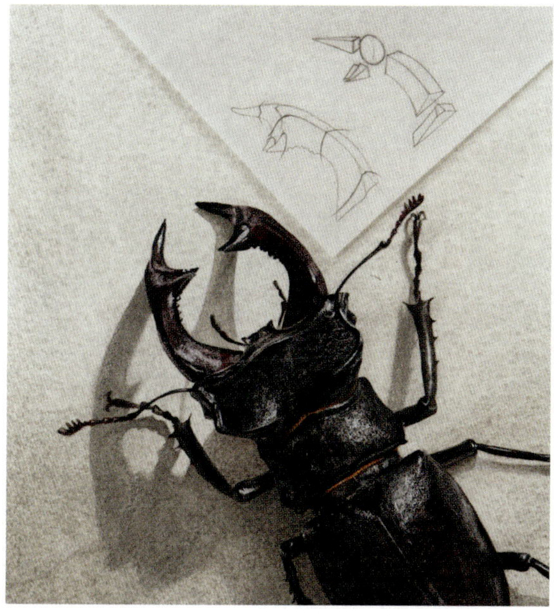

SCALE. Experiment with the scale of your subject so that the primary elements of your composition have importance without taking over. A smaller focal point lets you have more subjects or background elements on the page. A larger subject appears closer to the viewer, and minute details can be created to help make it look more realistic.

DEPTH. As you paint, keep in mind that elements in the foreground typically have intricate details, crisp edges, vivid color, and high contrast. Therefore, if you intentionally create the background with increasingly blurred outlines, muted colors, and limited value range, you convey a greater sense of space between the subject and its surroundings.

EMPHASIS. Value, color, line quality, and subject placement dramatically influence the weight, balance, and hierarchy of compositional elements. Look for the level of importance each element has within a composition. As your artwork transitions from a drawing to a painting to a refined illustration, you might notice a shift in subject focus or in the overall layout. Your observations can help you identify and apply the appropriate techniques to achieve the desired level of emphasis in the finished piece.

LIGHT SOURCE. The type of light cast onto the subject affects not only the look of the subject's features but also the shadow that it creates. Even when a light source is not shown in a reference image, you can deduce the light's direction, quality, and distance simply by looking at its effect on the subject. Taking time to consider light cues can help you create consistent shadow angles, define anatomical forms more precisely, and place the subject in a believable environment.

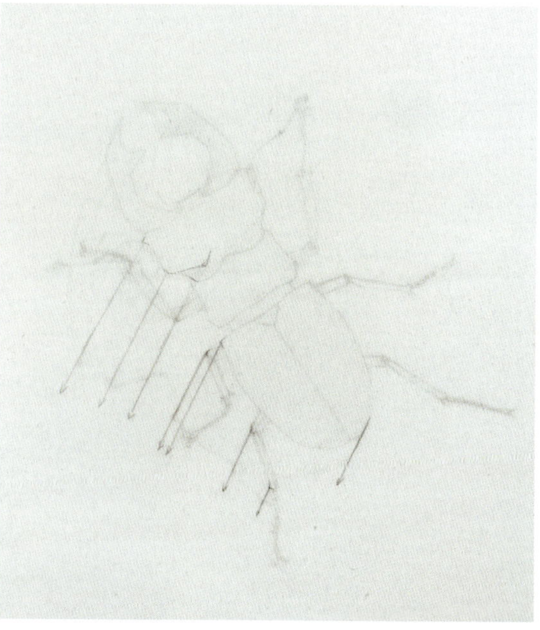

Pay attention to the relationship between the subject (positive space) and the background (negative space). If there is too much negative space in a composition, the subject can get lost on the page; with too little negative space, the subject looks crowded. Consider how close the subjects are to one another and to the framing edge, and whether you want to allow them to overlap one another. Strive to use the entire composition to draw the eye to different points of interest and create more visual balance while keeping the subject the most important.

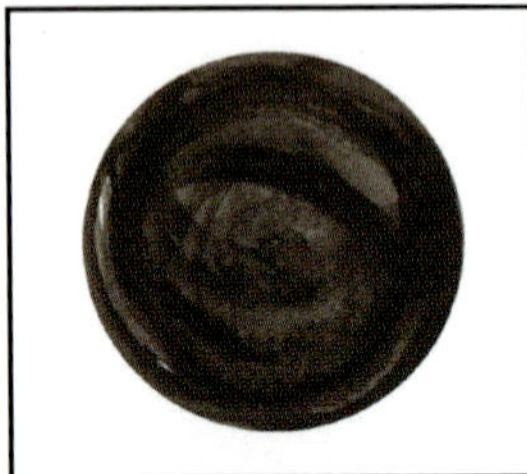

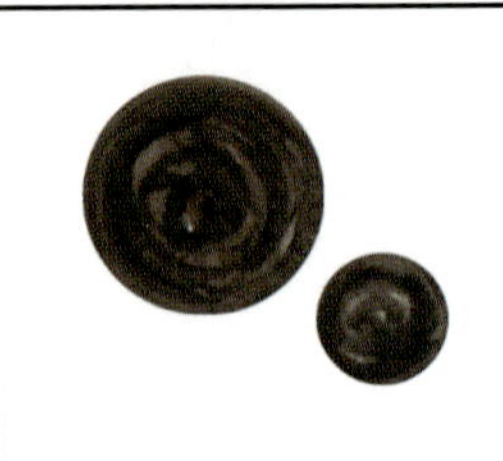

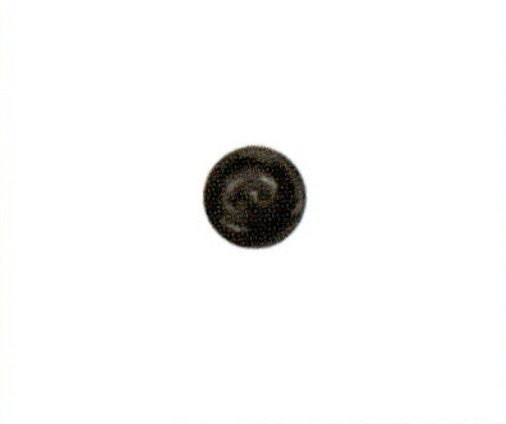

USING TEXT. Text can be an aesthetic and informative compositional element. You can include observations, species identification, personal narrative, anatomical features, and more, but be aware that this text will be as much a part of the visual quality of your artwork as the illustration. Apply the same design principles that you used to place an insect subject so that your words enhance your artwork conceptually and visually. For that reason, lines of words as well as the choice of script should be considered and applied with care. I find it's best to keep text simple, clean looking, and clear. You can always use a piece of tracing paper to lay out the lines or blocks of text before you work on your artwork.

Preserving Your Work

ADDRESSING WAX BLOOM. The pencils recommended in this book will produce a wax bloom over time, which appears as a white film over a color. It is most visible on dark colors. If this happens, gently wipe a soft, clean rag over your artwork to remove the film. To avoid the bloom altogether, spray your artwork with drawing fixative upon completion. Be sure to use the fixative outdoors or in a well-ventilated area.

STORING YOUR ARTWORK. Place completed illustrations in a protective enclosure such as a portfolio or in flat file drawers. If you choose to make your own enclosure or separate your pages, be sure that the material you use is acid-free (or even archival). Keep your artwork in a dry room with minimal temperature fluctuation. Another storage option is to frame pieces. Whether you choose a ready-made frame or go to a custom framer, consider using glass with an ultraviolet (UV) protective coating to reduce fading and other UV damage that may occur over time. Whichever option you choose, by taking care of your artwork, you preserve the results of your creative practice, beautify your space with nature art, or generate an extraordinary gift.

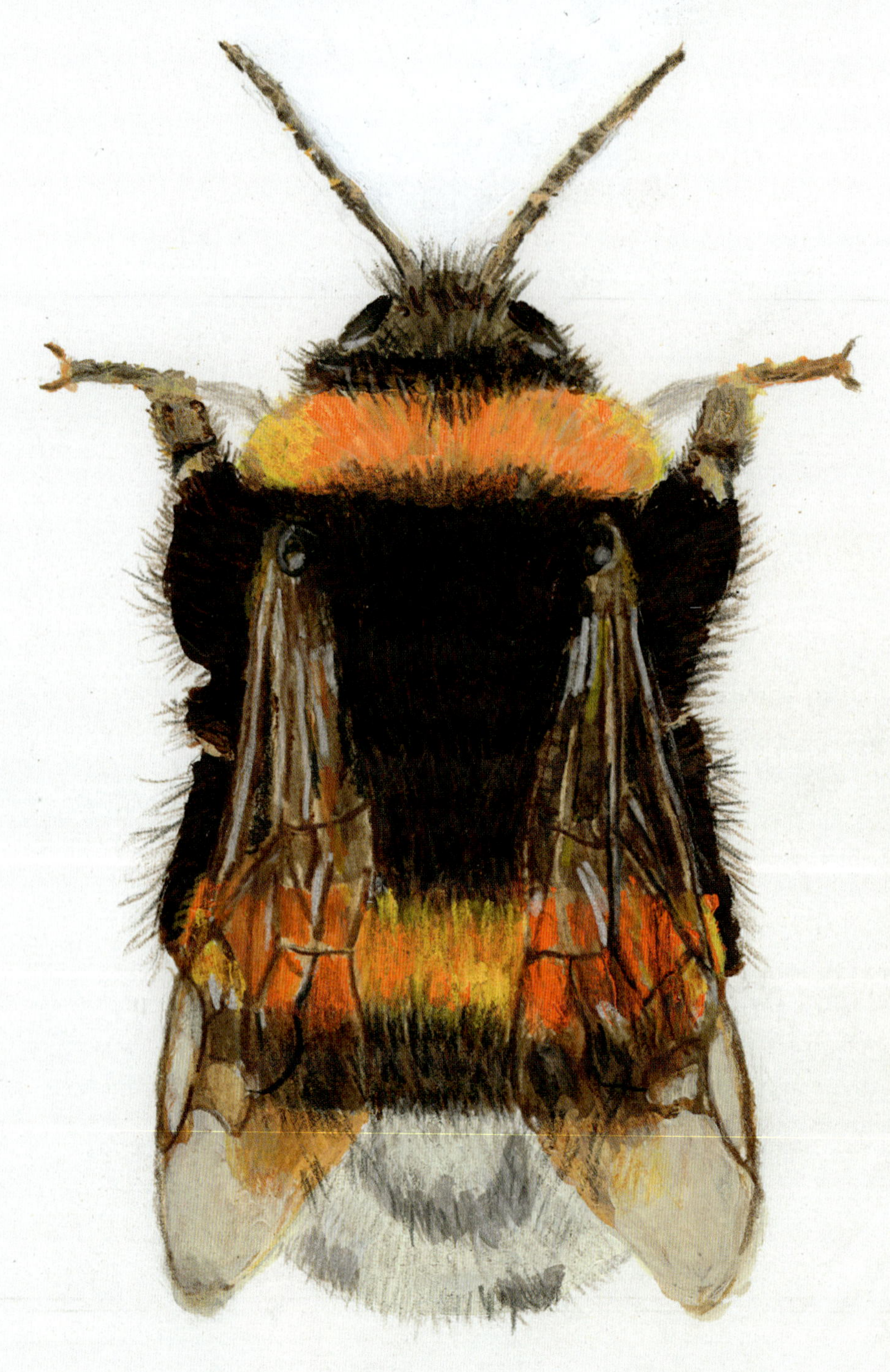

Linda Magnuson

LEVEL I

FOUNDATION SKILL BUILDING

The projects in this section are designed to strengthen your core creative skills, establish a supportive process, and streamline your practice. Each project has been crafted to help you achieve success from the very beginning of an illustration through to its completion.

In the drawing stage, you will learn how to start quickly, measure proportions accurately, and add anatomical details that make the subject look incredibly realistic. Then you will learn ways to make an insect appear to have volume and density. Finally, you'll apply techniques that refine anatomical forms, boost highlights, and create the surfaces of smooth shiny beetles as well as fuzzy bumblebees.

As you progress from one project to the next, you'll use your skills to add a surface below your subject and create a sense of atmosphere around it. Tips along the way teach you how to minimize mistakes and address issues when they occur. Each project builds on the previous one, exploring new techniques, offering helpful tricks, and giving you time to incorporate newfound skills into your practice. In combination, they assist you in developing a creative foundation that you can rely on while you craft beautiful, interesting, and incredibly lifelike insect illustrations.

Between projects are casual Nature Breaks. These are opportunities to explore the natural world, observe three-dimensional references, and create art from life.

SEVEN-SPOTTED LADYBUG BEETLE

COCCINELLA SEPTEMPUNCTATA

Ladybugs (aka lady beetles or ladybird beetles) are native to Europe and East Asia. They were introduced to North America because of their ability to protect agricultural crops from damage by other insects. The bright red color of the seven-spotted ladybug is a signal to predators that it contains a chemical that can be poisonous if consumed. I selected this composition because of the iconic color of the beetle, the symmetrical layout, and the accentuating highlights that make the beetle look like it is ready to fly off the page to the next garden.

 SEE REFERENCE PHOTOS ON PAGES 308–309

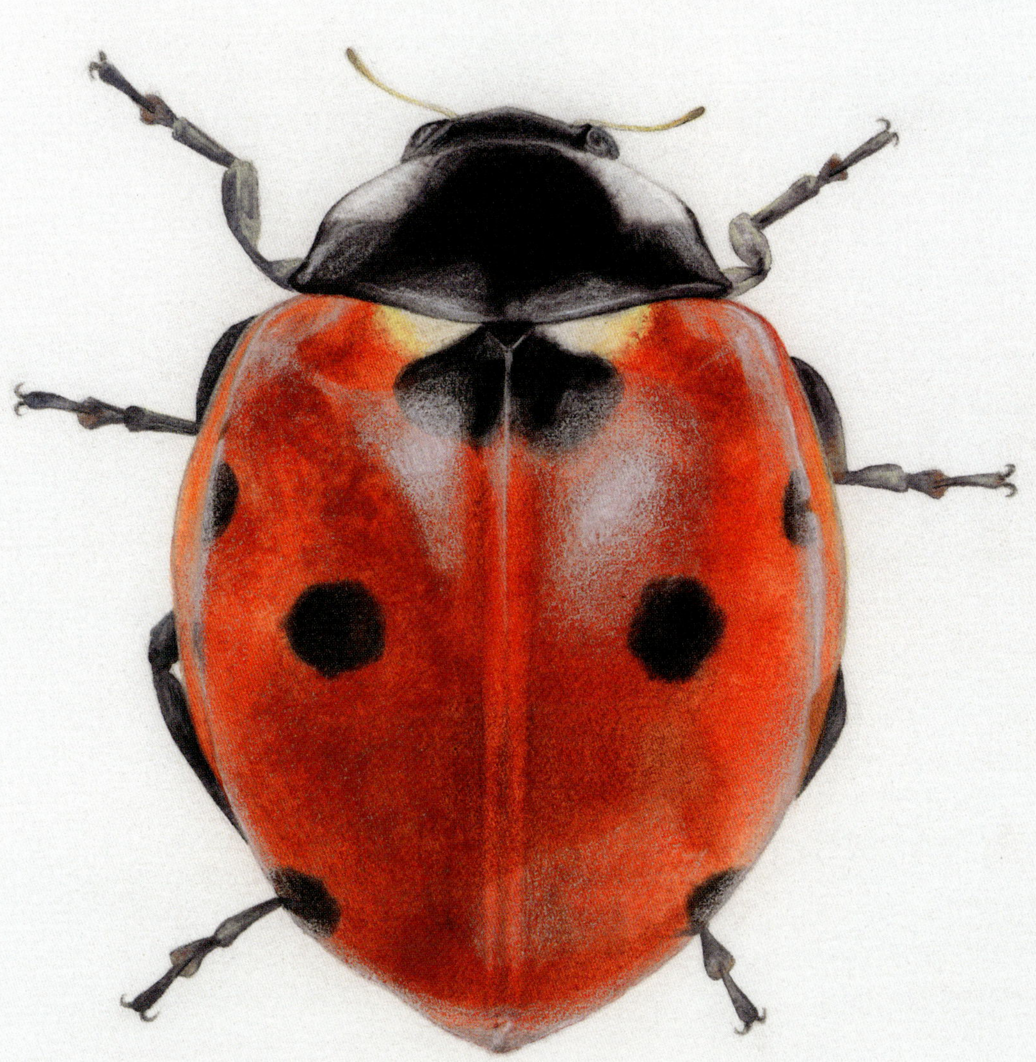

ACRYLIC
PAINTS
☐ burnt umber
☐ cadmium red
☐ cadmium yellow
☐ Mars black
☐ Naples yellow
☐ permanent green
  light
☐ titanium white
☐ Titian buff

BRUSHES
☐ sizes 0 and 3 round

COLORED
PENCILS
☐ 10% French gray
☐ 50% French gray
☐ 70% French gray
  (optional)
☐ black
☐ black raspberry
  (chocolate, sepia, or
  dark umber can also
  be used)
☐ burnt ocher
☐ cream
☐ dark umber
☐ jasmine
☐ scarlet lake
☐ terra-cotta
☐ white

ADDITIONAL
MATERIALS
☐ HB artist pencil
☐ ruler
☐ eraser
☐ artist tape
☐ tracing paper
☐ acrylic retarder
☐ paper towels or
  clean rag
☐ drawing board
☐ water container
☐ fixative (optional)

DRAWING

1 Prepare your workstation. Create a space, free of clutter, where you can set up your materials. Then place your watercolor paper, cut to size, on your drawing board. Draw a faint measured line ¼ inch from the edge on all sides and use this as a guide to create a boarder with artist tape. Be sure the tape edge is securely attached to the paper and the board.

A To begin your composition, decide where you would like to place the insect on the page. Use the HB pencil, with very light pressure, to create a straight line that will represent the midline of the beetle. Look at the ladybug reference images on pages 308 and 309. Now indicate the size of your beetle with two marks on the midline, one to represent the tip of the head and the other at the end of the abdomen. The scale of the beetle in your drawing might be quite different than the reference image—that's okay. I made the beetle in my illustration 6 ¼ inches long.

Look back and forth from the beetle on the reference image to your paper and envision the beetle on your page, then quickly create a gesture of the overall outline. Within a minute, you'll have a beetle form in your composition. Guesstimate the proportions as best you can, and keep your lines light enough so they can be easily erased. Next, draw a small vertical line that is only slightly darker than the gesture lines to indicate where the sides of the beetle are located.

B Now measure and mark the proportions so you can adjust the gesture to match the reference image. You can do this by using the thumb-and-pencil method: Place your pencil horizontally on the reference with the tip of the lead at the midline and your thumbnail at the side of the beetle. Hold this measurement and turn the pencil vertically to see how many times this measurement fits along the midline from the base of the abdomen to the tip

of the snout. It should be about a third of the total length. Now repeat this on your drawing to make sure the proportions are the same. Unless your beetle is the same scale, you will need to adjust your thumb to the midline-to-side dimension on your drawing. If the proportions of your gesture are different from the reference, adjust the length of the midline on your drawing so that your measurement fits about three times. When you feel confident the length-to-width ratio is the same as the reference image, mark each increment starting from the bottom of the midline.

Though the thumb-and-pencil method may seem complicated at first, this process makes it easier to correctly locate and draw anatomical features, helps you avoid complex issues, and makes your insect appear more realistic in the end. Take your time when measuring; it is worth practicing on these simple forms so that you can easily apply this technique on more advanced subjects.

2 Review the reference image and locate the section that is equal to the top segment on your drawing. Notice the line where the black thorax (the middle section, between the head and abdomen) meets the red abdomen. If you imagine the segment on the midline further divided into thirds, you should find the thorax-abdomen near the one-third mark. Move to your drawing and add a light dash to this spot. I suggest you use slightly longer dashes to indicate anatomy placement so you do not confuse them with the marks that simply divide the line. Remember to keep your lines as light as the pencil will allow.

Locate the line between the head and the thorax. Since the head is so small in comparison to the first segment, you can divide the space that was just created between the tip of the head and the base of the thorax. Return to the reference image and imagine this space divided into quarters. The head should be located within the uppermost quarter. Your thumb might move to

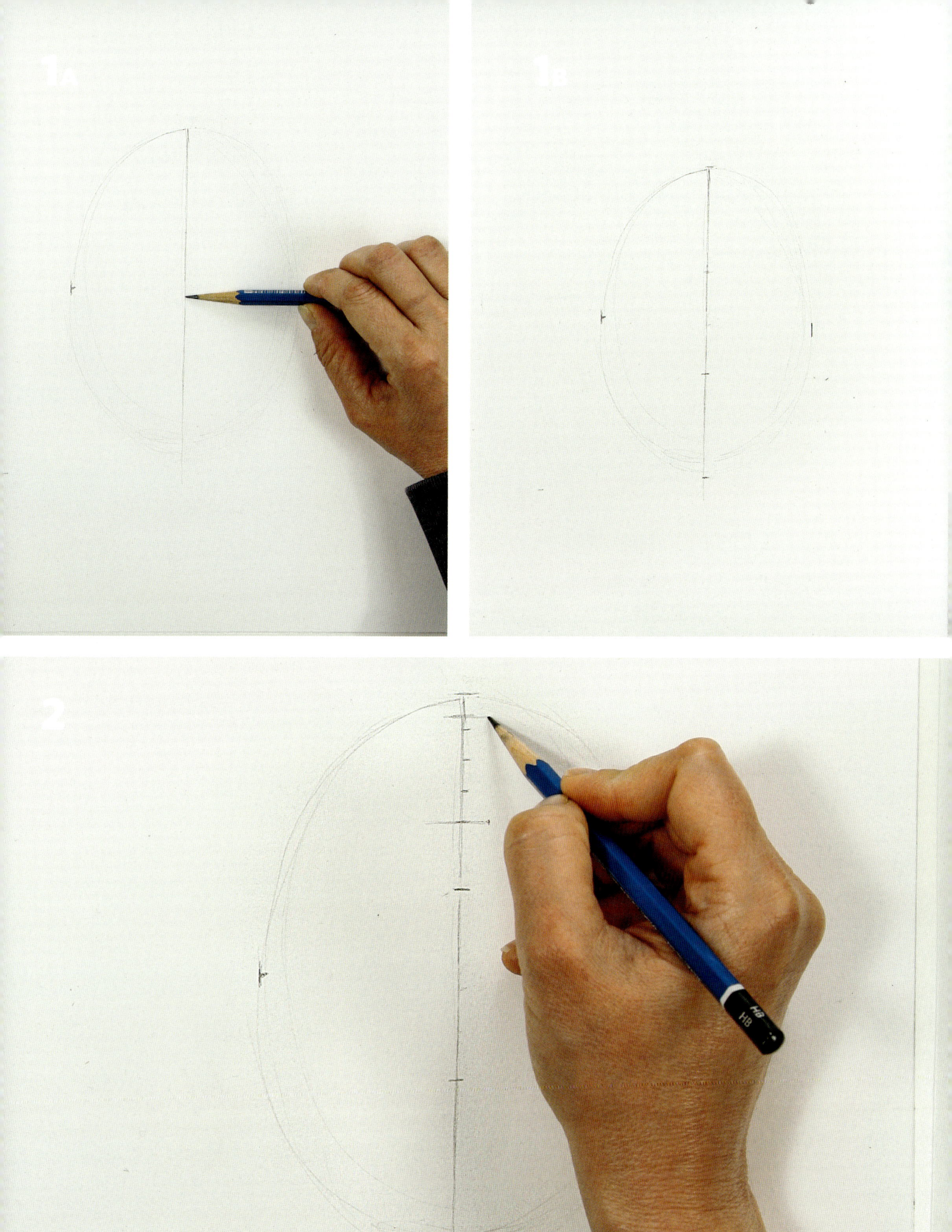

1A
1B
2
HB

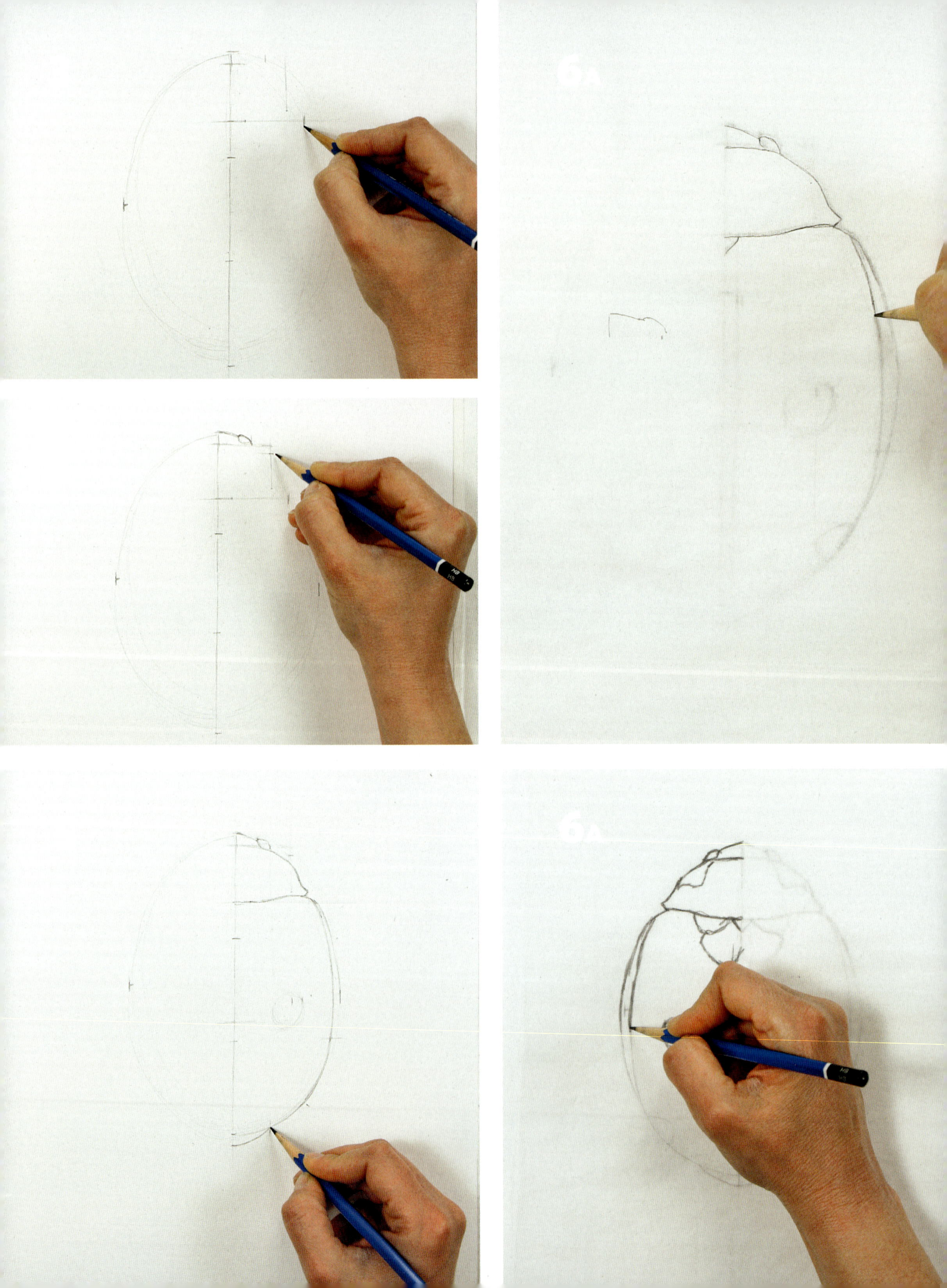
6A
6A

the pencil tip to assist in this visualization. Mark this placement on your drawing. All of the vertical measurements are now complete.

3 At this point, you may find it helpful to extend the vertical line that indicates the side so that the drawing's midline-to-side dimension is easy to see at any point along the beetle's body. Since the design is symmetrical, you can mark a single side and transfer the marks to the opposite side with tracing paper.

Look at the reference image and measure the width of the head using the reference's midline-to-side dimension. If I imagine this measurement divided into thirds, the outline of the head ends around the one-third mark. Move to the area on your paper where the head will be drawn, divide the drawing's midline-to-side dimension into thirds, and add a quick vertical line to mark the edge of the head. Repeat these steps to determine the widest part of the thorax, which lands on the two-thirds mark. Since the side of the thorax curves, it's helpful to approximate where the center of the curve is located. In my drawing, it's placed at the halfway mark. You can also determine the size of the eye by dividing the width of the head in the same manner as you've been dividing the midline-to-side dimension. It may be tempting to sketch the shape of the outline, but I encourage you to continue adding these reference points first. They help you visualize the *entire* outline when you draw the contour, not just a single section, and they give you a greater ability to draw accurate forms.

Your drawing now has all the information you need to create the outline shape without having to worry about placement or proportion. This was a big step. Congrats!

4 Start drawing the outline of the beetle's upper body. Be sure to look at the reference image every few seconds to visualize the shape of the line on the page. When a segment is finished,

pause to check the overall accuracy of the shapes and proportions against the reference before you move on. Make sure these lines are slightly darker than your reference marks yet still erasable.

5 Now study the abdomen in the reference image. Notice the subtle details: the slightly rounded corner near the thorax, the small flange on the side, the spot in the center, and the highlight that turns the end of the abdomen into a half circle above a rounded triangle.

Return to the drawing. If you locate the spot in the center of the wing, it will be easier to see the overall shape of this larger form. To do this, start with a quick gesture of the spot. Use the midline to confirm the spot's vertical position and the midline-to-side dimension for the horizontal location. On my drawing, I divided the abdomen in half vertically and found that this point aligned with the bottom third of the spot. Then I noticed that the left side of the spot was conveniently positioned directly below the side of the head. When you have the spot positioned correctly on your drawing, refine the shape of the outline.

Begin to outline the form of the abdomen, maintaining light pressure on your pencil. When you are just over halfway down, turn your paper so that you can create the quarter circle at the bottom and maintain a comfortable hand position. Be sure to leave space for the triangular form at the very end, which I found was about the width of an eye. Also, it is important to keep the arc light where it connects to the triangle so that there will be a seamless flow from one shape to another after you paint. Next, draw the triangular shape. When you are finished, follow the midline to the top of the abdomen and create the tiny triangle, called a scutellum, that sits between the wings. Your outline is complete. Excellent work.

6 **A** Now you can erase all your reference lines, with the exception of the midline, and remove extra marks on the page so that each form has only a thin, smooth pencil line around the perimeter. Take a sheet of tracing paper, lay it on top of the drawing, and replicate the half beetle as precisely as possible with a single pencil line. Your pencil pressure should be heavy enough to make a good transfer but not so hard that you leave an impression in the paper. Be sure to include the midline so that realigning your transfer sheet will be simple. Now flip the tracing paper, align the midline, and double-check that the width of the beetle appears to be the same as the width in the reference image. If you find discrepancies, shift the position of the tracing paper slightly. If this does not alleviate the issue, take the time to make any necessary adjustments to your drawing and then re-create the transfer sheet. This extra tweaking, though it may seem tedious, can make a huge difference in the finished piece.

When you are ready to transfer the image, secure the tracing paper with a piece of artist tape, hold it to your page, and trace a few lines near the edge. Without letting the tracing paper shift, peek underneath it to be sure that you've successfully transferred the lines from the back of the tracing paper to the page. If the paper moves before you are finished, it's best to erase the lines that transferred and begin again. When you've finished, peek again to be sure the transfer is complete. If so, carefully remove the tape from the page and set the tracing paper aside. There you have it—a whole beetle on your page with half the effort.

B Compare this new side of the beetle to the reference image. Adjust any areas that are similar but not perfectly symmetrical in the reference. For instance, you'll see that the spots are actually slightly different shapes. If you add these slight natural differences to your drawing, the insect will look more realistic. Once you've reviewed each line, add all remaining anatomical details on

both sides of the midline and erase the midline on the head and thorax. Before you move on, be sure that the value of the remaining drawing lines appear dark enough to see through a water wash but light enough to blend into the illustration when it is complete.

7 A To draw extremities of the beetle with accurate proportions, measure in the same way that you did to create the body. I usually start with the leg farthest from my dominant hand. To begin, determine the predominant angle of the leg by laying your pencil directly on top of the reference image and aligning the edge of the pencil with the angle of the leg. As you do, let your pencil also overlap the beetle's body so that you can look for other features that intersect this line. I found that the corner of the white spot on the thorax and the left side of the scutellum are all connected. Use this information to create this line on your page.

Next, find the length of the leg. Since you have already confirmed the proportions of the beetle, it's possible to use a measurement other than the midline-to-side dimension to mark these small features. I chose the width of the spot on the left to determine the length of the legs. If you measure the upper leg from the edge of the thorax on the reference image, you should find that the first length ends just beyond the tibia, while the second length lands just shy of the claws. Use your measurement of the spot to mark these points along the diagonal line on your drawing.

Before you draw the anatomy of the leg, look at the shape of the negative space around the leg on the reference. This helps you observe the actual form of the leg and lessens any confusion created by foreshortening. Create a quick ten-second gesture of the whole leg on the page. Then, starting close to the body, draw each part of the leg out to the claws. Check width measurements as

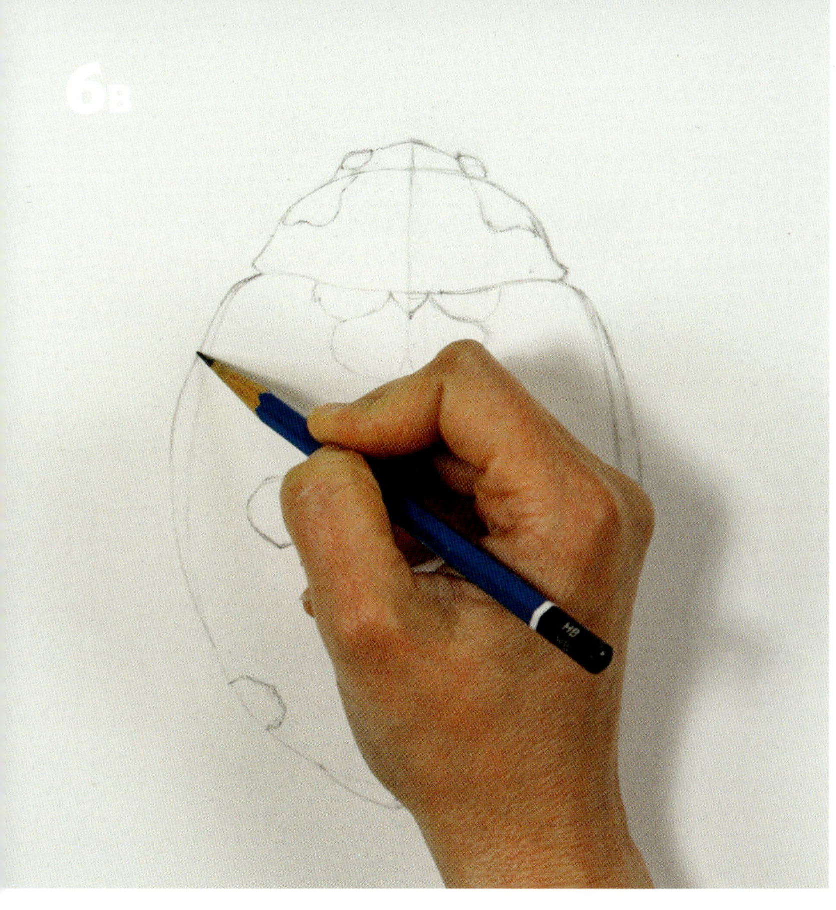

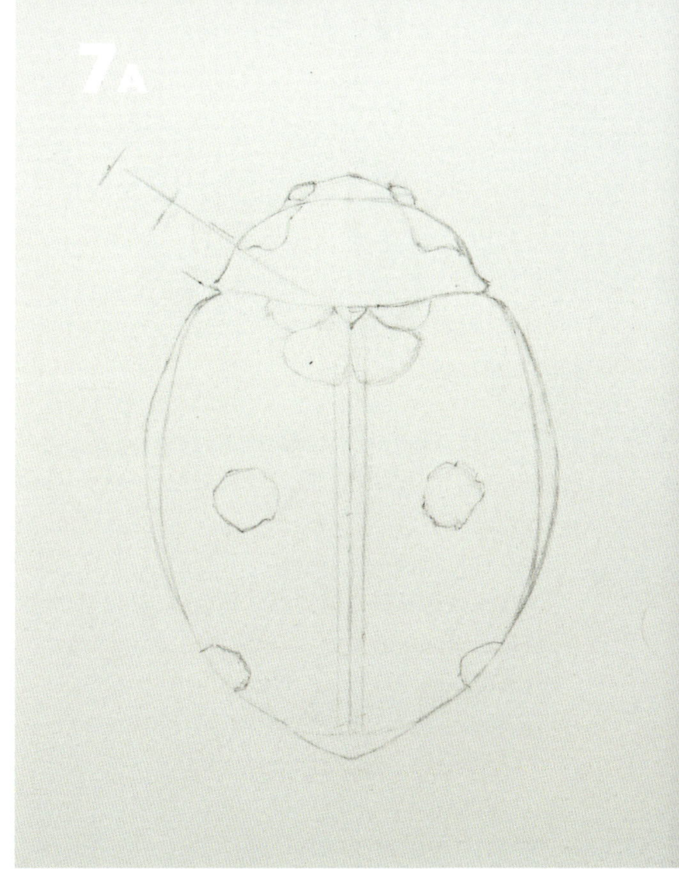

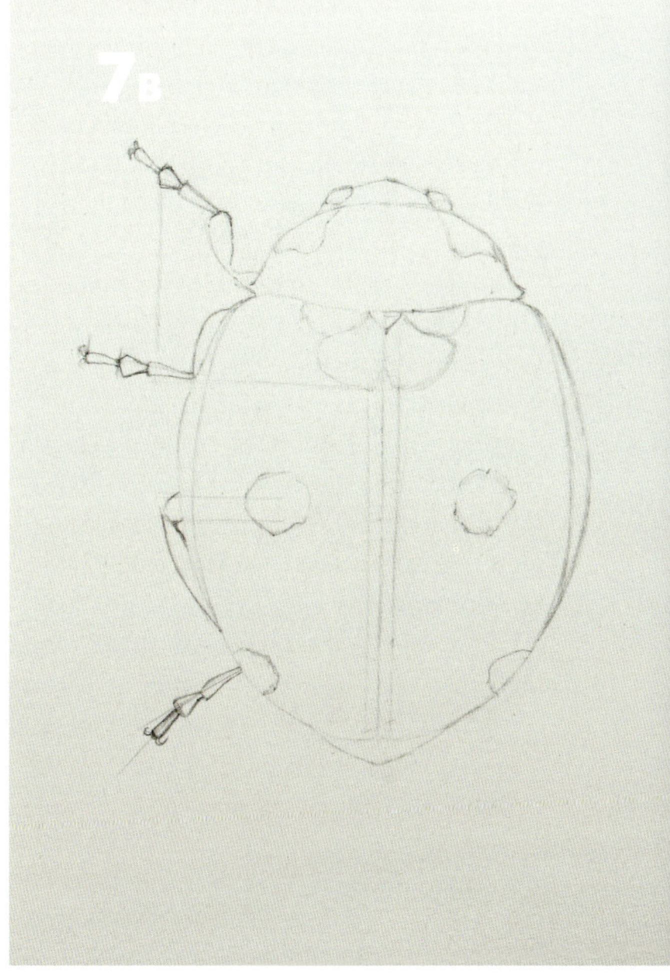

you go. Since this is such a small distance, I used the length of one eye to measure. When you draw these shapes accurately on your page, you create the illusion of depth, and your beetle will appear slightly elevated. Because of the dramatic angle you are seeing the shapes from, you may find portions of the leg are much shorter, thicker, or more tapered than you expected them to be. In general, if your drawing is lacking depth, check the accuracy of the extremities.

B After you have drawn the leg, erase all extra lines. You might draw vertical lines from the top leg to help determine the anatomical placement of each leg below. Though you might assume a transfer sheet would come in handy to draw the remaining legs and antennae, I recommend you take the time to draw each one individually. It's a relatively simple way to add character to the beetle and, simultaneously, to your composition.

You did it! The drawing portion is complete.

PAINTING

1 **A** Transition your workstation by setting your drawing materials aside and arranging your painting supplies. This quick reorganization can make it easier to locate items quickly, avoid unintentional marks or spills, and keep supplies in good condition. Be sure that you have clean water to work with while you paint.

Apply a pea-sized amount of each listed paint color along the side of your palette. Using a size 3 paintbrush, mix Mars black paint with a small amount of titanium white paint in the center of your palette to create a very dark gray. This color will appear black when you apply it to the paper and will enable you to further darken this area using colored pencil later in the process. Add one drop of acrylic retarder to the paint mixture to slow the drying process. Dip your brush in water and dilute the paint mixture until the pigment merely stains a scrap of watercolor paper with a rich, dark color. (If the layer of paint is too thick and dries with a sheen, you'll have difficulty applying colored pencils on top.)

B Use a size 0 paintbrush and fill the entire outline of a single leg with a thin wash of water, just enough to make the paper glisten evenly. Avoid the claws at this point, because you can create a more defined tip if you add them with a sharp pencil later in the process. Before the wash dries, use the same size paintbrush to place the black mixture in the darkest areas of this leg, and allow the color to bleed into the highlighted areas so they are slightly lighter. When this leg is finished, repeat these steps to complete the lower legs on this side of the beetle only.

C Next, add a similar wash of water to the entire thorax, including the light-colored spots. Now carefully add the black mixture to the center and edges of the thorax. Avoid the boundary of the light-colored spots until the rest of the thorax

has paint so that the amount of bleeding into this area is minimal.

D When the thorax has dried, use the same technique to darken the head, being careful to leave the small highlight along the thorax and the lighter areas on the eyes. Next, paint the spots on the abdomen, so that their placement can be easily seen after you add the red paint. Instead of adding a wash to the entire abdomen, you can either paint directly on the dry paper or add a wash that overlaps the outline around each spot and blend the color into the surroundings. To show you the difference between these two techniques, I used a wash for the spot on the right and created a hard edge for the left one. Finally, paint the remaining legs on the other side of the beetle, starting again with the top leg. Let all paint areas dry completely and replace rinse water if needed.

2 **A** With the dark areas complete, you can more accurately discern the colors and values of the wings. In this step, we'll create all of the paint mixtures in advance so you can seamlessly focus on painting. You might need to add a little water to the black paint mixture to keep it workable.

Use a size 3 paintbrush to combine cadmium red paint with just enough permanent green light paint to lower the saturation slightly. Add a drop of acrylic retarder to this base color, then divide this mixture into thirds. Leave one the original color, add some cadmium yellow paint to the second to create a bright red color, and stir in a bit of burnt umber to the final third for a dark red mixture. Paint a sample of each color on a scrap piece of paper, hold the colors over your illustration, and compare each one to the colors in the reference image. If the white of the paper is distracting, apply the red paints along the edge of the swatch and hover it over the black of the thorax. Make slight color adjustments to each paint mixture, if needed. Next, quickly mix the yellow paint color

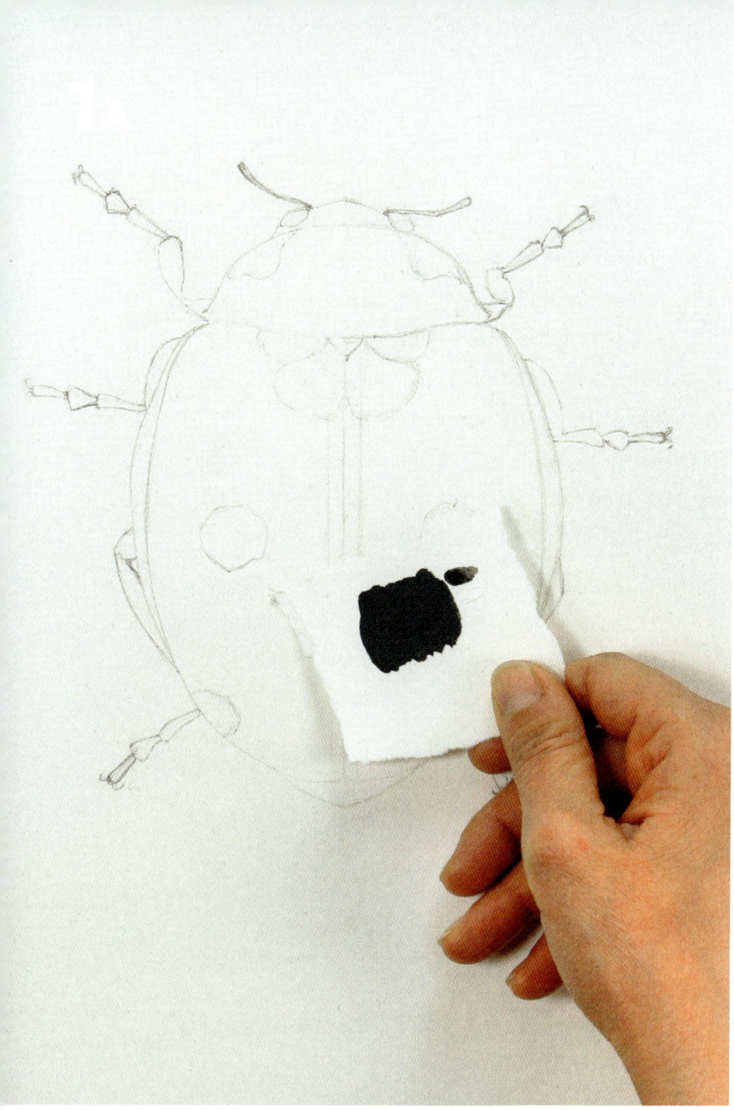

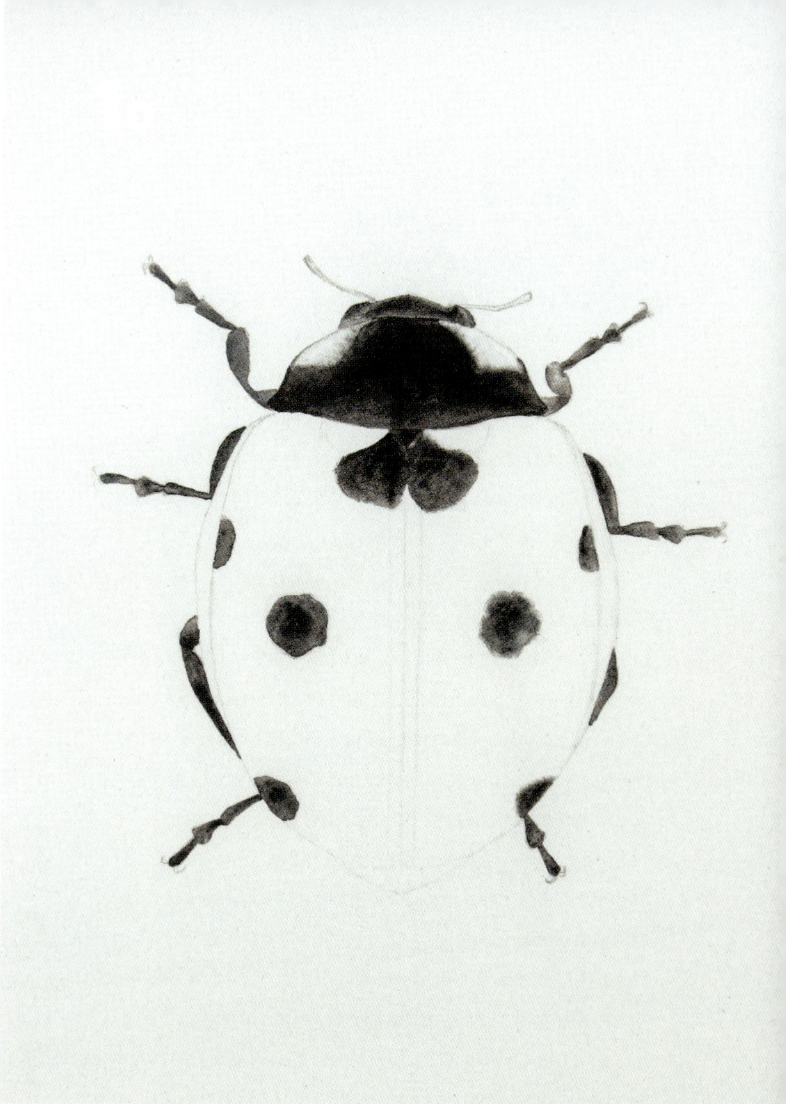

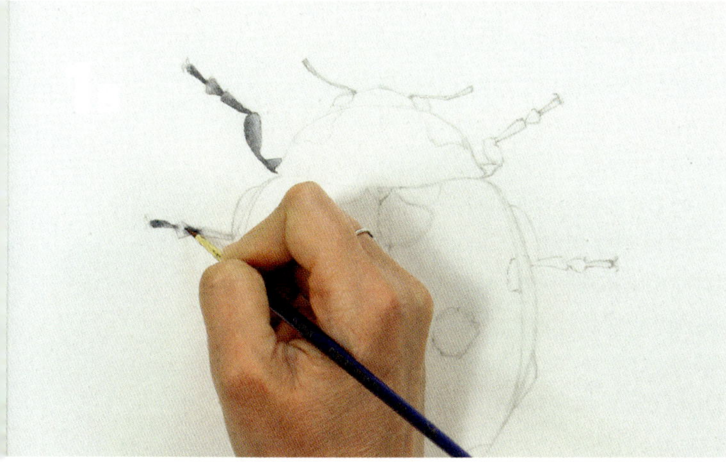

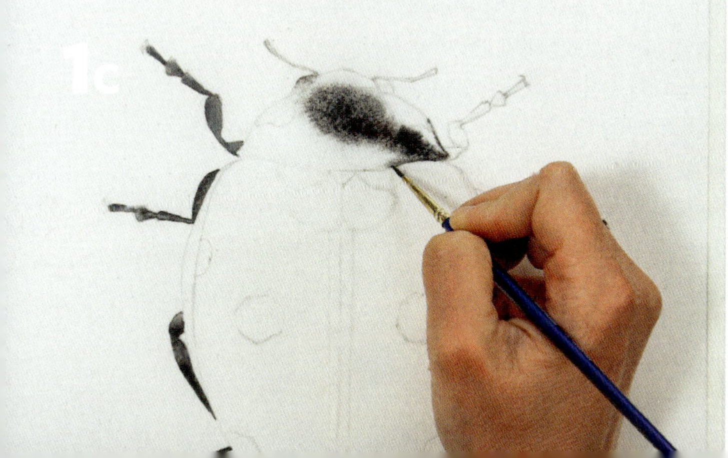
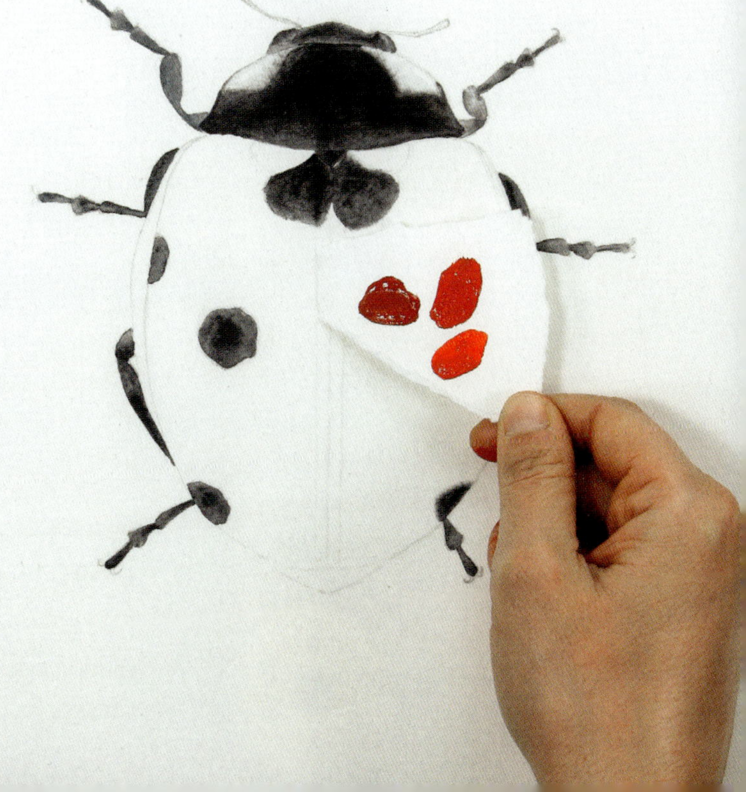

that borders the light-colored spots by combining Naples yellow with cadmium yellow and then adding a small amount of titanium white. Place a small separate amount of black paint on the palette and add water to achieve a consistency similar to that used for the legs. Finally, place a tiny amount of Titian buff paint near the side of your palette, just enough to cover the two light spots on the abdomen.

B At this point, the black paint on your beetle should be completely dry. Grab a size 3 paintbrush and brush a water wash over the entire back of the beetle, covering all the spots. Be careful to coat right up to, but not over, the boundary line. If water begins to pool in any area, soak it up with a separate clean, damp paintbrush.

Since this is a large area with several colors, strive to work quickly and glance at the reference image often. First, use the yellow mixture to paint the arcs that will divide the light-colored spots from the red. Then immediately fill the spots using a bit of Titian buff paint. Although you will need to let this area dry slightly, you can add a small amount of water to keep the rest of the wings glistening. When the light-colored spots start to turn dull, apply the bright red paint mixture in an even coat to the rest of the abdomen, including the dark spots. At this point, ignore the highlights entirely because you will add them later using colored pencil. As you approach the light-colored spots, notice how much the color bleeds. If the red begins to spread into the yellow area, use a clean, damp brush to remove the excess color.

C While the red paint is still wet, add your mid-tone red paint mixture to the center of the wings, toward the end of the abdomen, and on the "shoulders," leaving the section between the midlines light. Continue with the dark red mixture to accentuate the lines near the midline, at the base of the abdomen, and anywhere else that should be painted a deeper shade of color, as indicated on the reference image.

D Before the red paint has dried completely, use the black paint mixture to make all seven spots more vibrant. Although the edge of the spots will blend slightly, you should be able to define the shape of each spot as you paint. At this time, you may want to darken the triangular scutellum, but be sure to leave a hair-thin line unpainted along the edges so that it will remain separated from the dark area on the abdomen. Allow the paint to dry completely.

Working with wet materials and drying time is not easy, but you did it. Great job. Now transition your workspace from paint to colored pencil.

LAYERING WITH COLORED PENCIL

1 A Carefully remove the artist tape so you can freely rotate your image as you draw. Ideally your colored pencils match both the reference image and your paint. But if the perfect color match is not available, refer to your color chart (see page 24) and choose the pencils that are best suited to your illustration. If your colors vary from those suggested, you might want to make a note of what you have replaced them with to avoid confusion later. Then sharpen the tip of each chosen pencil.

B It's best to work on the main part of the beetle first and save the more refined anatomy for the end. Use a ruler and the terra-cotta pencil to refine the three midlines in the lower section of the abdomen. Vary the line weight of all three, so that they become lighter toward the thorax. Use the terra-cotta to blend the two outer lines into the surrounding area on either side of this midsection. As you work, notice the placement of highlights, and avoid these areas so that the white pencil will stay pure and not mix with red when applied. Use the black raspberry pencil to emphasize the darkest

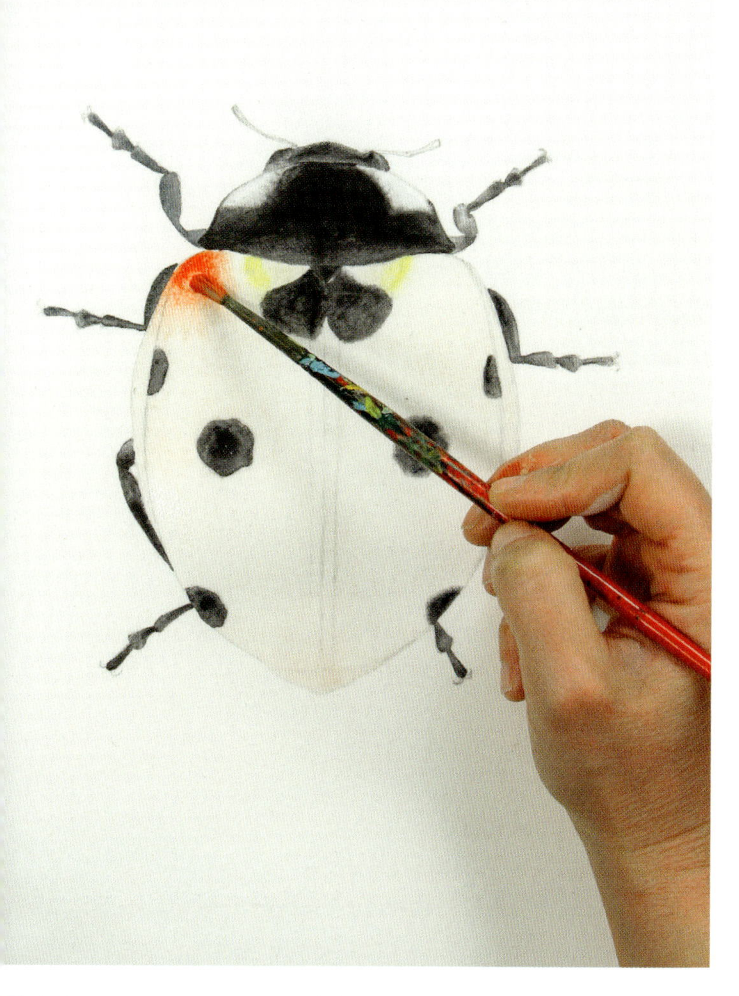
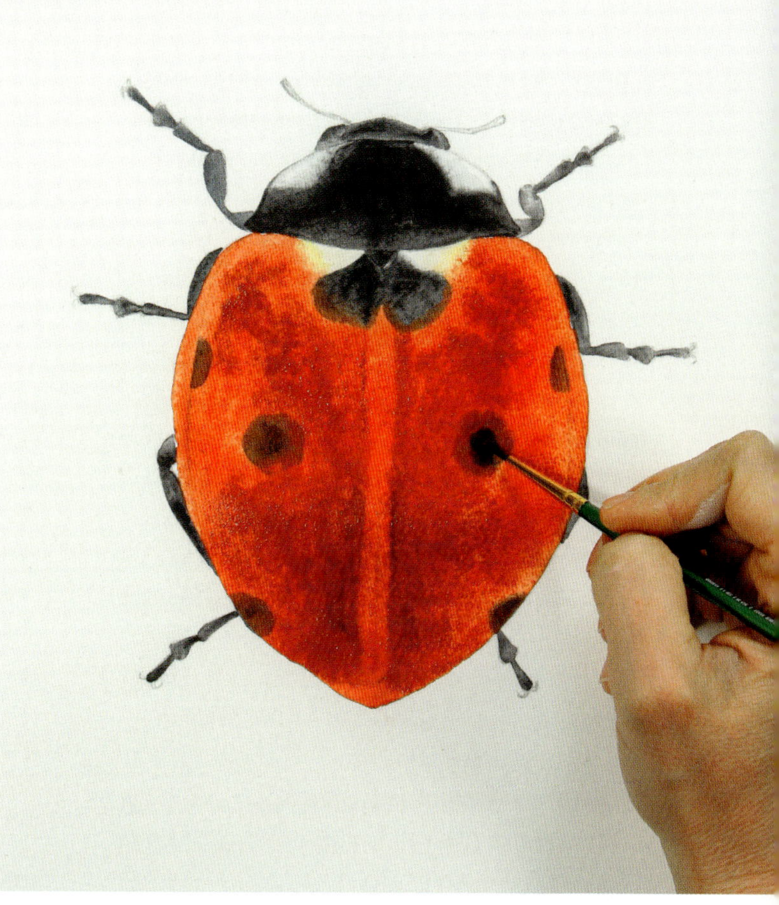
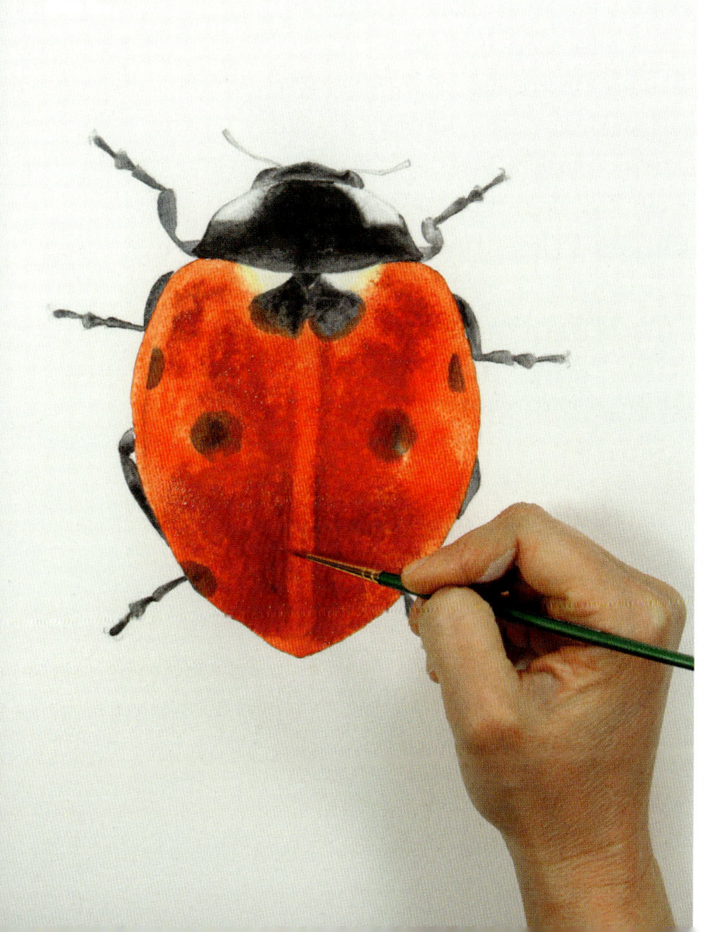
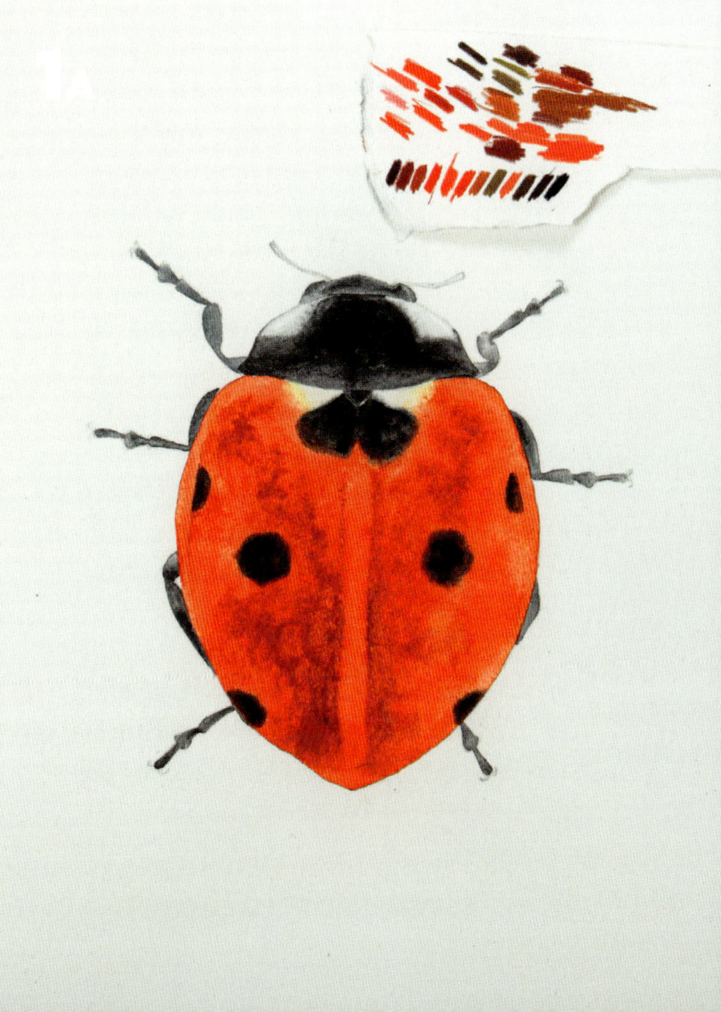

areas of the midlines, being careful to keep your pressure light, as this color can easily become too dark. At this point in the process, avoid using an eraser, which can pull up the paint beyond repair.

Periodically hold your picture at arm's length, blur your vision, and compare your work to the reference image. Look for other areas where you can apply additional pencil to your drawing.

C Switch to using the cream pencil, and add a thin line along the edge on both sides of the upper half of the abdomen, to separate the red from the black on the legs. As you work around the abdomen, begin to fade the cream pencil color into the red. Then switch to the scarlet lake pencil and add the red-orange color to the flanges on the insect's sides. Rotating your page lets you draw these refined arcs with a comfortable hand position. Continue with the same pencil to brighten the red in certain areas, such as the area that borders the white spots or the area to the side of the black dot in the center of each wing.

D Switch to using a light gray pencil, such as a 10% French gray, to add highlights to the sides, center, and other areas where the light is reflected. You might create an overall shape first and then fill it in. Be sure, however, to keep the outline almost invisible so that the line disappears completely as you fade into the surrounding area. If you use the side of the pencil lead, the tooth of the paper will make the wings look realistically textured. If you switch to the point of the pencil where the highlight is brightest, it will fill in depressions in the paper and create a shiny look. When working on the highlight at the bottom of the abdomen, allow the gray to go all the way to the end of the painted area so that this area starts to blend into the surrounding white paper. This enhances the illusion of the curve while de-emphasizing the area so that the upper body becomes the focus of the composition. Now switch to using the pure white pencil to add the "hot spots," blending the white into the gray. Return to using the 10% French gray pencil to

create a smoother transition to these bright highlights, if necessary.

Before moving on, hold the paper at arm's length. Take a moment to look at the highlights you've created, this time *without* comparing what you see to the reference image. Are there any areas you might adjust to make the beetle look more real or refined? I added more of the cream pencil to the sides, dark umber to the end of the abdomen, and small highlights at the top of the midline at the edge of the scutellum. This additional finesse, though seemingly small, can enhance the lifelike quality of your beetle.

When you have completed the abdomen, move into the thorax to create the highlights using the same techniques and colors.

2 A Now that the highlights are finished on the main portion of the body, use a sharp black pencil to enhance the back edge and sides of the thorax. As you draw, let the line weight lighten toward the head. Move to the eyes and enhance them in a similar way. Review the reference image again and look at the painting on its own to see if the center of the thorax, the abdomen spots, or any other dark areas need adjustment.

Before you work on the legs, carefully erase any pencil lines that are visible beyond the paint, but leave the claws in place. While you are drawing, your hand will often be on top of the beetle's body, so you might place a piece of tracing paper on the illustration to protect it. Hold this paper in place while you draw to prevent smudging.

B When you are ready, use the cream pencil to add all the leg highlights. Allow your pencil pressure to create a range from dim to bright highlights. Next, use a medium brown pencil, like burnt ocher, for a touch of color, especially on the second segment.

You are nearly there. As you add the final touches, slow down and finesse with care so that these details enhance your beetle illustration.

Keeping the pencil point very sharp, use a dark gray, such as 50% French gray, to draw the claws

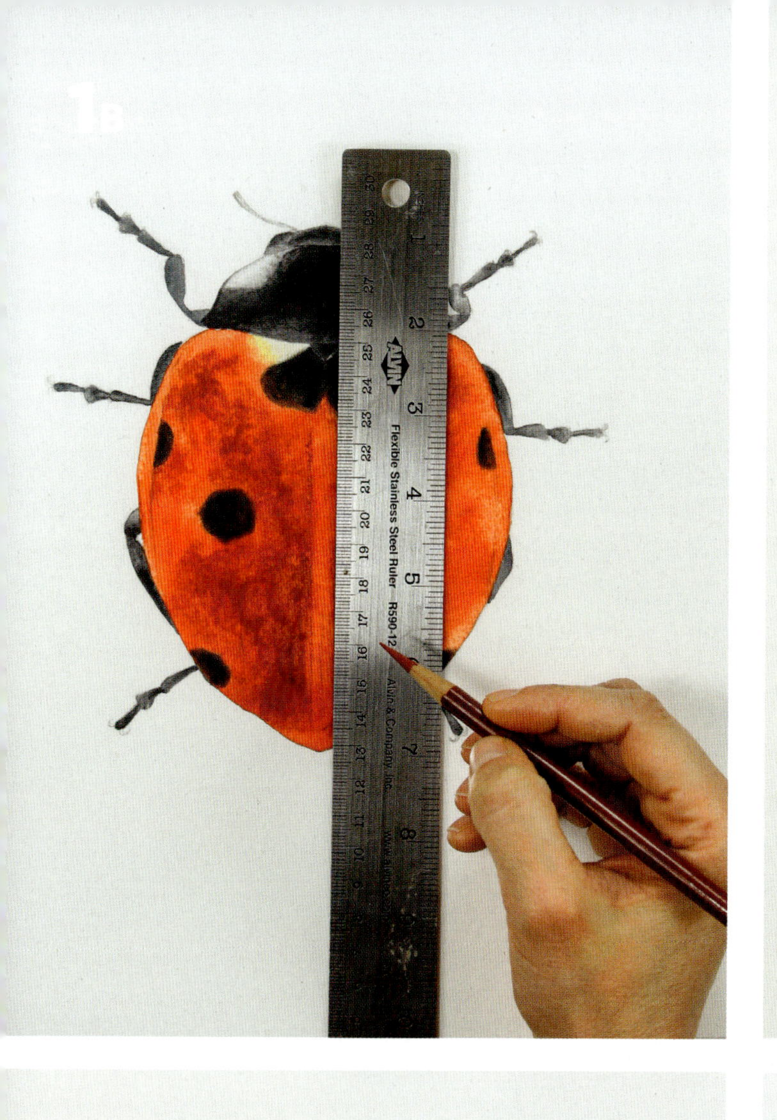
1a

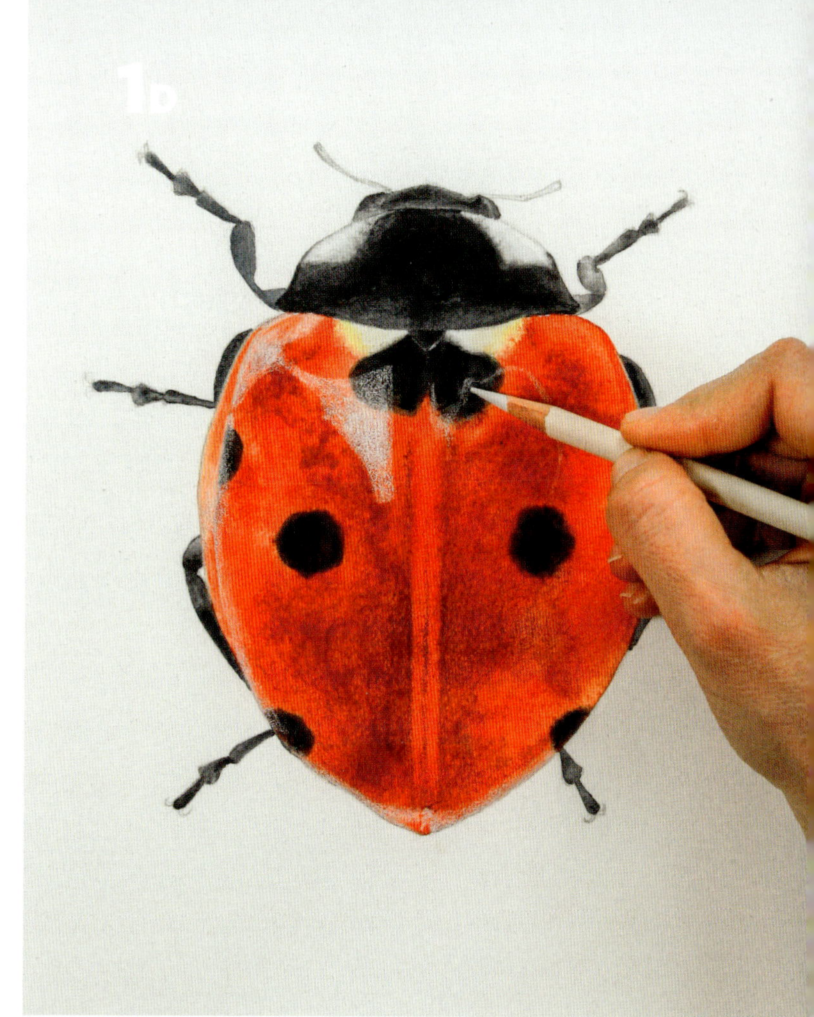
1b

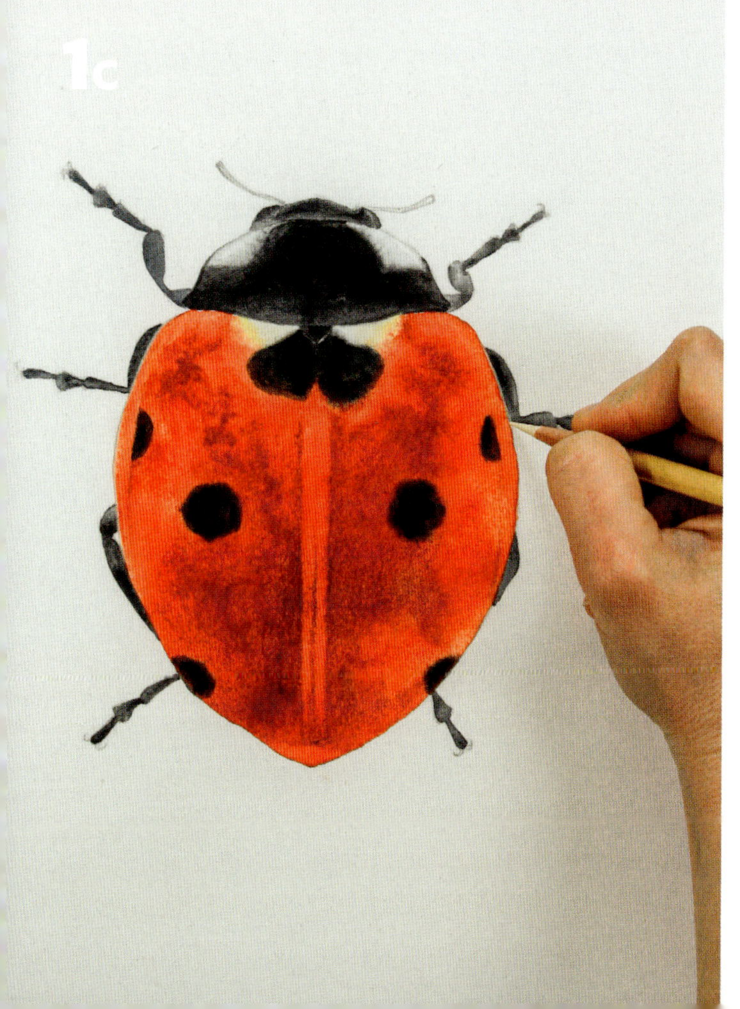
1c

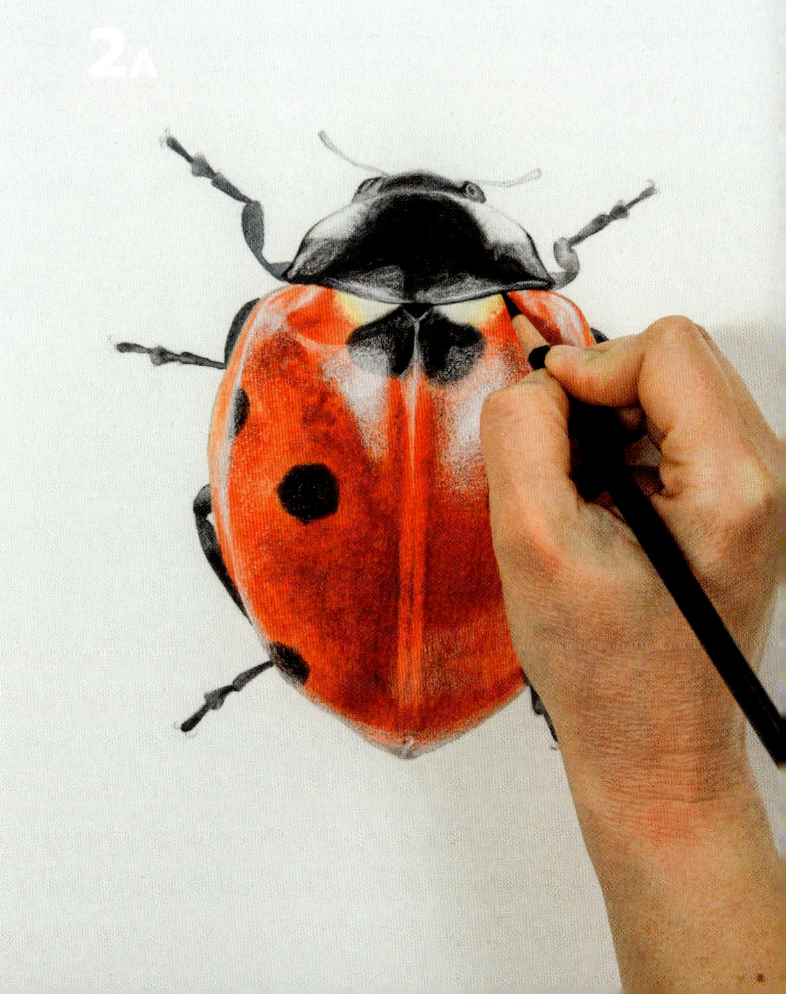
2a

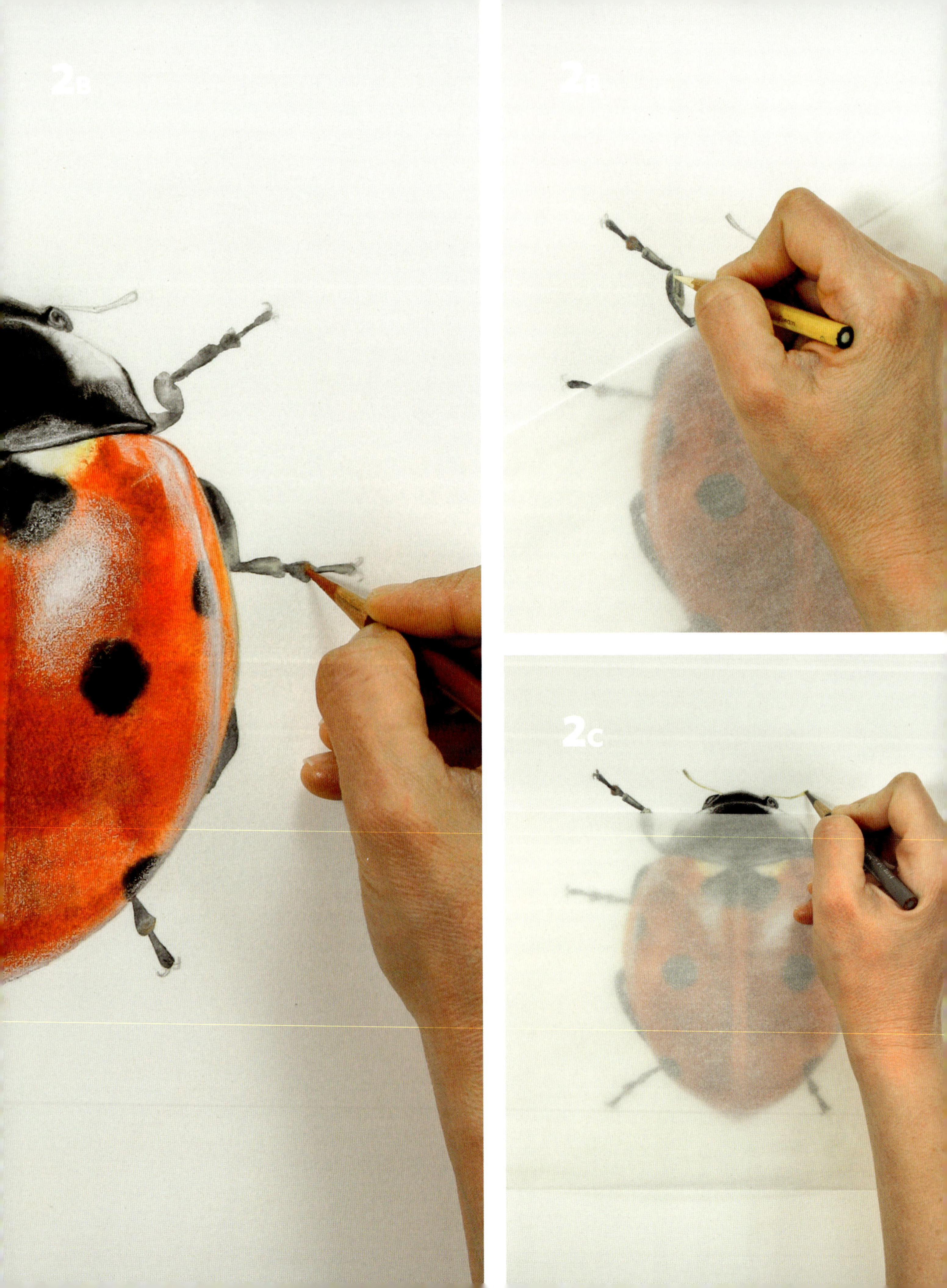

2b
2a
2c

and to clean up the edges of the legs. You may find that the 70% French gray or black is more effective in certain areas. Because it is such a strong color, use this deep shade carefully and sparingly.

C Now move to the antennae and erase the pencil marks enough to leave only a ghost of a line behind. Use the jasmine pencil to fill in both antennae. Keep the color lighter toward the base and darker at the end. To further enhance the ends, use the 50% French gray pencil and a bit of burnt ocher to smoothly transition from one color to the other. You can also add a small shadow using the 50% French gray pencil, with a very sharp tip, to draw a thin line along the side of the antennae closest to the body. This will emphasize the volume of the extremities.

Carefully look over the entire drawing. Compare it first to the reference image, and then examine on its own to see if anything can be added or adjusted. It was at this point in my project that I noticed the tiny dark reflection of the legs that shows on the wings. I added these reflections using the 50% French gray and black pencils.

As you work on these finishing touches, be mindful of the tendency to continue adding more and more details and, as a result, never finish a piece. For this reason, I only add significant details that slipped past my earlier observations. If you sense that your illustration is finished or starting to look overworked, trust your instincts and stop embellishing it. Sign the front, date the back, and spray with fixative, if desired.

Congratulations on completing a beautiful work of art. This is a great accomplishment!

NATURE BREAK, OBSERVATION

AMONG THE FLOWERS

By observing the anatomy of living insects, you can make your drawings more lifelike. This Nature Break is devoted to seeking out an abundance of butterflies. It's time to nestle in among the flowers.

LOCATION: Find a large garden, in full bloom, or locate a butterfly house in your area. You may need to request permission to work in the garden, but I find many public gardens and large exhibits welcome artists.

MATERIALS: When I sketch in a populated place, I often bring only a pencil, a manual pencil sharpener (with a waste catch), an eraser, and a sketchbook.

OBSERVATIONS: Notice both the energy level and behavior of the insects. Also consider the light and temperature of the environment. Now look more closely at the butterflies. How do the shapes of their anatomy express that they are alert or relaxed, young or old, about to move or in flight?

PRACTICE: Begin to create one- to three-minute gesture drawings. If the butterfly moves before your sketch is complete, leave the drawing unfinished and start another. Can you capture the essence with only a few lines? When you are warmed up and if your subject continues to pose, add more details and work toward a finished drawing. If you evolve the drawing evenly, rather than focus on just one part of the anatomy, every area will be at the same level of completion when the butterfly moves.

If the garden offers a species identification key, jot down the common and scientific names of the butterflies in your sketchbook before you leave.

REFLECTION: Look for areas in each drawing that express aliveness. Think about the techniques you used to achieve that quality, and how you might utilize those strategies in your work when you are unable to observe a living subject.

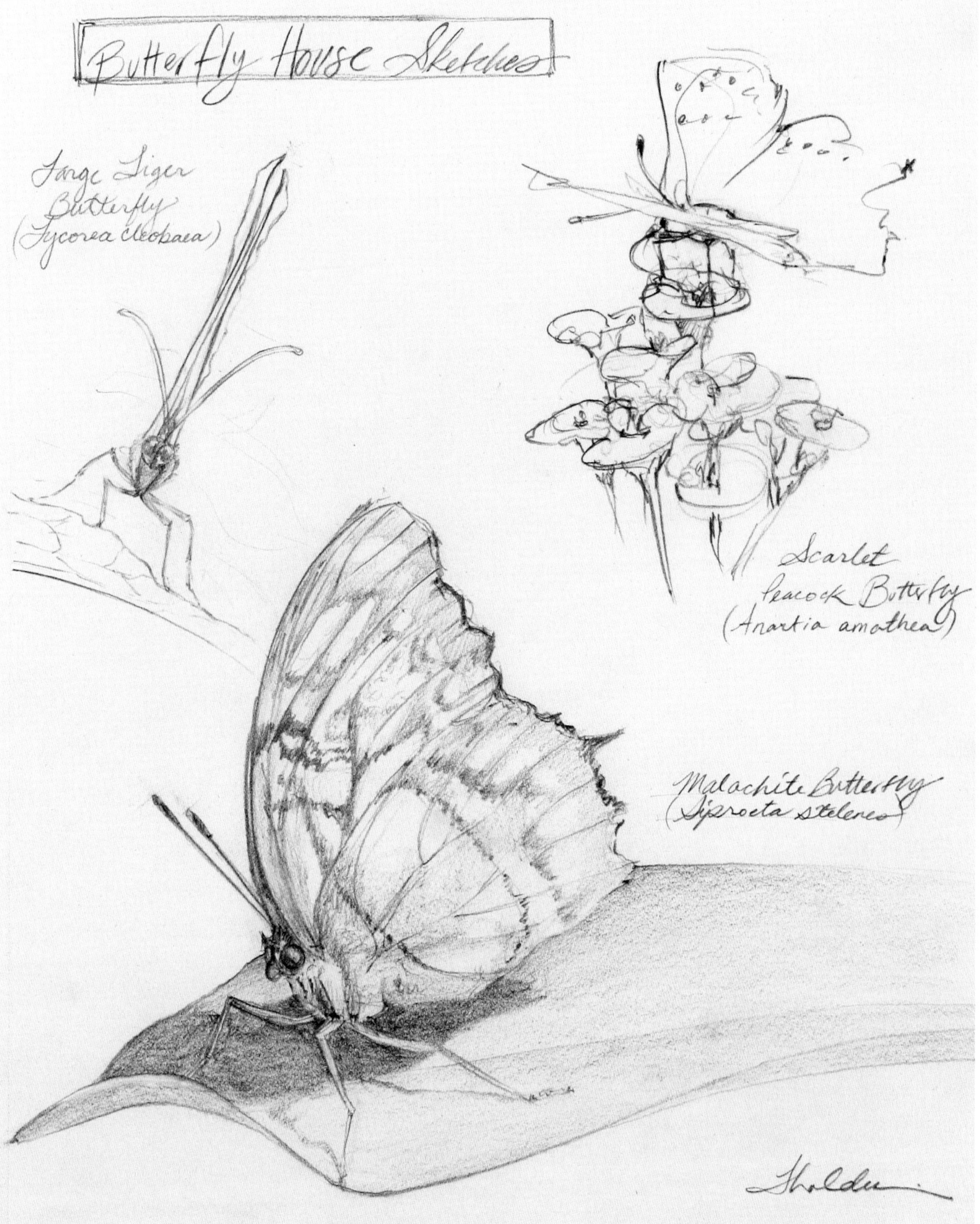

Butterfly House Sketches
Large Tiger
Butterfly
(Lycorea cleobaea)
Scarlet
Peacock Butterfly
(Anartia amathea)
Malachite Butterfly
(Siproeta stelenes)

OLD WORLD SWALLOWTAIL BUTTERFLY

PAPILIO MACHAON

Like many species in the Papilionidae family, old world or common yellow swallowtails are known for their striking and distinctive patterns. The early stages of the caterpillar exhibit incredible mimicry as well. Their coloration brilliantly resembles bird droppings, which offers them protection from predators. Although this species has a wide distribution in northern and western North America and across Eurasia, it is uncommon throughout its range. Similar to many commonly seen swallowtails, the adults have bold tigerlike markings and a dusting of color in the dark sections on their wings. You can replicate the teeny blue and yellow scales by utilizing the texture of the paper and by shifting the position of the pencil in your hand. The black-and-yellow patterns, though they appear complex, give you the ability to divide the large expanse of each wing into smaller sections, which will help you replicate the overall proportions more accurately. You'll be able to paint the subject in layers, which greatly simplifies the creative process.

 SEE REFERENCE PHOTOS ON PAGES 310–311

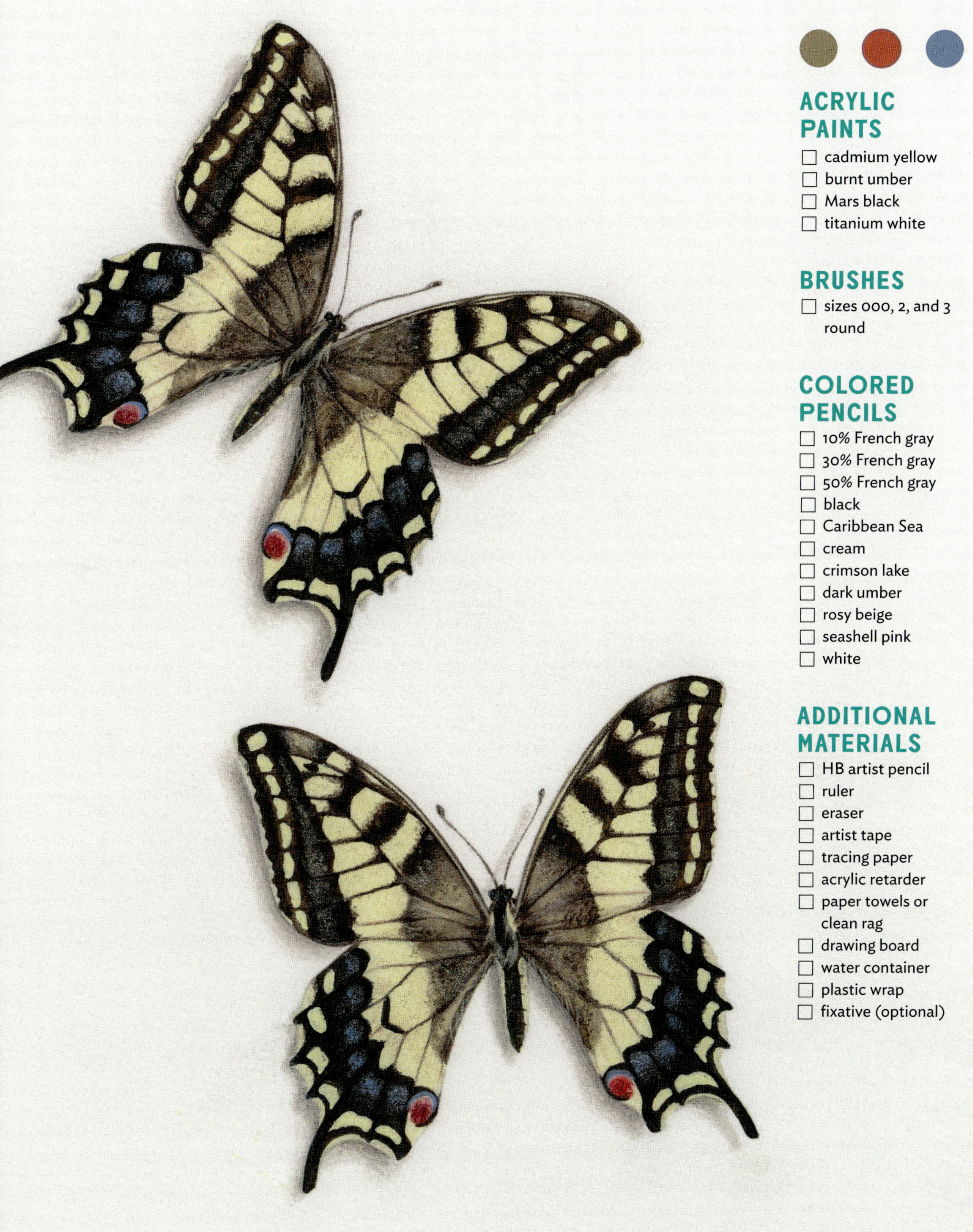

ACRYLIC PAINTS

- ☐ cadmium yellow
- ☐ burnt umber
- ☐ Mars black
- ☐ titanium white

BRUSHES

- ☐ sizes 000, 2, and 3 round

COLORED PENCILS

- ☐ 10% French gray
- ☐ 30% French gray
- ☐ 50% French gray
- ☐ black
- ☐ Caribbean Sea
- ☐ cream
- ☐ crimson lake
- ☐ dark umber
- ☐ rosy beige
- ☐ seashell pink
- ☐ white

ADDITIONAL MATERIALS

- ☐ HB artist pencil
- ☐ ruler
- ☐ eraser
- ☐ artist tape
- ☐ tracing paper
- ☐ acrylic retarder
- ☐ paper towels or clean rag
- ☐ drawing board
- ☐ water container
- ☐ plastic wrap
- ☐ fixative (optional)

DRAWING

1 **A** Prepare your workstation by securing your paper to a drawing board with artist tape and aligning the tape to a faintly drawn ¼-inch border. Then decide if you would rather have one large butterfly in your composition or a couple of smaller butterflies of the same size. Choose where to place your subject on the page. Lightly rough in the overall shape by drawing a midline for each butterfly, then create a quick one-minute gesture drawing to lightly indicate the placement of the body and wings. Take a moment to look at the overall composition; make adjustments if needed. With just these few steps, your artwork is well on its way and you can start to refine the proportions.

If you have two butterflies, work first on the one closest to your dominant hand. Start along the midline and add a dash to mark the location of the tip of the head and another to mark where the abdomen ends. Study the reference image to find the place where the thorax turns into the abdomen. I found that it was located close to the midpoint of the body length. Draw a small arc on your paper to indicate this placement. If your subject is positioned at an angle, you might need to turn your drawing board to keep your hand in a comfortable position.

B Since this butterfly design is symmetrical, you will have the option to mark the wings on a single side and transfer the image to the other side using tracing paper. Either way, locate the line that divides the wings where they meet the body. I found that the wings were attached halfway between the arc of the thorax and the end of the head. Draw a small horizontal line to the side of the midline and erase the initial gesture lines in this area so that only this new line remains.

On the reference image, notice that the head is located a little less than halfway between the wing line and the top of the head. Mark this location on your page.

C Extend the midline above the head and beyond the abdomen, drawing these lines using light pressure so that they can be erased completely at a later time. Using the thumb-and-pencil method (see step 1B on page 40) on the reference image, with the body length as your measurement, determine how many lengths it takes to arrive at the highest part of the wing. I found that the top of the wing was one and a quarter lengths above the head. Adjust your measurement on your pencil to the body length of the drawing, mark one and a quarter lengths up on your midline, and draw a horizontal line from the midline to where the tip of the wing will be drawn. Do the same for the lowest part of the hindwing and the end of the wing's tail. I found the base just after half a length and the tail just before three-quarters of a length. You have completed the vertical dimensions on your butterfly.

2 **A** To determine the width of each area, start with the body, since it is centrally located. Use the reference image to compare the width of the body to the length. I found it to be half of the length of the thorax. Return to your paper, place half of the thorax length on your pencil, turn your pencil horizontally, and mark the sides of the body on your paper.

B Next, on the reference image, align the side of the pencil to the outer edge of the wings and study the contour with one eye closed. Notice that the midsection of both wings is an equal distance from the midline. This would be a good location to measure. See how many reference body lengths it takes to arrive at this line—I found it close to one and one-quarter lengths. Mark this dimension on your page, then draw a vertical line parallel to the midline. Since the tip of the forewing is just beyond this line, you can easily guesstimate the location with vertical or angled marks.

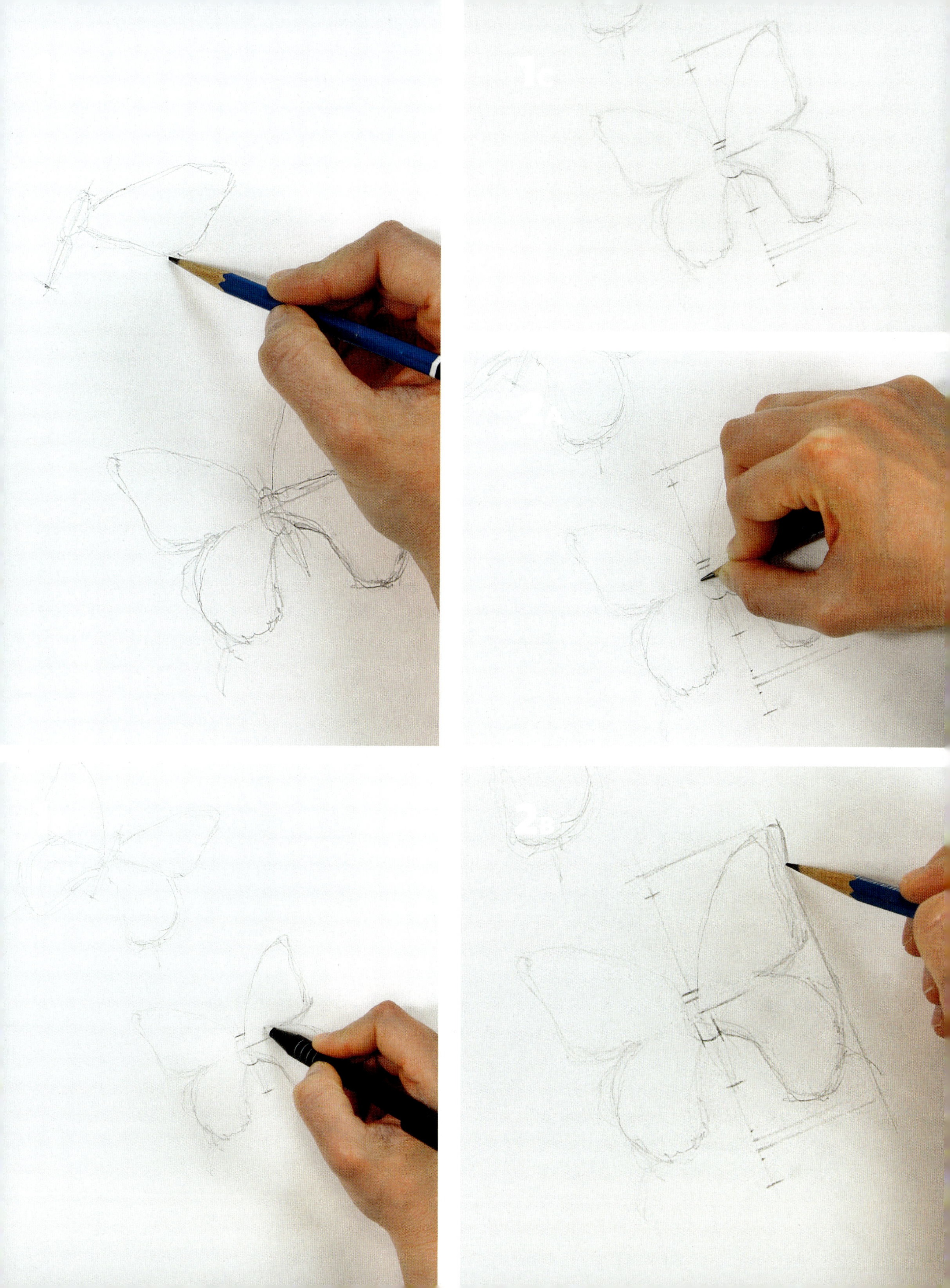

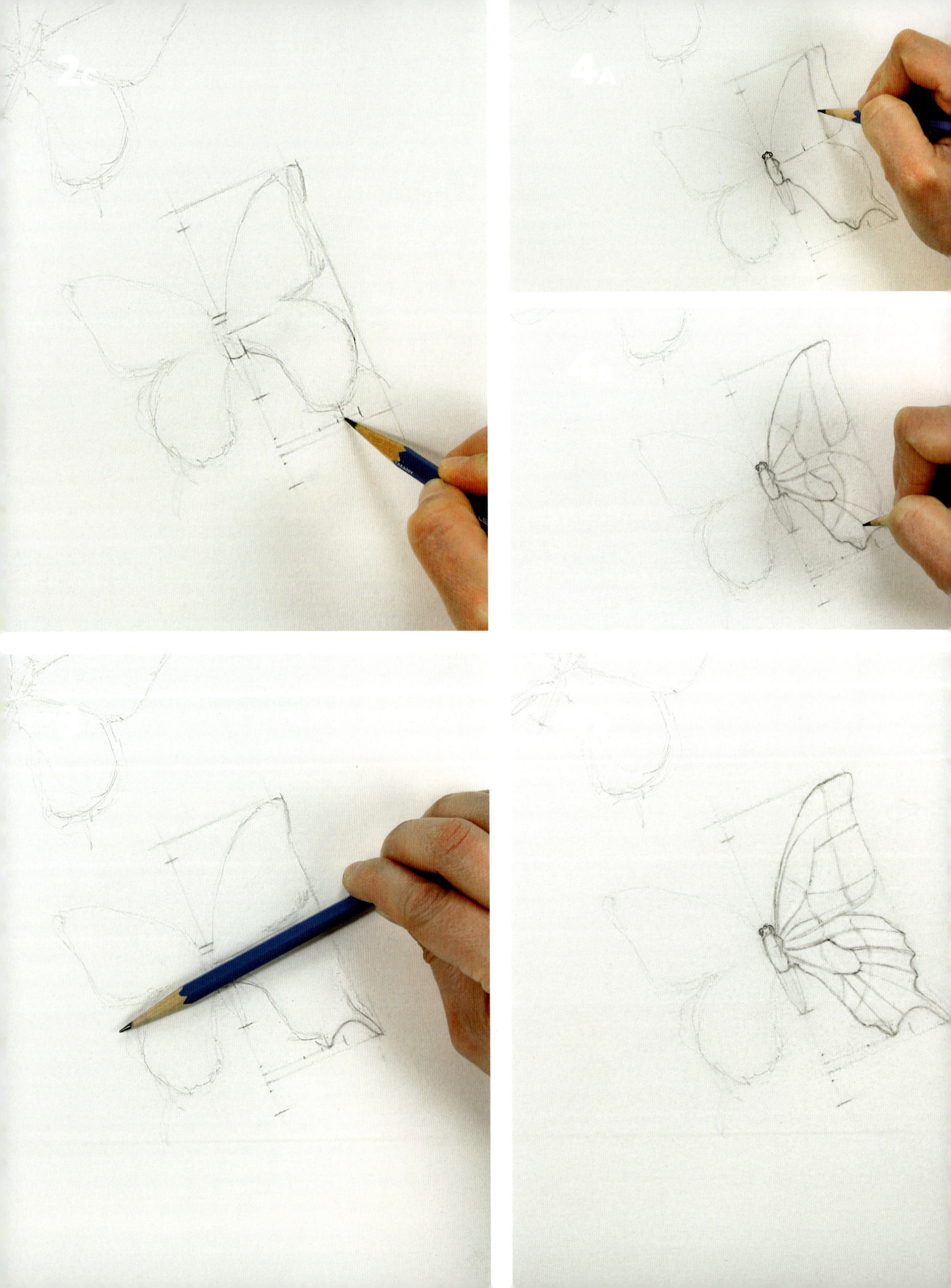
2c
4A
4B

C To define the inner edge of the hindwing, determine the distance between the midline and where the base of the wing begins. I found that it is just past three-quarters of a body length. Place a small vertical mark on your drawing to indicate this location. Also, notice that the tip of the tail aligns with the tip of the forewing. You can measure one and then indicate the other's location simply by drawing a quick vertical line.

3 Find the angle of the line between the wings. Place the reference image so that the butterfly is in the same orientation as your drawing and hold your pencil above the image at the correct angle. Then, without changing the position, pull the same angle over to your drawing. Let your pencil hover over this area so that you can imagine the line on your page, then quickly use the pencil to re-create this angle on your drawing. Repeat this step to be sure that the angle and placement of this line is accurate.

Measure, from the midline, the point where the wings come together and start to overlap. Add a mark to your page to indicate this placement, then pull the downward angle of the hindwing from the reference image to your drawing page. Before you move on, erase all gesture lines in this area. Hooray—the proportions are now complete!

With height as well as width marked on your page, refine the outline of both wings. Allow each wing's negative space to help you replicate the form. Now rough in the shape of the body. Since the body is thin and slightly asymmetrical, draw the outline on both sides of the midline.

4 **A** To draw complex wing patterns, it is helpful to group finite details into large simple shapes. For instance, notice that the wing patterns on this butterfly are divided into three vertical bands with a yellow section in the center. You can mark the place where each band intersects the outline of both wings and then draw the overall shape of each band.

At this time, you can also add the dominant vein toward the center of the wing to determine the placement of other veins. Though you may be tempted to add all the remaining details, pause at this point to reexamine the outline of the forewing and make any needed alterations.

B To add the veins, again divide the overall space first. On the hindwing, start with the vein in the center that extends down the tail and, on the forewing, group two or three cells together. For my forewing, I noticed that the smooth arc that separates the top two cells is roughly equal to the next two cells and that there is a triangular shape created by the bottom two cells, so I drew these veins first.

As you work, observe the shape of each line and the size of each cell on the reference image. Also, look for the alignment of each detail in relationship to the midline to help you position them appropriately.

C Now that the veins are in place and the patterns are grouped together, it is easy to place the tiger stripes and spots in the correct locations. When both wings are complete, check each area to be sure that the overall form, size, shape, and placement of the patterns are correct. Make adjustments as needed. Since antennae are often expressive and can add individuality, I typically wait until both sides of the butterfly are complete to add them.

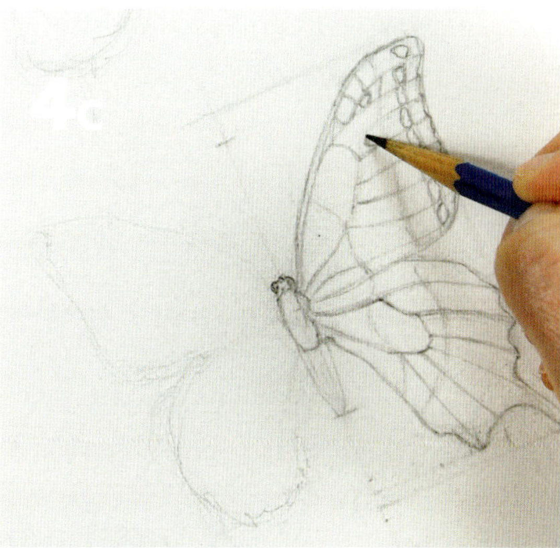

5 **A** It's time to transfer your lines to the opposite side. Erase any remaining gesture lines but be sure to leave the midline in place. Take a piece of tracing paper, lay it on top of your drawing, secure it with artist tape, and trace each line with your pencil. Flip the tracing paper so that the pencil marks are facing the drawing paper. Align the midlines, secure the tracing paper, and draw over each line to transfer the image to your page.

Compare your drawing to the reference image: Are there areas on the second side of the butterfly that differ slightly from the first? Darken your lines on your drawing if needed. The lines for the interior patterns and veins must be dark enough to be seen through a layer of yellow paint, but the outline, where the yellow meets the background, needs to be light enough for the paint color to conceal it.

B If you have a second butterfly, extend the midline slightly on both ends and only mark the tip of the head and the end of the abdomen. Then erase your gesture lines except for the very tips of the forewings. You can reuse the same transfer sheet to replicate both sides of the butterfly or, if you prefer, you can create an entirely new one and transfer the whole butterfly at once. Either way, be sure to include the midline. When your transfer is complete, set aside the tracing paper to reuse at a later time..

Now all you need to do is add both antennae to each butterfly with light pencil pressure. That's it, the drawing portion is complete. Transition your workspace from pencil and prepare to paint.

PAINTING

1 In most compositions, I typically paint the insect's dark dominant color first because it provides an immediate visual structure. In this composition, however, the pattern is so complex and the yellow areas have such even coloration throughout that it's easier to apply the yellow paint first and simply layer the dark pattern on top.

Using a size 3 paintbrush, combine cadmium yellow paint with titanium white on your palette. When you feel that the color is light enough, paint a small amount on the end of a scrap piece of paper, hold it over your drawing and compare it to the reference image. Add a drop of acrylic retarder and enough water so that the pigment becomes a richly colored stain when applied to the watercolor paper. You can draw a few lines on a scrap piece of paper with your pencil and apply a layer of paint on top to be sure it is thin enough. If not, add a little more water.

If your subject is similar in size to mine, switch to a size 2 paintbrush and carefully add a water wash to the area of the wings farthest from your dominant hand. Apply the yellow paint mixture to the entire area, right up to the outline, with the exception of the circle where the red dot will be added. Continue until all of the butterflies have a layer of yellow. Let the paint dry completely. (Cover the yellow paint on your palette with a small amount of plastic wrap to keep the mixture usable for later, if needed.)

2 **A** Return to your size 3 paintbrush to mix a new color in a dry area of your palette. Combine burnt umber with Mars black paint to create the dark brown for the upper wings. Add a drop of acrylic retarder to the mixture, then separate a portion and add more Mars black to that portion to create the darker brown color for the sides of the lower wings. After the paint dries on your scrap paper, draw a line with the black colored pencil to be sure that it will be discernable on your illustration. If the paint mixture is too dark, simply adjust the value using burnt umber.

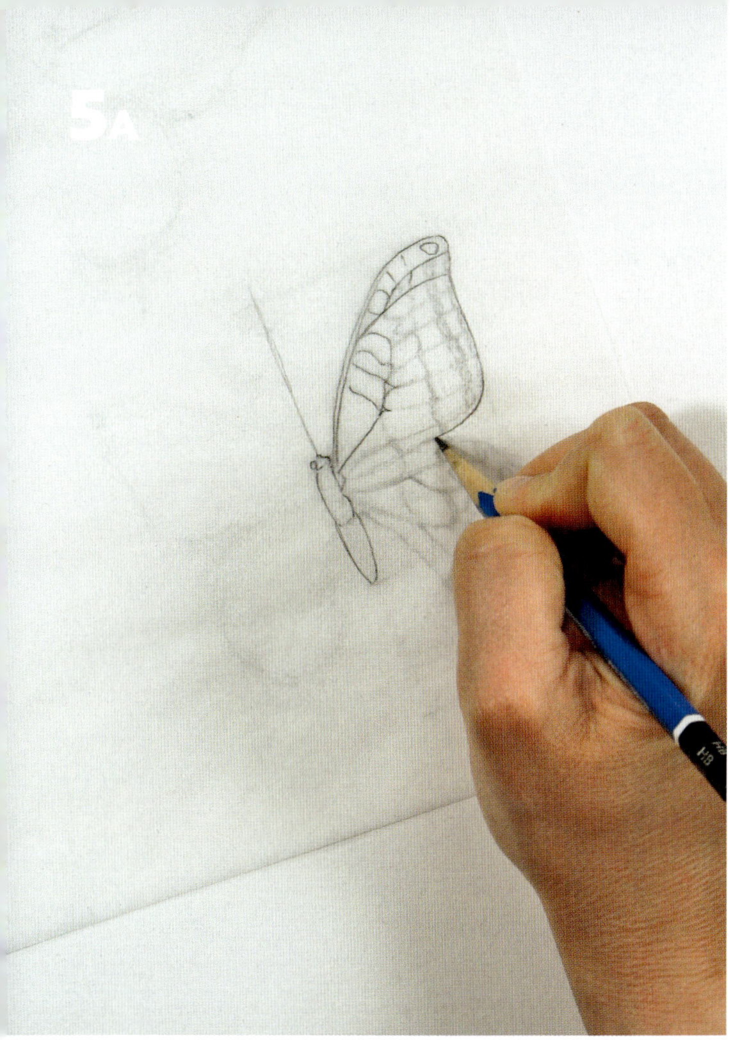

5A

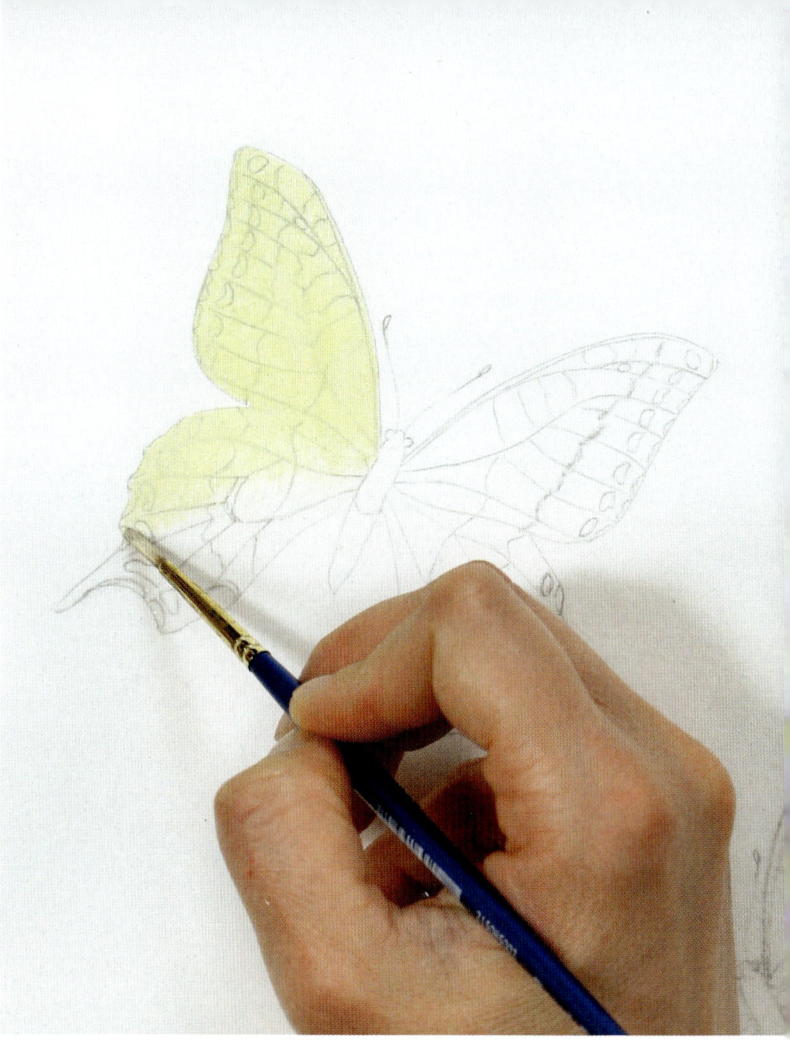

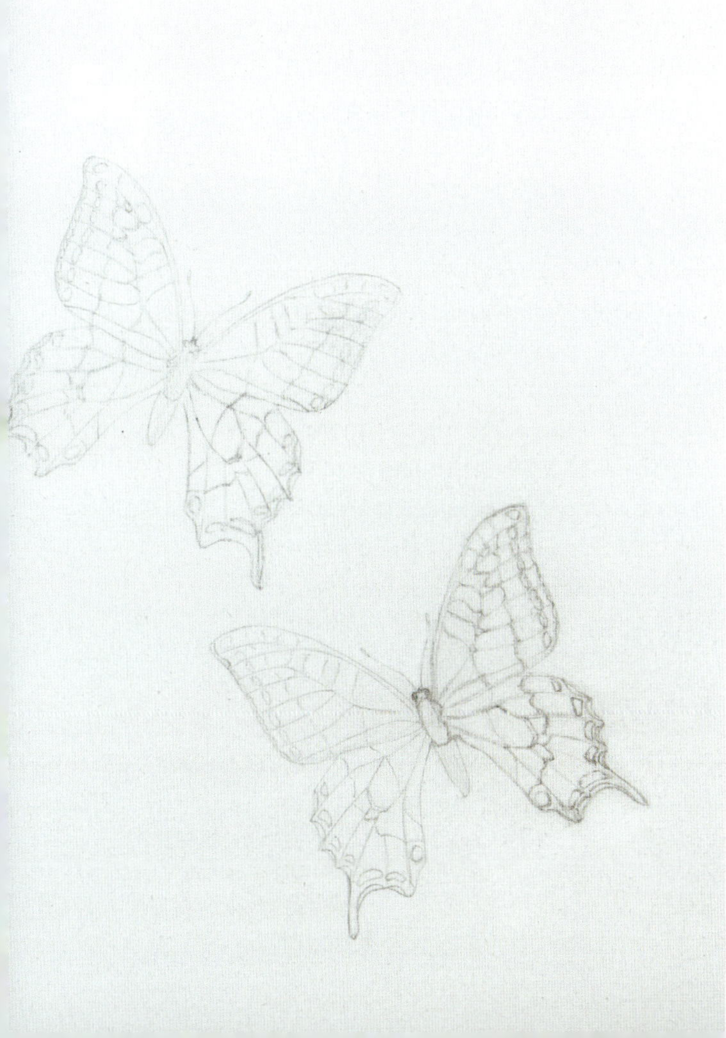

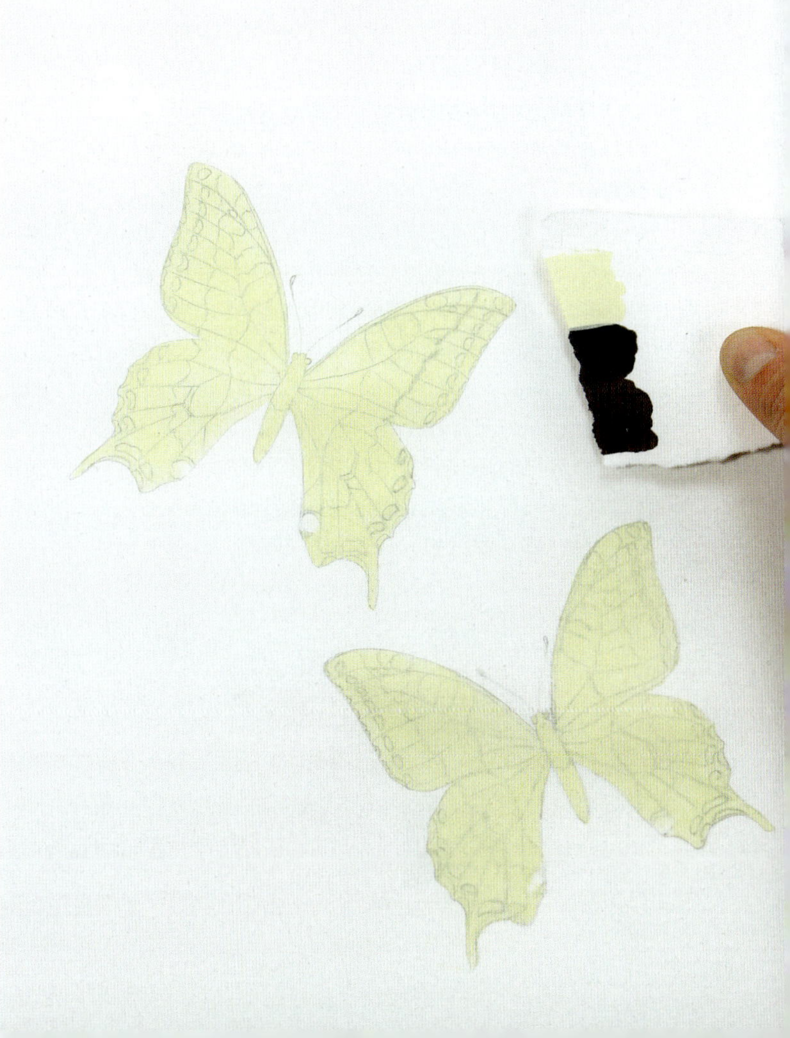

B Apply the paint mixture using an extremely small paintbrush, such as a size 000. Paint one wing at a time, starting at the edge of the forewing farthest from your dominant hand and working in small sections. If you would like to create a hard edge around the dark areas, you can apply the paint directly to the dry surface. In my illustration, I added a water wash, being careful to avoid the areas that would remain yellow. When the wash was beginning to dry, I applied the paint mixture so that I could create a subtle gradation into the surrounding color. If you need a lighter brown, dilute the pigment on your paintbrush with some water and then blot the excess on a paper towel or clean rag.

Some of the edges of the dark areas are speckled with scales as they transition to yellow. To create this effect, you can either stipple using the tip of your brush or wait and add these details in colored pencil later in the process. Either way, be careful to keep this detail small and subtle.

C Before you work on the hindwings, I recommend you complete the forewing on the opposite side and fill in the body.

On each hindwing, apply a water wash only to the light brown section near the body and a small portion of the yellow band, then apply paint to this area. When you paint the dark band along the border, the dry paper will enable you to paint cells individually and leave a hair-thin space between where the veins are located. As you work, you may need to clean your brush occasionally or add water to your palette to keep the paint from drying out and becoming unusable.

D Congrats, you have completed the first butterfly! If you included a second butterfly in your composition, repeat this process. Then let the paint dry completely.

3 Assess the perimeter of the yellow areas—it will be nearly impossible to make any corrections with a light colored pencil on top of dark paint. To adjust the shape or size of these sections, either use the dark brown or yellow paint on your palette. If you need to create another yellow paint mixture, be sure it matches your swatch. (Let the paint sample dry on the swatch before comparing the color to confirm it's an accurate match.) For such small adjustments, you can omit the acrylic retarder and simply touch up the areas with a size 000 paintbrush.

The painting portion is complete! Remove the artist tape and transition your workspace from paint to colored pencil.

LAYERING WITH COLORED PENCIL

1 **A** Begin by working on the forewings, then move to the hindwings. Instead of completing one wing at a time, as you did when you were painting, repeat each process on the opposite wing as you work so that the pair is built up simultaneously.

To begin, use the dark umber pencil with a sharp tip to add the brown veins and define the perimeter of the brown areas, which may need to be smoothed or further stippled. Sharpen the pencil again and define the edge along the interior of the forewing. Rotate your paper as needed to create crisp lines and smooth arcs, and to keep your hand in a comfortable position. Then switch to using the seashell pink pencil to draw in the light veins.

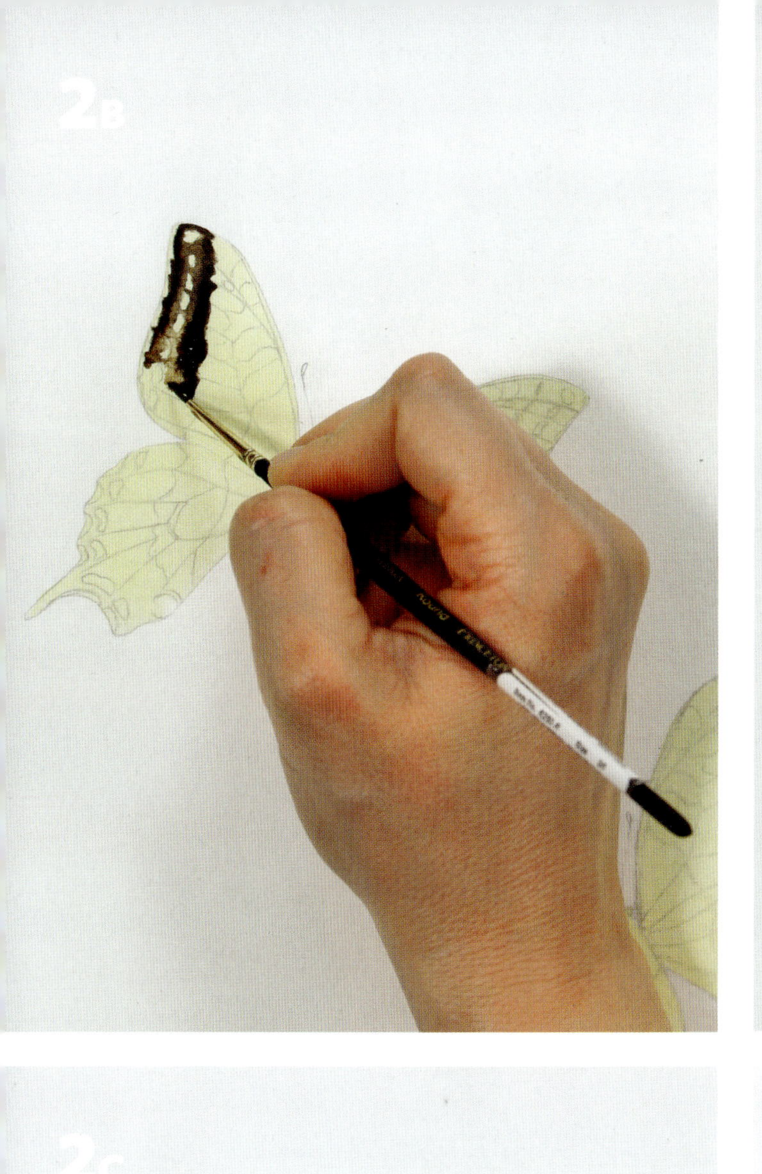
2B

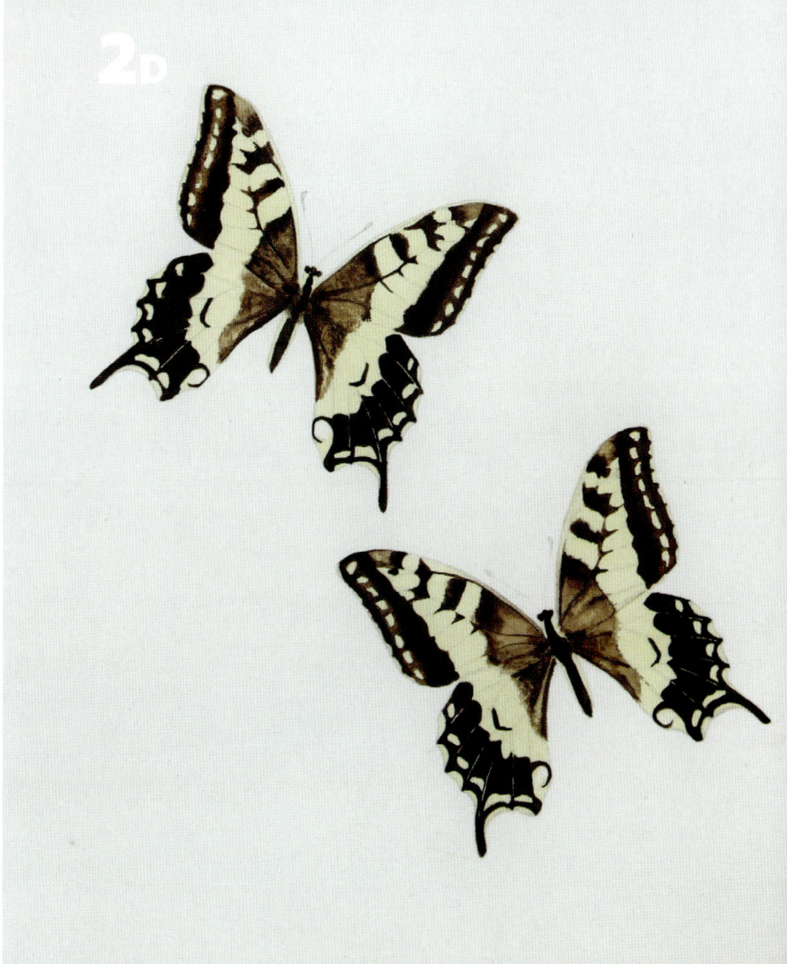
2D

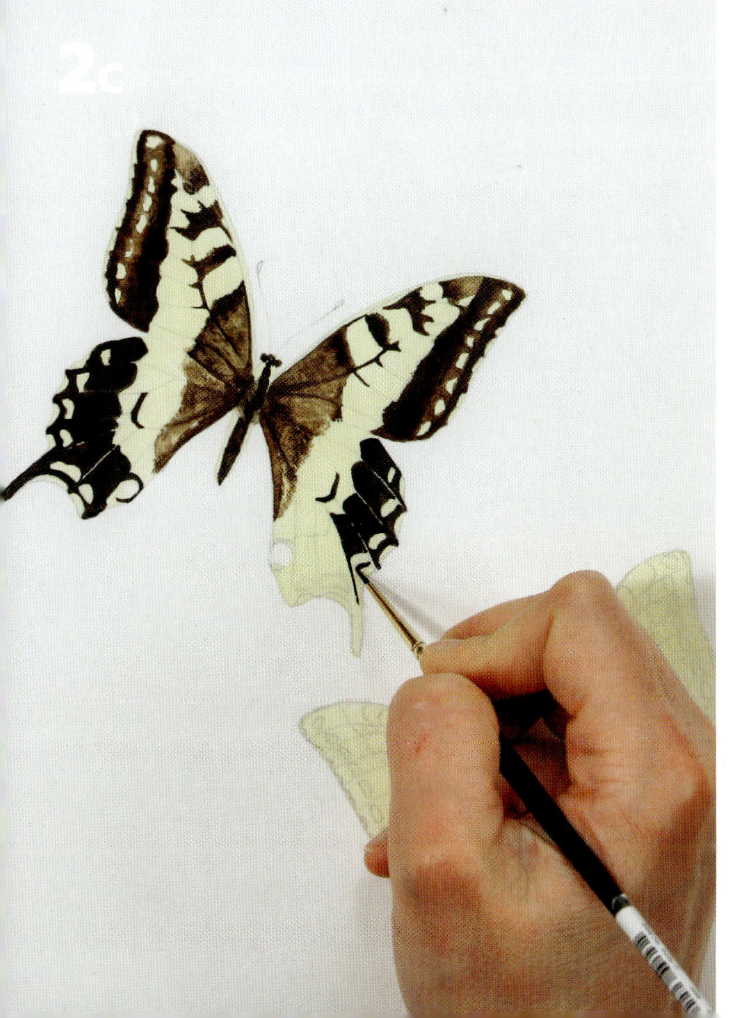
2C

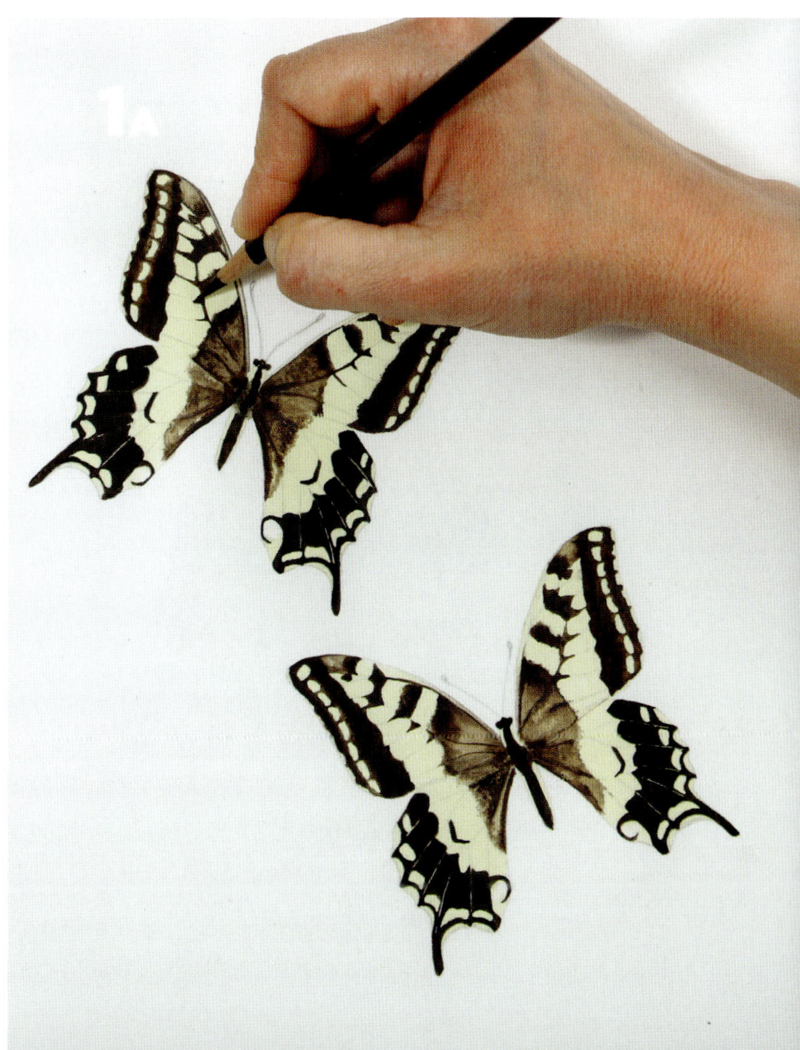
1A

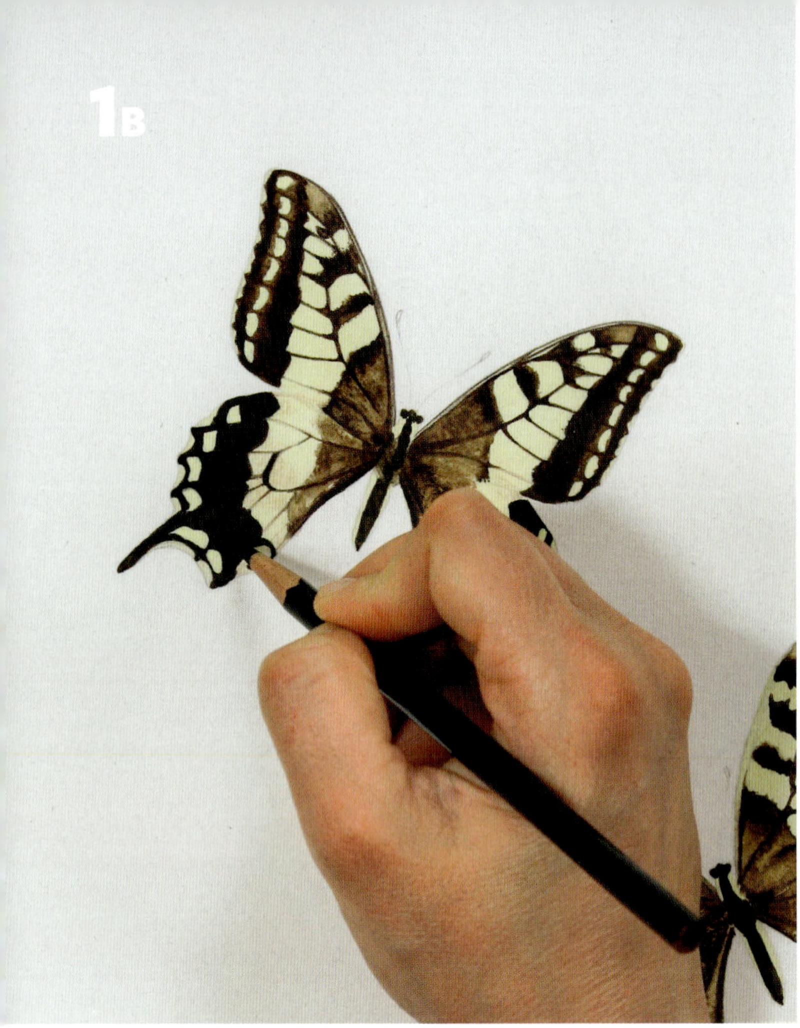

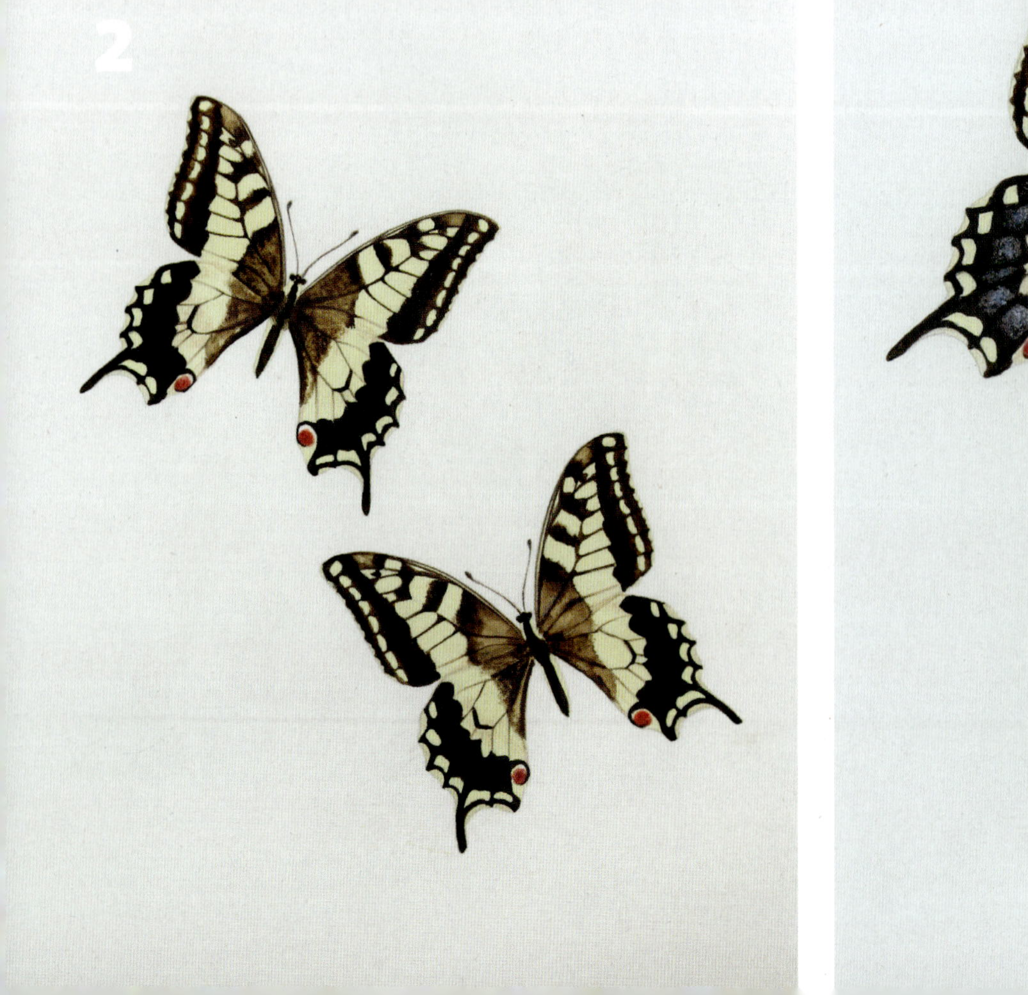

1B
2
3A 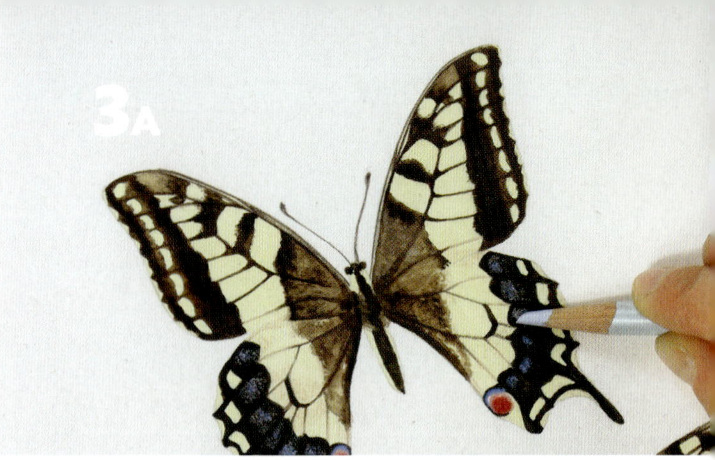
3B 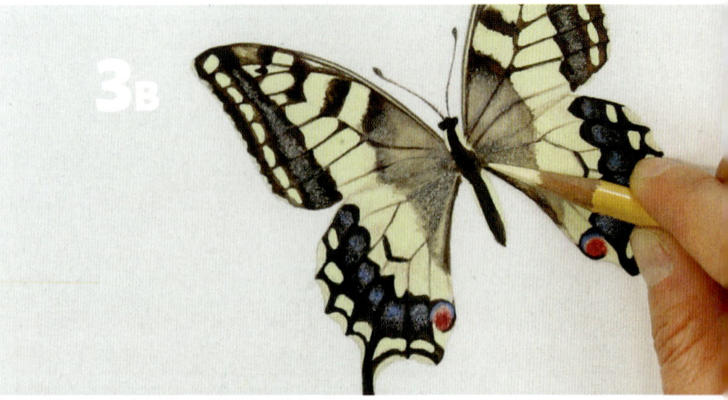
3C

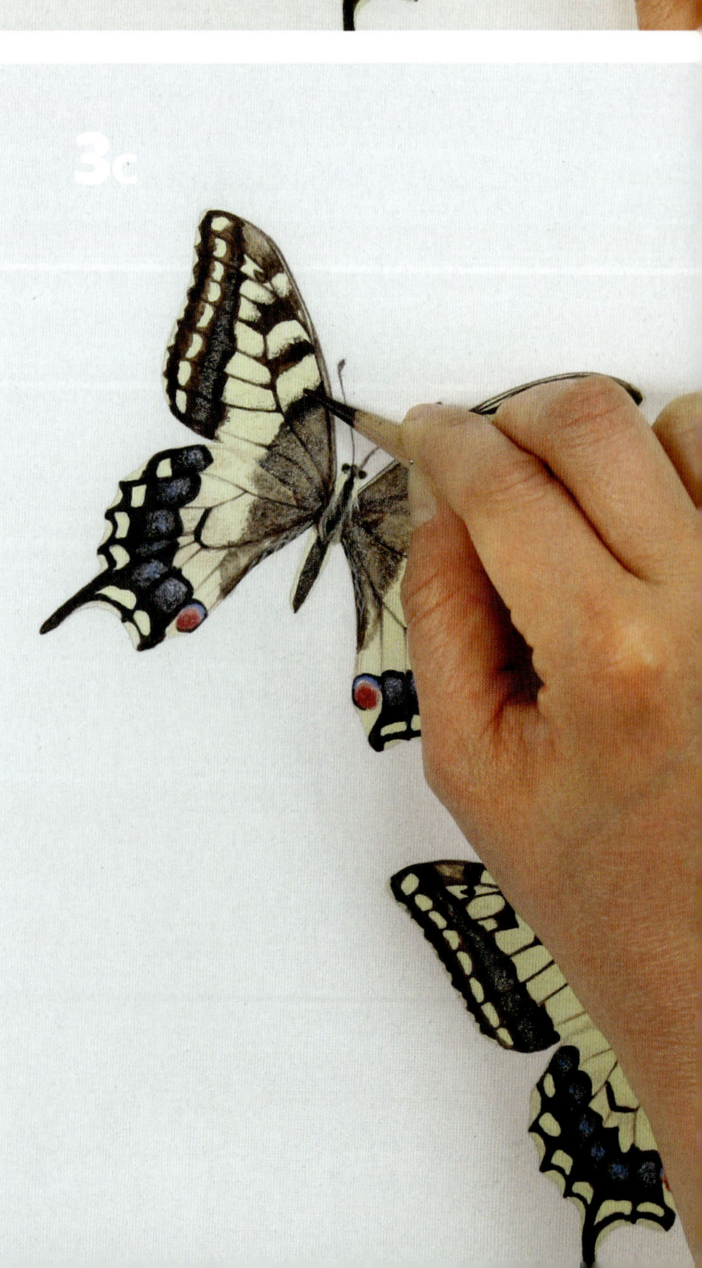

B Continue working with the seashell pink pencil for the veins on the lower wings and in select areas of the yellow cells to slightly mottle the hue. Add the dark umber pencil to the veins near the body. Switch to using the black pencil to create the veins in the dark brown section. Take a moment to appreciate how much cleaner and well defined these few details make your artwork appear.

2 Draw in the antennae, using the dark umber pencil with a very sharp tip to create a line in one careful stroke. Then, add the club to the end. If the line needs to be darker, go over it, but be sure it reads as a single thin line. You can switch to using the black pencil to further darken the end.

Move to the lower wings to create the eye spots. Start by using the crimson lake pencil to form the reddish circle. Create an arc above the red using the Caribbean Sea pencil, but leave a space where you will apply the rosy beige pencil in between. If you prefer to mix paint instead of using specific pencils, you can apply the colors in this small area using a paintbrush.

3 **A** Notice on the hindwing how the dark area of each cell has powdery light blue with slightly darker blue toward the center. Use the Caribbean Sea pencil with light pressure to make the darker blue. Then turn the pencil on its side so that the length of the lead can graze the texture of the paper and emulate the appearance of powdery blue scales. To avoid forming a flat section on the lead, rotate the pencil often as you work.

B Continue to look back and forth at the reference to add these minor details; however, focus on the overall look instead of attempting to draw every dot. Switch to the cream pencil and use the same pencil-side technique on the dark areas of the forewings and the light brown section close to the body on both wings.

C You can use the dark umber pencil to add scales to the yellow areas and to further integrate the stipple along the border of the brown areas. At

this point, you may want to turn your pencil vertically and use a very sharp tip to draw some individual scales. You may find it helpful to work with the cream pencil in these areas, too. Occasionally hold your drawing at arm's length to see how these changes influence the composition as a whole. If any scales stand out or distract from the overall pattern, adjust them so that these details only enhance the overall pattern and add to the realism of the butterfly.

Return to using the dark umber pencil to embellish the veins toward the body and add any dark details needed on the thorax or abdomen. Switch to using the black pencil to accentuate the dark brown areas in the hindwings.

4 At last, you can add the final details to the butterfly. Use the cream pencil, with a very sharp tip, to indicate a few wispy hairs just inside the inner edge of the hindwing. It will look more realistic if you alter the direction of the hairs slightly. Then move to the body and use medium pressure to add hairs to the thorax and to the light areas around the eyes on the head. You can also add a small amount of the black pencil to the body to accentuate the forms near the eyes. Use the burnt umber pencil to create the suggestion of segments on the abdomen.

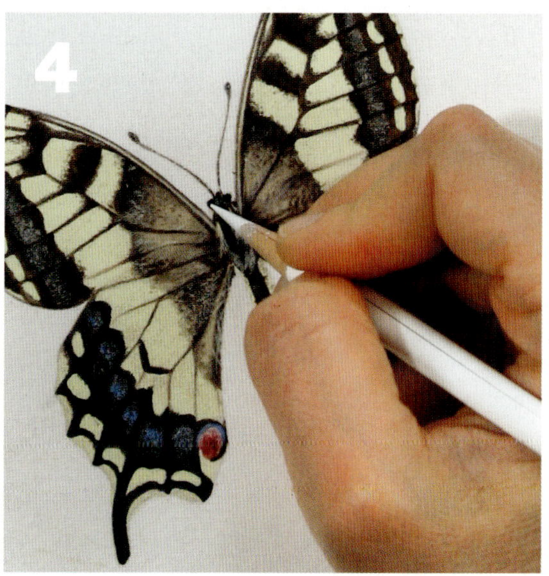

Now for the simplest yet most crucial detail: Take a very sharp white pencil and add a single white dot to the top of each eye close to the body. Try to do this with a single movement. Pause to be sure it looks like light reflecting off of two round surfaces and adjust only one if they seem too close together or need to be more aligned. Voilà, you have just brought the subject to life!

Compare each area of the drawing to the reference image and make adjustments as needed. Then compare one wing of the butterfly to the other to be sure that the steps were completed on both sides. Now hold the artwork at a distance: Are there enhancements you can add that are not in the reference image but that would make the insect look more realistic?

Congratulations on all you have accomplished. If you would like to add more depth to the composition, proceed to the next step to incorporate a shadow. On the other hand, if the piece feels complete, simply skip to step 7 to add one final touch.

5 The shadow in this composition has hazy edges, which indicates a muted light source. The distance of the shadow from the butterfly suggests not only that the light is located high above and toward the front of the butterfly but also that the butterfly's wings are about ¼ inch above a flat surface.

If your butterflies are posed at different angles, choose one to replicate the shadows found in the reference image. Start by using the 10% French gray pencil to create a very light outline where the dark part of the shadow begins, about ⅛ inch from the edge of the insect. Now fill in the outline with the pencil at full pressure all the way up to the edge of the butterfly. Blend the pencil outward from the outline by gradually lightening your pencil weight to quickly transition back to the color of the paper. Stand back from your drawing to determine if you have accurately replicated the shape of the edge. Next, draw a line along the edge of the butterfly where the shadow is the darkest using the 30% French gray pencil; blend this line into the lighter gray. This not only makes the shadow appear as if it gets darker under the butterfly but it differentiates the wing from the background, particularly the yellow areas. Repeat this step using the 50% French gray pencil if you want to darken the shadow a bit more. Keep your pencil weight light at first so that the shadow doesn't become too dark. Take a moment to see how this one detail makes the butterfly appear to be resting on a surface. Befriend shadows—you won't regret it.

6 Since the shape of the shadow in the reference image is the same as the edge of the butterfly, to create the shadow for the second butterfly you simply shift the shape of the edge in the opposite direction of the light source. For this piece, I'm assuming that the light source is far away, like the sun, so the angle of the shadow will be in the same direction on both butterflies.

Using the 30% French gray pencil, either draw the outline freehand or create a transfer sheet. If you choose to use tracing paper, simply trace the actual edge of the butterfly, flip the page, and shift the line about ⅛ inch from the outline of the butterfly. When the shadow appears to be of a similar thickness and cast in the same direction as the first butterfly, retrace the line to transfer the marks to your page. When the outline is complete, follow the steps used to create the shadow on the first butterfly.

Take a moment to appreciate your work—you just created this shadow without using a reference, and you imagined a light source far from the plane of the page by using the information in the image. Though the shadow in this composition is minor, this technique will greatly help you going forward.

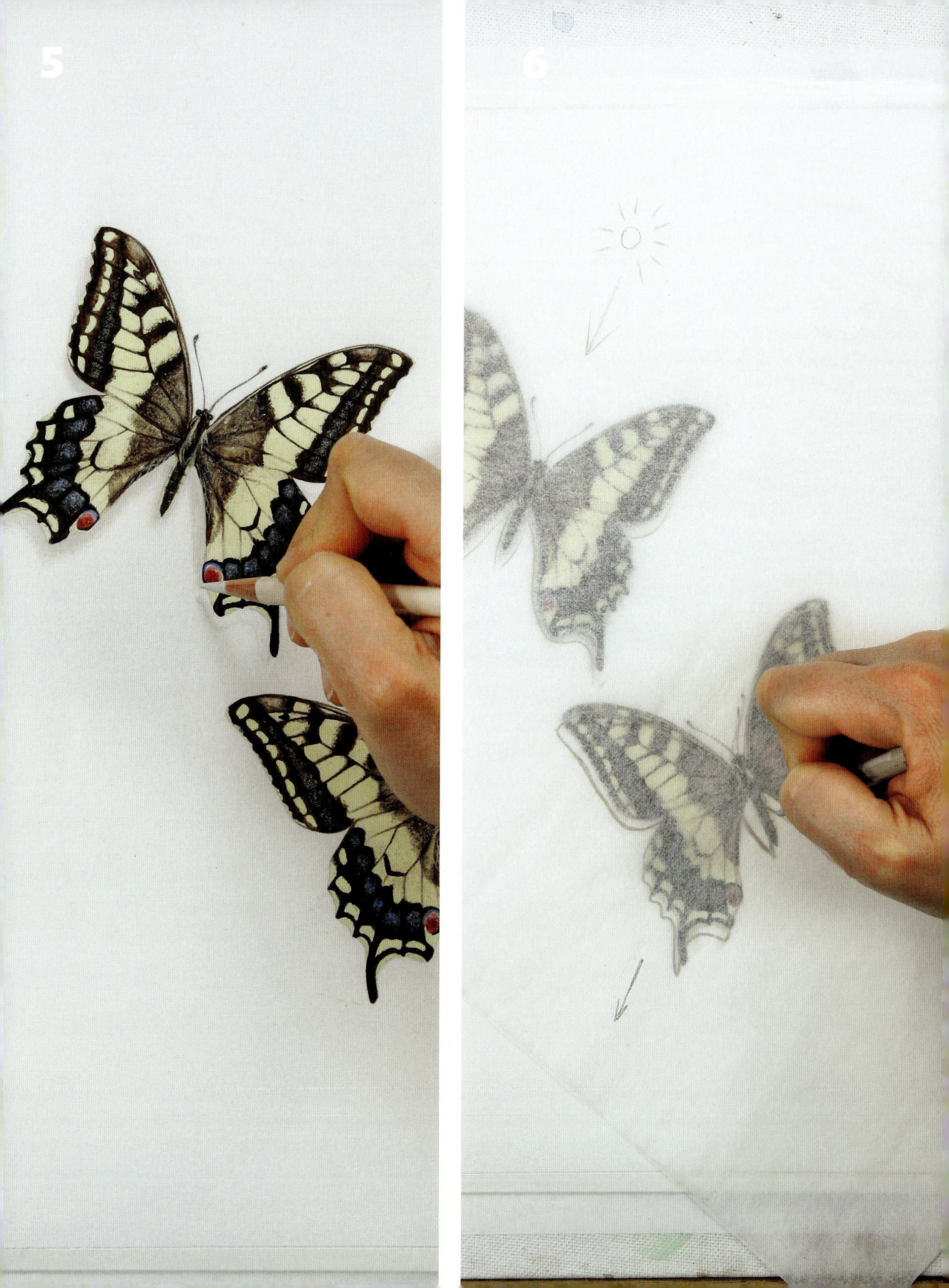

5
6

 The yellow areas along the edge that are not over the shadow are close in value to the white background. To differentiate them slightly, take the rosy beige pencil with a very sharp tip and work along the outer edge to darken the outline slightly. As you work around the wing, adjust your line weight to avoid a solid line and instead help the subject appear more dimensional.

You're done! Sign the front, date the back, spray with fixative (if desired), and celebrate.

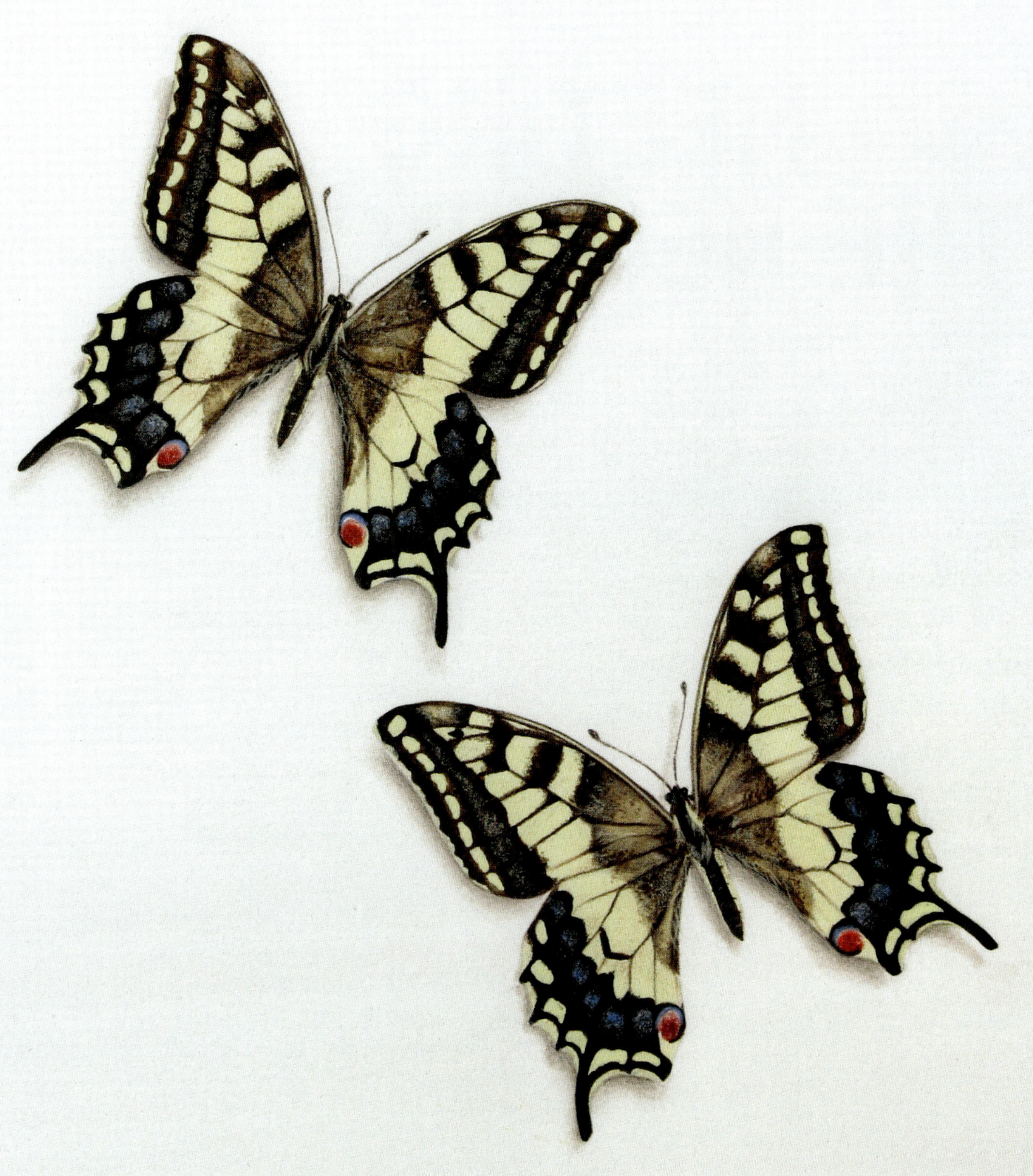

MEETING THE NEIGHBORS

The ways in which the natural world grows, struggles, thrives, and interacts can go unnoticed. This Nature Break is devoted to exploring the undercurrent of nature that is close to home. It's time to meet the neighbors.

LOCATION: Choose a place that feels close to where you live or work. This spot might be as near as your doorstep or as far as a few miles away. Regardless of the distance, make sure that you can spend an extended amount of time sketching, preferably without interruption.

MATERIALS: Sketchbook, HB pencil, and colored pencils.

OBSERVATIONS: Spend about five minutes simply taking in your environment. What do you notice first, and what becomes apparent after watching for a bit? In your mind, identify the natural elements, both living and nonliving, that are in this area. Recognize their different behaviors, abilities, anatomy, and other qualities. Notice the interactions and relationships between them, and be aware of your own human presence as you witness them.

PRACTICE: Warm up with quick gesture drawings, a few to a page, to capture the essence of the elements you have seen. Then turn to a clean page, choose one subject to focus on, and create a finished piece.

REFLECTION: Consider the world that you've just observed. What discoveries did you make? Have your observations shifted the view you have of your neighborhood? Review the artwork you created to both appreciate your achievements and acknowledge the unrepeatable moments you've experienced.

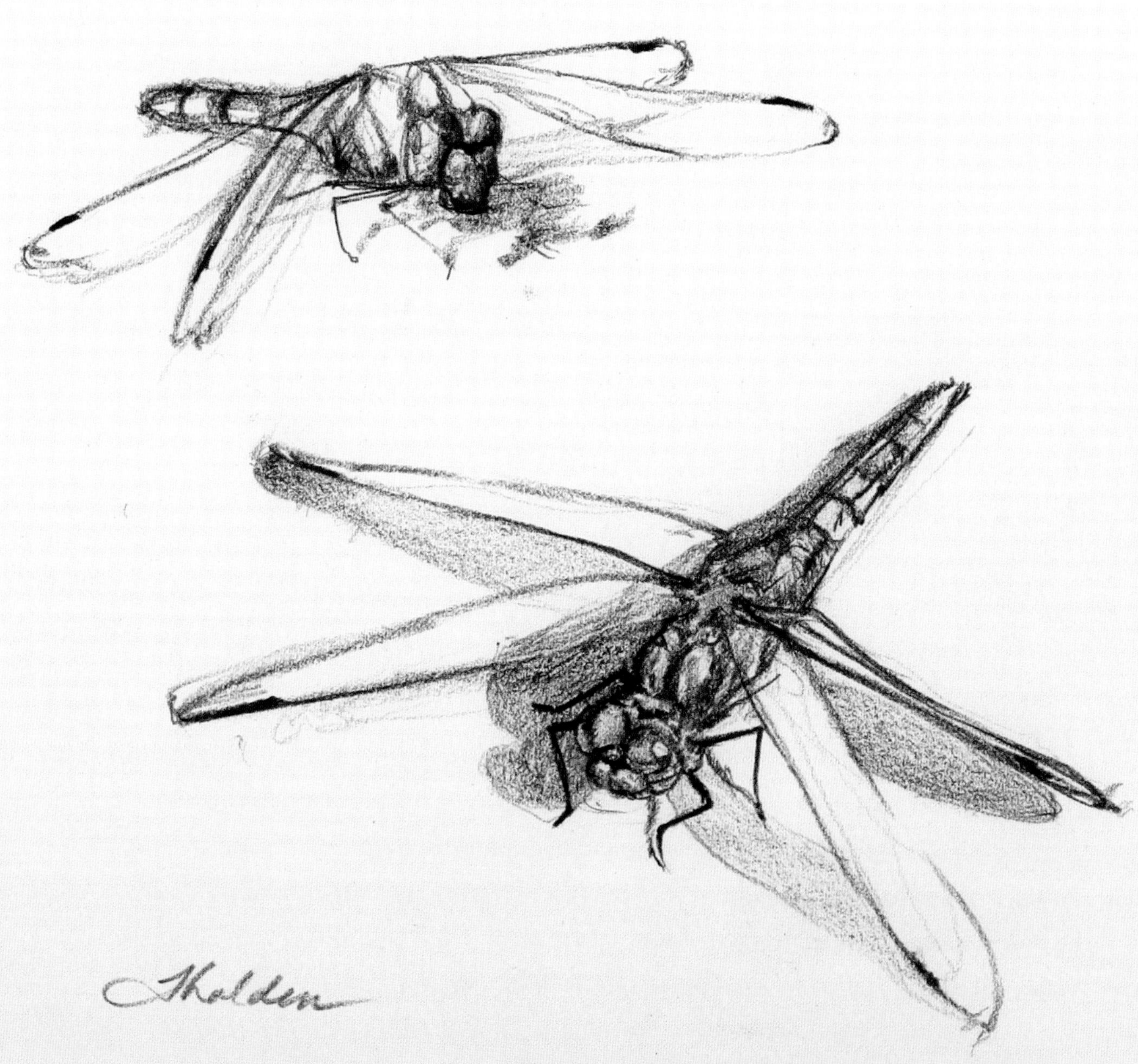

SPURGE HAWK MOTH CATERPILLAR

HYLES EUPHORBIAE

The spurge hawk moth caterpillar was introduced to the United States to voraciously eat a plant, called leafy spurge, with sap that can harm cattle and horses. When mature, the caterpillar ventures underground to pupate and will turn into a large day-feeding moth. In this composition, I am delighted by the caterpillar's dramatic shape and by the sense of space conveyed by the foreshortened forms. You can replicate this sense of depth by paying close attention to the overall structure and the placement of specific surface patterns. Once you sharpen the outline that distinguishes foreground from background, it's almost as though you could just reach right into the image.

SEE REFERENCE PHOTOS ON PAGE 312

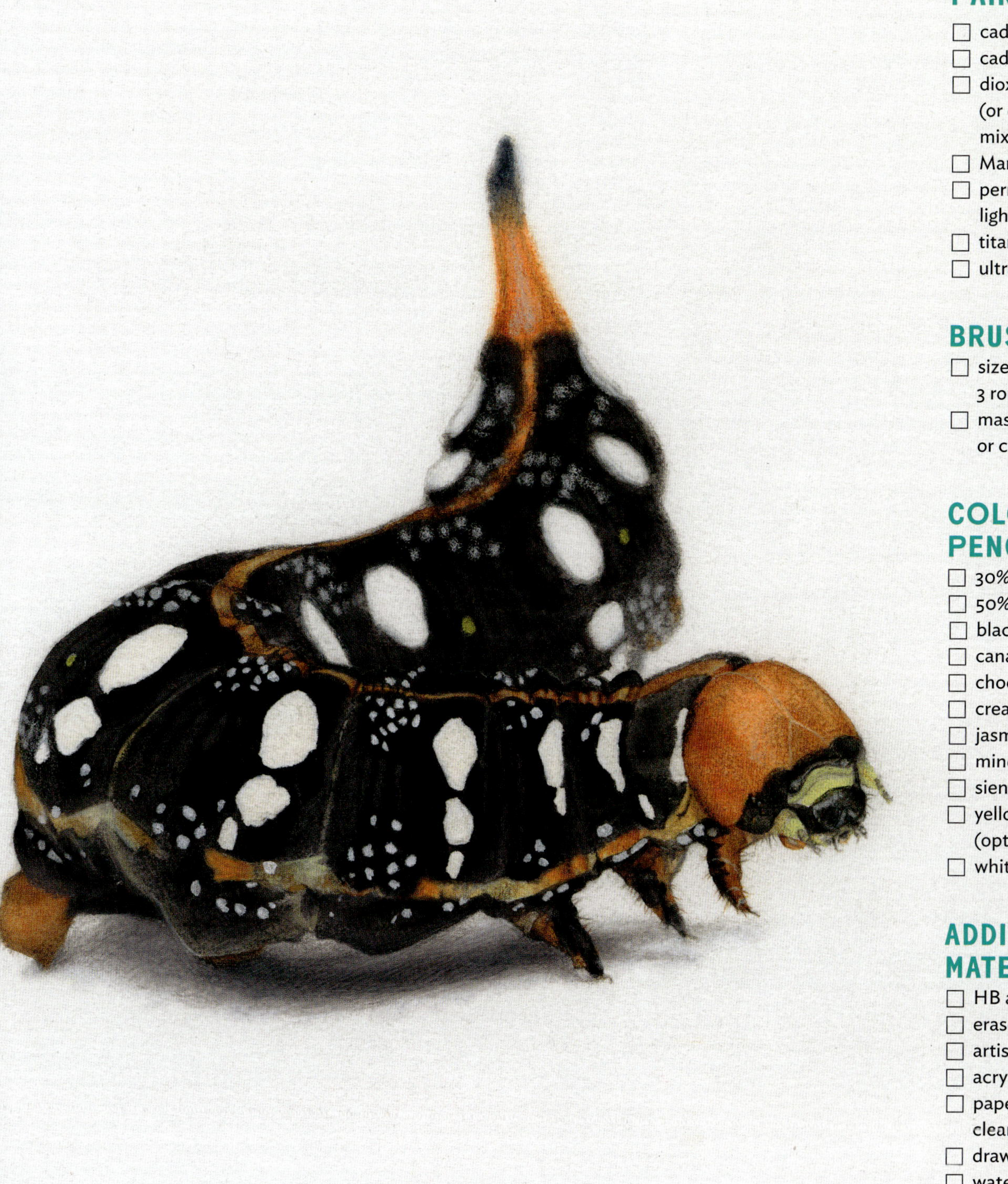

ACRYLIC PAINTS

- [ ] cadmium red
- [ ] cadmium yellow
- [ ] dioxazine purple (or dark purple mixture)
- [ ] Mars black
- [ ] permanent green light
- [ ] titanium white
- [ ] ultramarine blue

BRUSHES

- [ ] sizes 0, 1, 2, and 3 round
- [ ] masking fluid brush or color shaper

COLORED PENCILS

- [ ] 30% French gray
- [ ] 50% French gray
- [ ] black
- [ ] canary yellow
- [ ] chocolate
- [ ] cream
- [ ] jasmine
- [ ] mineral orange
- [ ] sienna brown
- [ ] yellowed orange (optional)
- [ ] white

ADDITIONAL MATERIALS

- [ ] HB artist pencil
- [ ] eraser
- [ ] artist tape
- [ ] acrylic retarder
- [ ] paper towels or clean rag
- [ ] drawing board
- [ ] water container
- [ ] plastic wrap
- [ ] masking fluid (optional)
- [ ] fixative (optional)

DRAWING

1 Prepare your workstation and tape your paper. Notice on the reference image that the subject's overall height is nearly equal to its width. On your paper, pencil in a quick square around the perimeter of the area where you would like to draw the caterpillar. Next, draw a gesture of the entire caterpillar, beginning with the front half.

2 Since this composition is asymmetrical, drawing a centered midline will not be useful. Instead, draw a vertical line where the tail-like horn is located; this will serve as the midline. You can use the height of the caterpillar's head as the measurement to determine the proportion of the rest of the body. Compare the height to the width of the head on the reference image. Move to your drawing, measure the head height with your pencil, and determine if the width is the same proportion as the reference image. If they are different, adjust the width to match, then define the overall shape of the head. Leave the details for later.

3 Use the head-height measurement to check the width of the caterpillar on the reference image. I found that the overall width was about three and a half lengths when measuring from the left side of the head. Return to your drawing and sketch a long horizontal line from the base of the head to the opposite side of your gesture. Use the drawing's head-height measurement to mark increments along this line. If the distance is too close or too far from the edge of your page, adjust the overall size of the head and remeasure. (Remember, careful tweaking now makes future steps easier and more accurate.)

4 With the horizontal axis line measured, you can mark all anatomical features above and below the line. Look at the reference image and either imagine or lightly mark the horizontal axis line on the image in the same location as your drawing. Then determine the location of the lower edge of the body and the end of the lowest leg using the head-height measurement. I found them around half and three-quarters of a length below the head, respectively. Return to your paper and mark both measurements. The lowest mark will become the base of your midline and the starting point for vertical measurements. Take a look at the reference image and, in the area where you have your midline, determine the caterpillar's overall height. I found that the very tip of the horn was about four and a half lengths up. As you measure on the reference image, notice the anatomical features that land at each interval: the midpoint of the front half of the body, the bottom of the large white dot, a bit below the orange horn, and the area where the very tip turns from orange to black.

Violà—you've just gained a new technical skill: knowing how to create a structure to measure anatomical forms on any dynamically shaped subject.

5 Return to the front half of the caterpillar and use the lengths along the horizontal line to locate and mark the segments of the body. You should find the end of the third section just before the first length, the mark for the second length just beyond the end of the fourth segment, and the third length close to where the fifth segment ends.

Next, add the back leg to your drawing. Place your pencil vertically on the reference image at the innermost and then outermost portion of the leg to see the relationship between the side of your pencil and the sixth segment. To locate the bottom of the leg, turn your pencil horizontally and notice where the pencil intersects with the midline. Once you have lines and dashes on your drawing that identify the correct location, look back and forth to the reference image and sketch the shape of the leg.

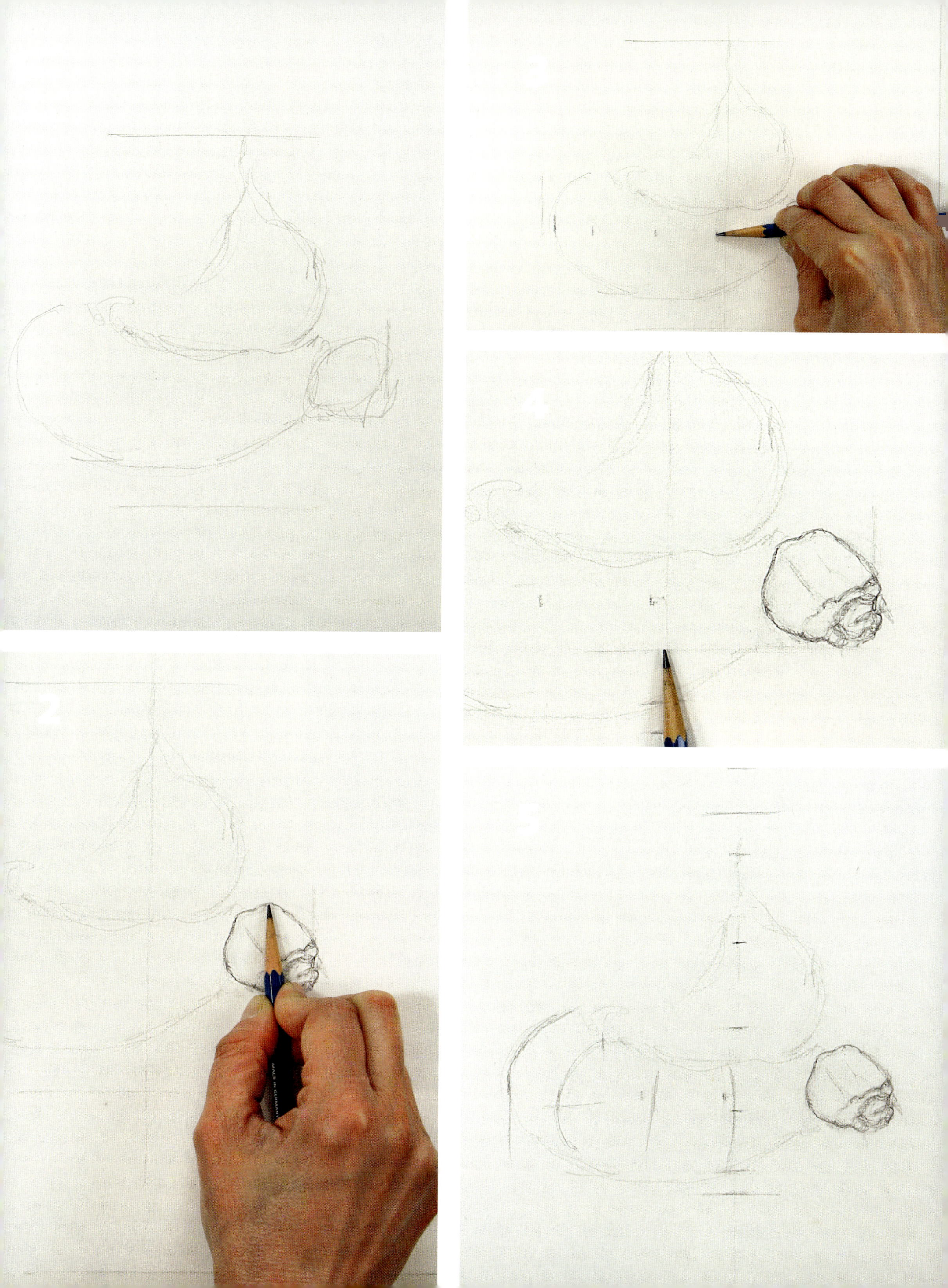

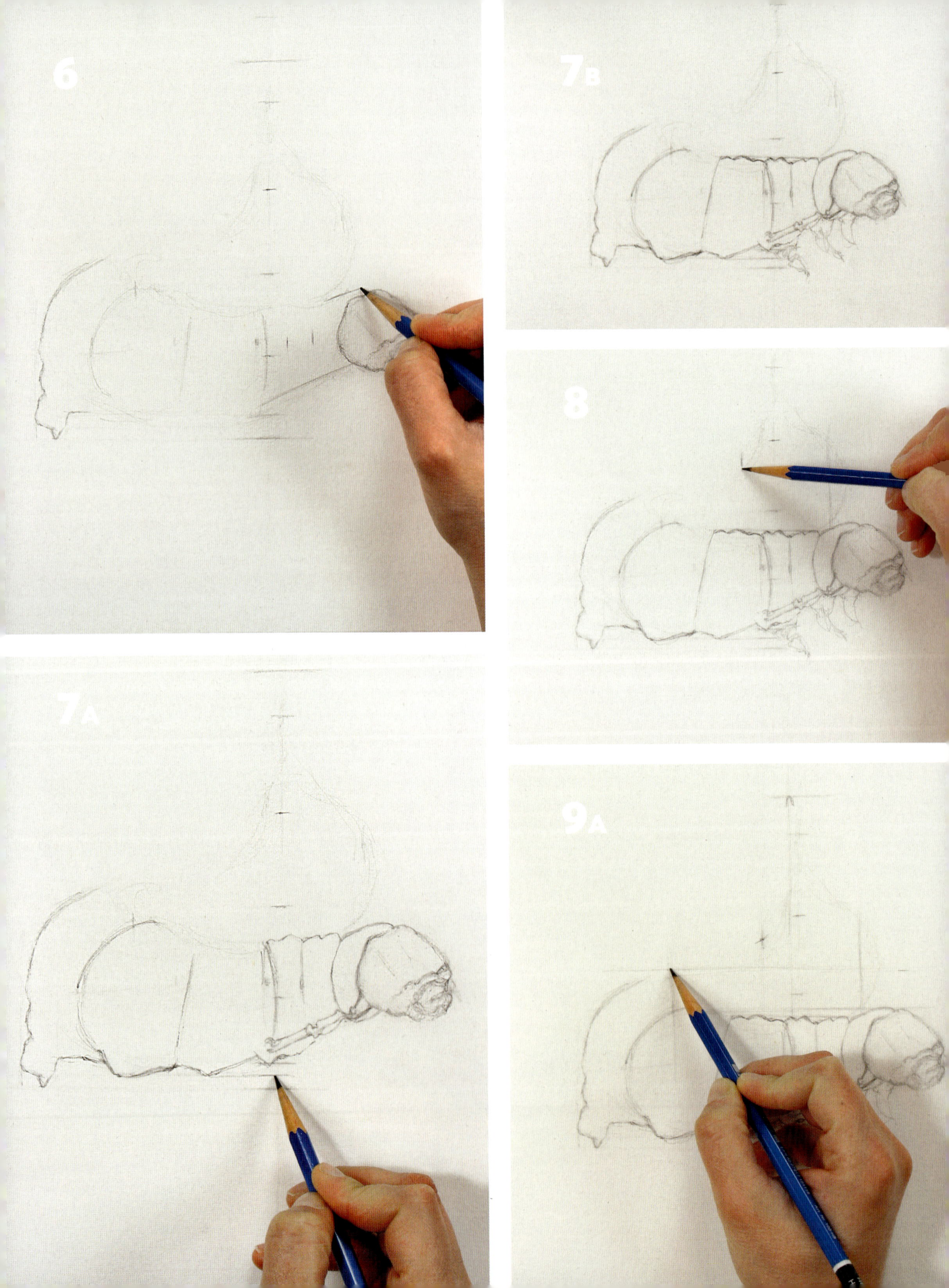

6 Move to the thorax. Looking at the reference image, I found that each segment was about one-third of the thorax. Using the side of your pencil, and with one eye closed, pull the appropriate angle from the reference image and transfer it to your drawing. Repeat this process to be sure that the angle is accurate. Use the same technique for the angle at the top of the first section as well.

7 A Locate the bottom edge of the fourth and fifth segments by placing your pencil horizontally on the reference image to see where it intersects the midline. On your paper, draw the horizontal line first, then create the bottom outline of both segments.

B Rough in the thoracic legs, just to help you see the overall form of the composition.

Move to the top of the fourth segment and add the upper outline. Notice that it is at the same height as the previous two segments. For now, leave the fifth and sixth segments as they are.

8 Review the reference image and shift your attention to the back half of the caterpillar. Notice the shape that the negative space creates. Also, recognize that the sides above the first and fourth segments are nearly vertical. Move to your drawing and add both of these vertical lines using the head-height measurement. Double-check that the distance between the lines is correct.

Find the horizontal and vertical position of the tip of the horn and draw it on your paper. Keep in mind that because the horn is angled slightly, the end may not be along the midline.

9 A Move toward the midsection of the caterpillar and observe how the outline rises slightly directly above the fifth segment. To find the height of this rise, use the head-height measurement in comparison to the top of the head. I found that it was half a length higher. On your drawing, it may be helpful to place a horizontal line from the top of the head to where you will be measuring. Place a simple mark just to indicate the shape of the rise.

B Before you connect the line of the rise to the beginning of the horn, jump ahead for a moment to draw the large white spot just above the fourth segment. Adding this feature now will help you create accurate proportions in this area of the midsection and ensures you have left space to add the caterpillar's patterns later in the process. Begin by drawing an angled line that represents the major axis of the oval. Mark the two ends, then sketch a quick gesture of the form. Use the head-height measurement to check the spot's proportions. I found that the height was half a length.

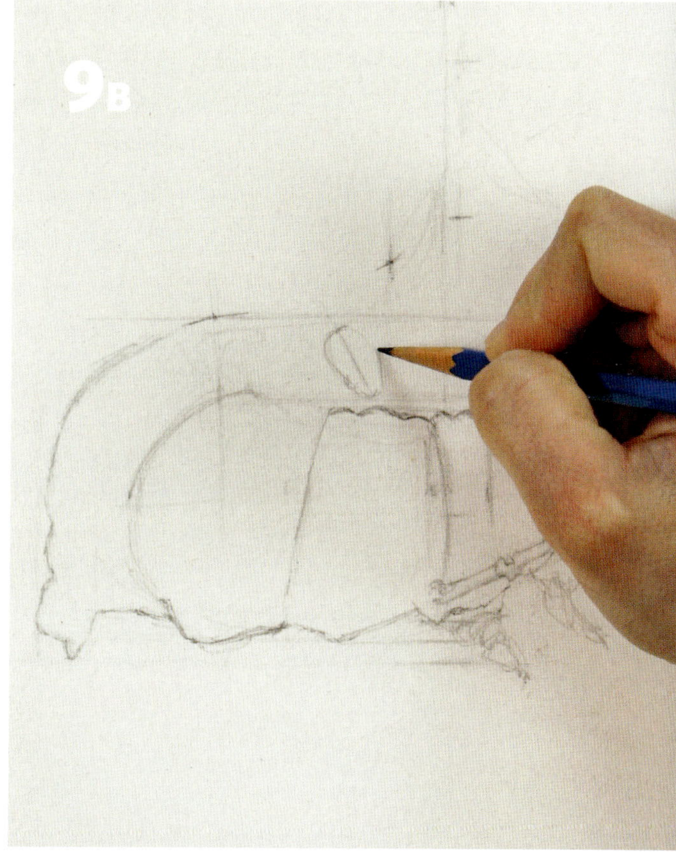

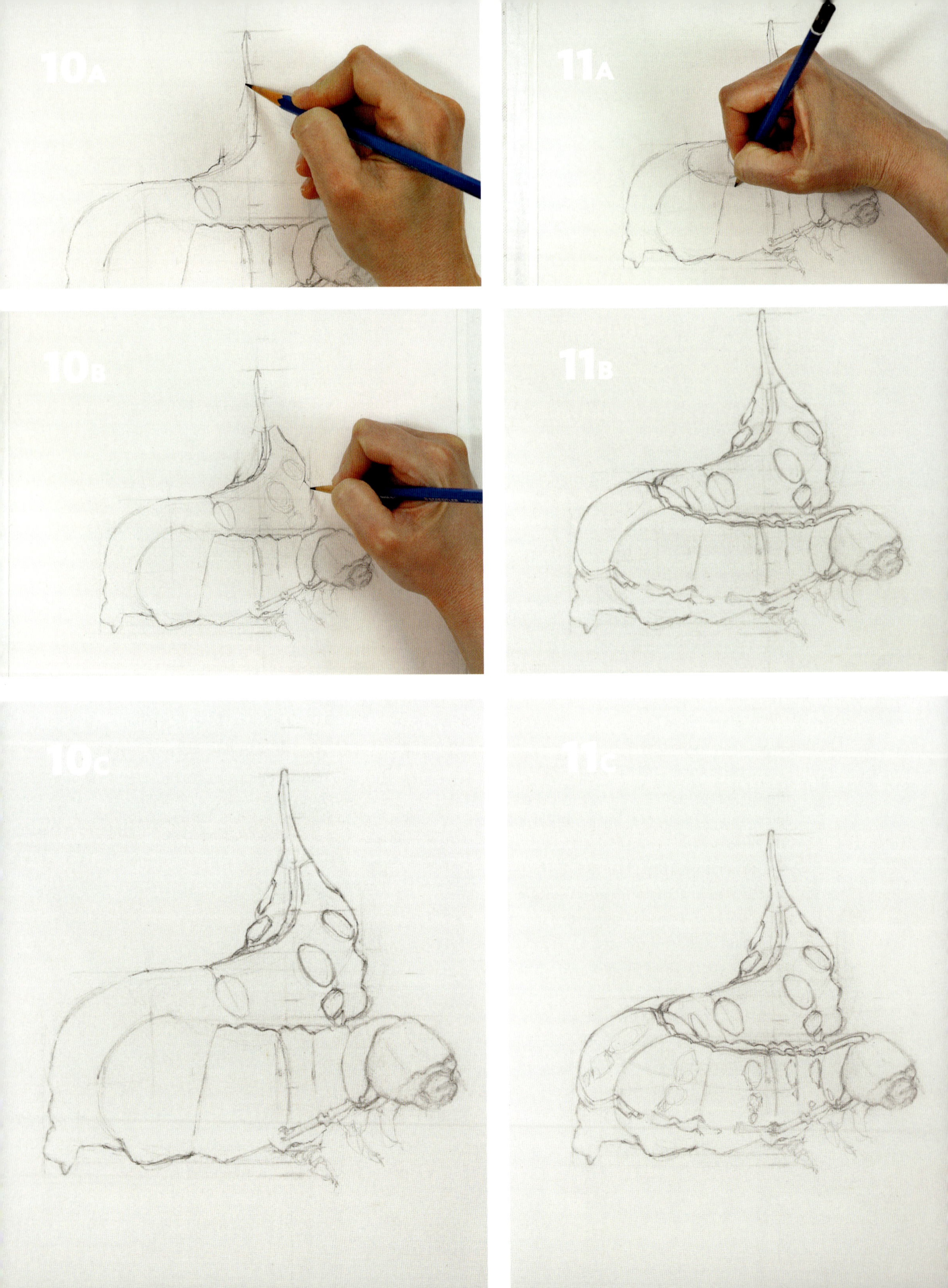

10A
10B
10C
11A
11B
11C

10

A A few additional key patterns near the horn can help you accurately visualize the overall midsection shape. First, create the orange stripe from the midsection up the center of the horn. Next, rough in the other two large spots on this side of the body using the same process you used to create the previous spot.

B With these details in place, draw the outline on the right side. Use the reference image, negative space around the caterpillar, and interior patterns to help you determine the shape of the form.

C Move to the left side. Since the outline is close to the stripe and the spots are partially hidden, draw the outline first and add the pattern afterward. When you are ready to draw the spots, keep in mind that they would appear in symmetrical pairs if you were looking directly down on the caterpillar. Imagining this view can help you place the spots more accurately on the page. Before you move on, review the overall outline as well as the shape of each spot and refine as needed.

In general, noticing relationships between anatomical forms is a simple and helpful way to quickly place elements in a drawing. It is another example of taking time in the beginning to set yourself up for success and is a powerful tool to have in your repertoire.

11

A Move back to the sixth segment to rough in the front half of this stripe. As you work toward the head, replicate the upside-down question mark made by the overall shape of this stripe.

B With the stripe in place, you can now locate the top of the fifth and sixth segments. You might rough in the partial spot on the inside of the curve to help with this process. Then rough in the lower stripe and refine the shape of both stripes.

C It's time to add the large spots in this area. Look at the relationship of a group of spots to its neighbors in the sections on either side. Draw a curved horizontal line to indicate where the base of each uppermost spot will be. Notice that the angle the three spots make on each segment is slightly different from the next. Now rough in each row of spots and refine each group.

12

Move to the legs below the thorax. If you imagine a line on the reference image that connects the end of all three legs, it would look like a small arc. Draw this arc on your paper, refine the leg attached to the third segment, then work toward the head.

Now that the rest of the body is in place, return to the head and refine the outline, if needed. Then lightly add the details of the face: the areas of color change, the antennae, and the location of the upside-down Y shape on top of the head. Look for the caterpillar's six tiny simple eyes, located just above the antennae.

Look at the entire drawing, check all proportions, and erase extraneous lines. Lighten your pencil lines on the back half so that you will be able to blur the outline with paint, then lighten the areas of the face where it is lightly colored.

You've just finished the drawing section of a difficult composition by considering the subject as a whole, utilizing the relationship between shapes to inform your drawing decisions, and visualizing the subject from a different angle. This is a huge accomplishment.

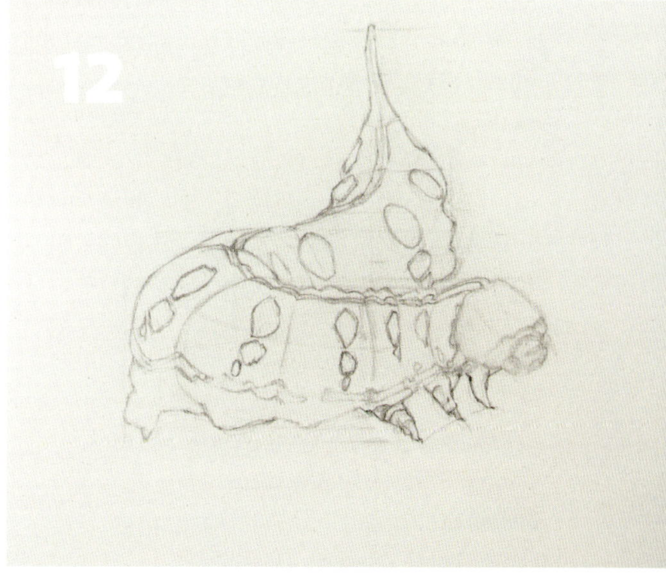

PAINTING

1 Before painting, you may want to apply masking fluid so that you don't have to work around the larger spots. Since the mask will create a hard edge, only coat the spots on the front half (you'll blur the edges of the ones in the back to create depth). Using a color shaper or small paintbrush designated for masking fluid, replicate the shape of each large spot. Be careful not to go over or under the drawn line. If you are unfamiliar with using masking fluid, feel free to apply a small amount to a scrap piece of paper, let it dry, and remove it to gain an understanding of the overall process (the instructions are in the next paragraph). Wash your paintbrush often so that the masking fluid does not dry on the bristles. Unlike paint, it will still harden in water. I recommend cleaning it against the inside of your water container, possibly before coating each spot. You can also wash it with a little soap immediately after you have completed the spots. If you use a color shaper, you can rinse the masking fluid off using water or peel it off after it has dried.

If air bubbles form on the coated surface, either pop them while the masking fluid is wet or wait until the fluid has dried to dab the area with a second coat. Skip the smaller spots that you will address later. Masking fluid dries translucent and shiny. Since the paper under any masked area will remain white, look over the area to be sure the masking fluid has created a solid layer and is only where you intend it to be. If you find an error, use an eraser to carefully pull up the edge and remove the dried masking fluid. Be aware of your pencil marks so you do not erase them accidentally.

2 Place Mars black paint on your palette and use a size 3 paintbrush to add water to reach a workable consistency. You could mix a small amount of color, such as ultramarine blue, into the black paint to match the reference image. Feel free to add a drop of acrylic retarder.

We introduce a new technique here—blurring painted edges—that you should practice on scrap paper first. When you are ready to work on your illustration, begin on the back half of the caterpillar and start with the left side. With a size 3 paintbrush, apply a water wash up to the stripe, avoiding the unmasked large white dots, and overlapping the outline of the caterpillar slightly. Then add the paint. Before the paint dries, take a clean, moist size 1 paintbrush and soften the paint edge around each spot, along the orange stripe, and around the perimeter. Clean your brush when needed. Repeat on the other side of the stripe. Keep in mind that the amount of blurring should lessen as you move toward the head.

There's a knack to blurring painted edges. If the paint fills the area, there was either too much water on the brush or the paint was still too wet. You can always sop up the extra water with the edge of a folded paper towel or clean rag. On the other hand, if the paint does not bleed at all, you either need more water on the paintbrush or the paint is already too dry. When the blended area begins to dry, you might notice a hard edge starting to form. If this happens, rinse and blot a size 1 paintbrush, and run it along the edge to create a smooth fade to paper in this isolated area.

3 To paint the front half of the caterpillar, work on one segment at a time and move *toward* your dominant hand. Apply a water wash to the segment you want to work on and the one directly ahead of it. Paint right over the masked spots, but avoid the portion above the upper stripe since it can be painted separately. Keep the value of your pigment even, since you will add the gray vertical stripes later with colored pencil. Before you move on to the next segment, and while the paint is still wet, use a moist, clean paintbrush to wet the lower stripe slightly and pull in some of the dark color so that the stripe becomes gray where needed. You could also switch back to the size 1 paintbrush and

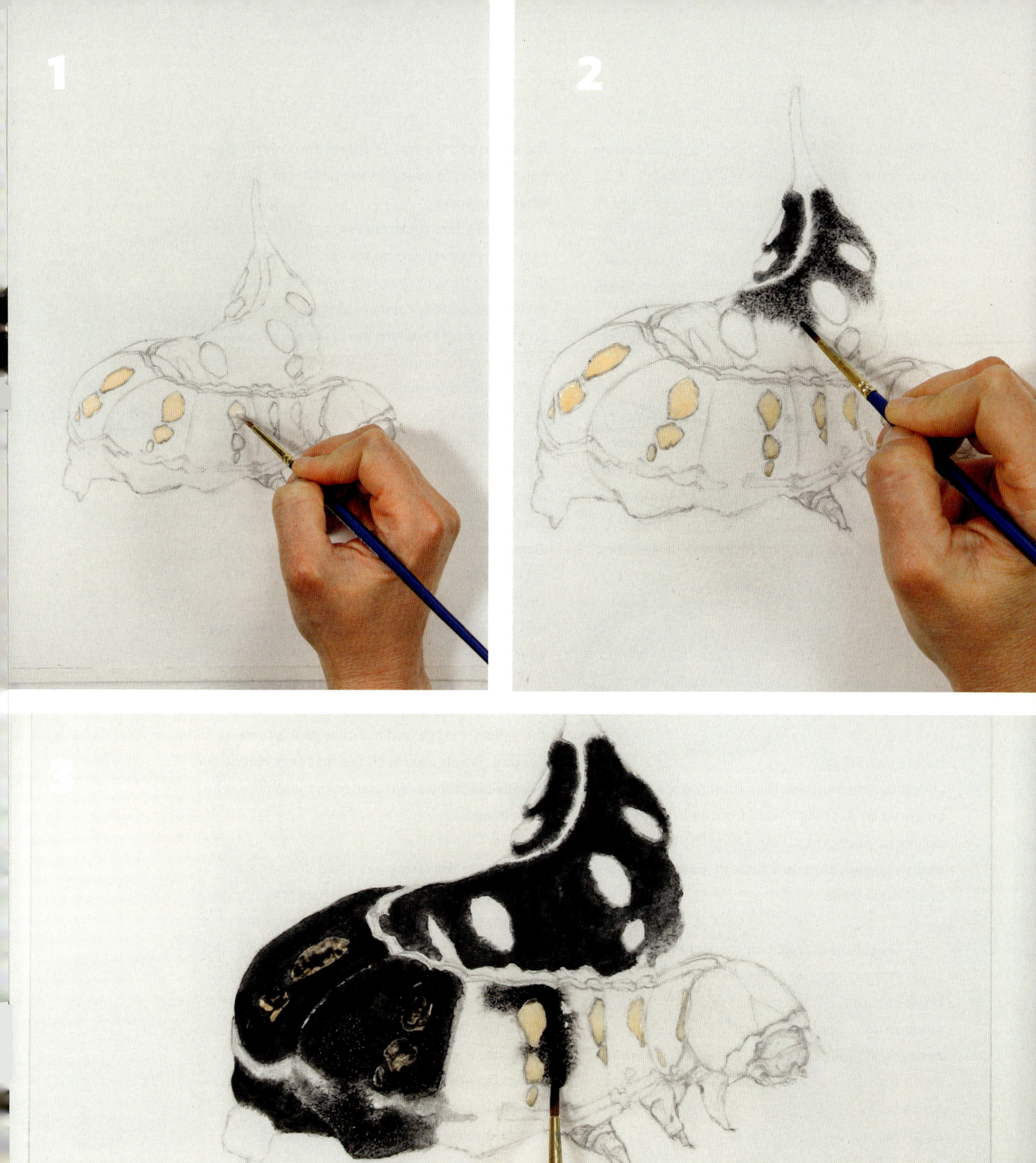

7 **A** All that remains to be painted are the isolated details. Work on the three thoracic legs one at a time, using the red-orange and blackened red-orange paint mixture. To create the tan areas, simply dilute and blot the pigment on your brush again.

B Next, work on the leg attached to the sixth segment. Do blur the edge all the way around. Now move to the leg that is mostly hidden under the body. You may need to add more Mars black paint to the blackened red-orange paint mixture to color this appendage. Blur the edge here as well.

8 To paint the lower stripe, mix your final color: the yellow found between the orange portions of the stripe and on the face. Combine cadmium yellow with titanium white paint, then add a touch of permanent green light and a miniscule amount of dioxazine purple paint to lower the brightness and make the color a bit cooler. If the mixture turns purple or green, start over and incorporate a much smaller amount of those colors. In the meantime, keep the other paint mixtures hydrated and usable.

With the paint prepared, apply a water wash and then pigment to one area of the stripe at a time, alternating between the yellow and orange paint mixtures. Dilute the pigment with water to create the lighter areas.

9 Now paint the yellow mixture on the face. Add a tiny amount of Mars black paint to create the slightly darker shade for parts of the frontal area and the end of the antennae. (The fine details will be created with colored pencil later.)

While this area dries, mix the black for the tip of the horn by combing Mars black and just enough ultramarine blue paint to create a slightly blued black. Apply a water wash to the end of the horn that slightly overlaps the orange and the outline. Then add pigment, blur the edges, and create a fade into the orange.

10 Examine the reference image and lightly mark the location of each tiny white dot only on the front half of the caterpillar with a white colored pencil. Then paint the spots that are in focus using titanium white mixed with water. Make sure the paint appears nearly opaque when applied to the page and allow the spots to dry with a hard edge. Begin at the top near the stripe and work downward, then move to the spots near the bottom stripe and work upward. Since some of the spots are duller than others, you may want to further dilute the white paint for those areas. When you are finished, remove the artist tape.

So far in this project, you've learned several new techniques: You made unpainted areas appear to be a surface pattern. You blurred paint boundaries to create a sense of depth. And by working with multiple colors simultaneously and diluting select pigments, you extended your color range. Well done!

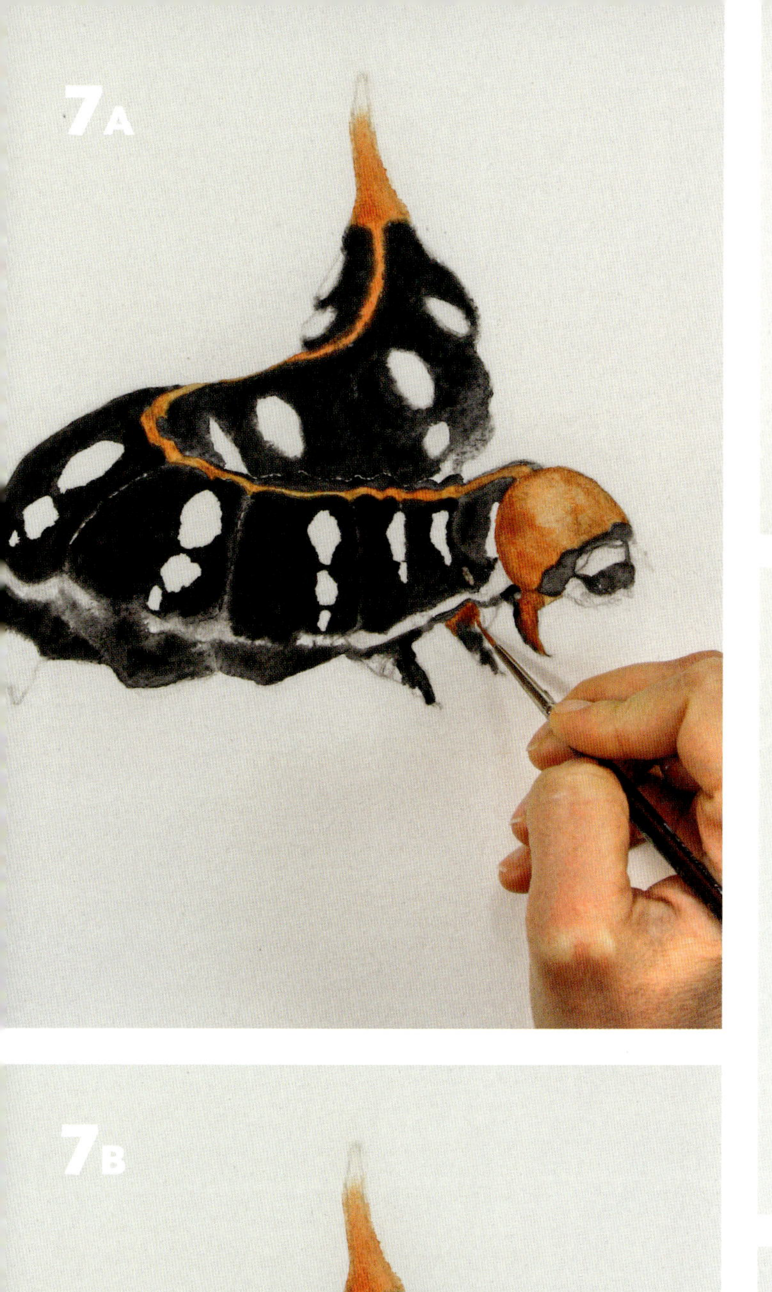

7A

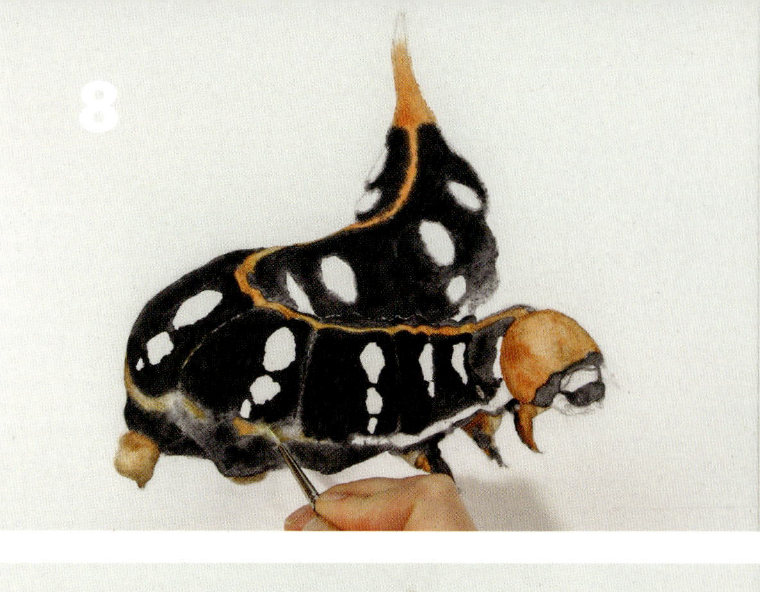

8

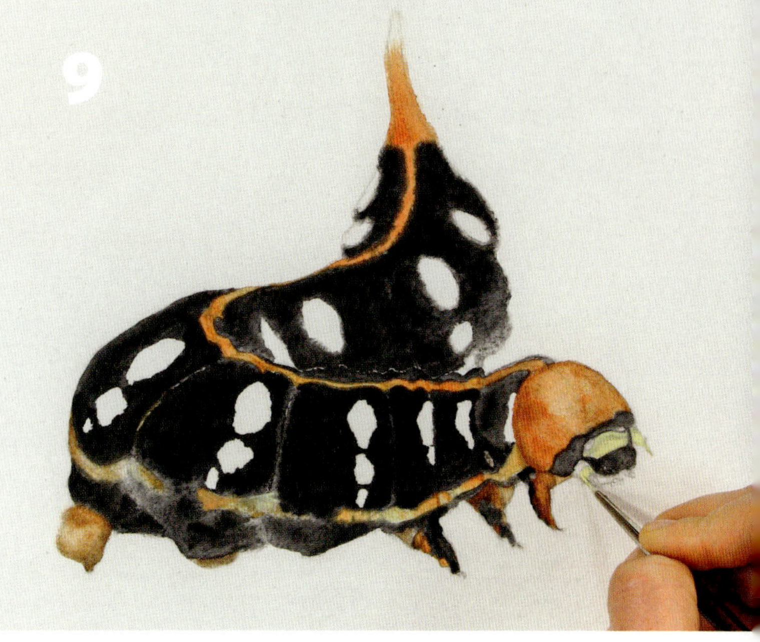

9

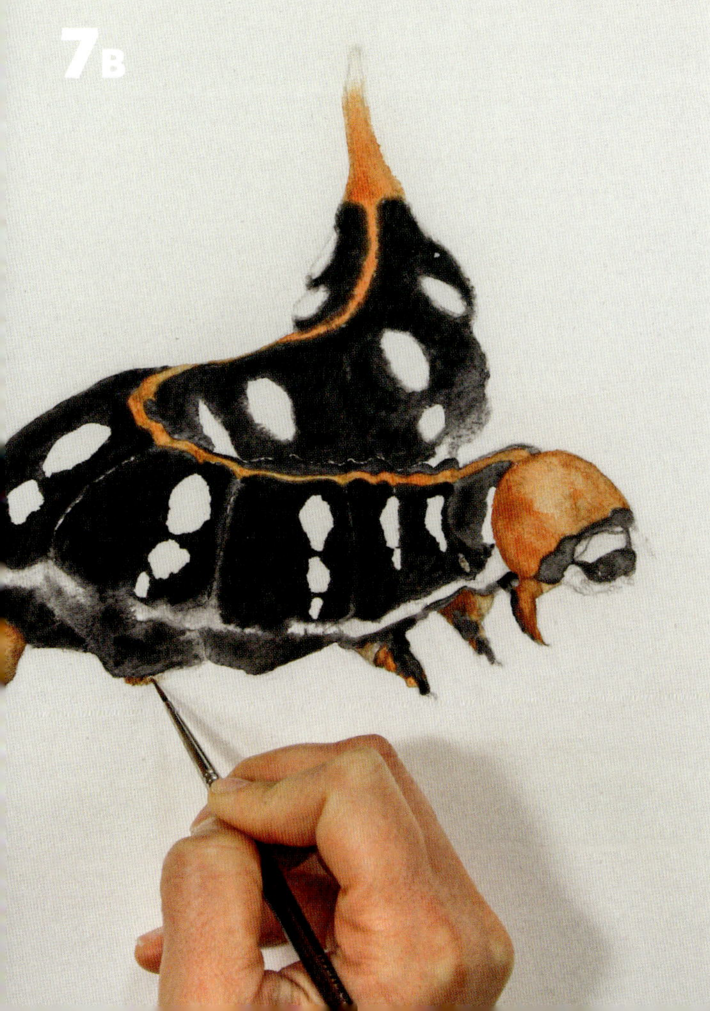

7B

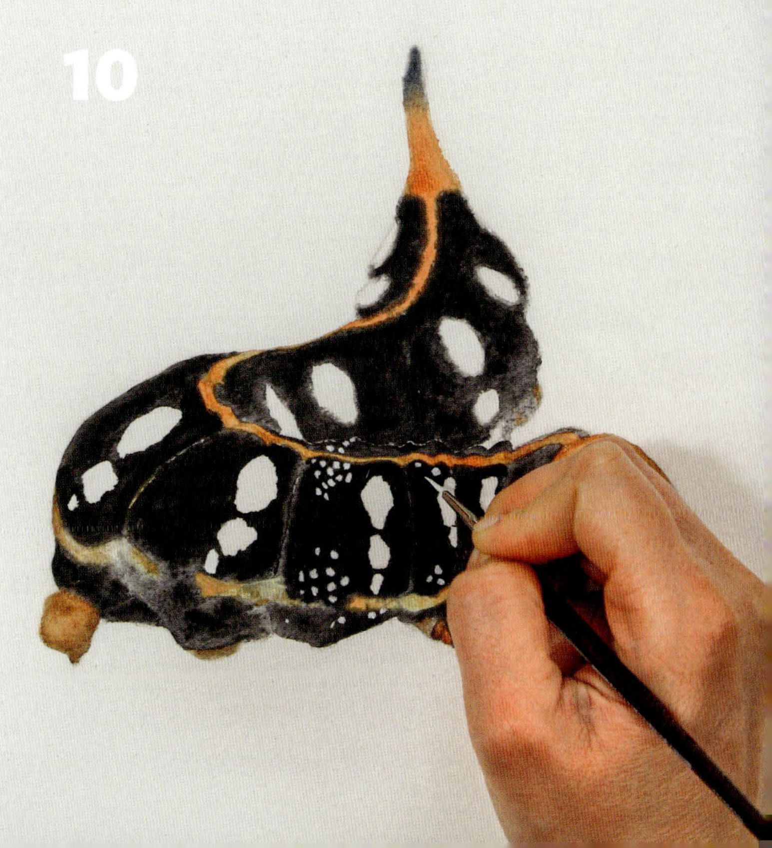

10

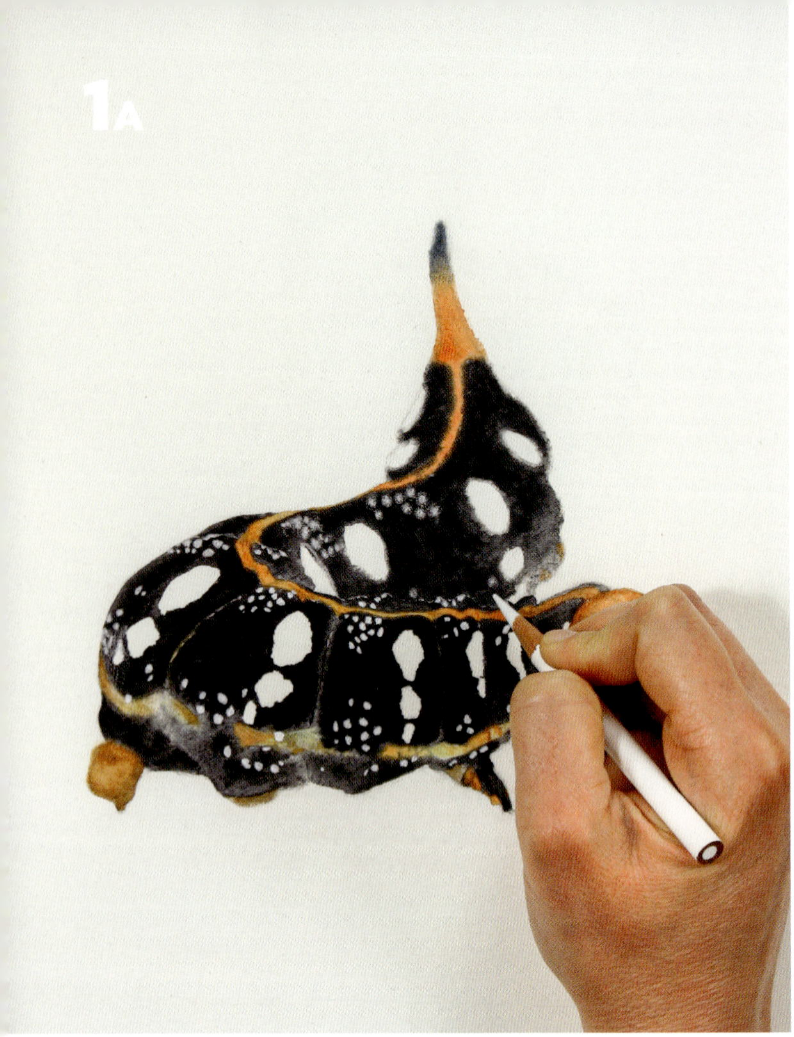

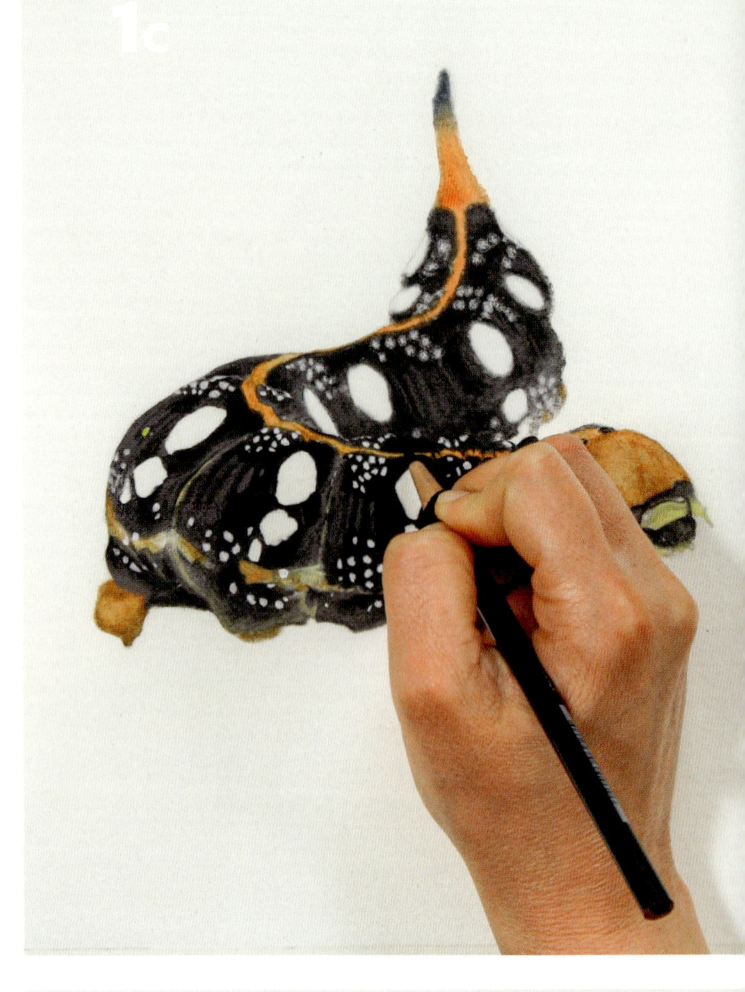
1A

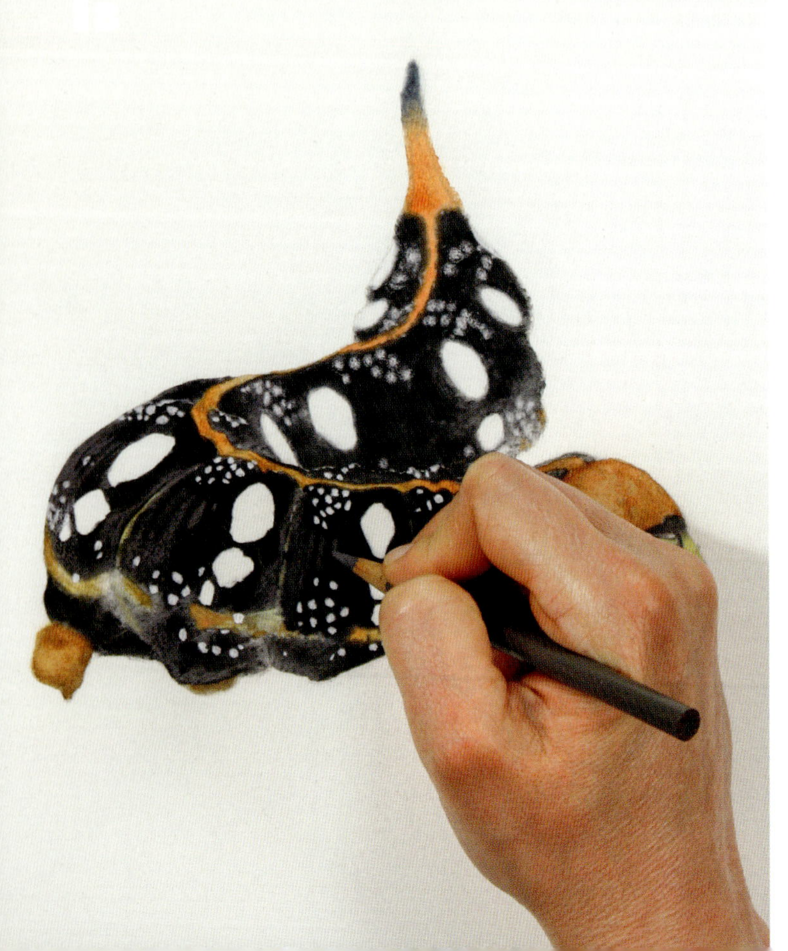
1B

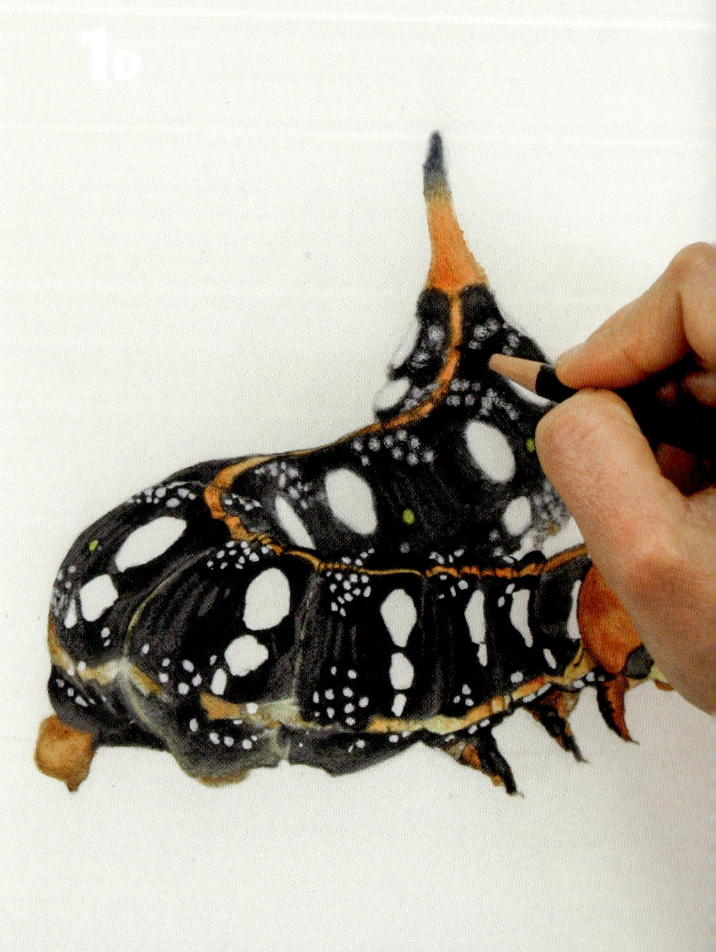
1C
1D

LAYERING WITH COLORED PENCIL

1 **A** Return to using the white pencil and add the remaining spots on the side and the back half of the caterpillar. As you work toward the tail, increase the amount of blur around each spot by circling the edge with very light pencil pressure. Pay careful attention to the opacity of the spots in each area.

On the front half of the caterpillar, if the large spots are jagged from the mask, use either a white or black pencil with a sharp tip to create a smooth, clean border. If you wish to blur the edge of the large spots, use a white pencil with a dull tip to go around the perimeter with fairly heavy pressure, overlapping the painted edge. Alternatively, use a black pencil, with a light touch, to transition from the outside in. Turn the drawing, as needed, to keep your hand in a comfortable position.

B Continue to work on the front half of the caterpillar in the creases on either side of the fifth segment where the gaps in the paint currently are. Use the jasmine pencil for the lighter areas and a combination of the 50% French gray and black for the darker areas. Then continue with the 50% French gray pencil to lighten the area below the lower stripe and add the vertical lines near the center of each segment. As you work, refine any rough edges around the outline and define the shape of the lower stripe. You may find it helpful to use black in these areas as well. Before you move on, use the chocolate pencil, with a very sharp point, to add the small line at the very end of each thoracic leg that creates a small claw.

C Move to the first segment and add black pencil in any areas that need to be darker than the paint. Be sure the area above the upper stripe matches the value of the section below, and adjust as needed to create continuity. If the outline in this area contains a hair-thin space, use the black pencil to fill in this line between the small spots that intersect it.

D To emphasize the ribbonlike qualities of the stripe, use either the black or the dark gray pencil to add the perpendicular shadow lines. To replicate the area that is in focus, refine only the edge of the stripe toward the front of the caterpillar.

In your illustration, look at the section on the back half of the caterpillar just above the third and fourth segments. If you fill in the area below the large white dots with black pencil, you create a greater sense of depth.

Keep it up, you're doing great!

Use the canary yellow pencil to add the small dots between the large white spots on the back half of the caterpillar. Blur the edge of each to match the section it is located in.

2 Move to the face. Use the black pencil to even the value of the dark paint and add shadows. Then switch to the white pencil and add highlights to the center near the yellow areas. Switch to the sienna brown pencil to add shading where the head meets the body and on the top of the head near the edge. A sharp tip can produce a smooth outline against the white. Where the paint is uneven, you can fill in with the mineral orange pencil. Then use the white pencil to add the light upside-down Y shape on the head and a black pencil to refine the edges along the body. These small details add a huge amount of realism.

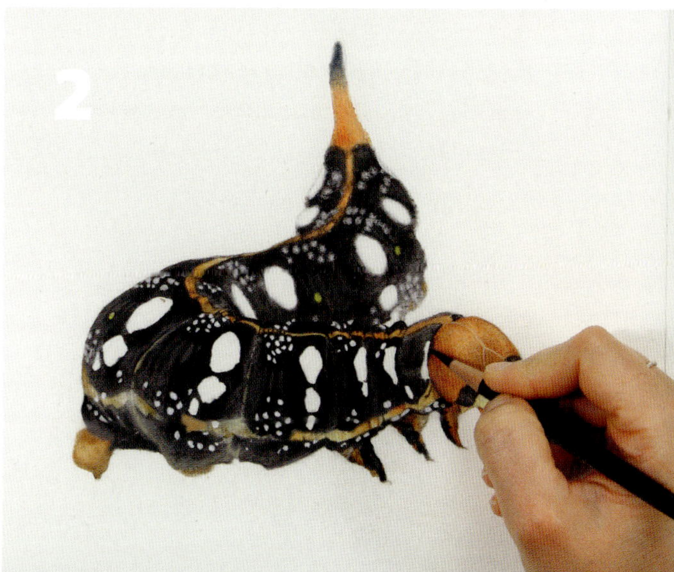

3 **A** Look at the shadow areas along the stripe. If a smoother transition is needed, use the sienna brown pencil followed by the mineral orange at the point where it changes from black to orange. Look at the reference image and the drawing on its own to determine the most realistic effect. When you reach the end of the stripe, use the mineral orange pencil for shadows on either side of the horn and the white pencil for highlights. If the edge needs to be blurrier, use the orange pencil with very light pressure. If there is a hard paint edge in this area that is not too dark, you may be able to soften it using the jasmine pencil, with a very sharp tip, directly on top of the dark line. Similarly, if you come across these issues in the black sections, use 50% French gray to blend and white to lighten the edges.

B Switch to the lower stripe and alternate between using the cream and the mineral orange or the yellowed orange pencil. If any dark sections are needed, use the 50% French gray and sienna brown pencils.

C Move to the section below the stripe. Use both the black and sienna brown pencils to darken the partially hidden leg. Make sure the edge of the caterpillar directly over this leg is slightly lighter; if necessary, use the white pencil along the edge to define it.

Nice work. Now you can place this incredibly lifelike caterpillar into a spacious environment simply by adding a shadow.

4 With the 30% French gray pencil, very lightly outline the form of the shadow underneath the caterpillar. Then fill in the shadow evenly. Next, blend the shadow outline into the white background using light pencil pressure around the edge, then apply 50% French gray to create the darker areas. Use a lighter pencil pressure to form a gradation around this area and return to the 30% French gray pencil to smooth this transition. Continue to darken and blend using these two colors until the shadow looks accurate and well integrated.

Note that your shadow will look more realistic if you keep your pencil marks uniform. Achieve this by making marks in the same direction or by drawing small circles throughout. Keep the marks close enough that you form a solid color or even gradation. To avoid accidentally drawing on the caterpillar, you can temporarily shift the direction of your pencil to follow along the perimeter. Then return to the previous direction to integrate the color into the surroundings. Build up value in layers and avoid erasing if possible, as erasures can interrupt the texture.

5 **A** If the texture of your paper interferes with the appearance of the shadow, you can use a colored pencil that matches the paper to smooth it out. In this project, you could cover the entire shadow in white.

B This will create a smooth surface, but one that needs further darkening. Use the 30% French gray, 50% French gray, and possibly the black pencil to deepen the value range to match the reference image.

Now that the section below the caterpillar is dark, you may wish to enhance the edge of the caterpillar so that it stands apart from the shadow. Simply use the black pencil along the dark edges and the white pencil on the light edges.

Notice how the caterpillar no longer appears to float in space but stands on a surface that you just created, and how the horn now appears farther back from the front half of the caterpillar's body. You are doing a wonderful job.

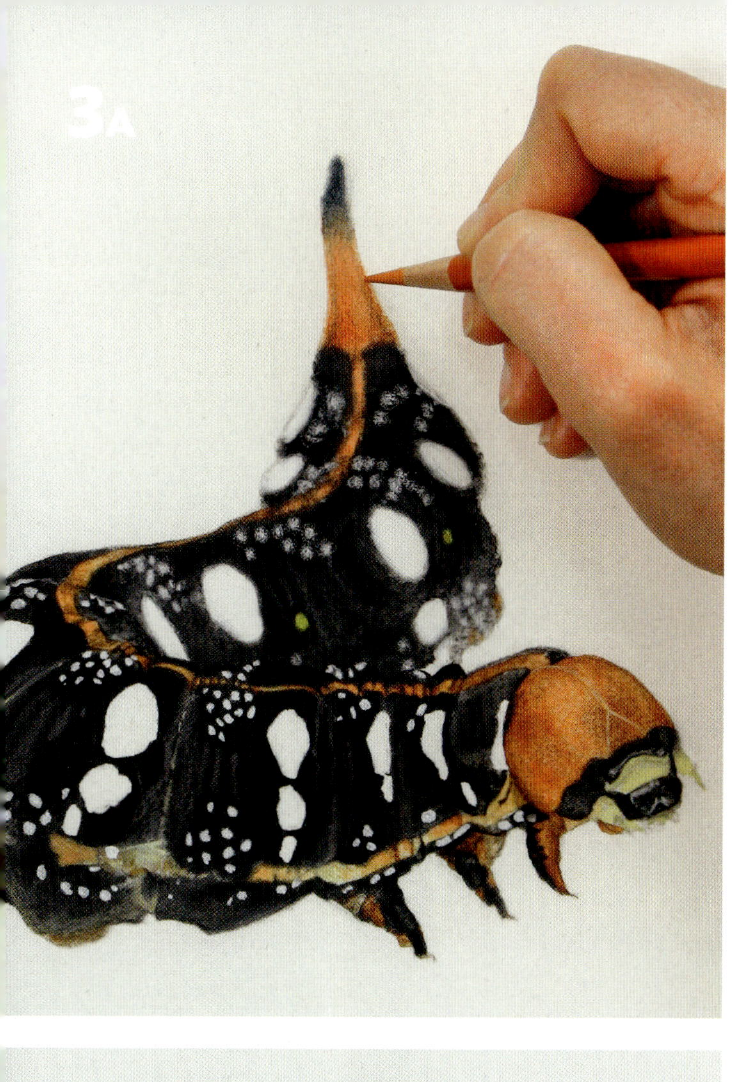

3A

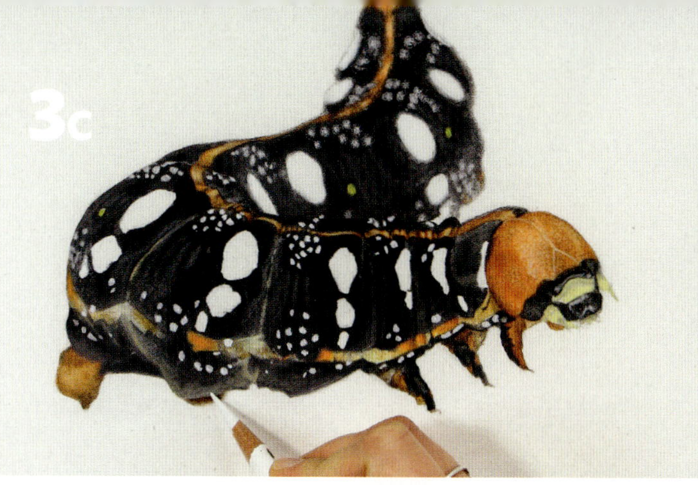

3C

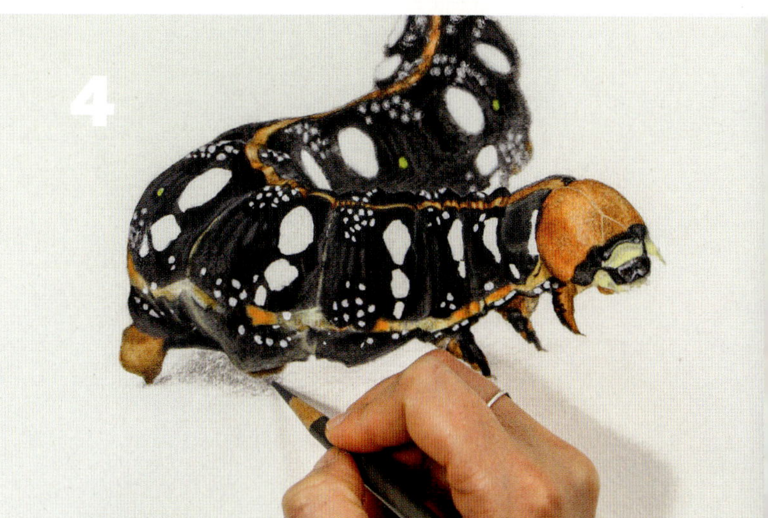

4

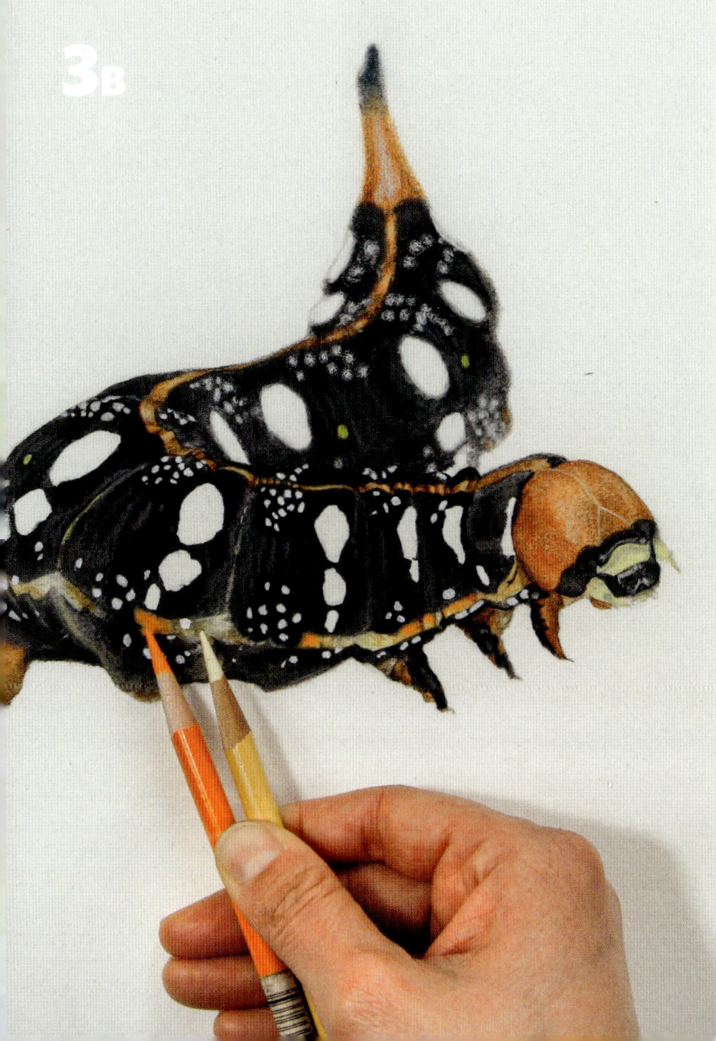

3B

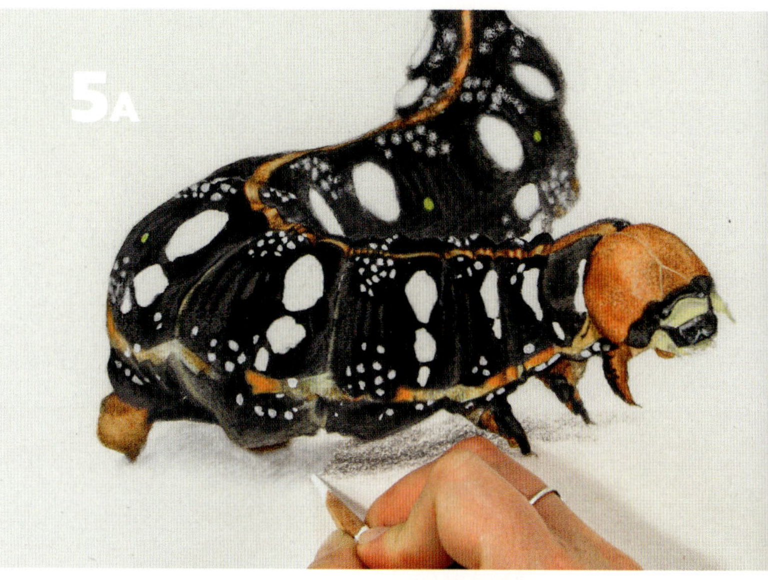

5A

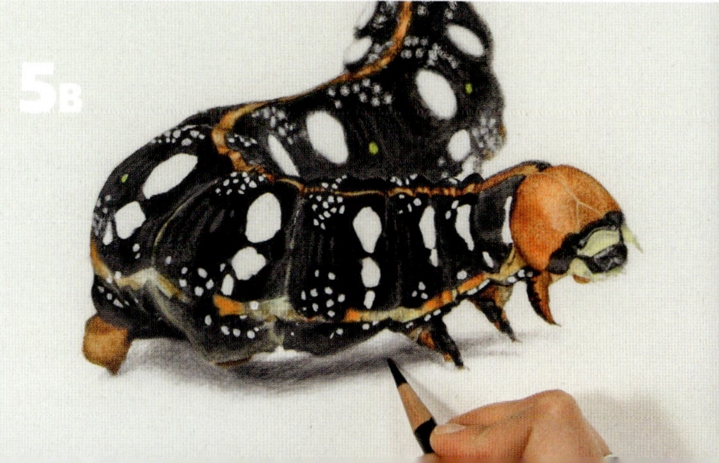

5B

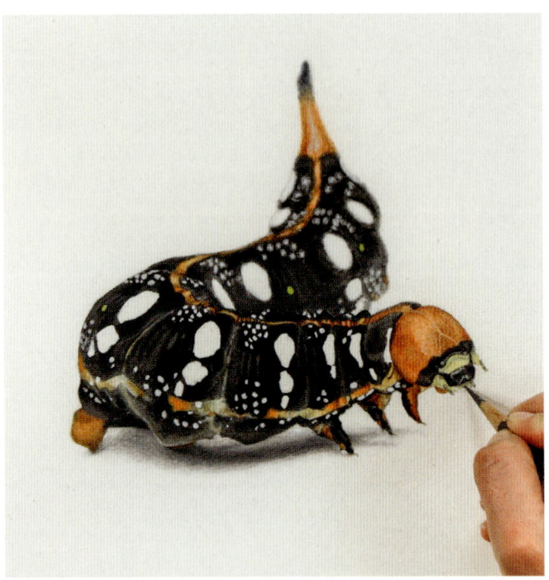

6 To finish the drawing, return to the caterpillar head and use the 50% French gray pencil to add the remaining details on the antennae and mouthparts. Also, look to see if you need to use the mineral orange pencil in this lower section. Check the rest of the head and add any final details.

Compare the entire illustration to the reference image. Can anything be added or adjusted? Do you need to make enhancements that are not in the reference image? As usual, sign, date, and spray (if desired) your illustration. This was a challenging composition. Take time to revel in your achievement.

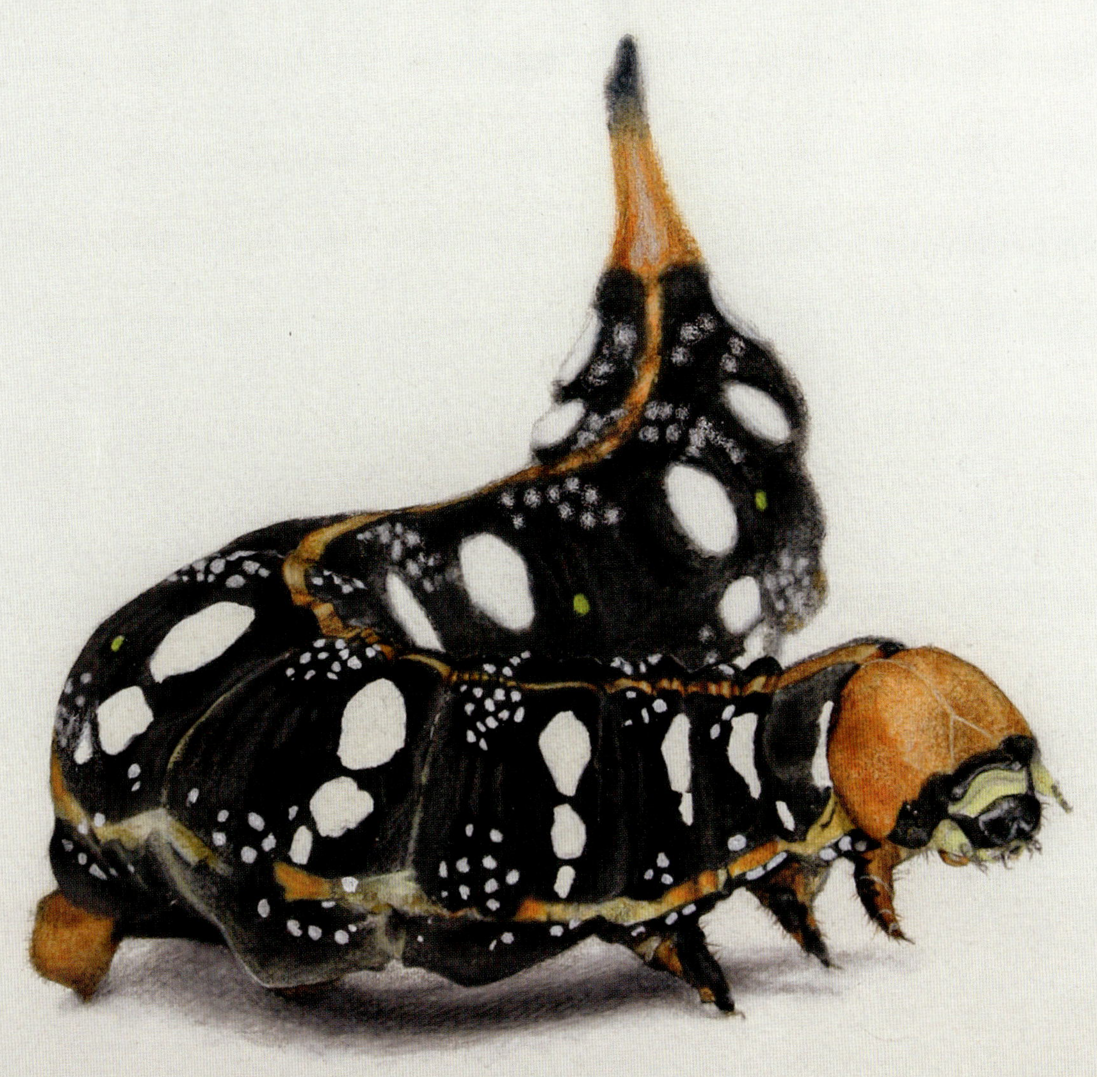

Shalden

LET NATURE COME TO YOU

This Nature Break is devoted to seeing what you can learn from a single spot when you slow down and let nature come to you!

LOCATION: Any place outdoors will offer some information about the natural world. Be sure that it is somewhere you can sit comfortably and remain still for ten to twenty minutes while you acquaint yourself with the surroundings.

MATERIALS: Sketchbook, your choice of art supplies, and a chair or blanket that can be easily carried.

OBSERVATIONS: Once you set up in a location, relax your body and witness the natural environment. Notice shifts in noise, movement, temperature, smell, or coloration. Consider the quality of each and how these elements might impact different species. If you find a creature, shift your vision between a focused investigation of it and a survey of the whole landscape.

PRACTICE: Select one of the natural characters you have been observing to become the subject of your artwork. Feel free to include the landscape in the composition. As you work, see if you can continue to be similarly aware of the activity around you.

REFLECTION: Before you leave the location, consider how you felt when you arrived and how your perception changed as you attuned to the environment. Did anything surprise you? More important, how did it impact your creative point of view?

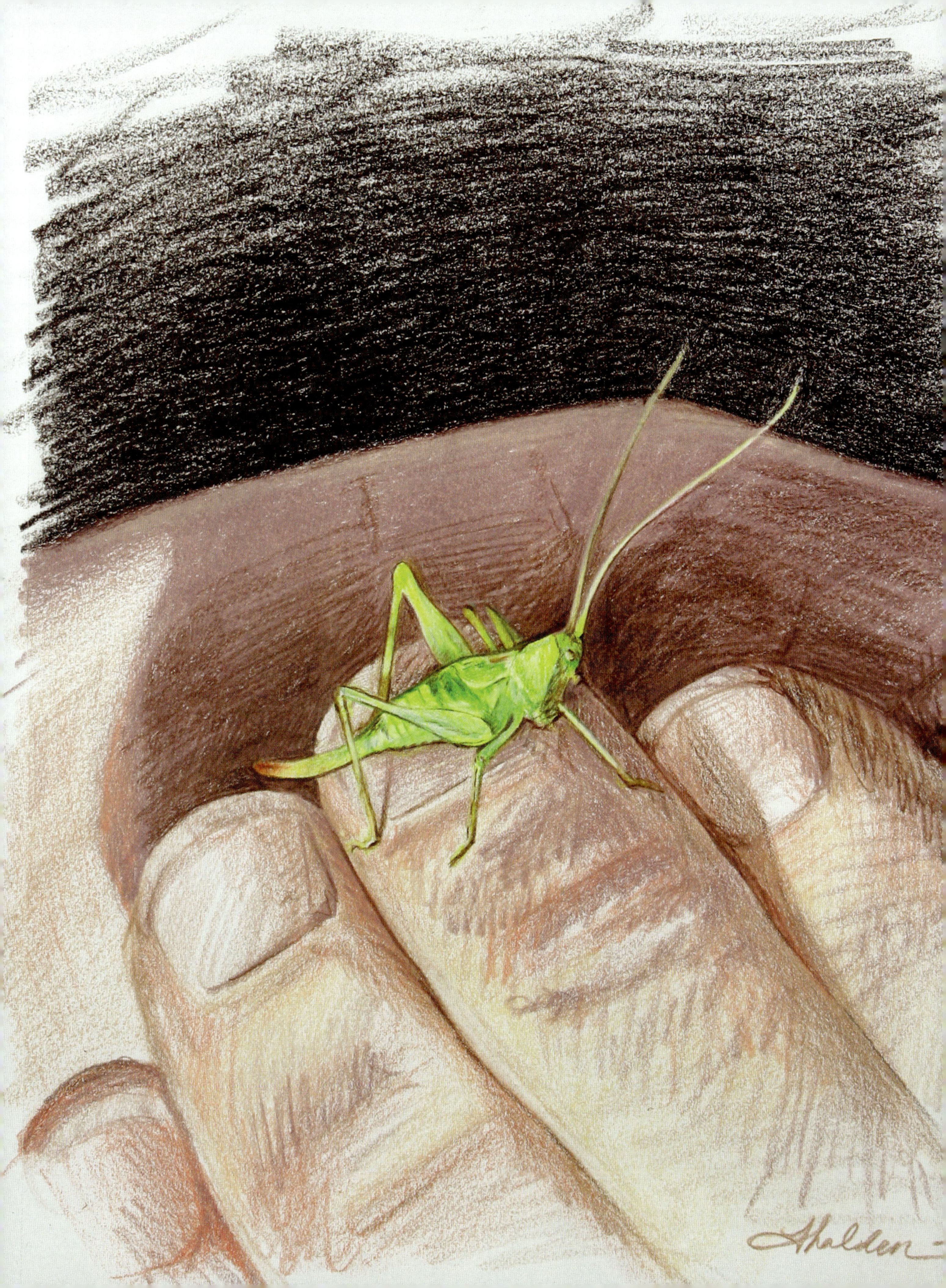

BUFF-TAILED BUMBLEBEE

BOMBUS TERRESTRIS

This particular bumblebee is a common garden visitor throughout Great Britain. It nests in large social units that consist of one hundred to six hundred individuals. They often establish their colonies in abandoned mouse nests. Although the end of the worker bee's abdomen is white, the queen bee has buff-colored hairs, giving this species its common name. I selected this composition for the textures it contains. You can create a voluminous amount of fuzz without having to draw every hair. And replicating the translucent wings comes down to applying certain colors so that they appear jagged while others are blended. By using both new and learned techniques, and focusing on one simple step at a time, you can make your bumblebee look as if it could move its wings and fly.

 SEE REFERENCE PHOTO ON PAGE 313

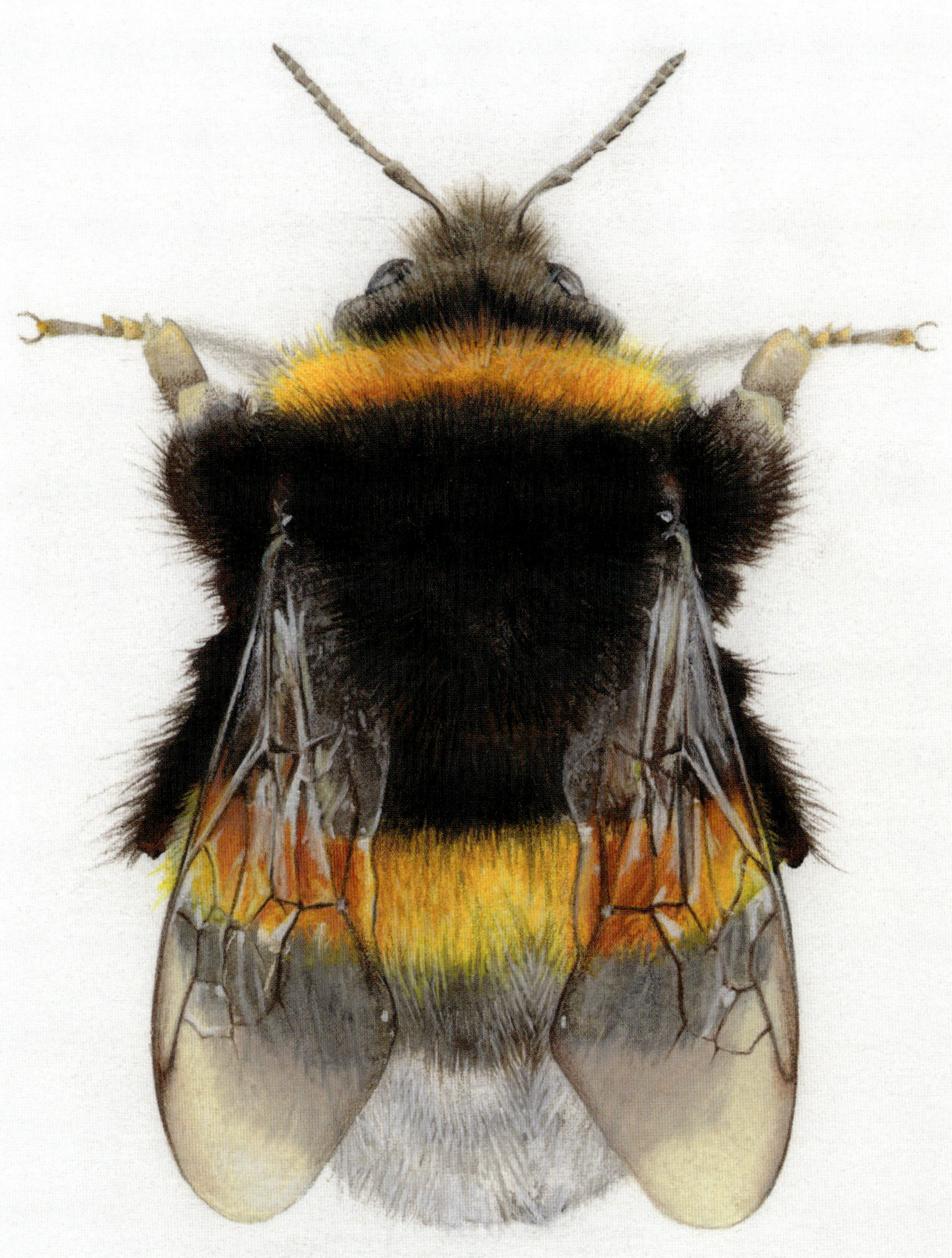

ACRYLIC
PAINTS
burnt sienna
burnt umber
cadmium red
cadmium yellow
Mars black
Naples yellow
Titian buff
titanium white

BRUSHES
sizes 000, 2, and
3 round

COLORED
PENCILS
10% French gray
30% French gray
50% French gray
black
burnt ocher
canary yellow
chocolate
cream
dark brown
goldenrod
jasmine
light umber
mineral orange
seashell pink
sepia
sienna brown
sunburst yellow
white

ADDITIONAL
MATERIALS
HB artist pencil
ruler
eraser
artist tape
tracing paper
water container
acrylic retarder
paper towels or
clean rags
drawing board
water container
plastic wrap
fixative (optional)

DRAWING

1 Make a quick yet proportional gesture drawing of the bumblebee's head, thorax, and abdomen, then add a midline. Decide how large you would like the subject to be, then mark the location of both the tip of the head and the base of the abdomen on the page with a dash.

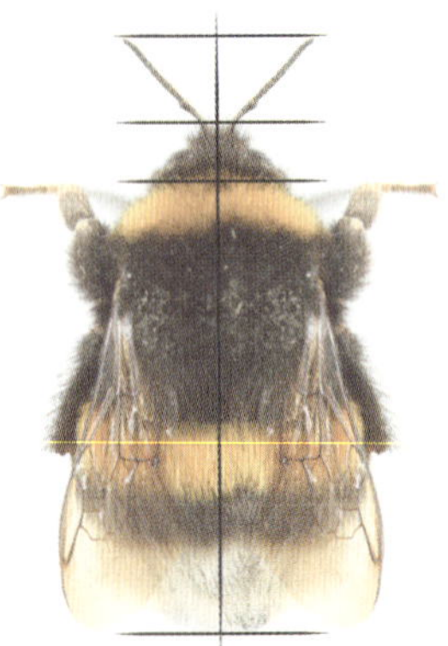

2 In this step, you will identify the measurements that can be used to establish your drawing's proportions, quickly test the options, and select the best one to work with. This process can train your eyes to quickly locate measurements whenever you view a new reference.

Any measurement can be used, but you'll save time if you pick one that is well defined in the reference image and that corresponds to the anatomy of the subject—perhaps the length or width of the head, thorax, or abdomen. Start by looking for a convenient feature located along the midline. In this reference image, I see three options: stripes, a vague division between the abdomen and thorax, and the length of the head. Since the abdomen is obscured by the wings, the best choices are the width of the head or the first yellow stripe, which clearly shows the width of the thorax.

You could stop here and simply choose either option. But you'll ultimately save time and effort by quickly comparing the two measurements. Use the thumb-and-pencil method (see step 1B on page 40) to place the width of the head from the reference image onto your pencil. Follow along an imaginary midline to see if the measurement lengths align with any anatomical transition points. Repeat this process with the widest portion of the yellow thorax stripe. Then select the measurement—head or stripe—that has the strongest relationship to the lengths and widths of the bee's anatomy.

3 A Since you know how many times the measurement will fit along the midline in the reference image, it may help to divide the midline on your drawing similarly starting from the base. Now you have the length of the measurement determined. You can then place the first full length on your pencil, rotate it horizontally, and mark both ends of the measurement feature with small vertical lines. Since this will be used to determine all remaining measurements, double-check that all the dashes along the midline match this dimension.

Your drawing should now have the width of either the head or yellow stripe defined, a midline that is marked with the lengths of your measurement, and a rough gesture of the head, thorax, and abdomen. During the drawing portion of this project, when you are instructed to measure on the reference image or your page, measure on your own first and then compare to the measurements mentioned to check your work. If you need more time or need to redo any step of this assignment, take it.

B If you have not done so already, measure the vertical location and width of the thorax stripe on the reference image and then mark your drawing. If you are using the stripe width as a measurement, you should find it is located about two lengths up on the midline; using the head-width measurement, it's close to three lengths up. Since the overall circular form of the entire thorax is slightly larger than the stripe, draw vertical lines to guesstimate this width as well.

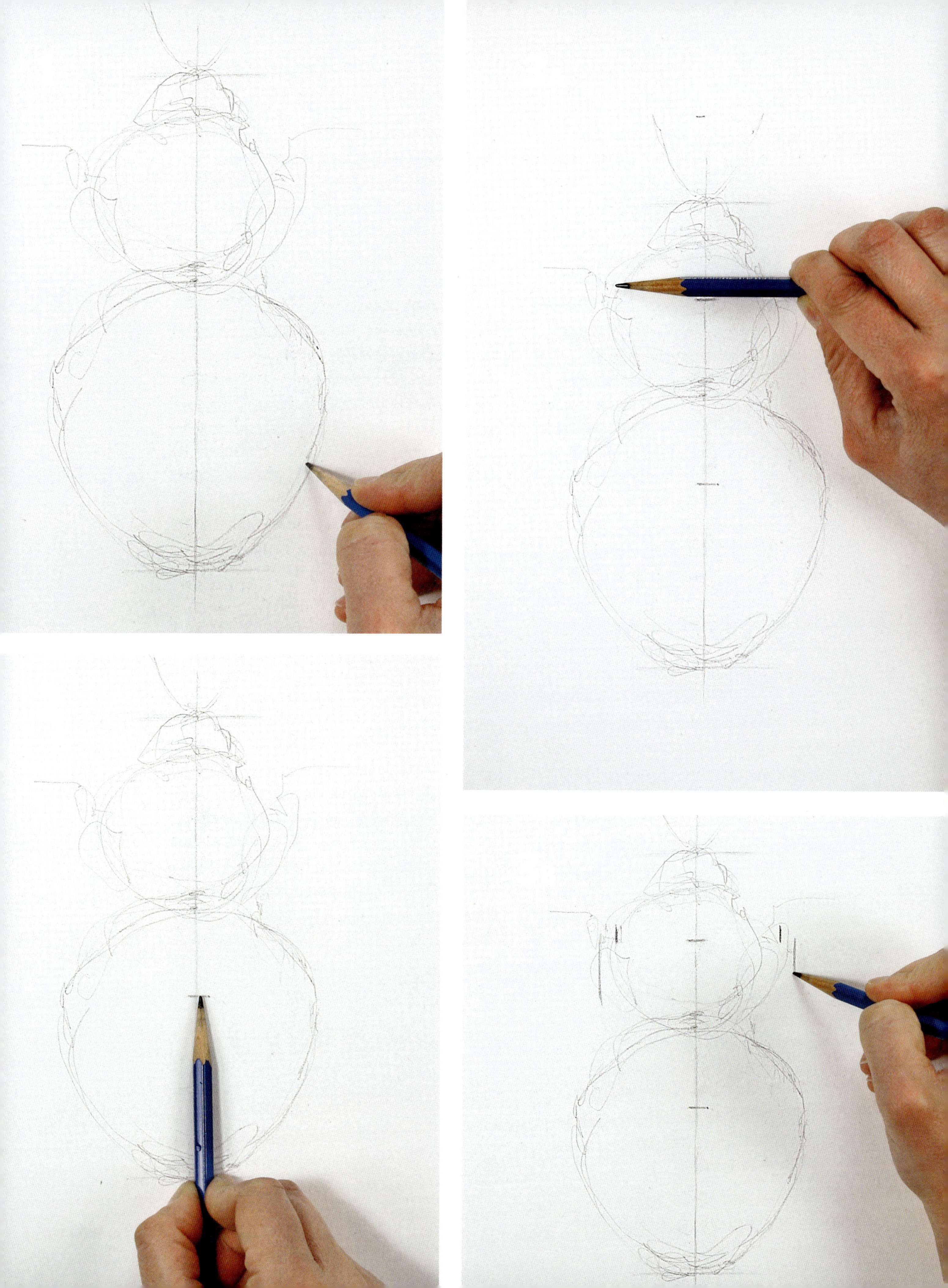

4 **A** To locate the top of the thorax, measure the thickness of the yellow stripe on the reference image. I found that the thickness of the yellow stripe (including fuzz and all) was about one-quarter of the stripe-width measurement and one-third of the head-width measurement.

B Now locate the bottom of the thorax. I found that it was situated either one-and-a-half stripe-width lengths or two head-width lengths up the midline. A horizontal mark at this location will also indicate the top of the abdomen. Since the abdomen appears to be equal in height and width, you can quickly mark the widest section of the abdomen. Then, if you have not done so already, find and mark the width of the head, which I found to be equivalent to two-thirds of the stripe-width measurement.

5 Now draw the bumblebee's outline. This composition is symmetrical: if you wish, draw one half of the bee and use tracing paper to mark the other half. Although the fuzz makes it difficult to see exactly where the body begins, do your best to create a line that follows the contour.

Check your measurements: holding your drawing at arm's length, compare the shape and size of the subject to the reference image. If your drawing is very different, retrace your steps to identify when the drawing deviated from the reference. Occasionally you can jump to a specific step, make a quick alteration, and return to where you left off. At other times, you may need to revisit each step and make many small adjustments. If your paper begins to wear from erasures, consider transferring the entire drawing to a new page. Sometimes, however—as I've learned from experience—it's simply best to take a deep breath and start the drawing over from the beginning.

6 **A** With the overall anatomical form finalized, locate the top and bottom of each stripe on the abdomen. Further divide the lengths already marked on your midline as needed.

B Lay your pencil horizontally on the reference image so that you see the arc and contour of each stripe in comparison to the straight line of your pencil. Notice that each also has a small peak near the center, close to the right wing. You might place a diagonal line on your drawing to mark each peak and the location of the end of the abdomen. Although I guesstimated the distance from the midline, I found that the diagonal seems to point toward the center of the head. Be aware that this may need slight adjustment after the wings are in place. Now draw the stripe lines on your page on both sides of the midline and, if needed, refine the shape of the outline.

7 To draw the angled antennae, lay your pencil vertically on the reference image: notice that the end of the antenna is directly above the end of the yellow thorax stripe. To find the height, compare the tip of the antennae to your measurement lengths along the midline and draw a horizontal line to indicate where the antennae will end. Look for the location where the antennae attaches to the head, then transfer the angle of each antennae from the reference image to your page. If you divide your angled lines into thirds, you can locate both the bottom portion of the antennae and the position of the fourth segment of the top section. Next, create the outline of the antennae and the remaining division lines. There are usually ten or eleven segments in this species.

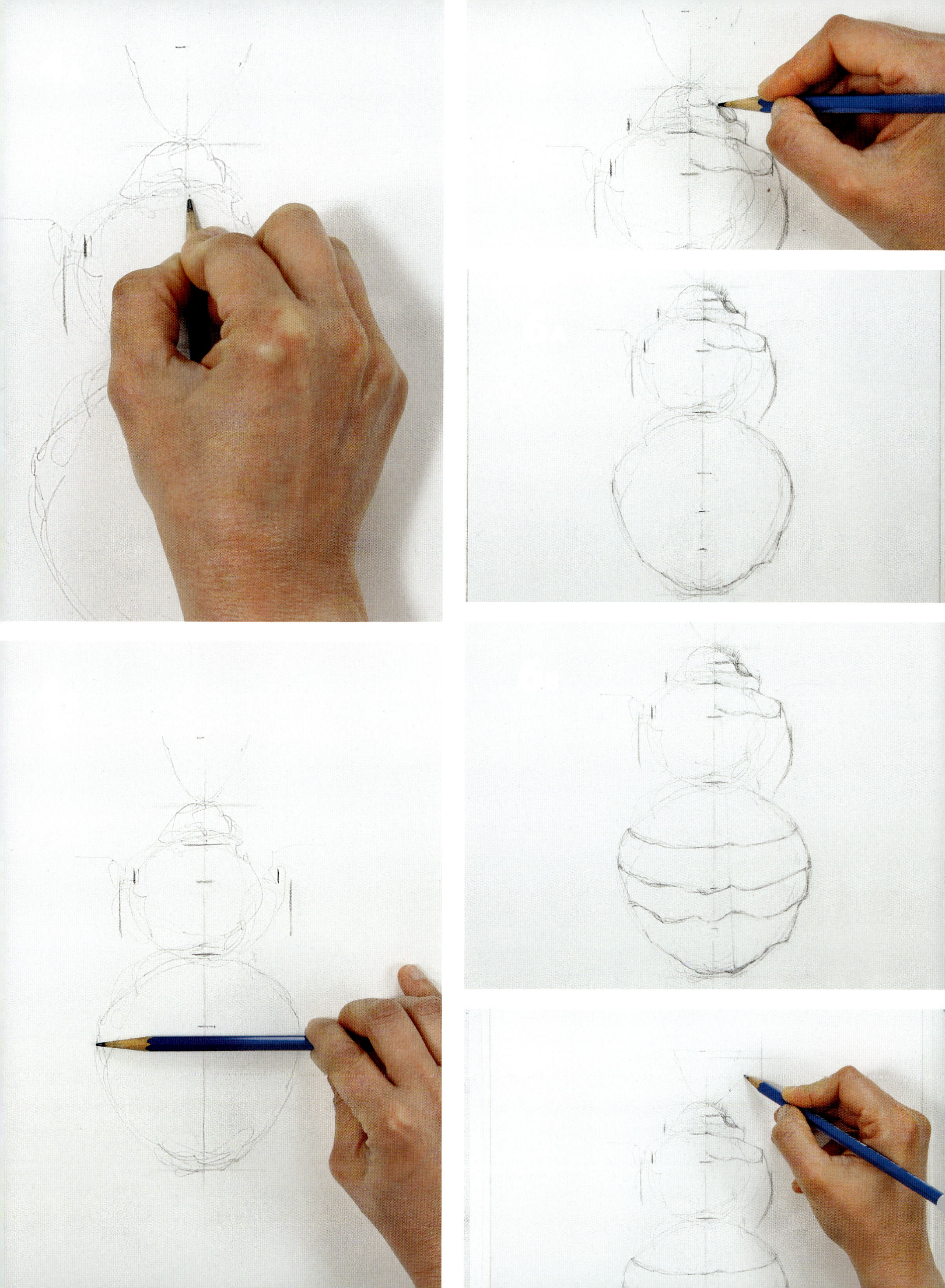

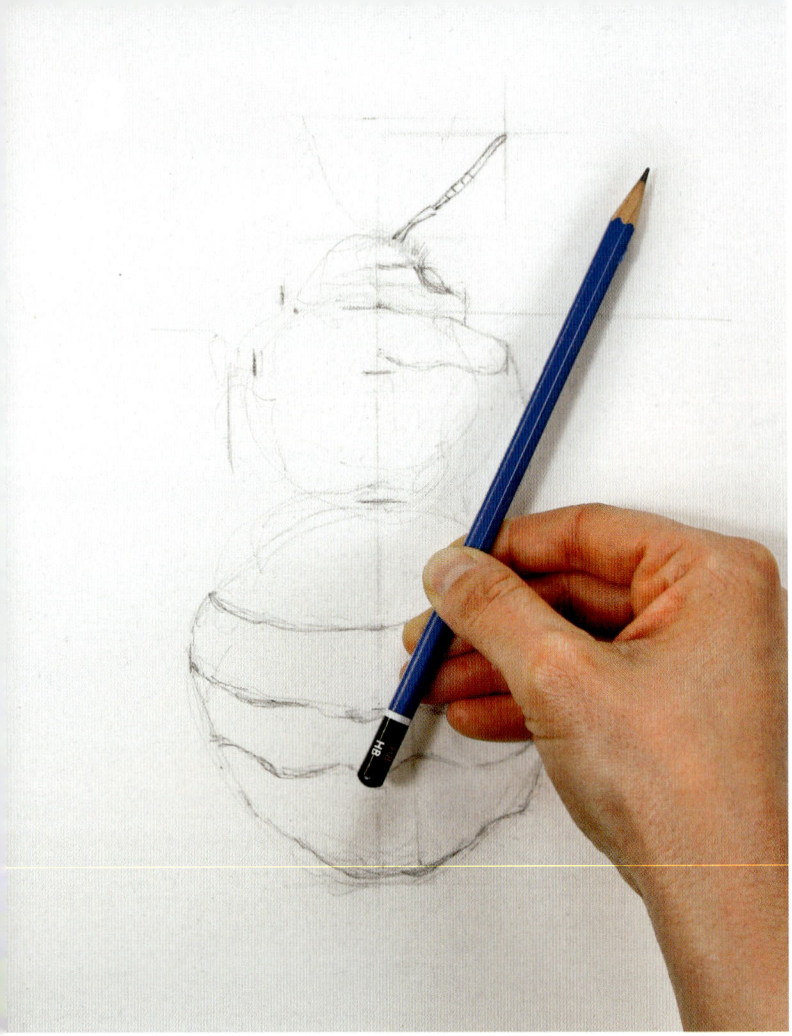

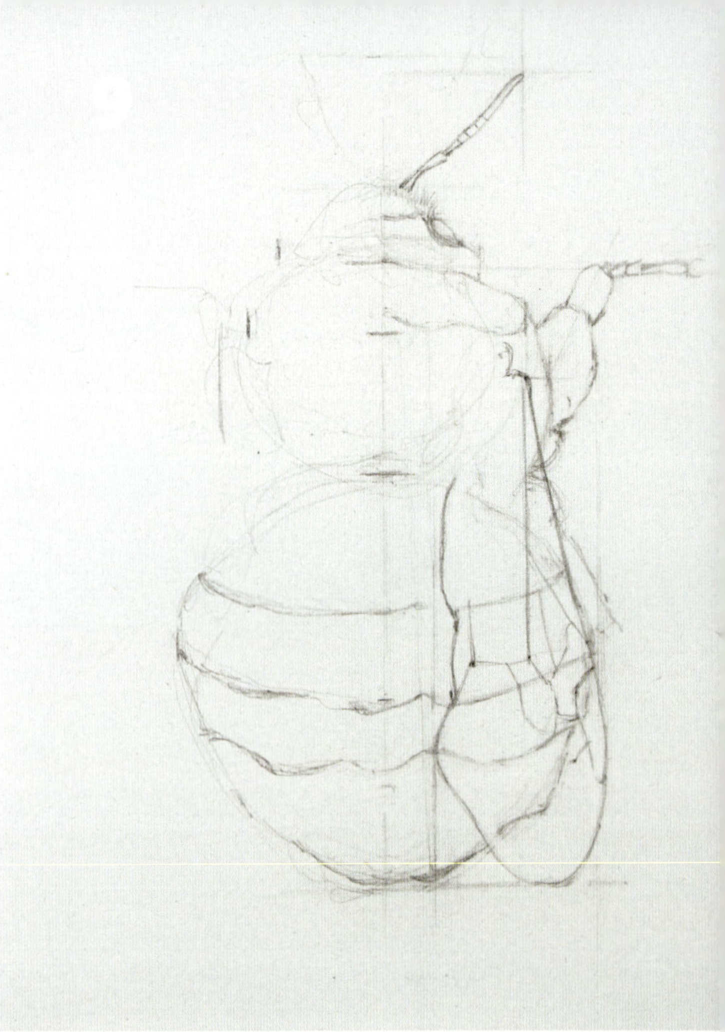

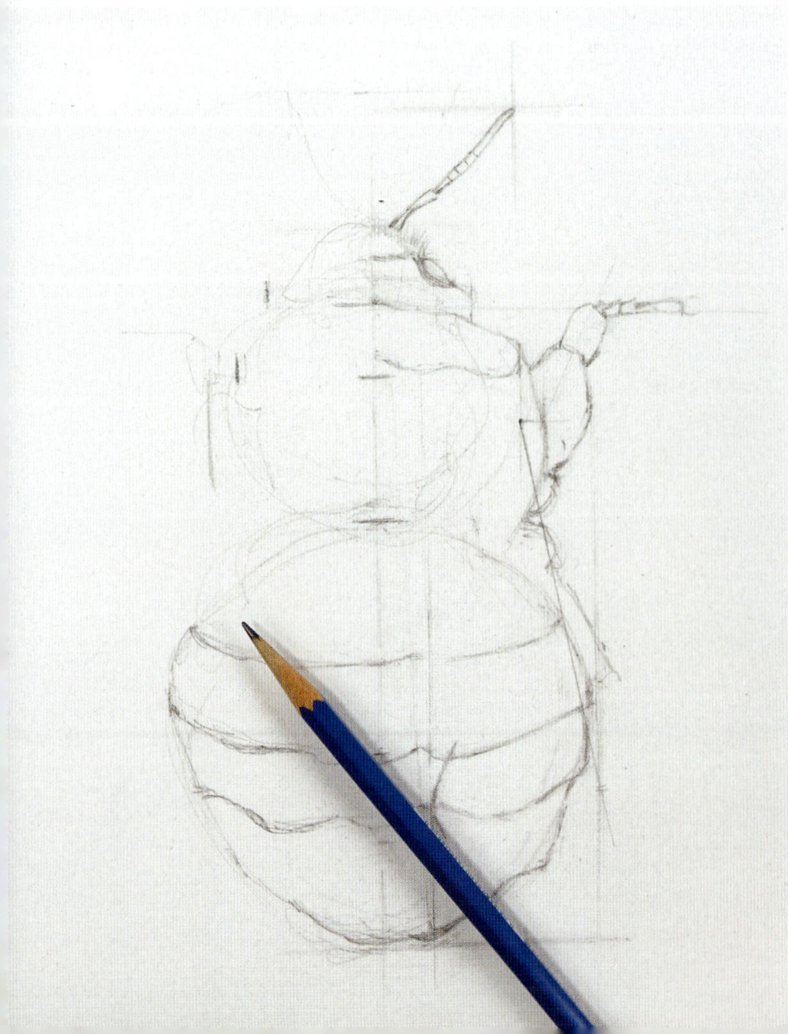

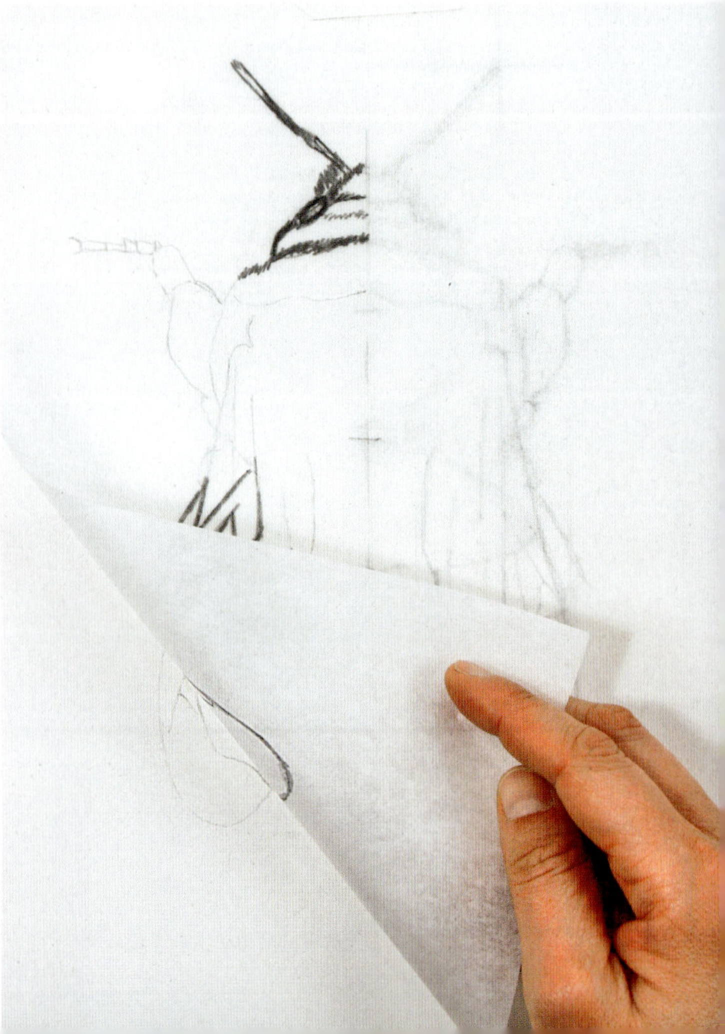

8 Measure and locate the correct position of the front leg and pull the angle for both the upper and lower portions from the reference image to your paper. Then draw a gesture of the overall form of each leg. To locate the point where the leg ends, place your pencil tip on the page where you think the claws begin, look back and forth from your drawing to the reference to confirm that the position is correct, and mark this location. Use both negative and positive space to carefully refine the outline of the entire leg so that you draw each foreshortened form correctly.

9 As you place the wing on the page, look for anatomical relationships. Notice how the end of the wing aligns with the bottom of the abdomen, the outside of the wing is under the side of the upper leg, and the inner wing lines up with the interior of the eye. Draw vertical and horizontal lines to indicate these correlations. Similarly, when you look for the location where the wing attaches, see if you can align this point to other features or angles. Now pull the outside angles of the wing from the reference image to your drawing and draw the curve at the wing's end. To create the contour along the interior side of the wing, use the location of the stripes and the thickness of the wing to determine the size and shape of each curve. Once you have completed the outline, add the veins so you will be able to see the underlying structure when you paint. Now that you have the veins in place, double-check the outline.

10 Make any final adjustments to the drawing and transfer the image to the opposite side. Remember to include the midline on the tracing paper and visually compare the width of the bee to the reference image before copying your lines. Then adjust the small details that do not appear to be symmetrical and either lighten or darken the pencil lines in preparation for painting.

PAINTING

1 In this project, the paint will differentiate edges that are fuzzy from those that are smooth. You will find the contrast between the two further emphasizes the furriness.

A Mix Mars black paint with burnt umber until it matches the color of the thorax. Use a size 3 paintbrush to add a water wash between the yellow stripes, on the upper legs, and along the inner side on the uppermost part of the wings. Then use a size 2 paintbrush to apply the color mixture. As you approach the wings or legs, watch how the paint bleeds so that you can transition back into the color of the paper before the edge of the wash; the idea is to avoid a hard paint edge in these areas. Be sure the pencil lines that define each wing remain discernable.

B When the paint has nearly dried, apply a diluted version of the brown mixture to the wings. Start from the base of the wings so that the paint can blend into the dark area, and paint in sections so that the veins remain white and visible.

Make a third version of the brown mixture by adding a small amount of Naples yellow paint until the color matches the value of the dark stripe on the abdomen. Wet the area with water to create three separate sections, then paint the left wing, right wing, and center.

2 Continue using this third brown color on the head. Avoid the eyes when adding the water wash so that you can create a hard edge along the perimeter when you paint the eyes later. In areas that should appear fuzzy—such as either side of the antennae and at the back of the head, where the dark fur blends with the yellow stripe—allow the water wash to go slightly over the outline. Then simply hold the paint-loaded brush between the eyes and let the color bleed outward to create the fuzzy edge. This color-bleeding process utilizes the natural interaction between paint and a wet surface to create a controlled flow. Enjoy creating these unique patterns while you emulate the look of the reference image. Paint the rest of the head and add a stripe of dark brown where the head meets the body. When this has dried a bit, apply the dark black paint to the eyes, making the color darker in the front and lighter toward the back.

3 To paint the end of the abdomen, mix titanium white paint with a small amount of Naples yellow. Study the reference image with blurred vision to discern the light, medium, and dark hair patterns. You can add slightly different amounts of the original dark brown paint mixture to create value variations. Working between the wings, apply the medium value first, then the light value, and finally accentuate using some of the dark-value paint mixture.

4 Move to the legs and create a paint mixture that matches the dark tan color found at the midsection. You can start with one of the gray paint mixtures used for the abdomen and add Naples yellow, titanium white, and just a touch of both cadmium red and cadmium yellow paint. Work with a size 000 paintbrush and keep the inner edge of the midsection white; you will draw in the light tan color with pencil later. Combine Naples yellow and titanium white paint to make a light cream paint mixture, and apply it so that it fades into the black. While the dark tan paint mixture is still wet on your palette, shift for a moment to paint the antennae. Since the area is so small, it is not necessary to use a water wash.

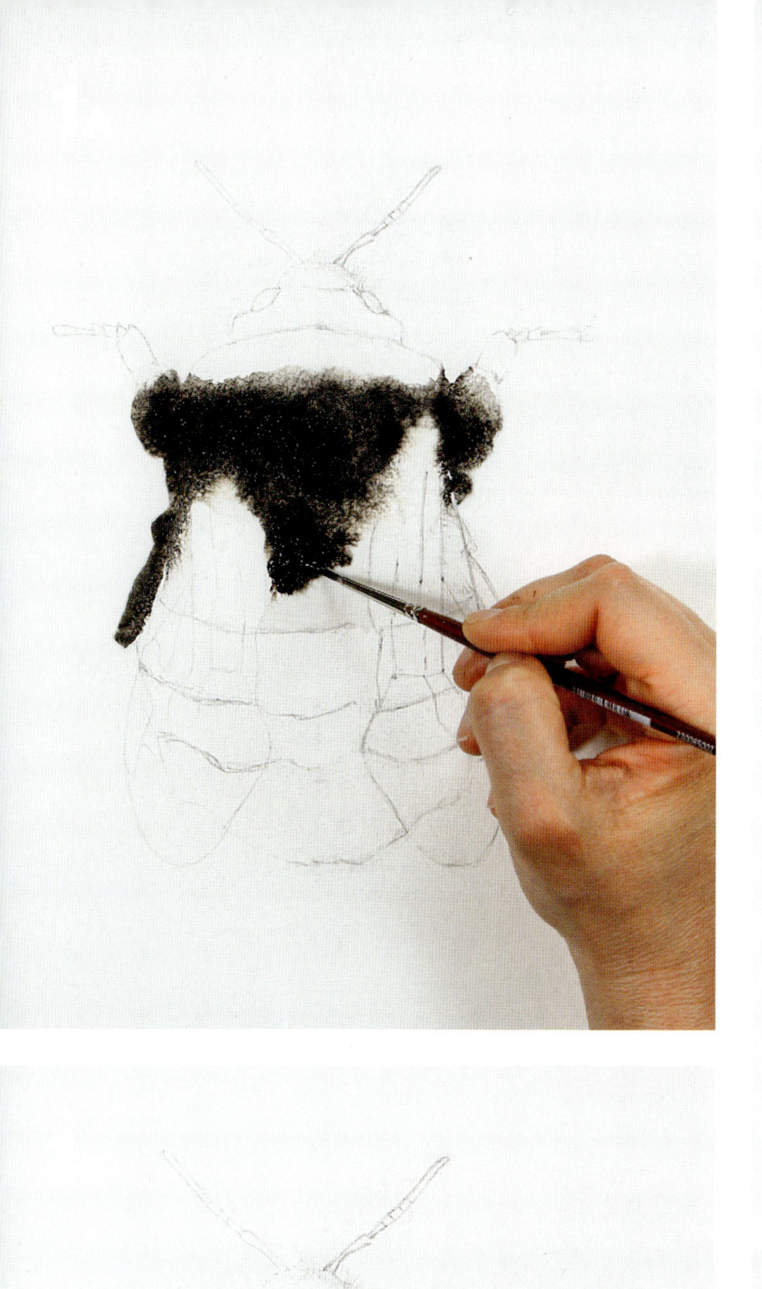

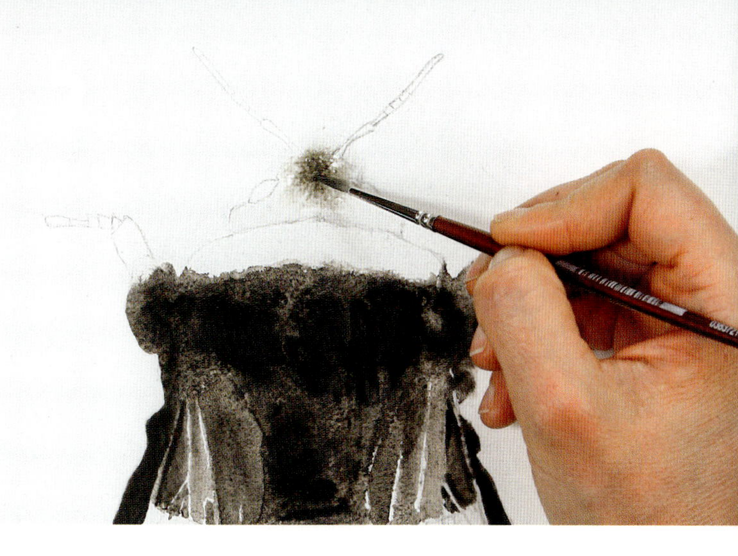

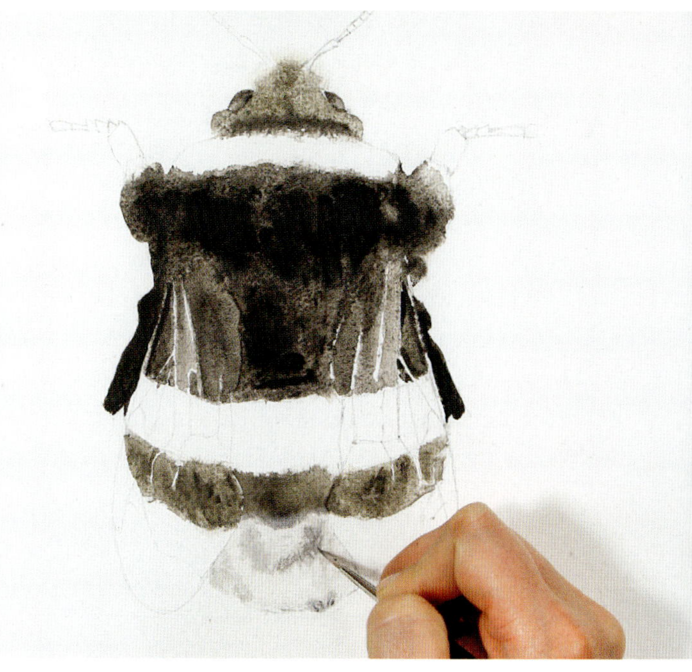

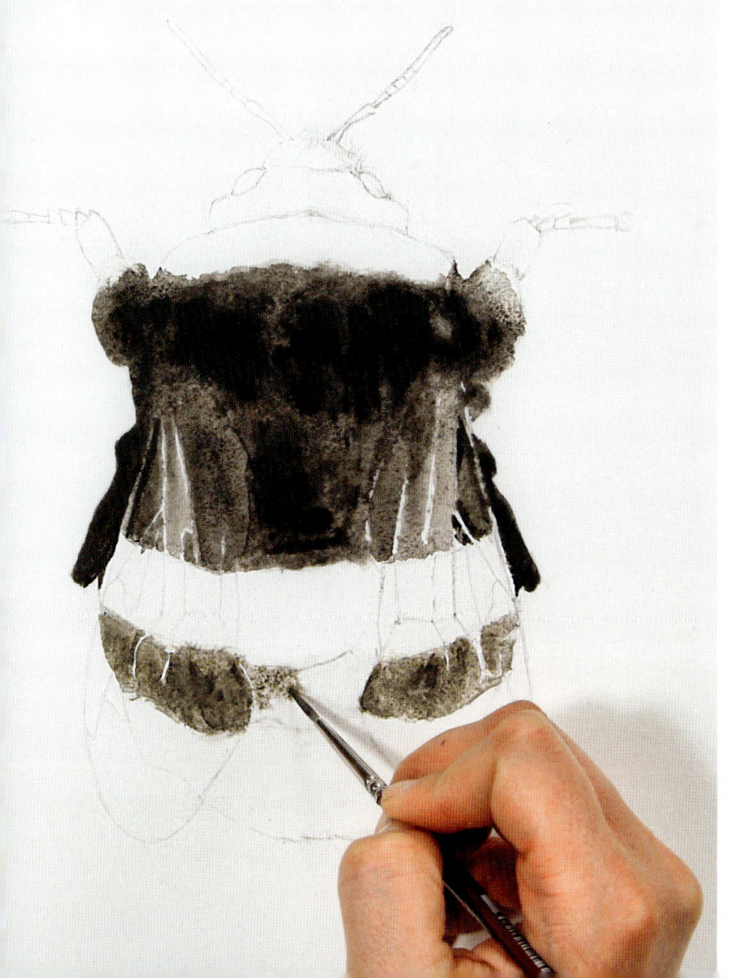

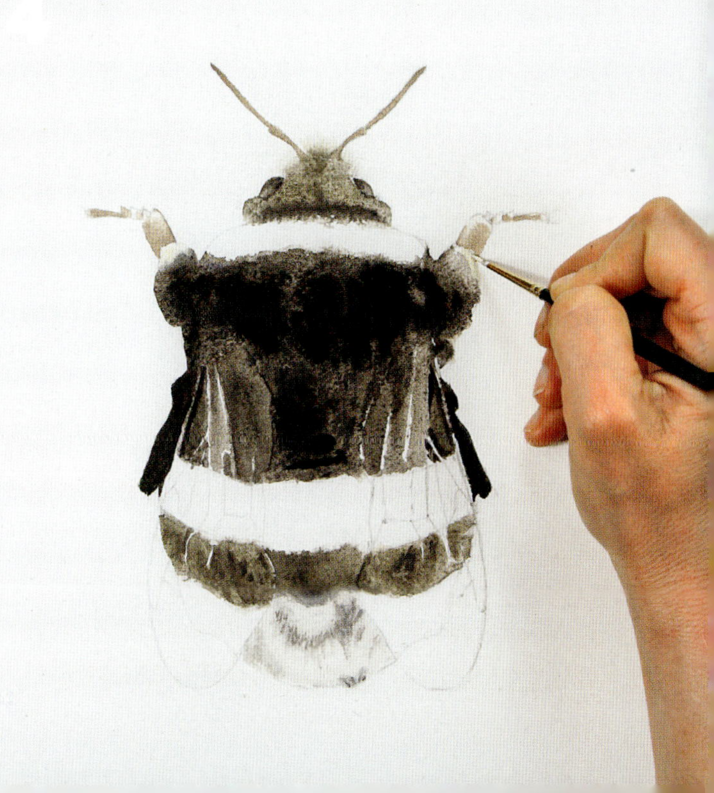

5 **A** It's time for some bold color! Using a size 2 paintbrush, mix the paint colors for the colorful stripes. For the lightest color, combine cadmium yellow and titanium white paint. For the mid-tone color, combine cadmium yellow with burnt sienna and add a touch of titanium white, just to bring down the saturation slightly.

When coating the thorax with a water wash, remember to allow the water to go slightly over the border all the way around. Start to paint in the center of the stripe using the mid-tone mixture. Then add the yellow mixture to the unpainted ends. Finally, switch to a size 000 paintbrush and add a thin blurred line using a dark orange mixture at the top and bottom of the stripe, right next to the black, as a transition from yellow to the darker color.

B Move to the yellow area on the abdomen. After wetting the area between the wings, begin by using the yellow mixture, followed by the mid-tone and then the dark orange paint mixtures. When this starts to dry, move to the wings, using the same method and adding more burnt sienna paint when needed. Continue to avoid painting in the veins, and make sure your paint is thin enough that you can see the pencil lines after the color has been applied.

While these colors are on your palette, add some of the mid-tone orange mixture to the lower leg segments.

6 To complete the wings, mix burnt umber with a bit of black paint to achieve a color that is just lighter than the veins on the wings. Have a small amount of Titian buff paint ready in a separate area of your palette. It is essential that these paints be highly diluted. You can always add a second layer to darken the illustration, if needed.

Add a water wash to the entirety of one wing. Use the Titian buff paint to create an arc that overlaps the end of the abdomen slightly; this will start to differentiate the wing from the background. Now switch to the brown mixture and paint the portion of the wing over the body, including the abdomen, to both integrate the veins and reiterate a wing resting on top of the body. Before the wash dries, select a very small paintbrush and apply the brown mixture along the outside edge of the wing to create the branching vein near the tip. You can add another layer to the edge to darken or refine it, if needed.

For the wing transparency to be convincing, every color inside of the wings must have the same value shift when compared to the section between the wings. To check this, look at the color of the wing over the white background: this will help you understand how much darker each stripe should be. If you find that the wings are too dark, however, you may need to add a bit more Titian buff paint to the section over the background. While this process is fresh in your mind, repeat these steps to paint the second wing.

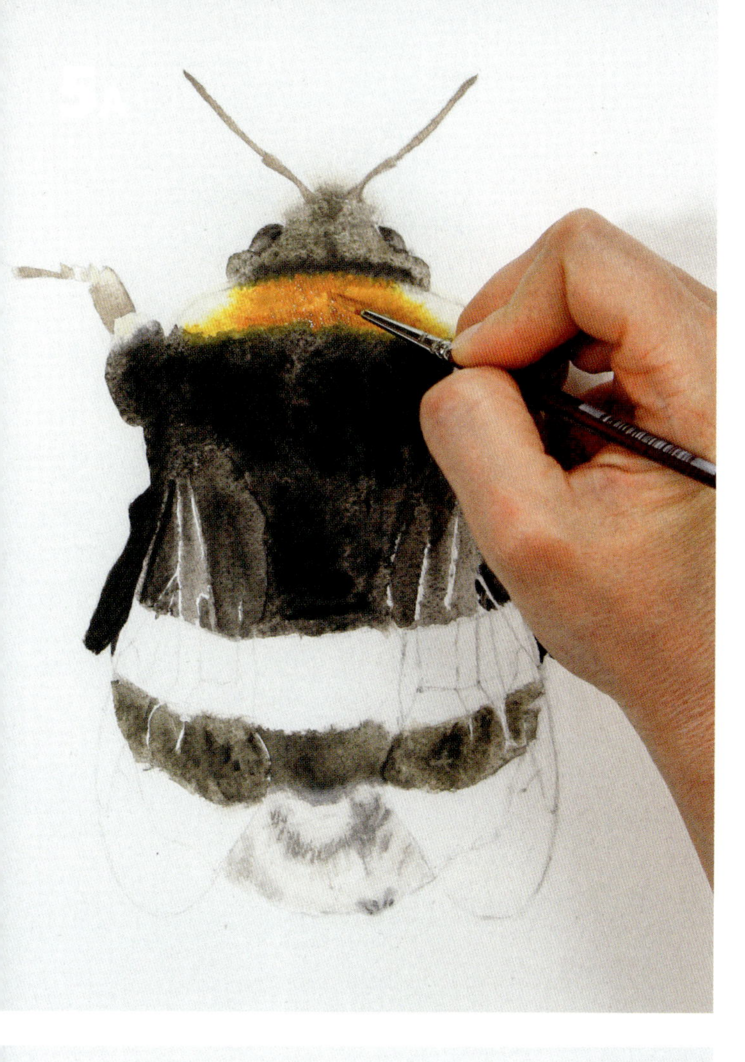
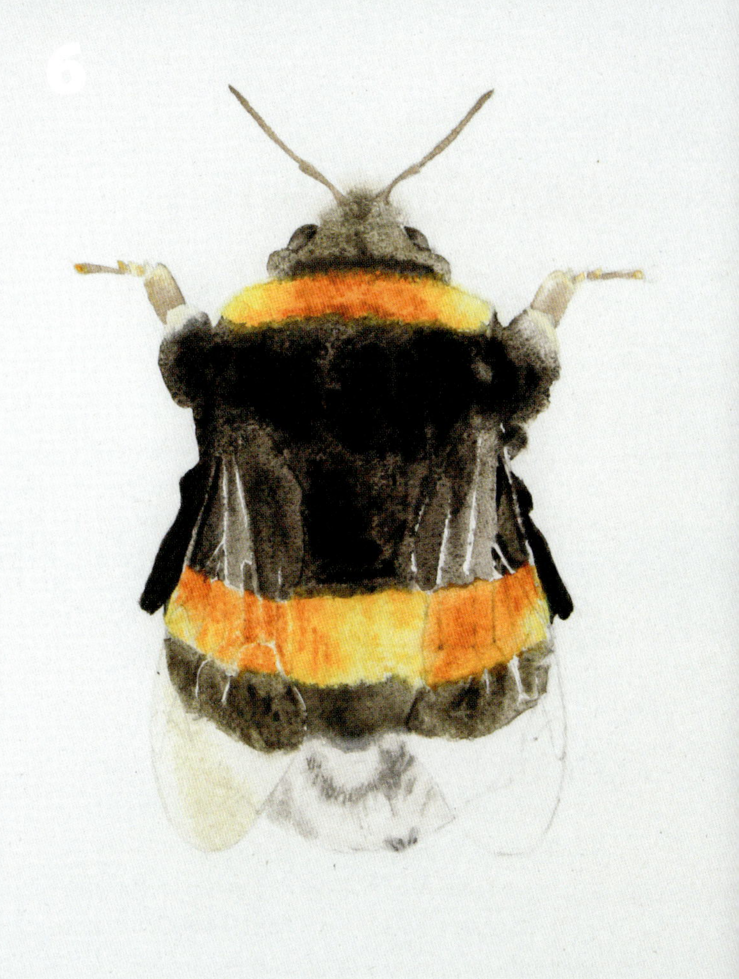
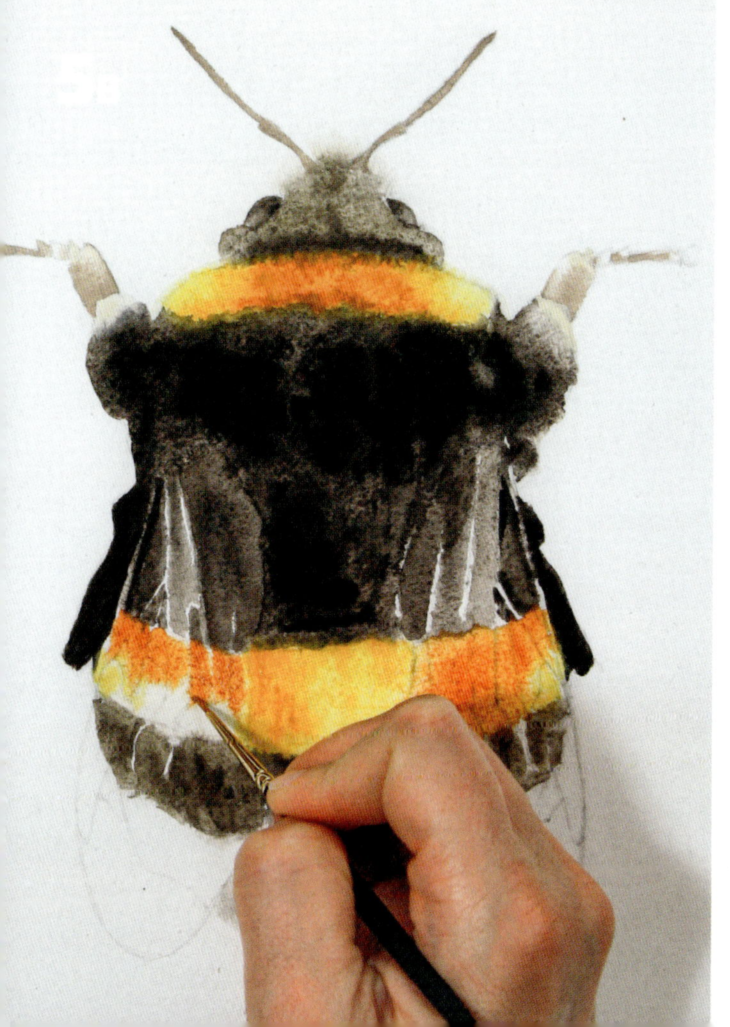
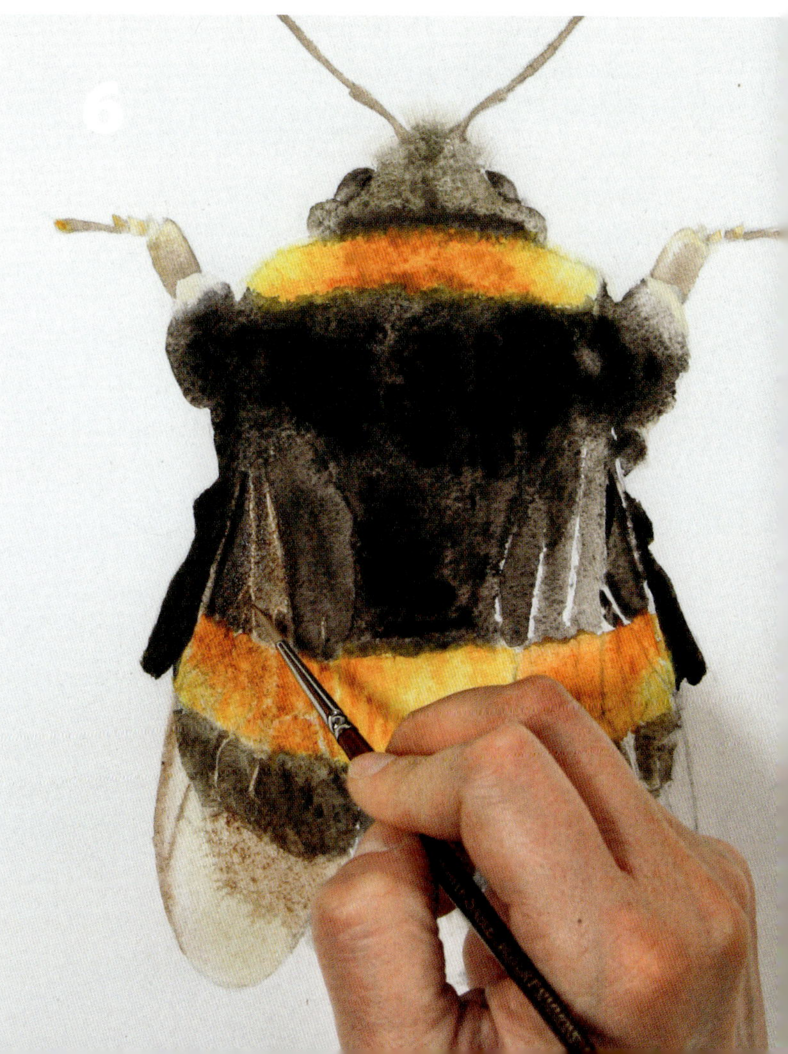

LAYERING WITH COLORED PENCIL

1 **A** When you are working with a lot of colored pencils, especially ones that have a similar hue or value, it's handy to create a swatch card with a sample of each color. You can even show the value range of each pencil by drawing a quick gradient. I keep the pencils on my workspace in the same order in which they are found on the swatch so I can locate colors quickly.

B To create the bumblebee hairs, start with the yellow thorax stripe and work your way down the body. Begin by using the mineral orange pencil, close to the midline, and flick the pencil toward the head. Keep your marks short, in a similar shape, and oriented in the same direction as the hair you see in the reference image, but allow them to be slightly different lengths, and occasionally vary the angle of some hairs for a realistic effect. Allow the paint to show through your marks except along the edge, which will need a solid layer of hairs to make the fuzzy quality of the bumblebee convincing. Repeat this process using the jasmine pencil toward the sides and also to speckle the middle section of the stripe. Jump to the outline along the side of the thoracic stripe and use the cream pencil to flick outward over the background. These slightly darker hairs will both emphasize the depth of fur along the side of the bumblebee and stand out against the white background. Now use the sunburst yellow pencil to add some orange hairs throughout the yellow area. Finally, use the sienna brown pencil to darken the stripe next to the black area of the thorax. Voilà, your subject is starting to look like a wonderfully fuzzy bee.

Though it may be tempting to work on the head now, wait! It will be far easier to make the head stand out from the abdomen when the body is closer to completion. And as you put in more time practicing your pencil technique on the body, you'll be able to apply more refined marks to this area.

2 Move to the front legs. Use the chocolate pencil to add hairs to the outer edges. Build up the hairs in layers by creating a row at the very edge and adding another layer a little closer to the interior. As you move toward the center of the form, add a few hairs oriented in the same direction. For the hind legs, continue using the chocolate pencil for the first layer and switch to the sepia pencil as you move inward. You might also add a hint of sienna brown at the end of the lower leg.

3 Begin working on the section of the thorax closest to the yellow stripe by using the sepia pencil to add a few layers of hairs. Add more hairs toward the interior, but keep the very center clear. I found it most advantageous to focus on the areas where the paint was lighter and chose to leave the dark areas blank.

Now switch to the black pencil and, using the same technique, draw hairs on the side of the thorax to differentiate this area from the brown legs. Also add more hairs in select areas where you have already used the sepia pencil to integrate the sides into the center of the thorax. If the wing needs more definition, shade the area between the wing and leg.

Now take a look at the reference image to determine where the thorax ends and the black stripe on the abdomen begins. Use the light umber pencil to draw a couple of layers of hairs at the base of the thorax, to define this separation. As you curve around and near the wings, switch to black and let your marks overlap the wing edge slightly.

You may notice a significant amount of pollen on the bumblebee in the reference image. Because this dust detracts from the fuzzy quality that I want to accentuate, I chose to exclude it in my artwork.

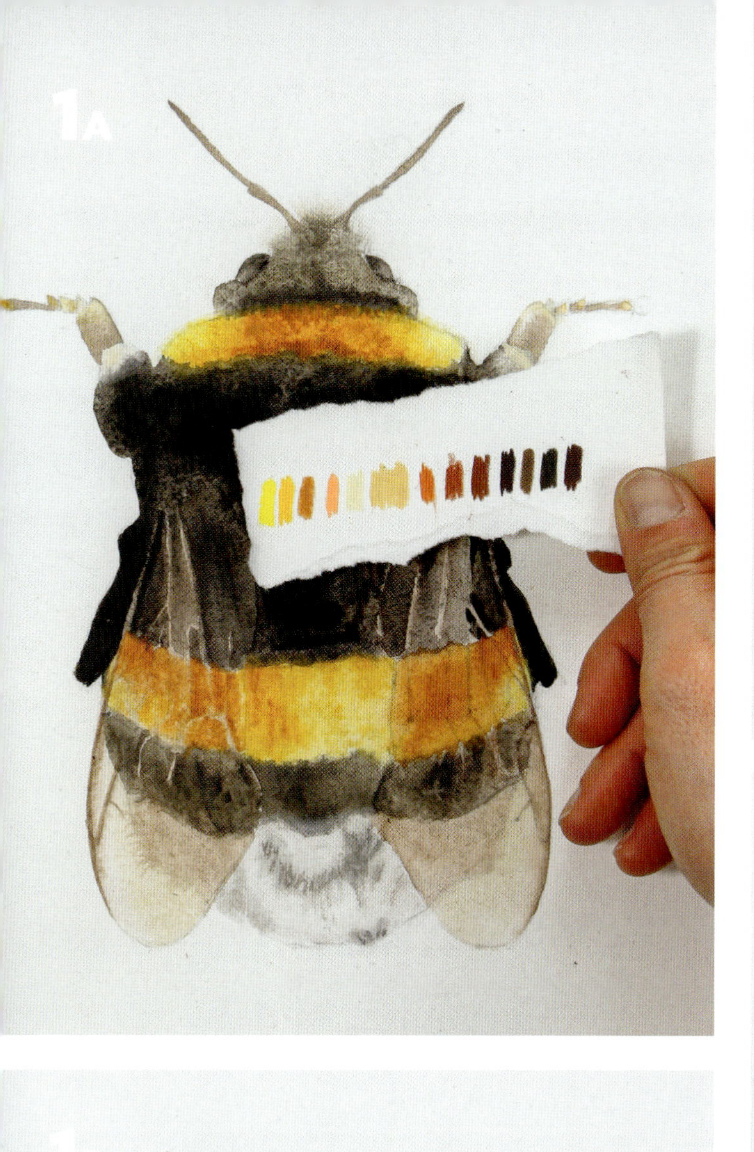

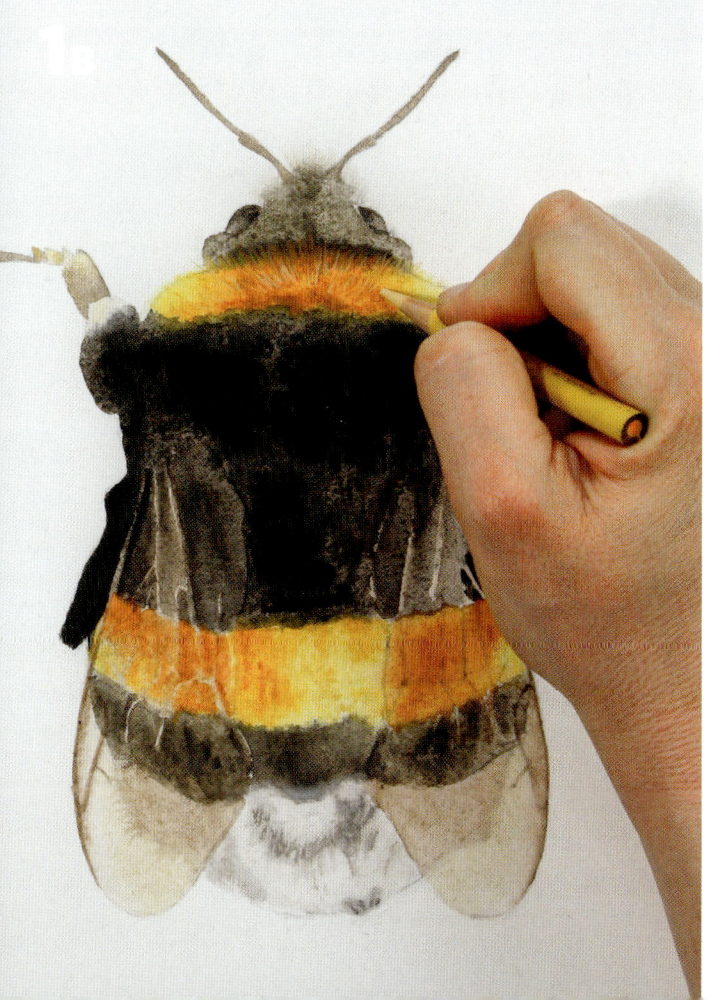

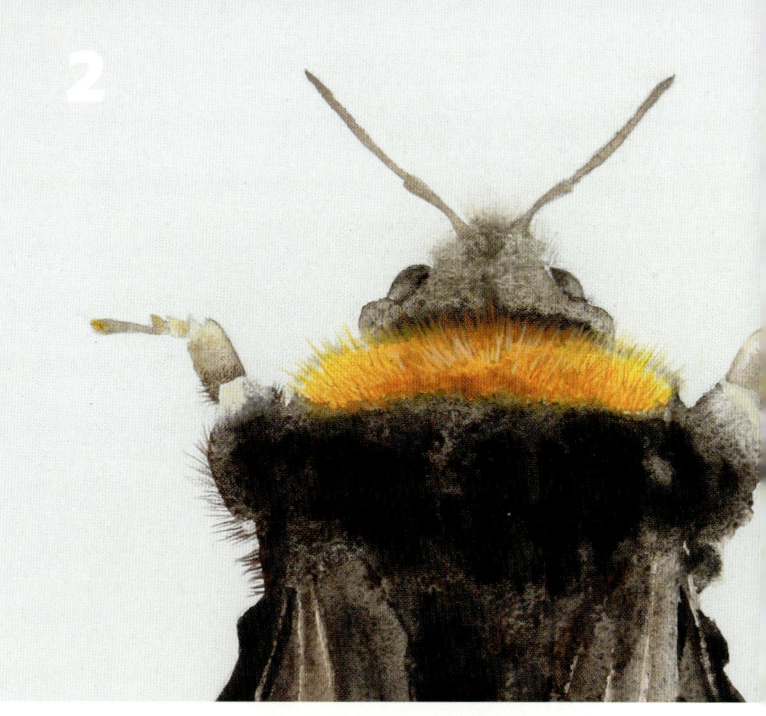

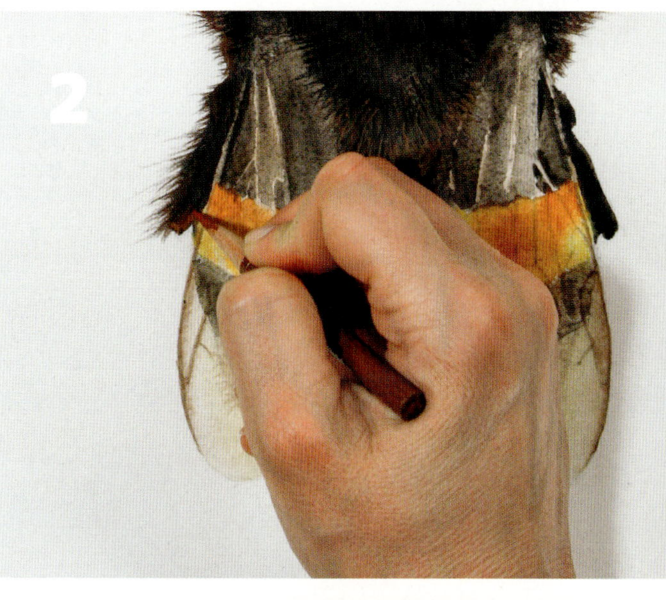

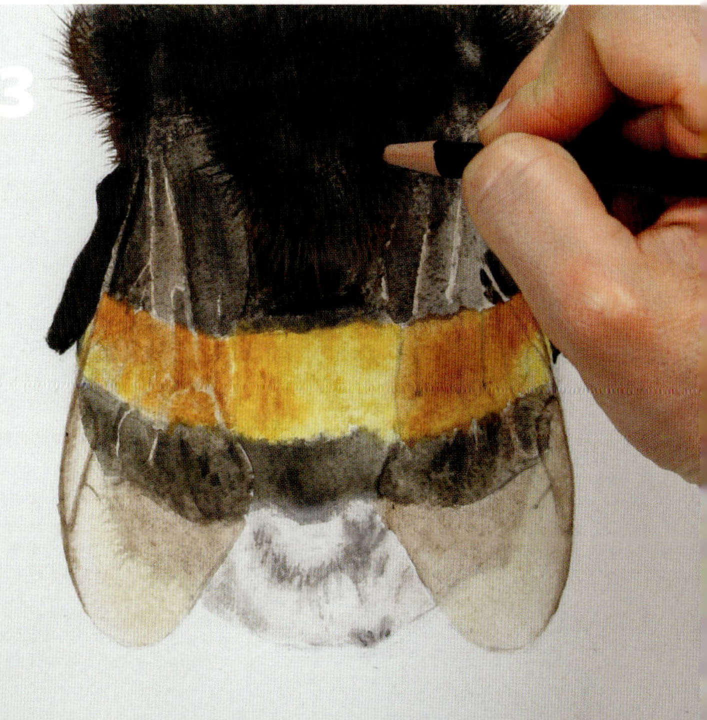

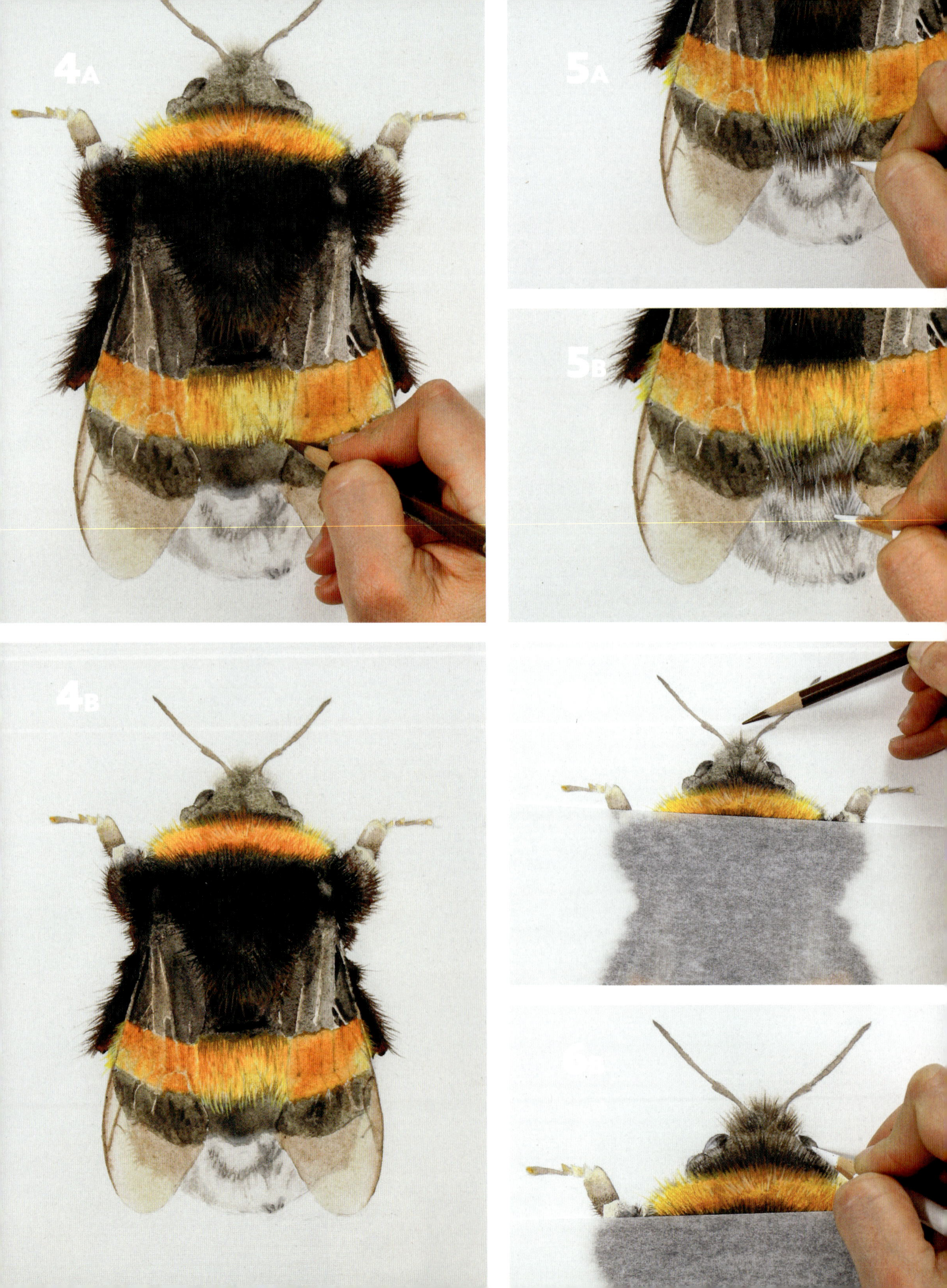
4A
4B
5A
5B

4 **A** Moving to the abdomen stripes, work only between the wings and start along the edges of the yellow stripe. Use the light umber pencil with downward marks for the top of the stripe and upward marks along the bottom of the stripe. Instead of being seen as hairs, these upward strokes actually create the negative space between yellow hairs. Allow them to be whatever shape is necessary to create little yellow downward-pointing triangles that match the hairs that were created using a single pencil stroke. As you near the peak toward the center of the stripe, pay close attention to the angle and pattern of the hairs.

B Next, work with the sunburst yellow pencil, followed by the goldenrod, to add orange hairs. Then you can apply a very light yellow to accentuate the points on the hairs at the bottom of this stripe. (I could not find a good pencil match, so I layered the cream and the canary yellow pencils instead.) Now move to the section of the stripe on the other side of each wing and add the small tufts of color that poke out.

Just above the yellow stripe, use the sepia pencil along the edge to add hairs that overlap the yellow. If you move closer to the thorax, switch to the black pencil. As you work, be sure to avoid the hairs that define the bottom of the thorax so the anatomy remains clearly defined. If needed, you can shade any uneven areas.

5 **A** Jump to the dark stripe on the abdomen. Using the light umber pencil, add a few strategically placed hairs to the light areas of this stripe. At the bottom of the stripe, use the white pencil to create the same upward motion used for the previous stripe.

B Move to the end of the abdomen. Use the 30% French gray and then the 50% French gray pencil to further integrate the darkened sections of paint into the white paper. Then use the white pencil to cover all of the dark areas with light hairs. Continue with the same pencils and similar downward strokes to accentuate the edge as well. Take

a look at your work and admire the fuzzy body you have given this bumblebee.

6 **A** Shift your attention to the head. Be sure to protect your work to avoid smudging (see page 27). Begin by adding hairs with the sepia pencil at the base of the antennae and along the back of the head next to the yellow stripe. Switch to the black pencil to further accentuate the area next to the thorax. As you work, emphasize the midline with a few longer hairs. You can add some light hairs with the seashell pink pencil, if needed.

B Use the white pencil to emphasize the highlights on the eyes. If you use the full value range of the pencil, it will be easier to visually describe this smooth curved surface. In my drawing, I chose to accentuate the eyes beyond what is seen in the reference image to heighten the emphasis. When the highlights are finished, line the interior edge of the eye with either the sepia or black pencil, skipping over any hairs that overlap.

C To complete the head, add highlights and shadows to the antennae. Use the cream pencil, with a very sharp tip, along the inner edge between the segments and the sepia pencil along the outer edge. At this point, the head—particularly the highlights on the eyes and the details on the antennae—should be the most prominent part of the drawing. (Later, the wings become the primary focus.)

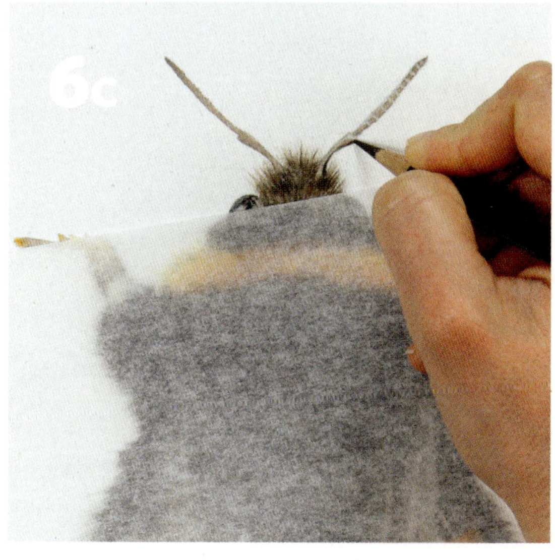

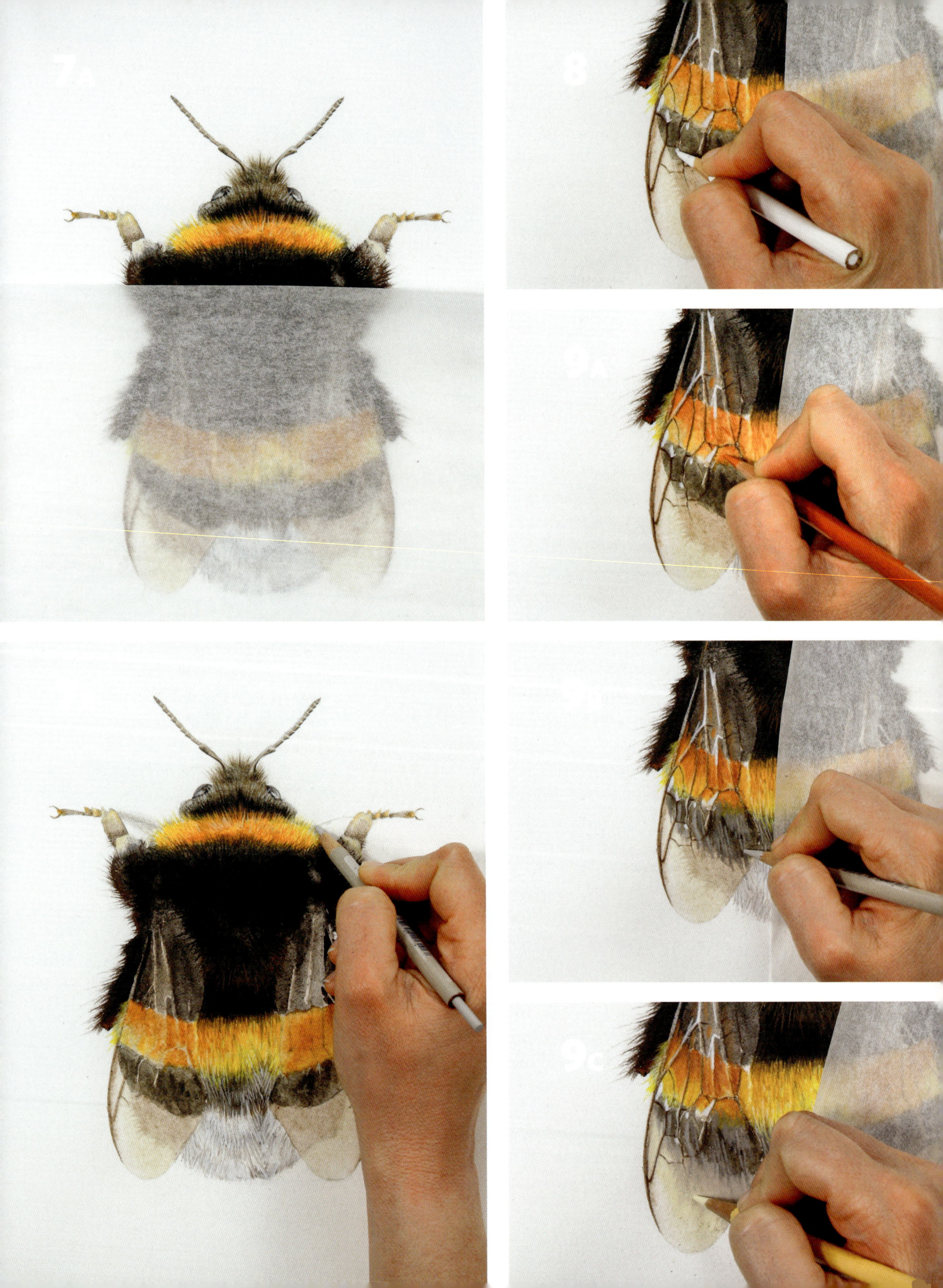

7 **A** Move to the legs. Apply a small amount of the light umber pencil to create claws and to define the base of each lower segment, where one connects to another. You might add some mineral orange or jasmine pencil to the ends of these segments to accentuate the paint color.

B To create the shadow cast by the legs, take the 30% French gray pencil and draw a single arc from the leg to the thorax to designate the center of the shadow. Use very light pressure until you feel that the arc is in the appropriate position. Then fade this line out on the top and bottom while further darkening the center of the arc. After adding the shadow, use the 50% French gray pencil to add more definition to the thorax hairs or edge of the leg, where the shadow meets the body. This helps make the shadow appear lower than the bumblebee.

8 Now it is time to give the entire drawing unity and pizzazz by adding details to the wings. For this part of the drawing, work with dull-tipped pencils and apply firm pressure so that the colors are rich in tone and easily blend together. My preference is to complete one wing at a time. However, since the anatomy and lighting makes the highlights on both wings identical, you might choose to do each step on both wings simultaneously.

Since white can easily be overtaken by other colors, it's good to rough in the bright highlights first and avoid these areas as you add other colors. As you locate these bright spots, you may find it helpful to redefine the veins in dark brown pencil.

9 **A** With this structure in place, begin adding color between the veins. Start on top of the yellow stripe using a mid-tone pencil, like mineral orange, then add burnt ocher and sunburst yellow. As you follow the coloration in the reference image, go back and forth between these three pencils to fill each cell. Instead of adding individual hairs, overlap and blend the colors together.

Before you move on to different colors, you might add mineral orange along the outside of the wing where it attaches to the body.

B Moving down the abdomen to the next stripe, use the full range of French gray pencils to add color to the cells and to replicate the slightly blurred hairs at the top and bottom of the stripe. A fairly thick layer of color and overlapping marks helps create this effect.

C Work on the last stripe using French gray pencils to add any dark areas. Look for the dark sections between the wings that would continue under the wing as well. Next, use the seashell pink pencil and cover the entire area of the final stripe. You will want to work in the same direction that the hairs are going and draw right over the dark marks. Now use the cream pencil to blend the edge of the stripe into the color of the wing over the background and continue outward toward the tip. It is important that this section of the wing be covered in a solid layer of pencil. At the edge next to the vein, layer the seashell pink on top of the cream pencil.

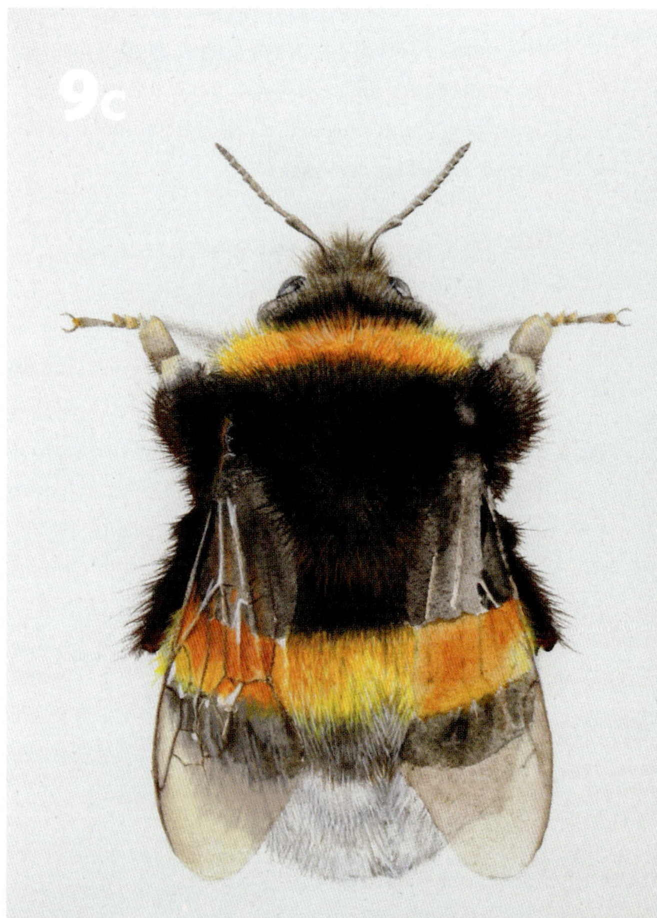

10 **A** Returning to the wing highlights, use the white pencil with a very sharp tip. Follow the reference image to make bold straight lines, stippled patterns, and small areas that are slightly lighter. Each highlight you add will help describe the shape of the wing and make the insect look more realistic, so take your time at this stage to observe carefully and apply accurate marks. Consider the shape of the anatomy and the position of the light source that is creating the highlight.

You might find it best to leave very thin highlights off altogether or create them by placing a color that matches the surroundings on either side to form a very thin white line between. When you have completed the highlights, switch to using the sepia pencil and define the veins using the same level of attention to their placement. You can also use the black pencil sparingly, particularly at the upper portion of the wing, to further illuminate the highlights and to articulate the structure of the wing.

B To accentuate the wing edge, use a fine white pencil line on the edges over dark sections, such as the upper wing, and use the sepia pencil on the edges over the light background. Avoid creating an outline here. Instead, allow the weight of your line to vary slightly. It will help if you blend the edge color in toward the interior of the wing, so that it does not appear as an abrupt edge.

11 Once you have completed both wings, look at your drawing at arm's length, and adjust any colors, highlights, or areas that would benefit from a smoother transition. Celebrate the finished work and honor the many new techniques you practiced: emulating texture with playful hairlike marks, blending colors with thickly overlapped marks, selecting a feature to measure proportions, and illustrating anatomical structure with bold, well-defined marks. In addition, understanding the principles of transparency will allow you to illustrate a great number of insects with confidence.

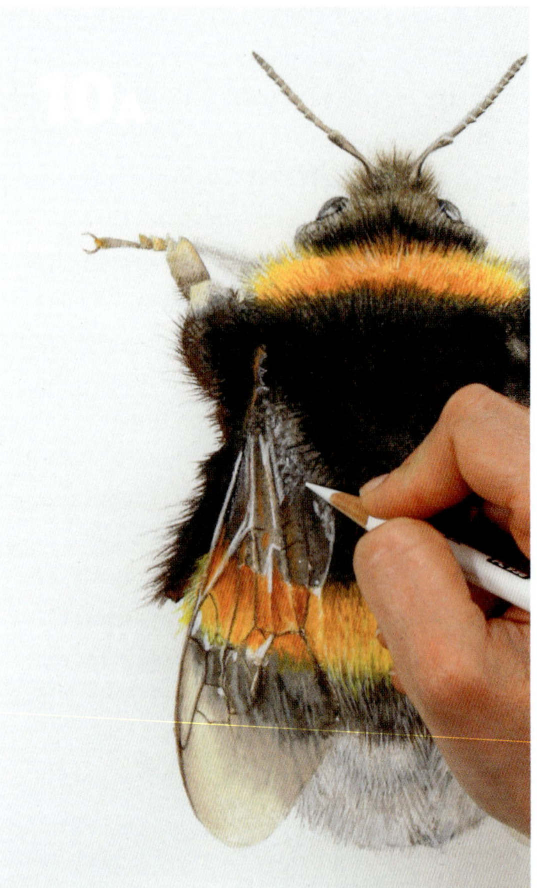

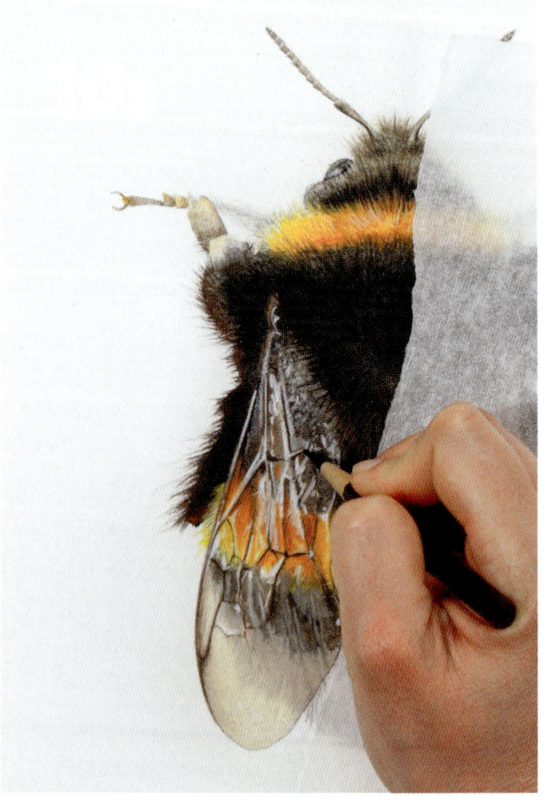

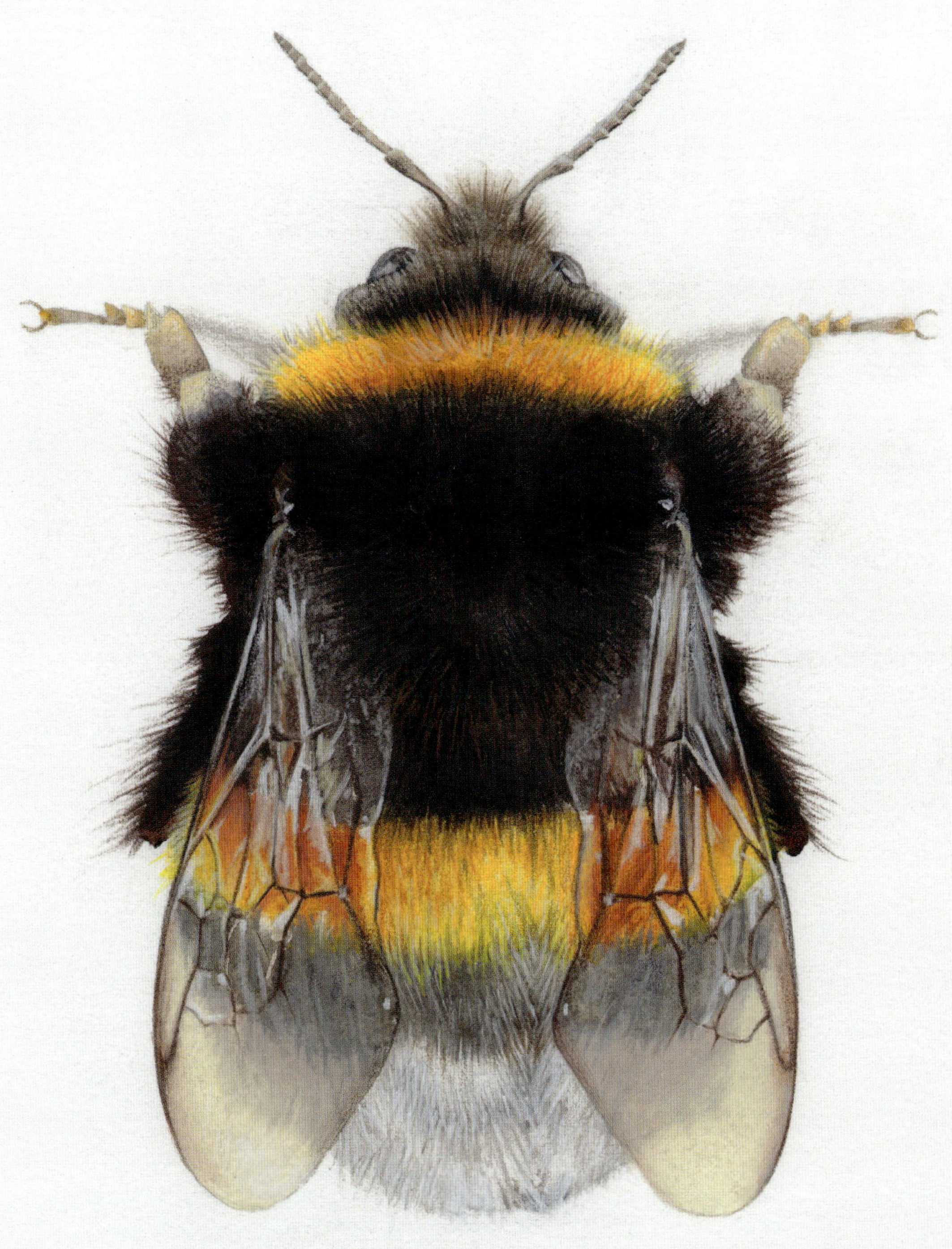

NATURE BREAK, OBSERVATION

● BRING THE OUTDOORS IN

For days when it's not possible to venture outdoors, this Nature Break is designed for bringing the outdoors in.

LOCATION: Set up a temporary indoor workstation that is comfortable, well lit, and away from distractions.

MATERIALS: Sketchbook and HB pencil. You might use paints, pastels, or another medium. You'll also need a subject to draw, such as a twig, shell, or seedpod.

OBSERVATIONS: You can either create a small still life on the table in front of you or simply hold your subject in your hand. As you decide on the position of your natural element, look at the shadows, highlights, and shapes created by both the positive and negative space. Then take notice of smaller details, such as the colors, textures, and patterns.

PRACTICE: If you are holding the subject, you can rotate its position to create many drawings. Alternatively, you could make gestural drawings, then work toward creating a single finished piece. If you choose to make a still life, you might begin with small thumbnail drawings to explore cropping possibilities. Then choose one composition to create on a separate page.

REFLECTION: How is the subject, and your artwork, different when you create indoors versus outdoors? How do you feel, both physically and creatively, in one place compared to the other?

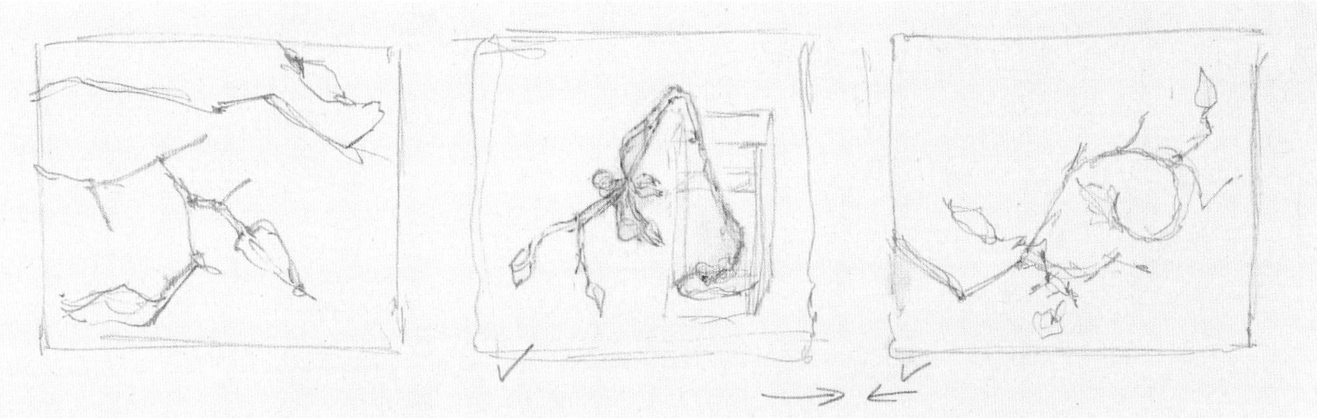

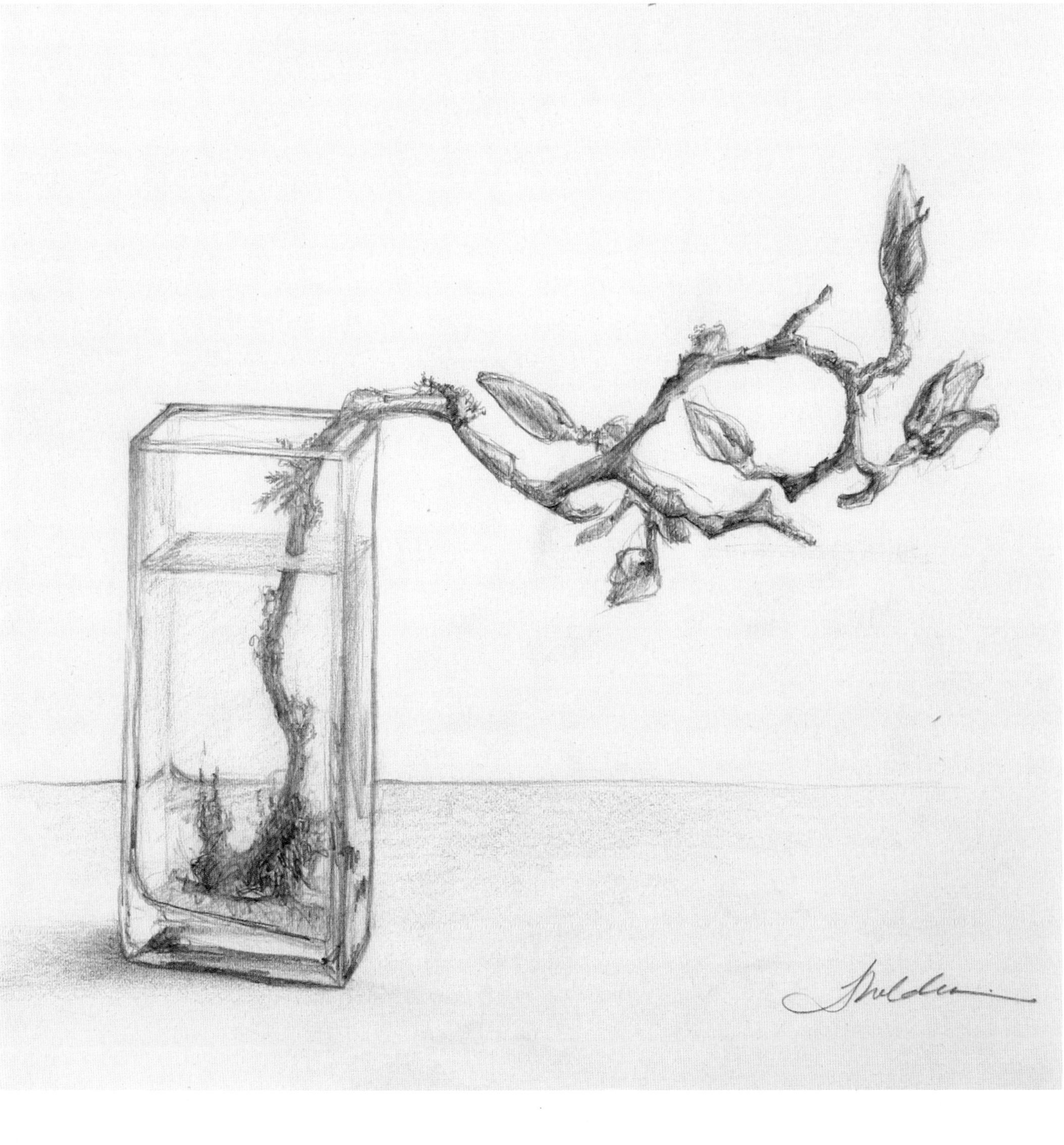

EUROPEAN STAG BEETLE

LUCANUS CERVUS

This stag beetle is widespread across Europe and is considered nearly threatened in some areas. It is best known for its antlerlike mandibles, which are used to ward off competitors during the mating season. I included this composition because of the dramatic light cast on the beetle that accentuates its complex anatomy, particularly the impressive shape of the mandibles. When you add a dark background, you make these bright areas appear even more illuminated. The addition of a painted shadow provides a wider range of techniques for conveying the three-dimensionality of the beetle, possibly to the point where it looks like an actual creature standing on top of your sheet of paper.

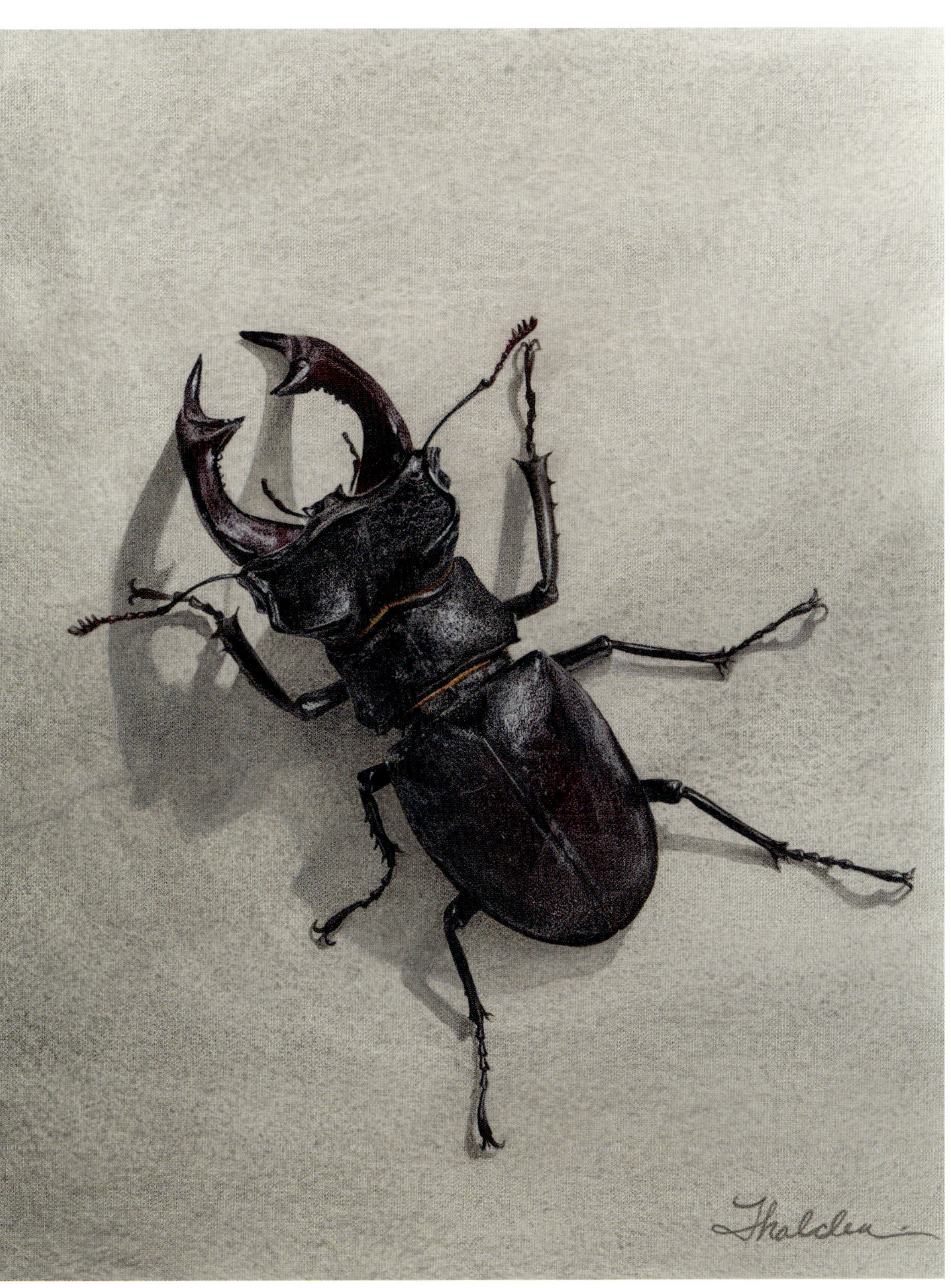

ACRYLIC PAINTS

- ☐ black
- ☐ cadmium red
- ☐ titanium white
- ☐ ultramarine blue

BRUSHES

- ☐ sizes 000 and 1 round
- ☐ size 12 filbert (or other large brush)

COLORED PENCILS

- ☐ 10% French gray
- ☐ 30% French gray
- ☐ 50% French gray
- ☐ black
- ☐ black raspberry
- ☐ light umber
- ☐ rosy beige
- ☐ seashell pink
- ☐ sepia
- ☐ sienna brown
- ☐ sunburst yellow
- ☐ white
- ☐ yellowed orange

ADDITIONAL MATERIALS

- ☐ HB artist pencil
- ☐ ruler
- ☐ eraser
- ☐ artist tape
- ☐ tracing paper
- ☐ acrylic retarder
- ☐ paper towels or clean rags
- ☐ drawing board
- ☐ water container
- ☐ plastic wrap
- ☐ fixative (optional)
- ☐ small container for a few tablespoons of liquid paint (optional)

DRAWING

1 Sketch the midline and gesture of the beetle on your page. Take into consideration both the length of the legs and the amount of visual weight that the shadow will add to the left side of the beetle.

Before you measure proportions, visually check the appearance of your gesture against the reference image. If you are creating an asymmetrical composition, make sure your drawing and the reference image are in the same orientation, so that you can easily compare each feature.

2 Now select a measurement that you can use to check the proportions. You might consider the length or width of the head, thorax, or abdomen. Study the reference image and use the thumb-and-pencil method (see step 1B on page 40) to test a few of these dimensions along the midline. Look for a measurement that can be easily multiplied or divided to measure all parts of the beetle's anatomy. Then measure outward from the midline to compare the measurement dimension to the width of each section of the body.

With the measurement selected, finalize the proportions in your drawing. Remember to first complete the dimensions of the anatomical form that contains the measurement and then measure downward from that form to correctly locate the base of the midline. If it's necessary to change the scale, adjust the size of your measurement and quickly redo your marks before measuring

the length and width of the remaining anatomical forms. If at any time the proportions you have drawn appear dramatically different than those in the reference image, be sure to pause, investigate, and resolve the issue.

3 **A** When you measure the mandibles, mark the place where the mandibles begin to angle inward as well as the location of the two points at the very end. Then measure outward from the midline at each of these points to mark both the interior and the exterior of the mandible. Transfer the outer angles from the reference image to your page. This technique gives you the ability to correctly measure both the length and width of appendages that are parallel to the midline without referencing another anatomical form on the page.

B Decide whether you would rather draw the entire beetle or transfer half of the image to the opposite side of the midline. Then begin to refine the outline of either the head or thorax. As you work, feel free to add referential lines, either parallel or perpendicular to the midline, to help you see the alignment of these forms.

C When you work on the curve of the abdomen, you can add the very subtle changes in the shape to help your subject look more lifelike. Be sure the overall shape of the curve is maintained when viewed at arm's length.

4 Once you have drawn both sides of the beetle, make any necessary adjustments to the shape or value of your lines and erase unnecessary marks. Leave the gesture of the legs in place.

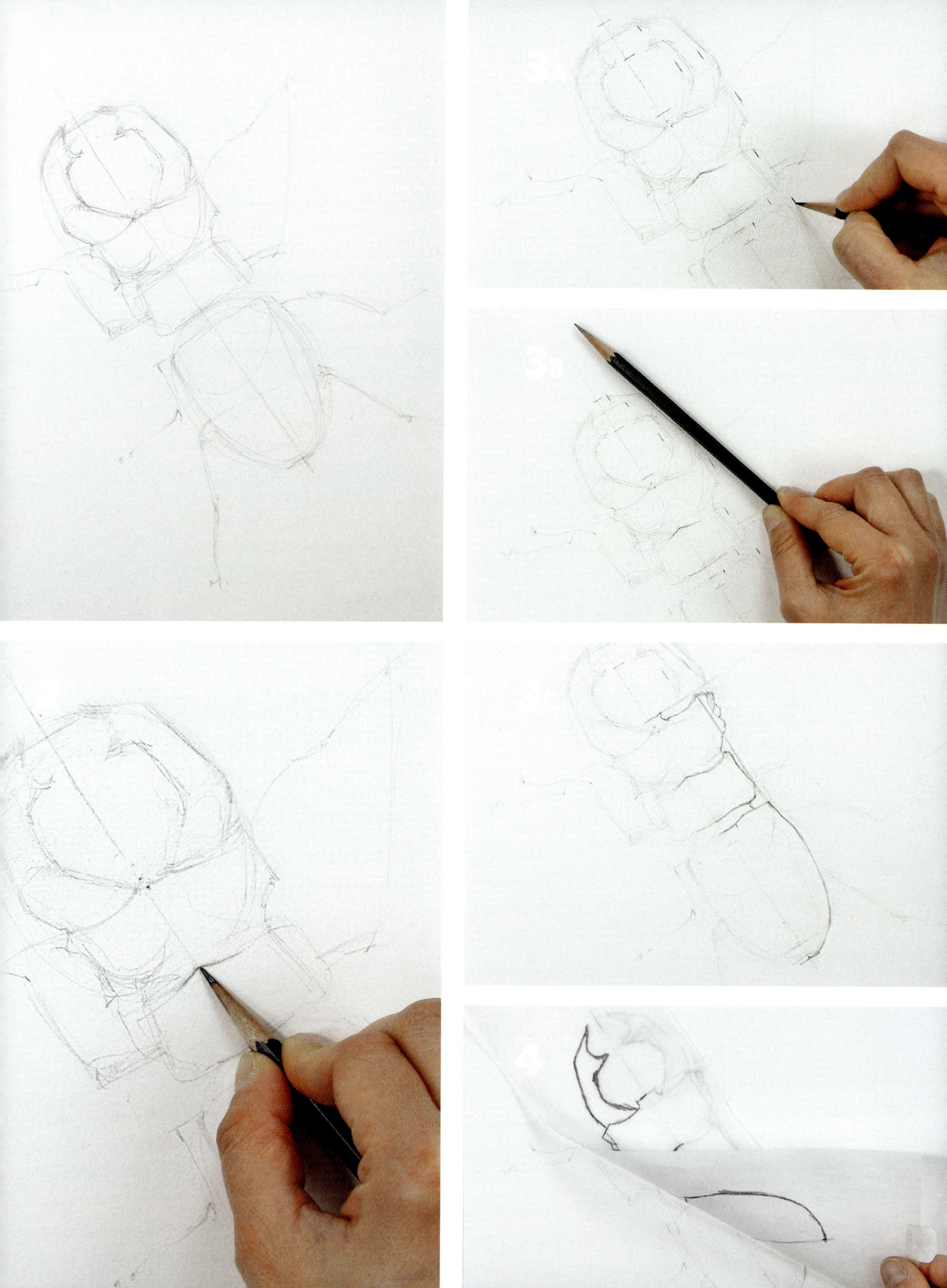

3A
3B
4

5 **A** This is a good time to add the small antennae-like palps, which are sense organs located between the mandibles. Next, work on refining the shape, angle, and location of the appendages along the side of the body. Remember to extend the midline past the end of the abdomen.

Start with the front legs or antennae and work in a zigzag pattern, completing each pair as you move downward toward your dominant hand. Mark the significant points along the length of the appendage. Then add additional vertical alignment lines, pull angles from the reference image, and measure the length of each leg segment. Next, add a midline down the center of the appendage and erase the gesture line. Rely heavily on the negative space to draw each form. Finally, add minor details such as the small segments, claws, and spiky tibial spurs.

B As you check your work and make final adjustments, examine each appendage both individually and as part of a symmetrical pair to ensure they appear accurate and realistic. Be sure the foreshortened parts of the leg are the accurate shape and at the correct angle to appear to recede in space. Since the legs are dark and will be coated in a layer of wash when you paint them, keep the outline a medium to dark value.

Remove all the lines that indicate the midline with the exception of the abdomen. Use a light circular motion when you erase to avoid streaks.

Double-check that the entire background has a similar value and the outline of the insect is uniform and dark in value.

Take a deep breath. You've completed the entire outline of the insect, and you've successfully drawn forms that extended into negative space, one of the trickiest parts of insect illustration.

6 **A** The shadow does not need to be drawn as precisely as the anatomy, so you can use the following techniques to work quickly and with accuracy. Consider the relationship between the beetle's anatomical forms and the shape being cast onto the surface. Lightly draw parallel lines that correspond to the angle of the light from each prominent anatomical feature. You can either draw these directly on your page or on a piece of tracing paper attached with a piece of artist tape. After studying this for a moment, add location marks to your drawing at the points where the outline of the shadow intersects with an appendage, meets the main body, or makes a dramatic turn.

B Refer to both the reference image and the angled lines as you carefully freehand the outline, drawing the sections that are easiest first. Rotate your page as needed. Keep your pencil weight just darker than the value at the edge of the shadow in the reference image, so that it will still be visible after you apply a wash but will disappear completely when you paint the dark gray shadow.

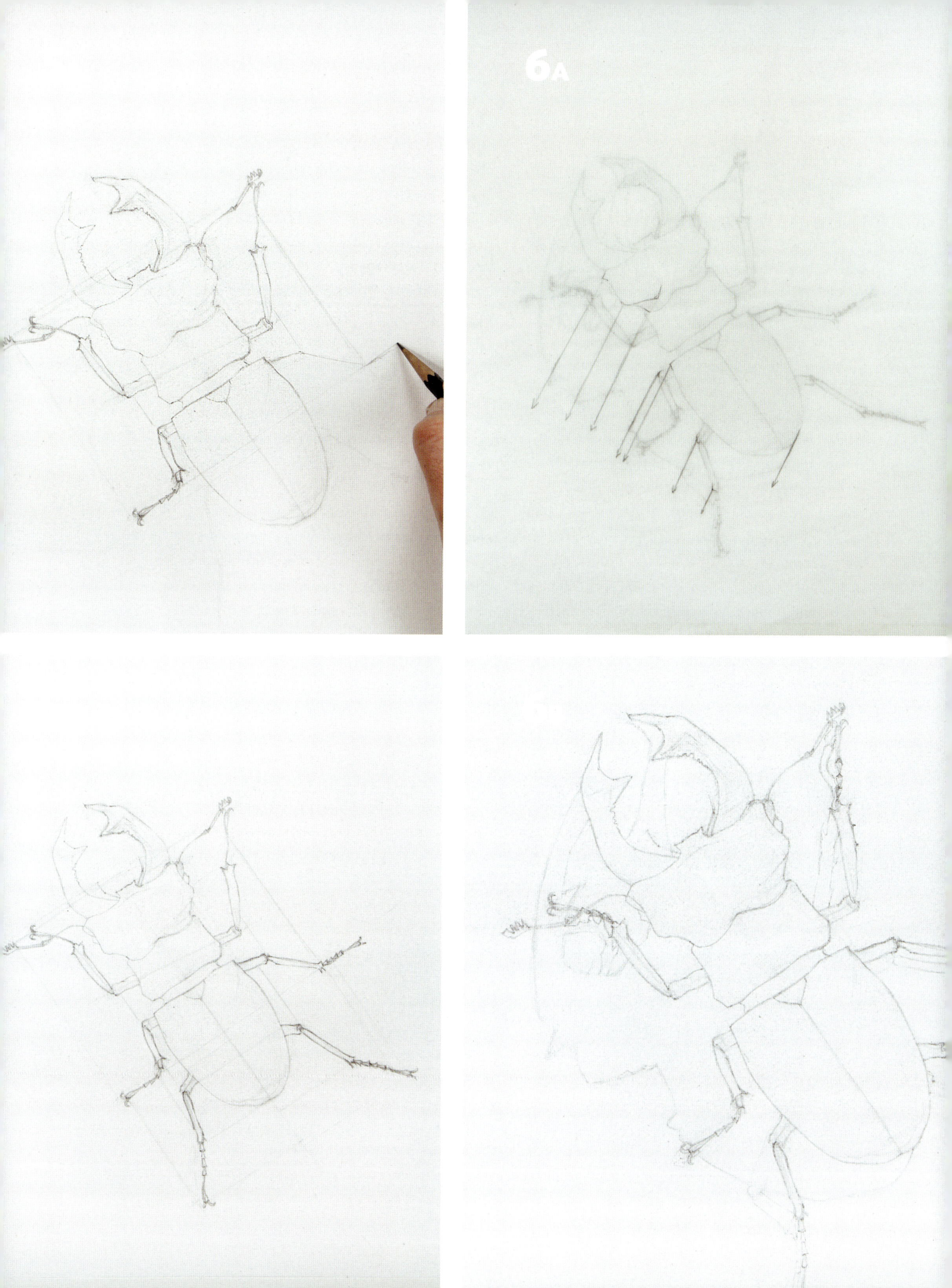
6A

PAINTING

1 If you are concerned about your pencil marks being lost, you can always copy your drawing onto a piece of tracing paper.

A I find it best to paint the environment first because the background color and value will influence the appearance of the subject. Start with fresh rinse water and use the black and titanium white paints to create a dark gray paint mixture on your palette. Separate this into three portions: one for the background, the second to paint the shadow, and the third to paint the body of the beetle later in the process. Cover the latter two with plastic wrap. Add water to the portion you will use to tint the background until it just becomes liquid. Although I tend to do this on my palette, this watery mixture can be messy, and you might feel more comfortable using a small container instead. Create a swatch of the tinted mixture to assess the level of translucency. Be aware that the mixture will become lighter when you apply it to the page with a wet brush, so it should be slightly darker on your palette than what you intend the background to be.

B Creating a background can feel daunting, but it is an opportunity to combine a desired outcome with the natural flow of diluted paint. You might take a scrap piece of paper and practice coating a large area evenly or creating a gradation. Strive to cover the entire area quickly, using as few layers as possible so that the paint can do its magic. (Reworking an area can result in an overworked paper and an unpleasant appearance.) Simply apply the wash and let it be. For this composition, keep the background transitions subtle so that the negative space does not distract from the subject.

Dip a paintbrush (such as a large filbert) in water, then pick up some of the gray paint mixture. Working from the top down, apply the paint to your page, covering every inch in a single layer. To create a gradation, simply add a bit more of the mixture to your paintbrush as you move down the page. For my composition, I first spread an even tint on my paper as if I was applying a wash, then I added a second layer using curved brushstrokes to darken the lower left corner. This emphasized the atmospheric environment as well as the light source coming from the opposite direction.

If the water creates puddles when you stop painting, carefully sop up a portion of the excess with the corner of a paper towel or a damp paintbrush. You might also find a speck of lint or a hair from the paintbrush in the painted area. You can attempt to remove these while the paper is still wet, although I find that they have little effect on the appearance and are easily removed when the paint is dry.

Now it is time to sit back and give yourself a pat on the back while the paper dries. With these few brushstrokes, you have created the environment in which your subject will reside. The page is no longer just a piece of paper but a window into another place. This exciting technique opens up enormous possibilities.

2 When the paper has dried flat, the penciled beetle outline should be clear, whereas the shadow perimeter lines may be just discernible. Redraw any lines that are too light or missing. If you use a transfer sheet, hold a pencil in your hand while you repeatedly lift the section that includes the area you need to replicate. By oscillating between the copied drawing and the page below, you will be able to visualize the missing lines and redraw them in small sections. If the entire drawing has been lost under paint, it will be best to hold the tracing paper still and retrace the entire image instead.

Acrylic paint is permanent after it has dried, which means you can paint the shadow directly on top of the tinted background at any time during the painting stage. I prefer to paint all the primary background elements—even the

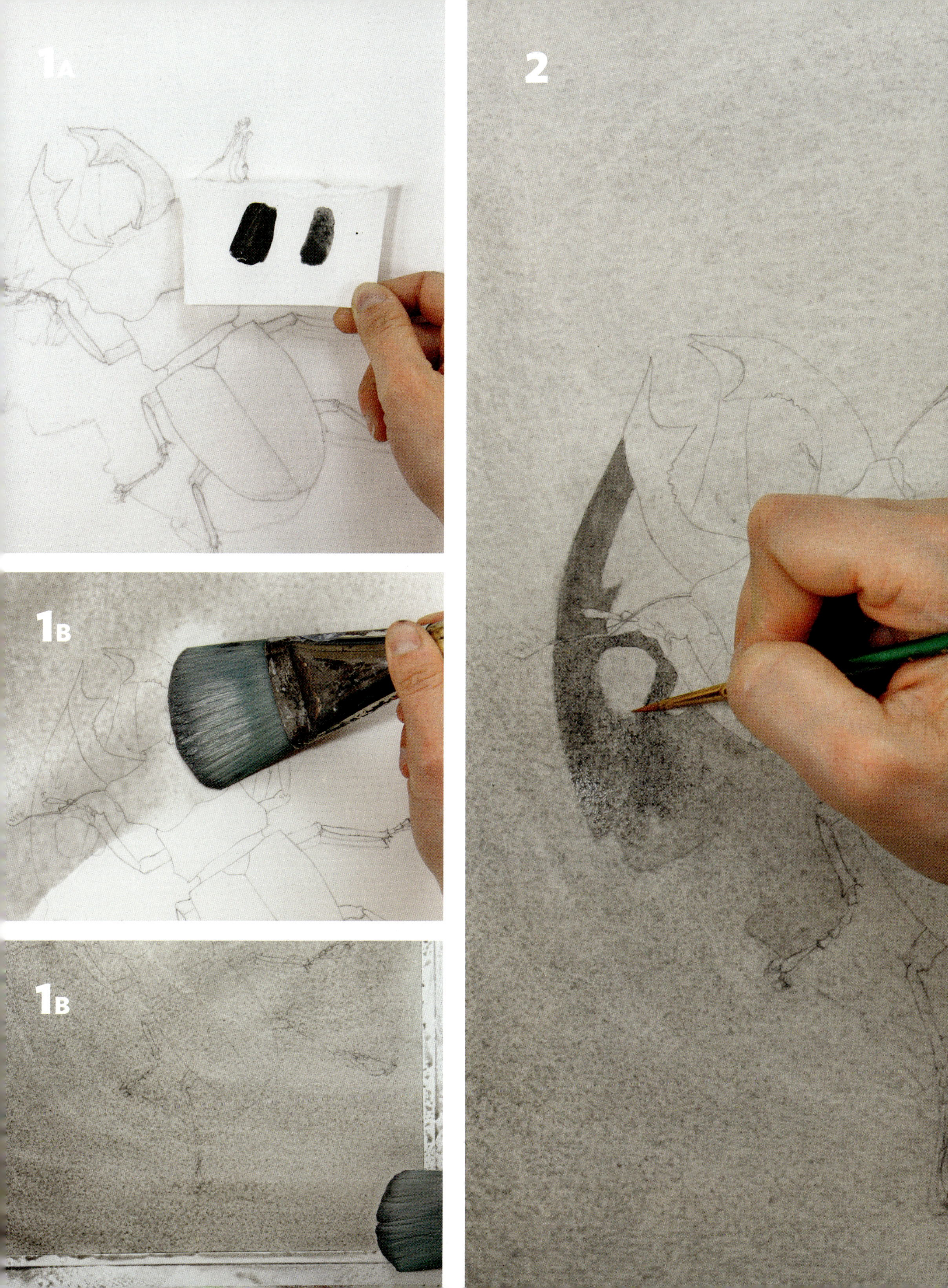
1A
1B
1B
2

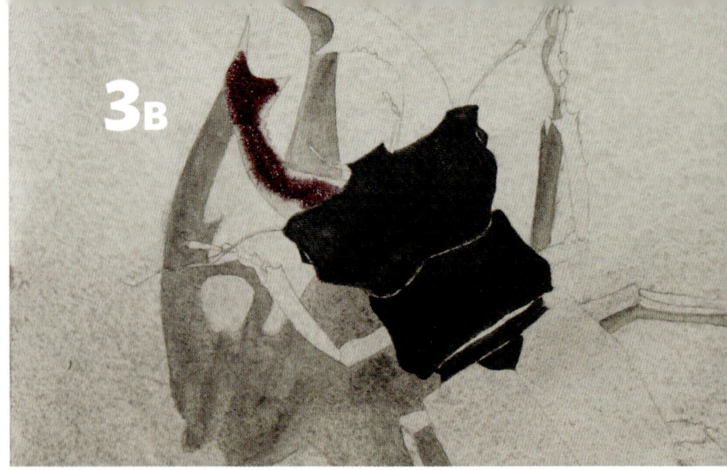

3B

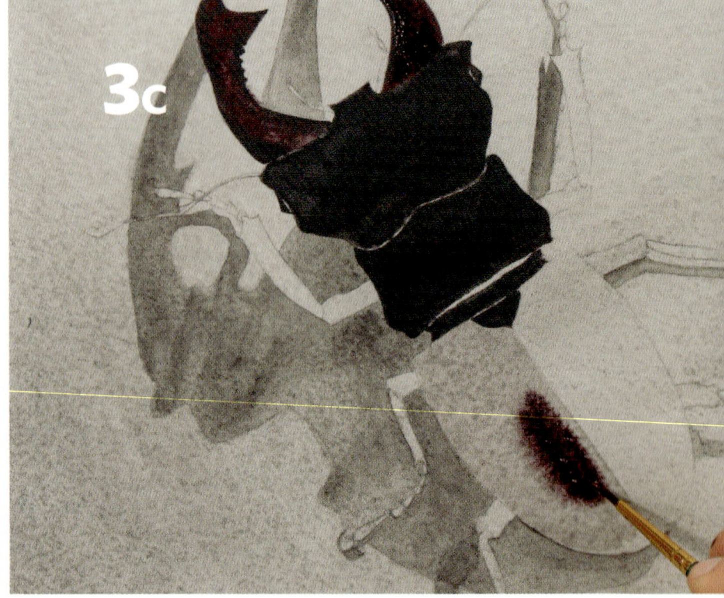

3C

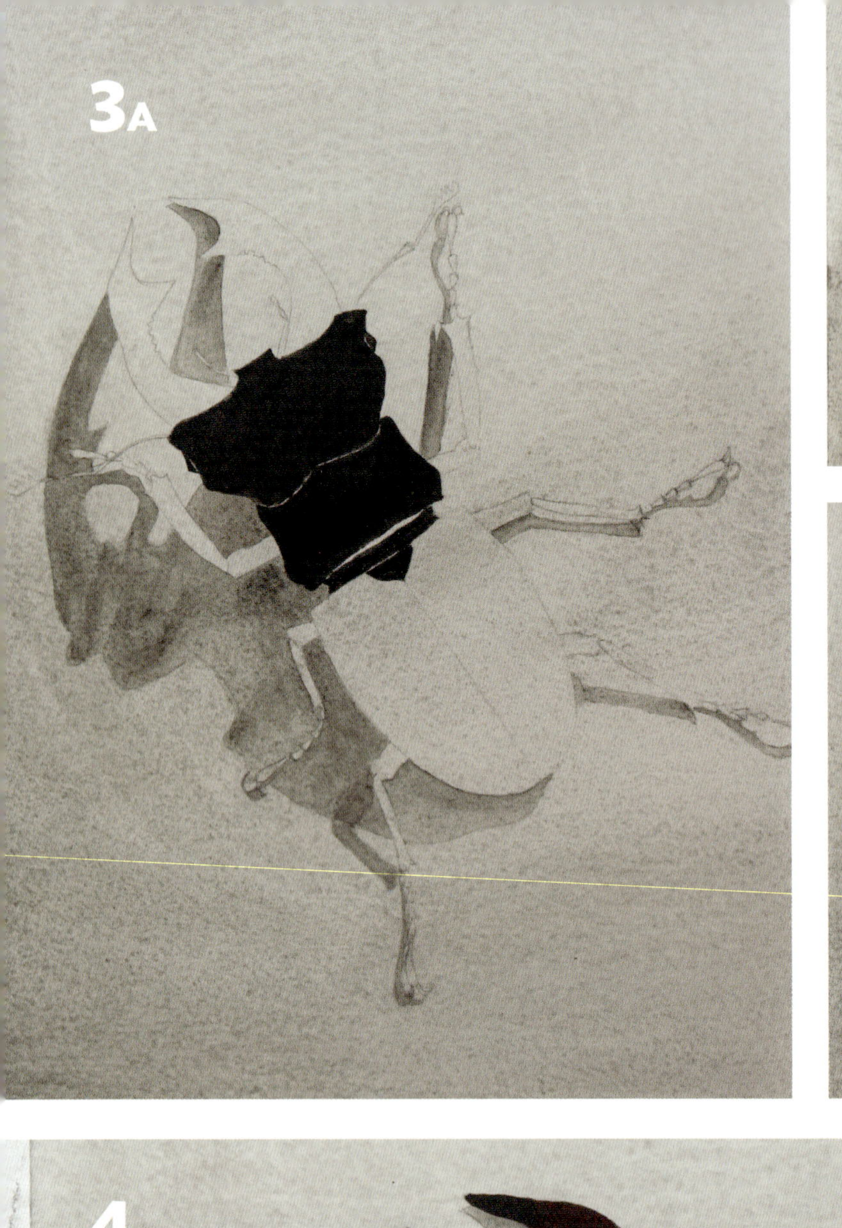

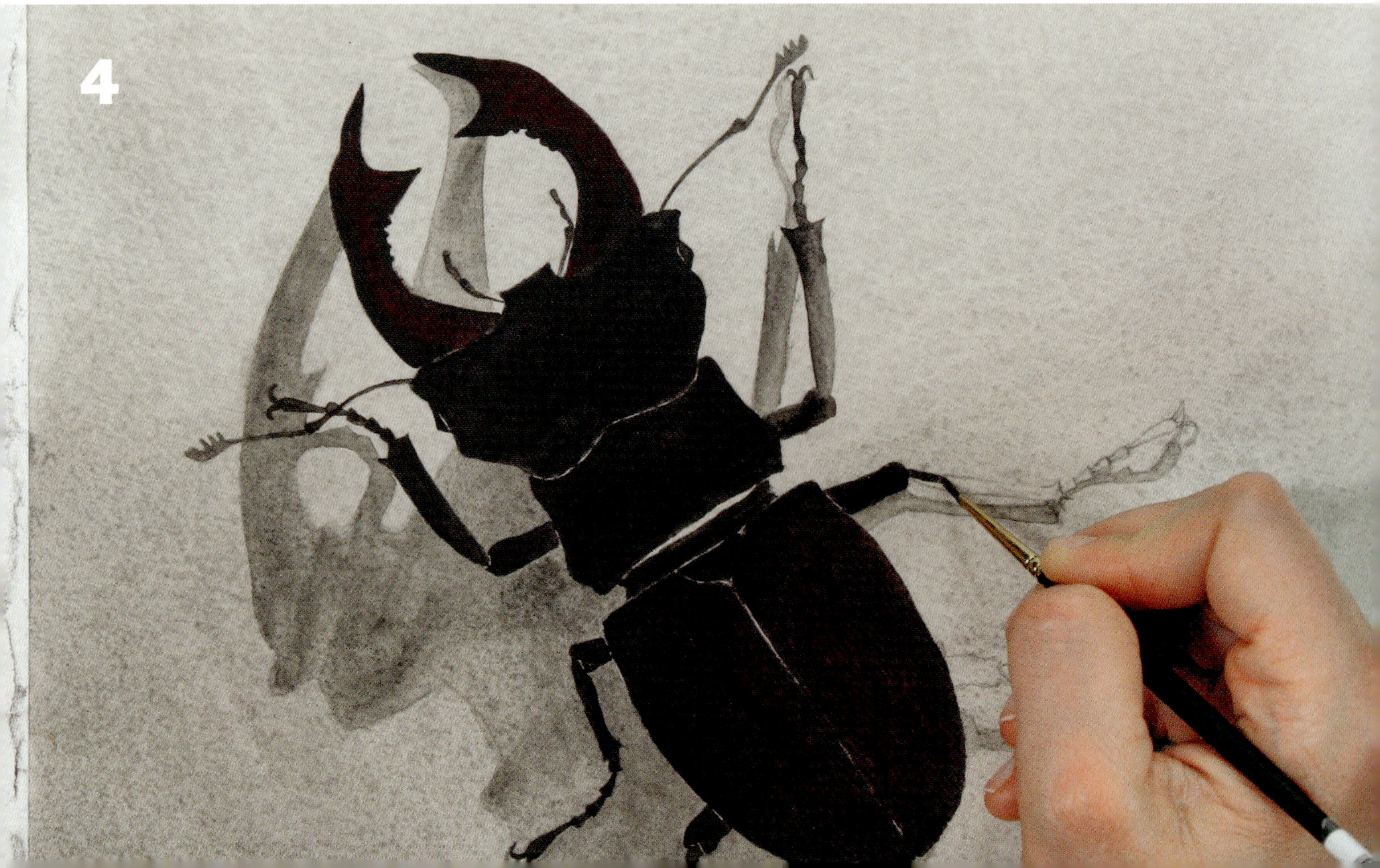

3A
4

shadow—before I make any color or value decisions about the focal point.

To add the shadow, first study the reference image to identify the subtle changes that appear within the outline. Pay particular attention to how the anatomical shape, thickness, proximity, and orientation of the beetle's anatomy affects the value within the shadow and creates variation in the level of sharpness along the edge. If you decide to include such variations in your shadow, keep both the range of value and shift in texture subtle to avoid an overly dynamic shadow that can distract from the subject and even appear three-dimensional. Since the antennae shadows are so light in value, you might wait and add this part of the shadow at the colored pencil stage.

Remove the plastic wrap from one of the black mixtures on your palette and hydrate the solution to a shadowlike value. Select a small paintbrush and add a water wash to the section of the shadow from the mandible down to the second leg. As you paint the section, working downward, the wash may start to dry toward the bottom; add a dab of water to keep an even glisten on the page. If you want to incorporate value changes in the shadow, first cover the section with an even tint equal to the lightest portion of the shadow, then add more pigment to darken select areas. Repeat this process, working from section to section. Do your best to match the value from one section to another and to blur the shadow's perimeter. Remember that you will be able to further darken the value, add details such as the antennae, and possibly even soften the edge of the shadow during the colored pencil stage.

Great job. Learning to create backgrounds is a significant leap in your ability to create spatial environments and make compositions more dynamic.

3 **A** When the shadow portion of your painting has dried, turn your focus to the subject. Continue using either the same or a slightly smaller paintbrush. Working on one anatomical feature at a time, add a water wash and then the original black paint mixture to the head, thorax, and scutellum. Be sure to leave dry the hair-thin spaces where your pencil marks are located on the page to keep the contour of each form visible. On either side of the thorax, you might want to make these dry areas a touch wider so that you are able to make the orange hairs slightly lighter than the surrounding anatomy.

B While this is drying, mix ultramarine blue and cadmium red paint to match the maroon areas on the beetle. Divide this mixture in half and add some of the black paint mixture to one portion to make a darker maroon. Using a very small paintbrush, add a water wash to one of the mandibles, leaving a hair-thin space where the mandible meets the head. Using the same paintbrush, paint the maroon areas. Then switch to an extremely small paintbrush to first apply the dark maroon, then the black mixture, around these areas. Remember that the highlights will be added entirely in pencil later. Then repeat this process on the opposite side.

C Select a small paintbrush to work on the abdomen, one wing at a time. As you have been doing with other anatomical features, divide the wings with a hair-thin space.

4 As soon as the paint on the body is dry to the touch, move to the legs and antennae, painting directly on the dry page. Starting at the top, paint all the legs that are in shadow, then repeat on the other side of the beetle. Leave the leg spikes and claws blank for now.

If you have not painted the shadow yet, allow the paint on the legs to dry completely and then follow the steps described earlier.

If the beetle you have painted looks extremely dark and incredibly flat, you are on the right track. Unlike the subjects in previous illustrations, much of the color, value, and dimensionality of this subject will be added in the colored pencil stage.

LAYERING WITH COLORED PENCIL

1 Adding colored pencil to this illustration will do more than just create sheen, texture, and color—it will communicate the topography of each anatomical form. Therefore, the placement, shape, and value of your marks have great significance in describing the surface of the beetle—particularly when you add highlights. As you consider both the quality and placement of these strategic marks, you advance your ability to interpret two-dimensional imagery.

Before grabbing your pencils, study the anatomical form of the mandibles in the reference image. Gather as much information as you can about the shape of the beetle and the reason for the size and intensity of the highlights.

See if you can differentiate the three spikes found at the end of each mandible. The first spike is located directly above the second, making it more difficult to perceive its individuated shape. Notice that some highlights are illuminated directly from the light source, while others are formed by light reflected off the surface the beetle is standing on.

Now look for overall highlighted areas on the mandible. I found three primary sections: the first, down the length of the mandible; the second, from the tip of the first spike down the wristlike form; and the third, the arc between the two lower spikes. Since there is a ridgelike line at the edge of each highlighted area, when you add these three simple lines to your illustration you immediately create all the structure needed to draw highlights with ease and accuracy.

The brightest highlights appear more as distinct forms rather than contributions to a gradation; I found it ideal to add them with the white pencil at this point. To create other highlight areas,

use the rosy beige pencil with varied pressure from full strength to barely touching the paper. You can always add a layer of white on top of the rosy beige to create a brighter highlight. On the other hand, if you need to tone down the value, use an eraser and carefully remove some of the pigment.

2 **A** Begin work on the beetle's head. Using the seashell pink pencil with light pressure, mark the location of the ridge around both the perimeter and the brighter mottled areas in the center. Then work from light to dark using the 10% to 50% French gray pencils. Periodically unfocus your eyes to blur your vision and observe overall highlight patterns. To create the mottled patterns, solid areas, and crisp lines, adjust both your hand position and the sharpness of the pencil tip to either exaggerate or de-emphasize the surface of the paper. Finish this area by adding the brightest highlights using the white pencil. Now simply repeat these steps on the thorax.

By including subtle contrast, such as a shift in texture, you not only boost the realistic appearance of your subject but also convey a high level of observation, intentionality, and skill acquired through your practice. As you work down the beetle's body, hopefully you will find that these techniques become easier and help you achieve rewarding results.

B At this point, you can either continue moving downward along the beetle to add highlights or pause to add the golden hairs above and below the thorax. Either way, use both the yellowed orange and sunburst yellow pencils to create the brighter hairs and the sienna brown pencil to render the darker sections. Begin each pencil mark near the thorax, flicking outward until you have fully covered the unpainted spaces with short, colorful hairs. You can refine the hair spikes and darken the sienna areas when you add shadows later in the process.

C When you are ready to add highlights to the abdomen, notice the many subtle value shifts on both wings. For example, the reflected light at the

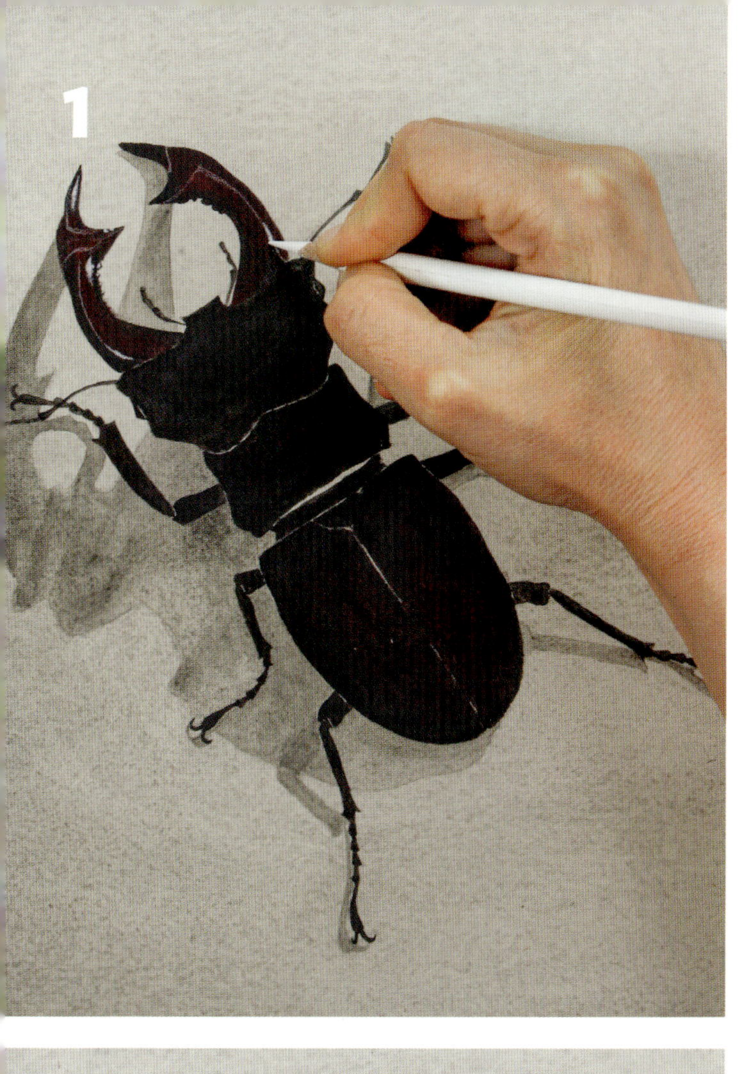

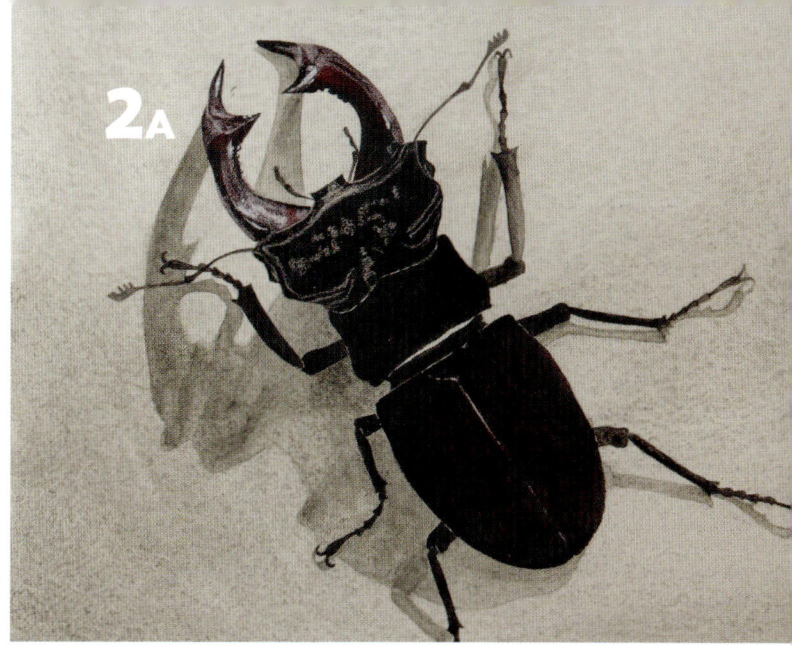

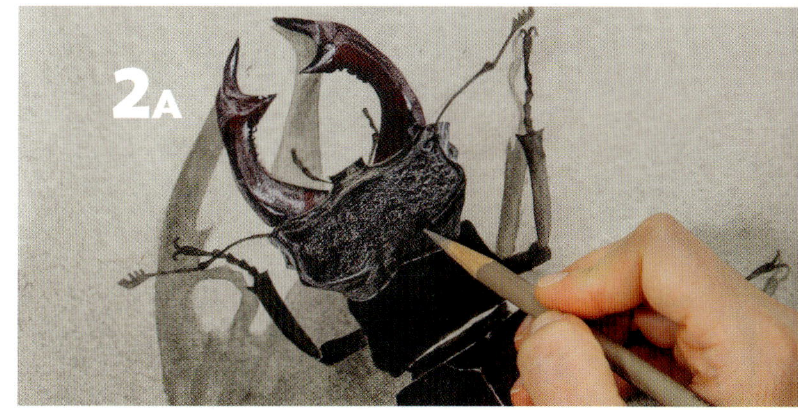

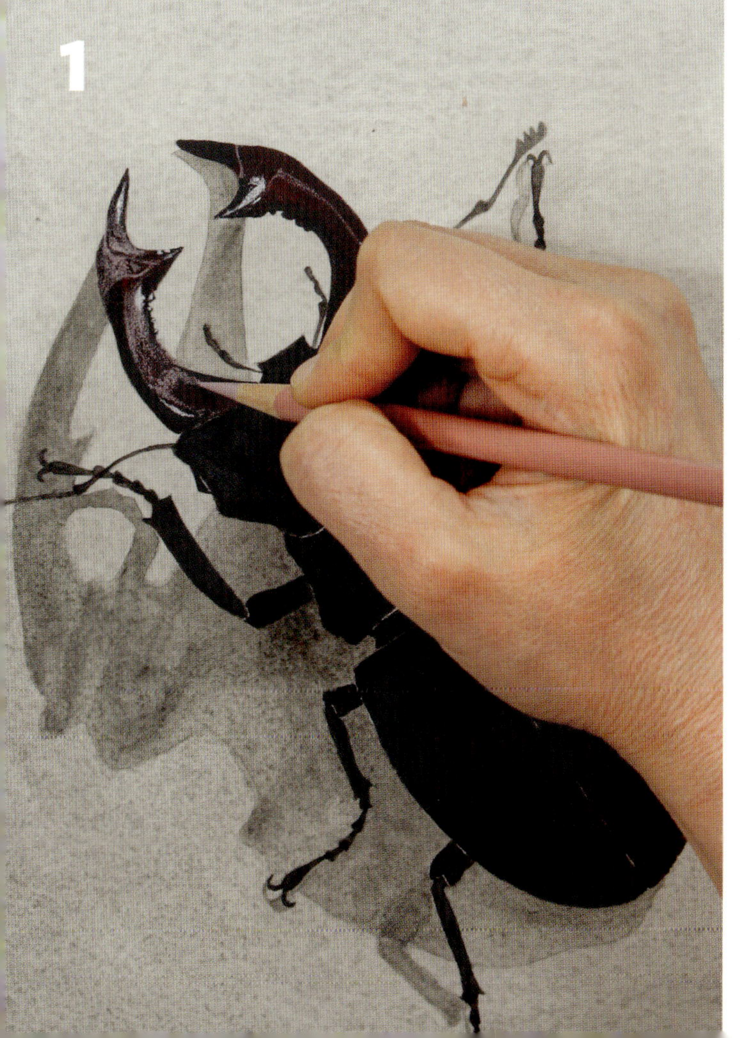

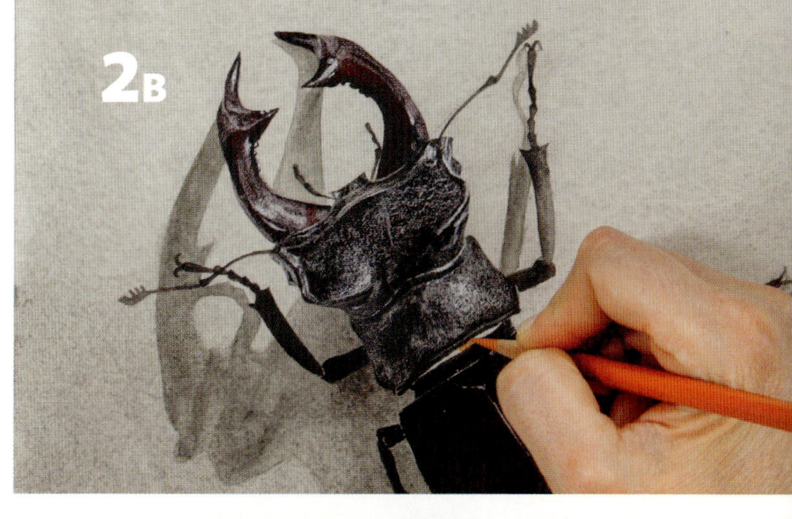

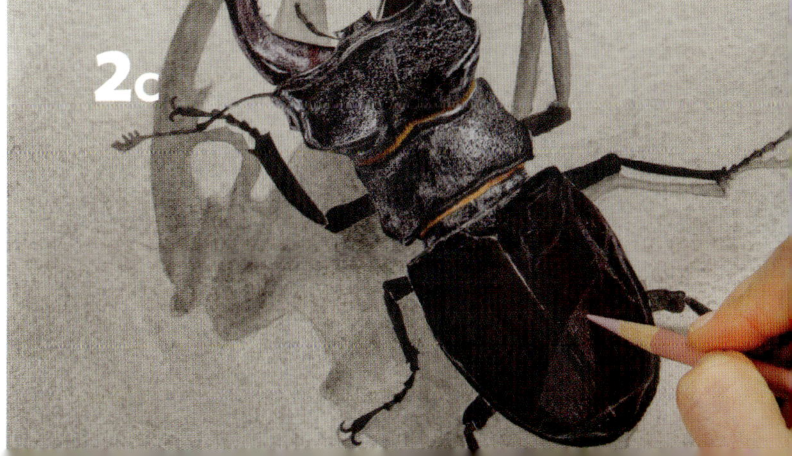

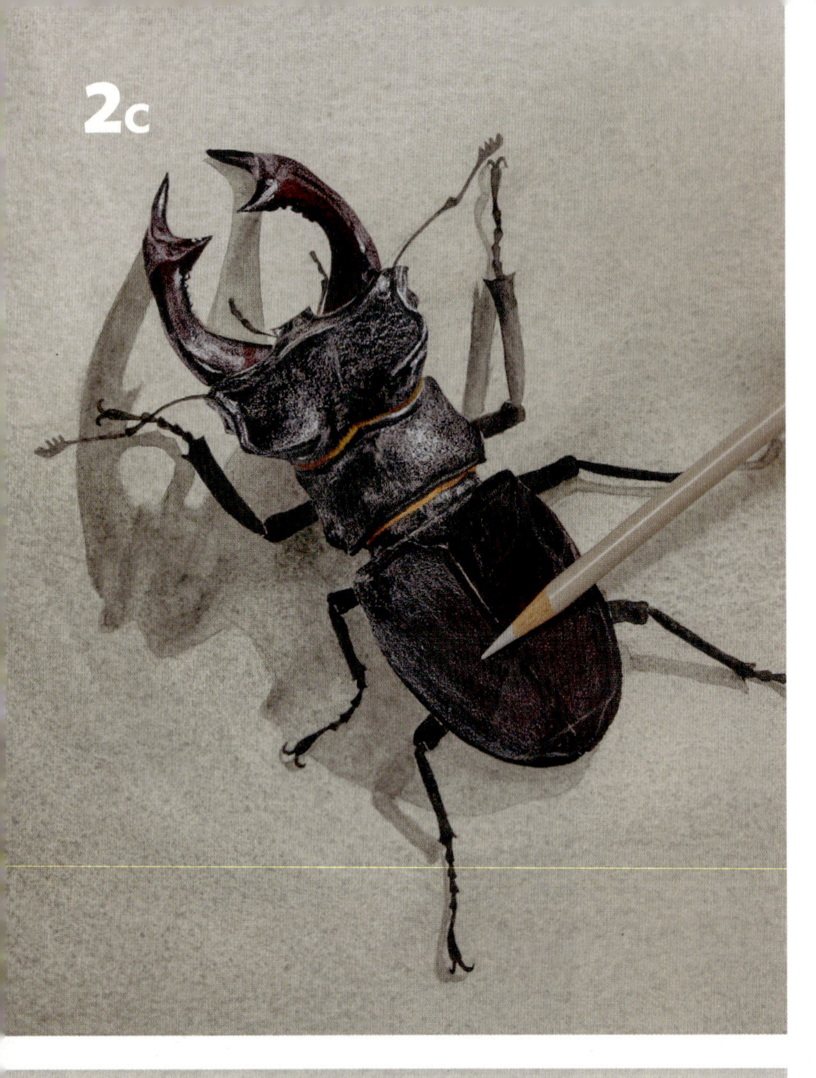

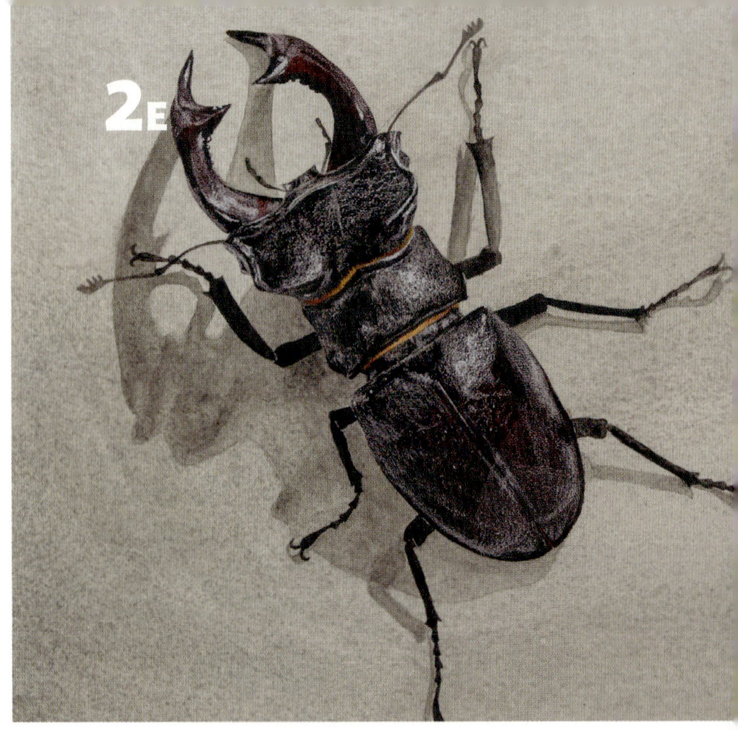

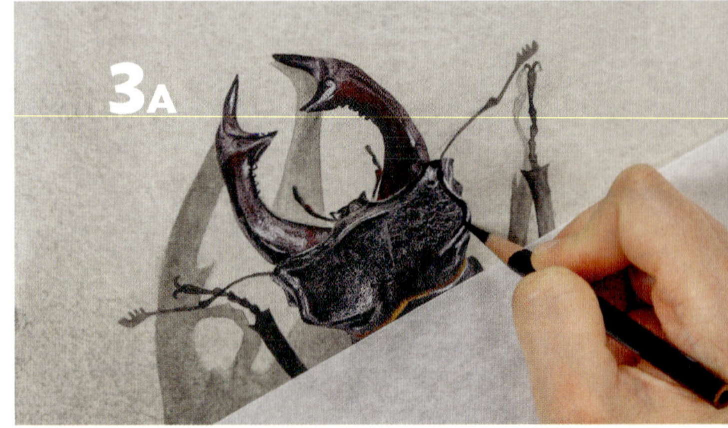

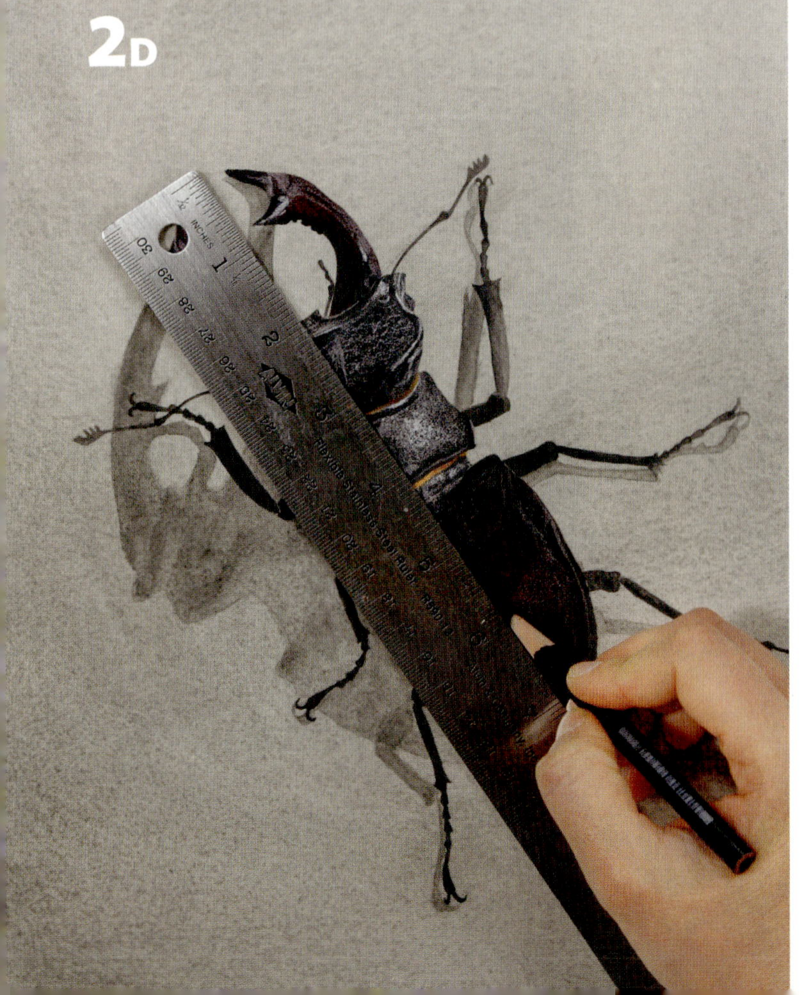

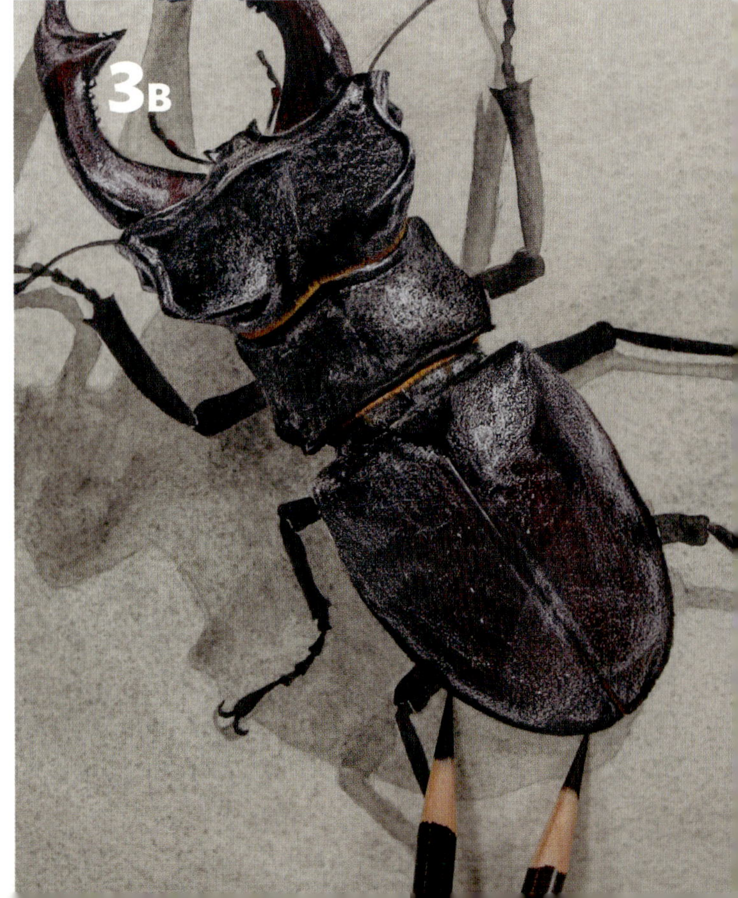

base of the abdomen creates an arced area that can be added using the rosy beige pencil. The vertical lines that make a very light pattern on the wings can be added using light pressure with a French gray pencil.

Now you can incorporate characteristics that make this beetle unique and the details that boost the three-dimensional quality of your drawing. For example, you can form the reflection of the hind legs, which darkens the edge of the abdomen, simply by erasing pencil marks in that small area. Search for the small specks of bright highlight as well as the tiny scratches located in random places around the abdomen. As you consider the hierarchy of the details to include, avoid those that would distract or be difficult to re-create at the scale you're working in.

D On the reference image, align a ruler to the line between the wings. You'll notice that the shadow, as well as the highlight, is straight. Although using a ruler is simple, drawing a single well-placed line requires finesse. The best way to achieve a great result is to hover your pencil lead just above the paper as you move along the length of the ruler to check where the drawn line will land. If the ruler casts its own small shadow in the direction you are working, either turn the page or move your light source so you can clearly see where the line will be placed.

Use the black pencil to create the shadow along the edge of the right wing. Since there is a hair-thin space of unpainted paper that separates the wings, I typically place this pencil line directly on top. Near the scutellum, it is difficult to differentiate the shadow along the right wing from the shadowed space between the wings, so I simply use a single line for both. If you choose to do this, let the line fade into the color of the paper at the point where the ocher underwings begin to show. Later in the process, you can return to this area and use the sunburst yellow pencil to add color to the abdomen.

E Before adding the remaining highlights, continue using the black pencil to draw a dividing line between the scutellum and abdomen that covers the blank spaces left after the painting process. If any white areas remain, fill in the gaps using a colored pencil, such as the black raspberry or sepia. Now with all of the blank paper replaced by dark colors, there is less contrast, and it will be much easier to envision the appropriate value and placement of highlights.

Return to using white and other neutral colored pencils to add all of the highlights to this area. Feel free to use a ruler to add the highlight along the edge of the left wing. Then look over the entire abdomen and add final touches. If an area in your drawing appears flat, blur your vision to double-check that the hierarchy of highlights is similar to the reference image and make adjustments as needed.

3 **A** Using the black pencil sparingly, add the darkest shadows to each section and along the edge of the body. Though you can start anywhere, I tend to begin at the tips of the mandibles and work downward.

As you add shadows to each section, you might keep the lighter colored pencils at hand so that you can quickly intensify highlights. To darken a highlight, either erase very lightly or carefully graze the area with the side of the black pencil lead.

When you get to the hairs at the top and bottom of the thorax, use the light umber pencil in the negative space around the brighter hairs and the black pencil in the shadows. Work between the hairs, so that the negative space refines the points of the hairs.

B Black may be too rich of a color to use toward the base of the abdomen. If this is the case, switch to using the sepia pencil to smooth the roughness along the edge. Using a slightly lighter color avoids creating an outline and contributes to the dimensional quality of the beetle. When you are finished, compare each section of the body to the reference image and make any final adjustments to the shadows or highlights.

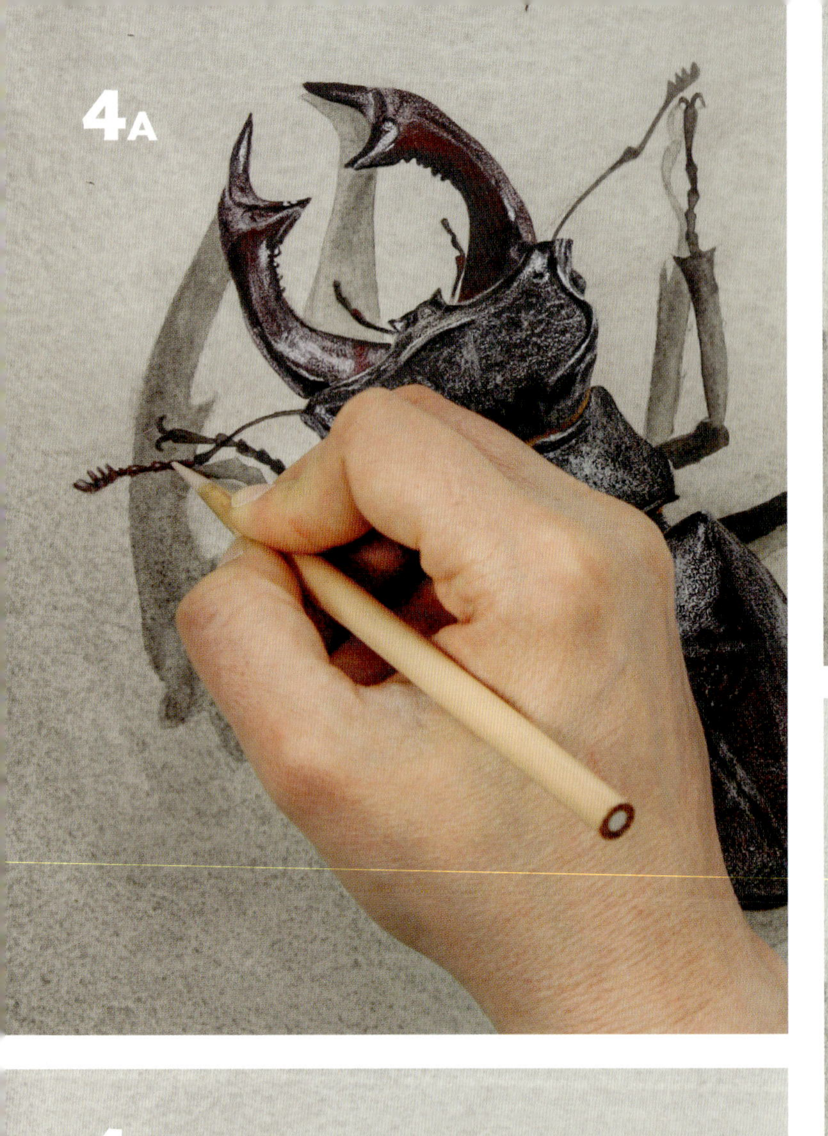
4A

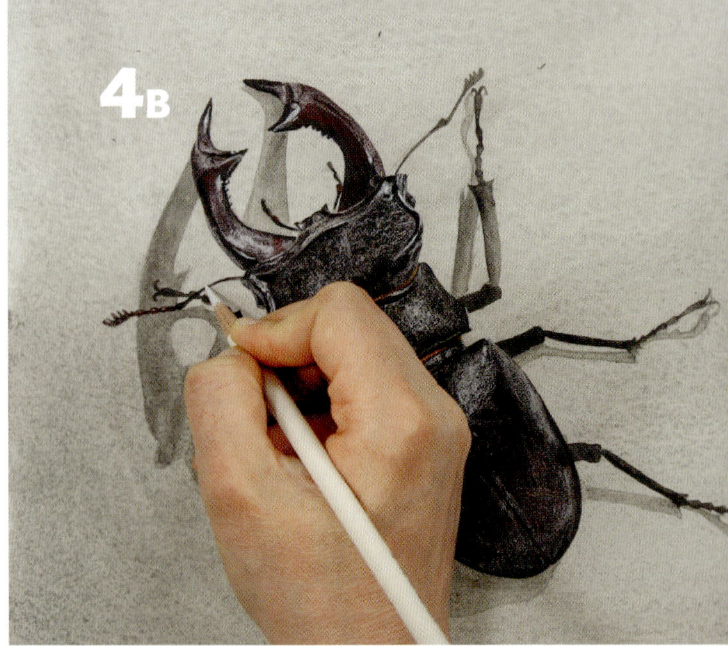
4B

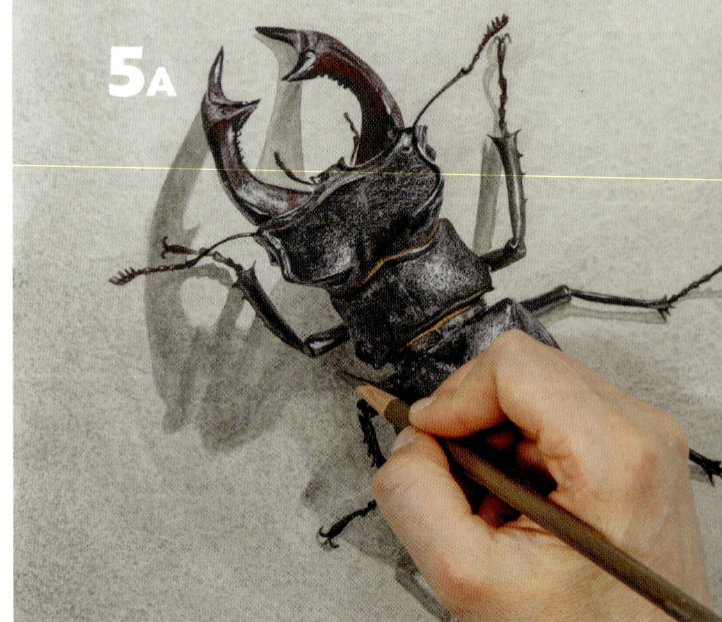
5A

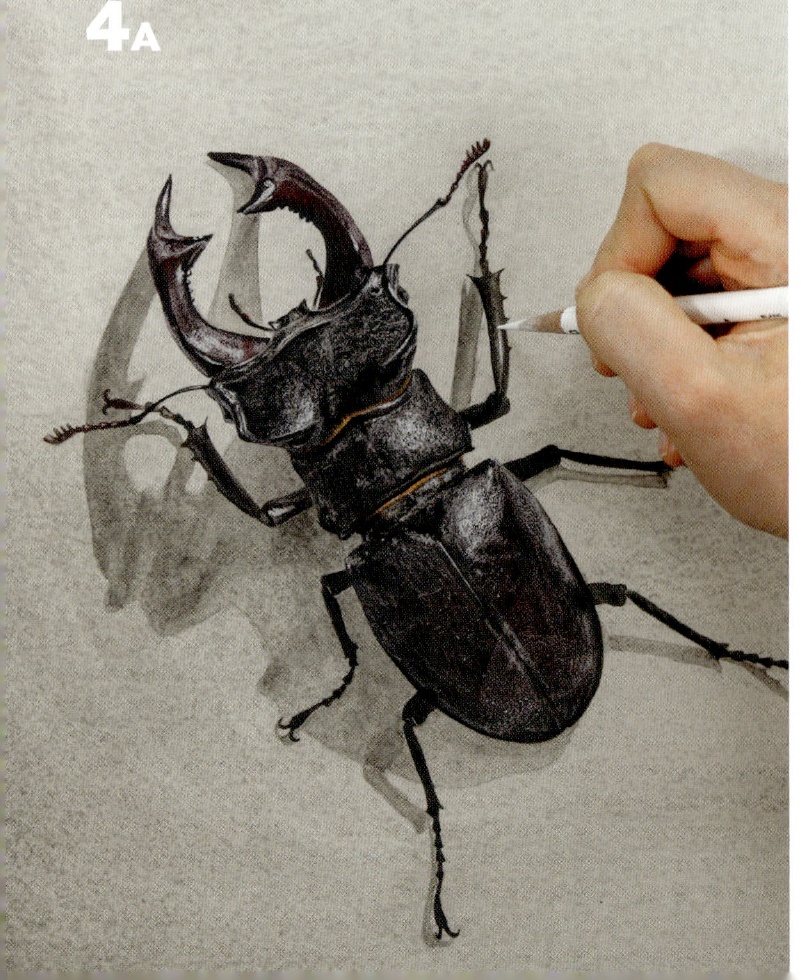
4A

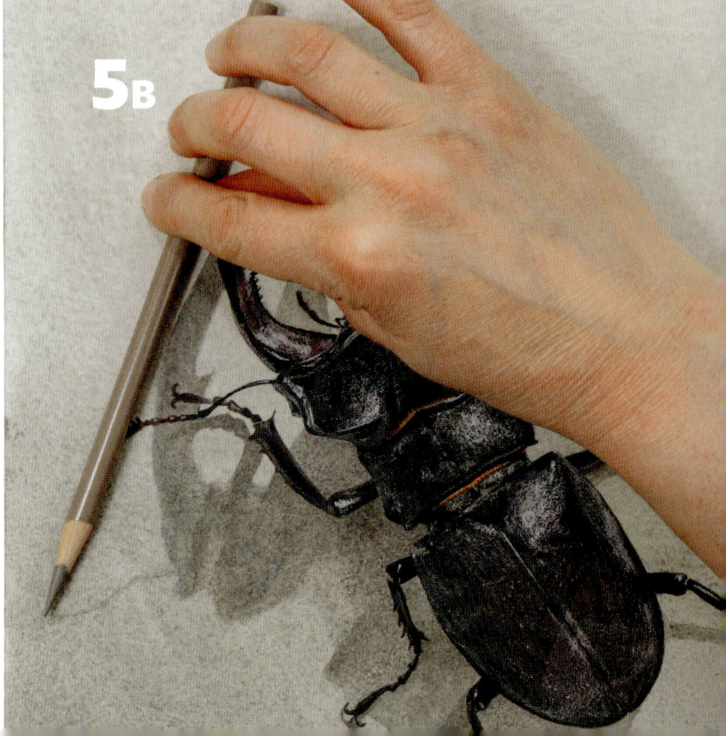
5B

4 **A** Now that you've completed the main body, you can select the best value to use for the highlights and shadows on the small appendages. Since the shadows are dominant, apply the black and sepia pencils first, followed by the French gray pencils, then the white pencil. The ends of the antennae and first set of legs are slightly more colorful, so switch to using the black raspberry and seashell pink pencils instead of the neutral. Take care when using the black raspberry; it will not erase well.

Work in the same zigzag pattern that you did when you drew the form and complete each leg fully before moving on to the next. At the base of each leg, pay close attention to value in order to recognize whether the leg or the body is darker and if there is a subtle line separating the two.

B Sometimes you might find that regardless of how sharp you make the pencil lead, the tip will leave only a ragged edge on the paper as the waxy lead stumbles over the paper's tooth. If you have a pencil color that matches the background perfectly, simply add a very thin pencil line along the outside of the outline. This alone might smooth the edge sufficiently. If you need to redraw the outline, you'll find that the waxy surface makes it easy to create a fine, smooth edge.

Being able to create an incredibly sharp line using colored pencil is an extremely useful skill. In this illustration, avoid applying this technique at the top of the antennae, because the black raspberry could appear as bright magenta when placed next to the light gray used in the background. You can test the colors on a scrap piece of paper to identify the ones to avoid. Whether you decide it is best to proceed or leave the edge as it is and move on, the important thing to recognize is that your skills are now at a level where you have these options.

5 **A** Switch your attention to the cast shadow in the background and begin to refine shapes and adjust the value. Make small circular motions using the darker French gray pencils to further darken or blend areas of the shadow. Determine whether the transitions between one area and another are smooth enough, and make sure that the value on either side of each leg matches. Use darker colors where the body is close to the surface. If the edge needs softening, use the 10% French gray or white pencil to stipple the boundary sparingly. If adding white begins to change the hue of the background, return to using the 10% French gray pencil or leave the edge as is. Give the same level of attention to the details of the shadow as you did to the beetle's anatomy.

B Now you can rough in the overall shape of the antennae's shadow. Hold your pencil at the same angle you used to draw the shadow of other prominent anatomical features and align the side of the pencil to the end of the beetle's antennae. Consider where the end of the shadow would likely be located along this line, add a mark to your page, and replicate the S shape from the reference image. When the shadow of the antennae is complete, check the entire shadow against the reference image and then on its own.

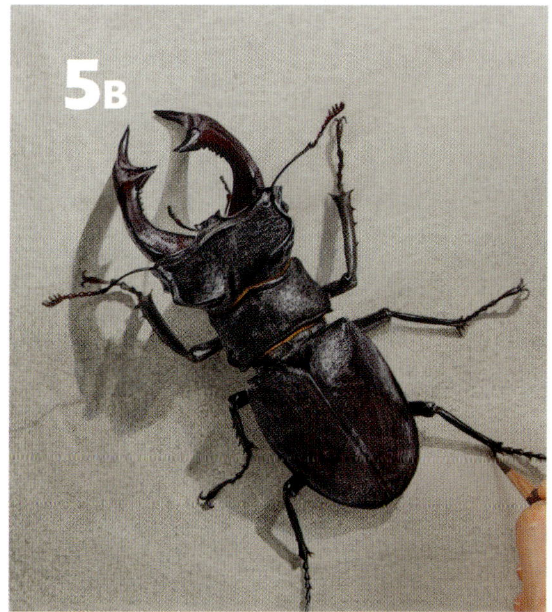

Celebrate finishing this illustration. Since this is the last assignment in the Foundation Skill Building section, acknowledge your hard work and accomplishments since you first opened this book. You now have the ability to draw a quick gesture, accurately measure proportions, cleanly refine an outline, correctly mix colors, paint a colorful base, and add intricate details with colored pencil. You can parade right onto the next section, where you will amplify these skills and present insects in dynamic environments.

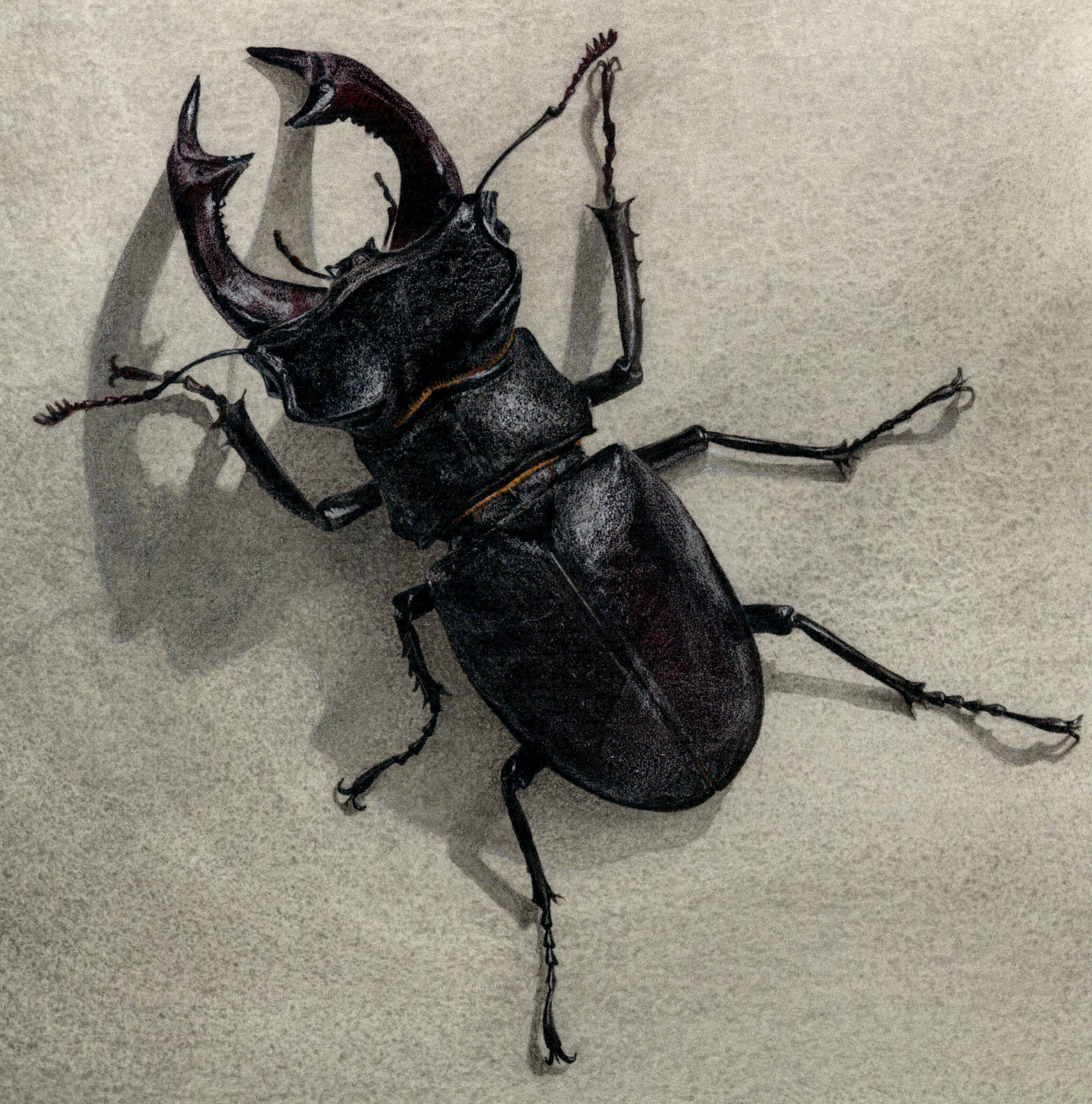

NATURE BREAK, OBSERVATION

● THROUGH THE WINDOW

Each time you sketch from the same vantage point, you observe and document the daily, seasonal, and yearly changes in your immediate environment. On occasions when venturing outdoors is not ideal, a window can offer creative inspiration. This Nature Break is devoted to connecting to the landscape while you are indoors.

LOCATION: Choose a window that is easily accessible and, if possible, from which you can see at least one natural element.

MATERIALS: You might set up a table and chair so that you can spread out your media. This is also a good time to use materials that would be difficult to use outdoors. On the other hand, you can set up a temporary workstation, as you would do outside, and simply sketch with pencil.

OBSERVATIONS: First spend some time just looking at the environment and acclimating yourself to the world beyond the walls of the building. Notice the elements, both natural and human-made, that can be seen from where you are sitting. Consider your composition. Perhaps you will use the window frame as a framing edge or focus on a single subject instead.

PRACTICE: When you are ready, begin your drawing. Since you have the luxury of being indoors, you might choose to add finite details to your subject and create a more finished work of art. You may even want to work on the artwork over multiple days instead of completing it in a single sitting.

REFLECTION: How did having a specific view affect your understanding of your subject? Did you find any surprising advantages or disadvantages to working indoors? If you worked over multiple days, how was your drawing or experience different from one session to another?

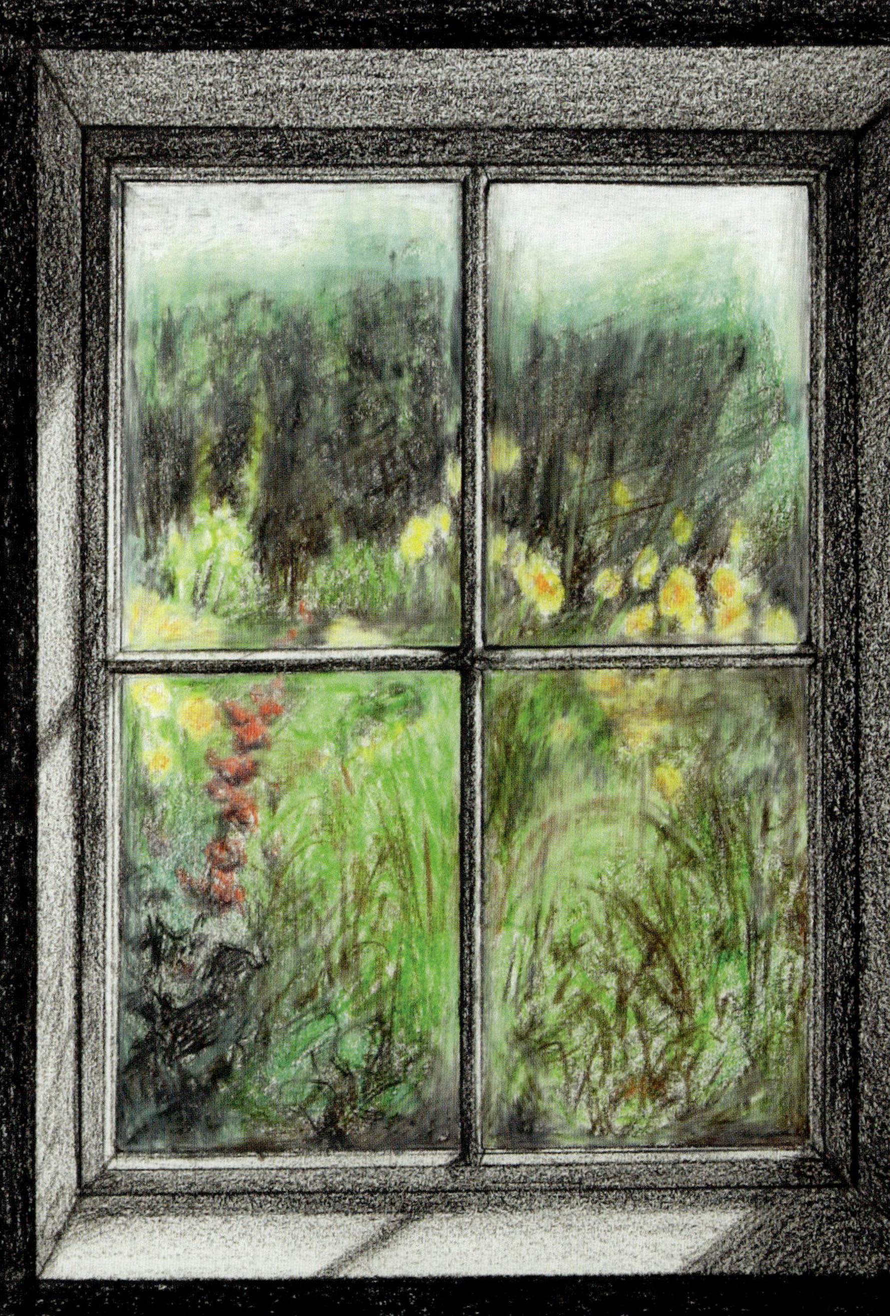

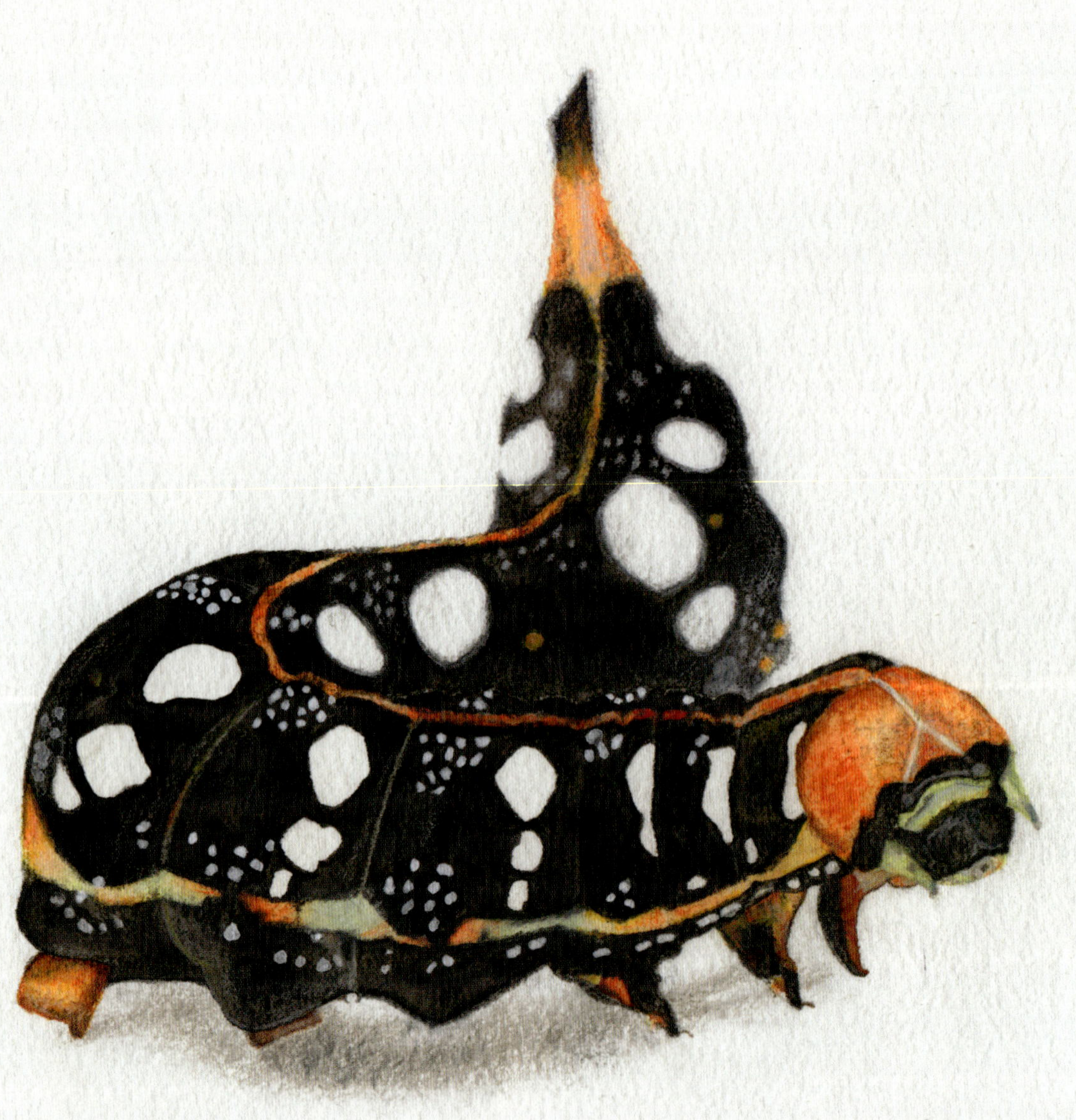

LEVEL II

COMPOSITION AND ENVIRONMENTS

"While I was illustrating this project, I came to befriend my caterpillar. Something got out of the way and it was coming to life. From the techniques I was learning, it seemed as if I was simply helping it emerge from the page. That was an emotionally satisfying aspect of the project! Working on this project helped me learn that most errors, which may seem like disasters at the time, can be compensated for. The final result is better than I could have imagined."

—Carol Orange, Creative Participant

This section builds on your creative foundation by expanding your skills with color interaction, units of measurement, and aesthetic composition designs. Creative tips help you give subjects the appearance of physical weight, illustrate forms in motion, and make corrections at a late stage in the process. You'll learn simple ways to draw complex patterns and to maintain accuracy when your subject is small in size or has sections hidden from view. You'll be encouraged to consider the illustration process as a whole, so that you can make the best choices within each step along the way.

You'll also find that the more commonly used materials and simple processes addressed in the previous projects are no longer mentioned. Brush sizes will be referred to more generally, giving you the choice of which paintbrush you would like to use to accomplish each task. As a result, some of the projects, material lists, and number of images may seem minimal, even though the illustrations likely require a similar number of items and an equal amount of time as earlier projects.

RED ADMIRAL BUTTERFLY

VANESSA ATALANTA

The red admiral (or admirable) butterfly has a nearly global range. The caterpillars, when they are not eating, create protective shelters in leaves either by curling a single leaf or connecting several together. The adults have a variety of food sources, including the nectar of flowers. I chose this composition because it explores botanical illustration as a secondary point of interest. The subtle variation of hue in the background, while simple to create, suggests the natural environment in which this butterfly thrives.

 SEE REFERENCE PHOTOS ON PAGES 316–317

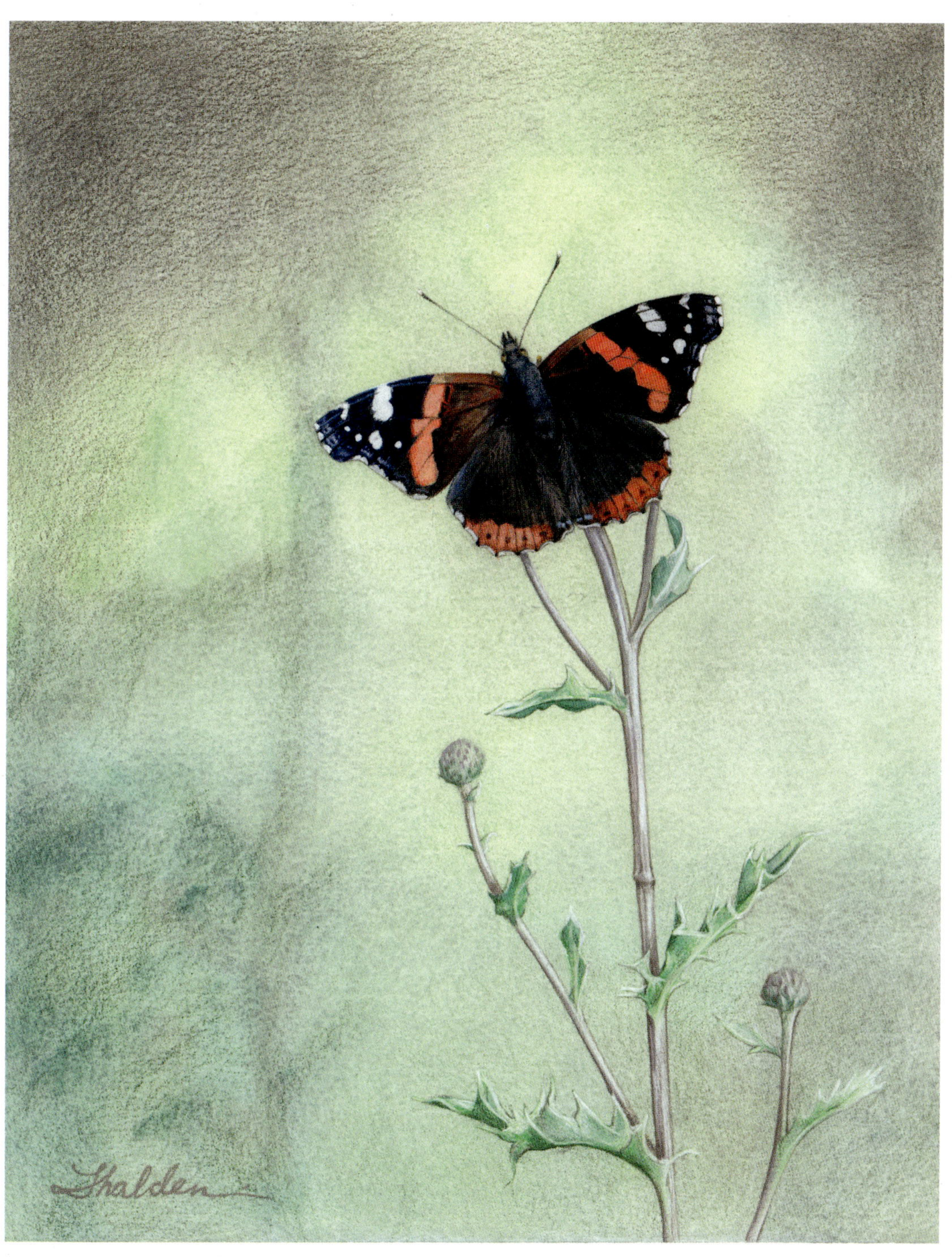

ACRYLIC PAINTS

- [ ] burnt sienna
- [ ] burnt umber
- [ ] cadmium red
- [ ] cadmium yellow
- [ ] Mars black
- [ ] permanent green light
- [ ] titanium white
- [ ] ultramarine blue

BRUSHES

- [ ] sizes 0, 000, and 0000 round
- [ ] size 4 round (or other medium brush)
- [ ] size 12 filbert (or other large brush)

COLORED PENCILS

- [ ] 10% French gray
- [ ] 50% French gray
- [ ] 70% French gray
- [ ] apple green
- [ ] black
- [ ] Caribbean Sea
- [ ] dark umber
- [ ] goldenrod
- [ ] indigo blue
- [ ] pale vermillion
- [ ] Prussian green
- [ ] rosy beige
- [ ] terra-cotta
- [ ] white

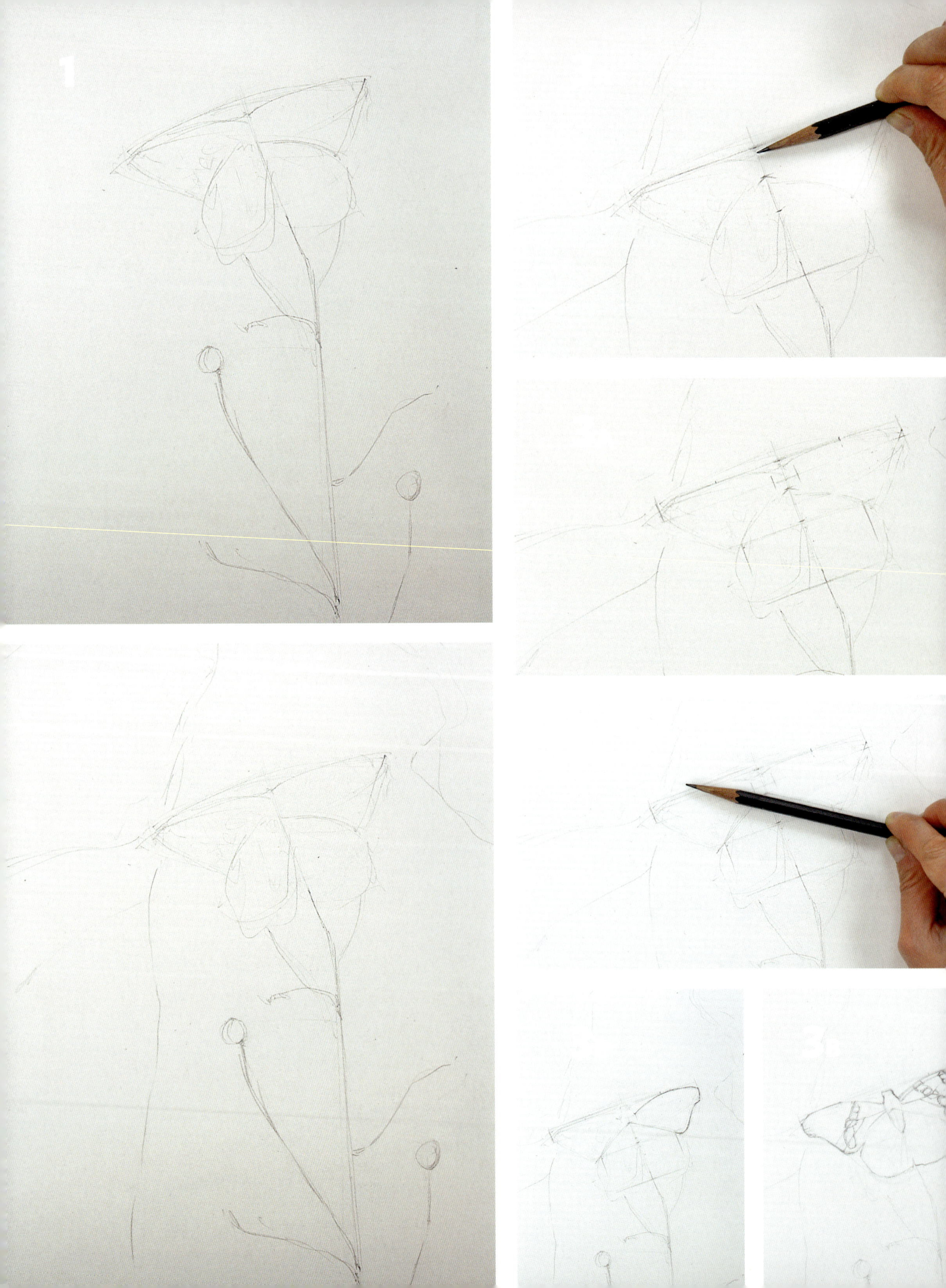

DRAWING

1 When you draw your gesture, place the butterfly first, then add the botanical. Since the plant stalk intersects the edge of the page and could distract from the subject, in my illustration I chose to extend the stem, lower the flower bud on the right side, and omit the smaller leaves and tiny mosquito. In the reference image, notice how the photographer achieved a similar effect by blurring the base of the plant. Making these types of compositional changes on your drawing draws the eye back to the butterfly. If I were working on a scientific botanical drawing, I would still take these design aspects into consideration but keep the anatomical details in place.

As an artist, when you choose to depart from a reference, you actively participate in creating the design aesthetics of the composition. While this offers both freedom and risk, it's a powerful opportunity to influence the way your drawing is experienced after completion.

2 Use lines that are slightly lighter in the background to indicate the location of the darkened upper corners and the dark stemlike line on the left. In this asymmetrical composition, your goal is to ensure a similar visual weight in each quadrant, without taking attention away from the focal point. In the reference image, look at the way value creates balance without disrupting the hierarchy. Look back at your page, imagine your drawing in full color, and consider if you need to adjust the placement of your gesture.

Learning to visualize a finished piece on a blank page is difficult. Simply choose what you think will work best, then see how it goes. Know that you can always adjust the amount of negative space and rebalance the composition by cropping the image after completion.

3 Return to the butterfly. Test a few measurements from the butterfly's anatomy to determine which one would be most useful to measure the anatomical forms.

A With your measurement, create a midline and mark the anatomical details along its length. I found that the head was easiest to measure if I ended it at the eyes. When you have completed the vertical measurements, mark the width of the body and the other horizontal measurements.

B Since the form of the insect is both small and simple, it may be easier to refine both sides of the butterfly simultaneously instead of creating a transfer sheet. Either way, draw the forewing first so that you can use the shape to help create the hindwing. As you draw the outline, patterns, and veins, remember to compare one side to the other and look for nuances in shape and positioning. You can draw the antennae now or wait, as I did, until the colored pencil stage (after the butterfly and the background have color).

If you are transferring the image, here's a little trick that will help you change the position of a wing quickly: After you align the sheet to the midline, transfer all lines except the wing that needs to be repositioned. Then rotate the tracing paper, while keeping the base of the wing in the same location, to slightly lower or raise the wing. All you need to do now is transfer the outline of the wing in the new position.

4 **A** When you draw the thistle, determine the intersection points along the stem and the overall length of each branch and leaf. Use the same measurement you used to draw the butterfly so that the composition's proportions are identical. Because the thistle is a secondary focal point, it's not necessary to measure every detail as you did with the butterfly.

Once your measurements are in place, pencil in the thickness of the stem. Since the leaves have a complex shape, take a moment to study their form in the reference image before you draw them freehand. Notice the shape of both the surface above and underneath and whether the edge is curled toward or away from the viewer. The more you understand the contour of the form, the easier it will be to capture it accurately in your drawing.

B Since the bottom of the stem is blurry in the reference image, use the upper leaves as a guide to determine the overall shape of the lower leaf and how it should attach to the stem. When you are finished, review your work, clean the drawing, and prepare the page for the painting stage. If you trace your drawing so that you have a copy of your work, mark the corners so that it can easily be aligned again.

You are doing great work! Having the ability to change design elements to make a composition even stronger and to envision a drawing while in the painting stage can be incredibly useful.

PAINTING

1 Because the background will be light enough for the butterfly to be painted on top, it isn't necessary to use masking fluid. While you could add masking fluid to the spots on the butterfly, I encourage you to use the paint method described here instead, so that you expand your technical versatility.

Create a base color that matches the light green in the background using titanium white, permanent green light, and cadmium yellow paint. Mix a bit more of this base paint mixture than you think you will need, so that you have the option to practice ahead of time. Divide the mixture into thirds. Leave one the original color, add some ultramarine blue to the second to create the medium green, and add both ultramarine blue and burnt umber to the third to create the dark green background color. If this last mixture becomes too neutral, add a touch of permanent green light. Dilute your mixtures but keep the value a bit darker than the reference image so that the colors will be accurate when you apply them on top of a wash.

Before you work on your illustration, you might practice painting the background by following these instructions: Tape a small swatch onto a separate portion of your workstation, add a thin, even water wash, and begin to add color. You must work quickly so that the entire page has an even glisten as you add one color and then another. Allow the colors to blend but avoid creating dramatic shapes, abrupt value changes, and hard edges—those could compete with the subject. This process should take only a minute or two from beginning to end. Be sure to have a paper towel on hand to use if the wash begins to run or pool.

Now that you have an idea of the process, begin your illustration. Aim to keep the background where the butterfly will be located a consistent value and the lightest green. Take a deep

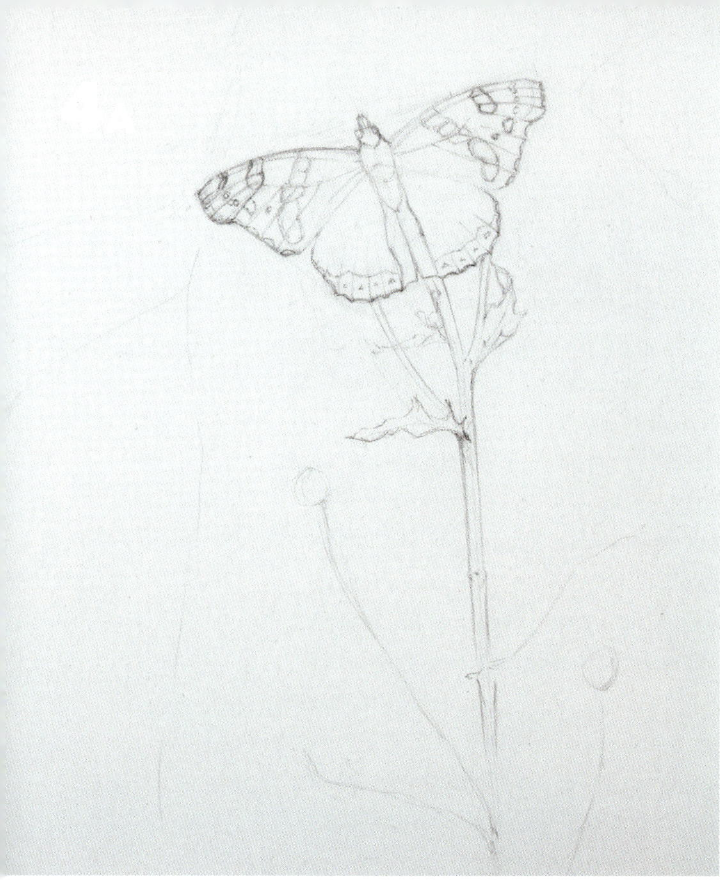

4A
4B

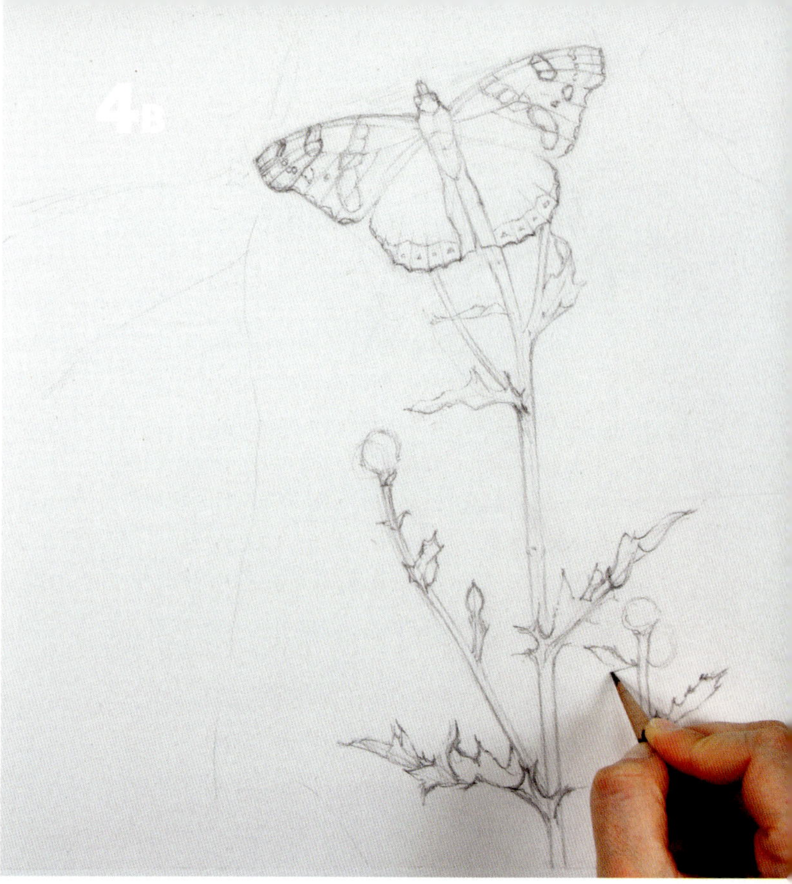

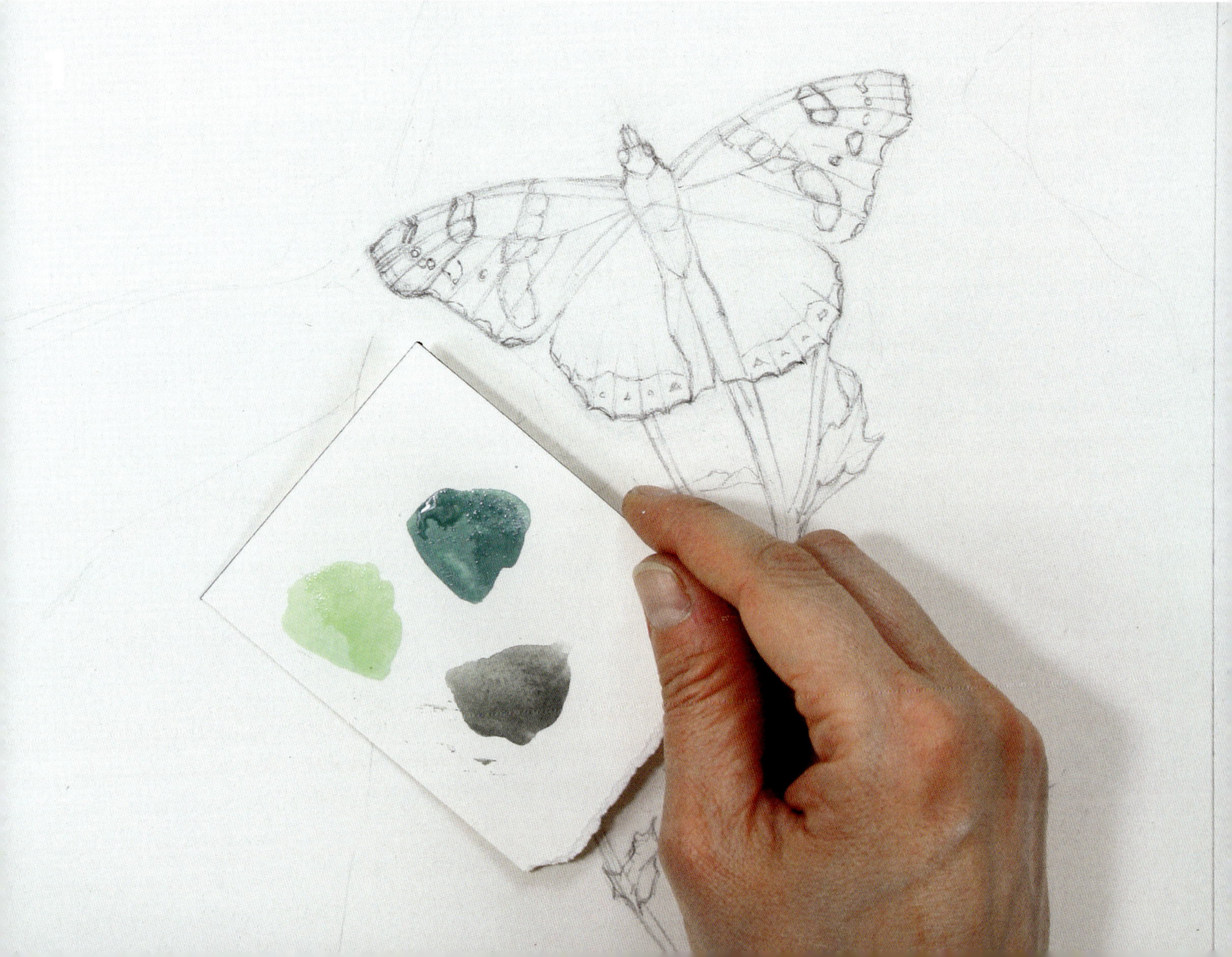

breath, let go, and have fun with this. However it turns out will be perfect.

2 **A** With a large paintbrush, add an even water wash to the entire composition. I used a size 50 filbert in the example, but any paintbrush above a size 10 is a great choice. Then immediately switch to a size 4 or larger paintbrush to apply the light green paint mixture to the lightest areas of the background. To keep the paint from drifting, put the painting on either a level surface or one that is angled slightly toward you.

B As soon as all of the light green areas are covered with paint, switch to using the medium green mixture and repeat the process. You can add more pigment to create slightly darker areas. As I paint each area, I like to combine blots, brushstrokes, and subtle variations to blend the colors together. Be sure that the edges of the paint are blurred and the style of the entire background matches. Work quickly so that you can avoid adding more water to the page as you work. If an area without paint begins to dry, use the brush you used to apply the wash and apply just enough water to match the rest of the page and continue.

C Next, add dark green to the upper corners. You might darken the corners to the degree in the reference image; that way you can skip the pencil step that my illustration required later in the process. With all the colors in place, you might use the light green paint mixture to further accentuate the lighter areas and create nice transitions between the darker areas. At this point, it's easy to over-work the background, so I suggest pausing your work to let it dry completely.

Sit back and rejoice in the accomplishment of allowing paint to spread and mingle with other colors to successfully create an environment for your subject.

3 **A** Now it is time to work on the butterfly. Although most of the butterfly is composed of variations of brown, closer inspection shows that the forewing tips are dark blue or even black. Select Mars black or burnt umber as the main color and add a little ultramarine blue to your mixture when needed. If you mix the paints close together on your palette, the mixtures can begin to merge and create even more nuanced colors.

Since the areas are so small, using a water wash should not be necessary. You can also apply the first layer of paint thinly, like a wash, and layer on top of it to darken the wings. Keep the value of your colors consistent and the veins unpainted. The highlights, as well as the blue accents along the edge of the wings, will be applied with pencil later; for now, they can remain dark.

B Since all four wings are slightly different in color and value, you can complete both wings on one side and then move to the opposite side. When you work on the body, leave the eyes unpainted for now.

4 **A** Selecting from the paints listed, create an orange mixture that matches the details on the butterfly's right wing. Notice the slight variation of color and value from one wing to another. In the lighter areas, you may need a mixture that has more white and less yellow. In heavily shadowed areas, you might add a bit of burnt sienna paint to darken the base mixture. Then select an extremely small paintbrush to apply the mixtures to the page.

B To complete the butterfly, add the white spots with your paintbrush along the tips of the wings. If you find that pure titanium white paint is too bright, lower the saturation by mixing in a miniscule amount of Mars black. To create the tiny dots and scalloped edging, gather paint on the very tip of an extremely small paintbrush. Take your time so that you can create each shape accurately. The brush can dry quickly, however, so pause to rinse it often. You might need to apply a second layer to achieve the desired color.

Although the butterfly is small, you've been able to create a subject that is very detailed. And the

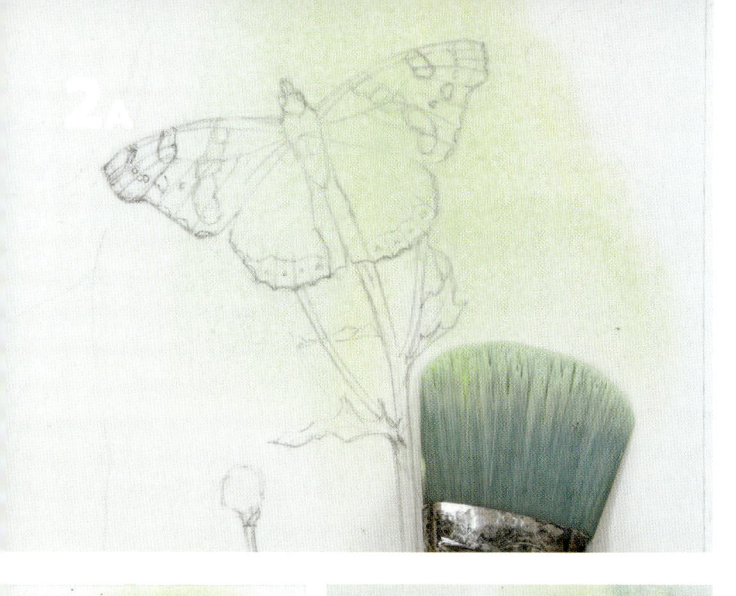
2A

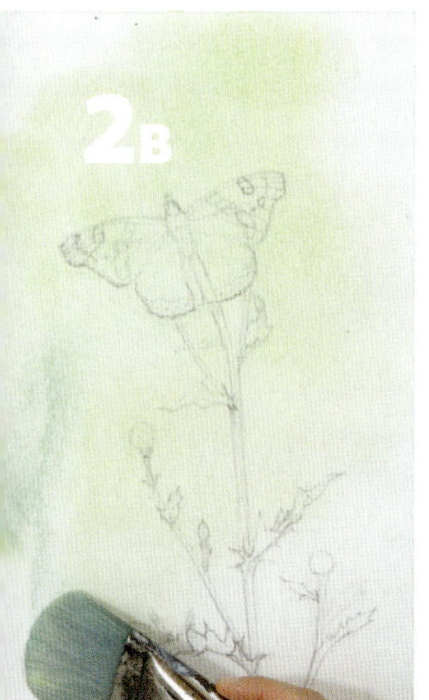
2B

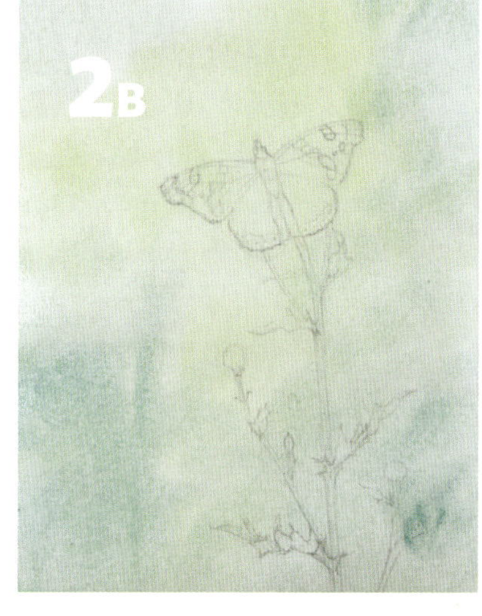
2B

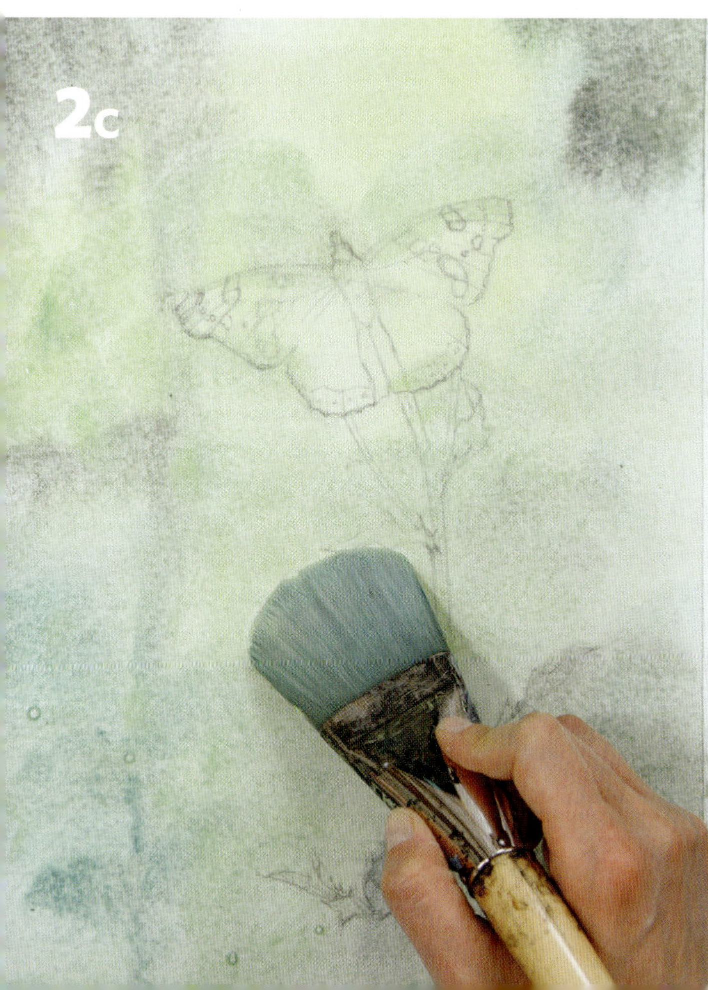
2C

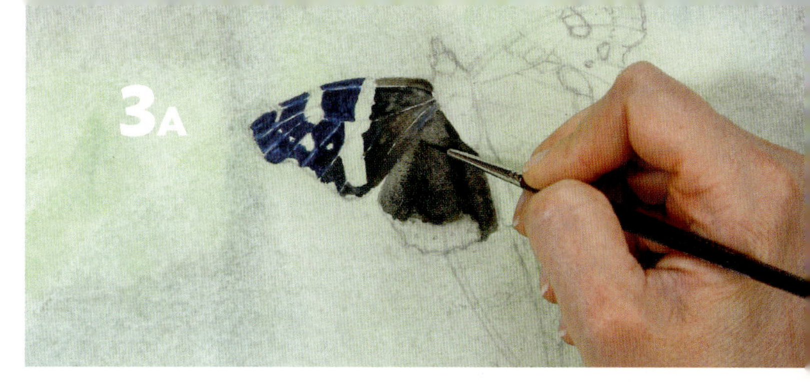
3A

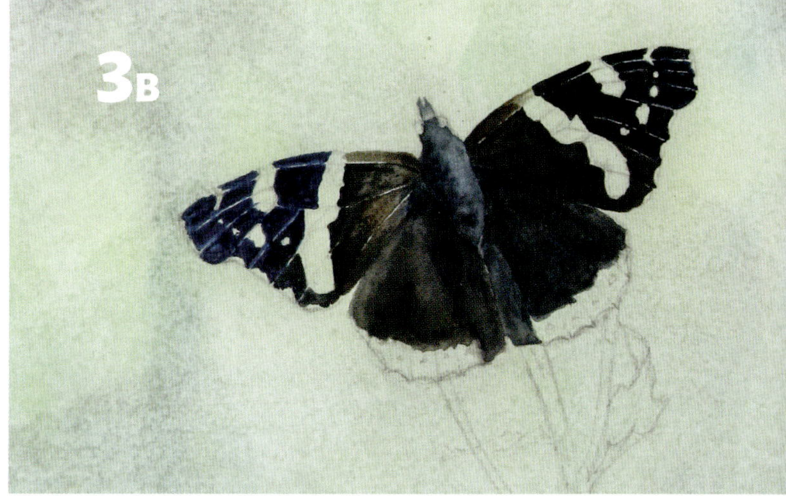
3B

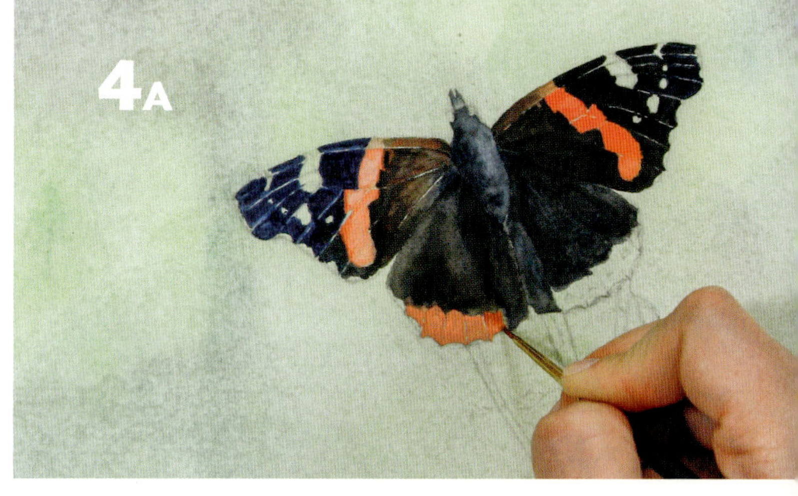
4A

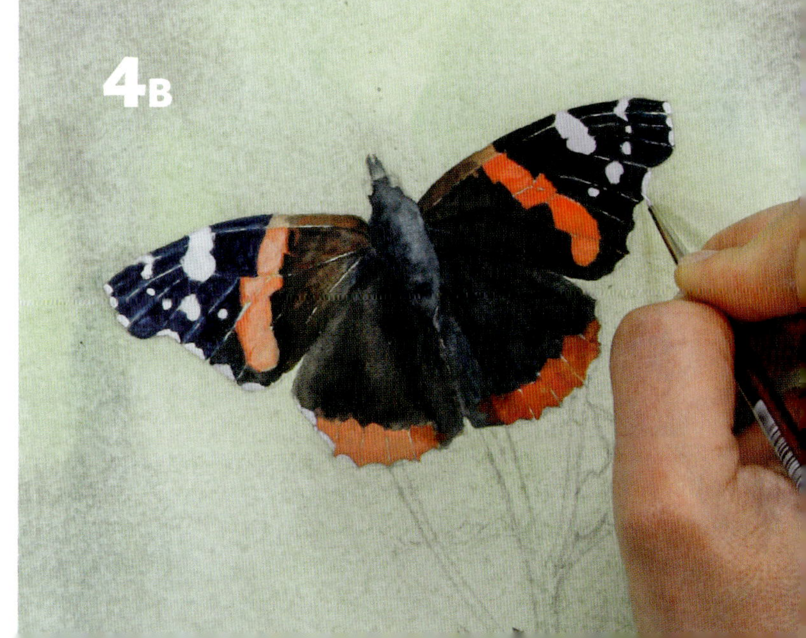
4B

subtle variation in value from wing to wing greatly enhances the lifelike quality. Now you can apply all of these techniques to create the botanical.

5 Create a light purple paint mixture that matches the dominant color of the stem. Some areas will need a bit more blue, white, red, or a touch of black paint, which can be added to a portion of the base color. When your mixtures are ready, apply the paint to the stem using an extremely small paintbrush. At the base of both the leaves and the buds, blur the edge of the paint so that it fades into the background color. Wait to add the purple to the flower buds until the green paint has been mixed. Until then, cover the purple mixture on your palette with plastic wrap to keep it usable.

6 Now create a base color mixture for the upper portion of the leaves. Since the yellow-green is available in colored pencil, it will be essential to add the blue-green in paint during this stage. Tip: If you add a sample of the apple green colored pencil to your paint swatch, you can use it as a reference when you mix the blue-green paint.

A Feel free to adjust the color by adding a small amount of blue or green paint to a portion of your mixture. Dilute the pigment to create highlights. Either leave the areas that will be apple green blank or fade the blue green back into the color of the background. Keep in mind that you can use a white pencil to further lighten these areas later in the process.

B Look at the flower buds in the reference image and determine the direction of the light source. To create the highlight on your page, you can either apply a wash to the entire bud before you add paint or paint directly onto the page and use a clean moist brush to fade the upper edge. Either way, use the green mixture to create a smooth light arc in the opposite direction of the light. You will be able to darken the shadow using a Prussian green pencil later in the process. Let this layer of paint dry before moving on.

C Remove the plastic wrap from the purple paint mixture on your palette and reconstitute it, if needed. Check to be sure that the value is the same as the green paint on the buds. Then continue the shadow on the upper half of the bud using the same gradation technique you used on the lower portion. Let the flower buds dry completely before you move on to the final painting stage.

D Utilize the remaining paint on your palette to add the details on the flower buds. Look at the reference image to locate a single diagonal line of dots that can be added to start the pattern on your page. Use the purple paint mixture to add *only* this line of dots to the upper section. You can use this first line as a guide for adding the rest of the purple dots. Next, switch to using the green paint mixture and continue painting the pattern on the lower section. Move to the second bud and repeat this process, then look over the composition to see if anything needs adjusting or accentuating.

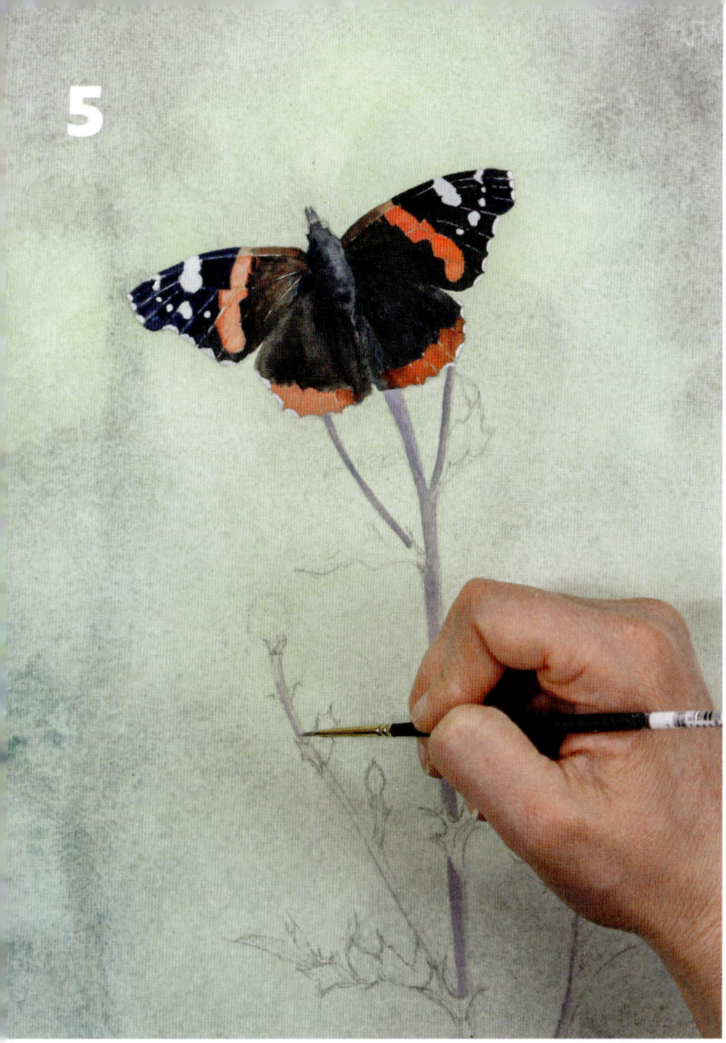

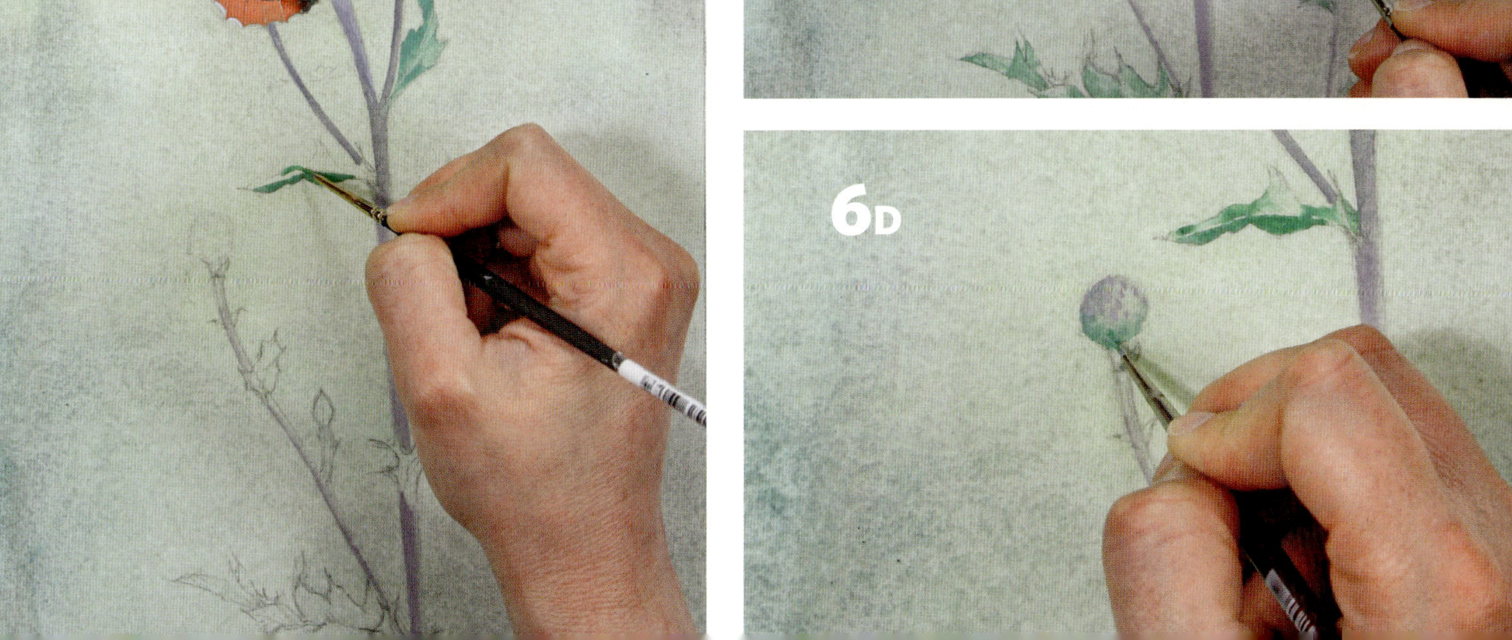
5
6B 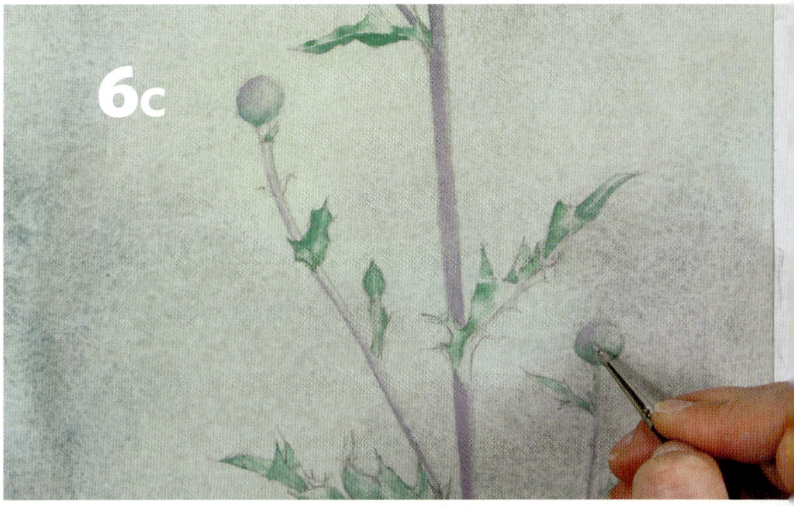
6A
6C
6D

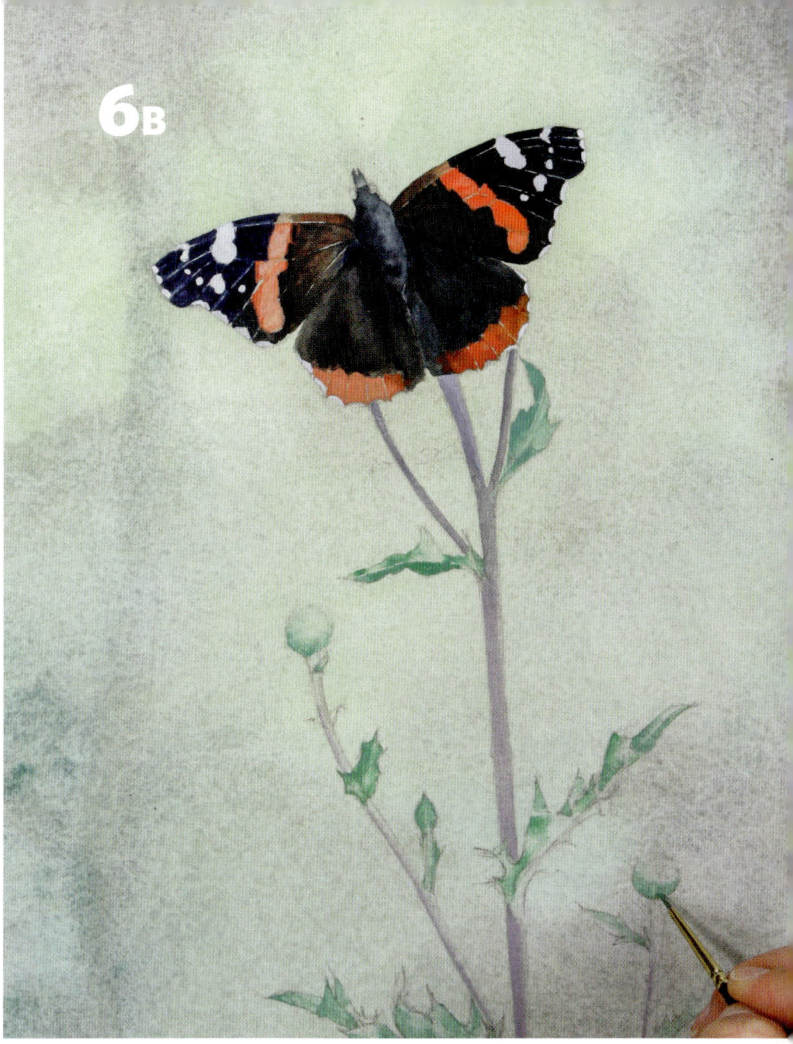

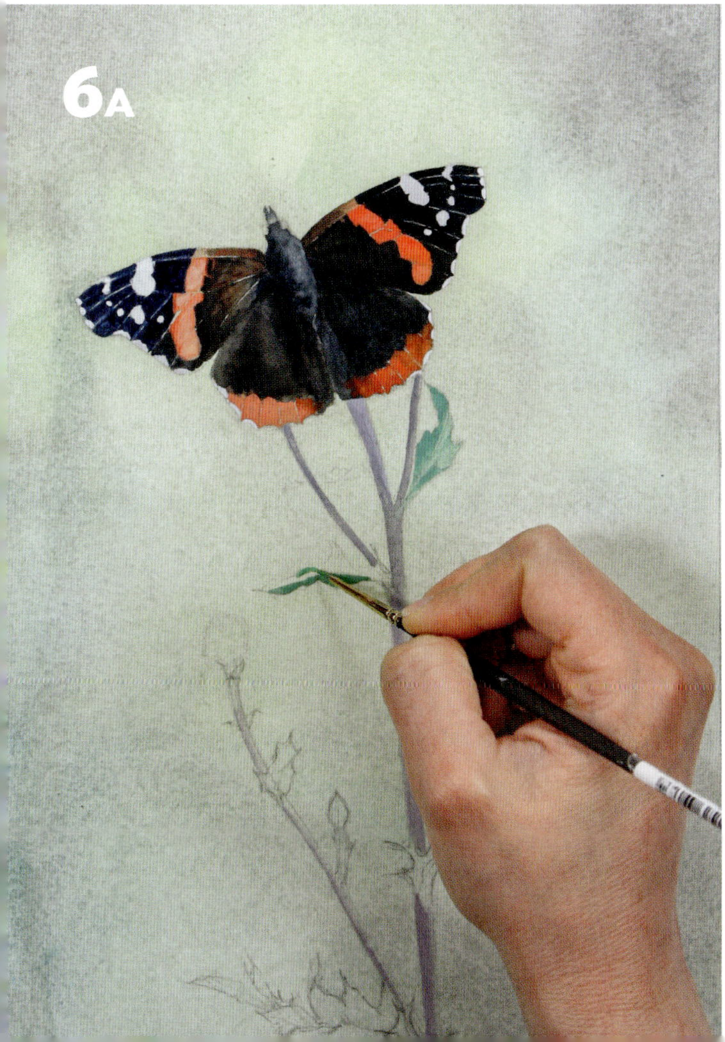

You've worked through many challenging tasks in this illustration stage. I hope it feels very good to think of all you've accomplished thus far.

LAYERING WITH COLORED PENCIL

1 Return to the butterfly to refine the details. Start work on the left forewing using the indigo blue pencil to indicate veins, darken or blend the coloration in the cells, and enhance the perimeter of the white sections. Add the light blue details using Caribbean Sea along the edge of the wing, and lighten select areas by layering white pencil over the blue. Move to the opposite wing. Since this wing is in shadow, some of the pencil colors will be different: use the black pencil to create veins and adjust the orange areas using the pale vermillion pencil. You will likely use the same colors along the edge. Then return to the left forewing and complete the veins near the body using the dark umber pencil. In my piece, I also used a small amount of the terra-cotta pencil to make the brown areas a bit more orange.

Before you move to the hindwings and repeat this process, apply a couple of simple yet effective tricks to finesse your work. Use an eraser along the sides of each visible vein to make them as thin as possible. There may be a slight groove between the painted areas to help you achieve this effect. Now look at the edge of the wings to see if the white areas are blending into the background and disappearing. If they are, select a middle-value French gray pencil with very light pressure to draw an extremely thin line along the outside edge of the wing. If the value of this line is just darker than the value of the background, you should find the white immediately appears to be part of the wing.

2 Use French gray pencils to add the fur located near the midline. Select a pencil with a dark value where the wings ripple and a mid-value pencil for the flat portions. To add bright highlighted hairs, switch to using the rosy beige pencil, keeping the pressure of your pencil very light. If the hairs lighten the overall area too much, come back in using a dark color and the same flicking motion.

Switch to the black pencil to create the dark area between the hindwings, simply flick the pencil from the center upward toward the hairs to create the dark spaces between the hairs. Continue and add the shadows to the top and outsides of the ripples. In my illustration, I decided to keep the shadows on the wings slightly lighter than those along the midline to emphasize both the continuity of each wing's contour and the difference in depth between the two areas.

Before you move to a different section of the butterfly, add the small blue detail on the hindwing using the Caribbean Sea pencil. That bright white horizontal line seen on the left side of the body is actually an exposed vein. Because it is difficult to understand visually and will be a distraction to the artwork, I chose to de-emphasize it in my illustration.

When you implement these simple yet intentional changes, even when your subject is relatively small, you express the technical authority you have with the medium.

3 Move to the body and use the indigo blue pencil, with light pressure in a small circular motion, to create the shadow areas. For the eyes, use the goldenrod pencil layered with the black pencil. Since the shadow is on the left side, be sure that you make the left eye slightly darker than the right. When you develop consistent lightning on forms, even in small details, you emphasize the three-dimensionality of the overall structure.

Look closely at the edge of the forewings near the head and you can see a small portion of the

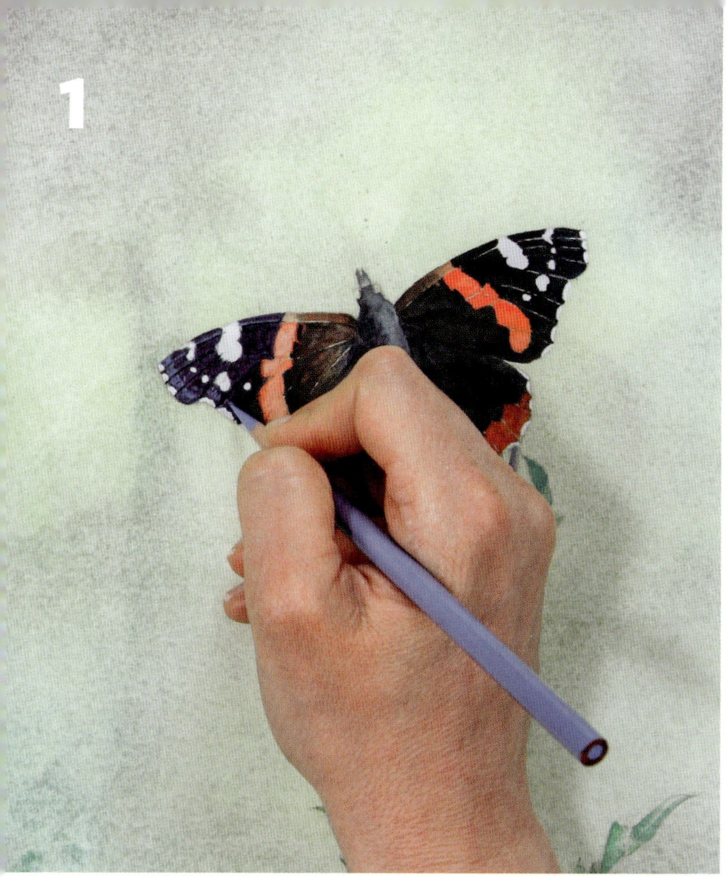

1

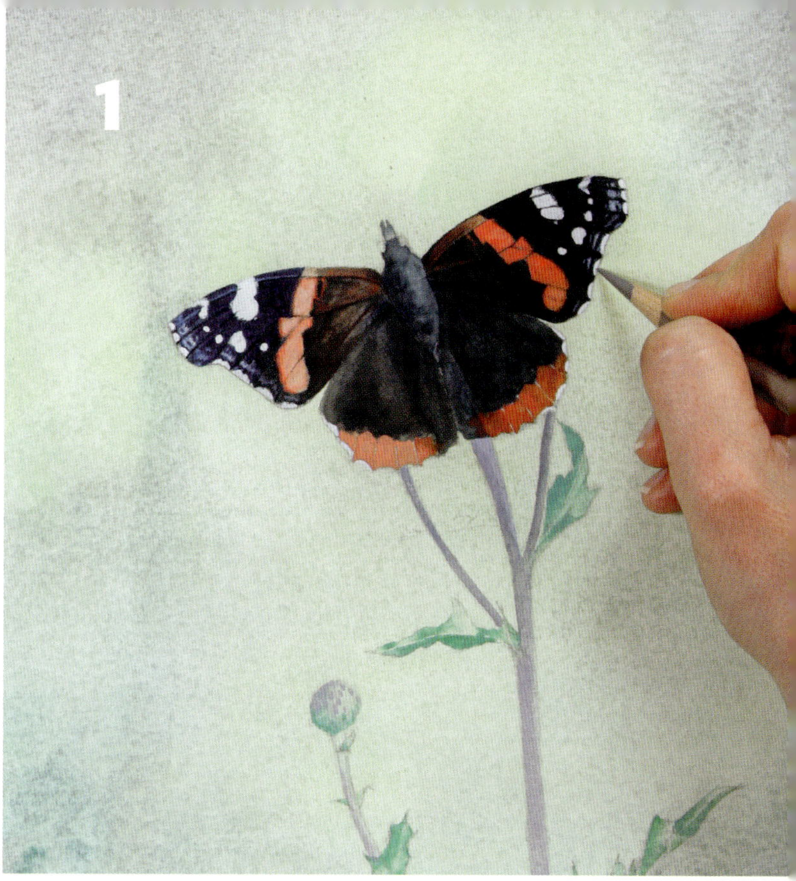

1

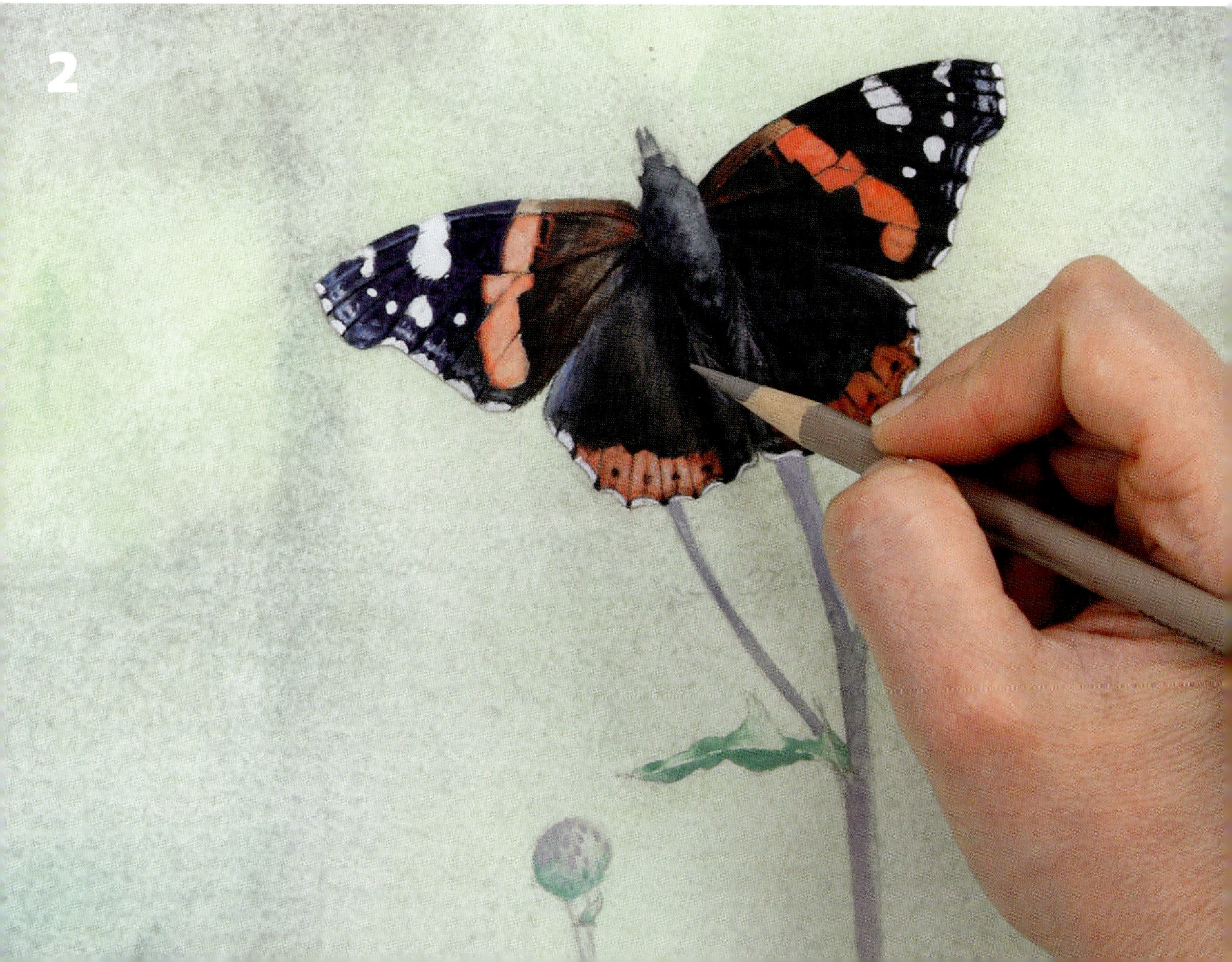

2

legs showing in the reference image. If you would like to add these, use one of the French gray pencils in combination with the goldenrod pencil. Then add a thin line using the black pencil along the edge of the wing to separate the two forms. In my illustration, I added the legs just before finishing the composition.

4 If you need to add the antennae, use an HB pencil and the same measurement you used in the drawing stage to mark their location and angle. To help you find the length of the club at the end, compare it to the size of the spots on the wing. Switch to using the black pencil and carefully add the line for both antennae, making the right one slightly darker, similar to the right wing. When you darken the club, leave a small section at the top for the light dot at the end, which can be added with a dab of white paint taken directly from the tube with a moist paintbrush. (Replace the cap on the paint tube and rinse that brush immediately to keep it from drying out.) Review the butterfly for any final adjustments.

5 **A** Return to working on the botanical. Use the 10% French gray pencil to add highlights to the stem. First add color to whole areas, then layer with crisp lines. Feel free to add highlights to the flower buds to accentuate the marks you made earlier. To enhance the dimensionality and differentiate the plant from the background, select a middle-value French gray pencil to draw a thin line along the left side of the stem. Use the white pencil to add bright highlights and the 70% French gray pencil to deepen shadows.

Since the lower portion of the stem is blurry in the reference image, use the color and value themes along the upper portion of the stem as a guide to create consistency throughout.

B Use a similar process to add detail to the leaves. For highlights, use the 10% French gray pencil followed by the white pencil. When you are ready to fill in the yellow-green sections, switch to using the apple green pencil. Allow this color to overlap the white to both reduce the intensity and integrate the color into the surrounding leaf. Now switch to the Prussian green pencil, layering it sparingly to enhance shadows, define edges, and further separate the plant from the background.

C If any hard lines formed in the background during the painting stage, this is the time to integrate them into the surroundings.

When I reviewed the composition, I decided to enhance the background using a dark-value French gray pencil in the upper corners and the Prussian green pencil in the lower corners. Since I darkened the background around the plant, I also accentuated the highlights and the shadows along the stem and leaves.

Anytime you want to add an even layer of value to a large area, such as the background, hold the pencil a couple of inches from the lead and create broad but controlled marks. Start at the top of the area and work downward, moving the pencil quickly with a back-and-forth motion. To avoid striping, keep your strokes close together and your pencil pressure consistent. Since your page should simply be getting darker, it will not be detectable if you need to work in another direction. It will also be helpful to keep your pinky finger on the page to give you maximum control and to keep the pencil angle consistent. To integrate color into a surrounding area, lighten the pressure of your pencil to create a smooth gradation. Pause after you complete every layer to reassess your result. Periodically unfocus your eyes and blur your vision to determine if the gradation is effective. If you choose to embellish the area where the leaves are, go slowly, and continue using the same technique as you go around the form.

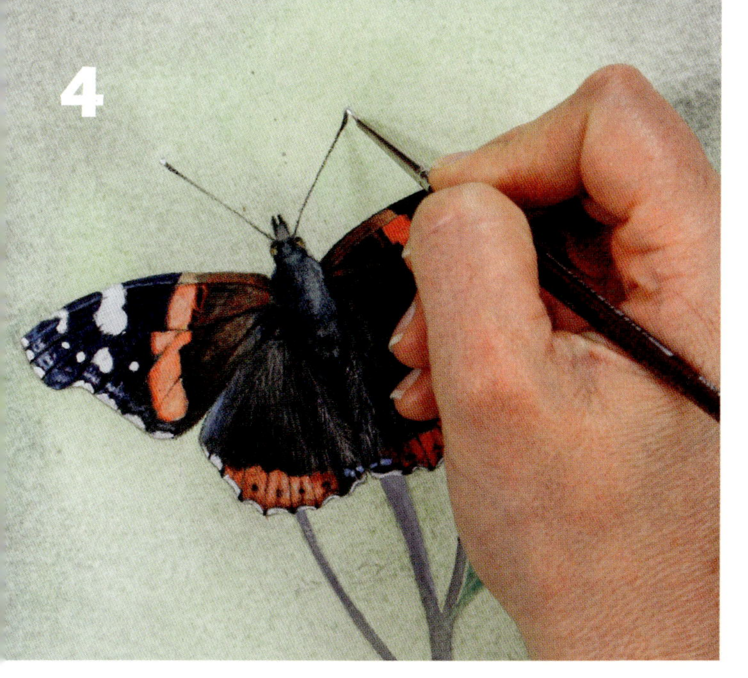
4

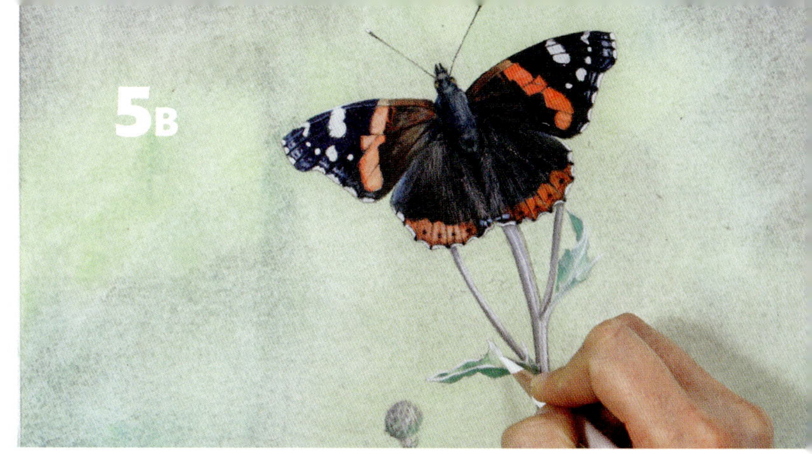
5B

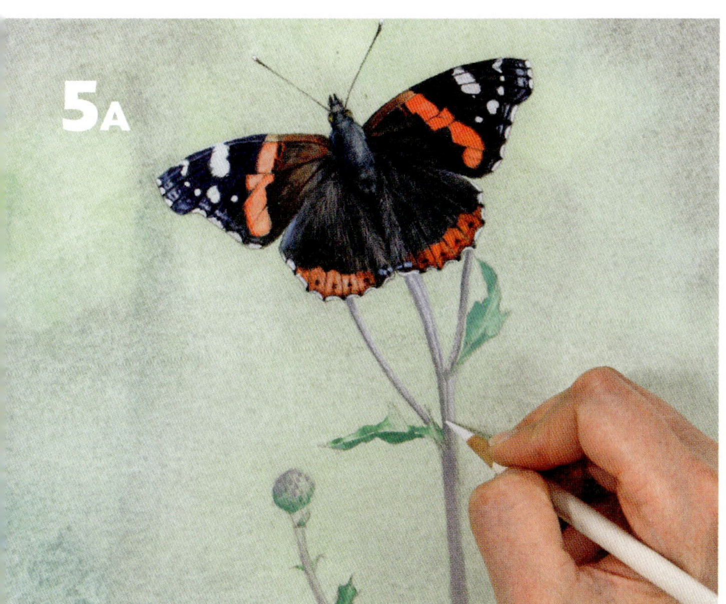
5A

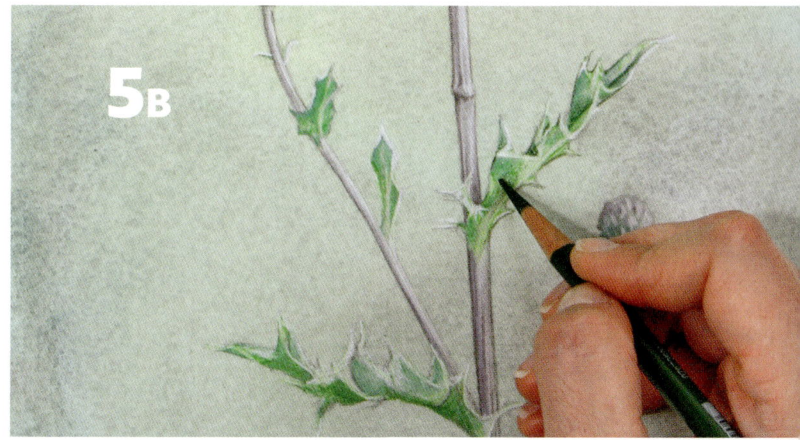
5B

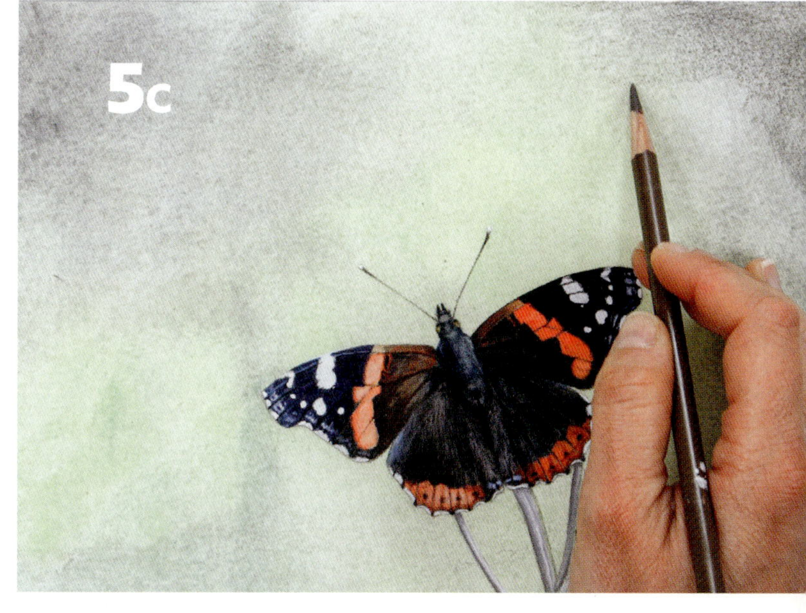
5C

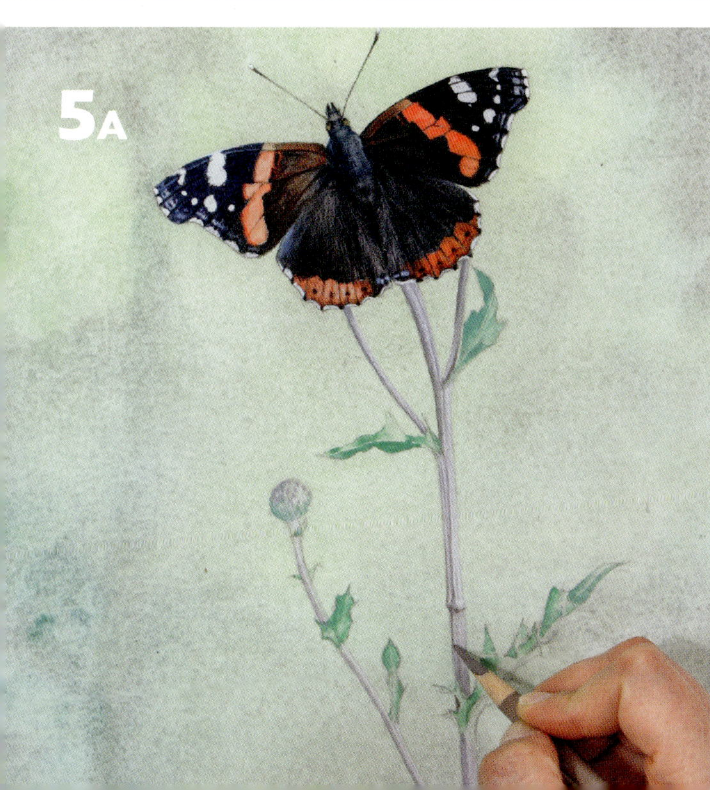
5A

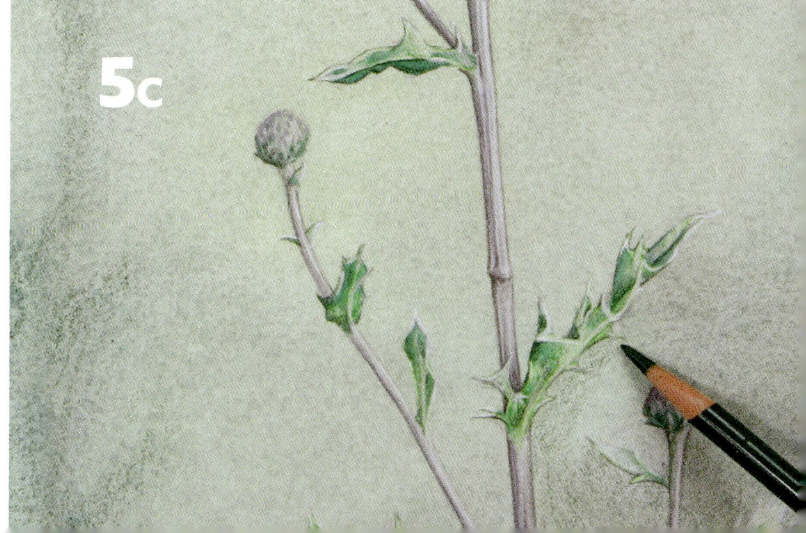
5C

You have successfully created a botanical illustration with nuanced detail. This perch you created for the butterfly adds complexity to your composition and hints at the natural habitat of this species. Nice job.

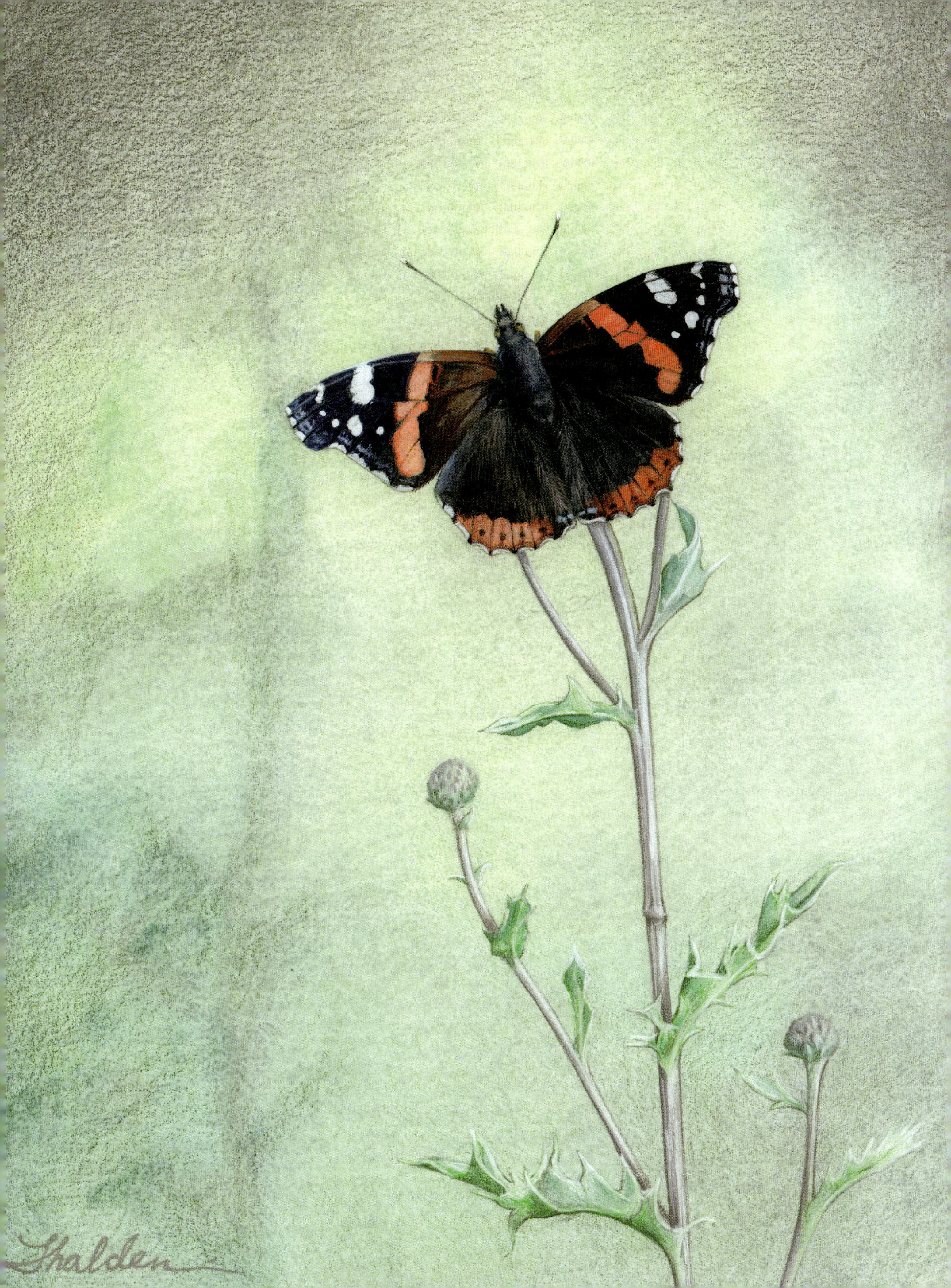
Shalden

COMPOSING NATURE

To make an aesthetically pleasing composition, both the contents and the framing edge of the layout need to have an aesthetic relationship. Using cropping tools can help you select designs and play with height, width, and negative space. This Nature Break is devoted to composing nature.

LOCATION: Choose a location where you can explore whole landscapes as well as up-close subjects.

MATERIALS: Sketchbook, HB pencil, and a seat. If you do not have cropping tools, either make them in advance or bring a ruler, pencil, scissors, and a piece of thick black or gray paper that is roughly 8 ½ by 11 inches.

PREPARATION: To make the cropping tools, draw a line, ¾ inch from the edge, on each side of the paper. Fold the paper in half lengthwise and then again widthwise. Unfold and cut along the drawn line. Then cut the exterior frame at each fold so that you have two pairs of L-shaped cropping tools (See step 1A on page 182).

OBSERVATIONS: Once at your chosen location, take a pair of cropping tools and place an L in each hand, facing one another. Flip one upside down, and overlap the two to create a frame with a hole in the middle.

PRACTICE: Close one eye and look through the viewfinder. Shift the height and width to consider what creates balance, beauty, hierarchy, or movement within a design.

When you find a composition that you are either attracted to or repelled by, hold both cropping tools in one hand and draw a small sketch of the composition. Label each sketch so you have an example of what does or does not work for you.

REFLECTION: Which compositions did you find most dynamic? What made a composition strong or inspiring to you? Can you tweak a composition to make it more appealing?

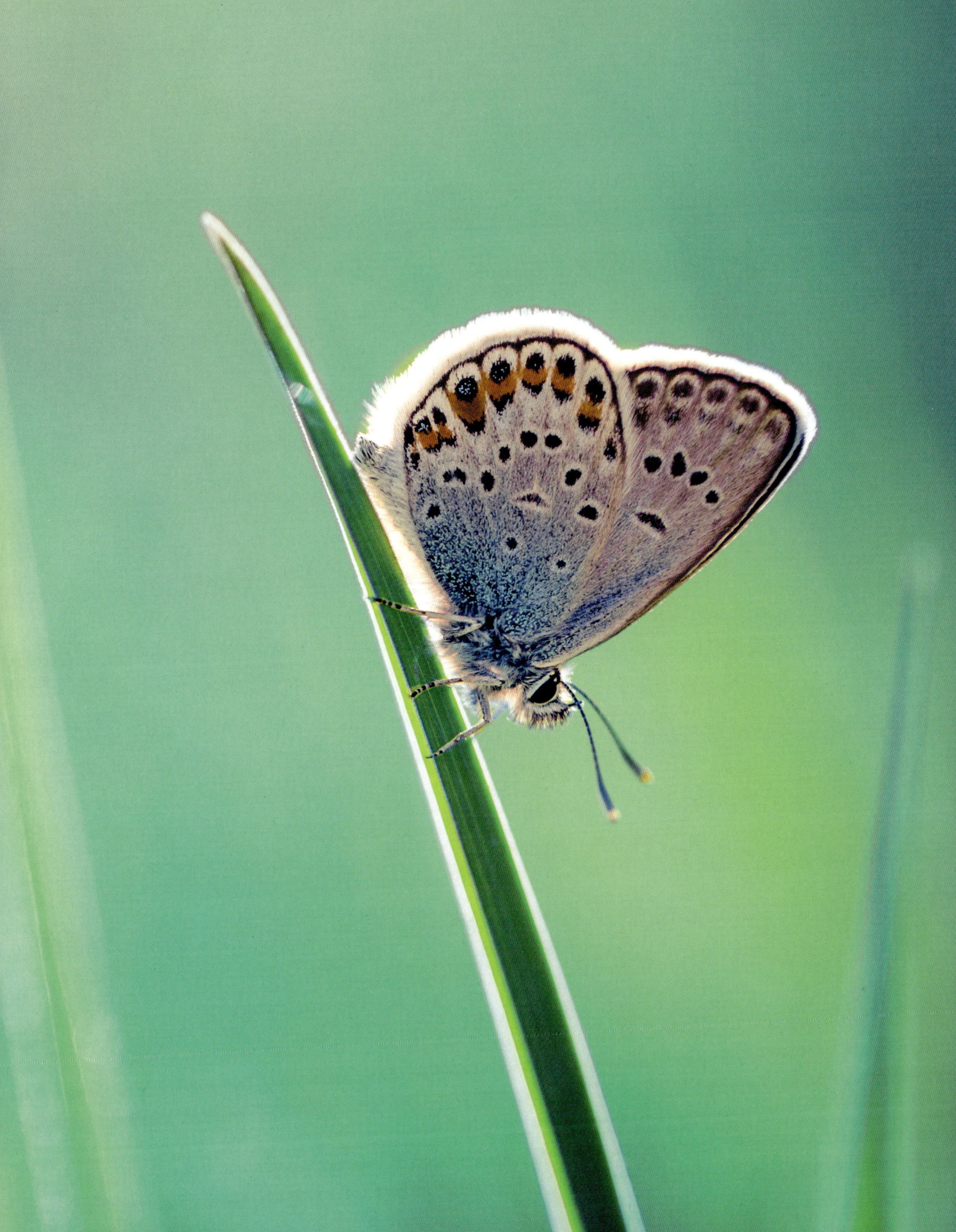

WEAVER ANT

OECOPHYLLA SMARAGDINA

Weaver ants live in the tropical and subtropical areas of Asia and Australia. They exhibit incredible teamwork and create elaborate nests made from leaves that they weave together with the silk produced by the larvae. They also farm aphids and their relatives to feed on the honeydew that these smaller insects excrete. The queen is greenish in color, but the workers, like the one in this composition, are a vibrant red-orange. I included this composition because it offers new techniques to explore: cropping an existing composition to make a new design, using both value and color to create balance in an asymmetrical piece, allowing the background colors to become a base for the foreground, and using diluted pigments or a gradation to suggest illuminated translucent forms.

SEE REFERENCE PHOTOS ON PAGE 318

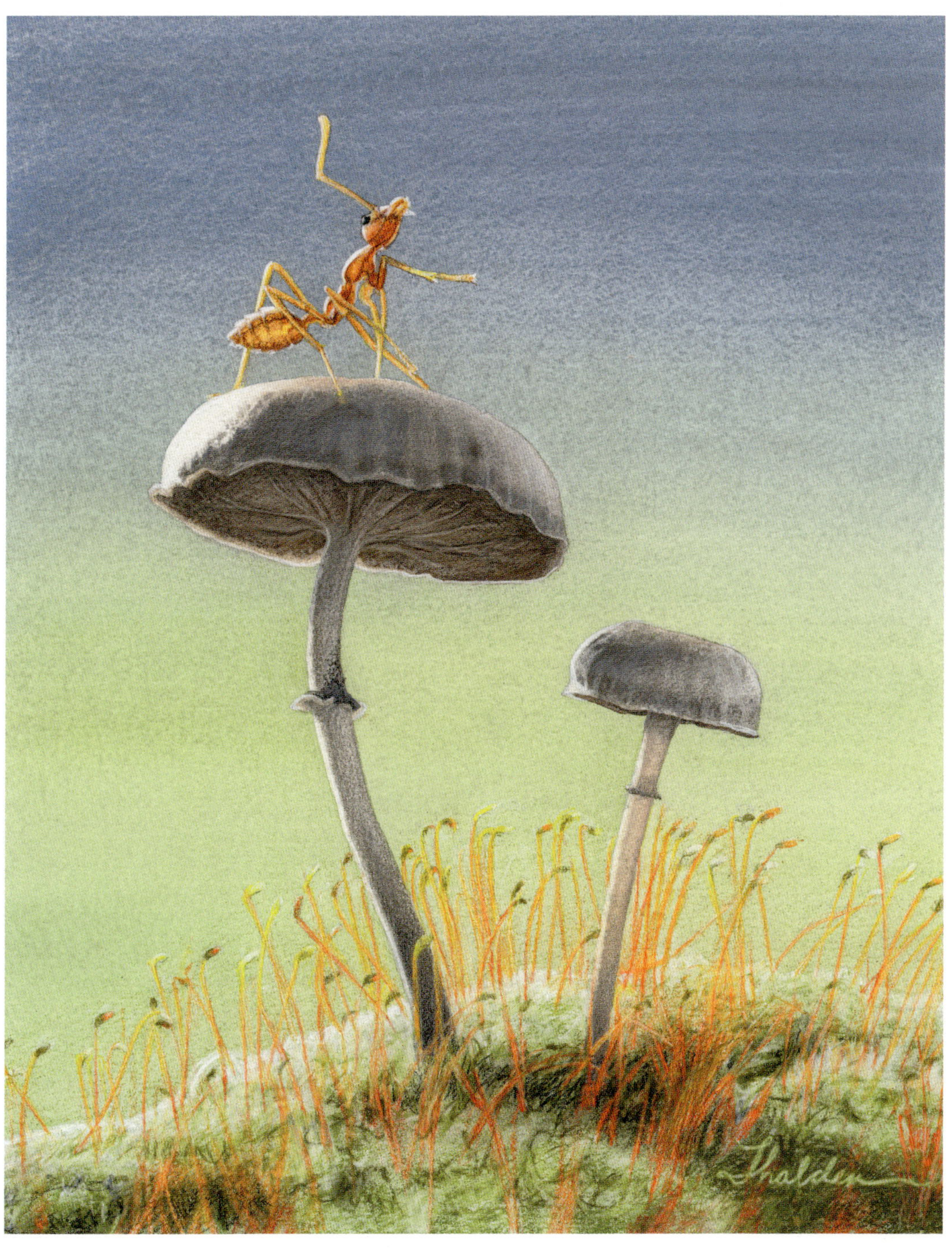

ACRYLIC PAINT

- [ ] burnt umber
- [ ] cadmium red
- [ ] cadmium yellow
- [ ] cobalt blue
- [ ] phthalo yellow green
- [ ] sienna brown
- [ ] titanium white
- [ ] Mars black
- [ ] Naples yellow (optional)

BRUSHES

- [ ] sizes 000, 2, and 3 round
- [ ] size 12 filbert (or other large brush)

COLORED PENCIL

- [ ] 10% French gray
- [ ] 30% French gray
- [ ] 50% French gray
- [ ] 70% French gray
- [ ] black
- [ ] burnt ocher
- [ ] canary yellow
- [ ] chocolate
- [ ] dark umber
- [ ] electric blue (optional)
- [ ] green ocher
- [ ] light umber
- [ ] lime peel
- [ ] moss green
- [ ] orange
- [ ] pale vermillion
- [ ] rosy beige
- [ ] seashell pink
- [ ] sepia (optional)
- [ ] sienna brown
- [ ] sunburst yellow
- [ ] white
- [ ] yellowed orange

ADDITIONAL MATERIALS

- [ ] masking fluid
- [ ] ruler

DESIGNING

Consider the composition's layout. Even though the subject is located on the far left side, this design has a nice sense of balance. In every quadrant, the location of colors, values, and subjects creates interest and movement. Notice how the orange color of the ant and the orange on the moss create a vertical balance, how the location of the isolated mushroom invites the eye to move over to the far right side, how the shadow in the upper-right corner relates to the mushroom's dark underside, and how the shadows on the ground add weight to the bottom of the airy layout. If you place your hand over one element, you'll see how dramatically the unity, emphasis, balance, movement, or rhythm changes.

You might choose to replicate the original orientation of this piece or you might take this opportunity to crop the image to create a new layout. The goal is to position subjects and incorporate enough negative space to both please the eye and address the elements of design.

If you would like to explore options, follow the instructions for making cropping tools located in the Nature Break at the end of the previous chapter. When you practice locating successful compositions within other compositions, you create unique designs while also refining your ability to compose space when your reference does not have a predetermined edge. Once you select a design layout, use artist tape to temporarily secure the cropping tools in place. Then quickly copy the design and framing edge on tracing paper. You might choose to keep the cropping tools in place so it's easier to visualize the composition while you are working.

DRAWING

1 Because of the multiple subjects and overall asymmetry of this composition, it's not convenient to measure along a single midline. Instead, you can use the grid method to help you locate the subjects on the page. The grid method enables you to draw one section of the composition at a time, create accurate proportions, and leave only minor tweaking for the refinement stage. To avoid distortion, the rectangles created by the grid on both the reference and your illustration must have the same height-to-width ratio.

Lay a piece of tracing paper over the reference image, secure the top in place, and mark the corners of your composition with a pencil. If you feel confident that the proportions of the page are the same ratio as the reference image, divide the composition in half both horizontally and vertically so that the layout is divided into quadrants. Then divide each quadrant into eight parts. Move to your page and draw the same grid using a ruler. Make sure that the lines are drawn lightly and will be easy to erase. To avoid confusion, you might make the secondary grid lines even lighter than the center lines.

Alternatively, you can create the grid on the reference image using 1-inch squares. Then draw a grid on your page using squares that are slightly larger or smaller depending on the desired size of your artwork. If you add headings to the margins of both grids, such as numbering each row and lettering each column, you'll be able to easily locate corresponding grid squares while you work.

2 **A** With the proportional grid on the reference image and your drawing, use the shape of the negative and positive spaces to create a gesture on your page. While you are drawing, keep your body relaxed and let your entire arm create the marks instead of working only from your wrist.

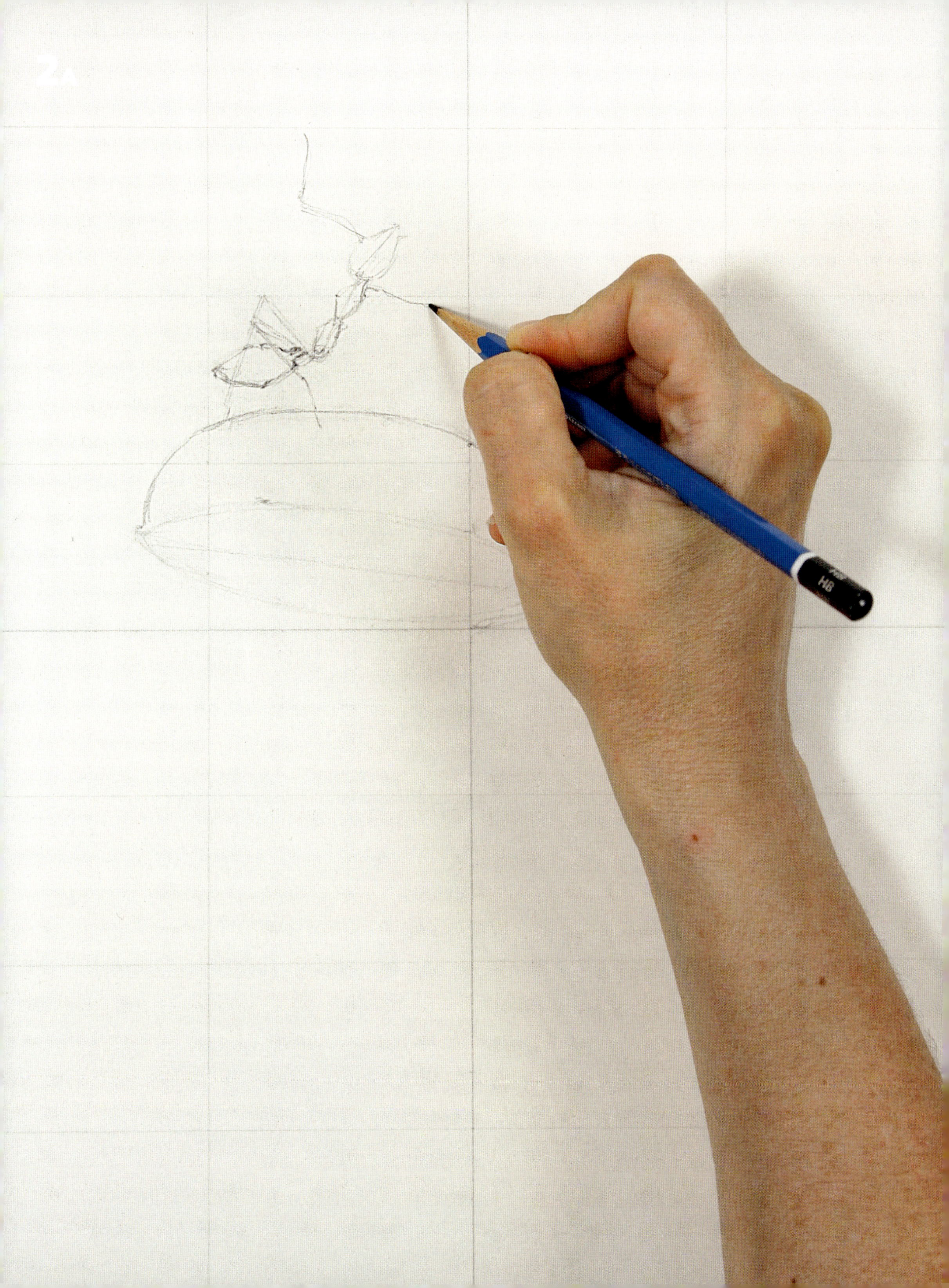
2A

Your goal is to quickly and easily create fluid lines. Adding a gesture drawing to a grid can help you to maintain an overview of the design and create a more unified drawing.

B Since the ant and the mushroom cap have the highest importance in the composition, draw them first. For the stem, you may find it helpful to create a temporary center line, like a gesture, to indicate the overall shape and location before you draw the contour.

After you draw the smaller mushroom, compare the width of the cap and stem to the larger mushroom to visually confirm the accuracy of the proportions.

C Once these subjects are in place, you might consider changing the contour of the landscape. I chose to raise the left side of the moss patch so that there was more of the surface filling the composition near the corner.

I also added a few of the darker ends of the moss spores to the drawing simply to provide a locator for the colored pencil stage. If you like, you can add lines to indicate where the shadows of the landscape will be placed. I preferred to wait and guesstimate these at the painting stage.

3 With the details refined and your drawing complete, erase the grid lines completely. Blend any bright erasure lines into the page.

Because the highlighted areas are located along the edge of the mushroom and ant, you will need to lighten the outline to the point where it is just visible. Then slightly darken any lines that are found within the mushroom caps or body of the ant so that they remain visible after the masking fluid has been removed. Keep the line that defines the landscape just light enough that you can see it through the background color. This way, you'll be able to easily interrupt the line anywhere you would like to place a vertical moss spore. Considering the process as a whole and making these intentional changes will not only assist you in

upcoming steps but also positively influence the finished artwork.

In this composition, the addition of color and value will dramatically change the balance and hierarchy of the overall design. Before you move on, take a moment to compare your drawing to the colorful reference image and notice the shift in the visual weight as well as the level of interest throughout the page.

PAINTING

1 The ant and the mushrooms have a different hue and value than the background, and they contain translucent sections, so it will be helpful to use masking fluid and paint these areas separately. Before you begin, double-check that the artist tape is securely attached around the perimeter of the page. Since you are masking a large area, work in a well-ventilated space.

If the masking fluid dries on the page while you are working, simply work in sections overlapping the previous area slightly. If air bubbles form, either fill or recoat them. When you reach the base of the stem, approximate the place where it meets the moss and create an uneven line.

2 While the masking fluid dries, mix three background colors on your palette: a mid-value gray for the top half of the composition, a slightly lighter green for the lower half, and a small amount of dark green to darken sections of the moss. Since the gray is so light, start your mixture using the titanium white and add a small amount of Mars black paint. If you left the composition uncropped, you might want to mix two different values of gray. Because I wanted to make the gray slightly cooler, I added a tiny amount of cobalt blue to the paint mixture. To make the light green

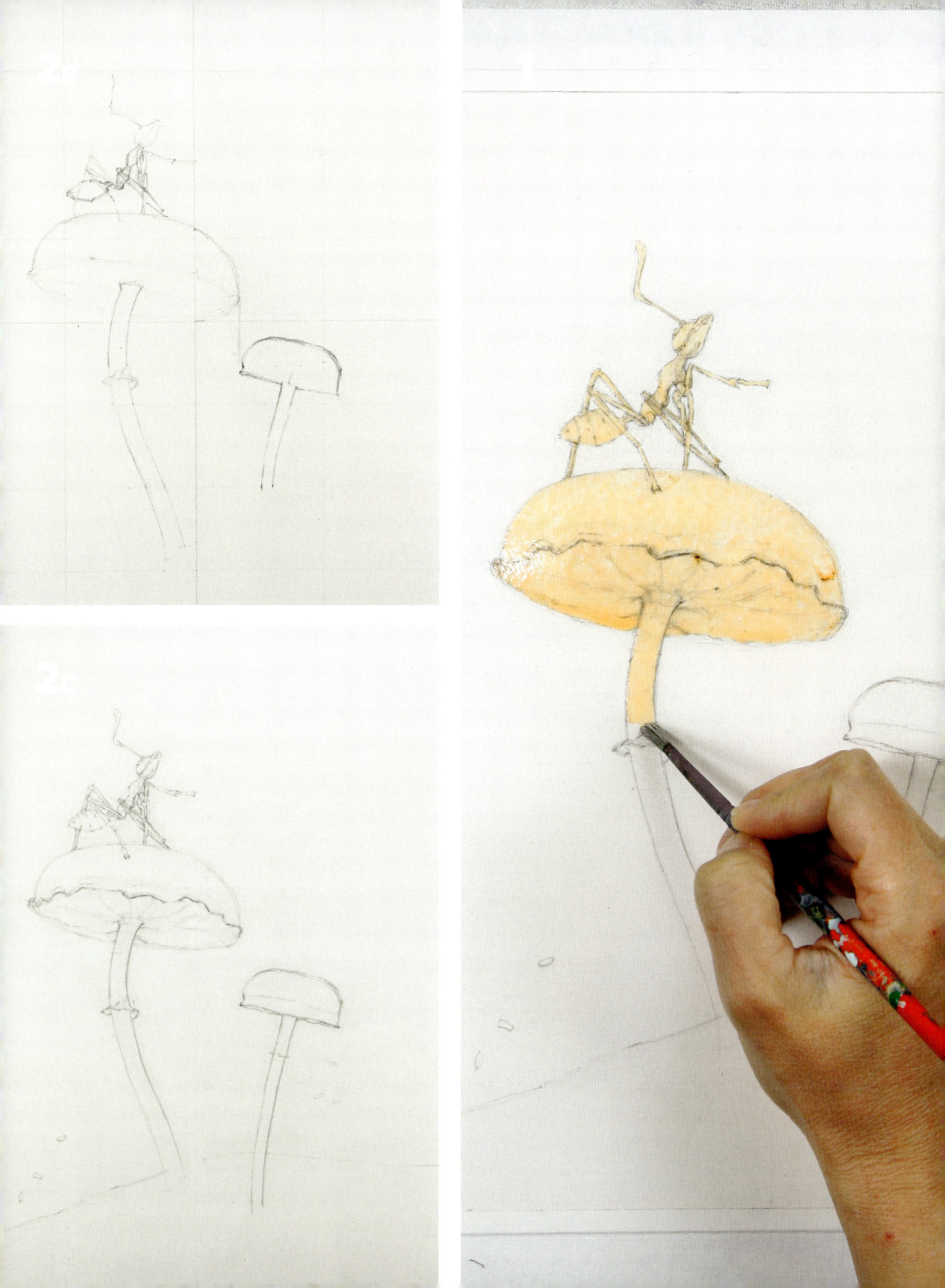

paint mixture, start with phthalo yellow green and add a small amount of cobalt blue and a miniscule amount of sienna brown paint to soften the phthalo's intensity. Separate a small section of the green paint mixture on your palette and add some Mars black paint until it matches the darkest areas of the mossy hill.

Before putting paint to page, coat a piece of scrap paper with the green paint mixture. Later, you can use this to test and select colored pencils to use as moss spores.

3 **A** If you have any concern about painting the color transition in the background, practice on a test sheet taped to a surface. Or jump right in! After adding a water wash to the page, start at the top and apply the gray paint mixture using long, horizontal brushstrokes. Keep the pigment solid near the top of the page, but when you get toward the center, do not recoat the brush—instead let the color fade out. Using a clean brush with a similar amount of water as the page, apply the green paint mixture about a third of the way up from the bottom and work up toward the gray. Let the colors overlap so that they blend into one another. You might repeat the gray from the top down to further integrate the colors. Then completely fill the lower section with the green paint mixture. I chose to disregard the small amount of gray in the lower-left corner of the reference.

Although you'll want to create a smooth transition between colors so that the background doesn't compete with the subject, ignore the pressure to get it "just right." On the other hand, if the colors or paper begin to look overworked or the transition is significantly different than what you want, it may be worth starting over with a new sheet and transferring the drawing. In my experience, sometimes it takes less energy to start over rather than continue with an illustration that is not working well; other times, it's best to accept and move forward. Anytime you arrive at a creative crossroads, simply consider the available options and determine which direction would be more beneficial.

B Before the background dries, use a small paintbrush to add shadows to the landscape, using your drawing or the reference image to guide your decisions. Add just a small amount of pigment to indicate the location of the shadows, then immediately return to each area to darken them further. By dabbing with the paintbrush, you can create the uneven and textural mossy surface.

At this point, you've successfully created a double gradation that suggests the sky and a vibrant landscape.

4 Once the background is completely dry, carefully remove the masking fluid with an eraser or—in areas with pencil details—by using a finger.

5 Decide on the base color to mix for the mushrooms. I first made a sample swatch with all my similarly colored pencils: rosy beige, seashell pink, chocolate, dark umber, sepia, and all the French grays. It seemed that all of these colors were present in one or both of the caps, on the undersides, and on the stems. Since none of these colors needed replicating in paint, I simply planned on creating a mid-tone for each area.

Mix a color similar to 50% French gray for the caps and large stem. If you'd like, create a very slightly purpled gray by adding a little cadmium red and cobalt blue paint. Once you have established the color of this paint mixture, separate a portion of it and add burnt umber until it matches the color of the ribs under the large cap. Then mix a paint color slightly lighter than the chocolate pencil to be used to paint the remaining area under the caps. If you need to lighten either brown, I'd recommend using Naples yellow, since the coloration has more warmth than the titanium white paint.

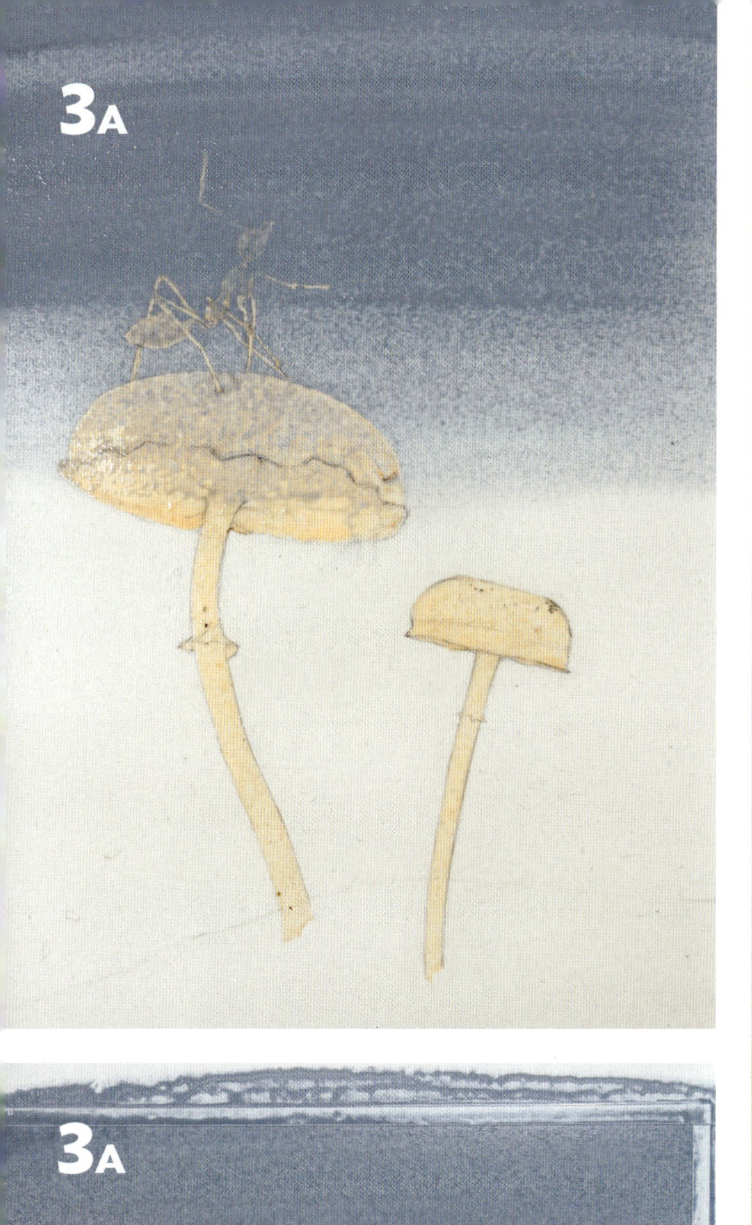

3A

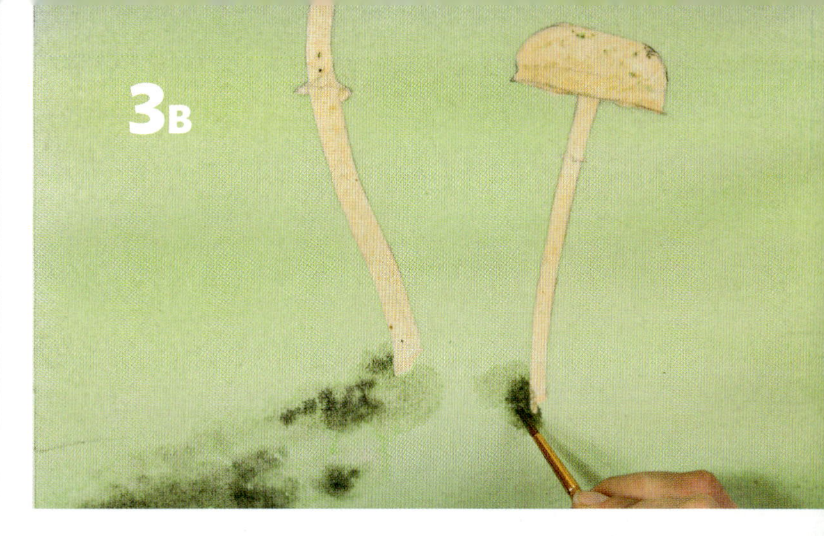

3B

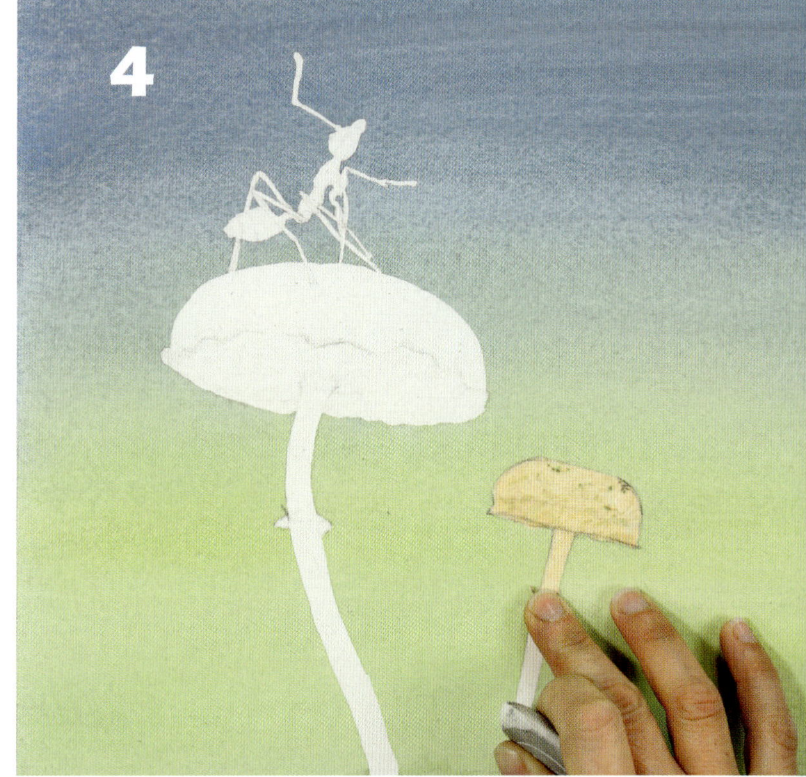

4

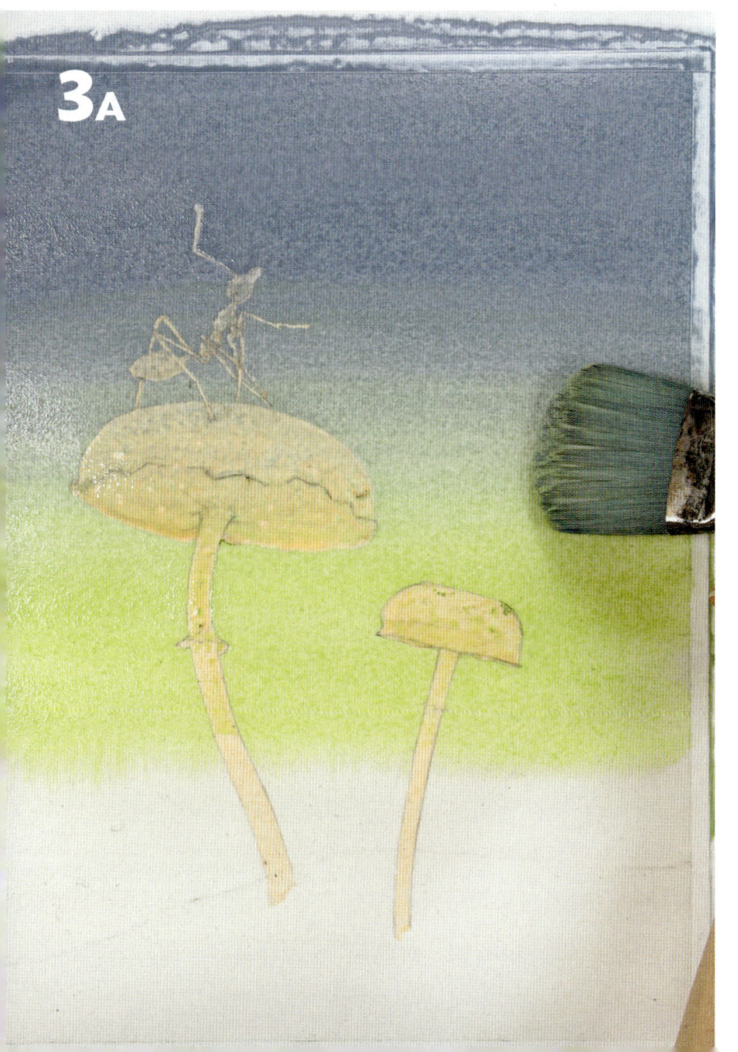

3A

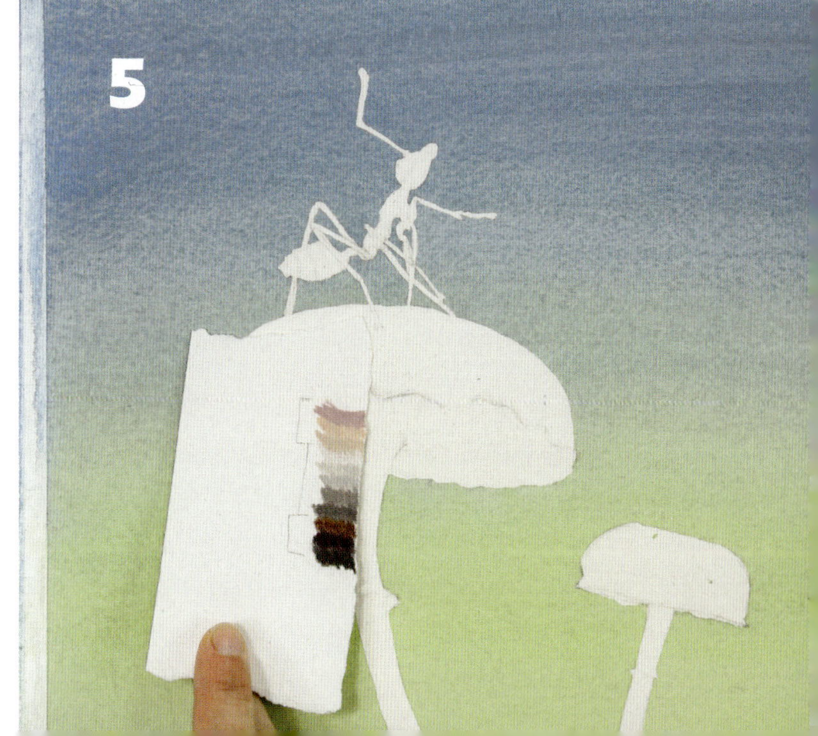

5

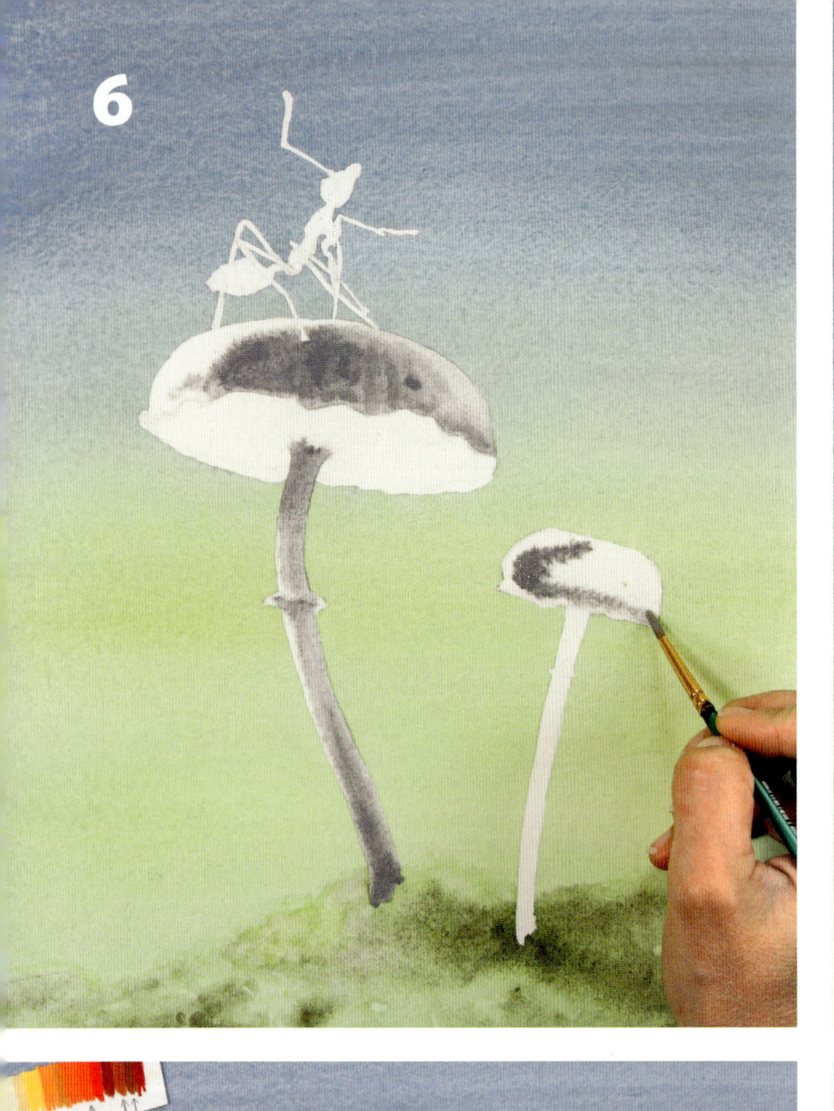

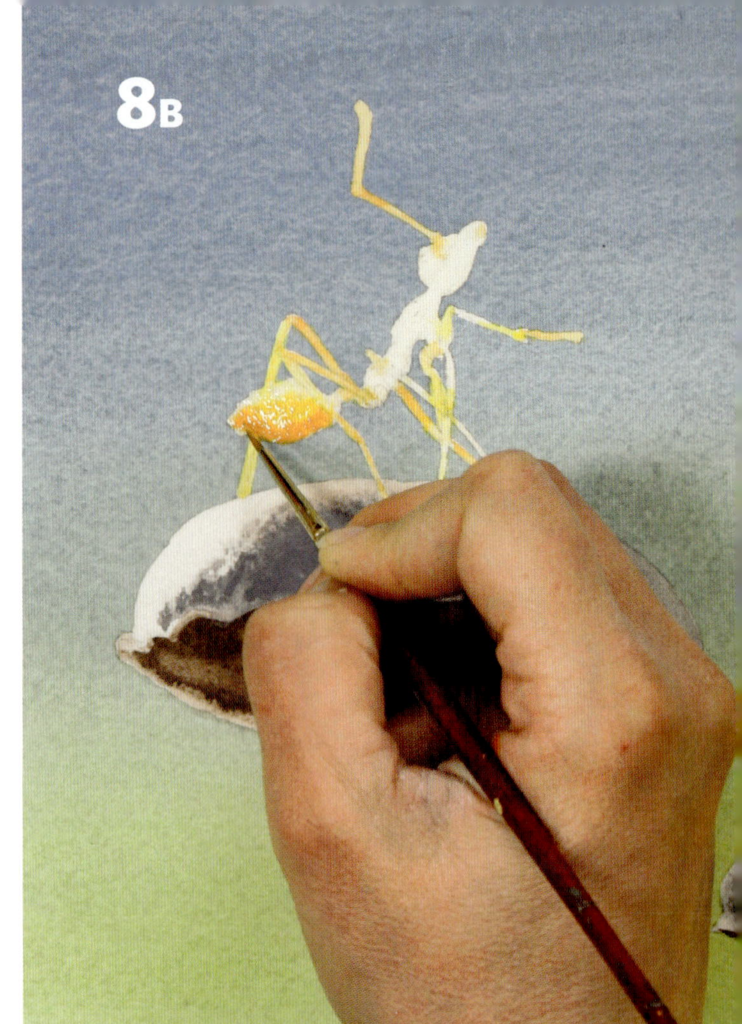

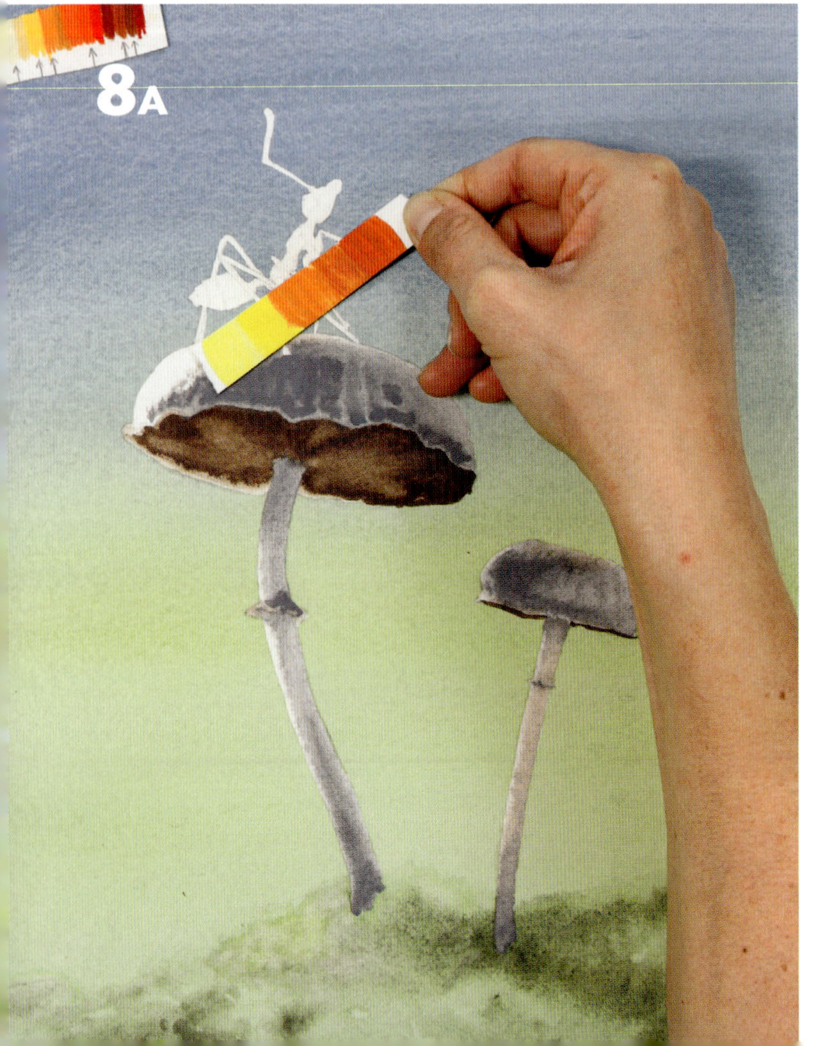

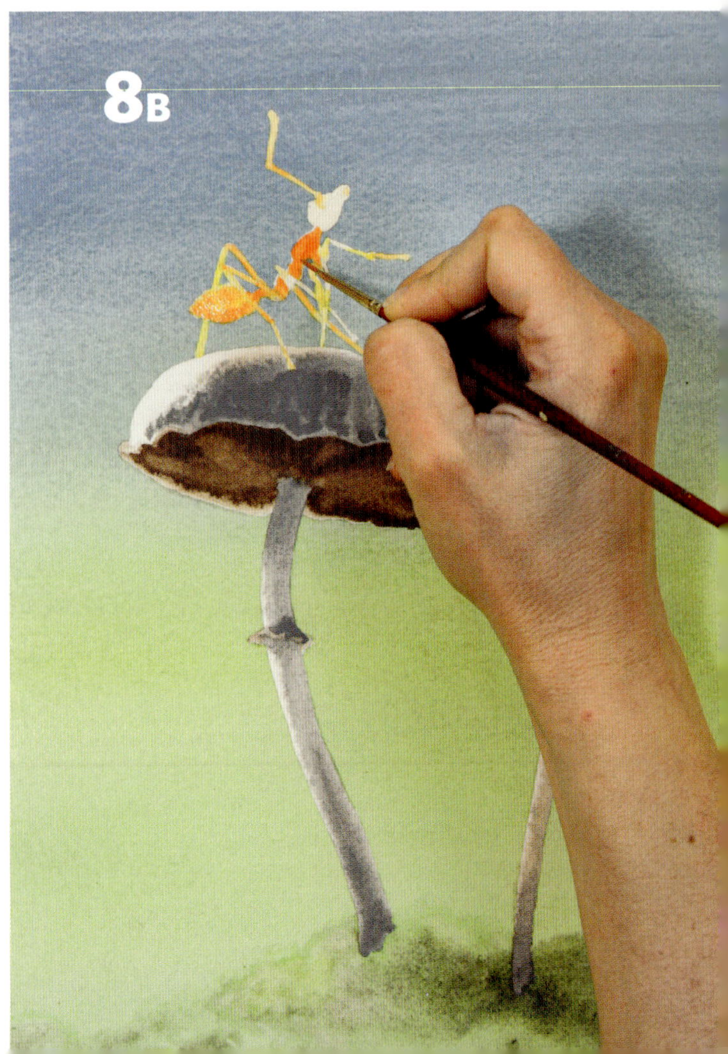

6 Now review the reference image to study how the forms are affected by the light sources. For example, the primary light source casts a shadow over the entire right side of the large mushroom cap; however, a secondary light source creates a subtle highlight along the edge. Observe the shadow on the stem created by the cap and the shadow under the ring along the stem and how both are equally important in describing the location of the primary light source. Also, notice how the highlight along the side of both stems is interrupted by these shadows, further describing the location of the primary light source.

Paint the mushrooms in sections so that you have time to add these value and color changes. To begin, make sure that your rinse water is clean so that the brightest highlight can remain white and add a water wash to the large mushroom cap. Then add pigment, but avoid the highlighted area on the far left so that the white of the paper itself creates the illumination. Next, either move to the large stem or work on painting the second mushroom cap. For now, leave the underside of the large mushroom cap unpainted.

For the small stem, a significantly diluted brown paint mixture will suggest an illuminated quality. Blot the paintbrush on a paper towel first so that you don't add an excess of water to the page. Before this dries, use the gray paint mixture to darken the base, the ring, and the shadow at the top.

In general, avoid overlapping the background as you paint because the translucent quality of the paint will allow the background to be seen through the mushroom and make the composition appear flat. If paint makes its way into the background, immediately blot the overlap with the edge of a folded paper towel, then plan on cleaning up any remaining color with colored pencil later.

7 Once the gray paint has dried, prepare the underside of the large mushroom cap for paint. The lower edge is both extremely light and right next to a very dark section, so you will need to adjust your technique to prevent pigment from pooling at the very bottom. When you add a wash to the area, simply leave the light sections dry, as if you were creating a hard edge. Then add the brown pigment and—before the paint dries but will no longer pool—come back in to blur the edge of the paint to create a very light brown. After the paint has dried completely, you might paint a second layer that alludes to the mushroom gills' structure.

If you cropped the composition and no longer have the dark section in the upper right to balance this deep value, you might make the underside of both mushrooms a bit lighter than the reference image. I did not realize this while I was painting my illustration, and I had to lighten this area significantly in the colored pencil stage so that it didn't attract too much attention.

Finally, in the center where the stem meets the underside, allow the brown to blur slightly into the gray to create continuity at this transition point.

Managing paint flow to make intentional value shifts gives you more control as you paint. You may not use this technique very often, but when it is needed it can be extremely helpful.

8 **A** Move to the ant and again consider which paint colors to use based on your colored pencil collection. I decided to create two base paint colors and make a spectrum of variation between them. I started with cadmium yellow and an orange mixture, with a small amount of sienna brown added to darken it slightly.

B Since the extremities are so small, you can paint multiple areas simultaneously. Use the lighter-diluted paint colors first and end with the darkest.

When the legs and antennae are complete, work on one part of the body at a time, layering colors similarly. You might find that your drying paper is an advantage because it allows you to start adding more finite details and create a more accurate base upon which to build. Leave the highlight pure white, although much of it can be created later in the process using a white pencil. Continue to tweak or to combine the colors on your palette as needed.

Although you might feel inspired to create the orange of the moss spores before completing the painting stage, I suggest that you wait to add them solely in colored pencil. The inherent value of paint would darken them too much, and they need to be light and intense to stand out against the background as they do in the reference image.

LAYERING WITH COLORED PENCIL

1 If there are any areas where the paint overlapped the background, clean them up first. Use the white pencil with a sharp tip to lightly cover only the overlapped section to blend it invisibly back into the background. If it is next to a highlighted section, use heavier pressure and incorporate it into the highlight instead. While I was adjusting the painting, I chose to remove a few small spots in the background using the utility knife technique described on page 30.

2 Begin working anywhere on the mushrooms. I started by using the white pencil on the caps. Then I switched to using the French gray pencils to lighten and blend the vertical stripes and to add the dark horizontal stripe near the edge on the caps. Keep in mind that the whole shadowed section should look integrated when you unfocus your eyes, so you might need to slightly adjust the value of the stripes. On the mushroom caps and stems, notice that the gray appears darkest not only along the shadowed edge but also next to the highlight. It is best to leave the base of both stems untouched and work on them after the moss spores are in place.

If you notice a subtle change in hue, refer to your color swatch to help you select the appropriate pencil to enrich these areas. If you'd like to add the light blue sheen on the right side of the mushroom caps where the secondary highlight is located, do this by applying the electric blue pencil extremely lightly, then layering it with white pencil. In my composition, I chose to leave the mushroom caps as they were, because I did not feel that adding the blue would enhance the realism and that it might instead blend into the background.

3 To begin your work on the landscape, practice making moss spores on a separate swatch of paper. If you made a green test sheet earlier, this is the time to use it. If you apply white colored pencil prior to using the oranges and yellows, it will brighten the colors slightly.

Create all of the long slender stalks and spores that are along the edge of the moss. Do not feel obligated to add every spore shown in the reference image. Similar to drawing fuzz on insects, the overall appearance of this composition is more important than creating an exact replica. I typically draw the spores that most stand out to me and then fill in between. Periodically, I look at the entire section and see if there are any areas that could use more spores or areas that seems too dense and could benefit from having some erased. It may help to add a few dominant spores lower down on the hill, but it's best to add most of them after the moss highlights and shadows are complete.

As you add the moss spores along the ridge, notice how the balance and interest of the composition changes. Look at the beginning when you have only added a select few, then again when the edge of the moss is completely filled in, and compare both of these stages to seeing them in full color later in the process. Simply by pausing to observe, you can witness the building of this powerful compositional element.

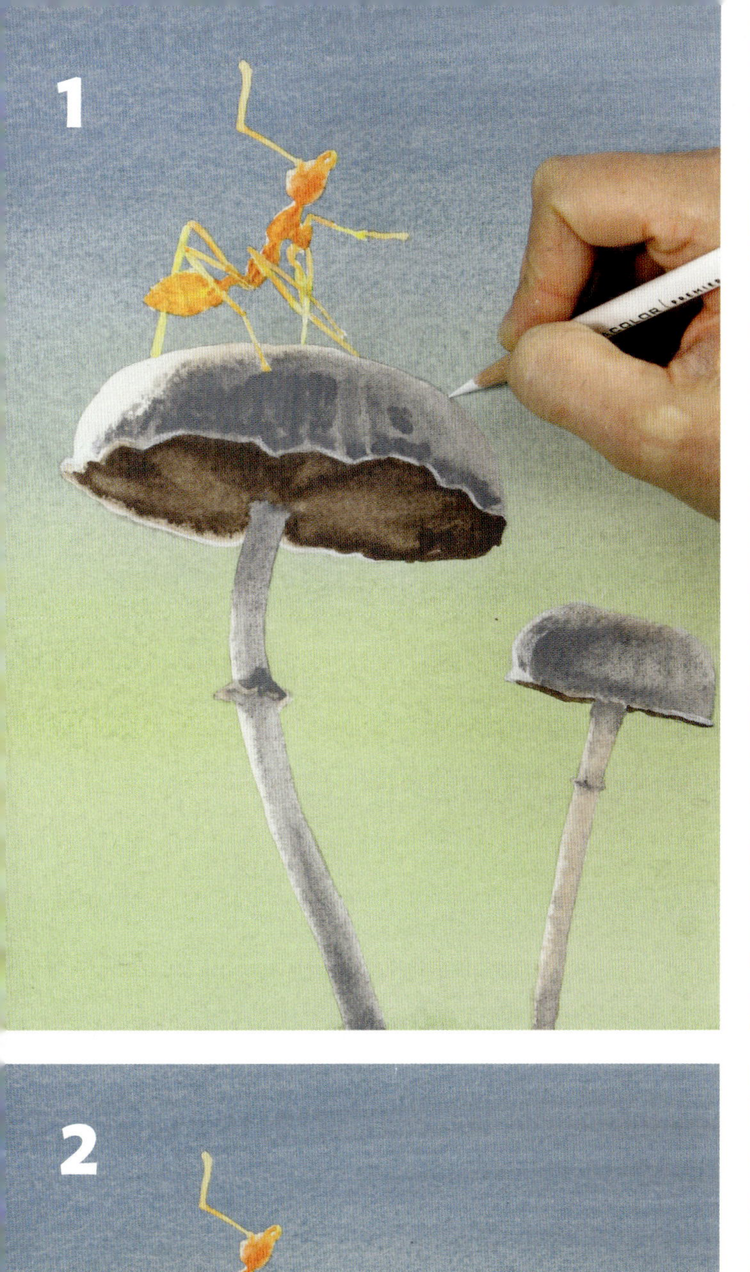

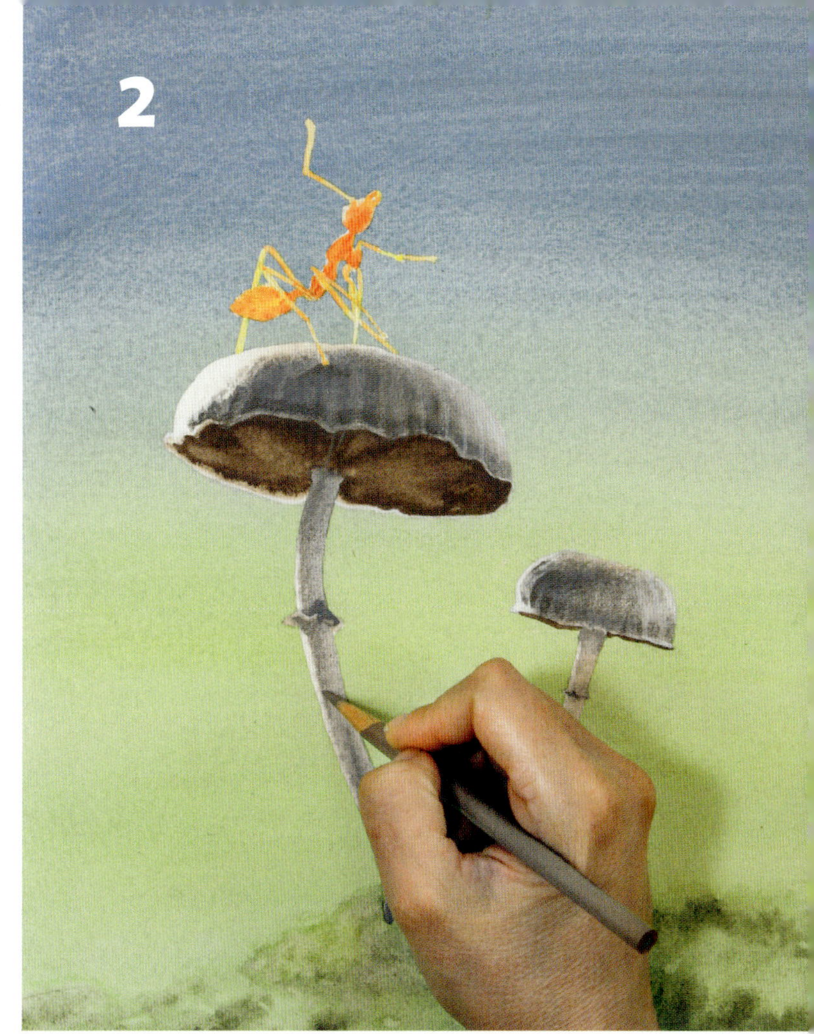

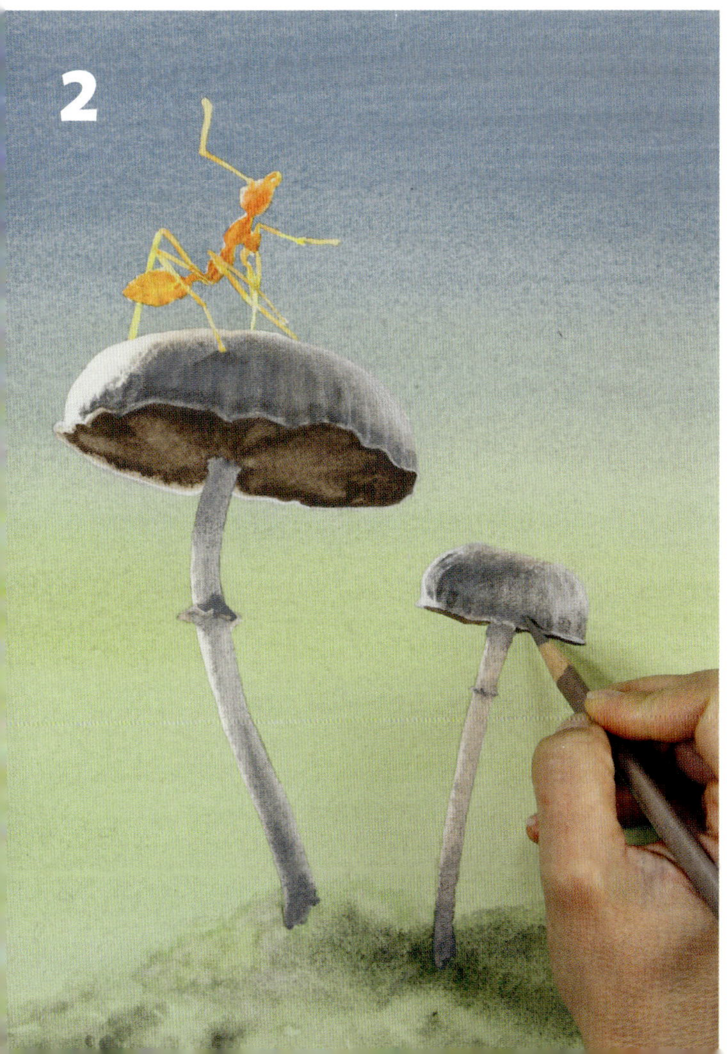

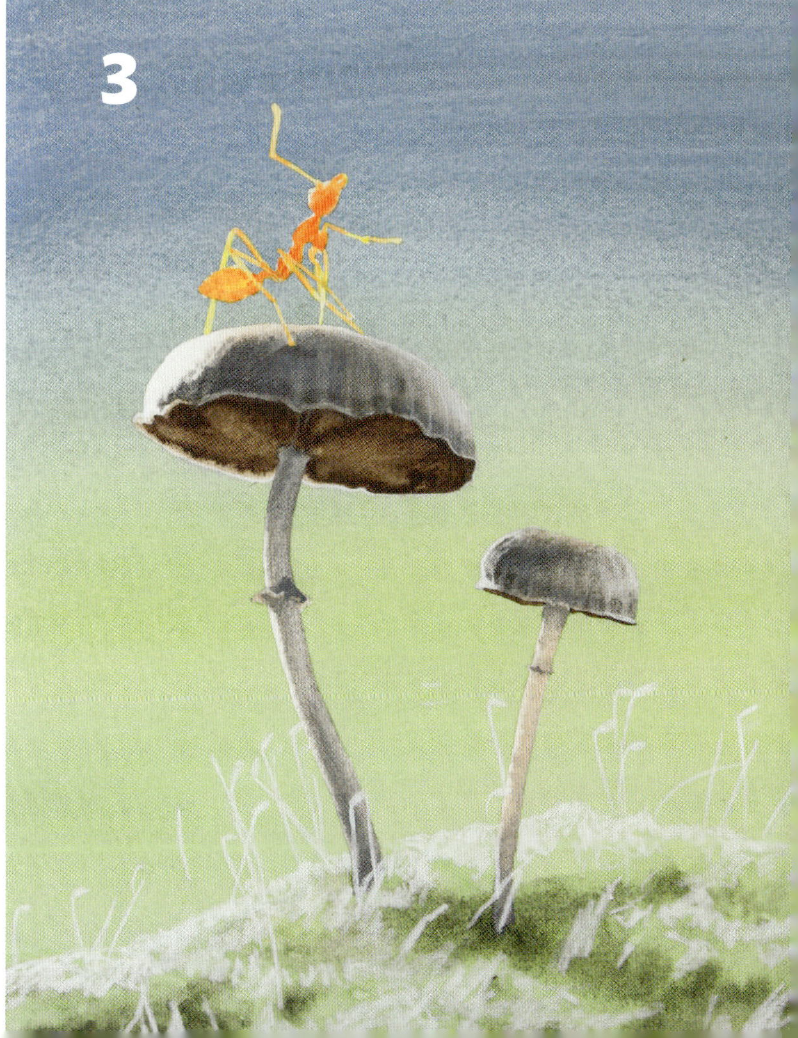

4 Shift your focus to the highlights on the hill. To emulate the texture of moss, use a fairly blunt tip and scrub your white pencil in an uneven and slightly disorganized fashion. Be sure that the edge of the mossy area is primarily solid white and that the highlights seem to relate on either side of each stem.

Next, use the side of the lime peel pencil to blend the highlight into the painted color of the moss. As you darken the mossy hill, feel free to return to using the white pencil if you need to replace or enhance the highlight in an area. Carefully avoid any white stalks you added earlier.

Then hold the lime peel pencil in the standard position and return to using the random scrubbing technique to add depth to the shadow areas. Then use the appropriately named moss green pencil to further darken these areas by using the same technique. Work on the shadows that describe the shape of the moss in addition to the diagonal shadow cast by the mushroom stems. If the dark green begins to overpower the highlighted areas, lightly use an eraser to tone it down, particularly in areas that transition from shadow to highlight.

Once the artwork begins to take on the appearance of a landscape, you can add enhancements without following the reference image. Maybe you use the eraser to pull some excess color out of the drawing. Maybe you go back and forth between colors to add texture and to shape the moss with highlight and shadow. Since the green moss is the least powerful element in the composition, this is a fun opportunity to question how realistic the landscape looks and test ways to enhance it relying solely on your wealth of knowledge. If you add too much contrast or details, you might change the hierarchy of the entire composition. If this happens, consider what could de-emphasize the area enough to direct attention back to the elements that are designed to be more prominent.

5 Return to using the white pencil and add the other spores that overlap the moss. Since some of the spores are further back and blurred, you can use a clean eraser to fade these areas slightly into the background. When you do this, you should perceive more depth in the foreground. You can also use the eraser to slightly blur the areas at the very bottom of the composition where the stalks will look more like orange patches. These techniques expand the use of an eraser beyond merely correcting mistakes, making it into a tool for drawing and creating.

6 To add color to the spores, use the yellowed orange pencil in the back and the orange pencil in the front. Then further accentuate the color near the tops using the canary yellow and sunburst yellow pencils. In the shadow sections of the moss, you might apply the pale vermillion pencil along the stems. Your goal is to keep the value similar to the background color and, with a steady hand, eliminate the white without overlapping the background, which would create dark areas. A small grazing of color will go a long way, especially toward the back of the landscape. I maintained a very sharp tip on my pencil and used just enough pressure to be in control of the line, moving from one side of the landscape to the other and back again. Be aware that the stems that are partially hidden behind the mossy mound will appear to end more bluntly than those that disappear into the moss. For more depth and integration of the stalks, use the moss green pencil to create mossy strands over the base of a few stalks in the shadow sections. Leave the dark tops blank for now.

Look at your work from arm's length to notice how powerful the spores have become in the overall composition now that they have color. Check to be sure that they do not have more importance than the ant.

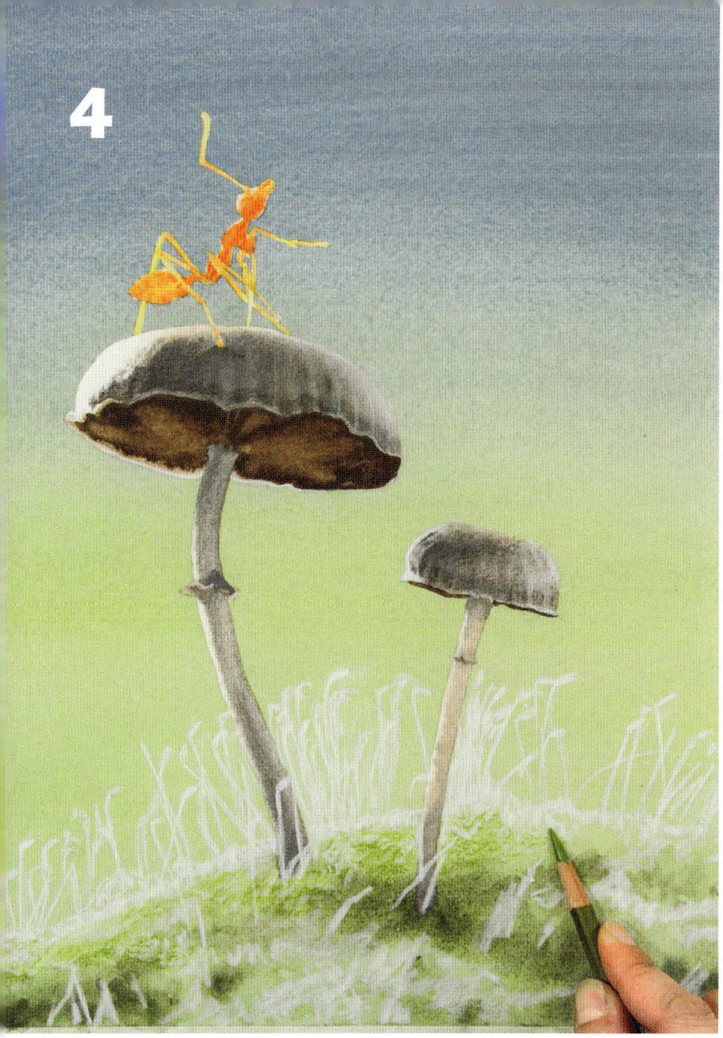

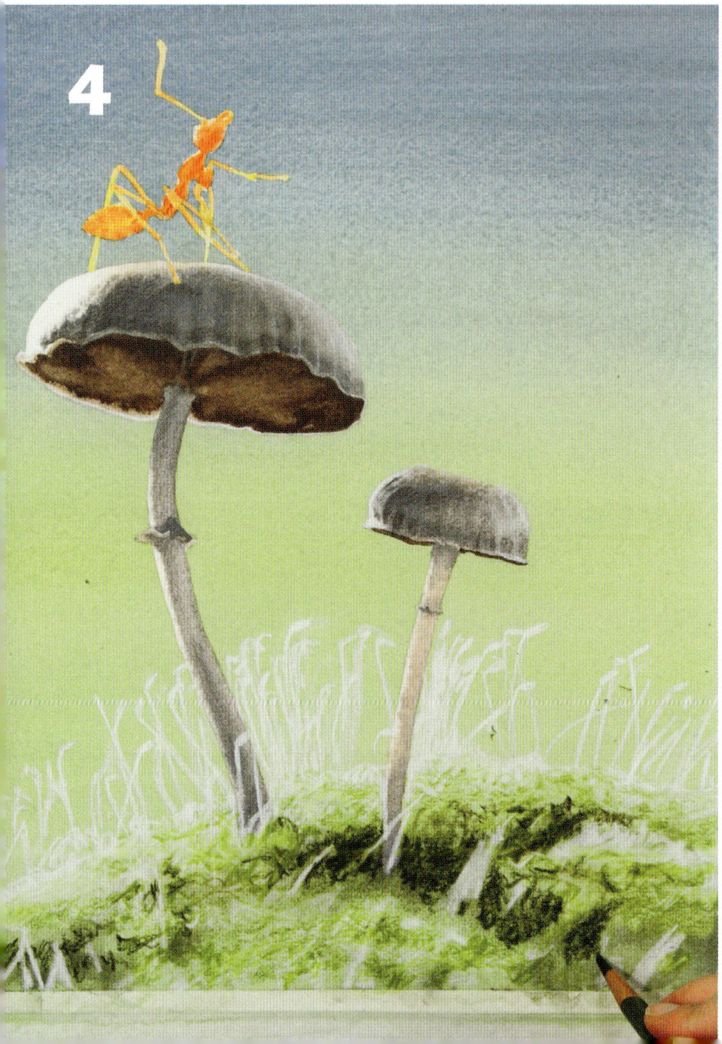

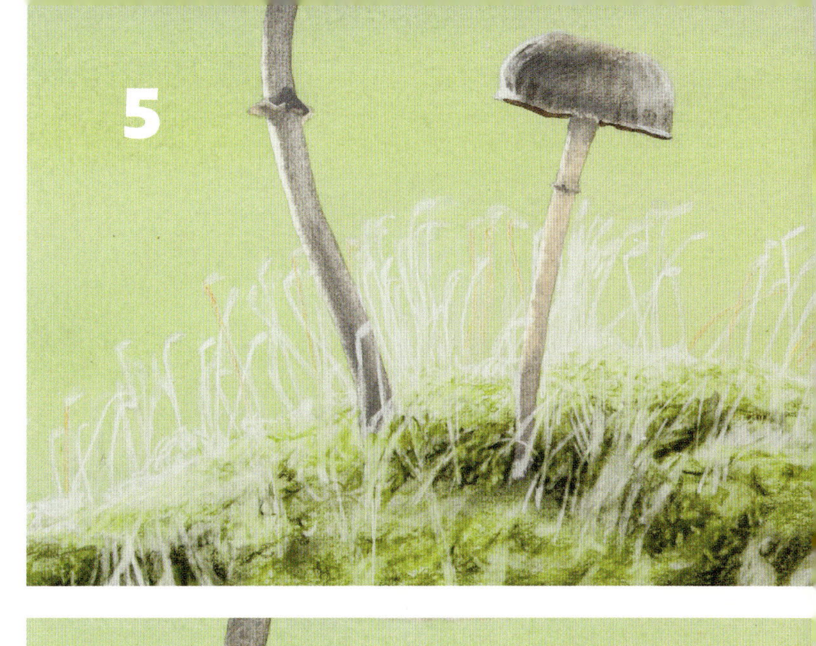

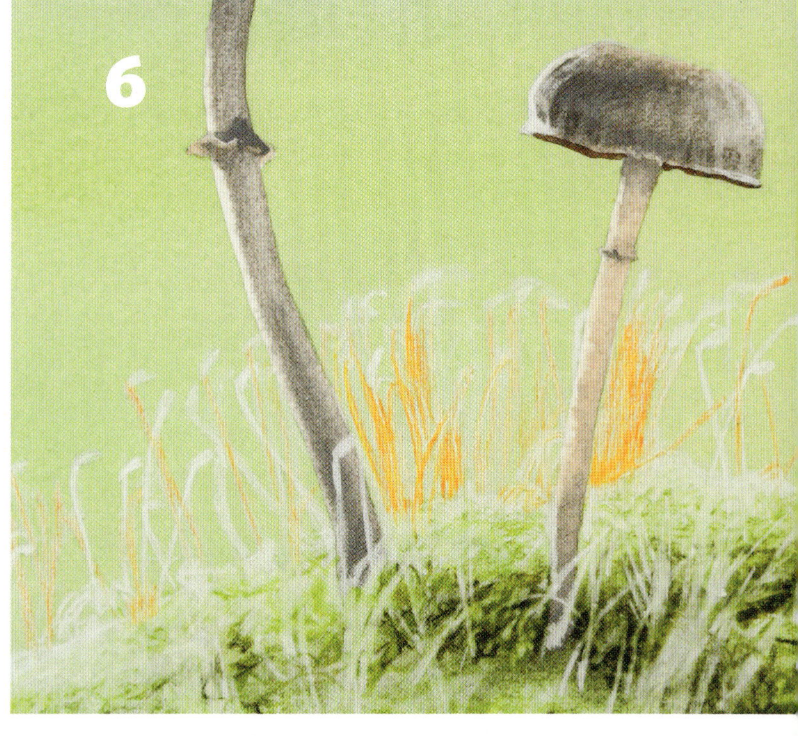

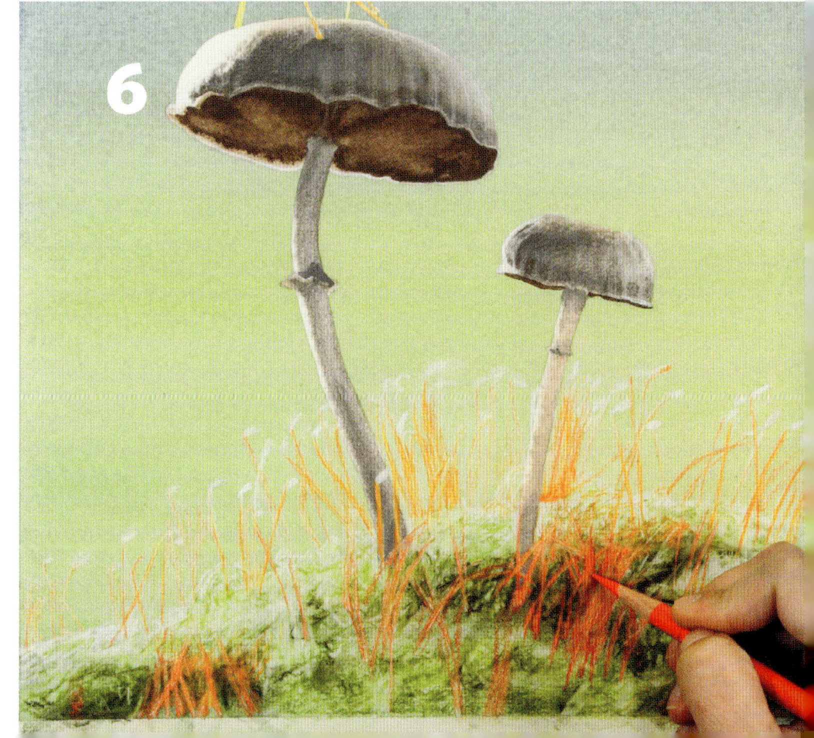

7 Move to the underside of the large mushroom cap. Use the seashell pink pencil to create the light gills and use either the light umber or sepia pencil for the dark gills. Look at the composition as a whole to decide how dark to make this area. If it is too light, the landscape will appear more interesting; if it is too dark, you'll have a distracting oval in the center of your page. I felt that a value similar to the moss shadows would give the mushroom gills an appropriate level of power while still being distinguishable. However, just before I completed the composition, I chose to lighten them further.

Next, darken toward the front edge of the gills to create further separation between the cap and the underside of the mushroom. When this is complete, work on the very top of the stem to blend, integrate, and create a smooth transition.

Be sure to make the portion of the stems near the caps slightly darker to reiterate the light-blocking forms above. Then enhance the shadow along the side of the stems and darken both bases around the spores. I used both middle- and dark-value French gray pencils and also applied the seashell pink pencil on the smaller stem. Finally, use the black pencil sparingly to add the dark areas above the ring on the stem, line the edge of the underside of the cap, and slightly darken the base.

8 At last it's time to work on the focal point. If any of the highlights were covered with paint, start by using the white pencil on the body, but leave the highlights on the head for later so they do not turn the eye gray when you apply the dark color. Then use the sienna and burnt ocher pencils to add details and refine the anatomy of the body. Move to working on the head, add the brown details, then draw the eye with an HB pencil. Be careful not to make the eye too large; measure to confirm that the proportion is in correct relationship to the head. Add the black areas to the eye. Now create all the highlights on the head of the ant except the highlight on the eyeball, which will be created in paint at the end of the colored pencil stage.

If the legs and antenna still need darkening, use the yellowed orange pencil. Add the dark umber pencil below the mandibles to create the line at the base of the head. In my composition, I also darkened the shadow side of each leg using the sienna brown pencil to better integrate them into the body. If you need to use your eraser, clean it after every use by rubbing the color onto a scrap piece of paper, so that you do not spread the orange pencil onto the background of your illustration.

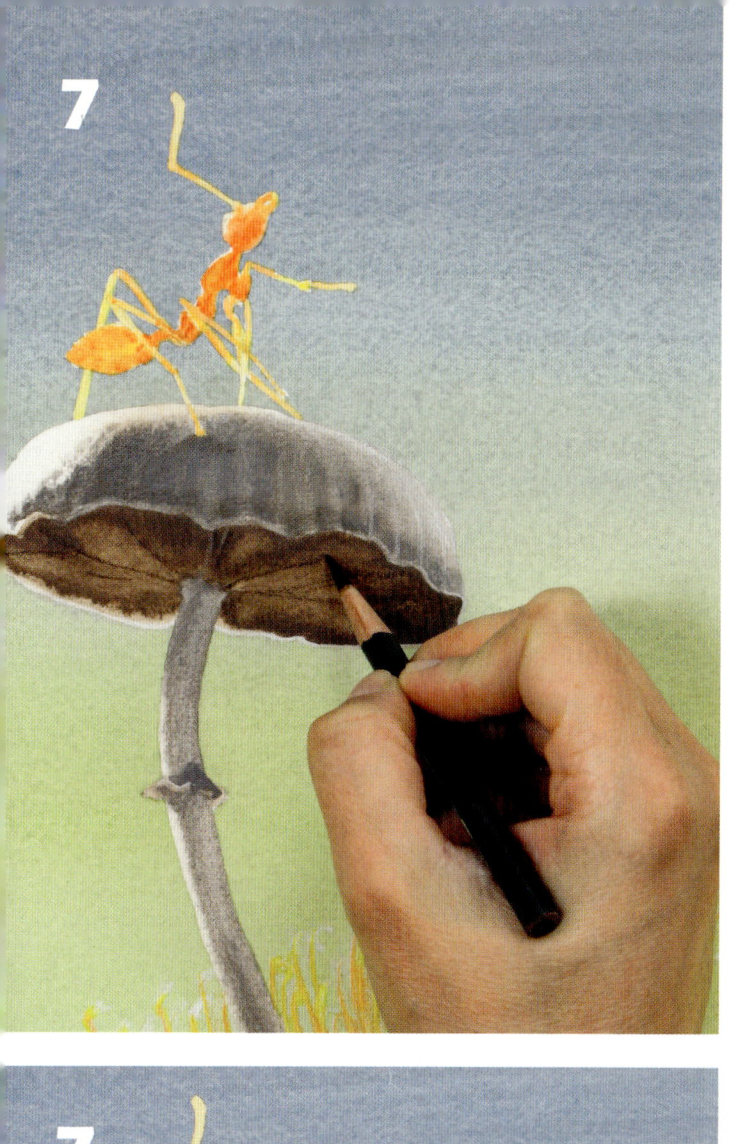

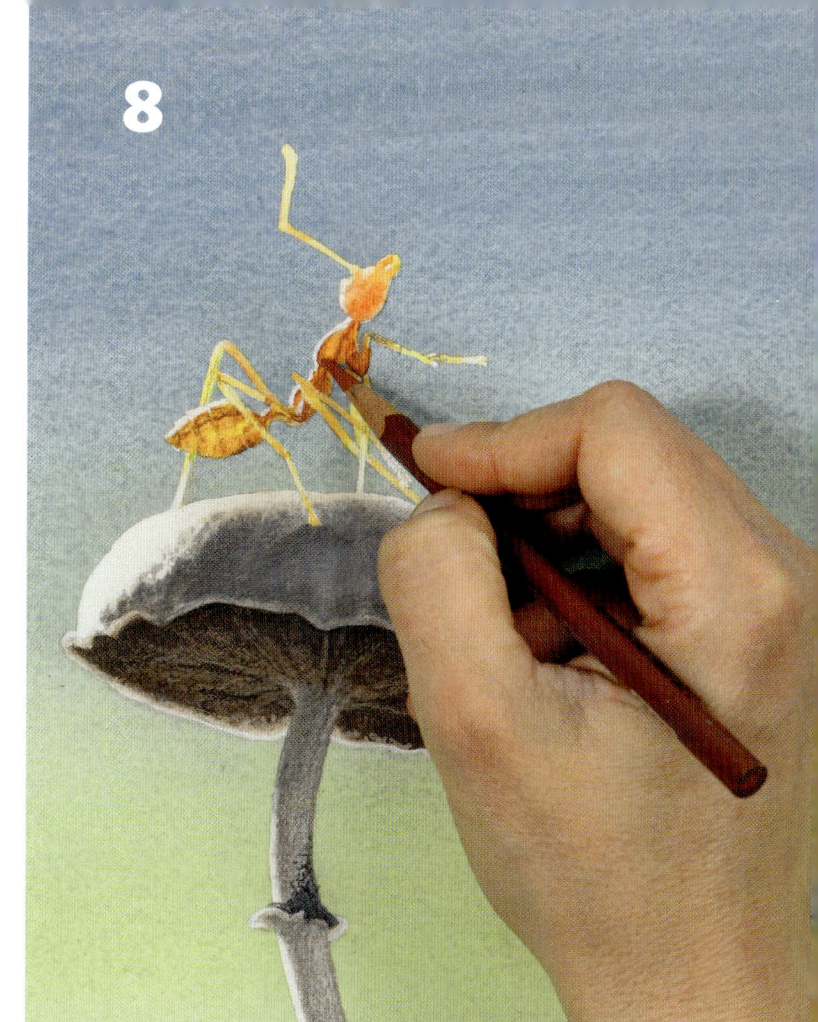

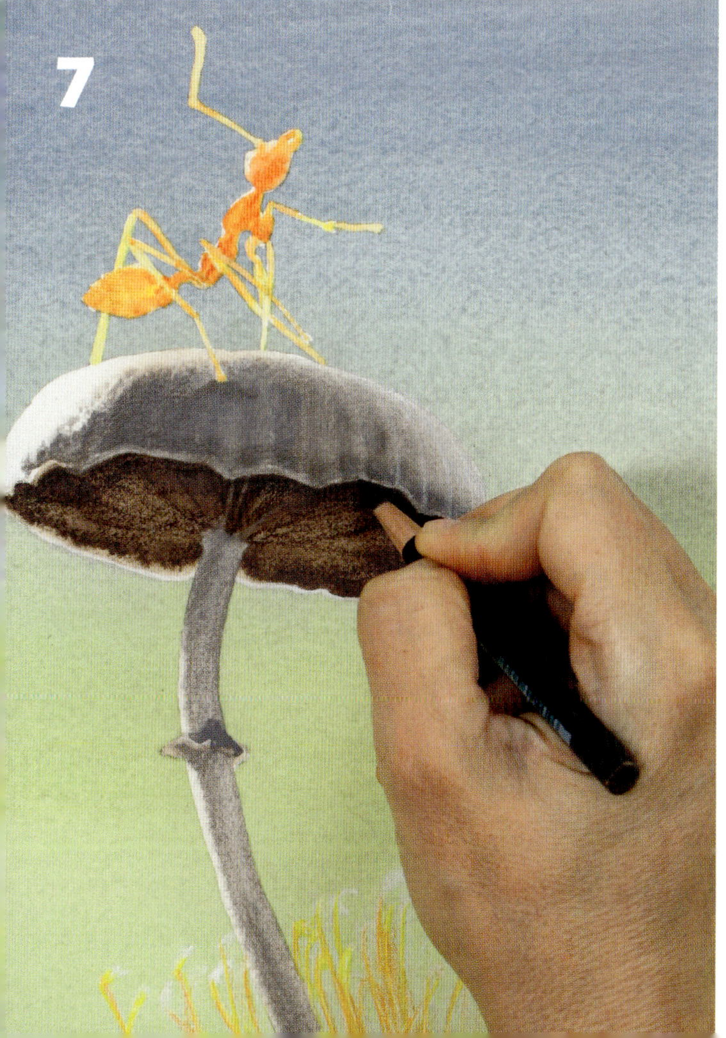

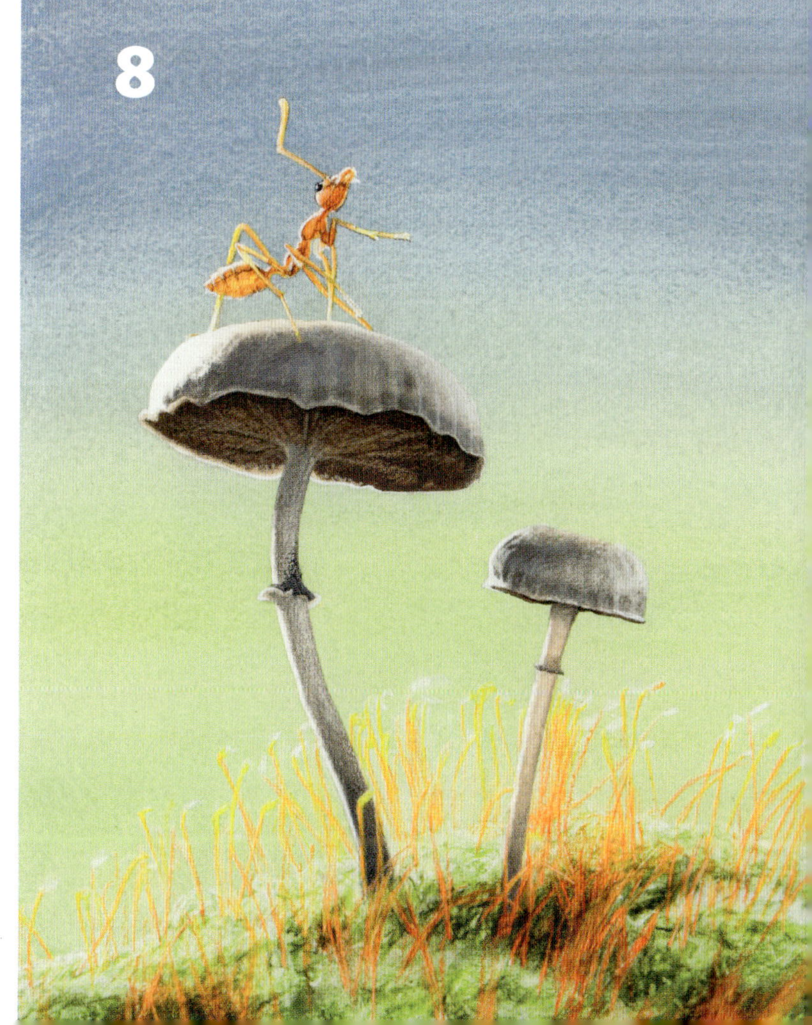

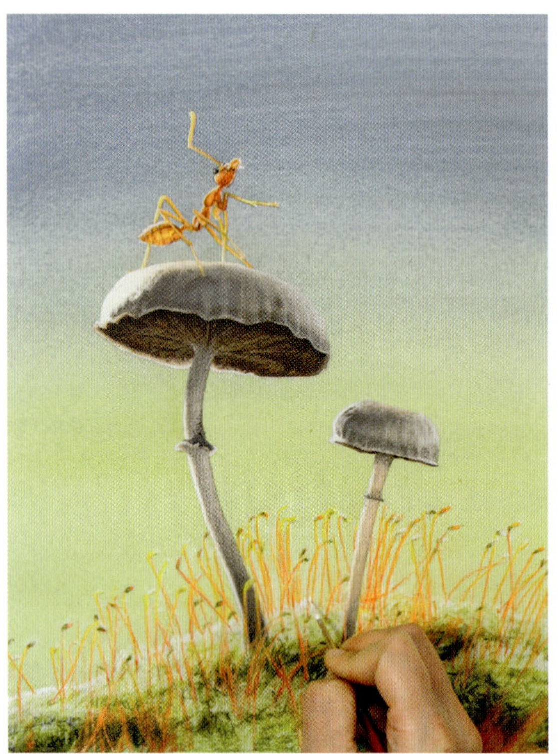

9 Once you have completed the ant, return to the spores to add the dark tops using the green ocher pencil and refine any colors that could use adjustment. I chose to darken some of the stalks so that they would stand out more against the background.

Looking at my composition from afar, I felt that the underside of the large mushroom was too powerful, so I both lightened it and also added a bit of black pencil to the moss shadows to create balance. I also wanted to make the highlight on the moss appear brighter. Since I had used the white pencil at full strength, I decided to fill titanium white paint in between the waxy pencil marks along the edge, which did the trick beautifully. Continue using the titanium white paint and move back to the head of the ant to add the highlight to the eye.

When you are finished, admire and celebrate this accomplishment.

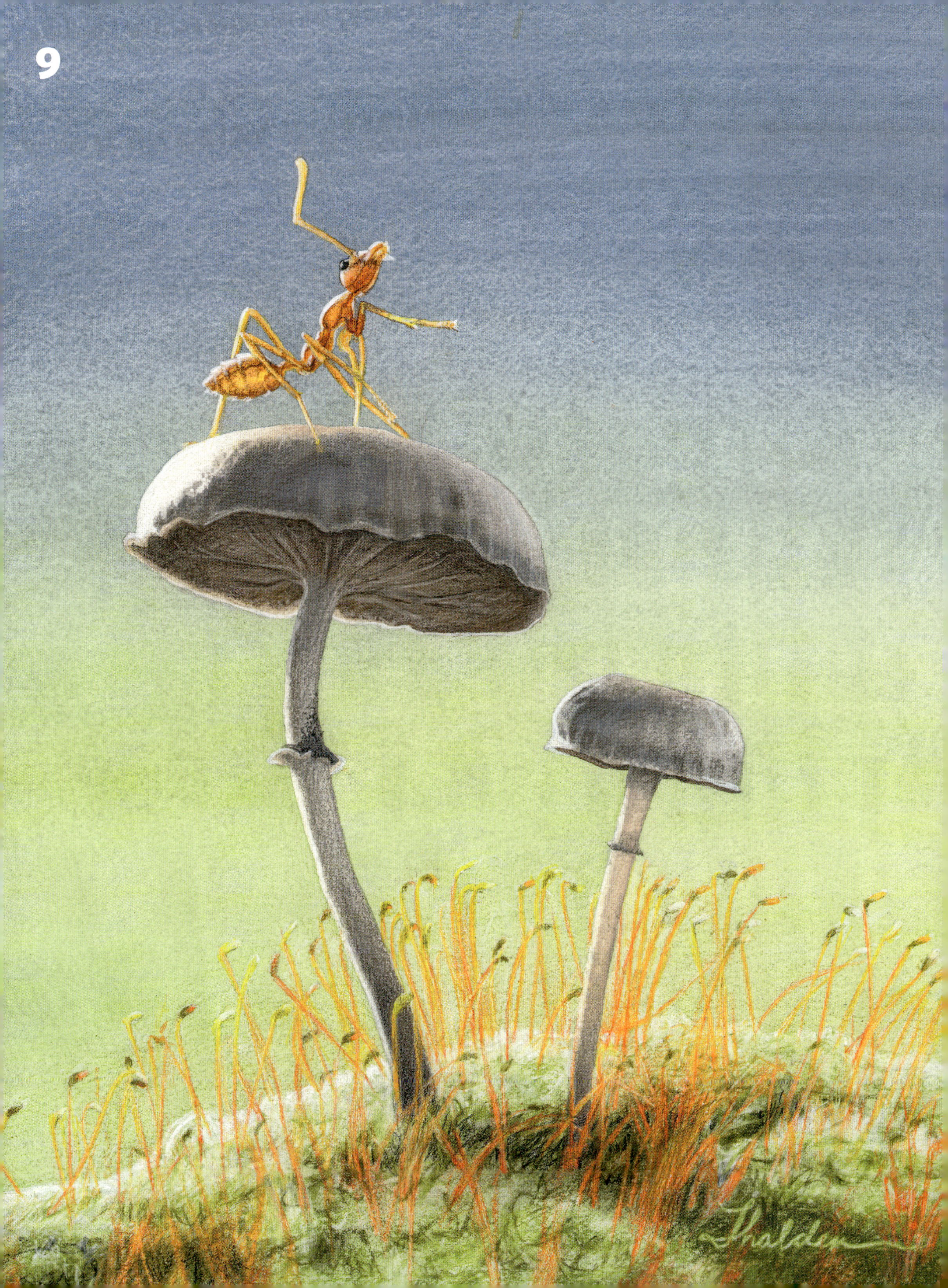

NATURE BREAK, TECHNIQUE

SHADOWS AND HIGHLIGHTS

The more you understand about how light interacts with a surface, the easier it is to convey three-dimensionality in a drawing. It is now time to focus on shadows and highlights.

LOCATION: Set up in a room with minimal or reduced natural light.

MATERIALS: Sketchbook, HB pencil, table lamp, and two groups of household items. For the first group, select objects in basic geometric shapes that are opaque and have a matte, patternless surface. A small cardboard box, a round piece of fruit, or a spice jar wrapped in paper might work nicely. For the second collection, choose household objects that are opaque and have different surface textures (one might be shiny while another is soft or fuzzy).

OBSERVATIONS: Place one item at a time near the lamp. Slowly rotate the object. Then change both the direction and distance of the light source. Notice the values, shapes, and areas of transition. Imagine this item as a drawing and consider what would make it appear realistic. Your goal is to find new discoveries that govern the relationship between light and objects.

PRACTICE: Describe and draw your findings in your sketchbook. Move from one object to the next and compare the similarities and differences between the forms. Create many examples on one page by drawing only the portion of the object that conveys each concept. When you document the items, small surface studies may be all you need to describe how light affects the curves, edges, sheen, texture, and other surface qualities.

REFLECTION: Review your documentation and consider which specific drawing techniques you can use in the future to convey roundness, sharp edges, grooves, softness, and other surfaces, shapes, or textures.

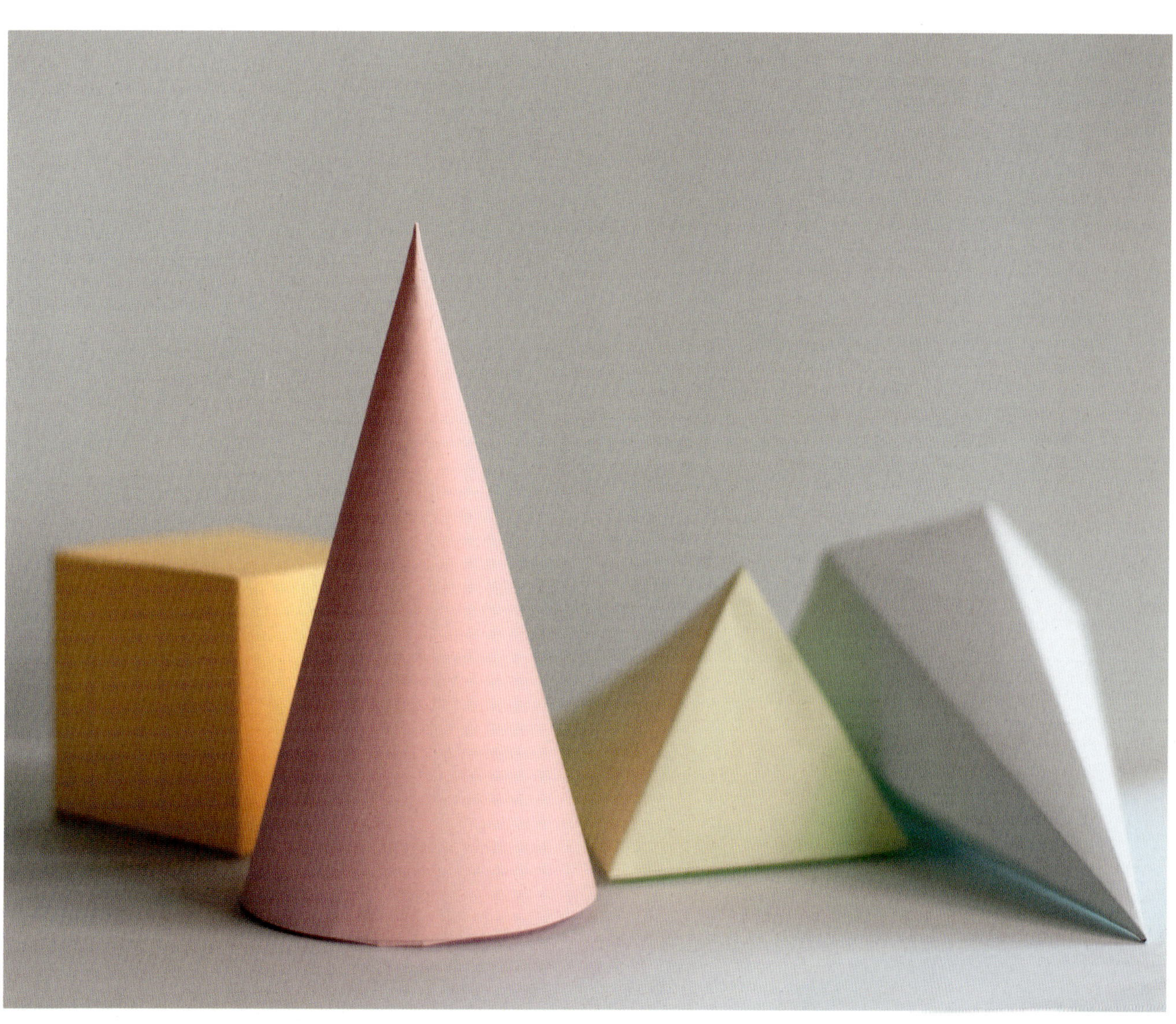

LUNA MOTH

ACTIAS LUNA

Moon moths are known for their beautiful circular moon-shaped eye spots and the long ribbonlike tails on their hindwings. It is believed that the tails serve as a form of protection by interfering with the echolocation of bats, one of their predators. The American moon moth, or luna moth, has wings that can span over 4 inches and are colored pale green. I included this composition for several reasons. First, the light wing color against the dark background creates a reverse contrast from the majority of the preceding projects. Because of this, value will be a primary focus in this piece. Second, by including multiple botanicals, you create a middle ground and emphasize the spaciousness of the composition. Third, you can work with the layout as is or take this opportunity to rearrange the subjects in a way that creates a stronger design.

SEE REFERENCE PHOTOS ON PAGE 319

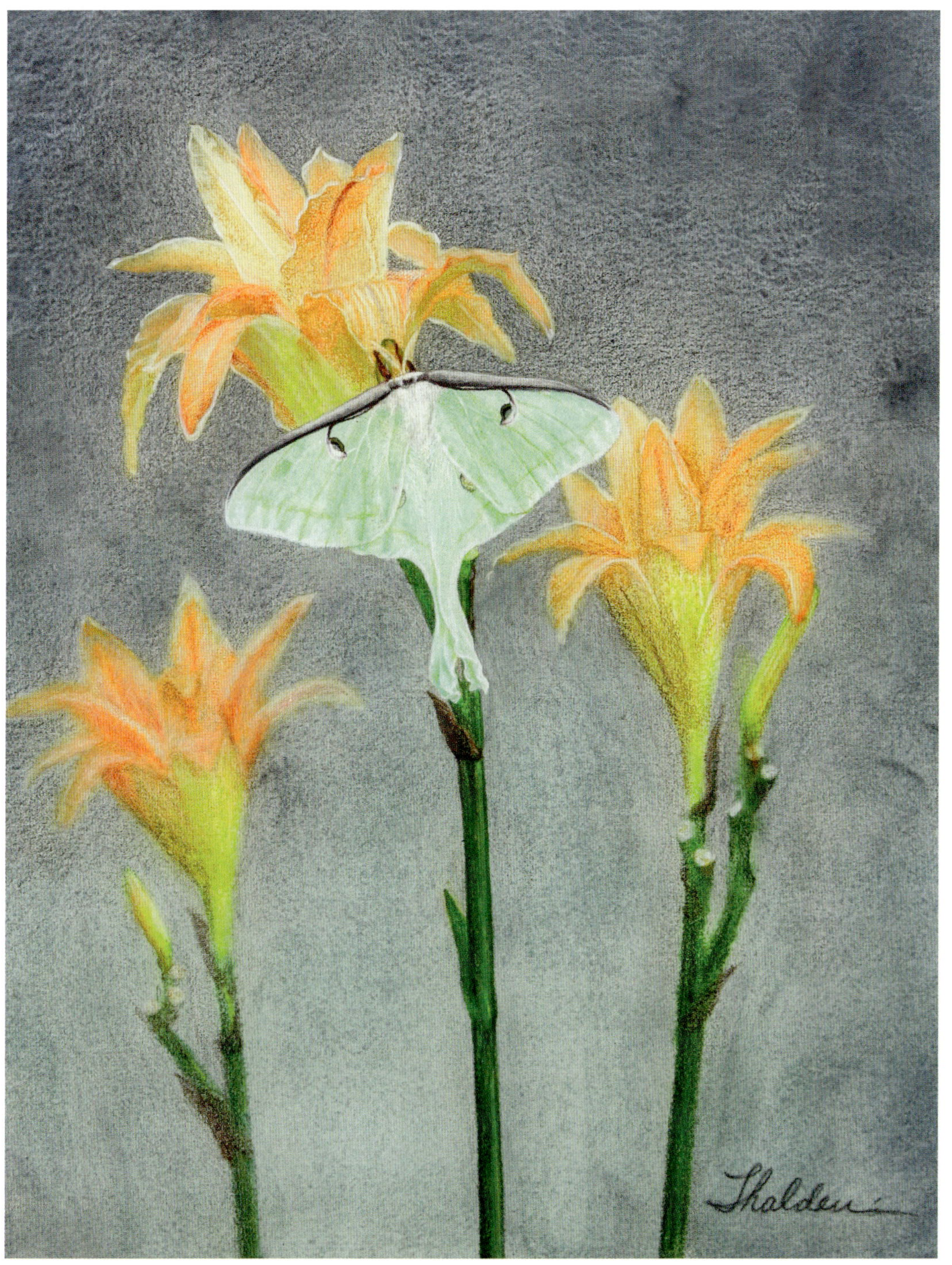

ACRYLIC PAINTS

- ☐ burnt umber
- ☐ cadmium red
- ☐ cadmium yellow
- ☐ cobalt blue
- ☐ Mars black
- ☐ Naples yellow
- ☐ orange
- ☐ permanent green light
- ☐ titanium white
- ☐ ultramarine blue

BRUSHES

- ☐ smaller sized brushes
- ☐ background brush

COLORED PENCILS

- ☐ apple green
- ☐ black
- ☐ black raspberry
- ☐ chartreuse
- ☐ chocolate
- ☐ cream
- ☐ crimson lake
- ☐ French gray (your choice)
- ☐ goldenrod
- ☐ lime peel
- ☐ orange
- ☐ pale vermillion
- ☐ Prussian green
- ☐ seashell pink
- ☐ sunburst yellow
- ☐ yellowed orange
- ☐ white

ADDITIONAL MATERIALS

- ☐ cropping tools

DESIGNING

1 **A** If you are interested in changing the design of the composition, begin by drawing a gesture of the current composition in your sketchbook. Place the central flower with the moth and then add the secondary flowers. Next, consider how you could reorganize these subjects. You might use cropping tools on top of the reference image or create a variety of gestures to visualize new dimensions and angles. Allow the proportion of height and width to be determined solely by the design. Each time you find a composition that might work, document it in your sketchbook. Either draw the framing edge directly on your gesture or create a small thumbnail sketch. In each design, consider the placement, size, and location of each element and the negative space surrounding them. If you want to make adjustments, create additional thumbnail variations on the following page to refine your ideas.

When you design, sometimes a single sketch is sufficient. Other times, it may take a series of sketches to arrive at a pleasing layout. Strive for a minimum of three finalized design options to choose from. Then select one to create your illustration.

B For my composition, I developed a design similar to the one on the far right, which made the stems more vertical but rotated the moth back to the original position shown in the reference image. Since I wanted to maintain format continuity in this book, I widened the framing edge and included all three flowers. When I did this, I found that the flowers looked too tightly packed together and were hard to appreciate, so I lowered the two on the side, knowing that I was taking on the challenge of drawing petals that cannot be seen in the reference image.

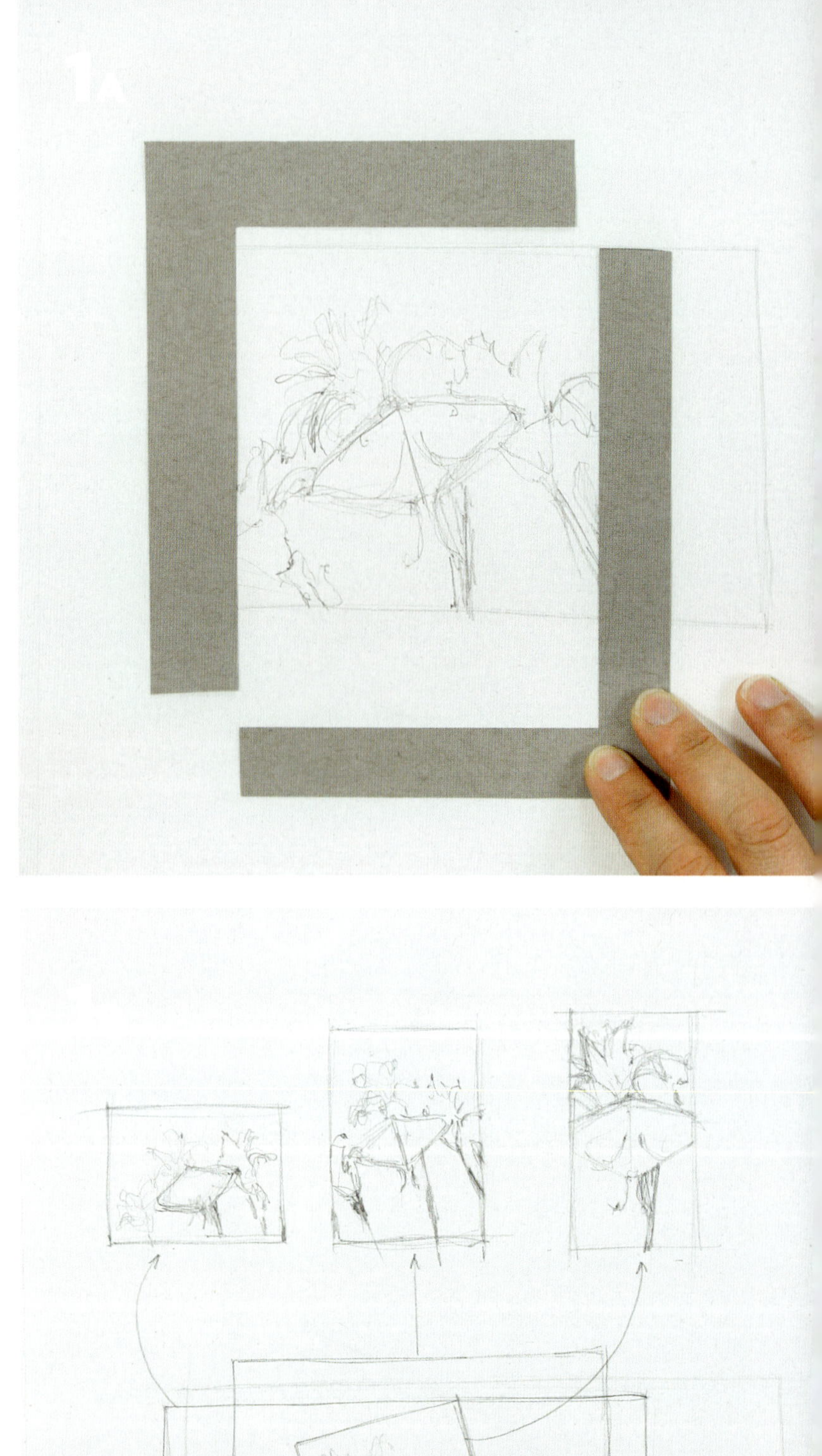

DRAWING

1 **A** Create a gesture of the chosen design on your paper. If your design is at an angle, like mine, rotate the reference image to match. At this stage, I first marked the location of the moth and secondary flower heads very roughly, then added the central flower with a bit more detail. Note that I enlarged the central flower on my illustration after the gesture was complete. I mention this simply to give you the option to make this adjustment before the refinement stage of your drawing.

B Now select a unit of measure from the moth to use for checking proportions. For my measurement, I used the distance from the tip of the head to the top of the tails.

Since the inner edges of the hindwings are not symmetrical, I simply extended the midline and observed how the edge of each wing corresponds. Study the shape of the tail in the reference image carefully so that you can render them realistically. (See also the image for step 8, which has a pencil overlay of the tail.) In my own drawing, I drew the tail on the left hindwing too short. You'll read about the repair later in the project.

When you refine the secondary flowers on either side of the subject, try drawing them with minimal measuring. You might include only overall distances and any particularly tricky shapes or proportions. It's best to wait to refine the central flower until after the moth is complete.

If your design entails drawing flower sections that don't appear in the reference image, look to the information that *is* provided to visualize the shapes. The lilies, for instance, are structured with whorls of three petals layered three times to form a six-pointed star pattern. One trick I use to create new petals is to duplicate a petal on tracing paper and adjust or flip it until it looks realistic in the area that needs to be filled in. You may

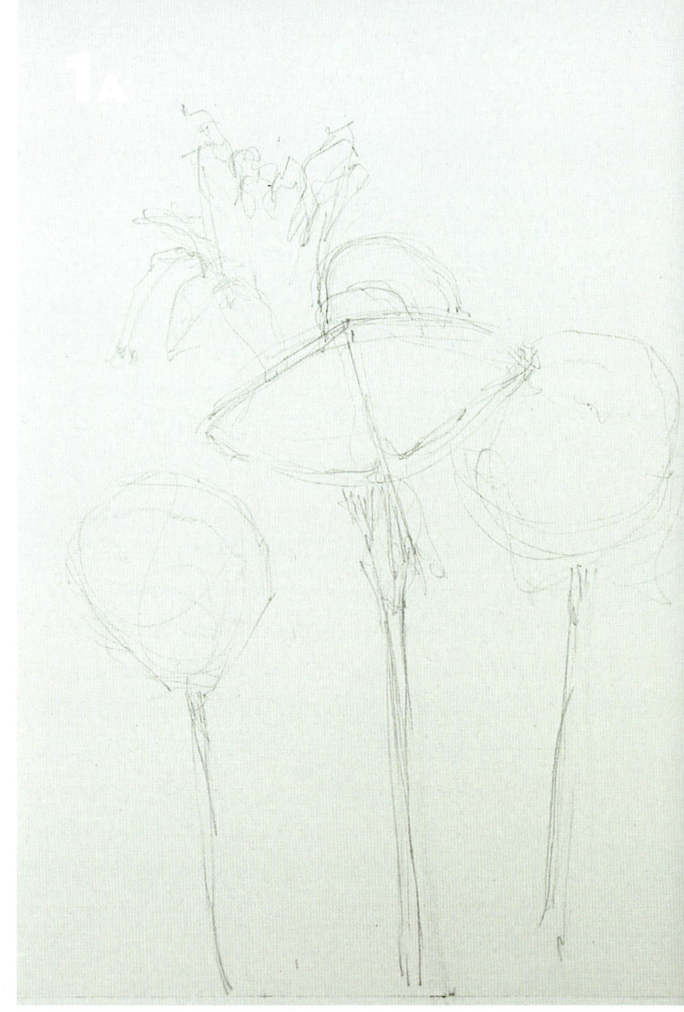

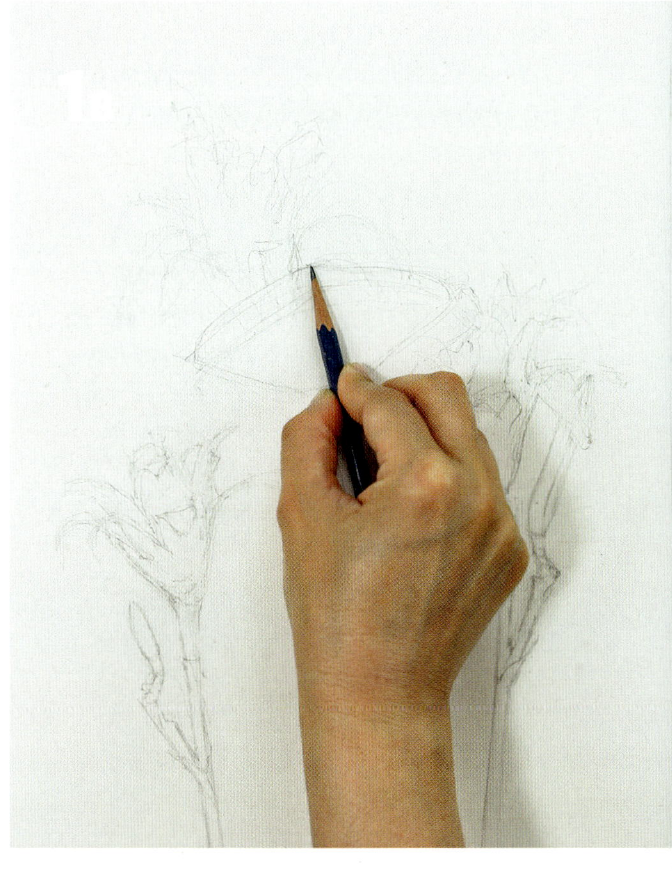

find that a simple size change or subtle line shift can make each petal look similar but not identical. Lightly draw the gesture as well as the refined outline of these petals so that you can rework them as needed.

Sometimes you may find that your illustration needs layout alterations that could not be foreseen in the design stage. Looking at my composition, I realized that I wanted the central flower to have more presence. Since illustrating begins with a gesture, I can easily redraw the flower slightly larger and higher up in the composition. Before I begin, I always copy my original gesture and mark the corners on tracing paper as a precaution. The change places both the flower and the moth closer to the viewer, thereby creating a middle ground where the other flowers are located. If you choose to make the same change, be sure to also widen the stem slightly to match the flower's proportions.

If you can tell that something looks off in your illustration but you can't identify what it is, take a very short break. Return with fresh eyes to look for areas that need adjustment. After making a change, if the result you achieve is not on par with other areas in your drawing, remember that you are in the process of learning a useful skill. Take your time and be patient with yourself.

2 **A** Since the moth was positioned at a slight angle to the camera when the reference image was taken, both sets of wings are foreshortened and slightly different sizes. Therefore, I found it best to measure the width of the wings first. I started with the right forewing, followed by both of the lower wings combined, then the left forewing. It may help with your accuracy to add the location where the wings start to overlap, the outline of the tails, as well as a horizontal axis line connecting the tips of the upper wings.

B Once the moth outline is refined, move to the central flower. When a subject is fairly large, a significant portion of the botanical behind it may be obscured. Instead of drawing the flower in two sections, which can result in distortions, use a sheet of tracing paper to draw the entire flower as if the moth were not there. Transfer only the lines around the moth to your drawing. This helps ensure continuity in your lines and proportions, which results in a botanical drawing that is far more believable. At this time, be sure to include the flower bud on which the moth is perched so that you don't have to add it later in the process, as I needed to do.

3 Make final adjustments to your drawing. Be sure that the flower tips that curve downward have enough space between the outlines to avoid visual discord. Pencil lines that outline the secondary flower heads should be dark enough to be seen when you are painting but light enough that you can create a fade into the background and emphasize their placement in the middle ground. On the other hand, the outline of all three stems will need to be dark enough to see easily through the background color. Because this design is an original, consider replicating the entire drawing on tracing paper before moving on.

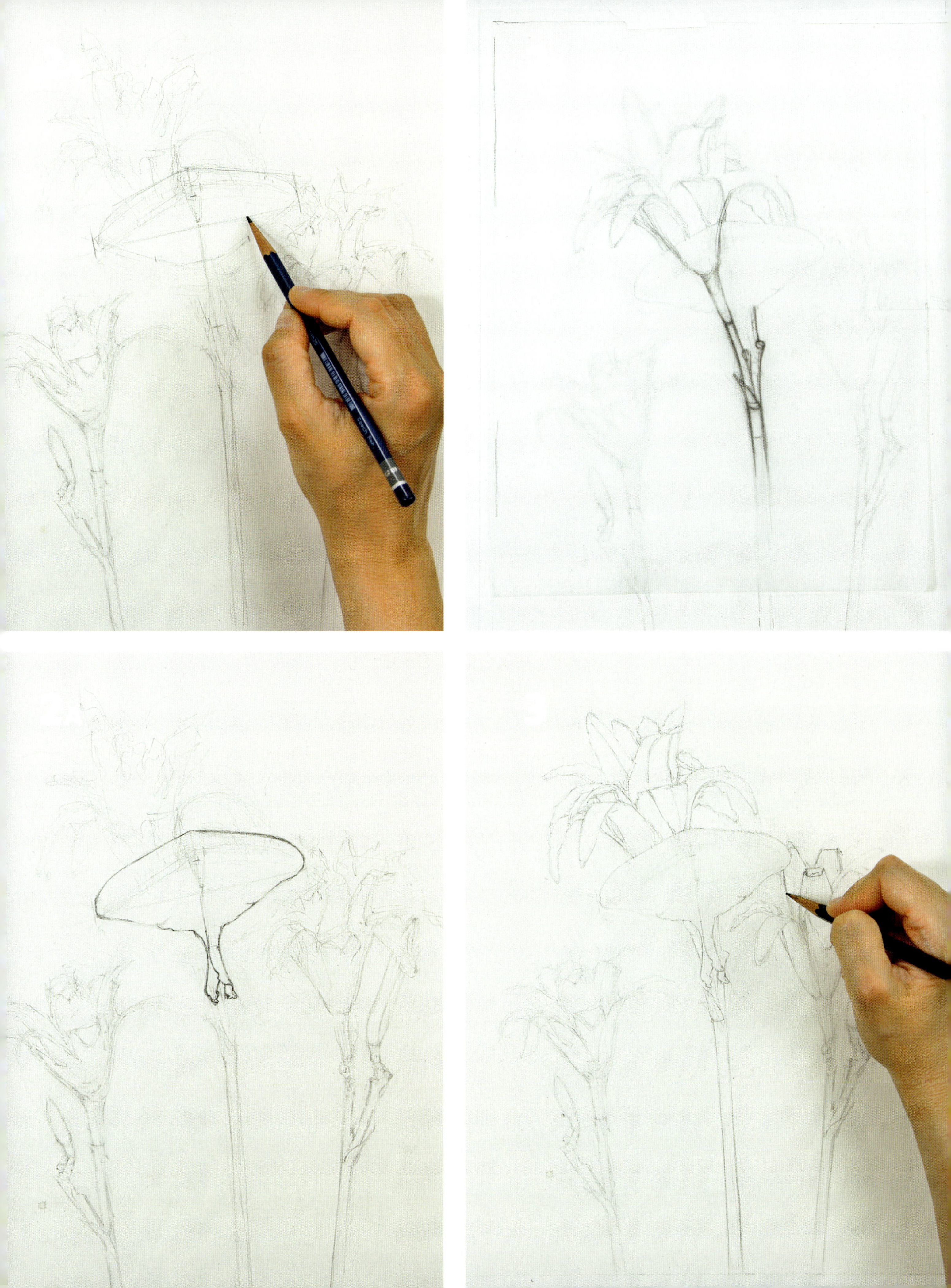

PAINTING

1 As you set up for the painting process, remember that masking fluid creates a hard outline and thus isn't advisable for use with the middle-ground flowers, since they will have blurred edges. The lily in the center does have crisp edges, but we'll use a different technique to make it dramatically different from the other flowers and interrupt the subtle yet realistic illusion of space. For these reasons, I chose to mask only the moth.

In this composition, the flowers are light against the background while the stems are darker. Therefore, the ideal background would have a value midway between the darkest part of the stem and the lightest values on the flower. Alternatively, you might prefer a value gradation with the dark value behind the flowers and a slightly lighter value near the stems.

2 Create a dark gray paint mixture on your palette. You can add some ultramarine blue to match the cool color shown in the reference image. If you want to include the reference image's light green patches, add titanium white and some permanent green light to one-third of the base gray paint mixture.

3 **A** Choose a brush size that is large enough to cover the background quickly yet small enough to place color between the petals. Keep a clean, folded paper towel in your nondominant hand and available in case any color begins to pool or bleed into the petals. Apply a water wash to the entire page. With the dark gray, start painting in the upper corners. Pay close attention to how much paint bleeds into the wash so you can guestimate the distance to keep the paintbrush from the subjects. Work quickly and keep the lower section glistening until the background is complete.

At this point, you can treat the edge of all three flowers the same. When you paint around the petals, it helps to use a series of V-shaped formations that start and end in the background instead of near the flower, so that the excess paint is more likely to bleed into the background. Let your brushstrokes add a subtle value pattern throughout.

B To create a gradation from top to bottom, begin applying the second color and continue down the page. You may need to return to an area to further integrate the transition. When you paint on either side of the stems, paint right up to the outline. If the paint bleeds into the form, just make sure some of the interior remains unpainted so that the stems are easy to locate.

4 While the beautiful background you created is drying, mix the base colors for the flowers. After reviewing my inventory of colored pencils, I chose to mix colors that are not in the pencil set to extend the illustration's color range. I created one orange paint mixture for the tops of the petals and another to use on the underside. Feel free to broaden your selection by creating more paint mixtures or other color variations until you create all the colors you're looking for. The goal here is to practice discerning and nuancing color value, hue, intensity, and temperature so that you can create color mixtures easily in the future. You also might try creating paint mixtures using colors that have an inherent dark value so that you can minimize the amount of black paint that you use. To create my color mixture, I selected a hue and added three other paint colors to cool, darken, and lower the saturation. Because of this, I only needed a miniscule amount of Mars black paint to further darken. Intentionally relying on the inherent value of your paints can make you more versatile as an artist and result in richer paint mixtures.

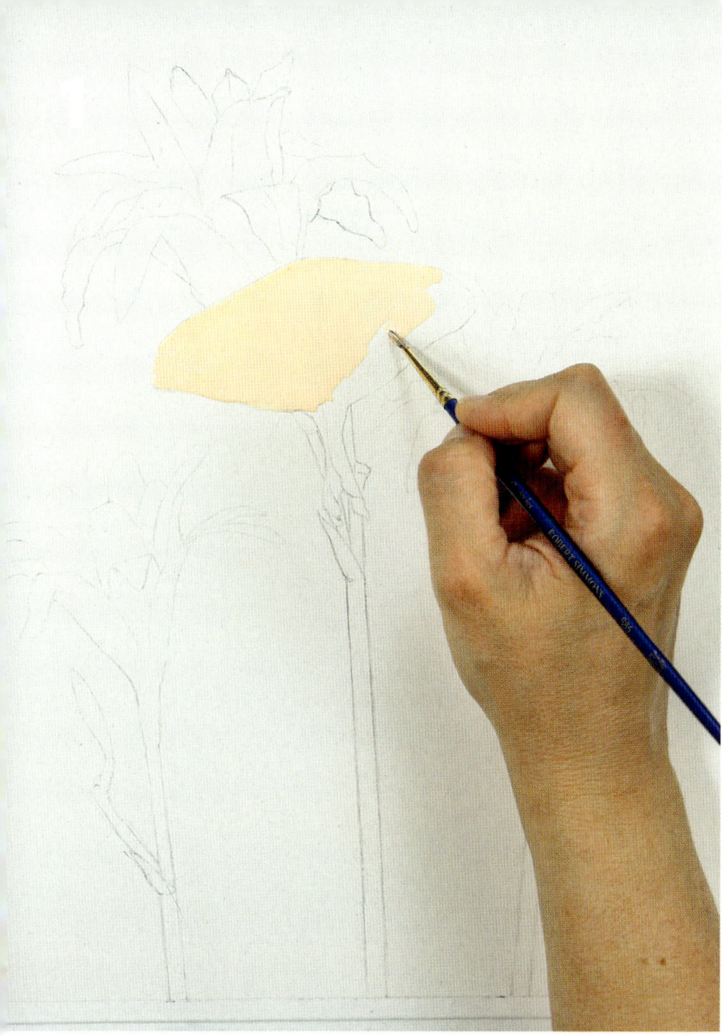

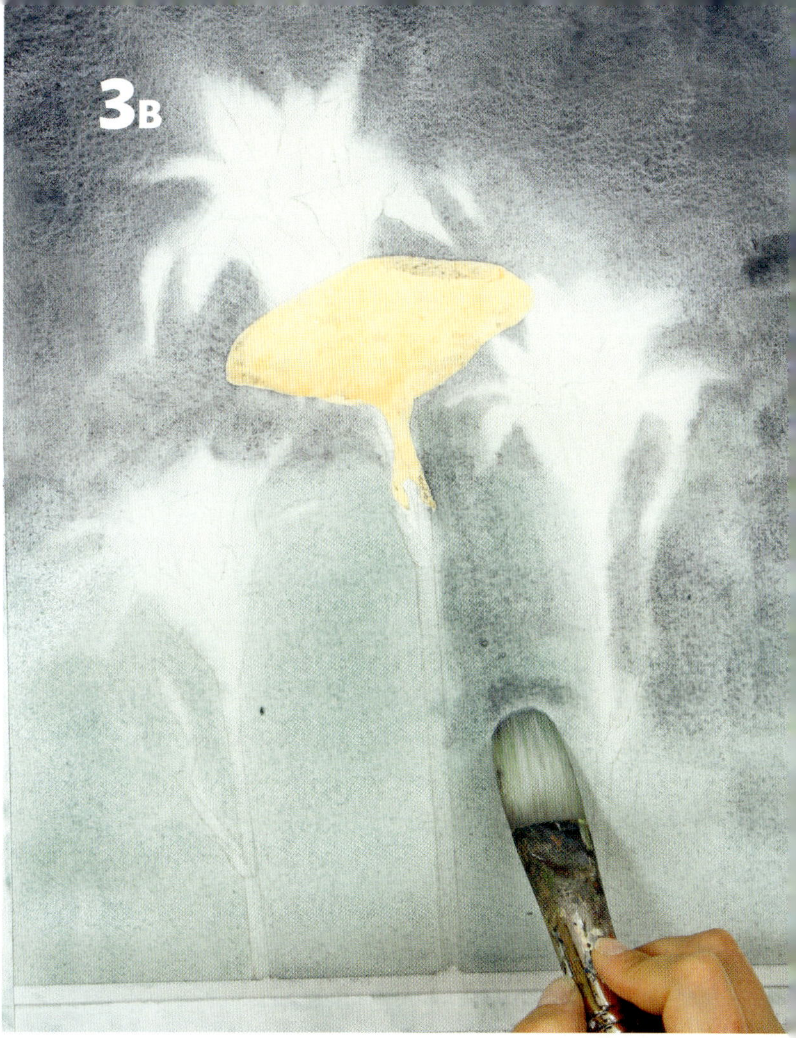

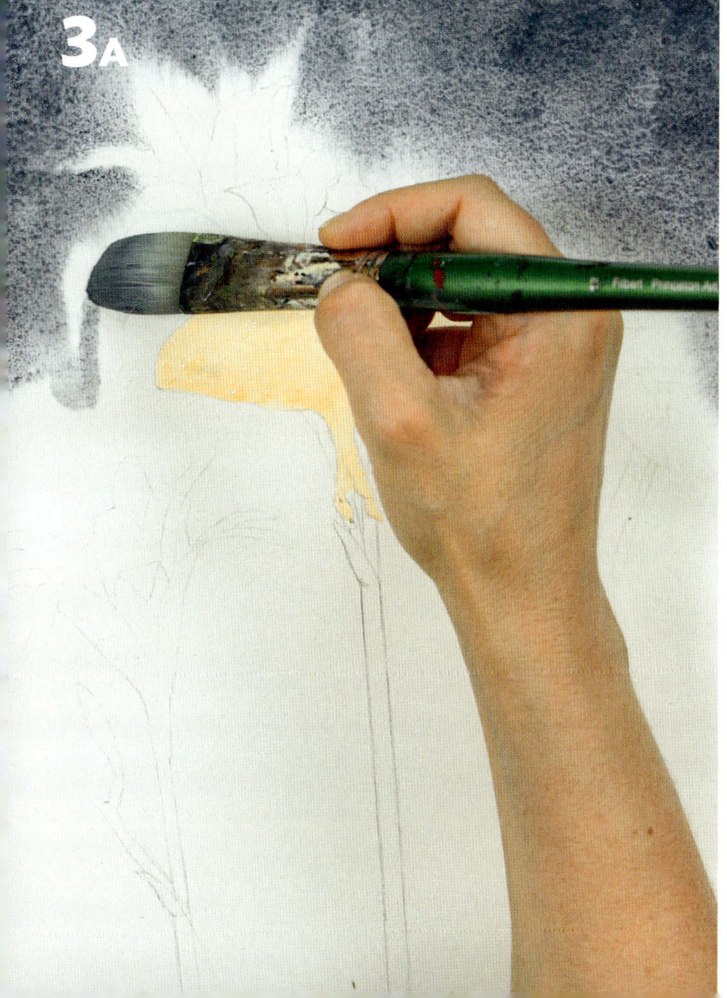

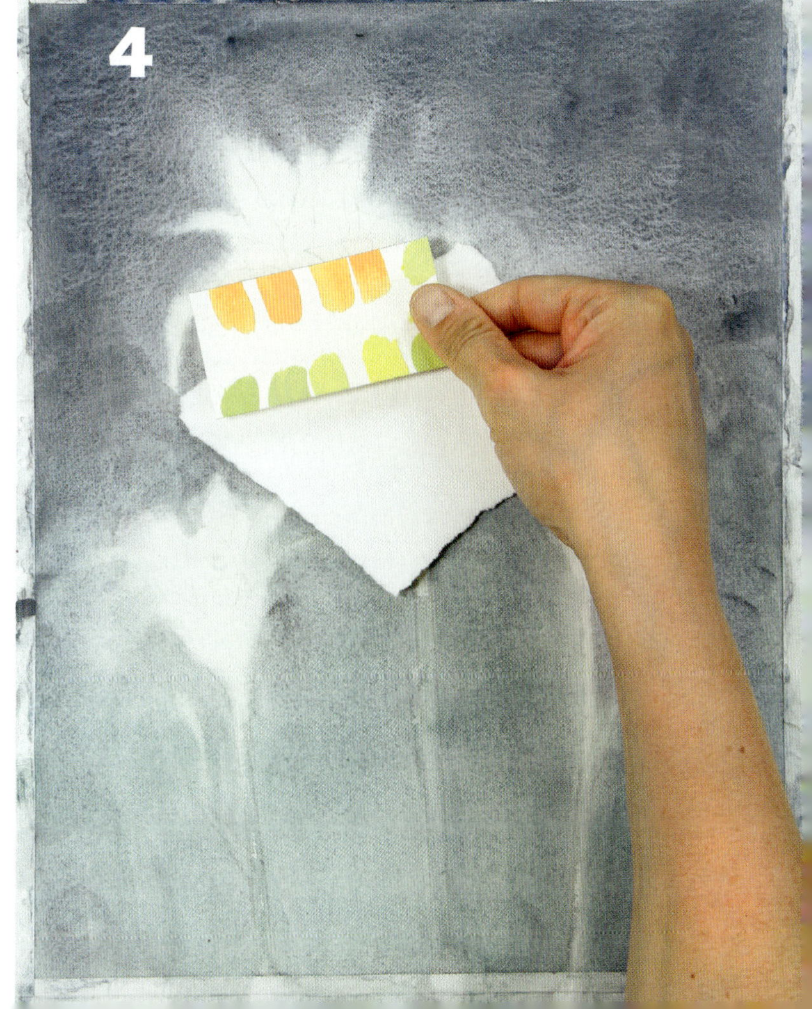

Now mix the color to paint the stems. You might challenge yourself by selecting your own paint colors to create a paint mixture that echoes the reference image's colors. If you would like to do this, begin now and read on when your mixture is complete. Your can compare your choices to the paint colors I used, listed in the next paragraph.

I formed the green base color by combining permanent green light with cadmium yellow, then adding burnt umber and a small amount of ultramarine blue, Naples yellow, and/or orange paint.

5 **A** Work on the two middle-ground flowers first. Consider the steps you will need to follow to achieve the results you desire. When you apply the paint to the flower heads, keep the value of both the yellow and orange lighter than the background.

B To create the stem, I suggest brushing a single stripe down the very center with a little extra on either side that gets filled with an additional stroke. Next, work on the flower in the foreground, then let the page dry completely. Consider the quality of the foreground flower's edges, and make the flowers in the middle ground a little blurrier.

6 Remove the masking fluid from the moth. Draw the details within the wings, keeping your lines very light. This is not as important along the leading edge of the forewings because of the darker value. You can also indicate the veins or the patterns of highlight and dark areas or, if you prefer, you can guesstimate the location while you paint, then be more precise in the colored pencil stage.

7 Since no colored pencil matches the wing color, you will need to mix all of the green variations in paint, knowing that you will be able to lighten them later with the white pencil, if needed.

First mix a light green base and adjust the hue slightly with Naples yellow and cobalt blue paint. Strive to match the darkest color in the center of the forewings. Divide this paint mixture and lighten one so that you have medium and light green paint mixtures to work with.

When you add a water wash to all of the wings, include the body so that you can create a soft edge where the wing and body meet. However, keep the eye spots and the dark stripe along the leading edge on the forewings dry. While the wash is still damp, use the medium-value paint mixture to indicate where the forewings overlap the hindwings. When you add the stripelike shadows on the surface, notice their relationship to the location of the veins in the wings.

By using painting techniques that you are already familiar with, you are able to re-create both a wavelike surface of delicate wings and the subtle illusion of translucency on paper.

8 **A** While the wings dry, mix a paint color for the dark area of the eye spots. My goal was to arrive at a value halfway between the black and the 70% French gray pencils. When you are ready, apply the gray paint mixture to the dark area of both forewing eye spots. Keep in mind that the colored pencil lines you will layer on top of this dark area later will significantly lighten the value of the eye spots.

B Now mix the dark purple to use along the leading edge of the forewing. Dilute a portion of the purple mixture until it matches the lightest color in this section and use it as a wash. It is easy for water to pool in these small sections, so be sure to blot the brush and check that the paper just glistens. Then layer less-diluted pigment to create a gradation toward the interior of the wing.

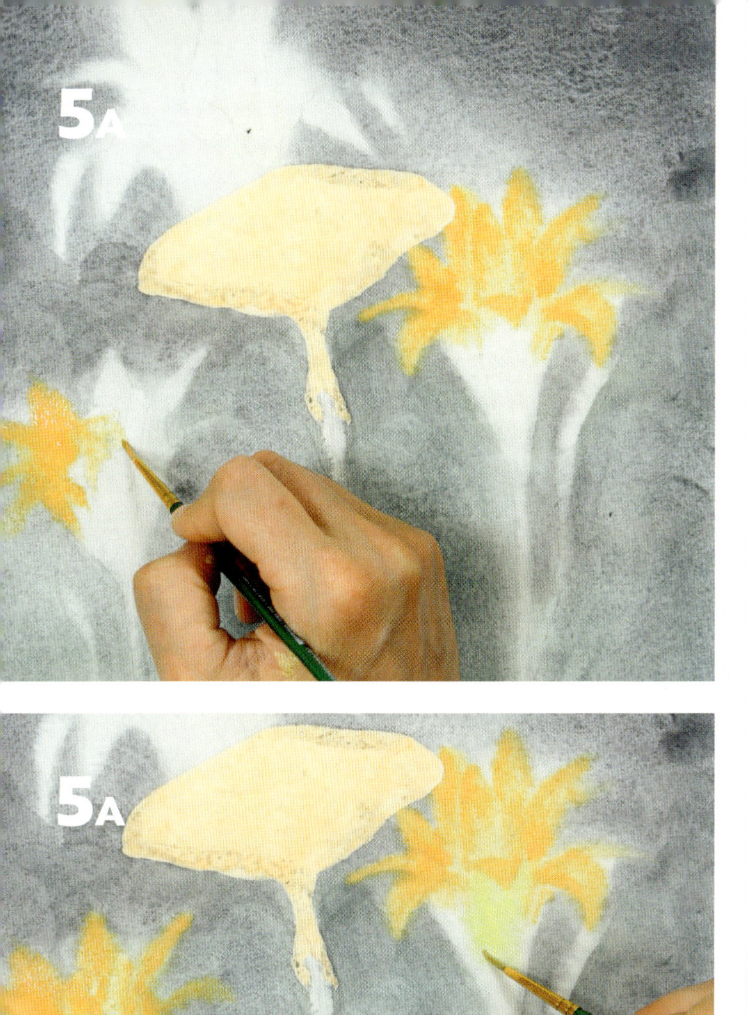
5A

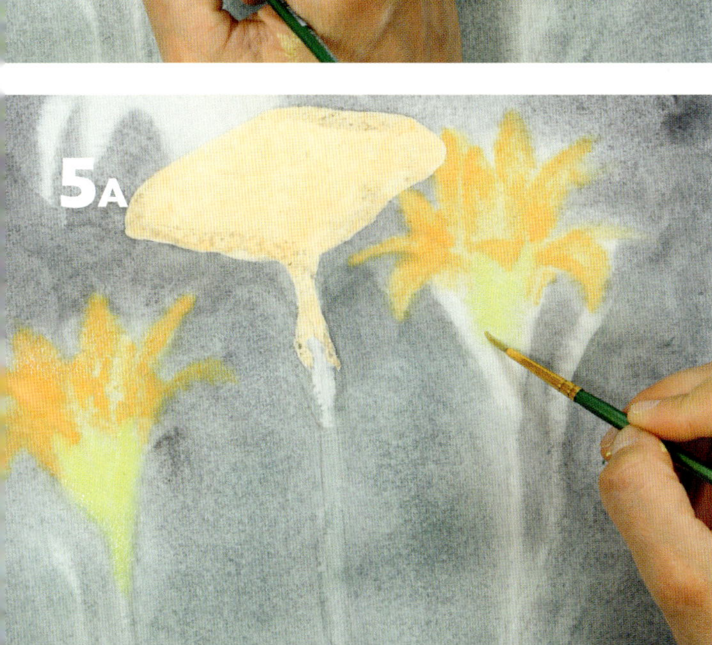
5A

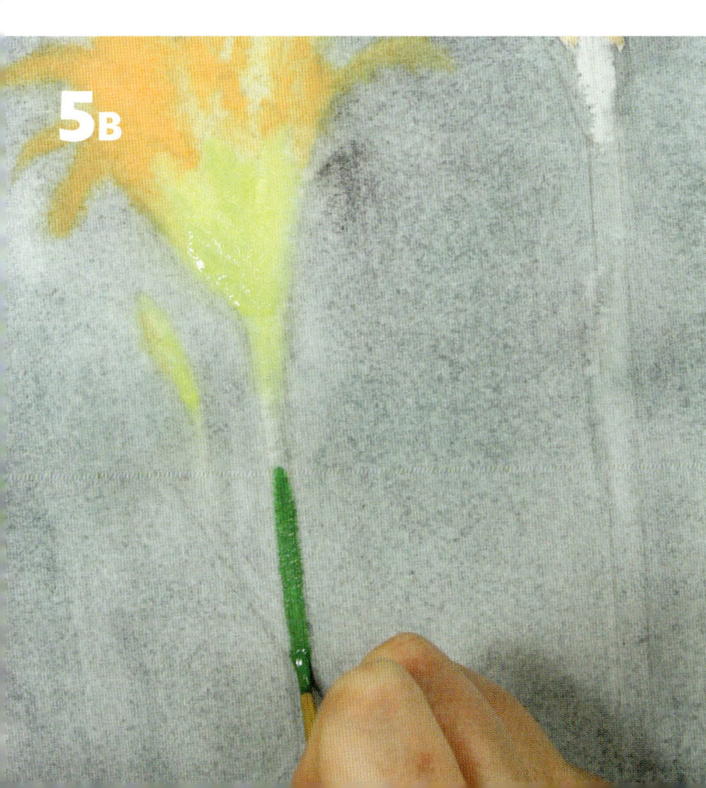
5B

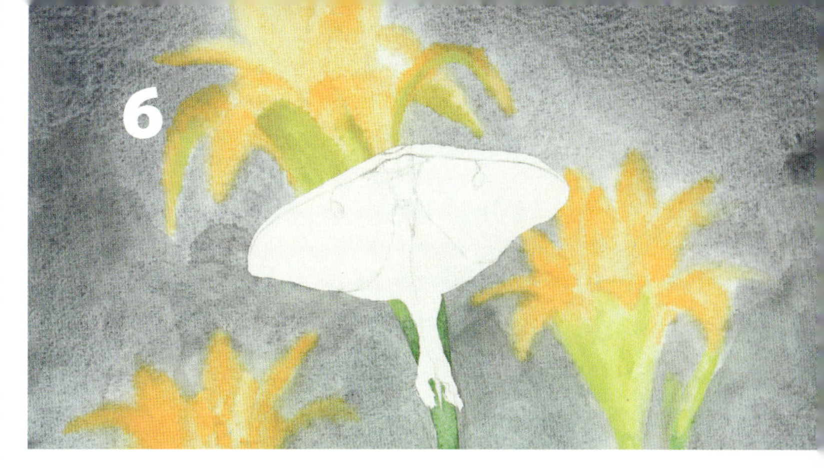
6

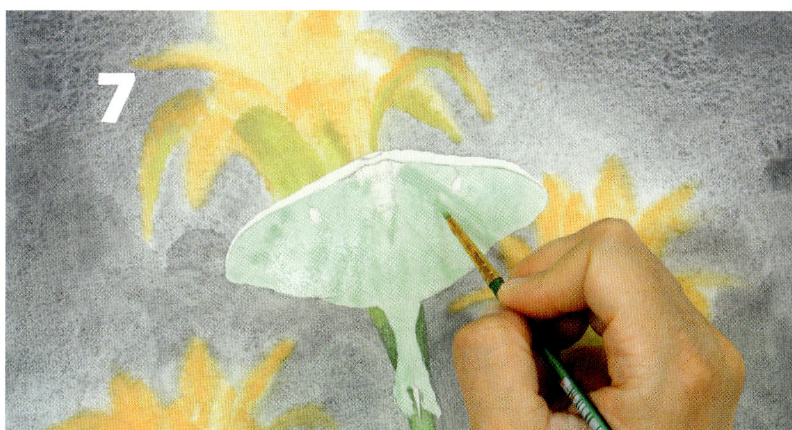
7

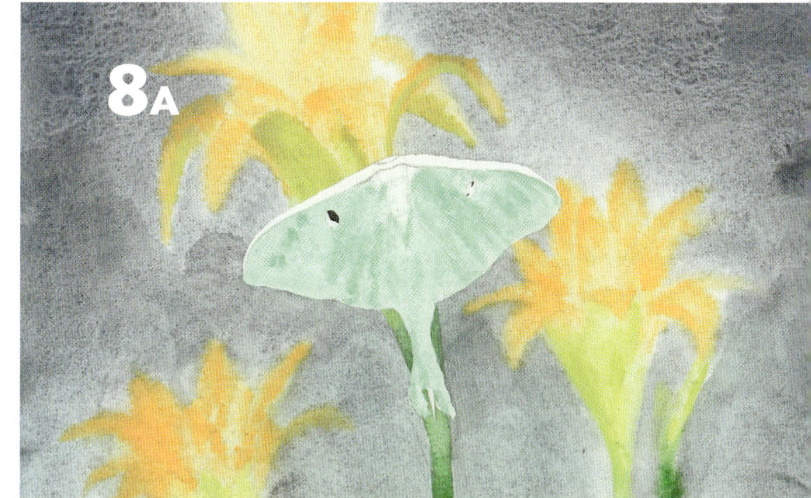
8A

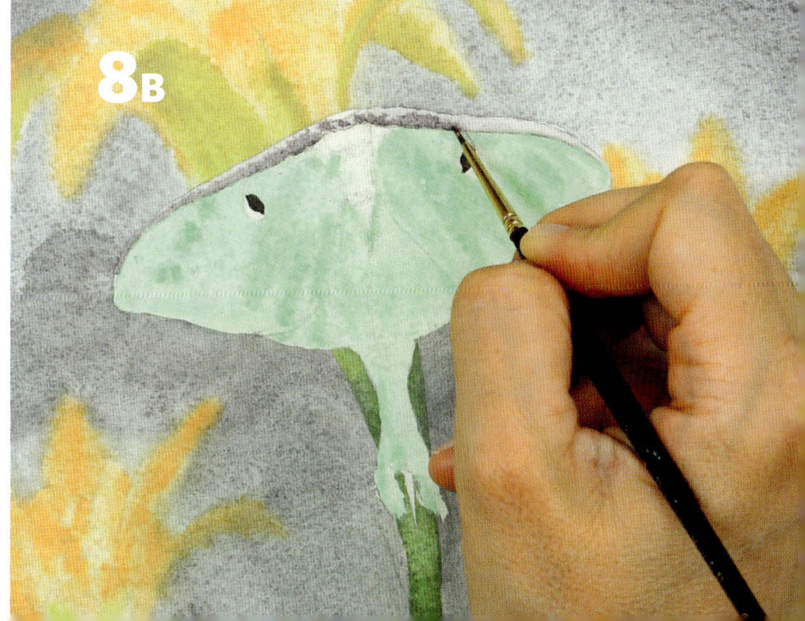
8B

LAYERING WITH COLORED PENCIL

1 **A** Create a swatch with a sample of each colored pencil, placing each block of pigment along the swatch edge with a little space between blocks. Use this to guide your pencil selections.

Now establish the level of detail in the foreground by working on the flower behind the moth. Start by selecting colors from the materials list that are in the mid-value range and work on the topside of the petals toward the front. When you define edges and begin to fill in areas, keep your pressure light so that you can still see through the marks. Use the cream pencil to lighten whole areas, and draw it along the edges to further differentiate the flower from the background. You can vary the line weight along the edge to emphasize the shape. Be aware that the cream pencil can be very powerful against the dark background; use this color sparingly at its full intensity. The crimson lake pencil can be used to darken the orange. To create the midline on the front petal that curves down toward the moth, you might consider using seashell pink.

Build up on all of the petals simultaneously instead of completing one at a time. Once again, unfocus your eyes and blur your vision to distinguish between colors on the reference image. To emphasize both unity and form, blend colors on each petal. Also, if you create a slight change in color and/or value on either edge of a petal, you help differentiate it from neighboring petals.

Leave space for the moth's antennae when you work on the flower, knowing that you may need to make some slight adjustments to the petal after you have completed the moth.

2 Now work on the underside of the petals. In addition to the colors you have been using, select a medium-value warm color to enhance and darken these shadowed areas. To locate the placement of details underneath the petals, it may help to imagine both the far edge and the midline as if they were not interrupted by the opaque petal.

In the very front, the base of the two petals overlap slightly. If you choose to suggest this subtle detail, use light pencil pressure to add the shadow and then re-emphasize the edge of the closer petal so that it is clear which petal is in front.

3 When the foreground flower petals are complete, work on the background around the flower to make the edge of the petals cleaner and brighter. Draw a solid but very light line just beyond the edge of the petal, then blend this line into the background using a small circular motion to match the stippled quality of the paint. Keep your pencil grip as loose as possible without loosing control to help make the transition between pencil and paint seamless and undetectable. Adding a second layer to match the value is better than creating an area that is too dark. If you don't have a colored pencil that perfectly matches your background, leave the edge as is.

If you'd like, you can make the edges of the closest petals more crisp with a sharp pencil line (I did not choose to do so). But keep the petals in back slightly blurred.

4 **A** With the foreground subjects clearly defined, you can work on the two secondary flowers. Look to both the reference image and your own painting to make colored pencil choices. In addition to the colors used on the central flower, I added the chocolate pencil to further darken shadows and the pale vermillion pencil to make the red areas more vibrant.

When you create areas of highlight and shadow, keep the direction of the light source in mind. Notice how each petal is curved, where the light falls on either side of the midrib, and which edge

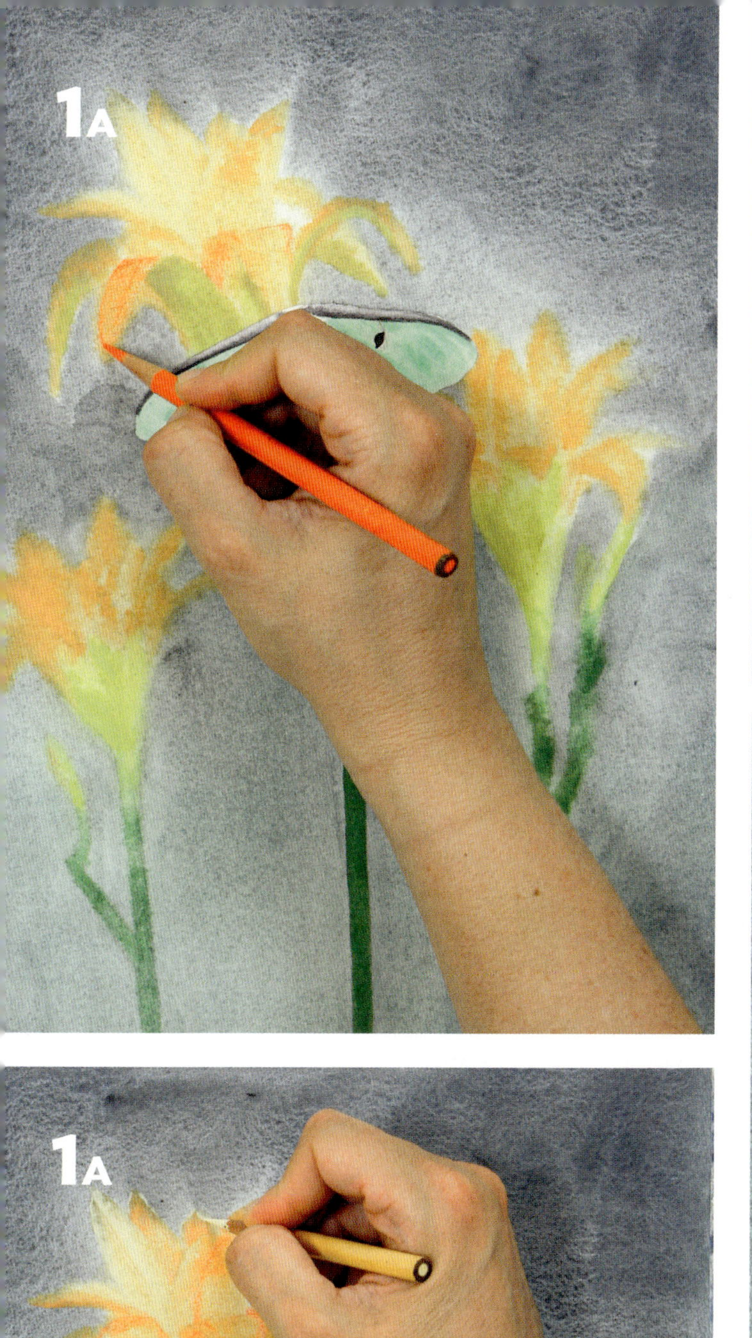

1A

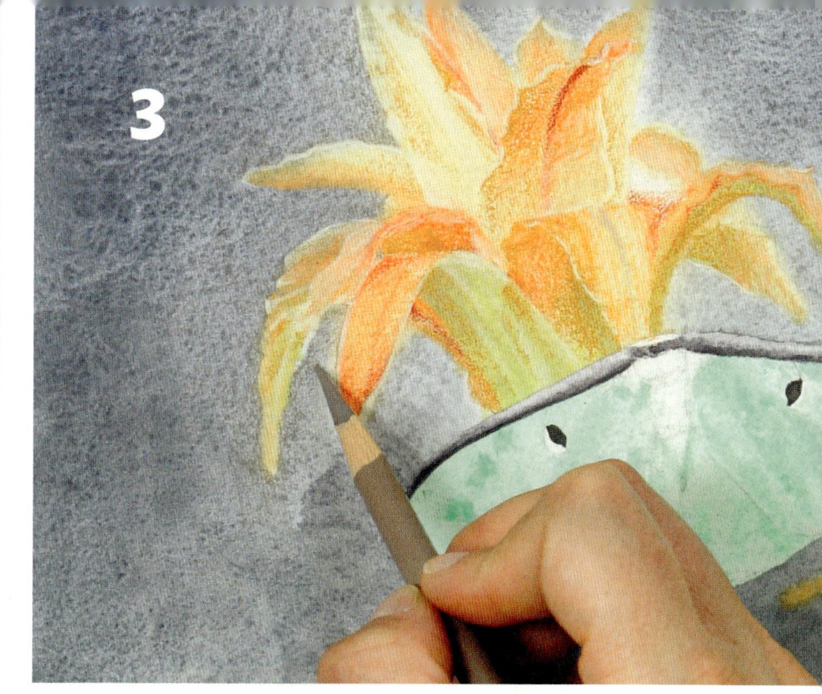

3

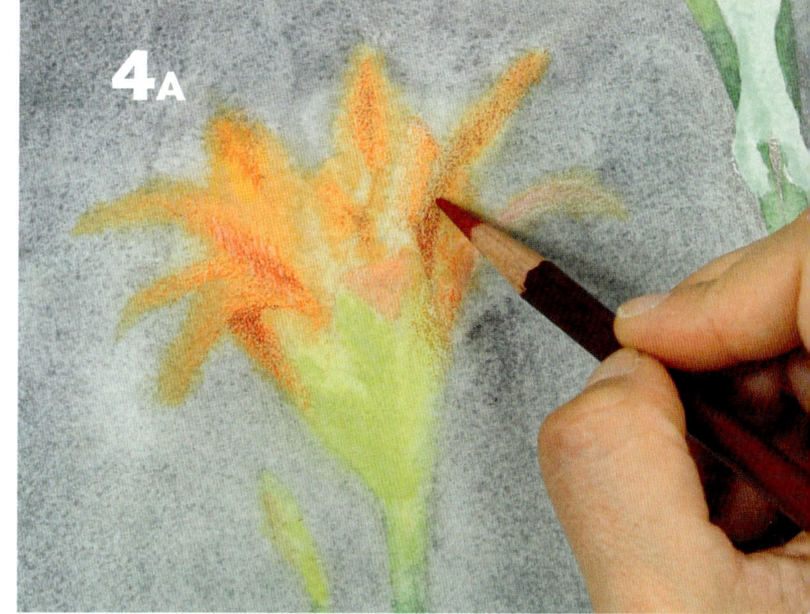

4A

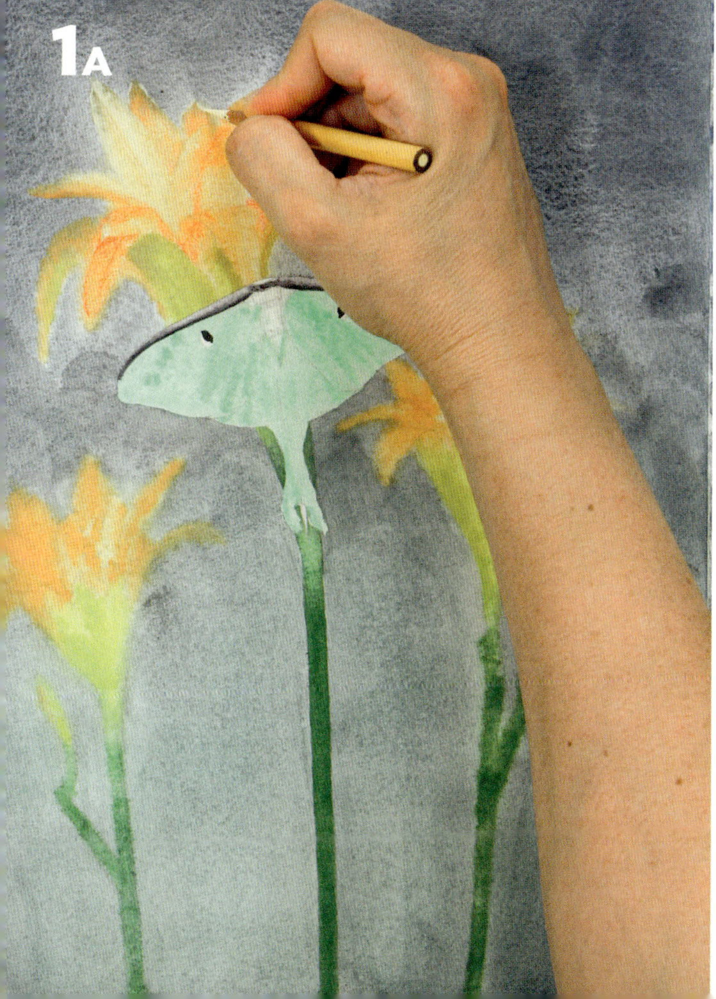

1A

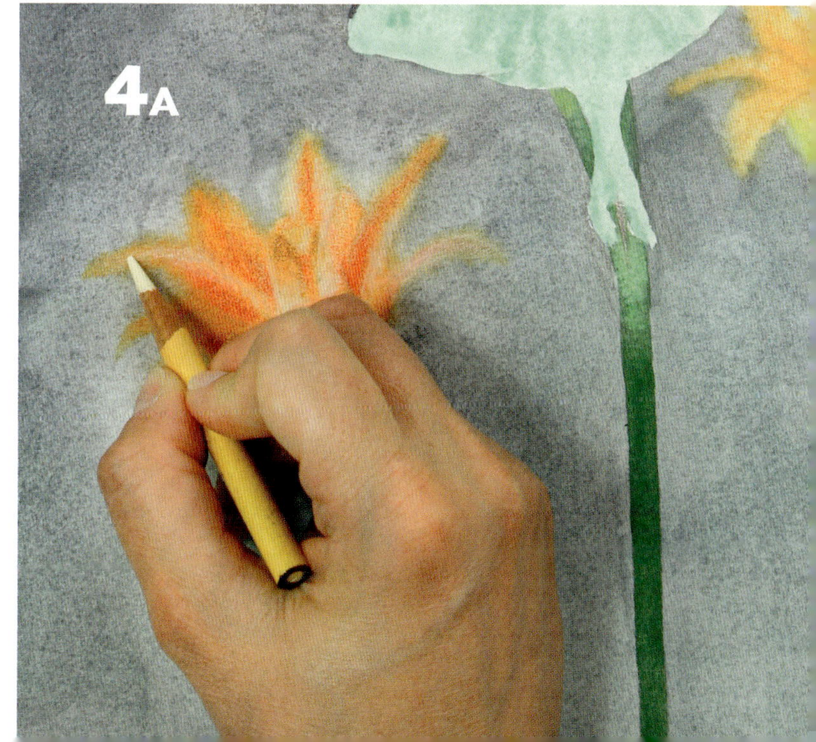

4A

is in shadow or has a highlight. Compare the flowers to each other to be sure the light treatment is consistent.

You can work simultaneously on both flowers or focus on a single one at a time. If you keep the tip of your pencil slightly rounded, it will be easier to blend colors smoothly into one another and into the background. It may help to use the same light circular technique that you used on the background around the central flower.

B In my illustration, I decided to bring the flower on the right closer to the foreground by making the blur around the edges a bit thinner. Once the flower heads are complete, darken the background around the flowers, if needed. For now, leave the flower buds and stems as they are.

5 Begin work on the moth—either on the antennae, the leading edge of the forewing, or the white features on the wings and body.

When you add the antennae, imagine a midline extending beyond the body. Compare the length to other established measurements on the moth. Since the subject is too small to draw the featherlike branches of an antennae, you can simply add a small arc to indicate the edge of the antennae on one or both sides of the central stalk.

Using your imagined midline, determine the location of the moth's head. The asymmetrical placement will help the moth appear dimensional, as if it is holding on to the flower instead of floating in front of it.

6 **A** To create the veins, select a colored pencil that is slightly darker than the wings. Do your best to ignore the value changes in paint and keep the lines light enough to erase completely until you feel confident that you have located them correctly.

B By looking closely, you can see that the veins are not always the same value. In these select areas, you can use an eraser to lighten the vein, draw the vein with the white pencil, or add a thin white line along side of the vein in the direction of the light source.

Then use the white pencil to refine the edges on both forewings. In the sections that are a bit rough, move the pencil back and forth to create a thin line of fringe.

Continue using the white pencil to add the highlighted ripples between the vein lines on the wings. Be sure to blend colors on either side so that you create a smooth transition from one shade to another. Anywhere that you find tight ripples in the wing, such as on the interior edge of the right wing, use a small eraser to create thin shadows by removing the white in parallel lines.

7 Select colored pencils to create the hairs on the body. Draw the lighter hairs first, then add shadows using an upward flicking motion. The body must look white with shadows and not gray, so keep your application minimal. Although they are not shown this way in the reference image, the wings will appear more defined where they overlap the body if you add a very slight shadow just beneath them. Then you can return to the edge of the wing and add the white hairs that are over the shadow. By adding these small enhancements, beyond what is seen in the reference image, you are further developing your skills in communicating the way that light can convey depth. You are doing a beautiful job.

8 Now add the highlights to the hindwings. First mark the hindwing eye spots with a very light pencil mark so that you can avoid these areas. Now add select hairs to emulate the overall pattern, paying close attention to the direction change near the body. Then fill in the remaining hairs.

To create the highlights on the folds of the tails, use the white pencil to draw a single line where the brightest highlights are found. Blend this line in toward the light source. I have included a pencil drawing so that you can clearly see both the

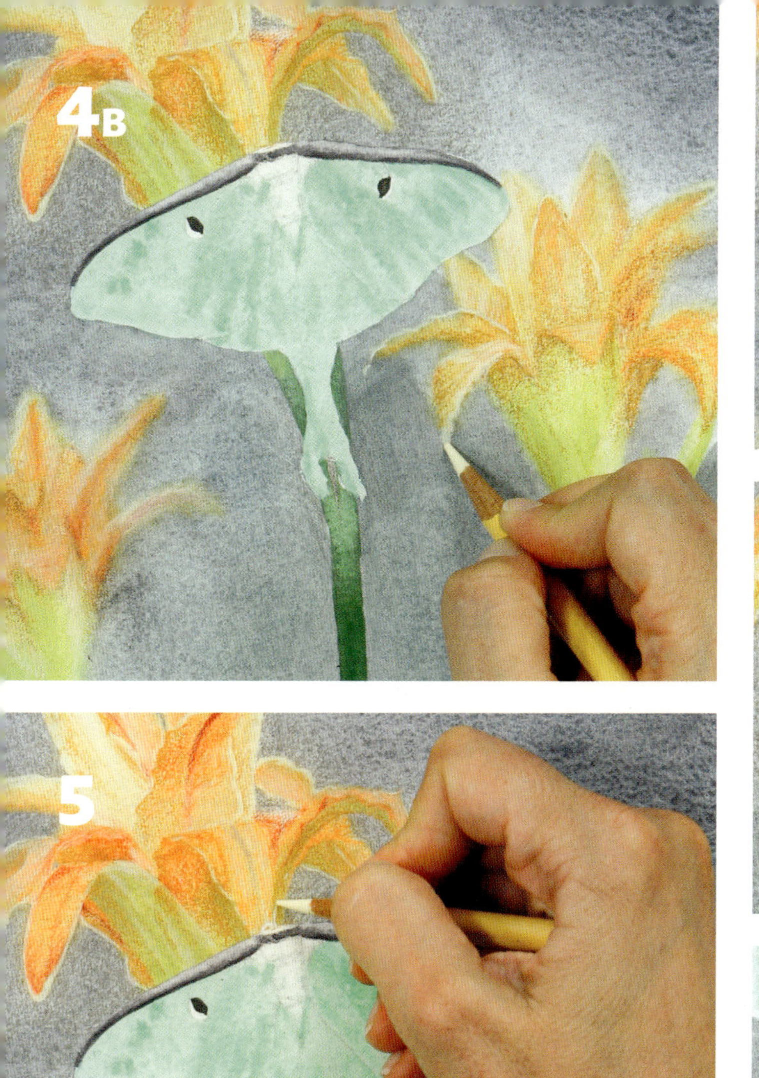

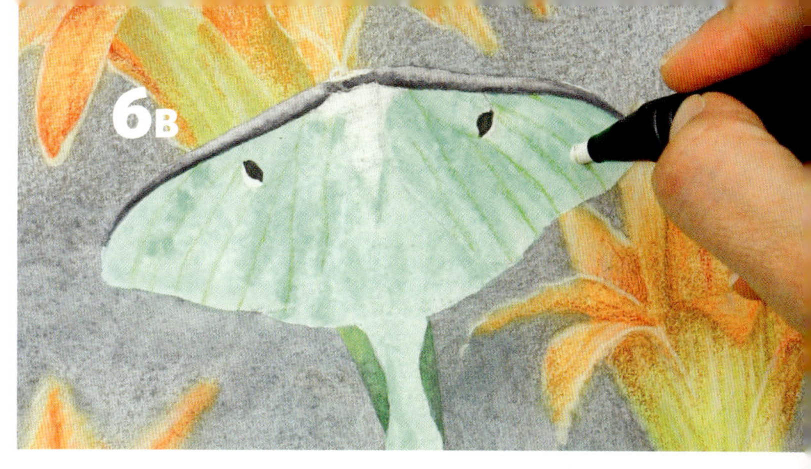

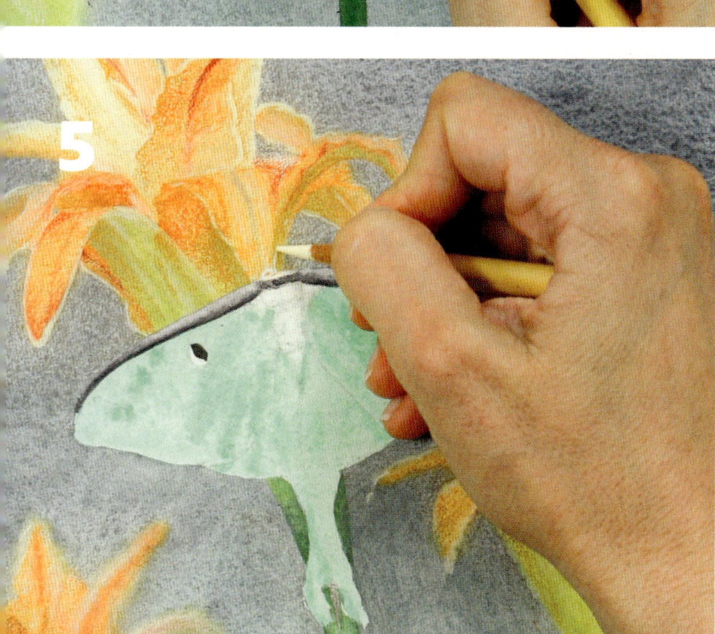

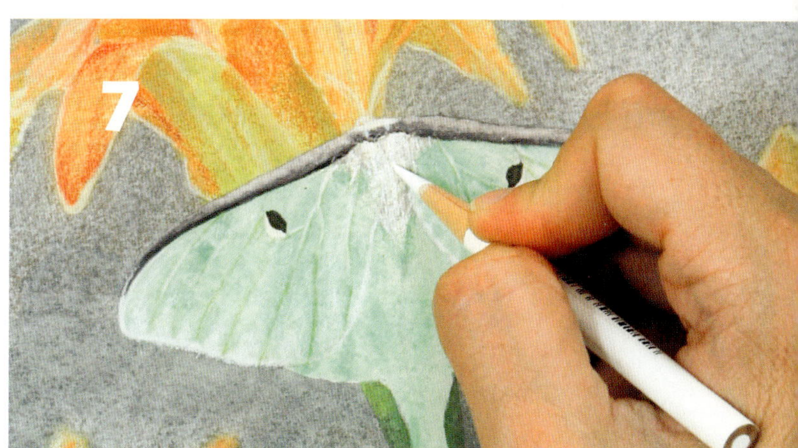

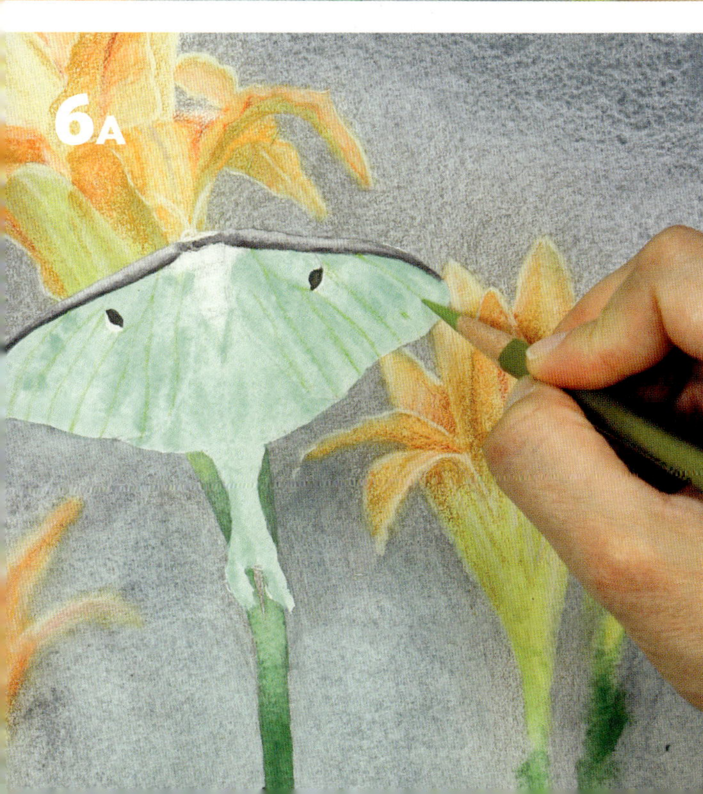

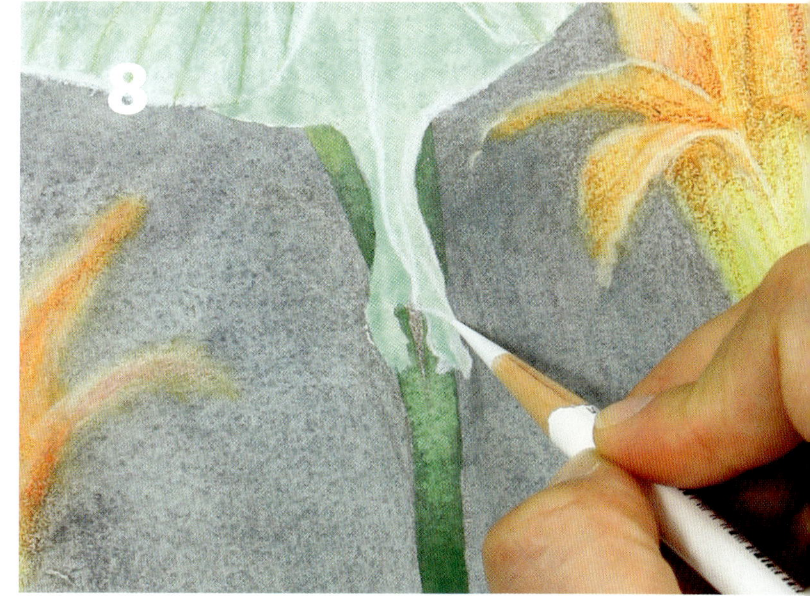

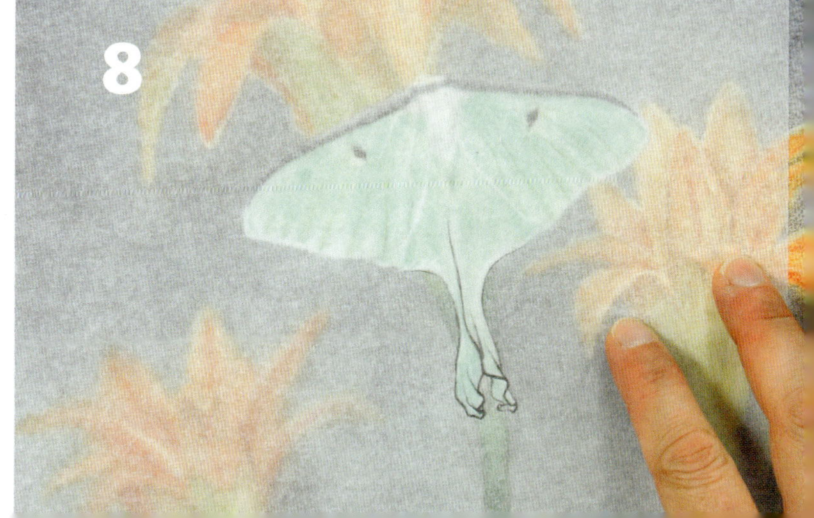

curves along the edge and a highlighted line that starts at the top of each curve and points toward the center of the tail.

This is the point when I noticed that the left hindwing tail needed to be extended. To resolve this, I erased all of the colored pencil in the immediate area, drew the correct shape using an HB pencil, and mixed a small batch of paint that matched the tail color. After the paint had dried, I simply picked up where I had left off and continued the process.

Even though you didn't need to make this repair on your own illustration, I encourage you to set your piece aside for a moment and challenge yourself to create a paint mixture that accurately matches the wing color. Allow a tiny amount of this new paint mixture to dry along the edge of a paper swatch and compare it to your artwork. Simply see how closely you can get to re-creating the original mixture. Since acrylic paint can appear slightly differently when dry, practicing color matching now can make future repairs a bit easier. (Have a paper towel and wet paintbrush nearby just in case paint accidentally gets onto the illustration.)

9 Move to the leading edge of the forewing. Use the black raspberry pencil to define the line along the shadow side, being sure to keep the gradation smooth. Add the "arms" that connect to the eye spots. Lighten the highlight, if needed, although you should keep it soft so that it does not begin to appear shiny. In addition to these details, I also like to add a very thin gray line, ever so slightly darker than the background, right along the edge on the highlighted side to suggest that the form is cylindrical.

10 Now add the colorful details to the eye spots. Since it is difficult to add all of the colors, even with the sharpest pencil, start with the predominant ones. On the forewing, I used the white pencil over the dark paint in the center, the sunburst yellow pencil to create the

line in the dark section, and the black raspberry pencil over the white pencil on the lower edge. You might want to test the black raspberry pencil on scrap paper before you begin—it can easily create an overpowering pink that does not erase well. Either way, work lightly and add color very carefully. Work on both eye spots simultaneously. Finally, you can clean up the upper portion of the eye spots with the black and the bottom area using the white pencil if needed.

Move to the eye spots on the hindwings. Since these are a secondary detail and in the shadow of the forewings, keep the colors subdued so that the edge and eye spots on the forewings remain more prominent. Select the colored pencils you would like to use. On my illustration, I used the goldenrod pencil to fill in the rings, darkened them slightly using the black pencil, and then drew a thin ring with the crimson lake pencil. Use the white pencil to reinforce the edge on the forewing above the spot. If the spots become too dominant, you can either slightly erase them or lightly and carefully layer them with white pencil.

11 Make any final touches on the moth. If you choose to darken the area where the wings overlap or deepen the shadow cast by the forewings, consider using the lime peel pencil instead of a neutral color. Also, notice how the left hindwing eye spot can be seen through the forewing. For this area of the illusion to be a success, apply the 50% French gray pencil very lightly, blend it into the surroundings slightly, and separate it from the lower wing with a pure white edge. On my illustration, I also lined the head and the interior edge of the antennae with an almost indiscernible dark line, just to help them stand out against the flower.

12 To refine the stems, start on the center stalk using the chocolate, cream, and black pencils for the browner areas and a variety of green pencils elsewhere. When you work

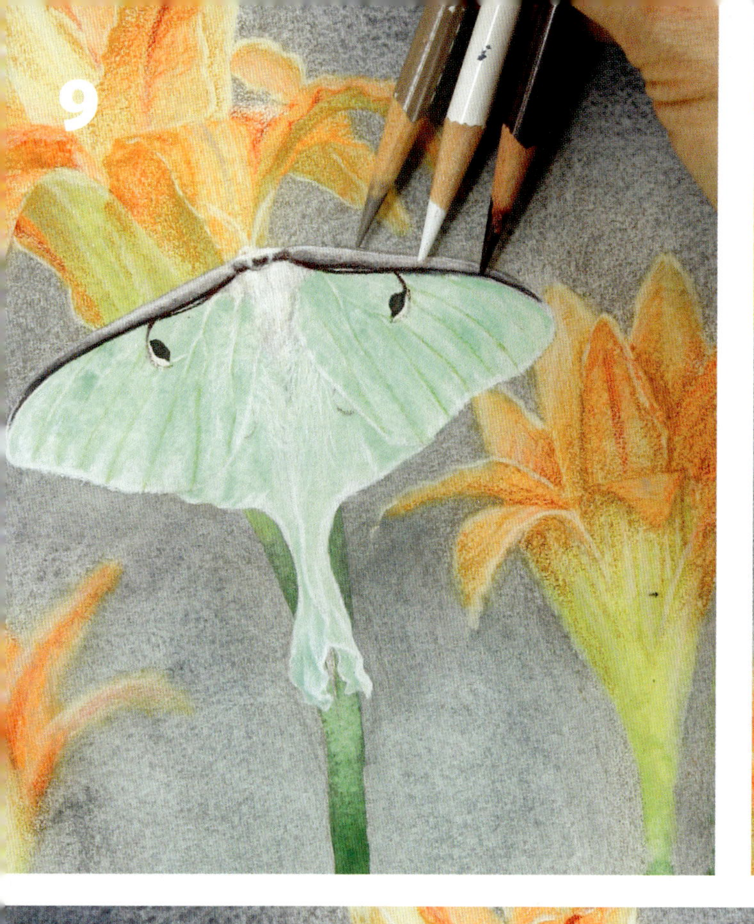

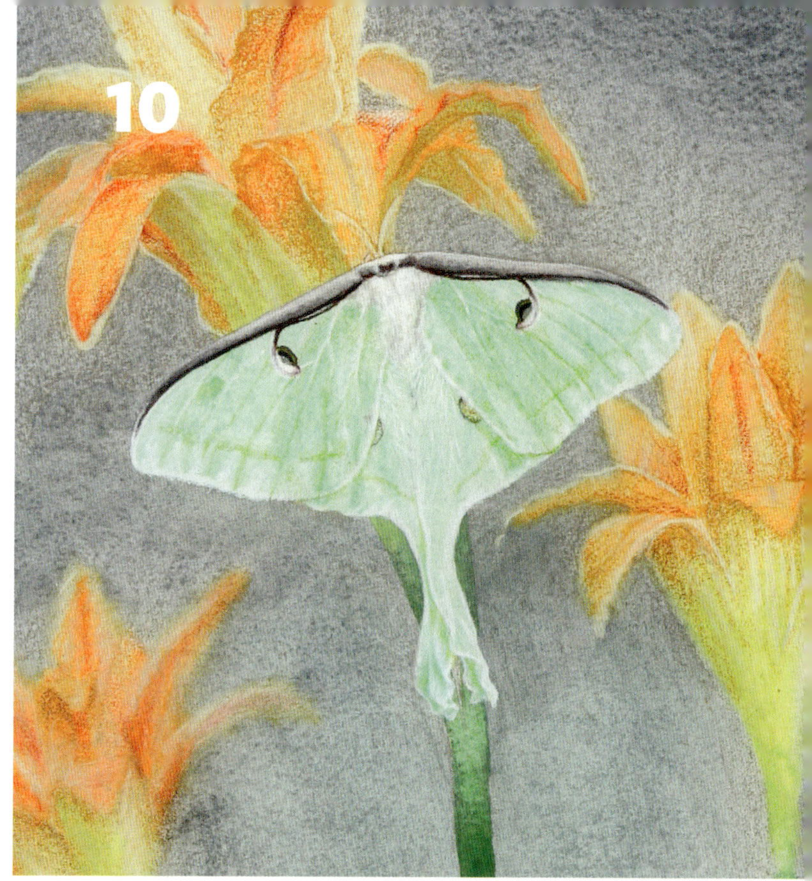

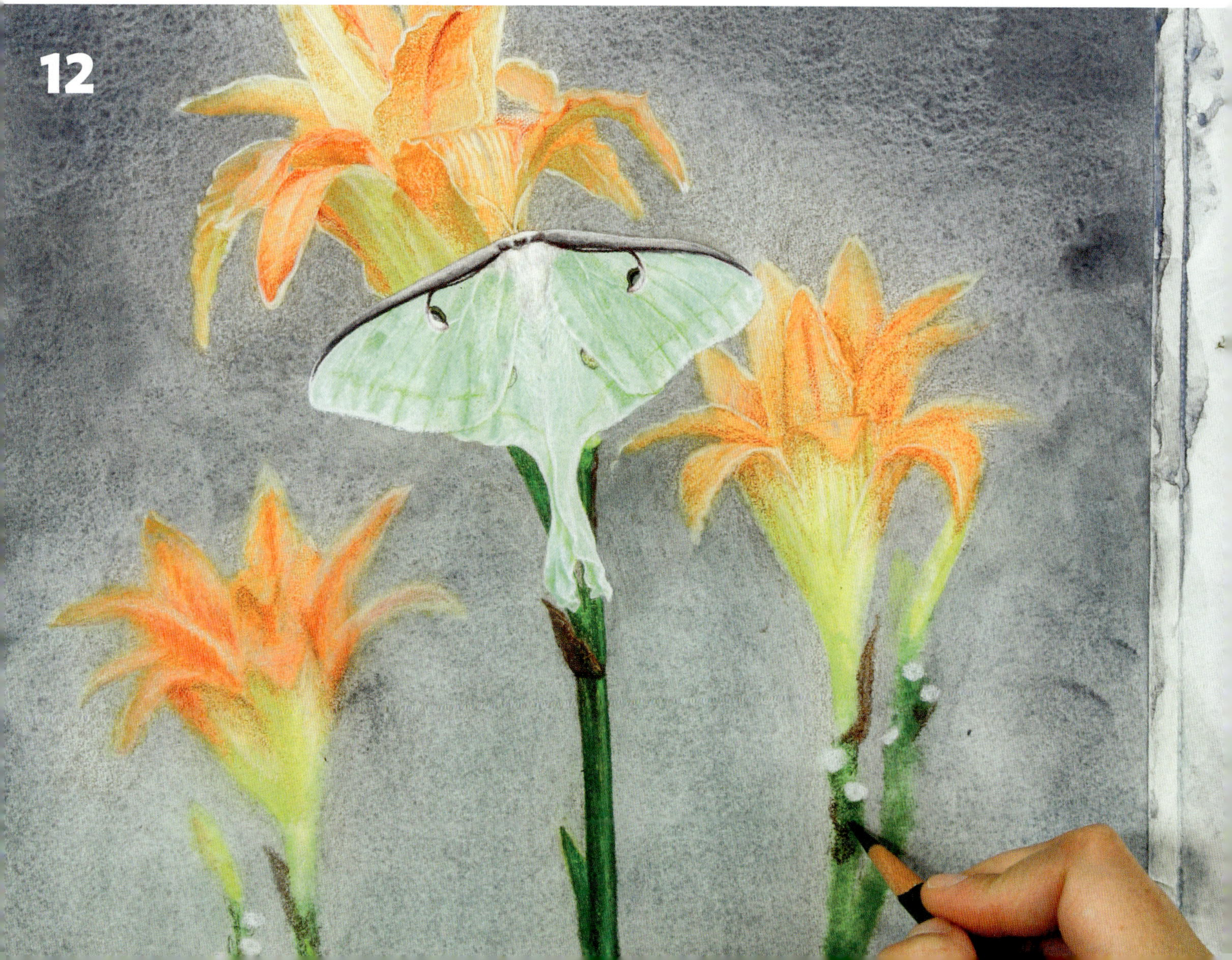

on the edge of each stem, be sure the level of
blur matches the flower it supports. You may find
it helpful to hold the selection of pencils in your
nondominant hand so that you can quickly rotate
between them.

Then refine the buds and, if you haven't already,
add the bud that the moth is holding on to. You
will likely need to enhance the shadows, highlights,
and level of detail on the flowers for the entire
composition to appear unified. You can also add
the moth's legs using the black raspberry and black
pencils.

13 To finish this piece, revisit the background and make any final touch-ups.
Admire your many accomplishments at each
stage of this project and how you can now achieve
an exemplary level of detail, subtlety, and accuracy.

This piece signifies the midway point of this book.
Think back to when you started and recount each
of the projects that you have worked on. Consider
the many challenges that you've worked through
and the skills you've gained. This expanded artistic
foundation will support your practice through the
remaining chapters.

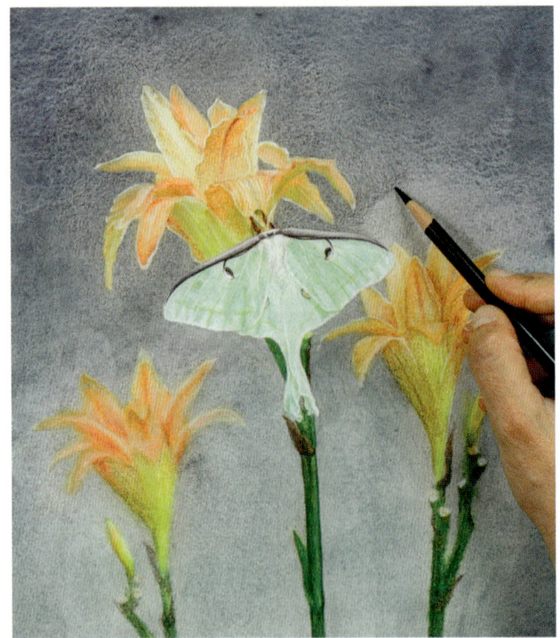

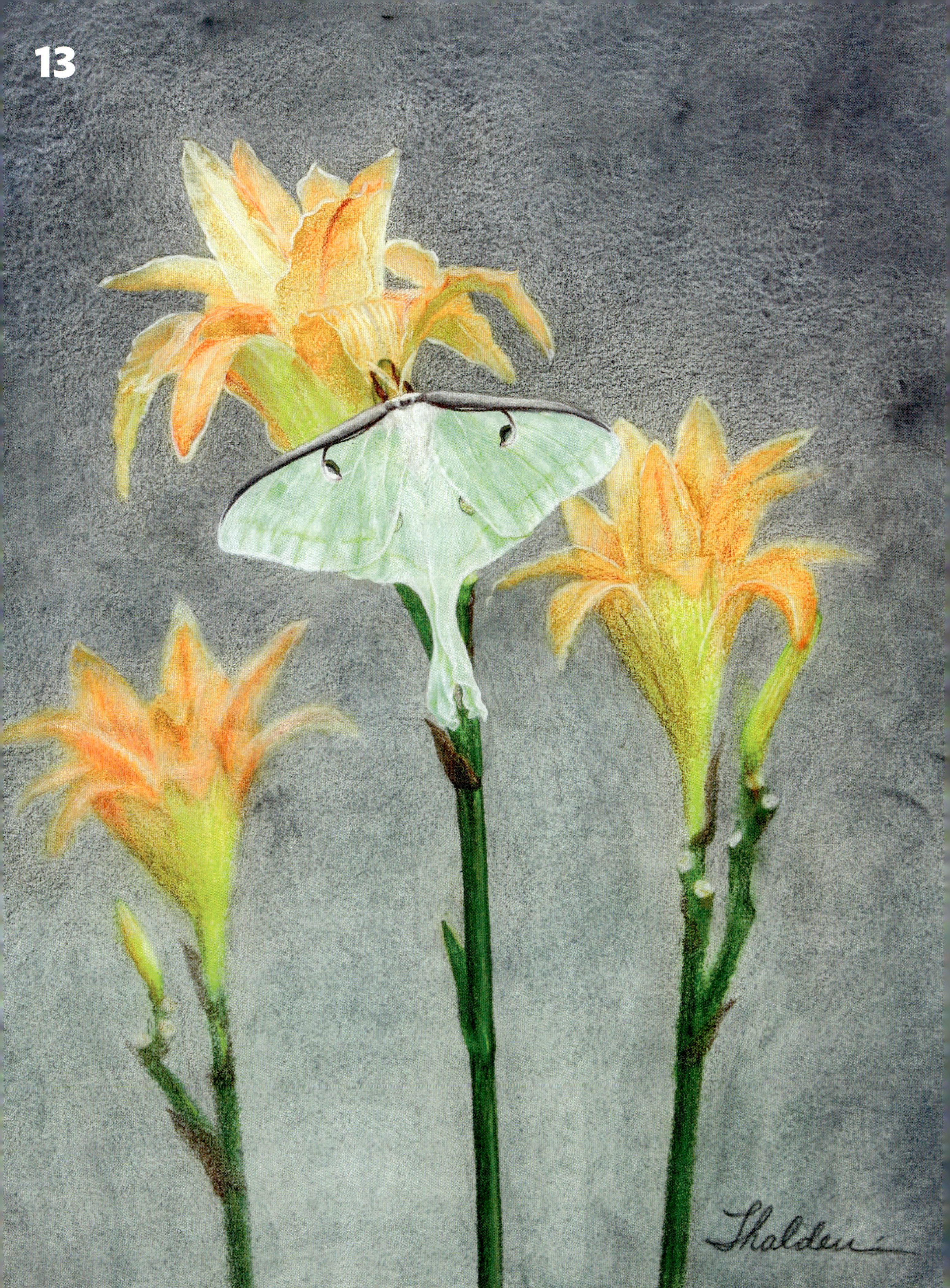
Shalden

NATURE BREAK, TECHNIQUE

COLOR INTERACTION

The hue and value of a subject can appear differently depending on the quality of surrounding colors. When you take this into account, you can make subtle and intentional adjustments to both emphasize the subject and increase the overall continuity of the composition. This Nature Break is devoted to exploring color interaction.

LOCATION: Set up an indoor workspace so that both the subject and work surface have consistent lighting.

MATERIALS: Sketchbook, pencil, colorful media of your choice, and selection of paper including black, white, gray, and a couple of solid hues. Select a subject that has a mid-tone value, particularly along its edges, and that is small enough to draw multiple times in one sitting.

OBSERVATIONS: Before you begin, take a moment to observe your subject. Pick it up, rotate it, and turn it over to simply notice the hue, value, and intensity of the colors.

PRACTICE: Place either the white or black paper under your subject and illustrate both the subject and a portion of the background in your sketchbook. When you have finished, switch the paper underneath your subject and make another drawing. Don't assume that you will use the same colors or values in your new drawing, but simply replicate what you see. Next, place a gray or colored paper under your subject and repeat the exercise. You can also change to a subject that has a vastly different value or color.

REFLECTION: Compare your drawings. In your sketchbook, describe how the value, hue, and intensity of the background affects the appearance of the subject in each. If some areas seem invisible against one background, consider how you could differentiate the subject. Imagine how this knowledge can help you illustrate a subject in a natural environment that has varying colors and values.

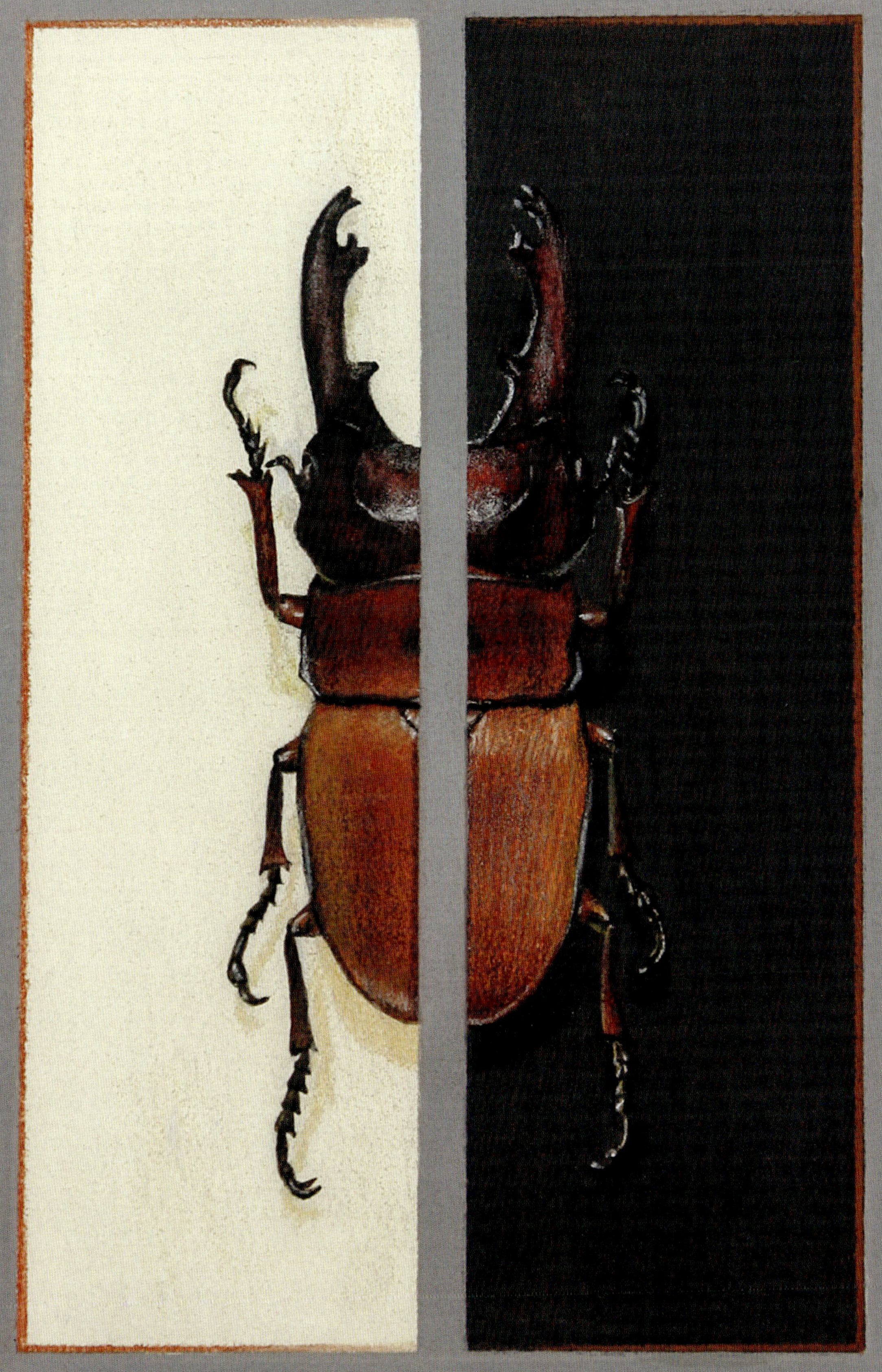

BUFF-TAILED BUMBLEBEE FORAGING

BOMBUS TERRESTRIS

Bumblebees often visit the same patch of flowers. They will even scent mark individual stalks that they find are either most productive or have been depleted of nectar. Their long tongues are perfect for extracting nectar from lavender flowers, a preferred food source. I decided to feature the buff-tailed bumblebee a second time so that you can rely on your knowledge of its anatomy while creating a transition from crisply detailed sections to blurred areas. The simple layout offers ample opportunity to consider the steps needed to create a successful creative process.

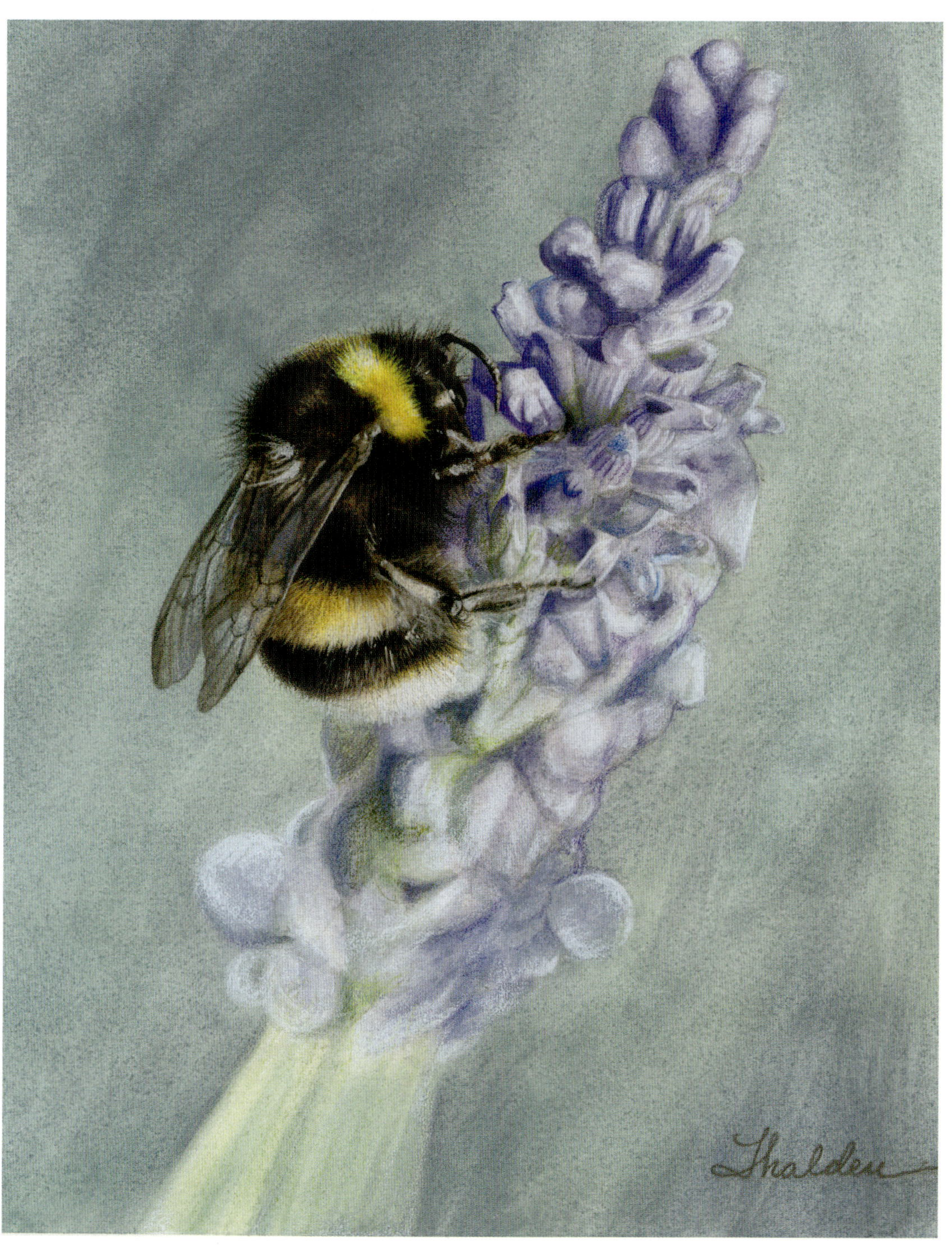

ACRYLIC PAINTS

- [ ] burnt umber
- [ ] cadmium yellow
- [ ] cobalt blue
- [ ] dioxazine purple (optional)
- [ ] Mars black
- [ ] permanent green light
- [ ] titanium white
- [ ] ultramarine blue
- [ ] yellow oxide

BRUSHES

- [ ] mixing brush
- [ ] wash brush
- [ ] painting brushes
- [ ] masking fluid brush or color shaper

COLORED PENCILS

- [ ] black
- [ ] canary yellow
- [ ] Caribbean Sea
- [ ] cerulean blue
- [ ] cream
- [ ] French gray (your choice)
- [ ] goldenrod
- [ ] imperial violet
- [ ] jasmine
- [ ] light umber
- [ ] lime peel
- [ ] moss green
- [ ] seashell pink
- [ ] sepia
- [ ] sunburst yellow
- [ ] violet
- [ ] white

DRAWING

1 Draw a simple grid consisting of two intersecting lines on both the page and a piece of tracing paper that has been secured at the top of the reference image. Next, draw the diagonal line that represents the midline of the botanical. Use the combination of the grid and the midline to place your gesture, but keep your lines loose, quick, and simple. Then test possible units of measure on the reference image.

2 A First, establish the location of the wings. Measure from the edge of the right wing (near the base, on the midsection, and at the tip) to the diagonal on the reference image. Once these marks are on your page, determine the width and pull the angles from the reference image.

B Mark the overall length and width of the bee in relationship to the structural lines. Unless the form intersects with a grid line, measure from the diagonal. Then measure details such as the length of the leg and the location of the stripes. You can now create the outline for the bee—or if you would rather, you can add a few basic measurements to the flower stalk first. When you add the veins to the wings, keep in mind that the anatomy will be parallel, even though the angle on each one will reveal a slightly different section of the wing.

3 To work on the flower stalk, start close to the bee and work upward. Return to the middle and complete the lower section. Continue to use the unit of measure, if you need to. When your drawing is complete, remove the structural lines and prepare for painting.

PAINTING

1 Look at the background that the photographer achieved in the reference image. Consider how you would like the background to appear in your illustration.

Notice how the similar colors and blurred quality of the pattern successfully enhance the focus on both the botanical and the bee, create subtle interest in the negative space, and hint at other lavender stalks. In addition, the dark areas near the top left and bottom right establish a diagonal that brings balance to the strong line created by the subject. These aspects of the photograph would be helpful to either retain or enhance.

Then look at the very light area located near the center along the right side of the composition. If you cover this area with your hand, you may notice how this isolated light area both creates an imbalance in the background and de-emphasizes the subject. To resolve this issue in your illustration, consider either darkening this area to match the surroundings or lightening other areas in the background. Visualize different options and select one that you think will create the most balance, movement, and emphasis in the composition. I chose to both keep the light area on the right and lighten the mid- to lower section on the left, thereby creating an additional diagonal in the composition. I also created subtle patterns in the dark corners, which added movement and abstraction to the background.

While this approach was my preference for this particular illustration, another time I might have chosen to emphasize both depth and realism by enhancing the suggestion of the other lavender stalks in the composition instead.

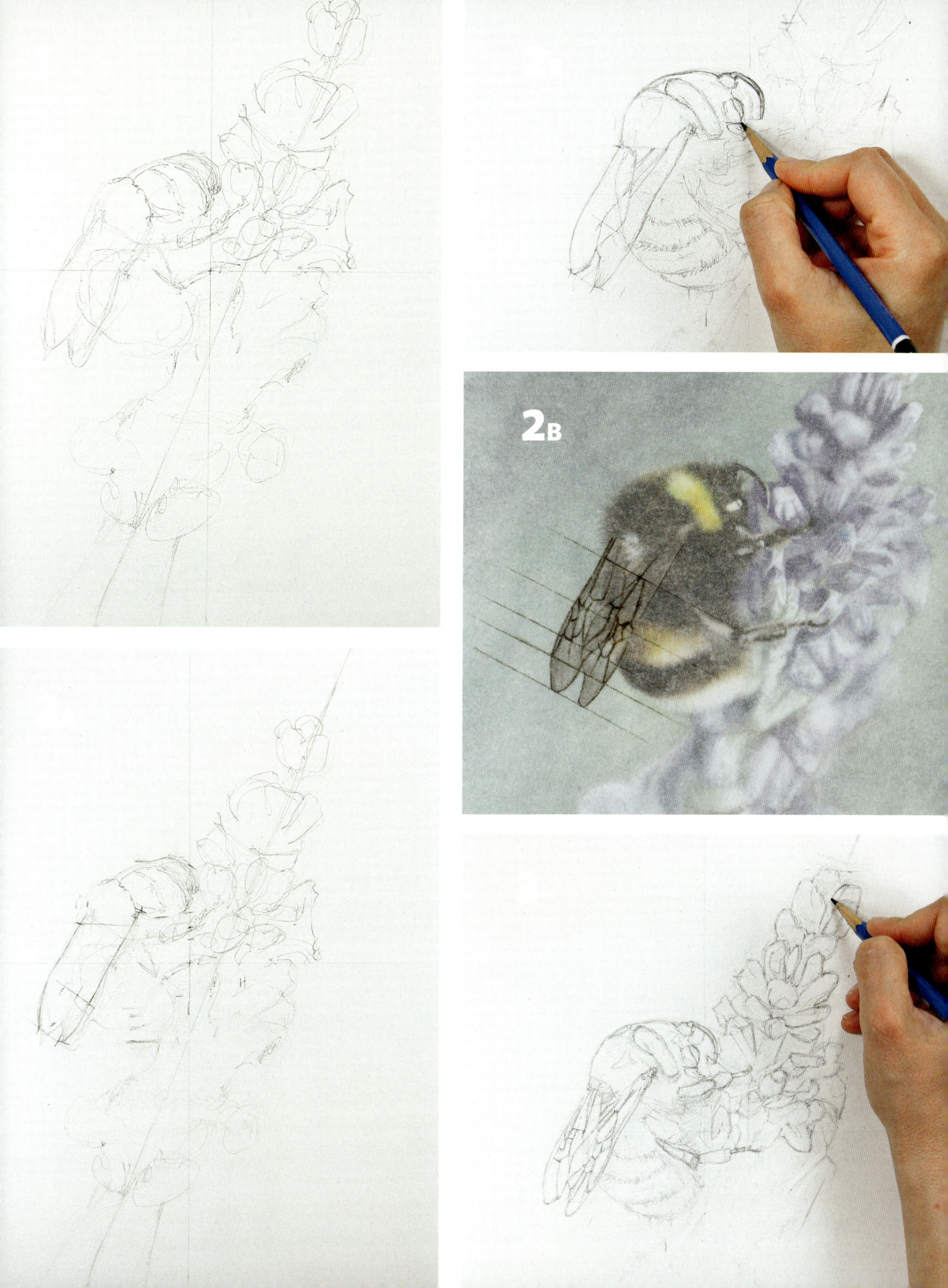

2в

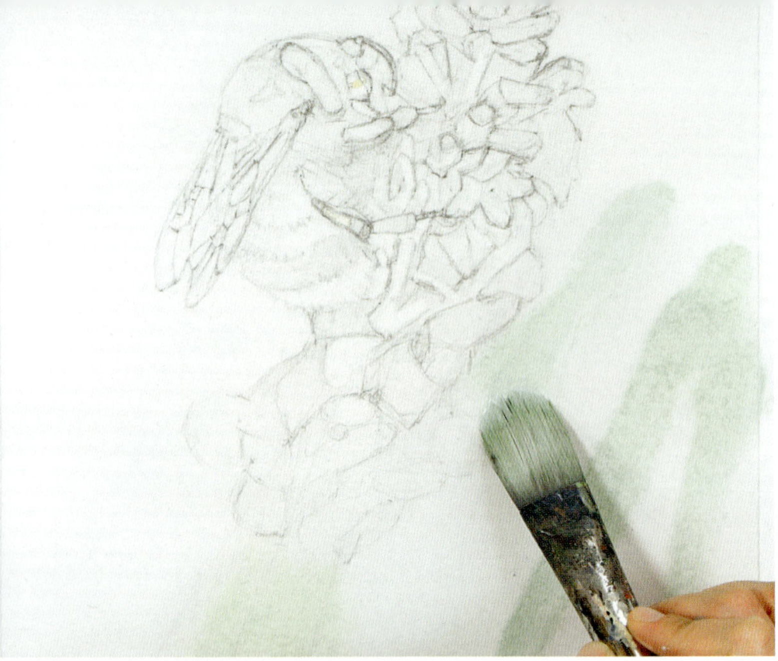

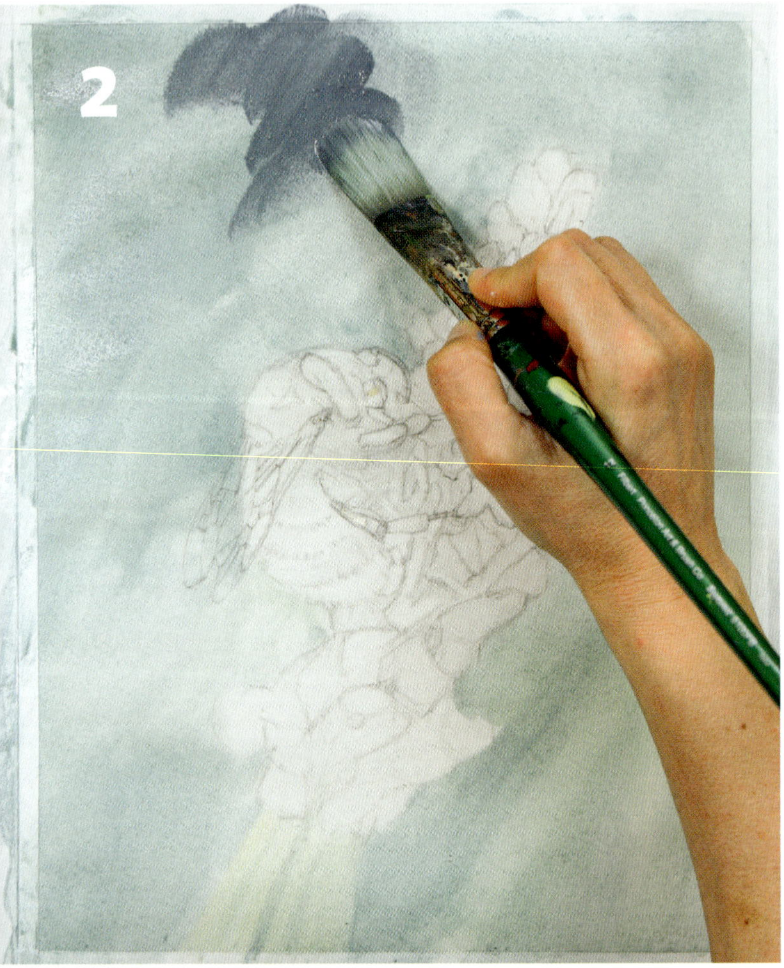

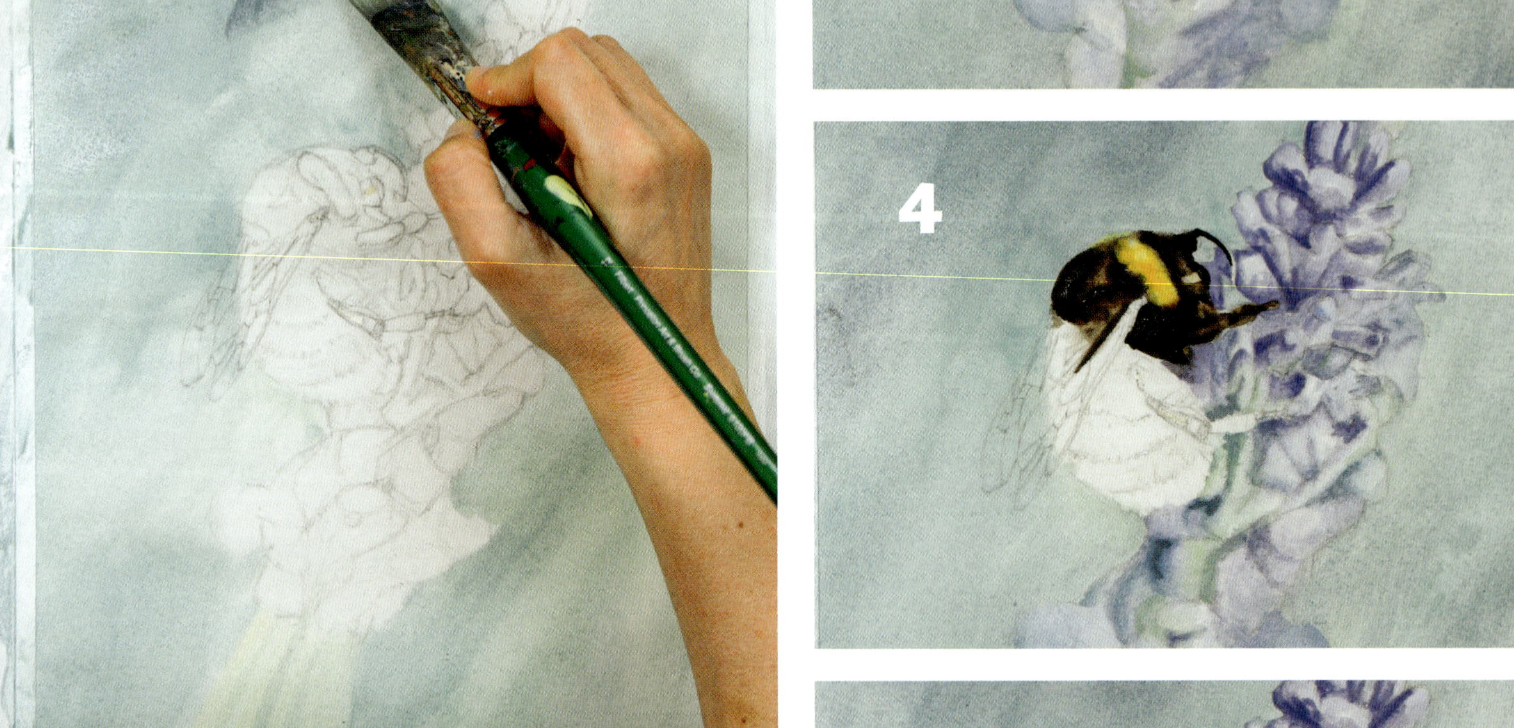

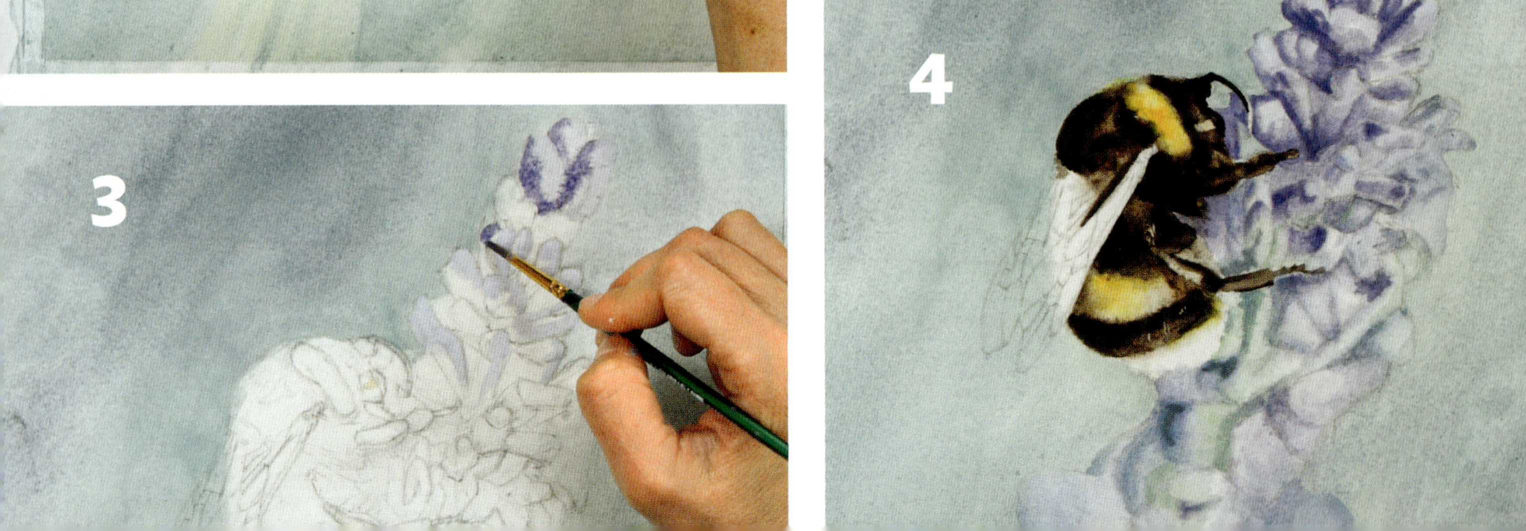

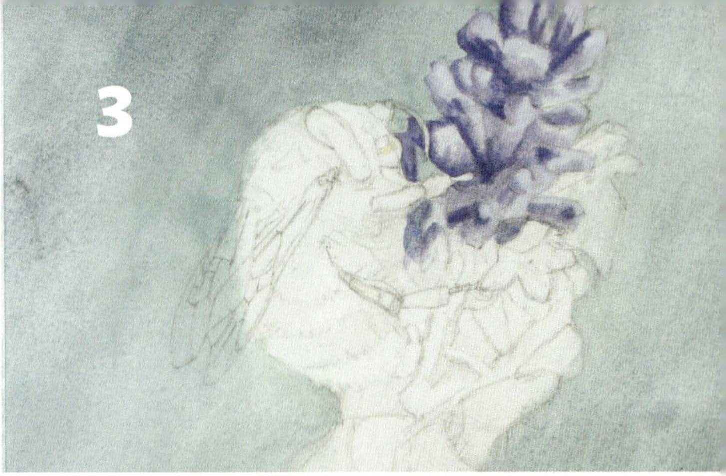

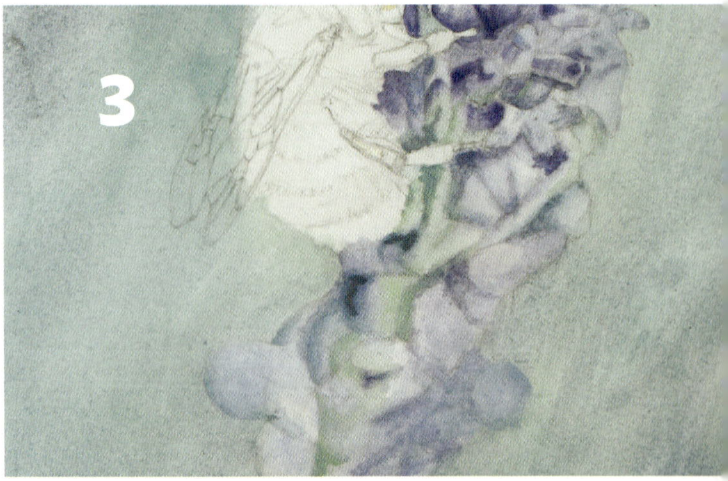

2 If you plan to use masking fluid to create the bright highlights on the bee, apply it now. Mix a base color for the background, then divide it into sections and create a couple of color variations. You can also mix the flower stalk colors at this time as well. Apply the paint mixture to the flower stalks first along with the other lighter colors in the background. You will also need some of the green you mixed for the stem to place among the flowers.

Begin painting, including the small island beneath the antennae and the portion of the bee's wings that overlap the background. After applying the last color, you can wipe the paintbrush on a paper towel and use the brush dry to help integrate select areas.

3 Mix a base color to use to paint the lavender flowers. Remember to take into consideration the colored pencils you have available. Create variations from the base mixture, including several value options and a very slightly blued hue to paint the petals at the bottom of the flower spike.

As you work down the page, you can paint a group of flowers at the same time as long as the light color is still wet when you apply the darker violet paint mixture on top. When painting the blurred areas of the flower spike, paint with as much care and attention as you would a crisp detail, otherwise the flower can easily become a jumble of random shapes and lose the ability to describe the subject.

4 Move to working on the bee. Before you mix paint, double-check that the masking fluid is still in place. Then mix the yellow and dark brown base colors.

Determine how you are going to paint both the translucency and dark veins on the wings. I painted the lines of the veins first, then added a slightly diluted color to the entire area, leaving the highlight areas lighter.

After you remove the masking fluid, you will instantly see the effect and begin to imagine the completed highlights.

LAYERING WITH COLORED PENCIL

1 Begin by refining the flowers that are in focus and close to the bee. I found that it was most helpful to work with multiple pencils on one flower before I moved on to the next. Your goal for the flowers near the bee should be to define structure and shape with highlights or shadows, to add pattern stripes, and to create smooth transitions from one paint color to another. In the blurred areas, the patterns are less important, if visible at all. Creating a thin layer with the white pencil can help to lighten or blur edges. After the violets are in place, you might want to add the greens and oranges with other pencils.

To maintain the hierarchy of the composition, periodically expand your focus to look at the entire emerging illustration. Know that if you avoid sharp edges and dramatic contrast changes on the flower stalk, you will reiterate the focus on the bee.

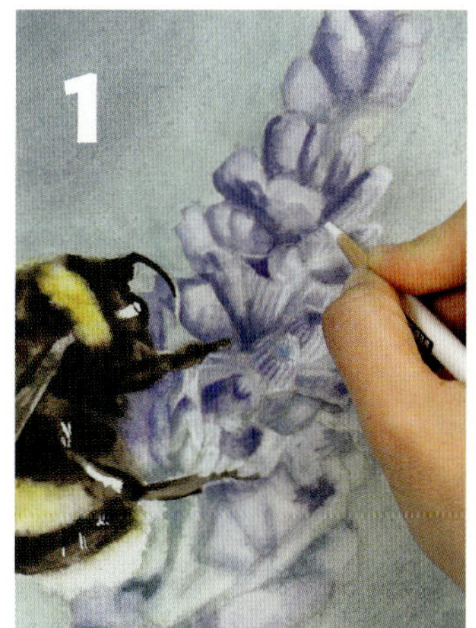
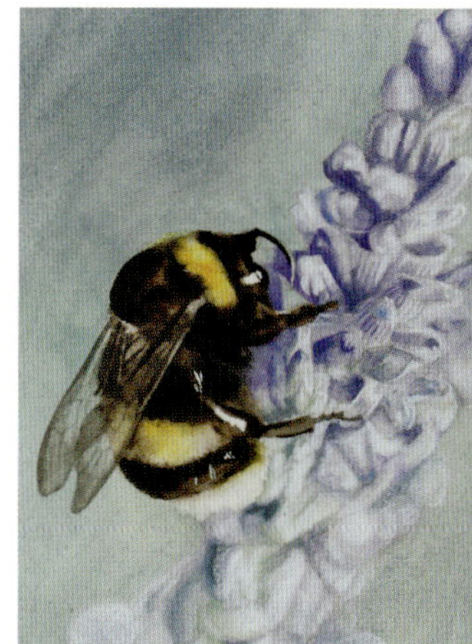

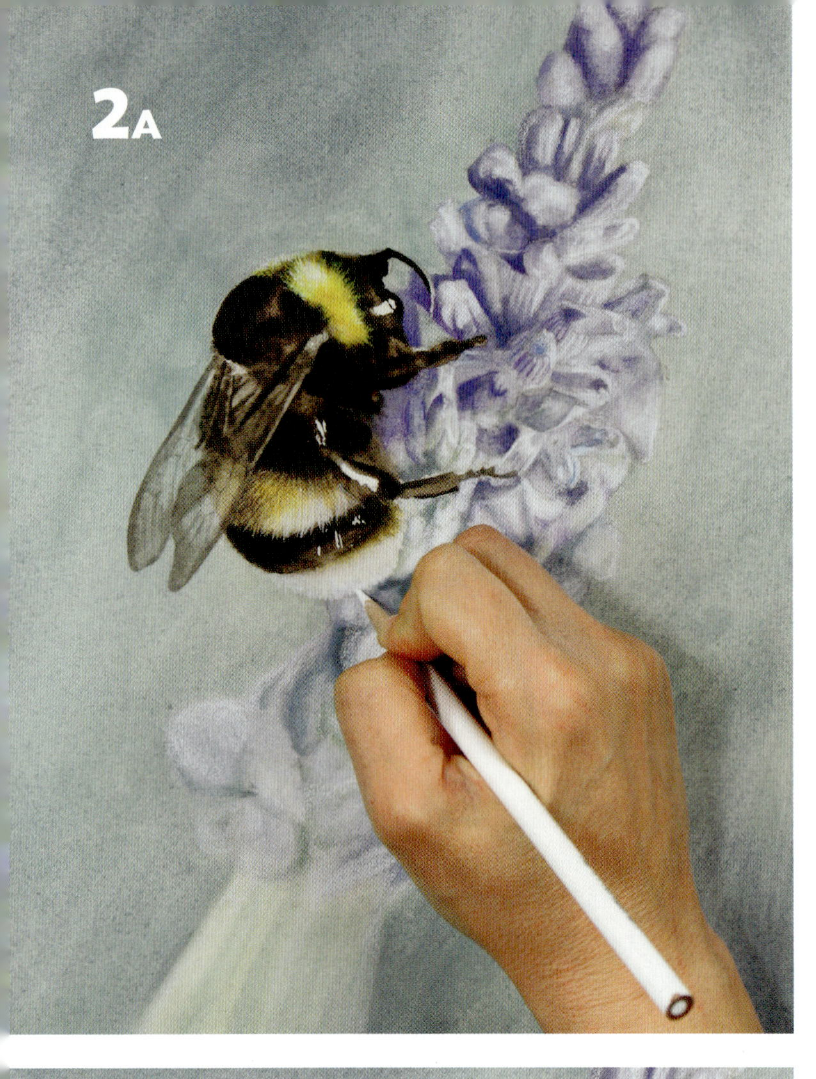

2A

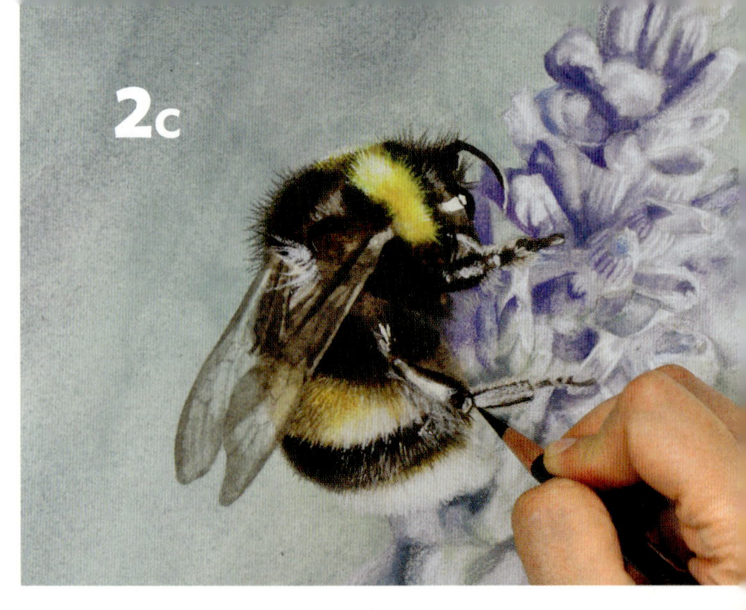

2C

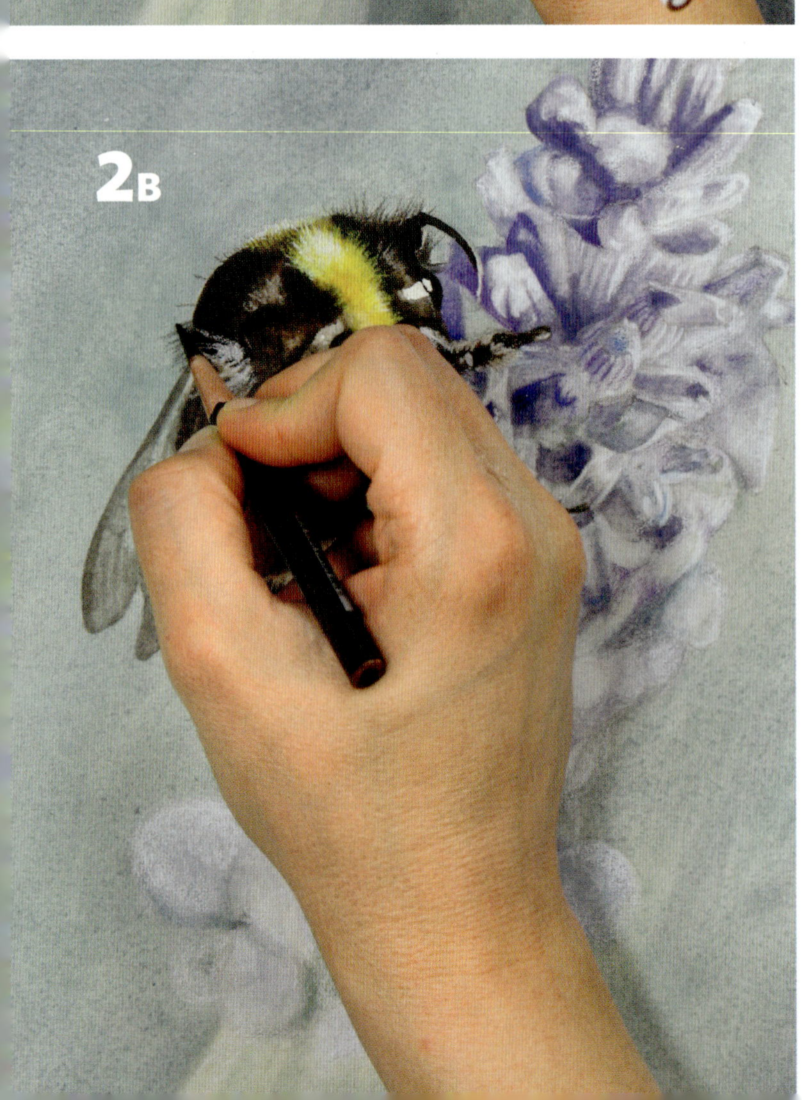

2B

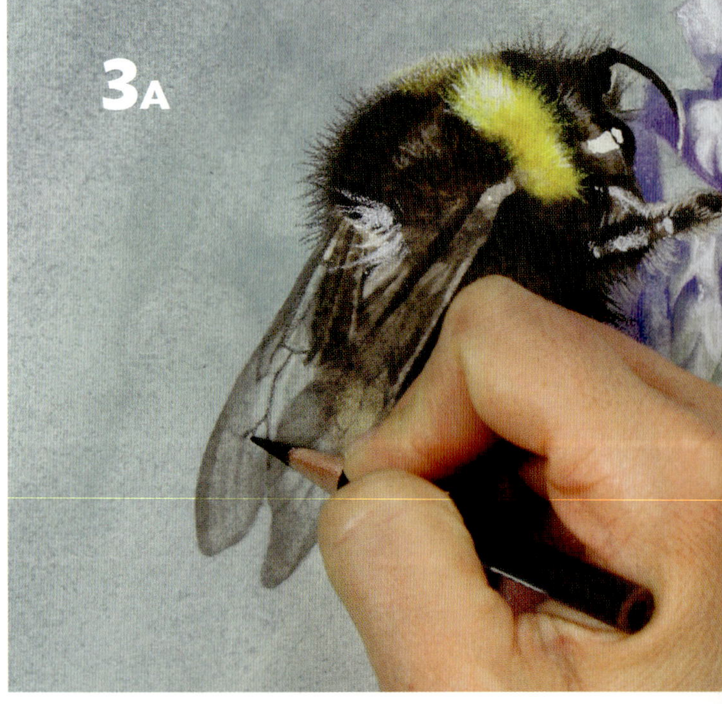

3A

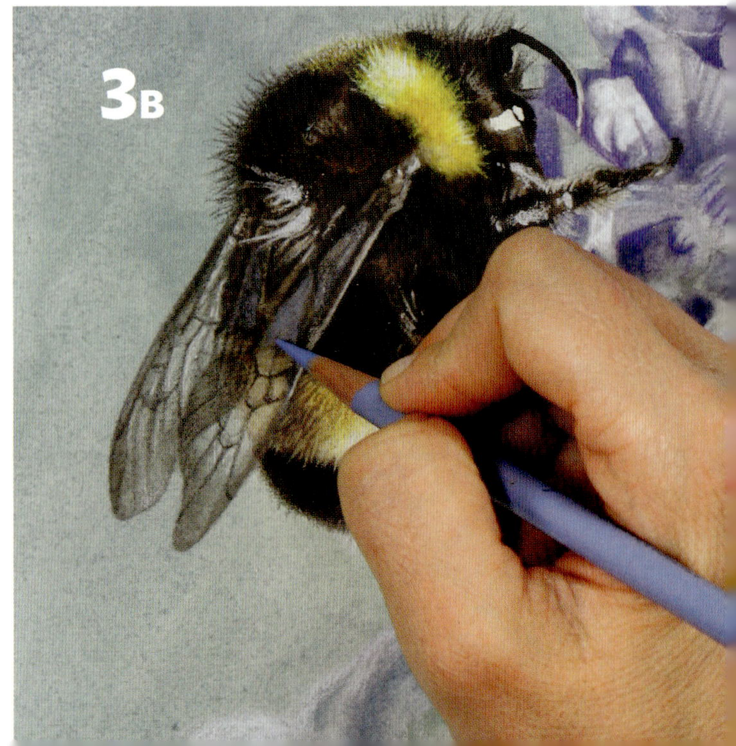

3B

2 **A** Move to the bee and add fuzzy details to the yellow and white stripes. Work with the lightest colors first. Gradually shift to using medium- and dark-valued colors.

B In the areas where the hairs are blurred, use lighter pressure and allow the colors to blend together more. Instead of using a flicking motion with your pencil, experiment with a light scrubbing motion perpendicular to the outline to create a slight haze upon which you can add more detail.

If you have any problem adding the hairs of the bee on top of the flower because of the colored pencil already in place, feel free to erase just enough space to add them. Then you can replace the flower color so that it can be seen between the hairs. When you move onto the dark stripes, continue to work from light to dark.

C Carefully blend in the hairs that were created with the masking fluid so that they look more like highlighted hairs than bright white islands. Now refine the legs, particularly the back leg that has the large highlight. If you cover the highlights with the seashell pink pencil, you can de-emphasize them, direct more focus to the head and wings of the bee, and add warmth to the color of the legs. You can also use a dark-colored pencil to adjust the width of these highlights and add fur around the edges of the legs. To soften individual hairs, use a light circular pattern at the base and then lightly erase the tips. If those areas need further adjustment, you can return to using the lighter colors or other French gray pencils. To adjust the width of the lighter stripes, use the sepia pencil to widen the darker areas slightly. Although you might want to use the black pencil to finish these areas, I recommend that you first work on the wings, antennae, and eyes to complete them to the level of the rest of the bee.

3 **A** Since there are no bright highlights on the wings, I added the veins first, then filled in the light areas using the white pencil.

B If you'd like, you can use a blue pencil to very lightly graze the wings to suggest the clear sky above the subject. Be sure that the blue pencil you use is of a similar value to the surrounding area. If it is too light, dark, opaque, or intense, it will start to look like the wing color instead of a reflection on a shiny, clear surface. In my illustration, I sometimes needed to lighten the blue slightly with an underlayer of 10% French gray.

C Switch to using the black pencil to add the final touches to the body and the eye. Use it sparingly and only to deepen the value in select areas or to convey a greater sense of furriness in the darkest sections.

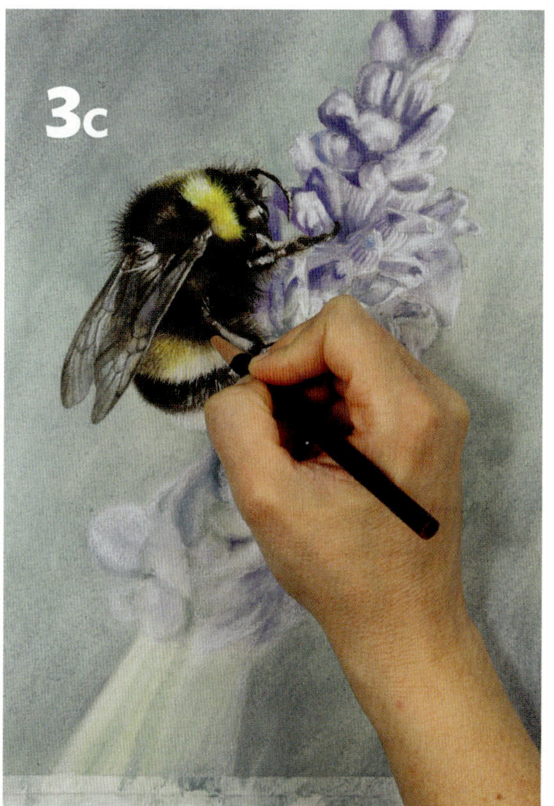

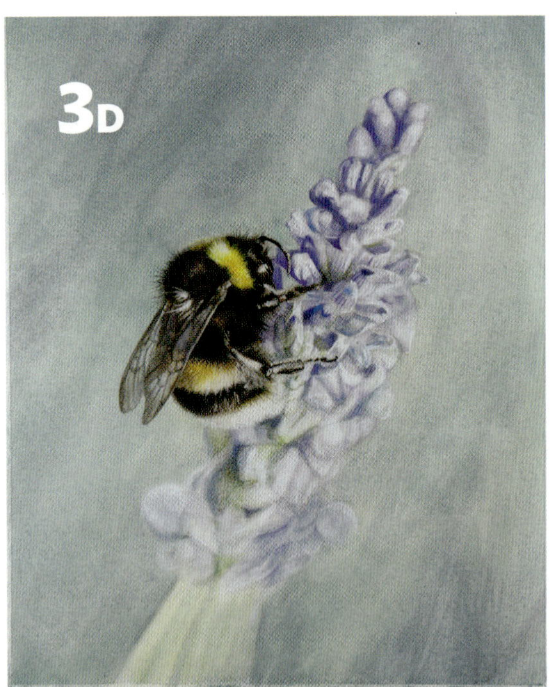

D Make any final adjustments to enhance the flower stalk, background, and bee. In this serene landscape, the dark and colorful bee is a powerful and dramatic focal point. Because of this, both the flowers and stem may need to be enhanced or embellished to create the visual weight needed to support the bee and to encourage interest in other areas of the composition.

When you are finished, celebrate this accomplishment, and admire the piece that you have created.

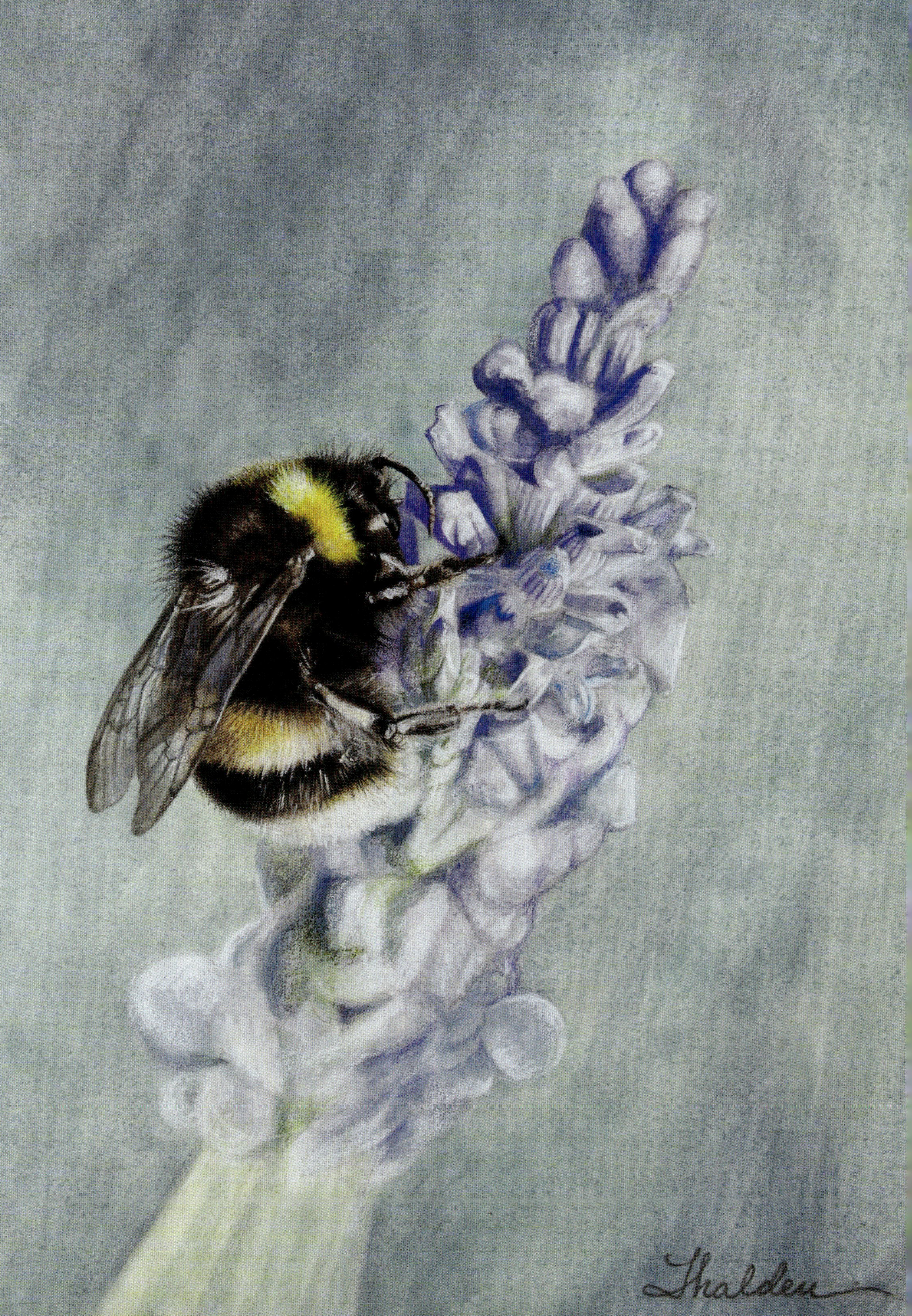

Thalden

● ROTATING SHAPES

Incorporating angled subjects or using foreshortened anatomy in your artwork can lead to spacious and dynamic compositions. If you practice drawing anatomical features in various positions, you can train your eyes to see the shape of the altered outline. The time has come to practice rotating shapes.

LOCATION: Choose a comfortable place to work either indoors or outside.

MATERIALS: Sketchbook, pencil, and a subject that has planes and/or rodlike forms. You might find it most beneficial to use a simple subject, such as a flat leaf.

OBSERVATIONS: Look closely at the subject in front of you. Begin to rotate it slowly and watch the forms change shape and size as they recede or advance.

PRACTICE: Draw a quick gesture of your subject at any angle. Include the outline of each anatomical form, but omit patterns and textures. Fill your page with various angles of the subject. Feel free to use the thumb-and-pencil method to compare the size of forms that are closer to those that are farther away.

REFLECTION: Which drawings appear most dimensional? If any seem to flatten out because the anatomy is distorted, look at the subject again to see if you can determine the cause.

Note: If you look straight down the center of a rodlike feature that is smaller than the distance between your pupils, such as the body of a dragonfly, it can appear as if it is split in two toward the front or the back. This is because each of your eyes will present a different angle that leads to a single point in the distance. When you are drawing, it is best to either position your subject in a different orientation or close one eye when you view the reference.

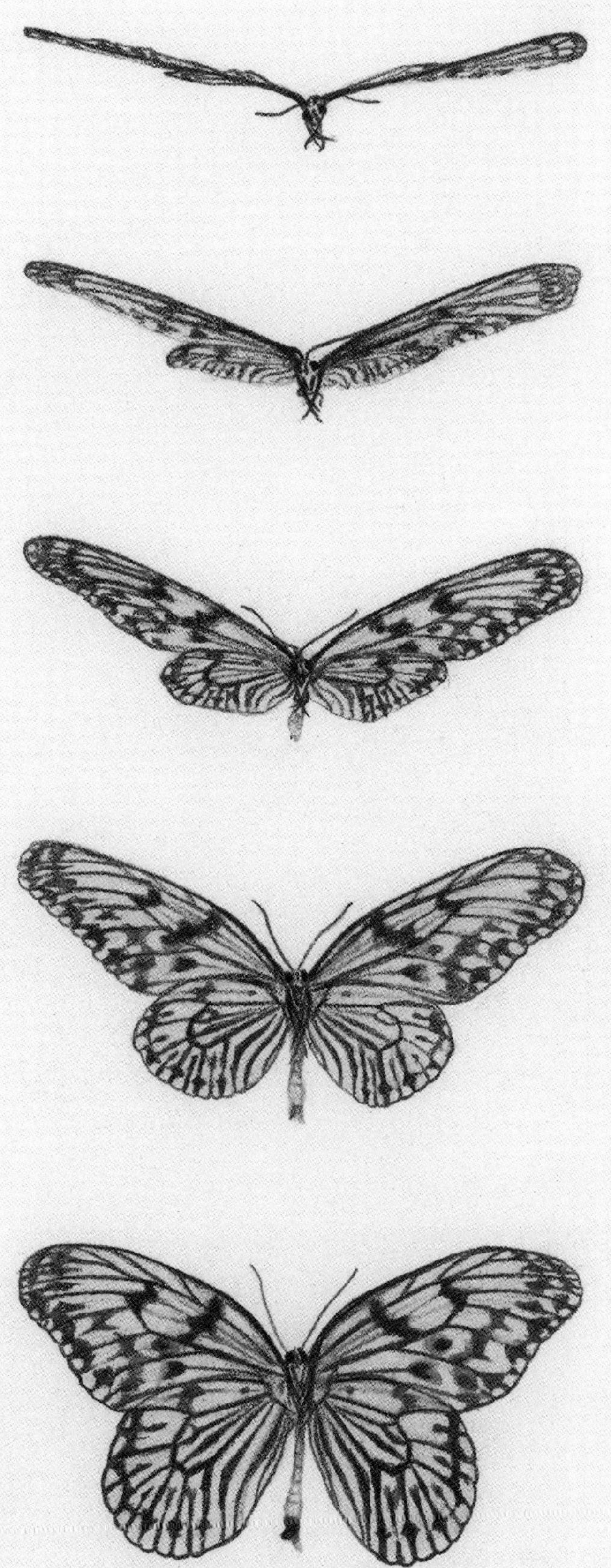

FOREST PIERROT BUTTERFLY

TARAKA HAMADA

The forest pierrot is a gossamer-winged butterfly found in Asia. Instead of surviving on plants, the caterpillars eat smaller insects, such as aphids. This predatory characteristic, in addition to the fluffy or "woolly" legs of the adults, identifies this species as a member of the harvester subfamily. The simplicity of this project's layout creates a powerful composition that will magnify details. In this regard, it will put your technical skills to the test both in application and in correcting errors. You will also learn how to simplify drawing the intricate patterns on the wings. And since the background color is solid with lots of space around the primarily neutral-colored butterflies, this is an opportunity to explore other exciting color options.

 SEE REFERENCE PHOTOS ON PAGE 322

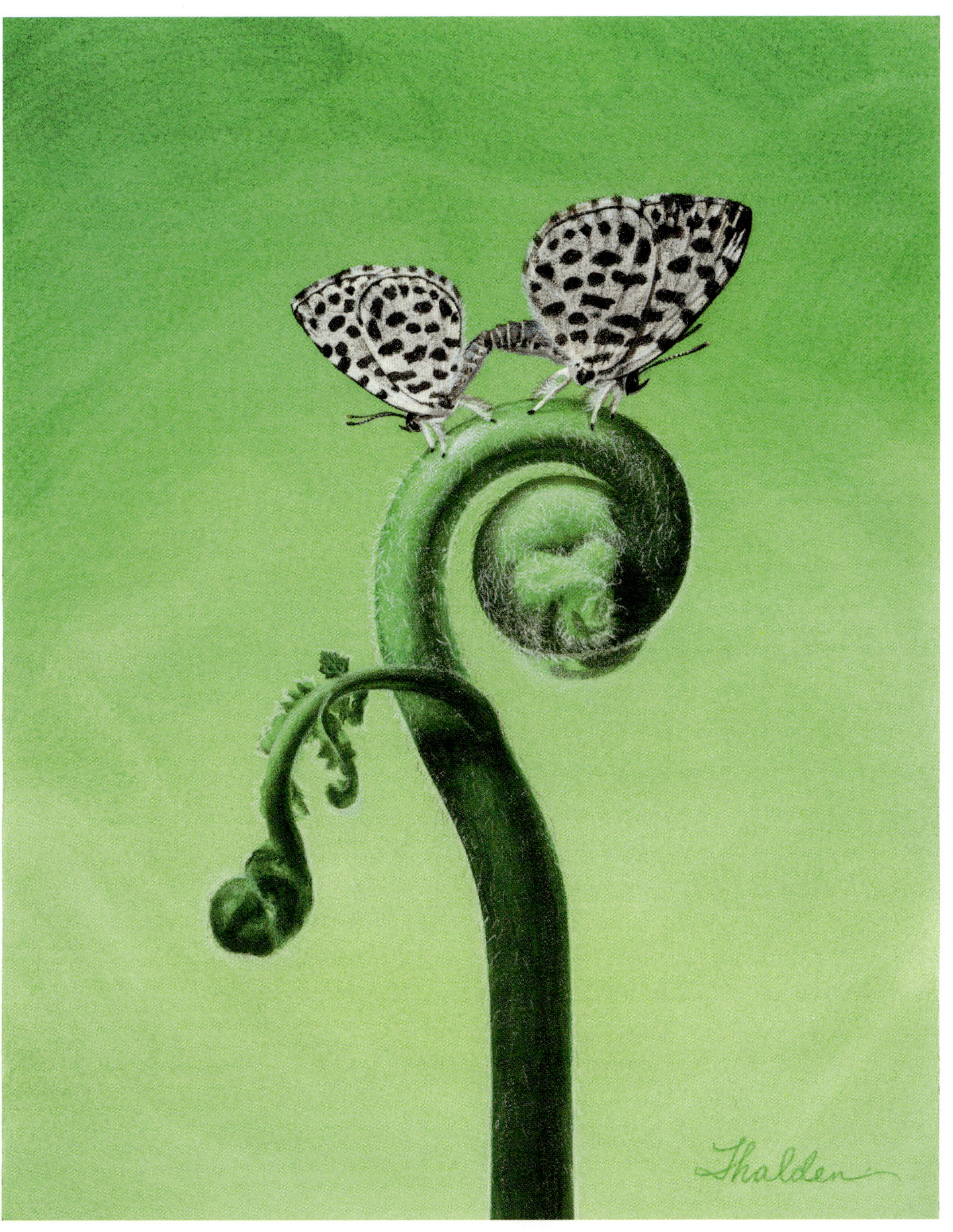

ACRYLIC PAINTS

- ☐ cadmium red
- ☐ cadmium yellow
- ☐ Mars black
- ☐ permanent green light
- ☐ titanium white

BRUSHES

- ☐ mixing brush
- ☐ wash brush
- ☐ painting brushes
- ☐ masking fluid brush or color shaper

COLORED PENCILS

- ☐ apple green
- ☐ black
- ☐ chartreuse
- ☐ chocolate
- ☐ cream
- ☐ electric blue
- ☐ French gray (your choice)
- ☐ goldenrod
- ☐ Prussian green
- ☐ white

PREPARING

In preparation for the Level III projects that will focus on complex techniques instead of sequential steps, try this exercise before you start the illustration: Look at this chapter's reference image and simply think through each step of the art-making process. More specifically, consider the sequence of actions needed to complete each stage of the process, including designing, drawing, painting, and using colored pencils. Although you will be instructed to write notes and identify decisions in future chapters, for now you have only the goal of simply familiarizing yourself with each layer of the illustration. That's it; that's the exercise. When done, read onward and follow the steps below. As you create your illustration, recognize the steps you identified in the exercise, note those you missed, and acknowledge the ones you would have done differently.

DESIGNING

1 If you'd like to make any design changes to the reference image, create them in your sketchbook. Since a change in background color, value, and pattern can influence the layout, you might want to test alternatives on scrap paper first. Follow step 1 of the painting stage for your trial runs, then return here to create your illustration's design.

A When I approached the design stage, my first goal was to create a vertical composition to orient the layout to this book's format. In looking at the vertical design in my sketchbook, I recognized there was too much weight at the top of the composition and a large area of negative space in the lower left. And so I decided to move the unfurling leaflet to a lower spot on the stem.

Anytime you need to relocate a single portion of a composition, you can always draw a fairly refined outline of the section onto tracing paper. Move the tracing paper freely over the gesture drawing to different locations on the page until you find one that's pleasing. Once I determined the placement of the leaflet in my illustration, I questioned its size and considered adding more than one. I marked the corners of the tracing paper and transferred the image to the page.

I decided to replicate the intense green background color of the reference because it offered a chance to use value and detail to both emphasize and differentiate the subject when you have a powerful background in a composition with a monochromatic color scheme.

DRAWING

1 Either test different units of measure and select one to use or create a simple grid on your paper. If you use a grid, be sure that a horizontal grid line passes through at least one wing on both butterflies. After you have drawn a gesture on your page, begin to refine the outline of the fern. To create the smooth curves of this plant, use your wrist, elbow, and shoulder to help create the shape instead of limiting your movements to your finger joints. Be sure to maintain contact with the page using your pinky finger or knuckle so that you have control while you are drawing. You may find that the line is easier to draw if you first rotate the page so that the curve you are working on is arced away from your drawing hand.

2 Before you refine the wings of the butterflies, add the spots. This might seem a bit backward, but establishing the spots will actually help you determine the overall shape of the form. Start on the large butterfly by measuring the length

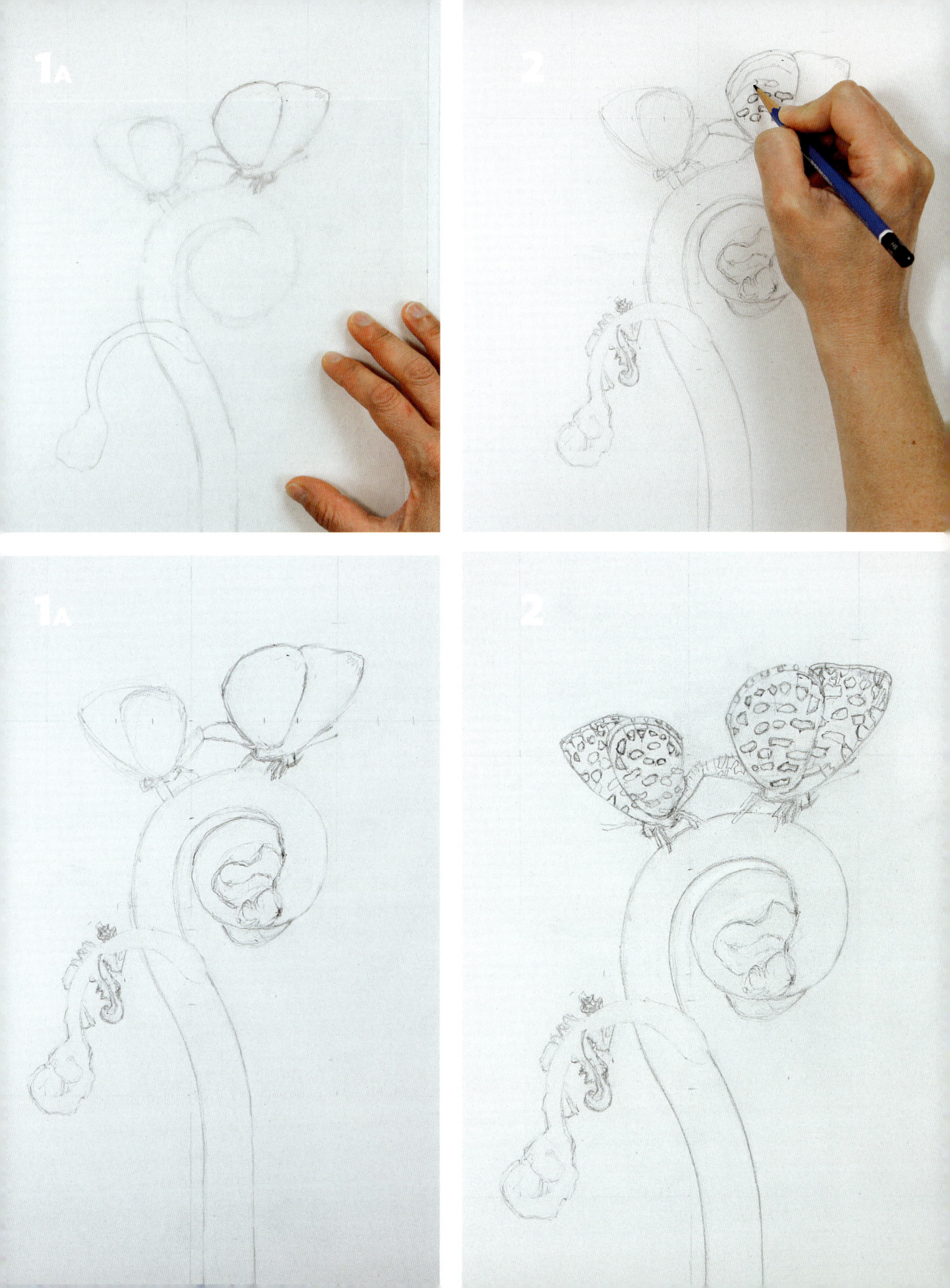

and width of the spots that fall along the grid line to establish the proportions accurately. If you are using a midline, create a horizontal axis line in this area on both the reference image and your page. After these spots are in place, continue working upward. You might find that it is easier to place the individual spots if you imagine the spots grouped in oddly shaped rows and draw a line to represent the center of each row.

PAINTING

1 **A** If you would like to use a different background color than that of the reference image, use your paints to mix a few color options and create paint swatches using small squares of scrap paper. Hover each swatch over the reference image so that it covers the background alongside the subjects. Aligning the swatch with the edge of the fern in front of either butterfly would work well. Next, isolate the new color scheme by looking through the circle created by curling your fingers toward your thumb.

Notice how the hue, value, and intensity of each color influences the characteristics of the fern and butterflies. When you find a color that is to your liking and emphasizes the subjects, mark the swatch and tape it into your sketchbook so that you can match the color when you mix paint for the background.

B Determine which colors to mix in paint and decide if you'll add masking fluid. On my piece, I didn't apply the masking fluid to the back legs of the small butterfly, as I should have, so I added them later using a utility knife (see page 30).

If you are keeping the green background as it appears in the reference image, you can create the gradation either by applying less pigment to the lower section of the page or by creating a slightly varied paint mixture. To create this intense and vibrant background, use permanent green light paint and adjust the hue using blue and yellow. If you need to darken the color, use a miniscule amount of cadmium red. To paint the fern, create a base mixture using the same paint colors and further darken a portion to create the shadows.

If you choose to work with a different background color, mix the amount of paint that you will need and make any variations that you would like to add to your palette. If you cannot decide between two different background colors, consider transferring your drawing to an additional page, painting both backgrounds, and selecting one after the paint has dried. It is going to be great—just go for it!

2 **A** At first glance, many would say that the butterfly wings are white. But if you prepare a light gray paint mixture, you'll be able to create subtle shadows and ripples on the wings. Leave any highlighted areas unpainted so that the color of the paper creates the bright sections.

B Similarly, I suggest mixing dark gray to paint the spots. You might notice that some of the small edge spots on the large butterfly are brownish; instead of mixing this color in paint, you may find it easier to enhance the color later using colored pencil.

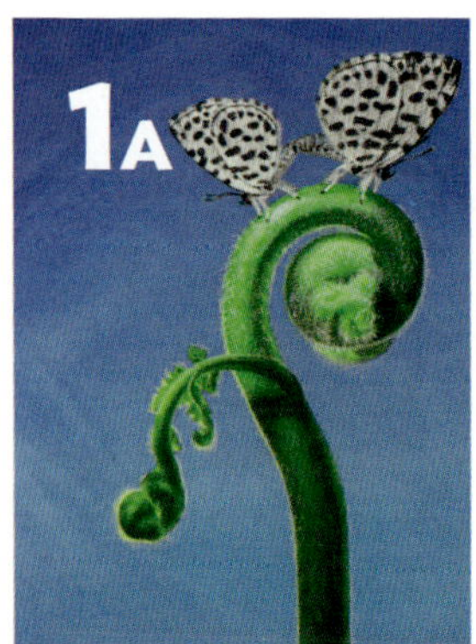
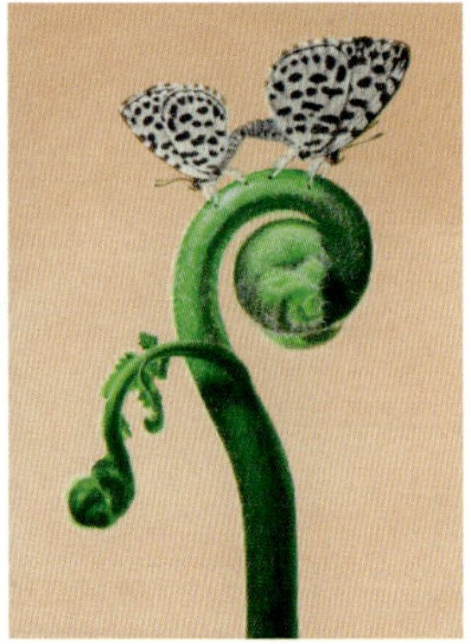

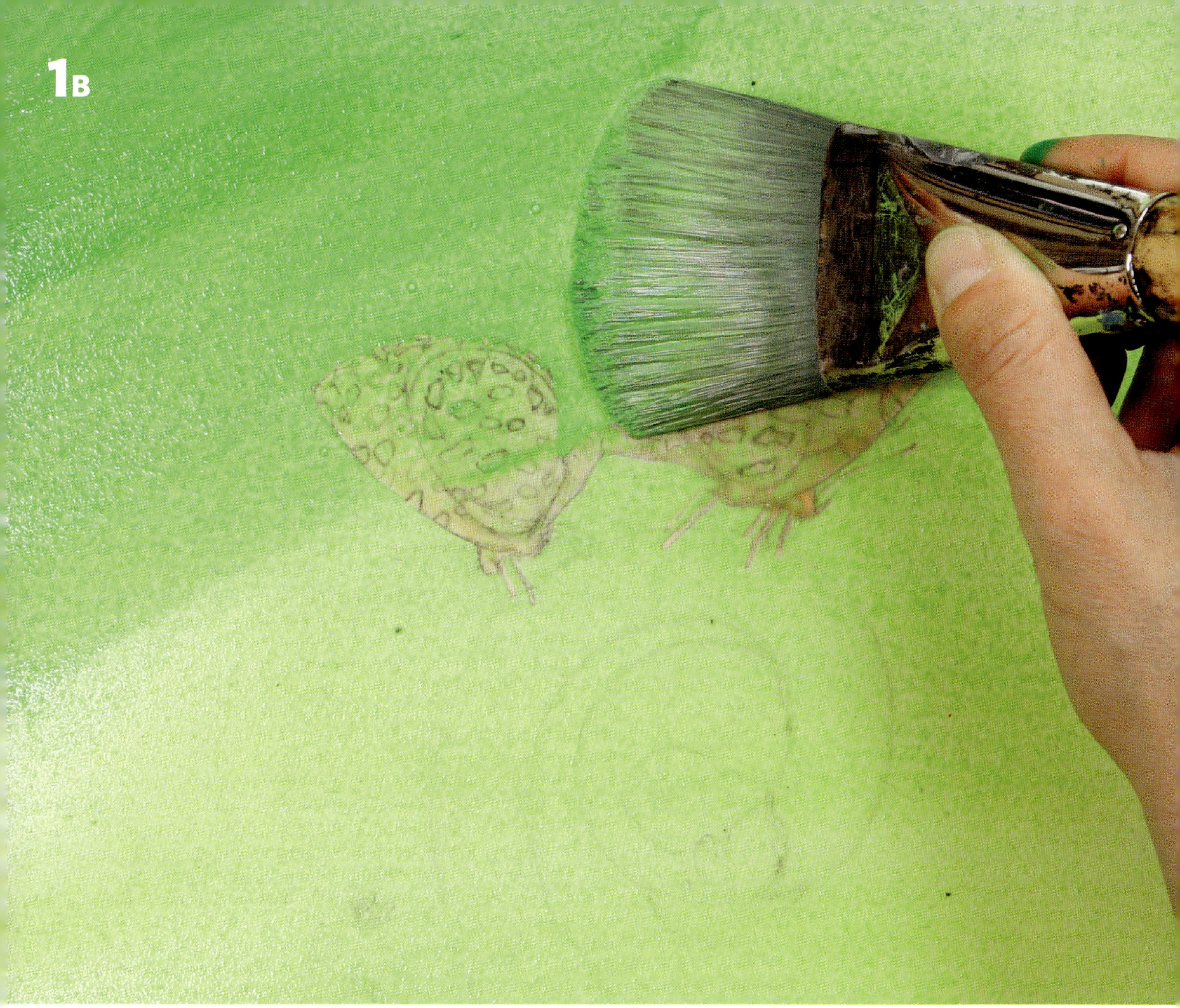

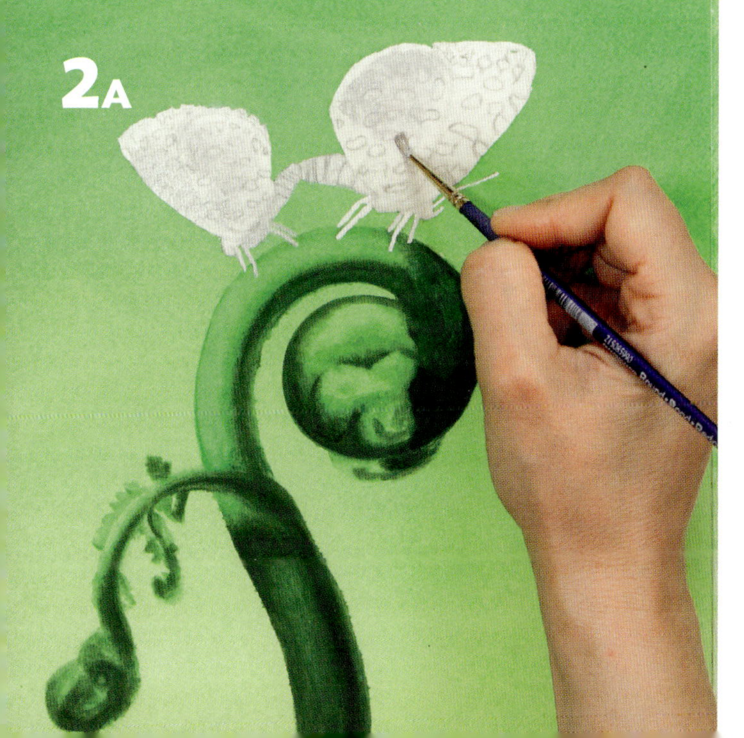

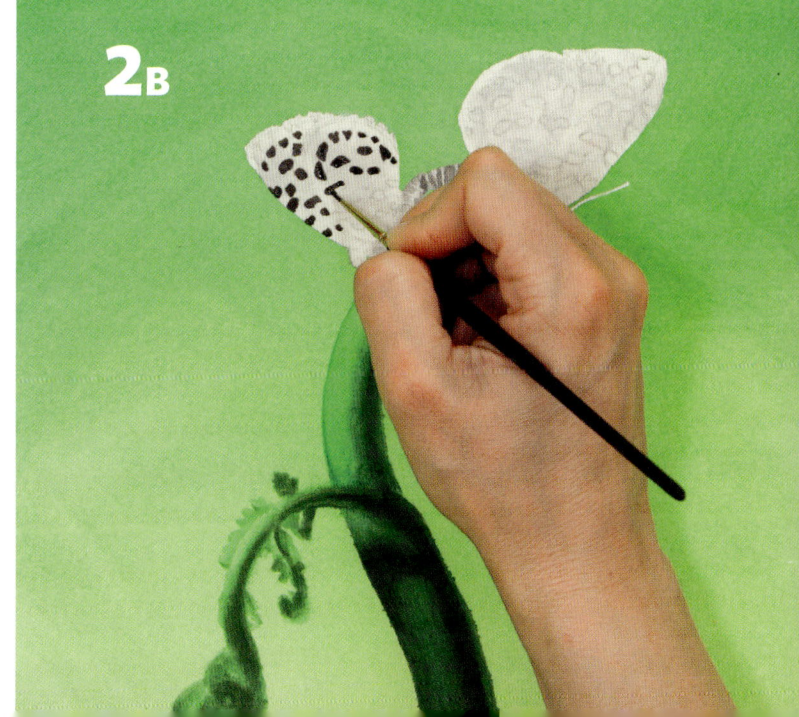

LAYERING WITH COLORED PENCIL

1 Take your time embellishing this composition. Every adjustment you make can have a significant impact on the overall appearance of this minimal design. Create a clean gradual curve, color match carefully, and apply details thoughtfully.

First, use your green pencils to even out the sides of the stem. If you find a color or combination of pencils that matches the background, you can work the area from both sides of the outline. Keep in mind that you might need to add the white pencil very lightly only as a base under a grazing of another color to match the luminosity. When you get to the top of the fern, draw a line along the edge where the far legs of the butterflies are hidden from sight behind the stem. Then add all the highlights and return to using the green pencils to darken the interior sections of both the stem and leaflet. At some point, you will want to pause to clean up the background using a variety of pencils.

2 With the shadows and highlights completed, turn to the hairs on the fern. Notice how they vary in different areas; many are very light, others are in shadow, and some are slightly colored.

A To begin, work on the leaflet using neutral colors to create the haze found in areas around the perimeter. Add a light line right next to the outline that is lightest near the fern where the hairs are most concentrated. Then use an eraser either to blend this halo into the background or to adjust its thickness.

B Next, add the individual hairs to the exterior of the fern head. Notice that the bottom and top of the fern head are both in shadow, but the lower perimeter hairs are light while the upper perimeter hairs are dark. I used varying degrees of Prussian green and very light cream pencils to create these. You may want to add a few hairs to the interior simply to help you envision the three-dimensionality of the form.

C If you use the side of your pencil to add a pattern right where the cast shadow begins, it will emphasize the direction and strength of the light source. Simply hold your pencil lead at the same angle as the light source and, right where the shadow ends, scrape the lead toward the highlight so that the texture of the paper leaves only specks of white. Then erase anywhere that this visual texture either fades or is absent. While you are working, pause intermittently to both consider your next step and acknowledge your progress.

D When you are working on the interior, it is best to use the white pencil for hairs on the darker areas, because the contrast makes the hairs appear even lighter there. Using a continuously sharpened pencil lead is essential for these details. Be sure to draw through the outline often so it seems as if the hairs near the edge have volume. Continue using these colors and techniques to complete the head of the fern. If the hairs become too light or need variation, you can lightly layer with a green pencil that matches the color under the hairs.

Move to the lower section of the stem. To keep the focus of the composition up near the leaflet and butterflies, add fewer hairs that are less intense than those added to the areas close to the focal point. First add a thin light line just beyond the outline anywhere the hairs are a bit highlighted. Then add the dark individual hairs along the perimeter. Lastly, draw the light hairs toward the center of the stalk.

Look over each area of the fern and either accentuate the hairs or use an eraser to decrease the overall intensity. You also might want to re-emphasize the shadows, particularly under the butterflies.

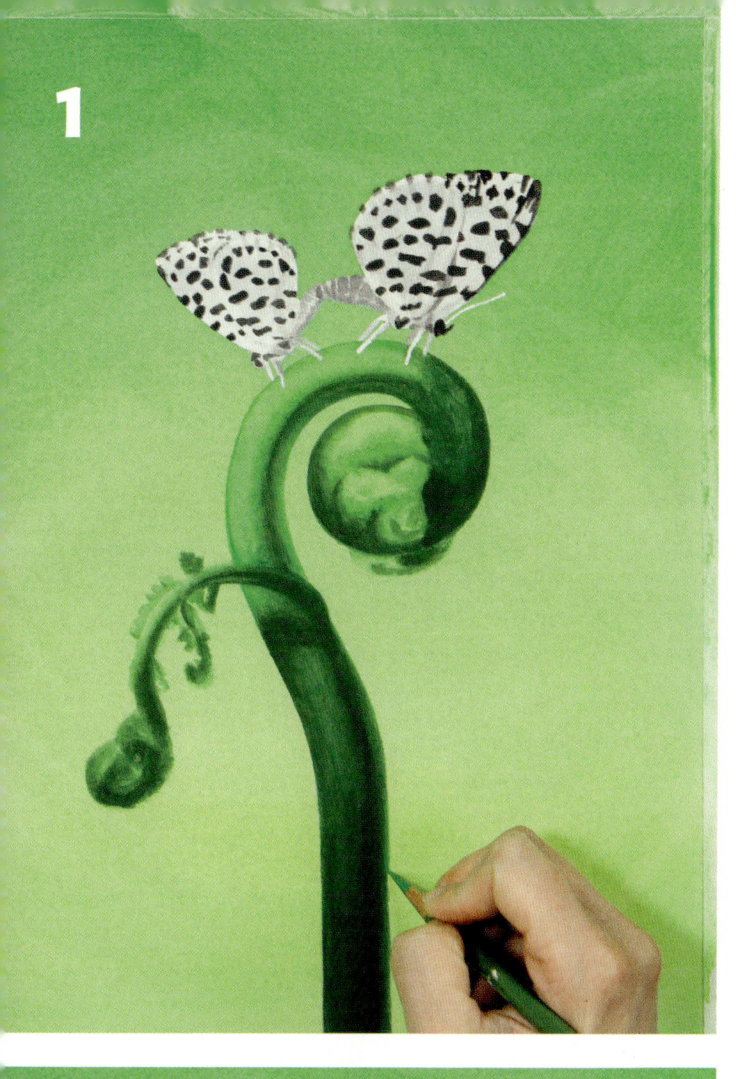

1

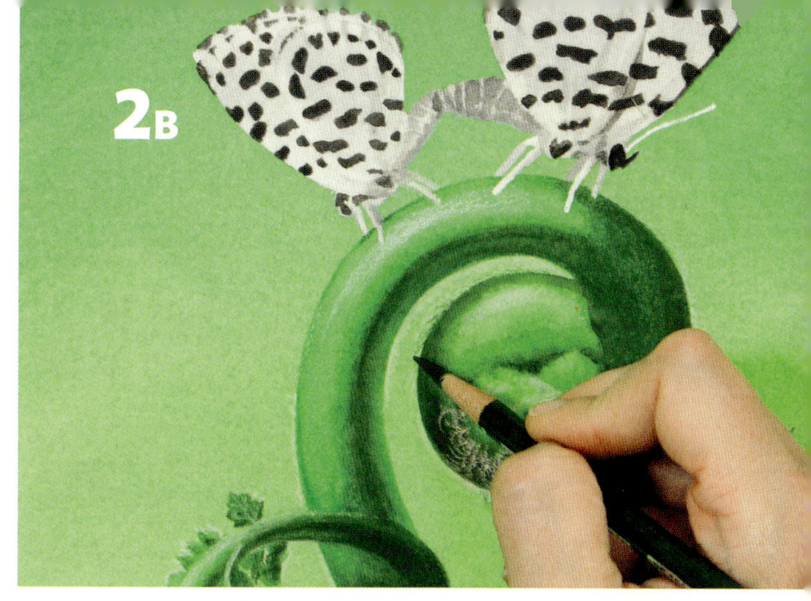

2B

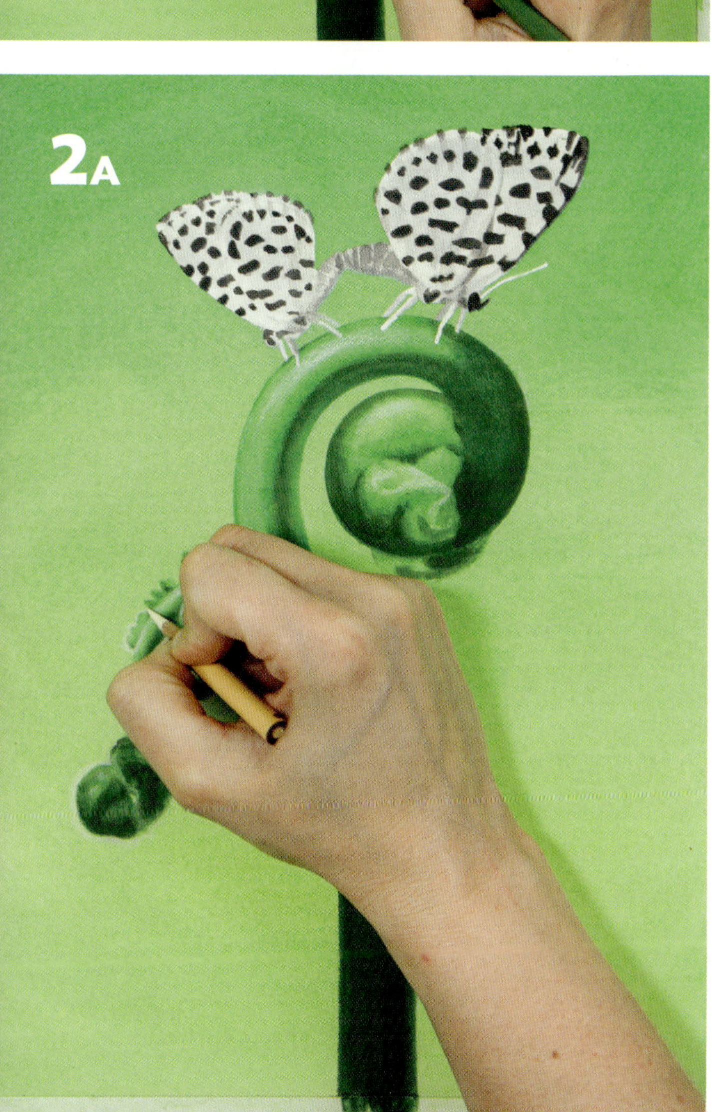

2A

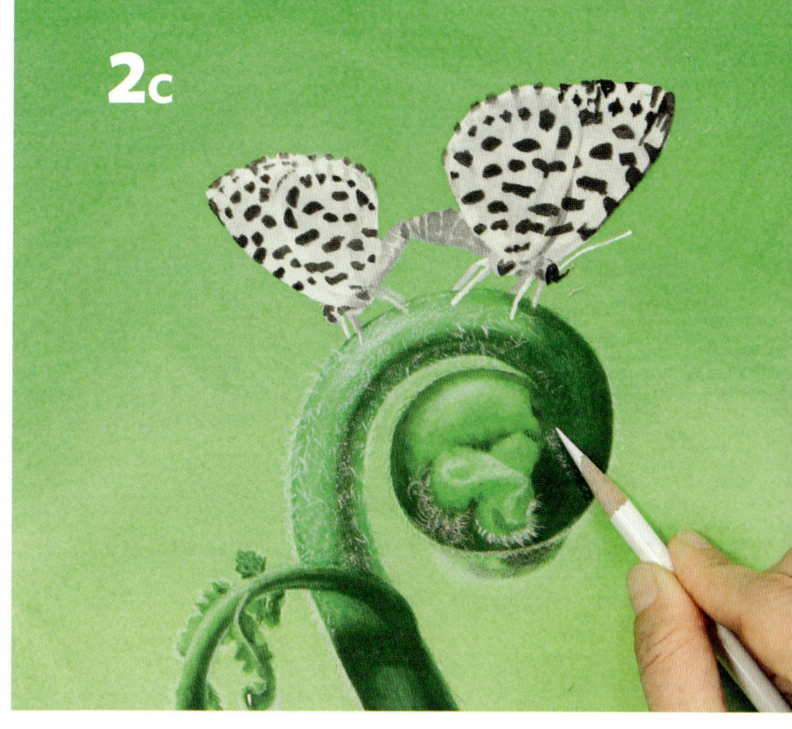

2C

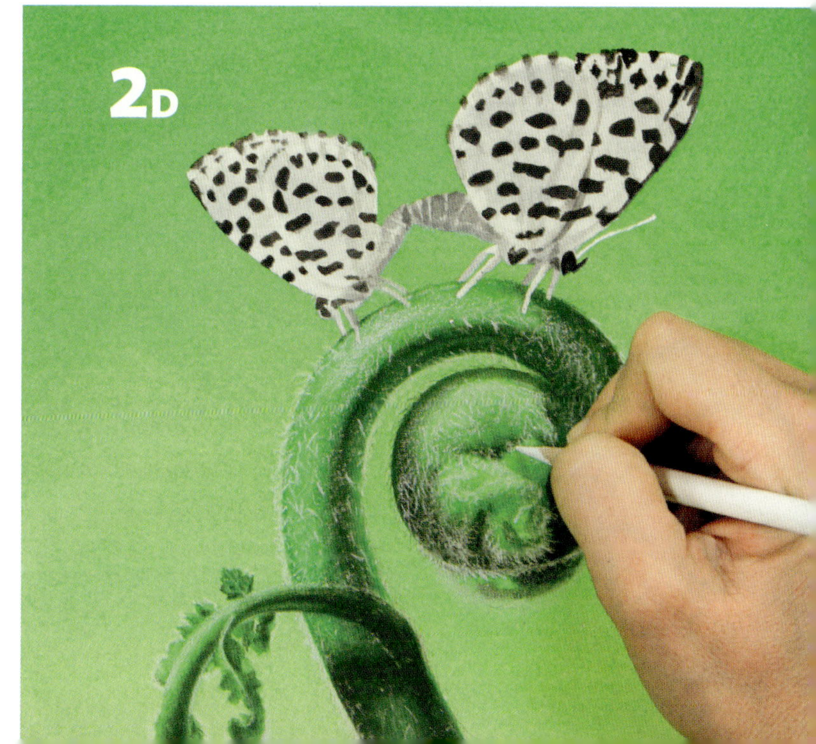

2D

3 **A** Work now on the details of both butter-flies. Start with the spots, then embellish the shadows on the lighter portion. To create the iridescence on the abdomen, add the white pencil first and top it with a layer of the electric blue pencil. Now create the fringe along the edges of the wings. On the larger butterfly, you might want to also use the chocolate pencil so that you can create the subtle stripe that runs down the center of the fringe. And with that, I want to take a moment to congratulate you on creating the iridescence. Although the area of iridescence is small, this new skill represents a leap in your creative practice.

B At this point, you can clean the lines on the legs and heads using the pencils you used on the background, then return to the neutral colors for the remaining details on the butterflies. When you add the feet, keep in mind that they should be angled slightly so that they appear to rest on the fern. This stance will give the drawn butterflies the appearance of having weight. If any of the feet seem to end right on the edge of the fern, I suggest that you adjust their location slightly so that the viewer understands the anatomy more easily.

C Now address the butterflies' small anatomical details. In the spotted section of the antennae, add the black dots before adding the white ones. To create the club at the end, use the cream pencil and, if desired, brighten using the goldenrod pencil.

D Turn to the shape of the eyes. If you want the shape more lifelike than the reference image, add some shadows and highlights. Use the black pencil to create a shadow around the lower section. Then, on the smaller butterfly, use undiluted white paint to add a single highlighted dot toward the top of the eye where the light would reflect. If you make a mistake, simply add a droplet of water, carefully wipe away the paint using a damp paintbrush, and begin again. Since the eyes of the larger butterfly are in shadow, you can use a French gray pencil to add this tiny highlight. Lastly, look at each section of the composition to add final details.

I took this opportunity to add some white scales to the dark spots. I added a bit of the chocolate pencil to the wings of the large butterfly along the edges. And I created a tiny shadow from each foot to the shadow underneath the body. Even though this detail was not in the reference image, I feel that it emphasizes the dimensionality and solidity of the butterflies.

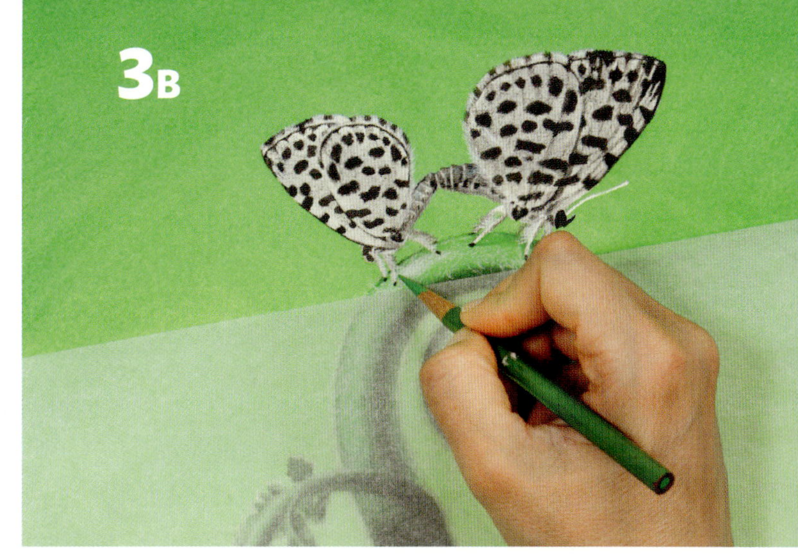
3B

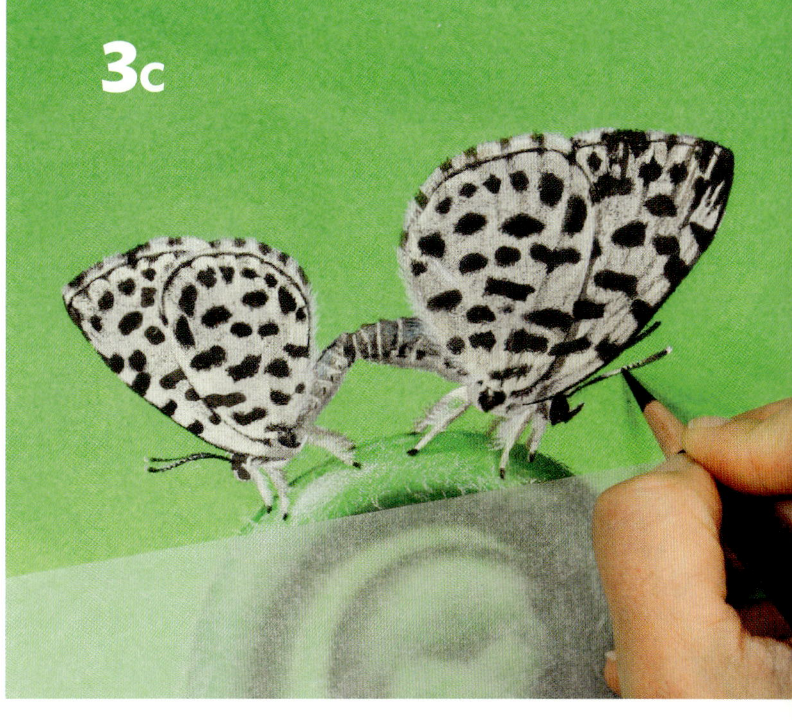
3C

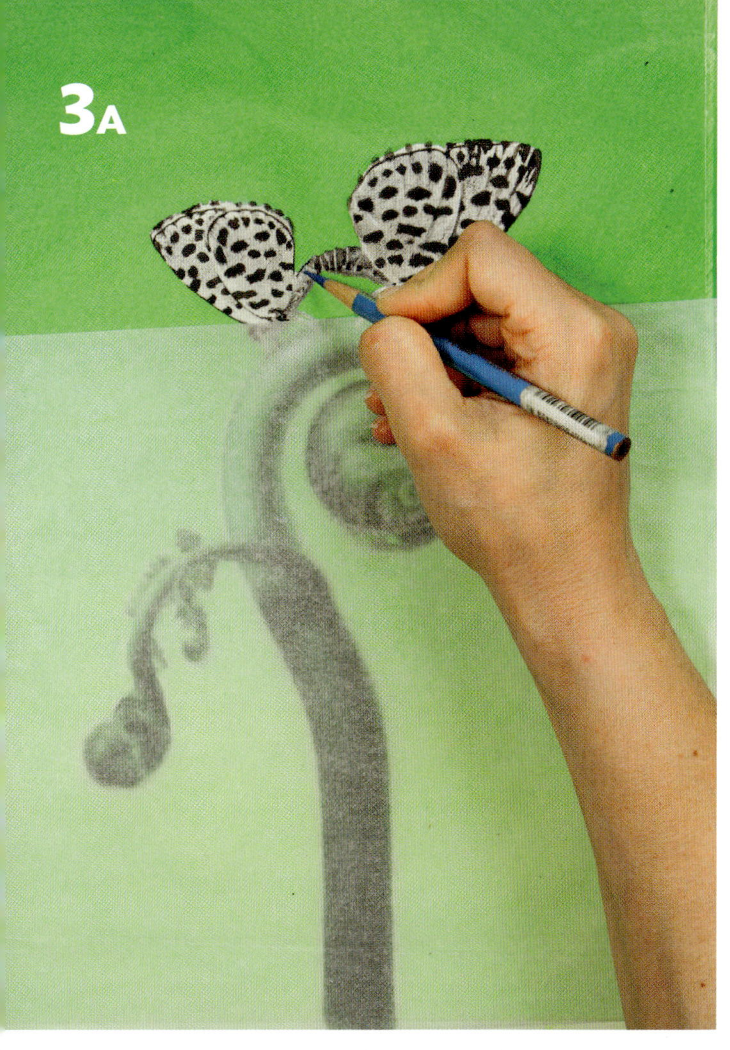
3A

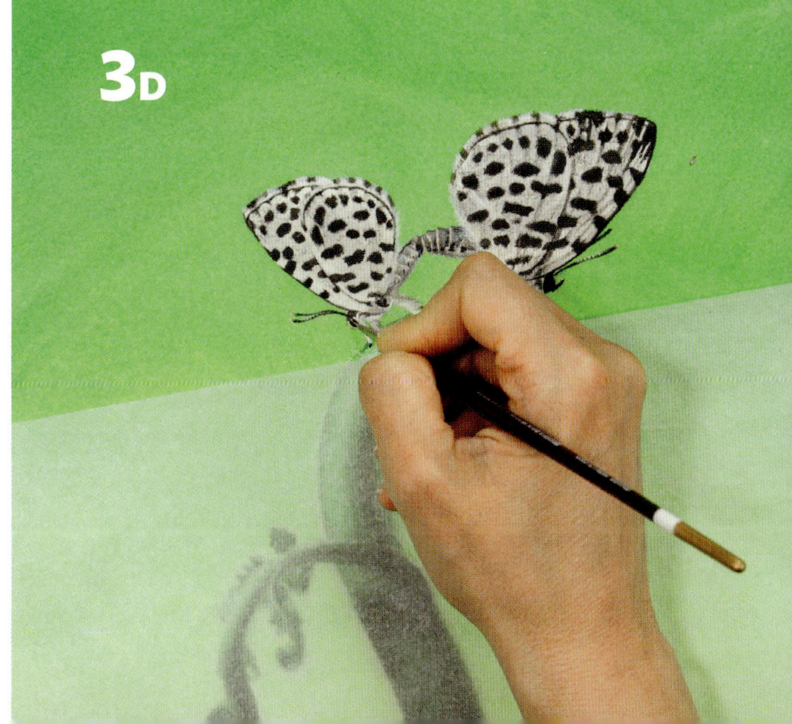
3D

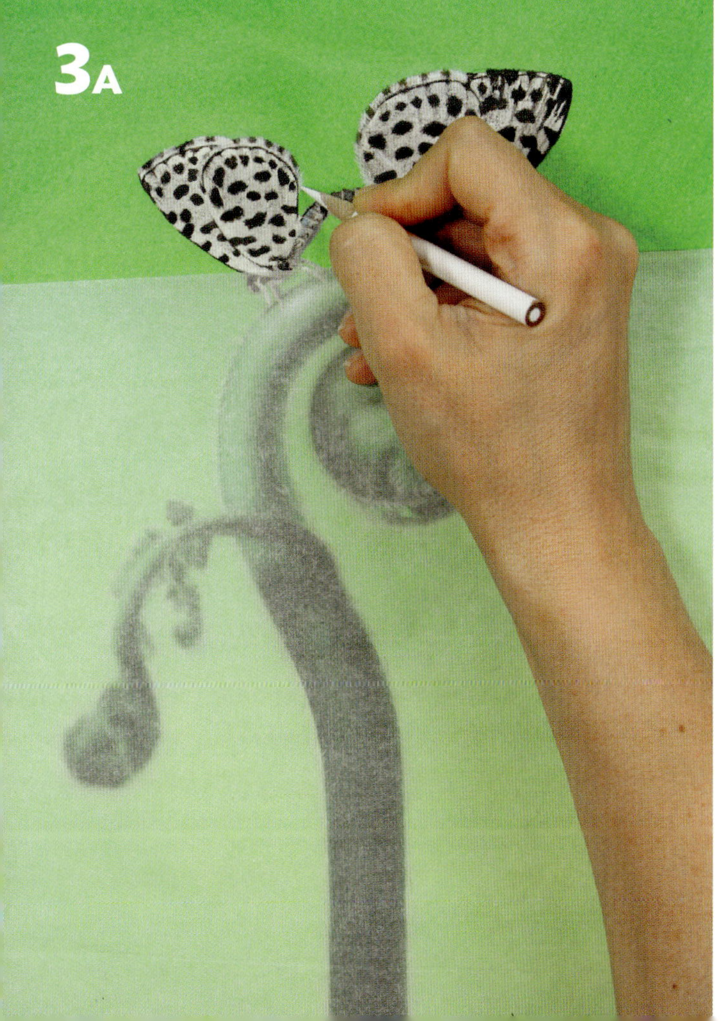
3A

You have done an amazing job on this illustration and on each Level II project. Now you have the ability to redesign compositions, maintain hierarchy with multiple subjects, place your subjects in an environment, add incredibly realistic details, color match using paint or colored pencils, give dimensionality to your subjects and so much more. I hope that you feel proud. Now you can venture into the final section of this book to strengthen your skills, develop a strong independent practice, and make your artwork even more dynamic.

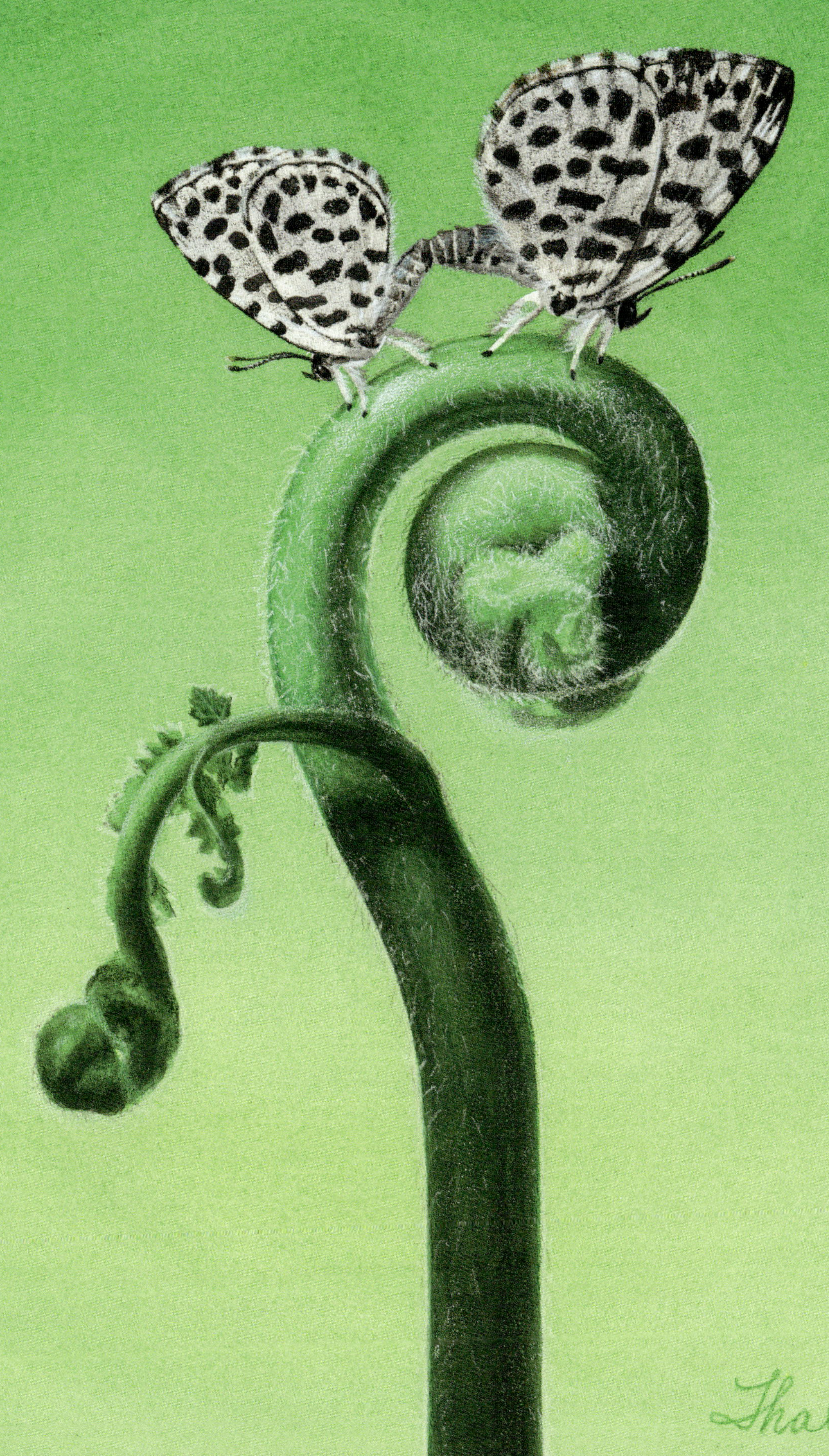

COMPLEX TRANSPARENCY

If you simply observe and re-create visual themes, you can turn simple patterns of varying color into cellophane wings, water droplets, or glass. It's time to advance your ability to create transparency.

LOCATION: Indoors using any light source.

MATERIALS: Sketchbook, HB pencil, colored media of your choice, and a variety of colorless objects that have different densities, thickness, translucency, and shapes. For example, you might use a plastic sphere, a glass vase, crinkled wax paper, and some water droplets on an opaque surface.

OBSERVATIONS: Place each of your items in front of you and simply look at the shapes and colors that define each form. It is important to differentiate what you are seeing. Notice if a highlight has a slight coloration, alteration in form, or shift in value. Also, compare how these qualities differ from those around the object.

PRACTICE: In your sketchbook you can either sketch each object and then label what you have observed or select two or three objects to arrange and draw as a complete illustration. Draw at least part of the background to emphasize the distortion created by the object. To keep transparency as the primary focus, place your attention on applying color rather than perfecting your drawing.

REFLECTION: Consider how realistically your drawings convey the actual object. First and foremost, does it look clear? Can you tell the level of transparency? Does the object look dimensional? Can you imagine its density? If you hesitate when answering these questions, compare the drawing to the object and see what would enhance that particular quality. Also, consider how highlights, blurriness, distortion, and color transitions affect the illusion. Then document these additional observations in a separate note, sketch, or illustration.

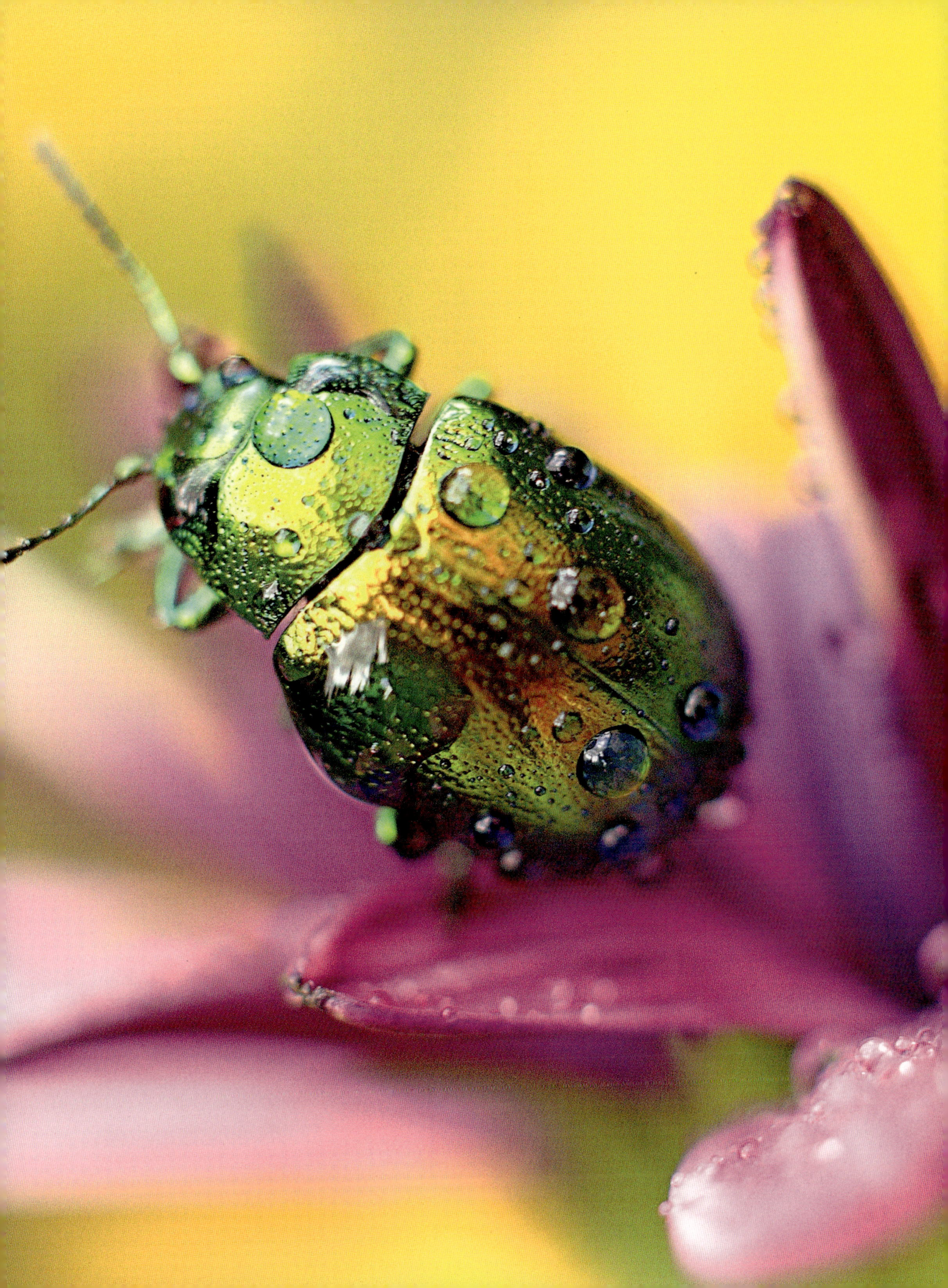

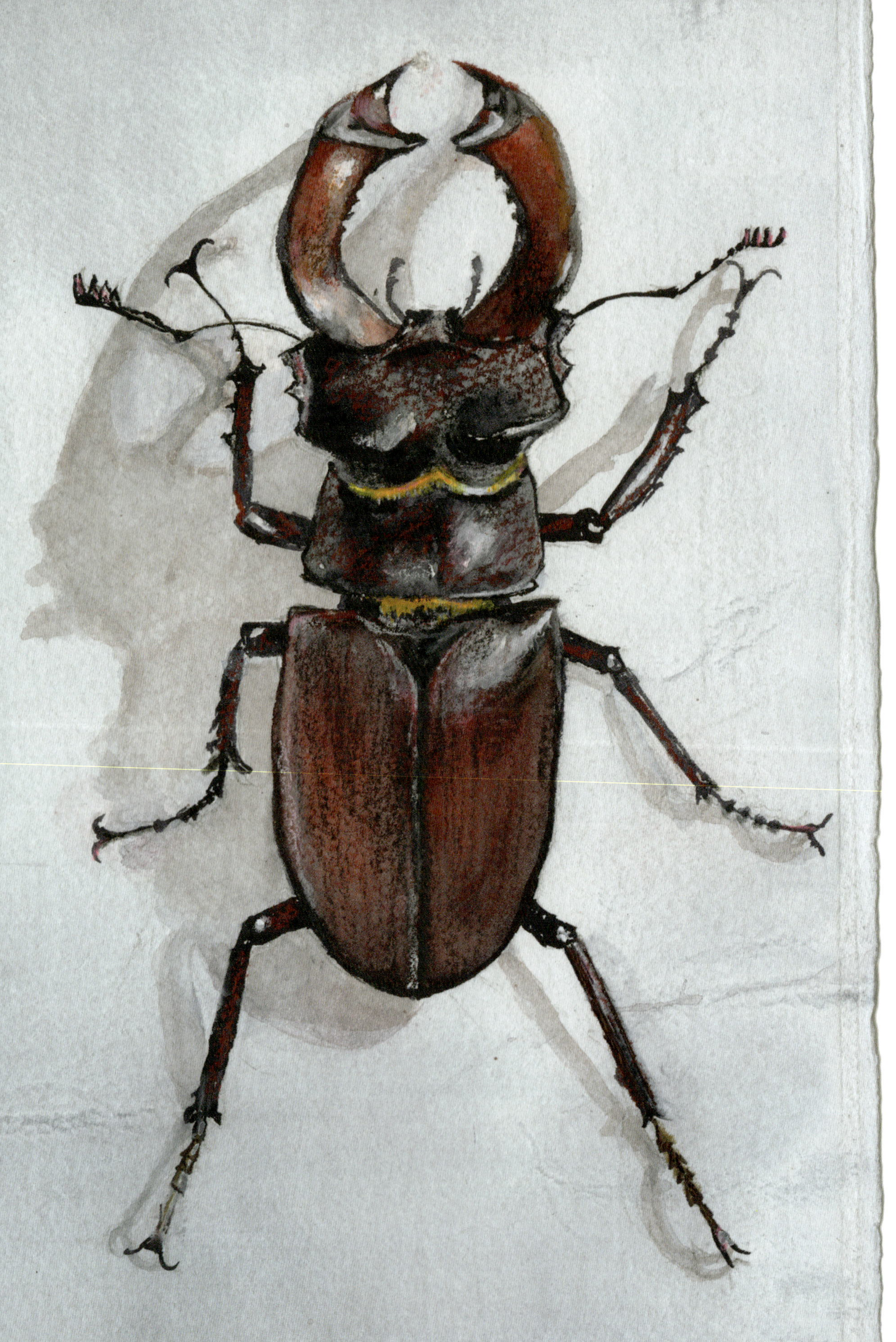

J. PARI-MUELLER

LEVEL III

ADVANCED TECHNIQUES

"I have gained an even deeper appreciation for the intricacies of the insect world—the varying shades of color, minute details on legs or antennae, amazing sheens and patterns."

—JoAnn Pari-Mueller,
Creative Participant

In this book, the term *advanced* refers to the abilities that you've already acquired. This level, therefore, is intended to help you season your skills, learn exciting new techniques, and address challenging subjects. Each project will guide you to progressively develop your own overall process for illustrating, so that you have time to build an independent practice that can support you far beyond the completion of these chapters. The problem-solving methods covered in this section are versatile. You will be able to apply the same process to any subject you are inspired to illustrate in the future.

The Level III projects focus on the creation of species with intricate surface patterns and elaborate coloration that are presented in lifelike environments. The step-by-step approach of previous chapters is replaced by a focus on specific topics. Techniques will cover painting style, fully developing a middle ground, adding elements mid-process, painting around large unmasked areas, and drawing complicated patterns so that they are easy to comprehend. Along the way, you'll develop original composition designs, use multiple references, and learn creative shortcuts. You'll also learn how to address common challenges that arise when illustrating insects. This will help prepare you for creating a subject in a complex position, working with a light source that is in a less than ideal location, improvising with a limited palette in your studio, or illustrating a surface that is unfamiliar or feels especially daunting.

You can return to the Nature Break exercises again and again to explore and apply your creative skills. You'll also have an opportunity to develop goals for your future practice.

PAPER KITE BUTTERFLY

IDEA LEUCONOE

This butterfly gracefully flutters through the coastal mangrove swamps in Southeast Asia and Australia. Its large, delicate wings inspired additional common names such as rice paper butterfly and large tree nymph. The slightly yellow color that appears on the wings close to the body distinguishes this species from others with a similar wing pattern. I included this composition because the butterfly wings appear as geometric planes at an angle. Illustrating these shapes can enhance your ability to incorporate subjects in extremely complex lifelike positions. Additionally, this composition offers you the opportunity to allude to anatomy hidden behind a slightly translucent form. You'll also learn tips for painting thin lines with great precision and further enhancing forms in the background.

 SEE REFERENCE PHOTOS ON PAGES 323–325

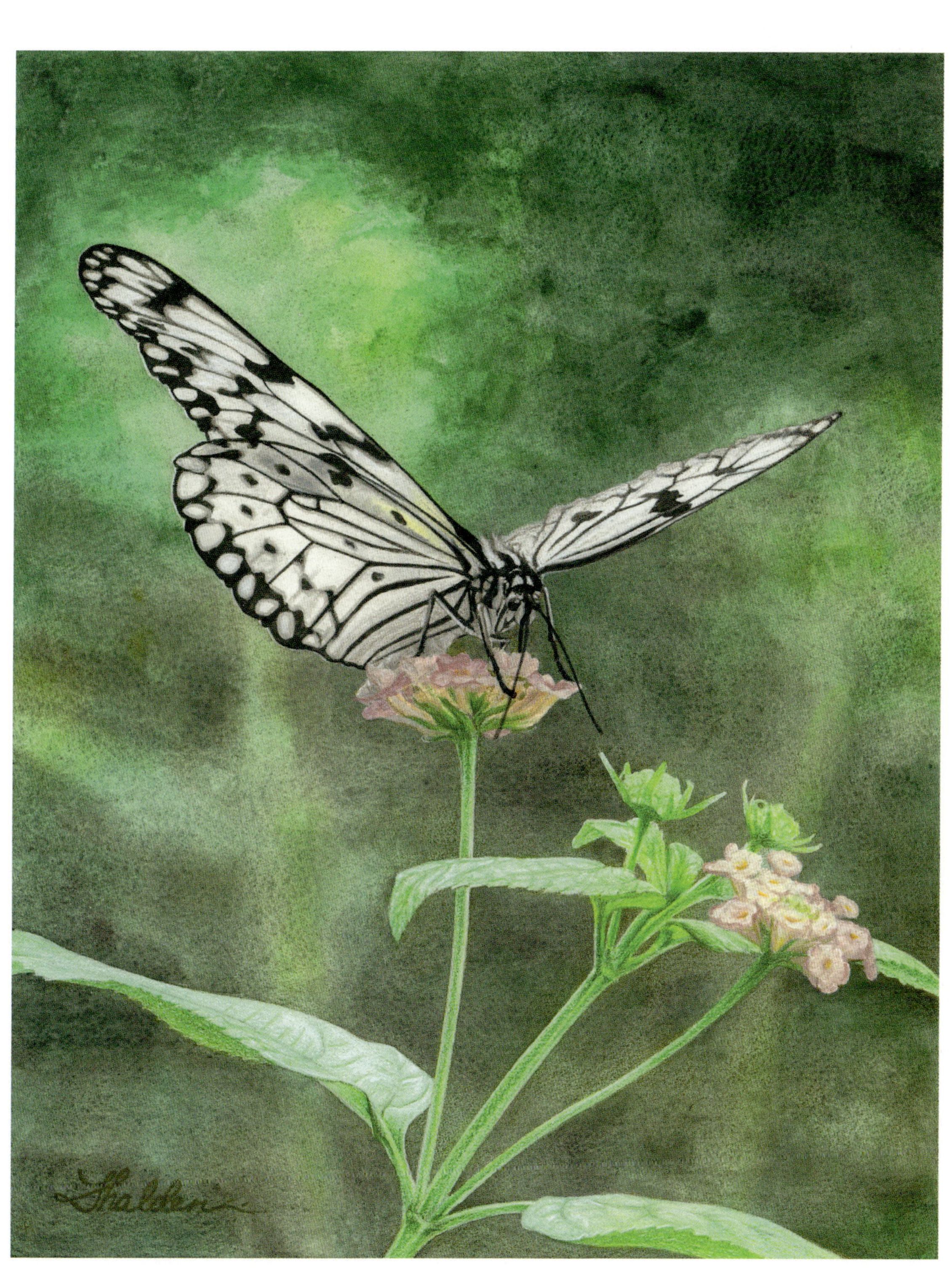

DEVELOPING YOUR OWN PROCESS

It's time to create your own sequential illustration steps! Begin by studying the reference image to consider each step of the process and to identify any opportunities for decision-making. The goal in this exercise is to help you avoid unanticipated issues that can interrupt your workflow or affect the appearance of your finished piece. Most significantly, you will be able to develop a preparation step that can support you in future projects. During this preview, jot down simple phrases, questions, or decisions in either your sketchbook or a digital document. Although you may need only a single word or phrase to describe each one, don't overgeneralize or skip any steps. You might include the process headings mentioned in this chapter so you know when to pause and read the content. After you finish each section of the outline, read the following questions to confirm that you have completed each portion before you move on. If you get stuck, it might be helpful to review a similar process in a previous project before you continue. Also, refrain from working on your illustration until you have completed this decision-making stage.

OUTLINE PART 1: DESIGN

Will you want to adjust the layout, color, or value to further meet either your creative parameters or personal aesthetic? Are there specific techniques or colors that you want to test or practice before you decide on a specific process?

OUTLINE PART 2: DRAWING

Which tools and materials will you need to set up your workstation? See if you can quickly identify a couple units of measure to test when you begin working. Consider whether or not identifying a midline and/or using a grid would be most beneficial to you. Also, consider the first measurements that you will need to have on your paper. Where will you begin and end drawing the outline? Which wing patterns could you add to further refine the outline of the wings?

OUTLINE PART 3: PAINTING

When you transition from drawing to painting, are there any items that you want to remind yourself to add or remove to accommodate using a different media? How and where will you begin painting? In what order will you need to create and apply each paint mixture so that every area has a base layer of color? If you decide to use masking fluid before you paint, when will you need to remove it? At what point will you pause to make a colored pencil key to help you decide which paint colors to mix?

OUTLINE PART 4: LAYERING WITH COLORED PENCIL

Are there any painting supplies that you want to be sure you put away or drawing tools you need to have close at hand? In what sequence will you refine the background, botanical, and insect? Remember to start with the more subtle aspects of both the composition and form and to end by working on the more pronounced details. Are there any areas of your artwork that you will need to protect while you are working?

OUTLINE COMPLETE

Take the time you need to prepare and consider this stage of the illustration process. With practice, these steps will become second nature. Eventually, you'll quickly grasp the process required to create any subject. At that point, you might only utilize this written exercise as a tool to address an area that is unfamiliar or potentially challenging. For now, consider both this illustration and the next as an opportunity to develop this aspect of your foundation.

When you are ready to begin your illustration, simply follow your own outline just as you followed the steps that were provided in previous chapters.

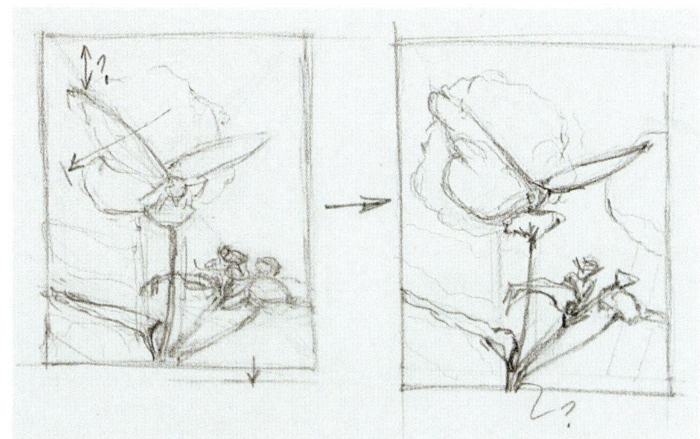

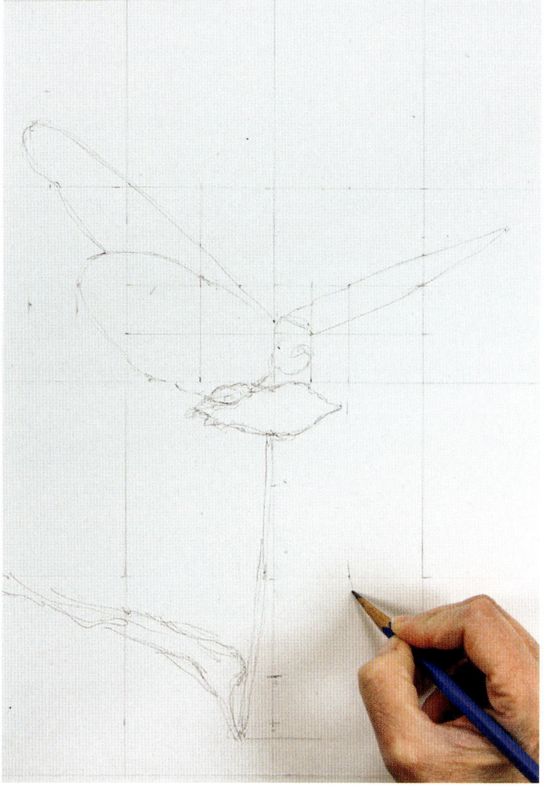

DRAWING HEAVILY PATTERNED WINGS POSITIONED AT AN ANGLE

Before you refine the shape of the wings, consider not only how they are attached but also their range of motion. Simply following this thought process can help you to draw forms that appear realistically connected to the body.

A When you begin to draw, first refine the leading edge of both upper wings, then add a quick gesture of the wing patterns. Next, work to refine a few key patterns that will help you determine the overall wing shape more clearly. You can then move on to fine-tune the remaining patterns. Don't be surprised if you need to oscillate between tweaking the shape of the outline and the patterns.

To avoid confusion, I want to point out a perplexing difference between the two upper wings in this photograph. At some point while you are drawing, take a moment to study the wing on the right. Notice how the very first vein, the long black line that leads from the body to the pointed apex, has side veins that angle toward the leading edge. When you compare this to the other wing, you will find this entire row of cells missing. I can only conclude that they are hidden behind the leading edge due to the photographic angle, which caused the black markings to appear next to the leading edge instead.

B When you draw the pattern on the lower wing, pay close attention to the color along the leading edge to help differentiate the shape of the anatomy from the surface pattern.

If you are using a grid to determine proportions, you might find it helpful to further divide individual rectangles located within the more densely patterned sections of the wing. When you are drawing in these areas, keep your lines very thin so that they are easy to identify. If you draw a line that is too thick, erase along the sides to sharpen it before you add more details.

While you create these intricate patterns, allow yourself ample time and patience so that you can achieve accurate results with greater ease. As you continue to work, incorporate intermittent pauses into your practice that allow you to acknowledge and celebrate what you have accomplished.

DRAWING THE COMPLEXLY PATTERNED BODY AND APPENDAGES

C The heavy patterning and downward-turned head make the body of this butterfly complex to draw. To begin, study the reference image so that you discern each anatomical feature. Locate the head, each leg, both antennae, and the thorax. Notice that both antennae intersect with other body parts, one with the leg and the other with the tongue. Still observing, see if you can differentiate the smaller details such as the mouth, eyes, and beginning of the thorax. Then look at the area where the wings attach to the body and the exposed section of the abdomen.

When you draw complex patterns on areas that have intricate features, continue to focus on the anatomy and simply use both color and pattern to enhance these features. If you were to merely replicate just the patterns that you see, the result could flatten the quality of your drawing, make the anatomy difficult to

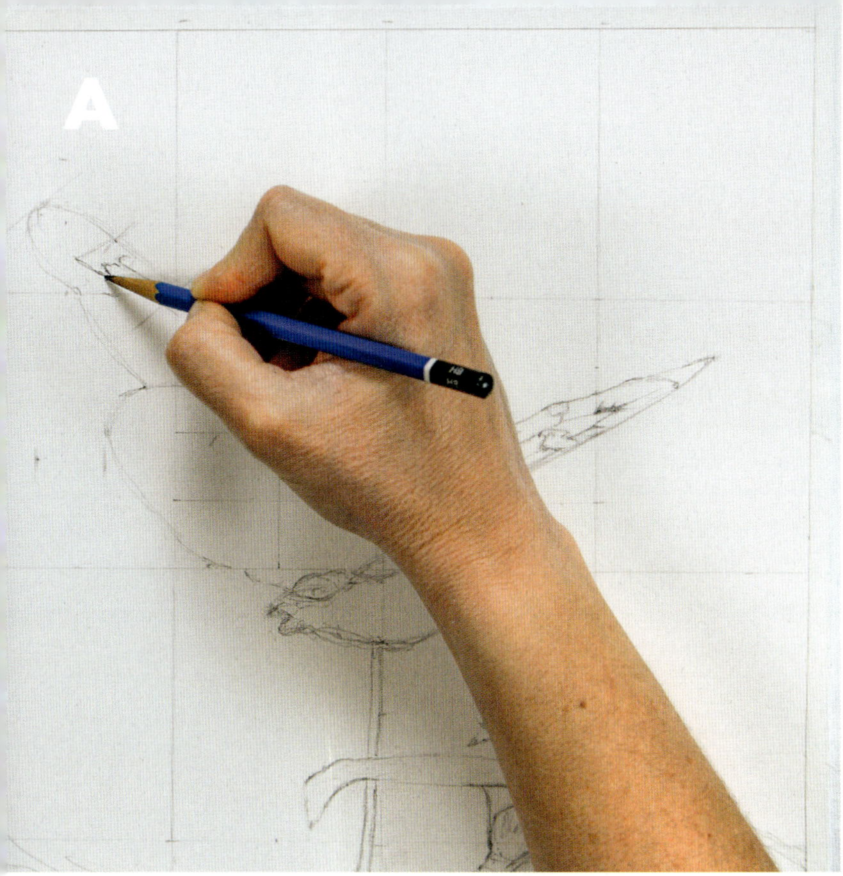

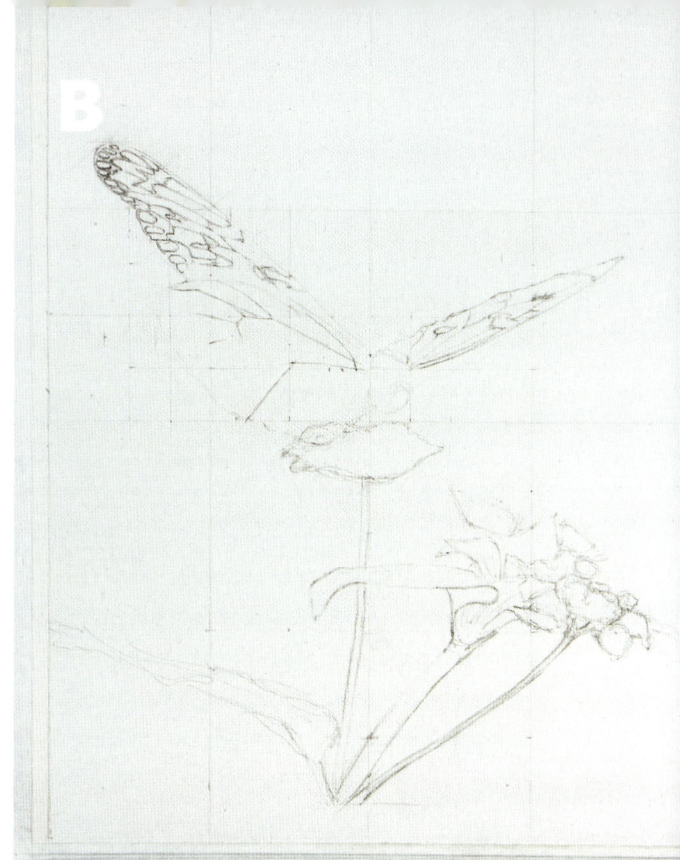

comprehend, and potentially cause you to miss important anatomical features. For example, notice the black-and-white stripe on the thorax that appears to connect the base of the legs to the eye. This species, along with others of its family, has reduced front legs that lie folded flat against its thorax. These creatures, which are categorized as insects, stand on only four legs. If an artist were to focus on pattern over anatomy when drawing this butterfly, it would be easy to imagine that this defining characteristic could be altered or omitted.

I suggest that you refrain from letting this consideration add pressure to your practice. Alterations, both intended and unintended, are certainly an inherent part of the creative process (even one's own creative style is in itself a modification). They are what give illustrations a special quality that a photograph simply cannot convey. It is helpful to remember that foundation concepts can support and guide you when you work with increasingly complex themes.

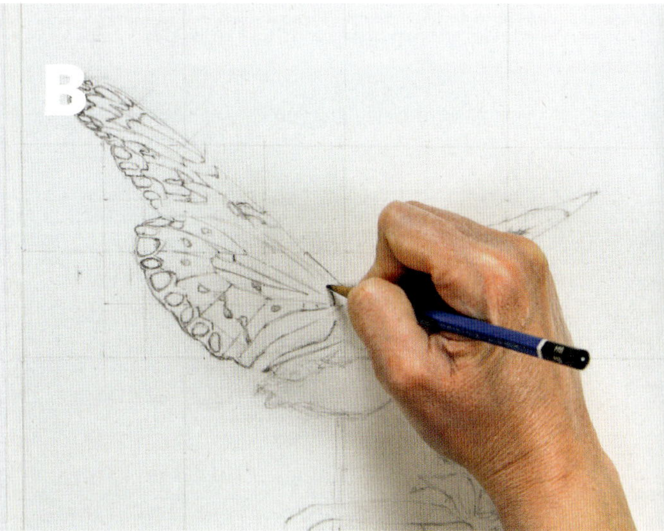

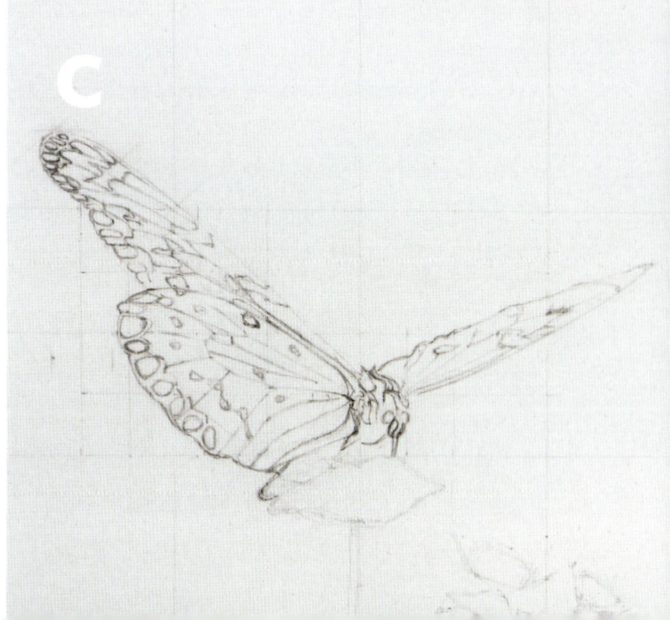

ADDING REFERENCES TO UNDERSTAND ANATOMY

In this reference image, the photographer intentionally blurred some areas, making it difficult to illustrate in these sections with great detail. In my practice, whether I am working on a commission, exhibition pieces, or creating personal work, I often include research in my process. If the subject is particularly complex, I view many images to fully understand the three-dimensional structure of the anatomy. I then select a series of images to use as references so that I can illustrate volume and details accurately. Also, unless you have been given permission to use images, it is important to focus solely on the specific qualities of the species to avoid duplicating any potentially copyrighted content of another artist.

In both the drawing and refinement stages of this project, it could be helpful to do a quick search on the lantana plant so that you can see both the shape of the stem and the location of the veins on the leaves more clearly. If you choose to extend the composition, as I did in my illustration, you might also study images that show the node at the point where the leaves come together. It might also be helpful to review the section of the luna moth project (page 183) where instructions are given to add sections that do not appear in the reference image.

Furthermore, anytime you notice something perplexing in a reference image (such as an insect standing on four legs only), doing a little research can provide you with a knowledgeable talking point to share with others after your illustration is complete.

DRAWING ANATOMY THAT IS PARTIALLY HIDDEN

As you study the reference image, imagine the body as if it were entirely visible instead of partially hidden by the wings. It may help to envision a central line bisecting the symmetrical sides to determine the angled position of the butterfly more clearly. The white stripe down the center of the thorax can help you to comprehend the line contour.

D Trying to visualize the full outline can help you draw the separate anatomical sections correctly in your illustration.

The visible anatomy will also offer evidence of forms that are concealed. In this composition, notice how the wings change in value and shape as they wrap slightly around the bulbous abdomen. Later in the process, adding these subtle details will help you to convey both the volume and lifelike presence of this hidden form in your illustration.

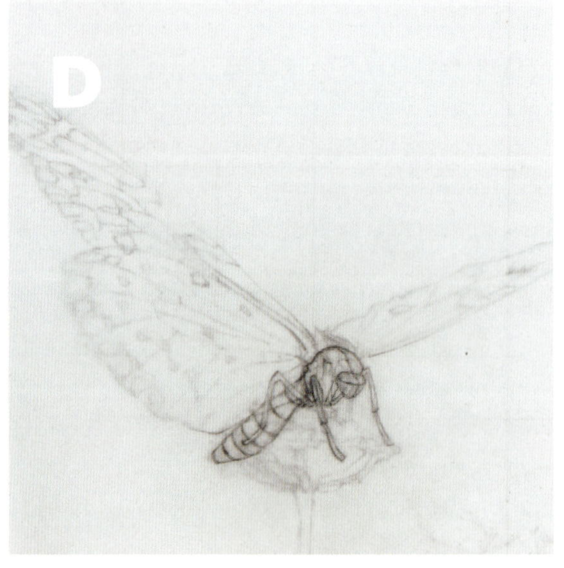

ADDING FEATURES

E When you are ready to add the antennae, study the reference image. Instead of focusing on them as two-dimensional lines on a flat piece of paper, try to envision the antennae curling out into space. This simple exercise can make it easier to create lines that appear dimensional. You can draw the antennae while you have a measurement structure in place, or you can wait until you arrive at either the painting or colored pencil stage. Regardless, be sure to first define the shape using pencil before you apply color.

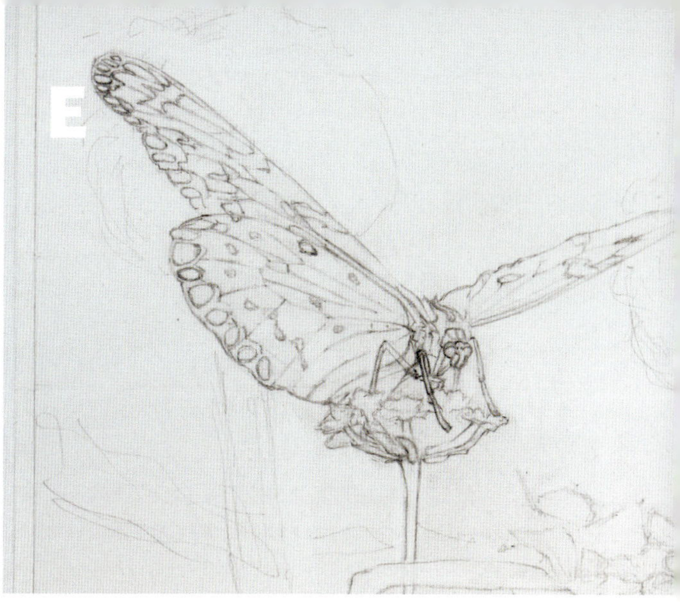

PAINTING THE BACKGROUND IN STAGES

F Since both the botanical and the background in this composition are similar variations of green, you'll need to rely on using hue, value, and clarity to create both depth and emphasis while you are painting. Since acrylic paint is not resoluble, you can create the background in two stages by applying masking fluid on top of the first layer.

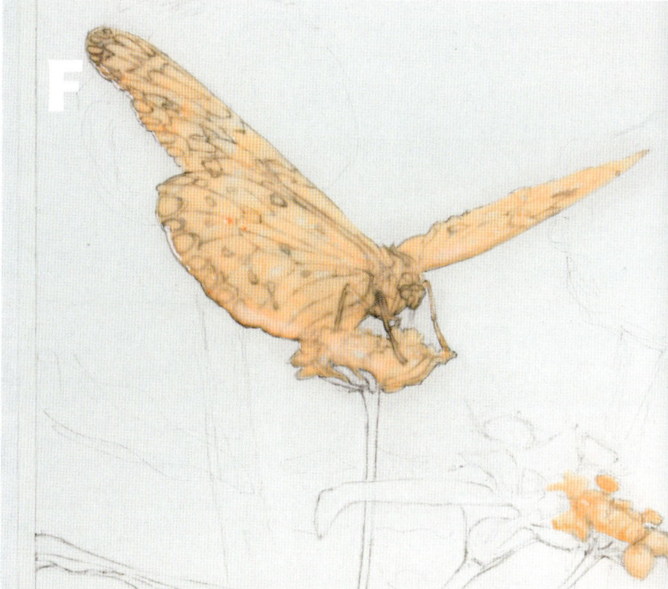

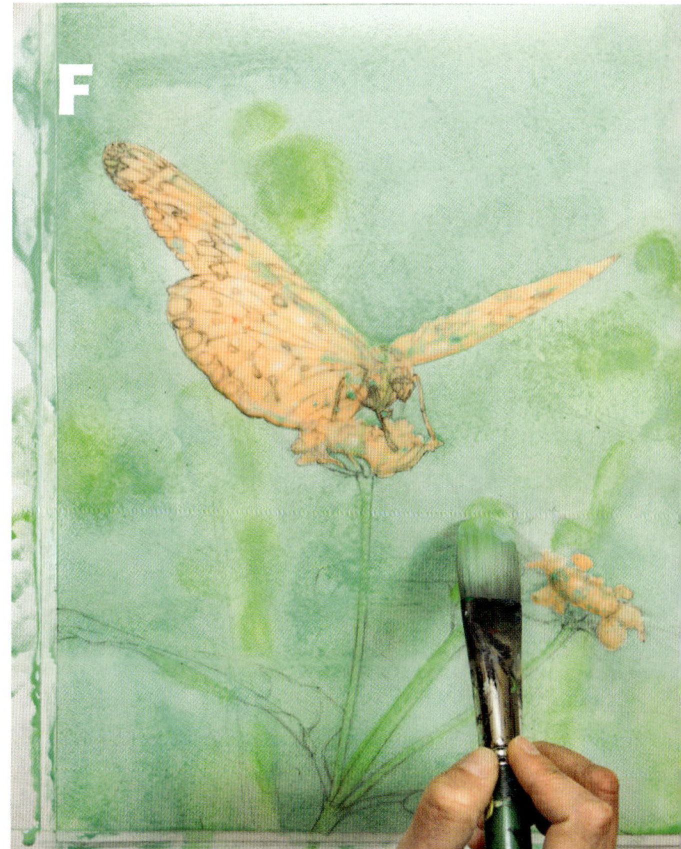

APPLYING MASKING FLUID ON TOP OF PAINT

G Before you apply the masking fluid on top of the first painted layer, you need to wait for both the paint and paper to air-dry completely. Depending on how much moisture is in the air, that could take around a half hour. To test drying progress, lay the back of your hand onto the paper to determine if it is still cool to the touch. You will know that the paper is ready when the surface is flat again and at room temperature.

Since the botanical is a large complex shape, the masking fluid will start to dry before you finish the task. If the leading edge dries while you are working, simply overlap it and continue onward.

After the masking fluid has dried clear, look for areas that may have been missed as well as any tiny air bubbles that need an extra dab of resist. To clearly see the area you have masked, change your position or tilt the work surface until the masking fluid reflects the light in your workspace.

PAINTING A SECOND BACKGROUND LAYER

H When you are ready to apply the second layer of paint, it's time to create a variety of medium to dark paint mixtures. After you have confirmed that the artist tape is still well secured, add a water wash to the entire surface, and apply paint only to the darker sections of the composition.

I As you apply paint to the surface, be sure that the colors, values, and hues are consistent from one side of the masked area to the other. Be aware that the masking fluid can cause the paint to pool in various locations. As always, watch for uneven drying and be sure to blur the perimeter of any area where the paint begins to develop a hard edge.

J When the paint on the surface of the paper is dry to the touch, you can safely remove the masking fluid.

CREATING A SUBJECT THAT APPEARS WHITE

First, compare the difference in value between each of the wings. If you quickly glance back and forth from the wings in the reference image to those on the white paper, perhaps you will be able to determine the subtle differences in both the value and hue of each wing.

K If you were to rely solely on the color of the paper, the unpainted subject could appear separate from the dark environment. If, however, you use a range of French grays to paint the wings, they will appear white in color against the dark background, thus creating unity within the composition. In addition, you will convey the anatomy, translucency, and the orientation of the subject to the light source. After you have finished painting, you will have the opportunity to adjust the value by using a white colored pencil.

To begin, mix a light gray paint that matches the shadow under the abdomen and add white paint to create a series of new mixtures of varying values. Be sure to create a yellow mixture as well. When you place your paint swatch next to a green section on your paper, the mixture will appear slightly different from the reference image because the

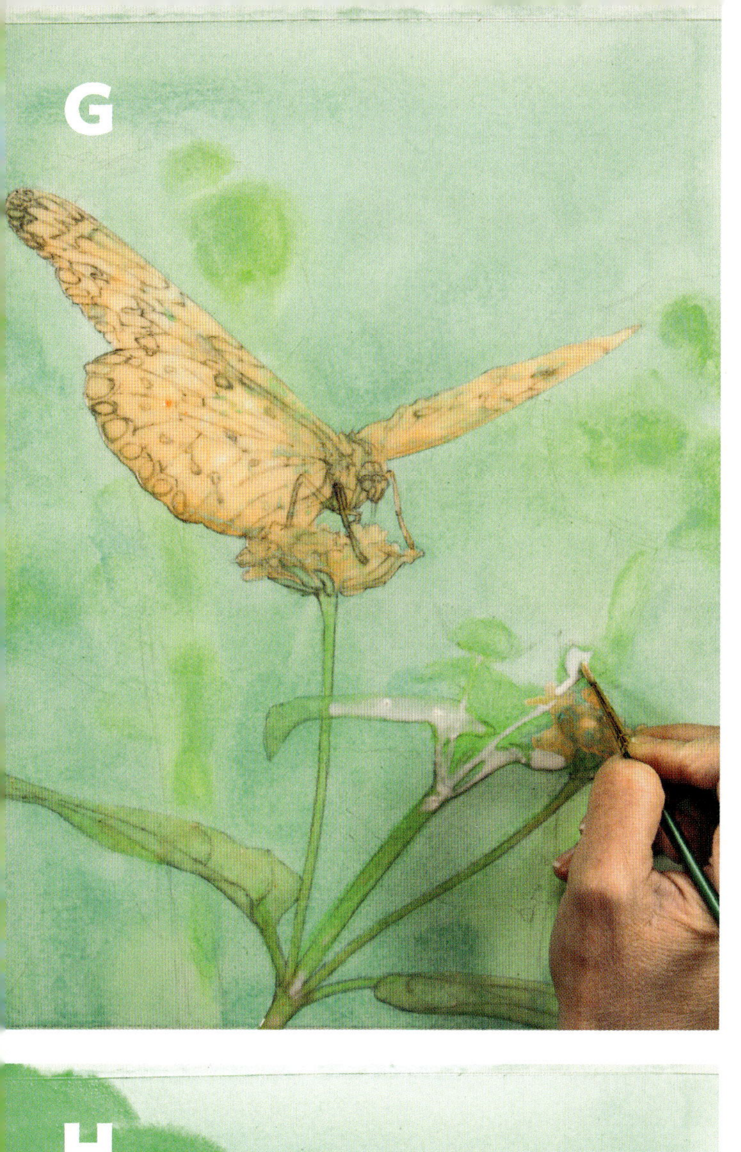
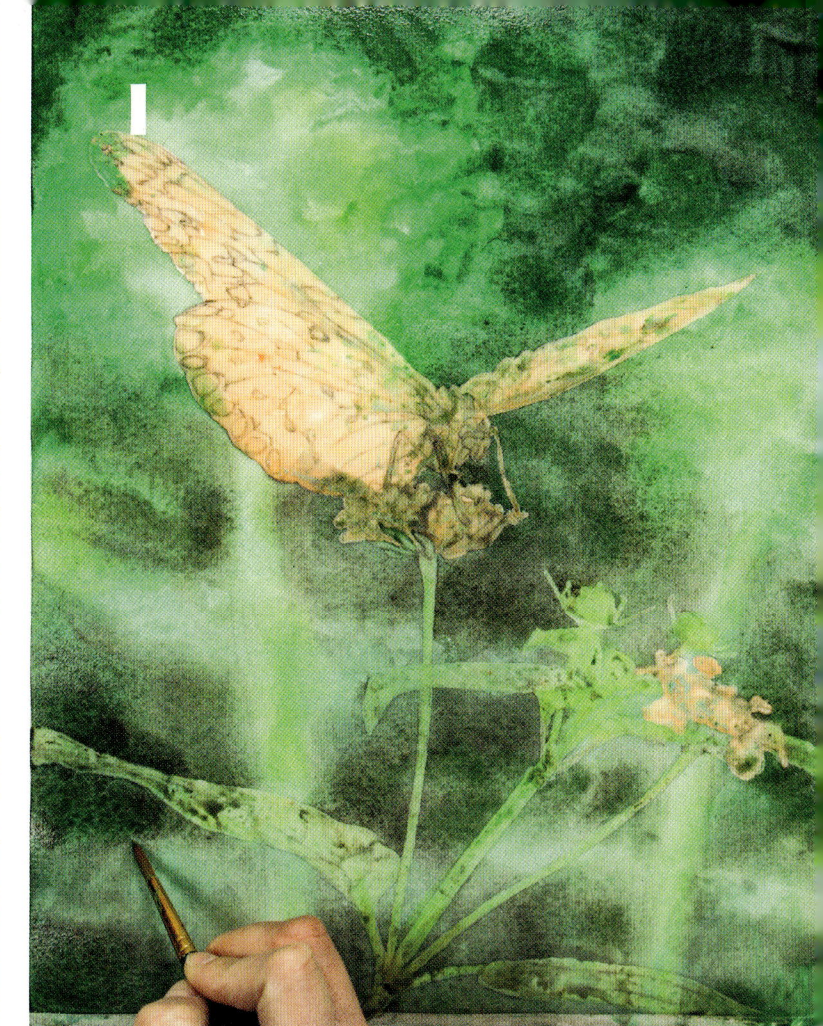
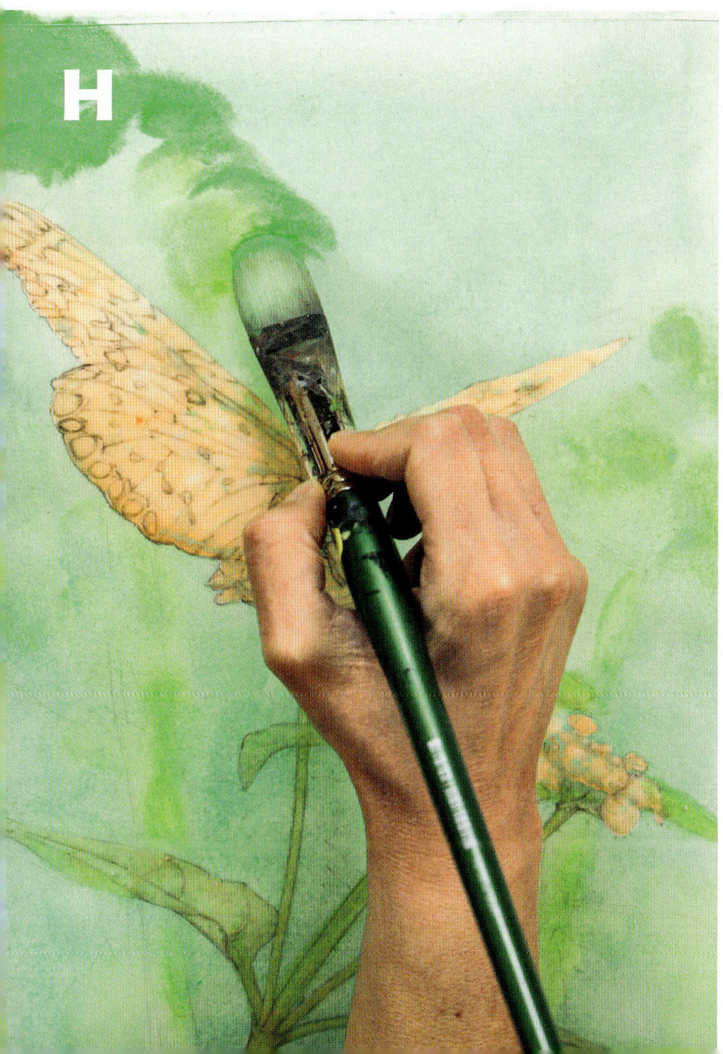
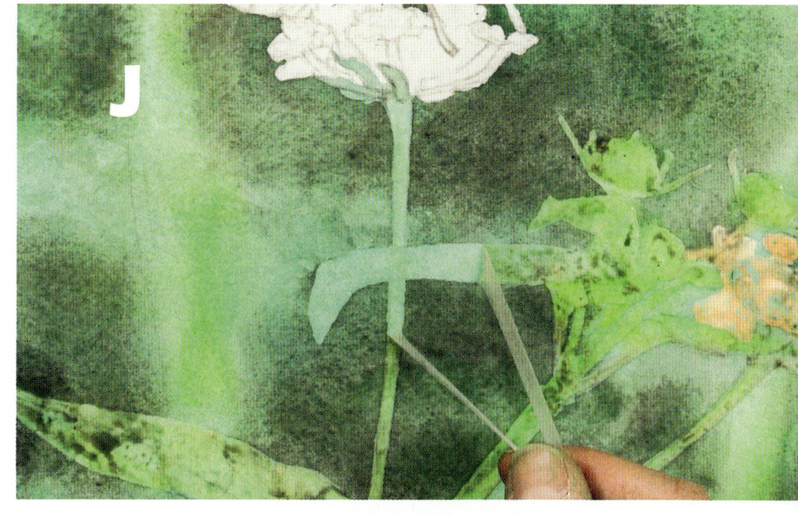
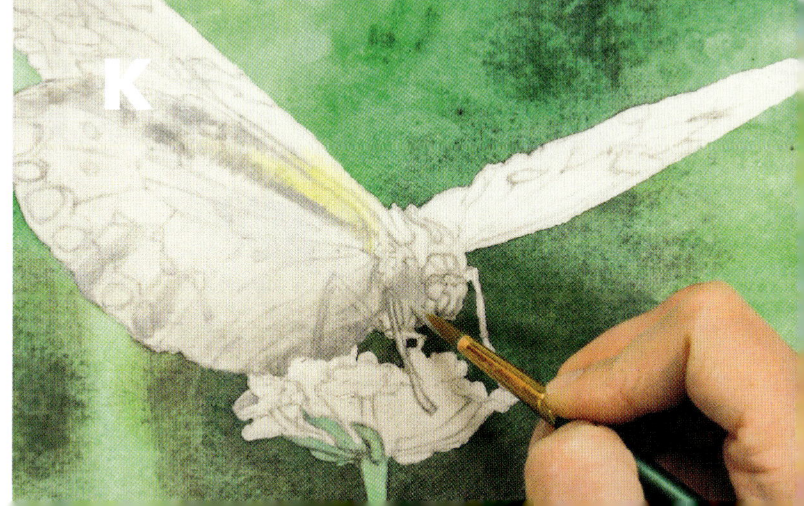

dark lines will not yet be in place. Simply do your best to match the color. When you add a wash to a portion of the anatomy, you can avoid overlapping the background by angling your head until the light in your workspace creates a glimmer on your paper.

While you use these techniques and finesse your skills, know that you are taking leaps forward in your creative advancement.

ESTABLISHING HIERARCHY WHEN THE SECONDARY FOCAL POINT IS A BRIGHT COLOR

L The unpainted flower clusters in the foreground will appear very bright, making it difficult to determine the value of the butterfly in comparison to the final composition. For that reason, you might want to paint the flowers before you finish painting the butterfly. Since there are so many colors within the flower clusters, it will be helpful to mix a variety of colors instead of painting with a single base color. When you paint the underside of the flower, remember to lower the saturation level of your paint mixtures.

In my composition, I chose to paint the lightest areas of the flowers light pink instead of white to place the appropriate amount of emphasis back on the butterfly. I also used a gray paint mixture that was slightly different than the hue I used on the butterfly to further differentiate the two.

MIXING NEUTRAL COLORS USING PRIMARY-COLOR PAINTS

To create the patterns on the butterfly, you can use paint, colored pencil, or a combination of the two. All are good options to explore. To help you decide which is best, consider the advantages as well as the disadvantages of using either medium, according to your own artistic strengths and current creative goals.

If you choose to use colored pencil, you may want to read the section on creating thin and ultra-smooth lines on page 246.

If you use paint, this is a great opportunity to mix primary colors to achieve a neutral gray. If you choose to explore this, begin by adding cadmium yellow paint to your palette, close to the amount of neutral paint you will need. Then add a small amount of cadmium red to create orange. Next, add a very small amount of both cobalt and ultramarine blue to either balance or darken the mixture. As you gradually adjust the color, assess the mixture you have created to determine whether it is lacking or abundant in one particular hue. Once you have created a neutral gray, use either water or white paint to replicate the value range you see in the reference image.

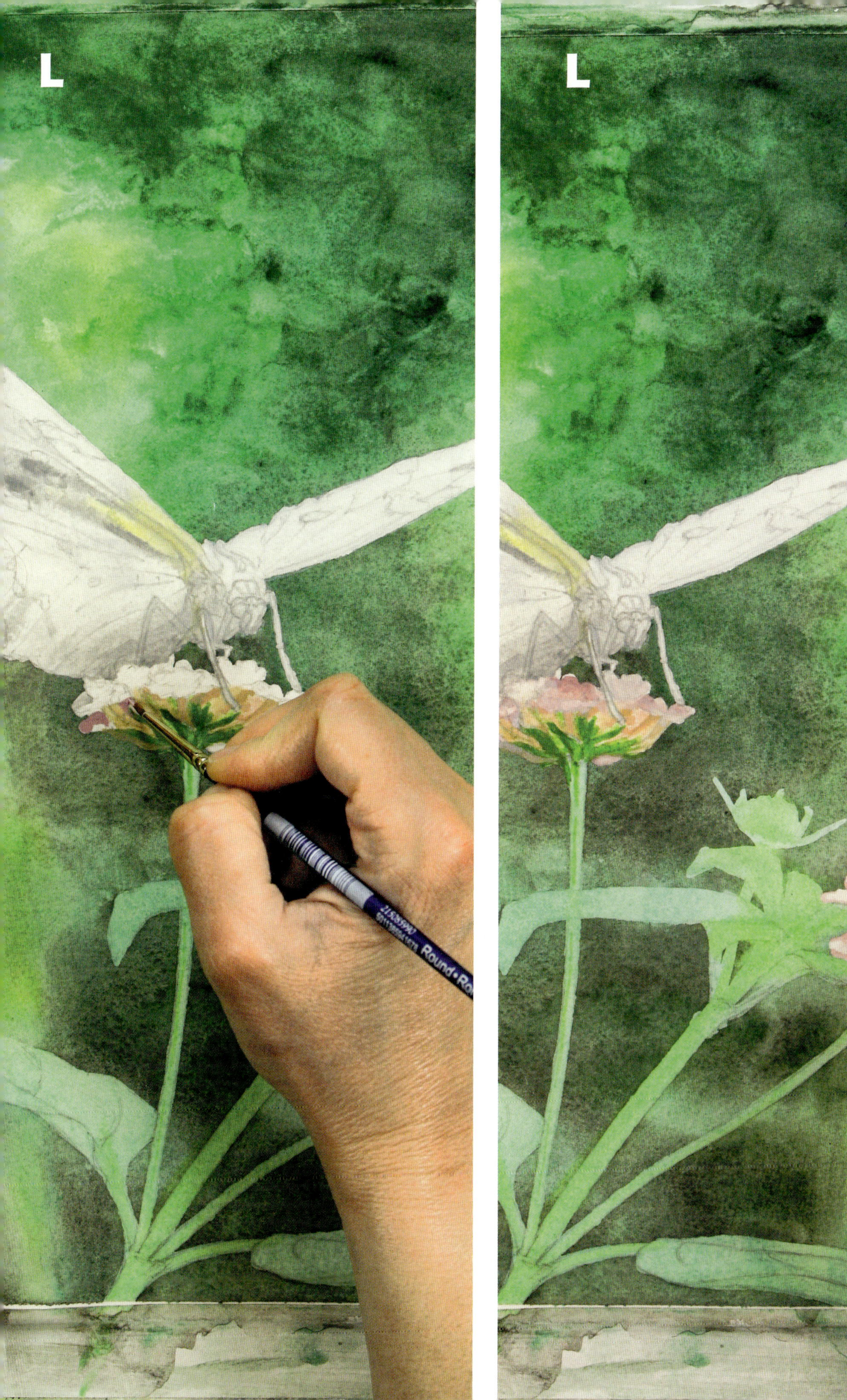
L
L

CREATING LINES AND ARCS USING PAINT

M Even if you choose to create the patterns using only colored pencil, you can follow these steps at any time to practice using a fluid medium to create straight lines and smooth arcs with a paintbrush. It may be helpful to read both this section and the one that follows on edge quality before you begin.

Select the smallest paintbrush you have and be sure that the bristles are straight and have a uniform shape. When you apply paint, maintain a steady speed, paint in one smooth motion, and commit with confidence. Maintain contact with the paper using your pinky finger, the side of your hand, or the heel of your hand. Rotate your wrist to create arcs; slide your hand smoothly across the paper to make straight lines. You may need to rotate the paper to accommodate the natural ergonomics of your hand motion. You can confirm the orientation by hovering above the paper and testing your hand movement.

Once you start to get the hang of it, begin to consider the location of the tip of the paintbrush before it touches the paper. This awareness can help you maintain control from the moment the paint meets the surface. Also, if you are painting a long or a particularly thin line, you might be surprised to find that your breathing can affect the shape you produce. You might try applying the paint during either a slow inhalation or exhalation.

Be sure to offer yourself the ease, understanding, and spaciousness you need to learn this technique. While you practice, know that you are building upon an already high level of skill and are beautifully refining your abilities.

EXPLORING THE EDGE QUALITY OF SMALL PATTERNS

It's helpful to think of the blurring technique as a spectrum that begins with dry paper or hard edges and ends with wet paper or soft edges. If, in this composition, you blur the edge of the patterns on the wings very slightly, you can convey a color change on the surface of a single form. To do this, first add a water wash to one wing and allow the glisten to fade completely before you apply the paint mixture. The paper fibers should be only slightly moist when you paint, which will minimize bleeding, give you control of where pigment is placed, and create patterns that appear a part of the wing. If you also choose to emulate the effect of the camera lens, which places more focus on the head of the butterfly, you will want to blur the edge even more in specific areas of the wing.

At some point, you might want to create an exercise for exploring how different moisture levels will affect the application of pigment. You could even design a labeled guide that you use in the future. To do this, you would create a spectrum of paint that ranges incrementally from pigment applied to dry paper all the way to a puddle of water sitting on top of the paper surface. You can also try varying the amount of water on your brush to see how the saturation of your paint mixture influences different points along the spectrum.

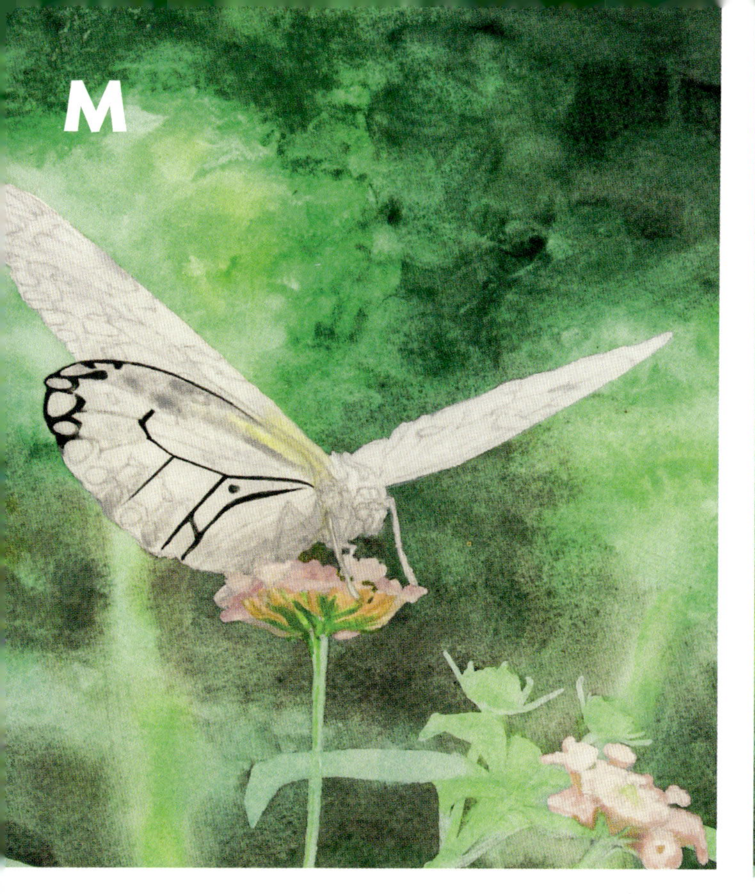
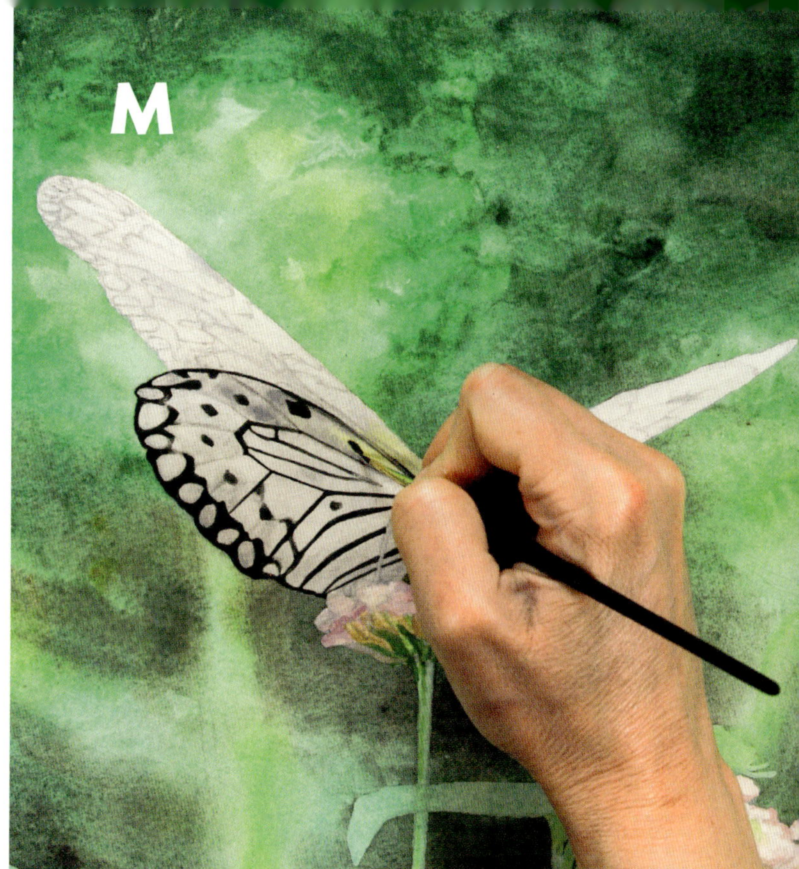

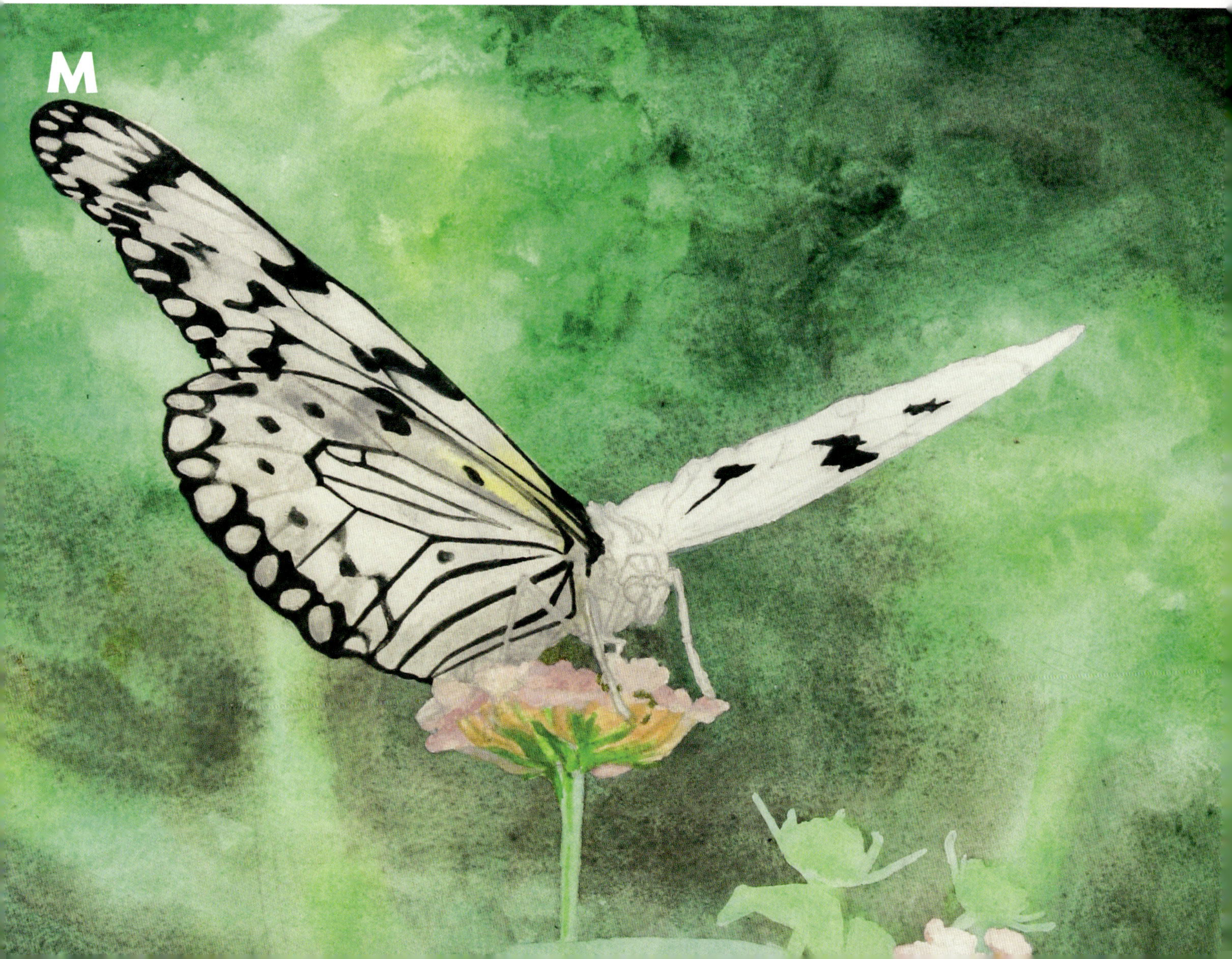

MAKING MISTAKES WHILE USING HIGH-CONTRAST PAINT COLORS

N Since the patterns on the butterfly are intricate, saturated, and surrounded by a very light color, it will be easy to make mistakes when you are painting. If this happens, strive to immediately remove pigment using water and a clean brush. If the pigment stains the paper, you will need to choose another solution for removing paint (see page 30). Although it is not generally easy to make this type of repair, it can be done.

Since I anticipated the likelihood of this happening, I simply expected that both error and repair were going to be an inherent part of this stage of the illustration. I had to redo several lines and periodically had to pause in the middle and start a line all over again. In addition, I made a conscious choice to repaint the left antenna in a slightly different location. I chose to accept the challenge of then having to camouflage the original line because it was incredibly thin, sat on top of

a colored ground, and was created using pigment that had been diluted. Had this error occurred while I was working on the wings, where the pigment is fully saturated and painted on a white ground, I would not have made this choice knowing that even my greatest efforts would likely stand out as an error in the final piece.

ILLUSTRATING BACKLIT BOTANICALS

Presenting the light source behind the subject is avoided in compositions because important features can be de-emphasized and the shading can make flat and round forms easily appear concave. When you have the challenge of creating a shadow on a botanical in the direction of the viewer, you can decrease these issues by gently lightening the darkest values. This will be especially helpful on the flower buds in this composition so that you can reiterate both the continuity of the gradation and the convex surface. The square stem of the botanical explains the fairly abrupt changes in value that can be seen in certain areas along its length. In general, when you add shadows and highlights, try to keep value changes as minimal as possible from one side of the stem to the other. This will minimize the potential to create a striped and flattened appearance. In addition, you can make the highlight on one side of the stem slightly wider or brighter than it is on the opposite side. This simple change will shift the shadow to one side, make the composition more dynamic, and translate the volume of the form all at once. As always, be sure that the overall shadowed areas appear darker than the highlights. If you find that the stem begins to appear as if it is glowing instead of backlit, try slightly reducing the highlight on the darker side of the stem.

As an artist, the more you understand the effects of light on complex forms, the more you will be able to convincingly convey that a form is oval, triangular, concave, creased, textured, translucent, or myriad other shapes and qualities, regardless of where the light source is located.

O Since the edge is along a painted line, you might want to enhance it using a guide instead of drawing by hand. While some artists might locate an adjustable ruler or search for the perfect French curve, I prefer to rotate a straight edge. To do this, place the ruler at the top of the curve and make a small mark. Then follow along the edge of the curve, rotating the ruler slightly and pausing to make additional marks that continue downward. If your marks are short enough, the line will appear round instead of faceted.

LEADING THE VIEWER'S EYE AROUND A COMPOSITION

It is important to understand that you have the ability to intentionally create flow through each quadrant of a composition. This can be achieved in the design stage by the placement, shape, and angle of each element within the composition. In the painting and refinement stages, these elements can be further enhanced or de-emphasized by adjusting the level of contrast and saturation.

Pause for a moment to consider the path your eye might travel when you look at each element in the reference image. It is reasonable to imagine that the powerful butterfly would catch your

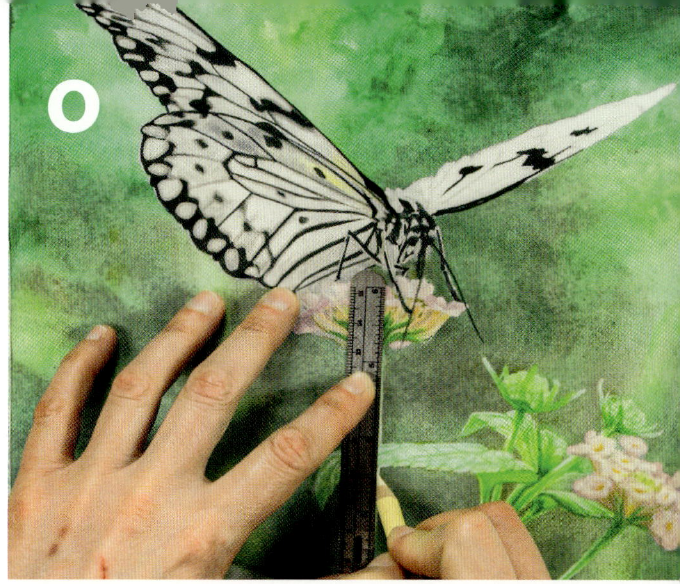

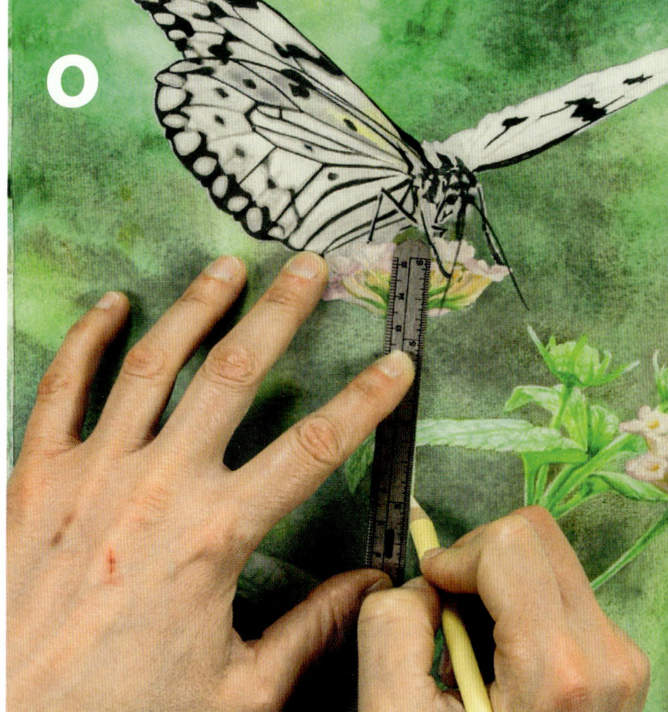

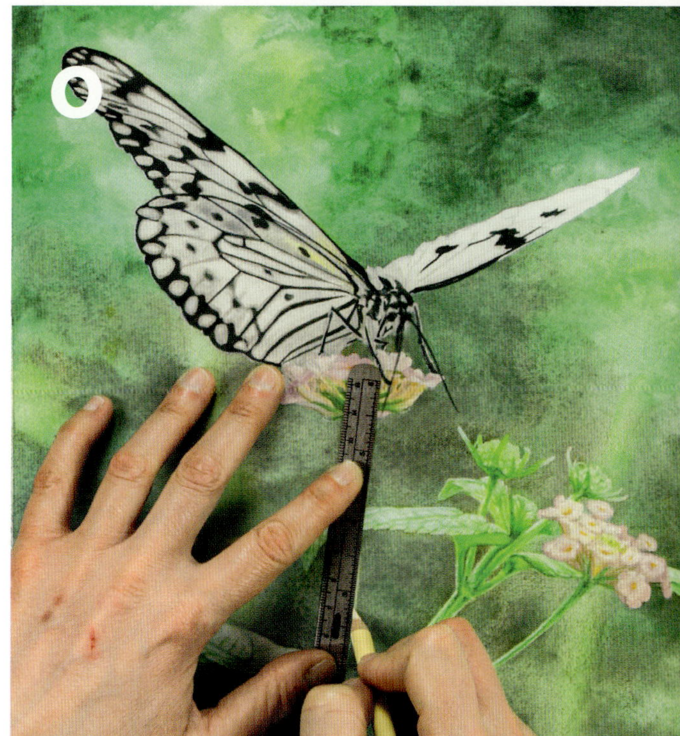

eye first. From there, you would likely look at the botanical, perhaps close to the lightly colored flower on the right side. At this point, your gaze might be drawn to the drooping leaf. If so, the path would skip over the lower right corner of the photograph and, instead, pour like a waterfall onto the highlighted leaf on the left side of the composition. The strong diagonal position of this leaf in the layout could lead your eye upward and right off the paper. Although the focal point is strong enough to pull your gaze back into the composition, it is not a smooth transition. Throughout this rather small visual circuit, I also felt that the large light form in the background seemed to become a distraction.

P In my illustration, I made many changes to enhance the composition and create a broader, more fluid visual circuit. I moved and darkened the background botanical and added another to fill the hole on the right. This alleviated much of the distraction, added side-to-side balance, and placed more emphasis on the butterfly. I de-emphasized the value of the drooping leaf and, as a result, it did not draw as much attention but still appeared realistically lit by the light source. Then I added a fairly bright leaf below to create interest in the lower right corner. When I did this, it became essential to avoid brightening the lower stem,

which could easily lead the viewer's eye off the bottom of the paper. Instead, I worked on the leaf to the left by brightening the lobe and darkening the end. My purpose for doing this was to encourage the eye of the viewer to continue up the diagonal, remain within the composition, and move smoothly upward to either explore the focal point or the background elements.

Anytime you examine the visual circuits within different compositions, you learn a great deal about hierarchy and rhythm. Although you can certainly play with the circuit in your own illustration, the visual exercise alone will help you to identify circuits and prepare you to create new ones in the future. At some point, you might want to review the projects in this book to compare the visual circuits you see in the reference images to those I created in the final illustrations. In addition, you can study various famous works of art to notice what path your eye follows. Consider what makes one circuit more successful than another. You might even ask others where their eyes led them to learn about both the similarities and differences of their experience when viewing a particular piece of artwork.

CREATING THIN AND ULTRA-SMOOTH COLORED PENCIL LINES

Q If you have chosen to create any of the wing veins using colored pencil, you will likely find it difficult to achieve a thin line that is both smooth and continuous. Select a colored pencil that matches the surrounding area of the wing. Draw

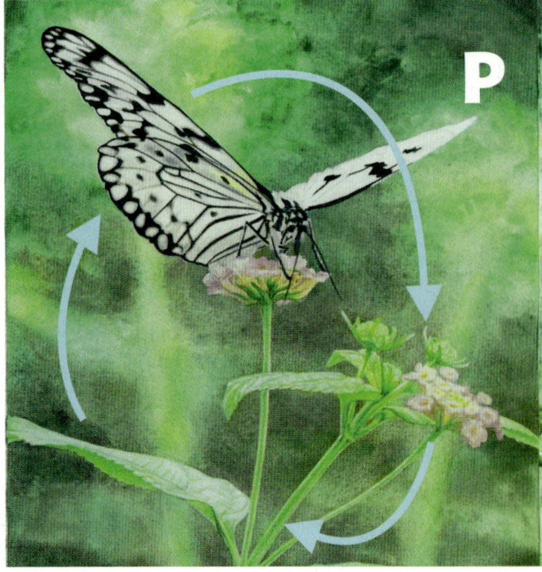

a thin, almost invisible line where you want the vein to be, then apply the dark gray or black on top. The resulting line you create should be extremely thin and very smooth. This technique, which has been offered in previous projects to refine outlines, is yet another example of how the skills that you already have can now be used in new ways to expand your creative abilities.

ENHANCING A COMPOSITION AT A LATE STAGE

Once all of the components of the composition are in place, there's always a chance that you might notice areas where you might like to adjust the value, color, or orientation. If this happens to you at a late point in the process, take a moment to consider whether it is best to honor your creative request or to leave the piece as it is.

Think about how important each modification feels to you, how significantly it will affect the illustration, and the level of risk involved. The next step is to imagine the challenges you might encounter and whether or not you think it would be wise to proceed. Revisiting the overall creative goals you are working toward can help you make a decision.

For this project, I suggest that you choose a single alteration to work on. Select one that will provide a slight amount of challenge but have a low level of risk. Then go ahead and take the leap.

Anytime you make an alteration, be sure you are prepared to accept any outcome. When a final adjustment turns out even close to what you envisioned, regardless of your previous experience or the level of risk you take, It should be considered a miracle and celebrated as such!

Good luck—I believe in you.

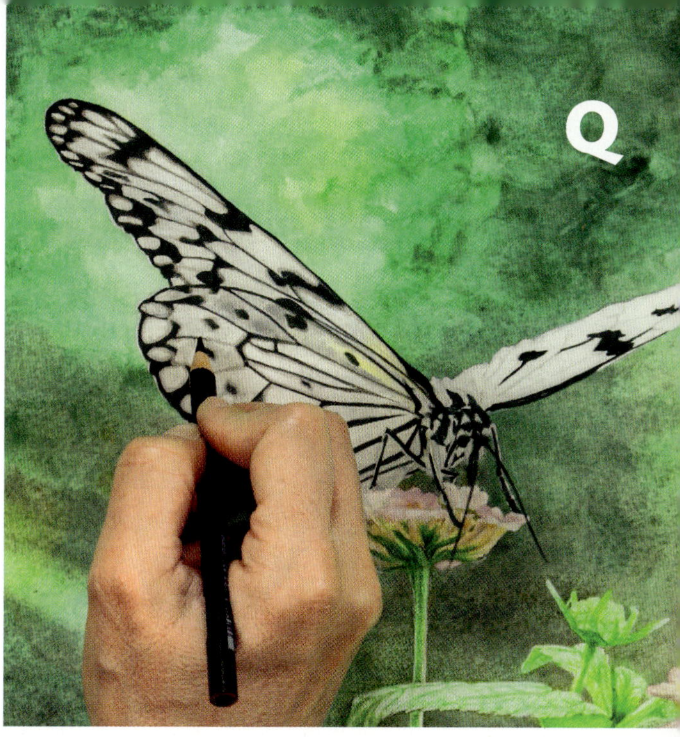

In my illustration, I wanted to make two changes. First, I felt that the color of the flowers could be more saturated. Admittedly, this would only add a minor amount of improvement to the composition. Still, this change felt moderately important to me and the risk seemed low enough to proceed without hesitation. My second request, however, had more to offer and much more at stake. I wanted to paint a dark translucent layer over the entire background to accentuate the botanical in the foreground and tone down the botanical in the background. My greatest concern was the potential of creating unwanted hard edges in the middle of painted areas. To minimize this possibility, I identified a route that would help me repaint areas more quickly and easily. I also had to ask myself if I was willing to remake the piece, which I knew would be disappointing as an artist and frustrating as an author. In the end, however, I agreed to take the risk. Throughout my career, I have needed to make similar decisions. The results have gone both ways; this time it worked well. Just as easily, I could have decided that the risk was too great and continued using colored pencils to darken a few select areas of the background instead. In my mind, both choices were of equal merit, even if the outcome and level of risk were quite different.

REVIEWING YOUR PREPARATION AND PROCESS

Now that you have traversed each step of the process, think back to when you first looked at the composition. Compare your preview to the steps that were actually necessary to successfully complete this piece. Simply take some time to reflect, so that you can refine, build upon, and personalize this preliminary stage of the process in the next chapter.

Consider: Which steps were helpful to you? What information could have been omitted from or added to your outline? Are there any techniques that you substituted for another? Also, revisit the overall sequence of the steps to think about a rearrangement in the future.

With each observation, you are further developing the ability to look at any piece and know immediately what you need to address, make important decisions quickly, be appropriately prepared to work, and achieve results you can feel good about. Great job exploring this foundation building skill.

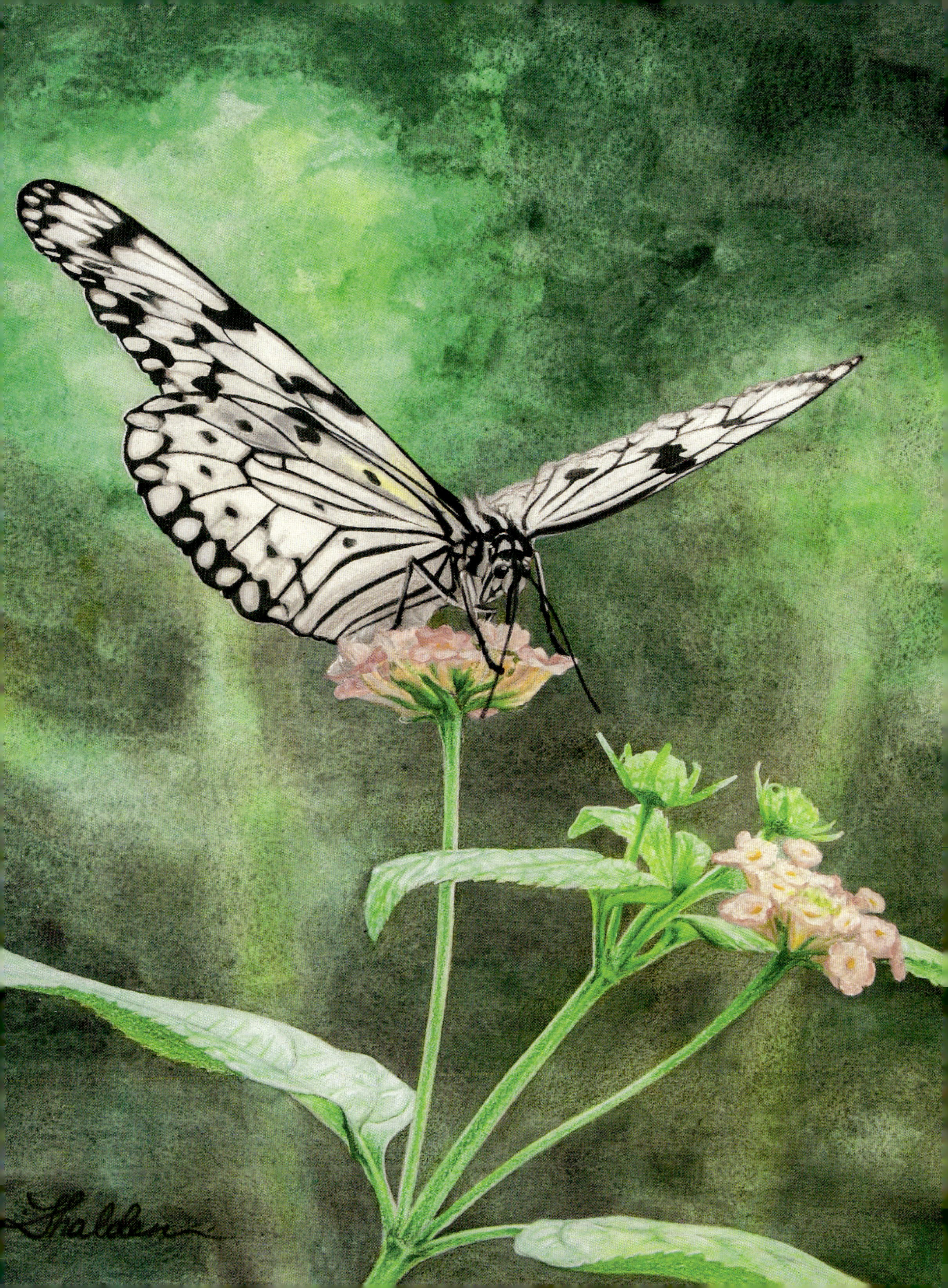

INTUITIVE ADVENTURE

When your artistic process is guided by personal insight instead of logic, your decisions about materials, location, and subject can be discovered along the way. This Nature Break allows inquiry and instinct to lead the experience. It's time to go on an intuitive adventure.

MATERIALS: Let your body and mind relax. Then silently repeat this question: *What do I need to bring to create artwork today?* Each time, notice whether a thought or an image comes to mind or if your eyes track to a specific object. Let this item be a part of your palette. You may or may not end up using traditional art supplies. Put all of your items in a carrying case and get ready to venture out.

LOCATION: Your next questions will determine your transportation: *Should I walk? Should I drive? Should I take public transit?* With each question, see if you can sense the answer. Then, at every opportunity presented by an intersection, a bus stop, or other crossroad along the way, also ask yourself: *Which is the best direction to go?* Of course, be conscientious of logistics and safety with your choices.

OBSERVATIONS: Whether you travel a few feet or many miles, recognize any new sites, interactions, and discoveries.

PRACTICE: When you have arrived at a location that could be a temporary art studio, take out your supplies. Ask questions to determine both how you might use your supplies and what being creative in this location could be like. Allow yourself the freedom to play, wonder, and explore creativity in a completely new way.

REFLECTION: What did you see, feel, and experience? How did this exercise change the way you engage creatively? Did you find any part of the exercise challenging? What have you gleaned that could inspire future artwork or another adventure?

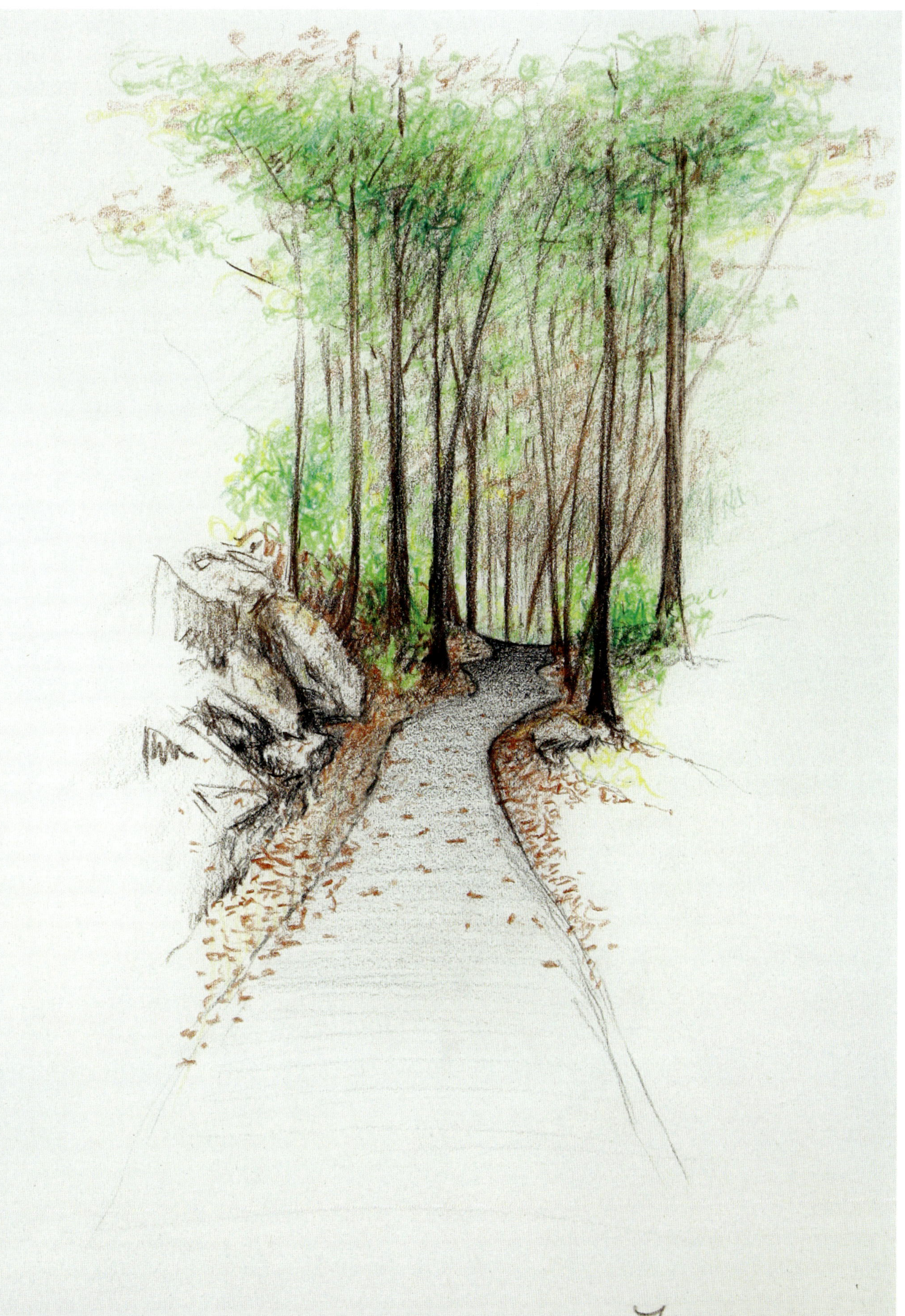
Thalden

SNOWBERRY CLEARWING MOTH

HEMARIS DIFFINIS

Hummingbird moths hover in the air as they feed on the nectar of flowers. Surprisingly, these moths can be seen foraging during the day. Their wings, which are nearly invisible while in motion, beat so rapidly that they can create an audible humming sound. Hummingbird moths even have long hairs at the end of their abdomen that they are able to fan out like the tail feathers of a bird. As their name implies, these moths are often mistaken for tiny hummingbirds. The snowberry clearwing is one of five clearwing moth species found in the United States. This species has the advantage of mimicking a bumblebee's coloration, fooling predators into thinking they can sting.

 SEE REFERENCE PHOTOS ON PAGES 326–327

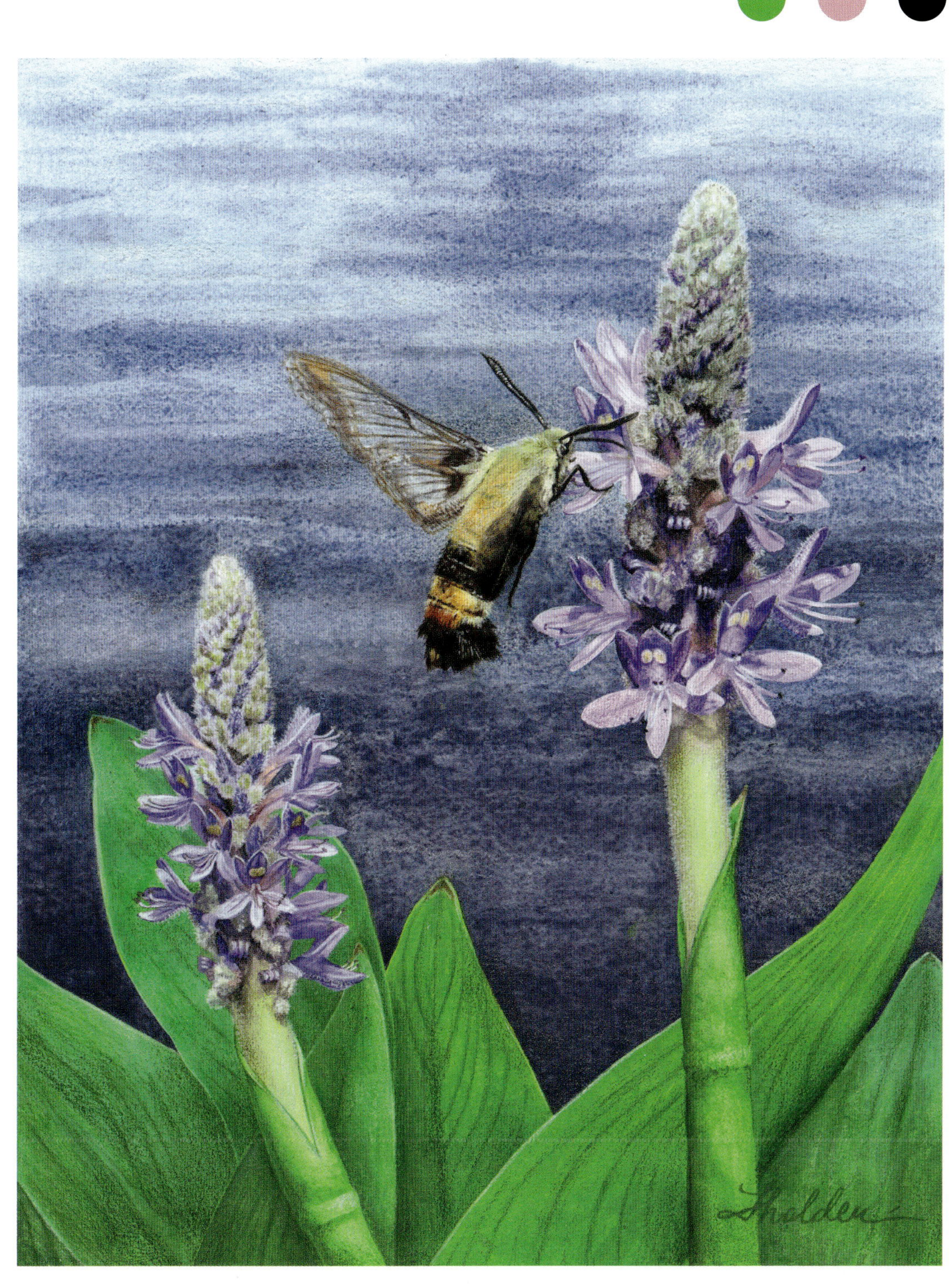

I have included several optional learning opportunities that address using multiple references, using a limited palette, re-creating the surface of water, and observing nuanced color variation. Since this project is already packed with information, I highly recommend selecting only one topic to explore so that you have time to integrate the information. In other words, you have the ability to determine how simple or complex the overall project will be, and your finished composition may look quite different than mine. Keep in mind that you can always read through the techniques and practice each one at a later date. Regardless of the journey you choose, I hope that you will have a chance to experiment, have some fun, and learn new skills as you progress through this project.

DEVELOPING YOUR OWN PROCESS: PART 2

Start by writing down every step you plan to follow within each part of your creative process. Remember that the purpose of this exercise is to free your mind so you can focus on the artwork itself, practice the steps so that they can become ingrained, and develop a successful routine for working through complex compositions in the future.

Reviewing the questions in the previous chapter may help you envision the best creative process to follow. Make as many decisions as you can ahead of time, and include moments when you will engage in exploration. For example, in the design stage, you might simply list, "reorganize the layout," "play with the background color," or "change the location and number of elements in the composition." You might also consider leaving extra space in your list so you can easily insert new process steps. Be sure to include the titles of each process provided in this chapter in your outline so that you know when to pause and read about the techniques needed to continue onward. As you write down each step, incorporate periodic pauses so you can take time to acknowledge and celebrate your accomplishments. If there is a task that you feel could be challenging, you might include an encouraging phrase that would offer some support before a process.

CREATING A BRAND-NEW DESIGN

When creating a new design, you may want to consider the balance, hierarchy, unity, negative space, and visual circuit of your layout in addition to addressing the overall dimensions. Keep in mind that elements that can be seen in their entirety will have greater visual importance than those partially concealed by another component in the design. To help guide your process, you can also review the design section in both the Weaver Ant and Luna Moth projects.t

A Begin by looking at the reference image to determine the areas you would like to retain. In my illustration, I wanted to keep the level of detail, the orientation, and the colors of the subject. I also recognized that the neutral value in the background worked well, and although I thought that the blurred spike was distracting, it seemed to successfully add a sense of special depth to the overall composition.

B Next, view the reference image with a more critical eye to locate areas you feel could be improved. For my illustration, there were four areas that I wanted to adjust: the blank section in the upper left corner, the visual discord at the top of the botanical, the weight in the bottom right quadrant, and the hierarchy of primary subjects.

GENERATING DESIGNS

C Now it's time to grab your sketchbook and brainstorm ideas for your new design. Start by documenting each concept by drawing quick thumbnail sketches. Be sure to leave a little space surrounding each sketch so that you can easily view them individually. Your compositions might end up looking very similar or be very different from one another. Fill up as many pages as you like, and add notes if it will help you remember specific details. You can either pause to develop ideas you feel have potential or simply mark them so that you can continue generating new concepts. This will help keep your mind free as you explore more possibilities.

RESOLVING DESIGN ISSUES

When problem solving, you can use the following technique to determine the degree to which each element has influenced the composition. Simply use a portion of your hand to cover a specific section of the reference image and, closing one eye, view the overall image as if the element is absent. Notice how the emphasis and balance has shifted, for better or worse, when this element is no longer there. For example, you can cover the insect to see how much more powerful both the botanical and the environment appear. You can then try experimenting with a different area, such as the blurred flower stalk or another portion of the background. Using this technique can help you to decide if an element should be relocated, removed, or remain the same. You can also use this technique to quickly determine how cropping one or two sides of the reference image would influence the overall composition.

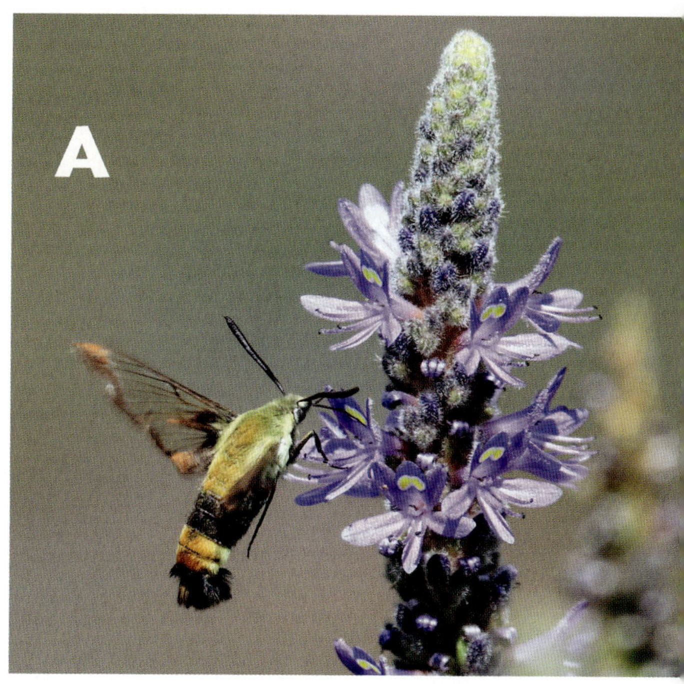
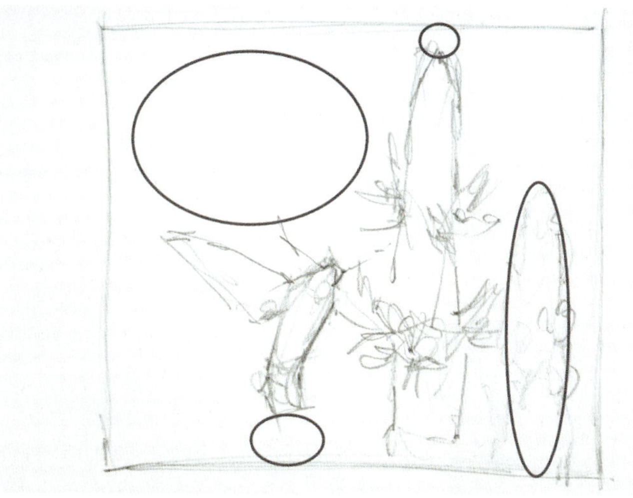
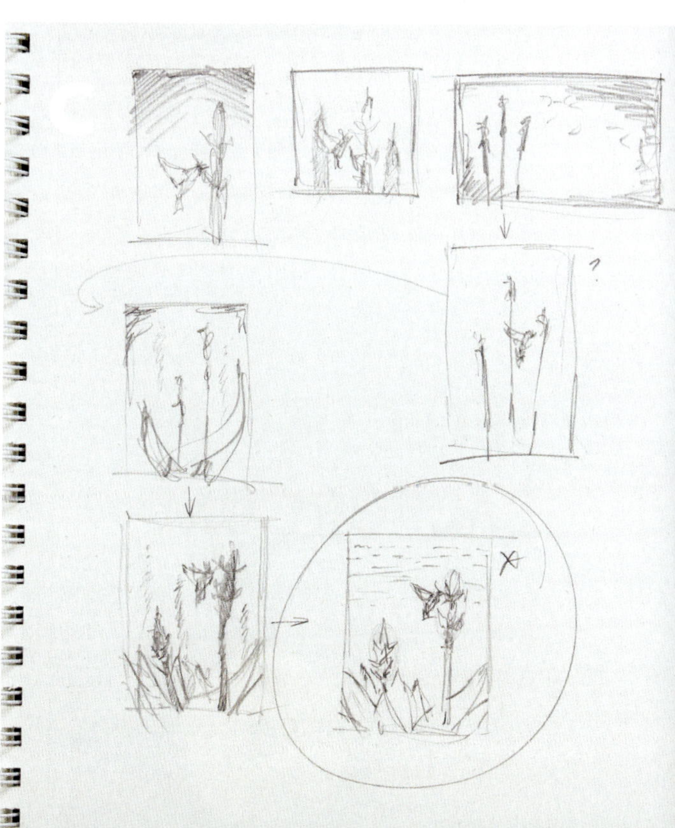

In the design stage of my illustration, I used this technique to explore hierarchy. When I covered the first whorl of flowers, I found that the lower whorl and the insect had more emphasis and, most important, the moth became the focal point of the composition. Although I could have removed a portion of the botanical or changed the value of the flowers, I decided to relocate the moth to the area with the most power. Unfortunately, this placed the focal point in the center of the design. My next step, therefore, was to work in my sketchbook to adjust overall dimensions and add other elements that would serve to widen the visual circuit in the final illustration.

To address the upper-left corner, I explored the idea of either subtly changing the value or adding visual texture to widen the circuit. I addressed my second concern by increasing the space between the flower stalk and the framing edge. To do this, I considered shortening the botanical, changing the overall scale of the subjects, or extending the framing edge. Last of all, I wanted to either remove the blurred flower spike or add more of them in other areas to create balance in the background.

After you have added a variety of design concepts in your sketchbook, you might want to review previous projects to see if there are other compositions that inspire additional options for you to choose from.

When you are ready, select the layout you want to use. You can then revisit your steps to see if there are adjustments you need to make. If you'd like, you can even select more than one concept and create a series of two or three consecutive illustrations.

SELECTING A BACKGROUND

If you choose to create a different background color, you might want to reread the section of the forest pierrot project (page 216), that offers suggestions for selecting an alternative color scheme. Consider the color wheel and determine which hues, values, and saturation levels would both support the subjects and enhance the overall composition. Feel free to consider colors that are more natural as well as those that would not be found in a natural environment.

For my illustration, one of the colors I selected was a blue with a low saturation. While researching the species, I identified the botanical as pickerelweed, which grows in shallow water. This inspired the possibility of creating a blue gradient in the background that emulated the surface of a pond. Using a muted color would help the subject stand out, and by incorporating a simple wave pattern, the visual circuit of the composition would also be enlarged.

ADDING REFERENCE IMAGES

Designing can often lead to the need for additional references. When you select photographs to use, pay close attention to the appearance of the subjects and compare them to the subjects in your original reference. There could be a difference in the environment, such as the amount of sunlight or wind, or it could be the exposure or color balance of the image itself. Since the background can easily become a distraction, I typically avoid using images that have complex textures, busy reflections, or high-contrast colors. It's also beneficial to look for photographs that have been taken from a similar elevation so that the viewpoint matches. Although it may take a while to find images that meet all your criteria, it will make the process of illustrating much easier and the outcome more lifelike.

Sometimes you can use only a specific portion of an image to meet your requirements. For example, an image of a mallard duck swimming among lily pads might not have seemed like the ideal choice for a background to use in this illustration. The section above the waterfowl in this image, however, was exactly what I was looking for. I knew that if I replicated the subtle ripples and reflected clouds at the top of my illustration, I could create a realistic environment as well as add interest to the upper left corner of the composition. I would also choose to exclude the lily pads so that the focus would remain on both the insect and pickerelweed. In addition, I could transition from realistic imagery to a solid blue background close to the center of the layout, which would make the subjects in the illustration appear even more pronounced.

It's always important to encourage the respect of artwork created by other fine artists and photographers. At any time you are searching for reference images, regardless of whether you will be selling your work or keeping it private, it is advisable to use photographs that are copyright-free, that have been purchased for use, or that you have taken yourself.

COMPENSATING FOR A LIMITED PALETTE

So often a product or color that you would otherwise depend on will run out, cannot be purchased, or is no longer produced by manufacturers. You will also find that there are hues, intensities, and values in nature that pigments cannot re-create. When this happens, problem solving and versatility can help you keep moving forward and continue to produce quality artwork. If you would like to give it a try, keep your goal achievable and test techniques before you apply them to the finished piece. As you strive to achieve high-level results, be sure to give yourself the support you need to learn and grow.

To provide you with an example, I chose to remove several key colored pencils while working on the flower spikes in my illustration. Another option that would have offered a similar challenge would have been to use only the six base paint colors: cadmium red, cadmium yellow, cobalt blue, ultramarine blue, titanium white, and Mars black. If you are up for a significant challenge, these would be good options, although just removing a single colored pencil or a nonessential paint color from your palette would provide a great learning opportunity. Because this was a playful challenge instead of one created by a supply shortage, it is important to mention that I only limited my palette on a small portion of the composition to keep the creative extension manageable.

Anytime that you are faced with the challenge of a limited palette, identify the process that you were planning to use and then brainstorm other means to produce a similar result. You may need to do some experimenting to be able to compare the benefits and disadvantages of each option. You might also give some thought to how heavily you would like to rely on one medium versus another to create density, hue, and detail. Whether you spend more time and effort in the painting stage or the colored pencil stage really comes down to appearance, availability of supplies, and personal preference.

I also want to let you know that to be engaged in a significant learning process at an advanced stage of your artistic development can be humbling. Other times, you may find that when you expand new areas, your experience enables you to figure it out more quickly. Either way, your practice can greatly benefit from exploration, experimentation, and ingenuity.

SIMPLIFYING REPETITIVE PATTERNS

D To draw the complex network of flower buds, first create the overall spiral pattern of both the upper lighter rows, which are younger buds, and the lower darker rows, which are closer to blooming. When you begin this way, it is much easier to draw an accurate shape of each bud in the correct location.

If you want to add more visual clarity to your drawing, you can slightly darken the older buds. Value can add anatomical discernment to your artwork and make it much easier for you to see specific sections or particular lines in your drawing. But be sure to shade evenly, otherwise the value can begin to resemble shadow, which would make it difficult to differentiate the actual shadows when you begin to apply color.

SEPARATING THE BACKGROUND FROM THE SUBJECT IN A DRAWING

E You can also darken the outlines around the small windows of negative space along the perimeter of the subjects where the background can be seen. If you look at the flower stalk on the left in my illustration, you can see that the accentuated perimeter helps to differentiate the flower petals

from the pond behind the subject. While I am drawing, I'm careful to keep the value of these outlines close to that of either the background or the shadows on the subject so that they become invisible when color is applied.

SETTING UP SUBJECTS TO APPEAR IN MOTION

When a portion of the focal point is blurred due to movement, you can begin to express these sections in the drawing stage so that it will be easier to understand how and where to apply color. Instead of using a single outline, you can use multiple lines to express either the thickness of the blur or the location of repeated edges. It may be helpful to keep one line slightly more dominant than the others.

Because the upper and lower wings on the left side of the moth blend together slightly, take time to identify and differentiate the separate outlines in your drawing. Since sections of the wings are also transparent, it will help you to draw the veins and the outline of each opaque section so that you know where the background color will be visible. **F** Astonishingly, the wings of a hummingbird moth move in a figure-eight pattern. The set of wings you see on the right are actually in the middle of this movement pattern. Toward the left of this area, you are actually seeing the top surface of the upper wing and, toward the right, you can see the underside of the lower wing. To add more confusion, the forms are all foreshortened and the contour is difficult to decipher. After you add the

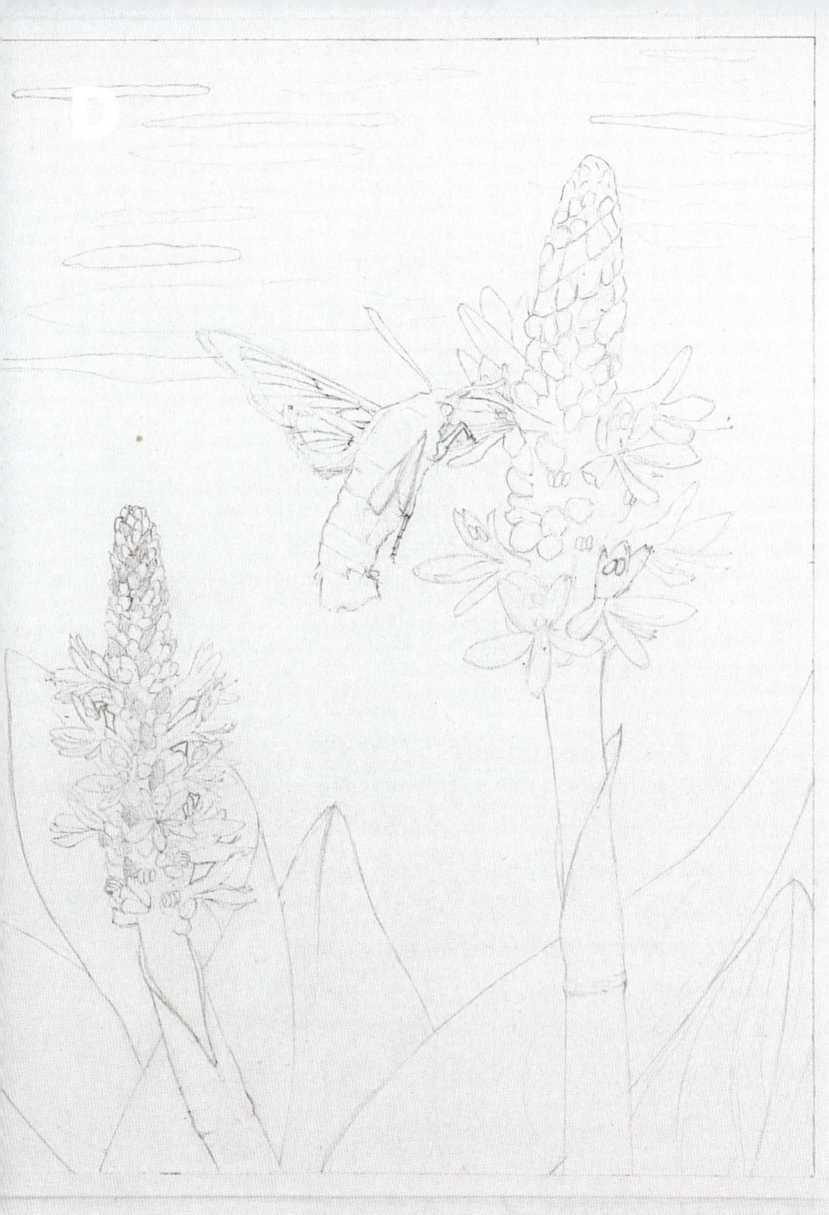

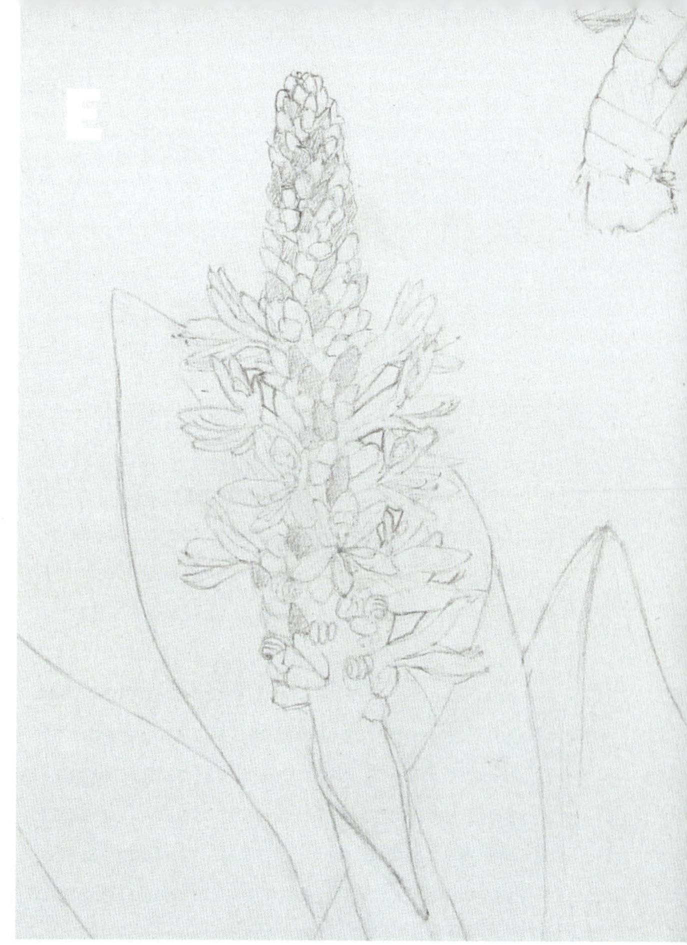

wings to your illustration, take a look at the entire insect to see if they appear realistic, and make adjustments as needed. In my illustration, I realized the correct position in the colored pencil stage, so I needed to pause, reassess, and redraw the wings accurately.

Taking the time to observe how complex forms are projecting toward or away from you, as well as how they are moving, will help you continue to draw accurately and convincingly.

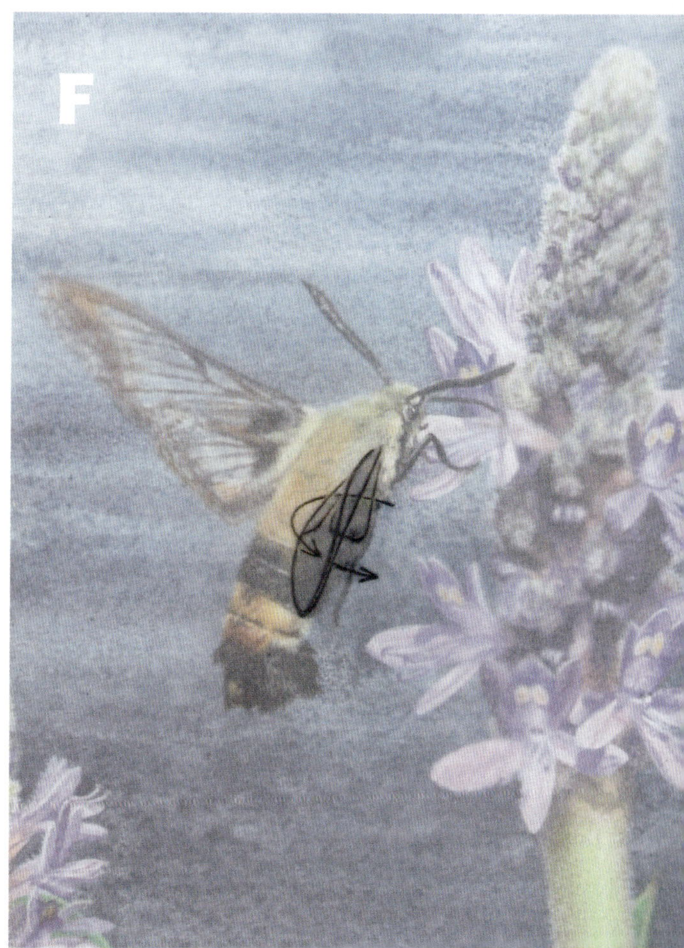

PAINTING REFLECTIONS IN WATER

When you are attempting to suggest spatial depth on the surface of water, keep this basic aspect of perspective drawing in mind: An object's height and width is relative to how far you are from it.

For example, take a look at the lily pads in the reference image of the pond. From the angle that the photograph was taken, the ellipses closest to the viewer, near the bottom of the composition, are both taller and wider than those farther away and located higher up in the composition. To see the incremental change more clearly, use the end of your pencil to compare sizes.

Even though the shape and size of ripples on water are not as predictable or defined as the lily pads, you can measure height in a similar way. By doing this, you can create a sense of spaciousness in the background.

PAINTING A BACKGROUND AROUND A COMPLEX SUBJECT

When you paint the background, there are many options regarding the amount of masking fluid you might use. To make your decision, consider both the design you are working on and the strategy that could offer you the most benefit. Whichever direction you choose, know that it is a good one to proceed with.

If your composition is more complex than usual, you might coat the entire subject prior to painting so that you can focus solely on the environment. If your layout is fairly simple, you might try to avoid using masking fluid altogether and see how it goes. Even keeping a small section unmasked may be enough to investigate this process.

Regardless of which technique you choose, painting around outlines can help you focus on the speed at which you apply paint, your ability to maintain a wet painting edge, and working carefully around outlines.

G In my illustration, I masked half of the composition just to provide you with a comparison of the two techniques. I would otherwise have chosen to leave all of the greenery unmasked and coat only the flower spikes and the body of the moth.

COVERING LARGE AREAS USING MASKING FLUID

When you use masking fluid over a large and intricate area, take your time and remember that it is most important to employ precision around the perimeter. Use the same color shaper or small paintbrush that you have designated for this purpose. Also, be sure to work in a well-ventilated area until the product has dried so that you don't inhale fumes. If you work outside, avoid having direct sunlight on the masking fluid.

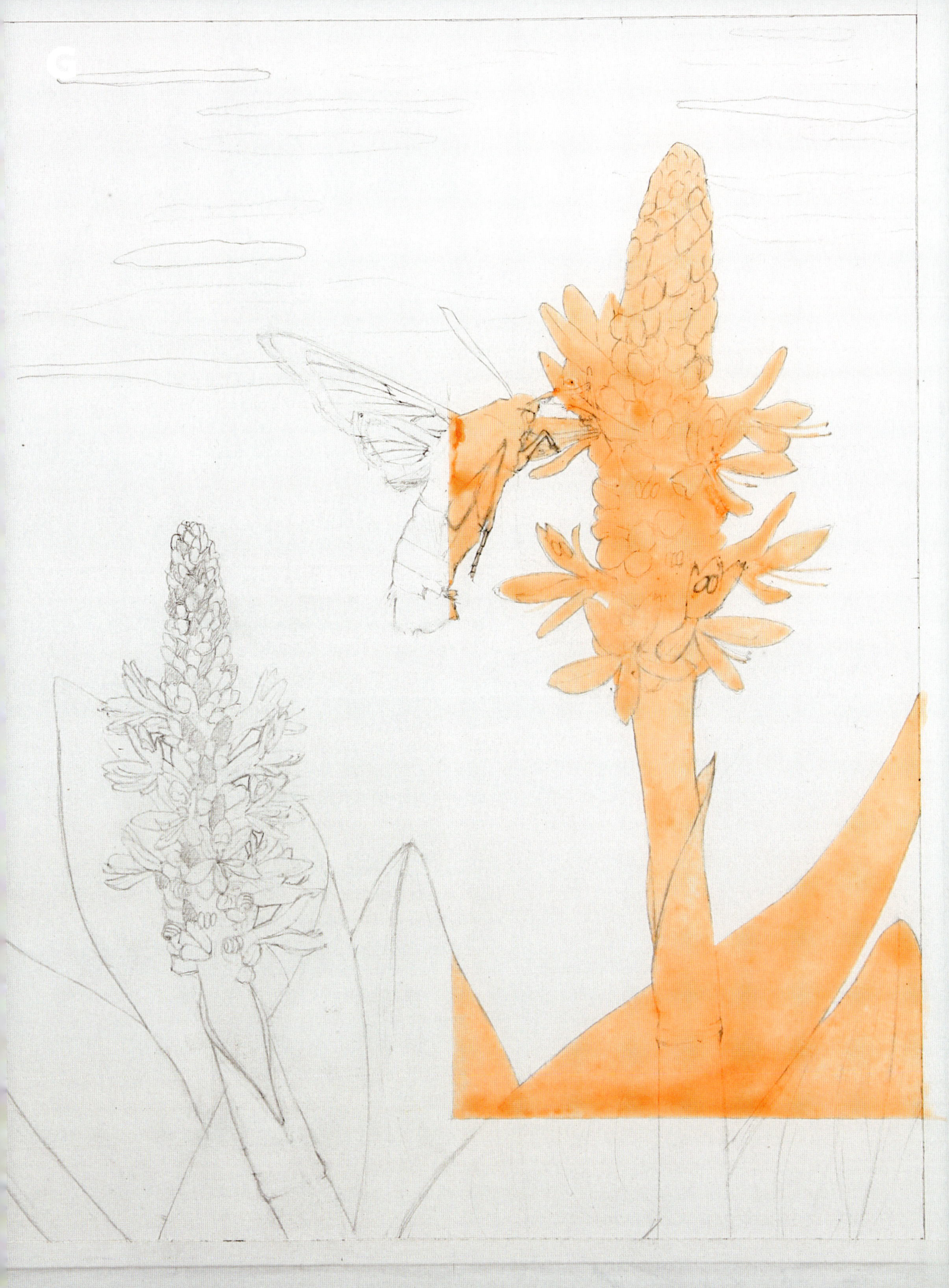

CREATING THE TRANSPARENT SECTIONS OF A WING

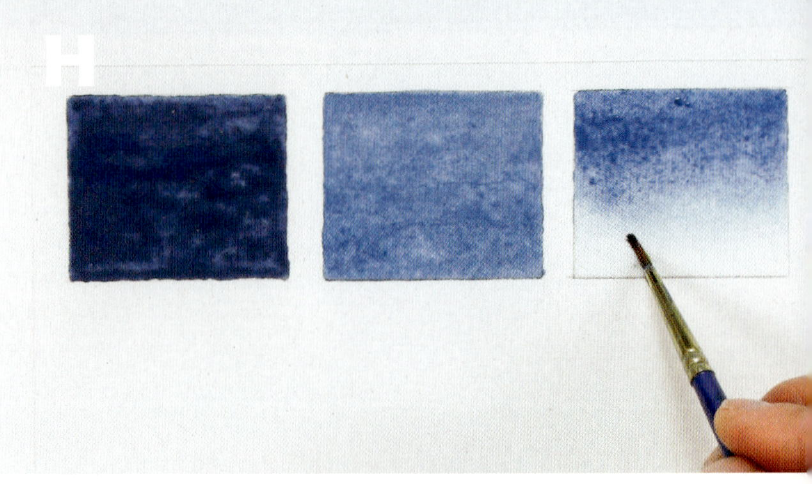

There are many ways that you can create the areas where you can see the background through wings. One option is to paint the wings when you paint the background. If you choose this technique, avoid the wings when you apply masking fluid. Be aware that this can create hard edges, so you will need to blur the edge with a brush or soften it with colored pencil later in the process. Another option is to leave the entire wing unpainted. Simply paint only the background and allow it to dry. Then, while the background paint mixture is still workable on your palette, you can create the wings independently. Further still, you could use colored pencils to create some or all of the coloration on the wings. Maybe you will think of yet another technique you can use.

AN EXERCISE FOR HONING YOUR PAINTING SKILLS

H Unless you have chosen to go with an unpainted background, this is a great opportunity to take your painting skills to the next level. This exercise is especially helpful if you create unintended hard lines or blooming in painted areas. To begin, draw small squares on a scrap piece of the type of paper you'll use for your final composition. Select a small paintbrush with a pointed tip and choose one square to work on. Without applying a wash, paint a horizontal line across the top, from the left to the right corner. Pick up your paintbrush and paint another line just below. Repeat this process until the remainder of the square has been coated in a single layer of paint. As you paint each line, fill in any gaps that the paintbrush has missed. Allow the top of the square to begin to dry while the bottom edge remains wet and workable all the way across so that you can apply the next line of paint. Your goal is to create a square that is a solid color, with no variation in either value or hue.

You can also apply a wash to practice creating an even gradation that fades back to the color of the paper or into a different color. It might also be fun to place a drop or two of water onto a square while it is drying to see how saturation level causes paint to bloom. This can help you learn how to control or encourage this effect in the future. If you become comfortable working at this size, try a square that is slightly larger. Eventually, you may find that working on a background—whether it has a solid color, patterns, a simple gradation, or loose gestural forms—is much easier and that the results are more in line with your intentions.

Of all the exercises offered in this book, this one has the simplest concept yet is the most difficult to achieve, regardless of your skill level. While you may reach the goal, the purpose is to have an exercise that can accompany your practice. Instead of having perfection as your aim, consider this exercise as creative maintenance or a great way to warm up prior to painting. Although you will improve with practice, be prepared for your results to also ebb and flow over time.

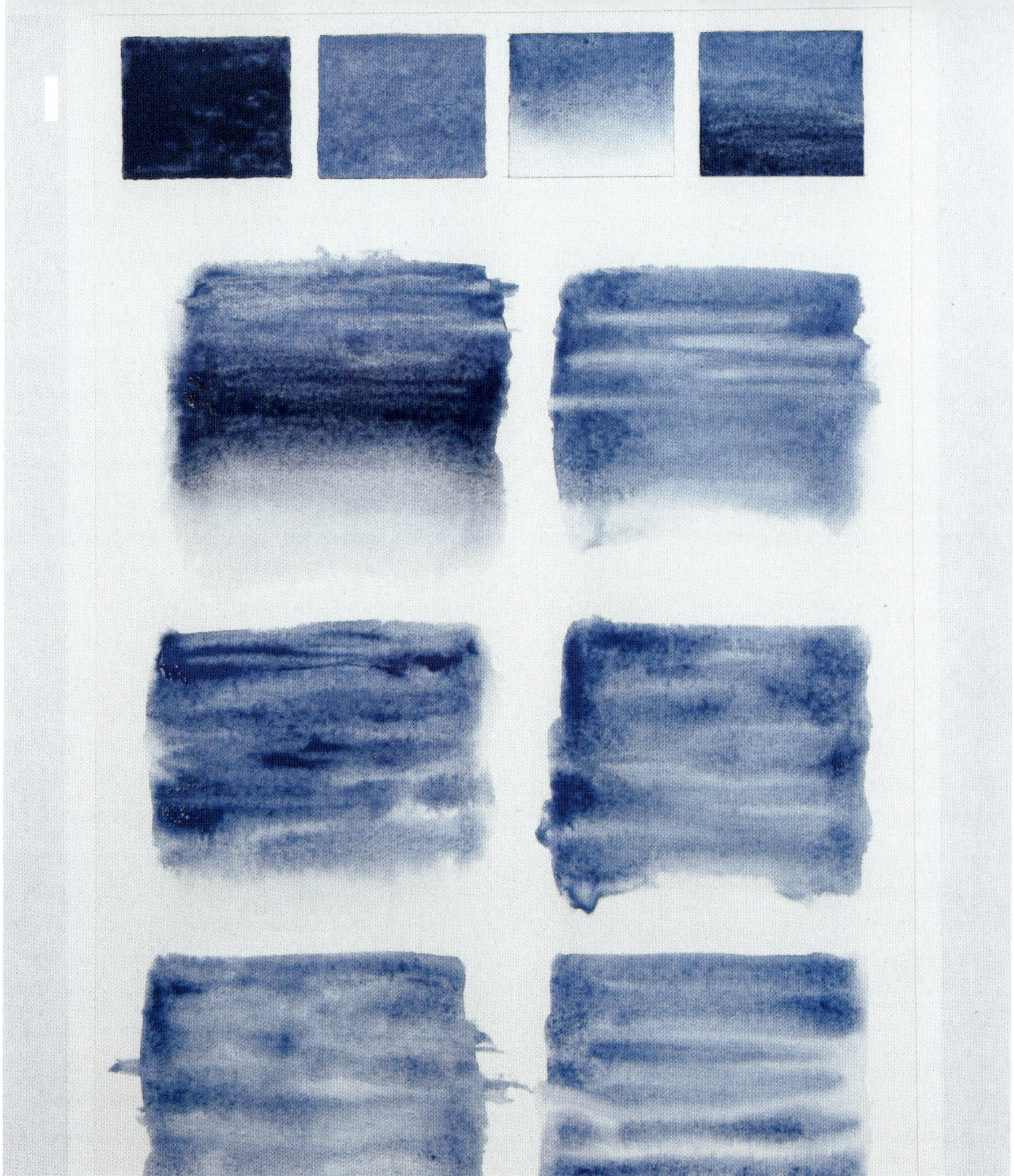

PAINTING RIPPLES IN WATER

I If your design includes a pond in the background, practice painting ripples on a scrap piece of paper. Start by creating both a medium and a very dark blue paint mixture. They do not have to match in hue. Then separate a section of both mixtures and combine them to create variations between the two. To begin, create a tinted wash to lower the level of contrast in the background so that it doesn't compete with the subject. Then paint long horizontal lines using the medium blue paint mixture. Make sure you are using a brush with a pointed tip so that you create points on either end of the lines as you touch the brush to the paper and lift it off again. You can paint these lines in varying lengths and stagger them so that they appear more realistic. Repeat where it is necessary to create darker lines. Let some of these lines intersect with the side of the area. When you feel more comfortable with this technique, try using the tip of the paintbrush to create thinner lines near the top and thicker lines as you work downward.

If the paint mixture is too diluted it can "bloom" on the page as the water floods over the surface. While this can be a wonderful effect to use in the future, for now simply try to work with the surface so that your lines all bleed evenly. On the other hand, if your paint does not blend in, you might need to add water to either the mixture or the paper. Try blurring your vision periodically to see if the water effect seems realistic.

Unlike that of creating detailed anatomical forms, this process is much more painterly. Therefore, you might want to replicate overall themes instead of re-creating the reference image. While I'm working, I try to remind myself that I am painting shadows and avoiding the highlighted tops of the waves, so that I don't get lost in pattern and end up flattening the illusion of space.

J I decided to paint the background in two stages so that I could focus on the complex pattern in the upper half separately from the intricate outline of the unmasked subject in the lower half. Whether you choose to paint in stages or all at once, create all of the paint you will need for the entire background at one time.

Apply a tinted wash to the upper third of your illustration and continue using a clear wash until you are just over halfway down the composition. Return to the top and, applying your learning from the practice session, begin to add horizontal lines using the medium blue mixture. When you reach about a quarter of the way down the page, begin to replace the lighter color with the medium blue mixture. Continue the same pattern, applying the medium-dark blue mixture on top, so that you create a gradation as you work down the page. Pay extremely close attention when applying a wash, and then paint, near areas that are unmasked so that you do not cover them by mistake. Also, make sure that the paint color and value match on both sides of the subject.

K When you get to the midway point, switch to the dark blue paint mixture that will be used in the lower section. If you are going to paint in two sections, allow this pattern to blur into the clear wash and let the upper section dry completely. When you are ready to work on the lower half, just add a clear wash that overlaps a small portion of the painted section and continue. Otherwise, simply work your way down the page, painting wider waves, alternating between using the medium and dark blue mixture and then the dark and very dark blue mixture.

L In my composition, the flower stalks divided the background into three sections. Since the portion in the center had the most detail, I quickly filled in the areas on either side. As I did so, I paused periodically to make sure that the edge of both the paint and the wash in the central area remained workable.

As you paint a background, you might have a desire to add or remove pigment. While it is possible to go back into the painted background, more often than not it will interrupt the flow of the painted pattern. In my illustrations, I do this both hesitantly and minimally. You may find it is best to wait until after you are finished painting to see if any adjustments, in either paint or colored pencil, will make the circuit more successful or keep the background from competing with the subject. If you choose to adjust the background while it is drying, always make sure that the amount of water on your brush matches the level of saturation on the page. If you accentuate the background in the colored pencil stage, be sure to use horizontal strokes so that the marks blend into the ripples.

To fill in the small windows created by the subject where the background can be seen, I either paint them in as I move down the page or wait until the main, complex area is complete before returning to fill them with the matching color.

Painting this background was a significant challenge, so congratulations on the results achieved.

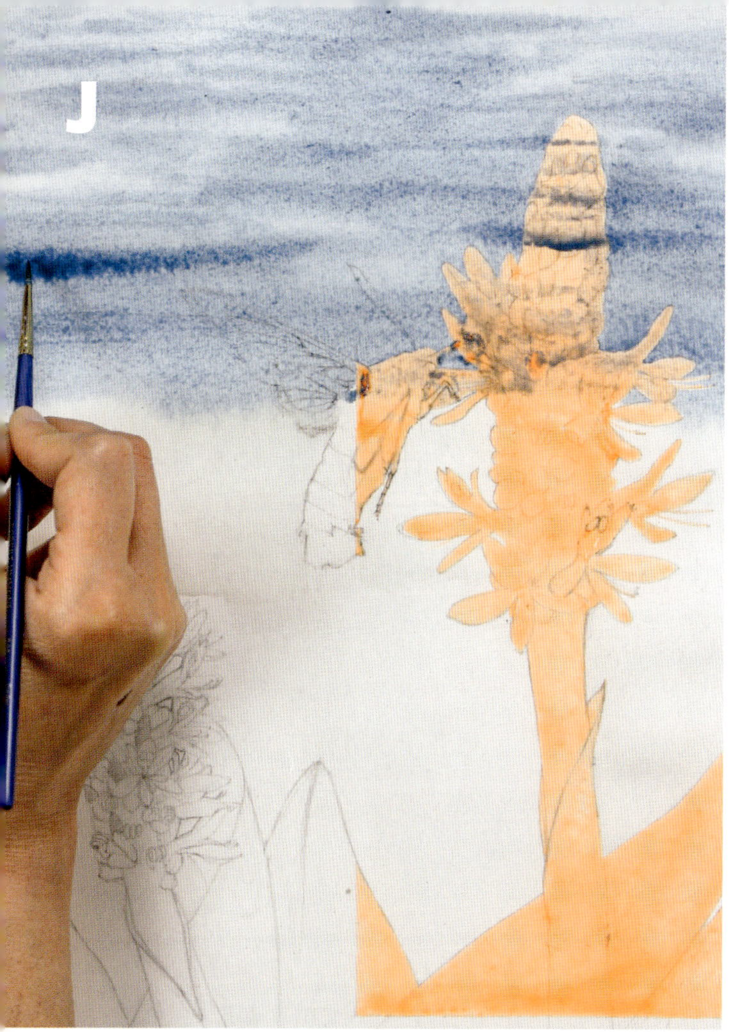

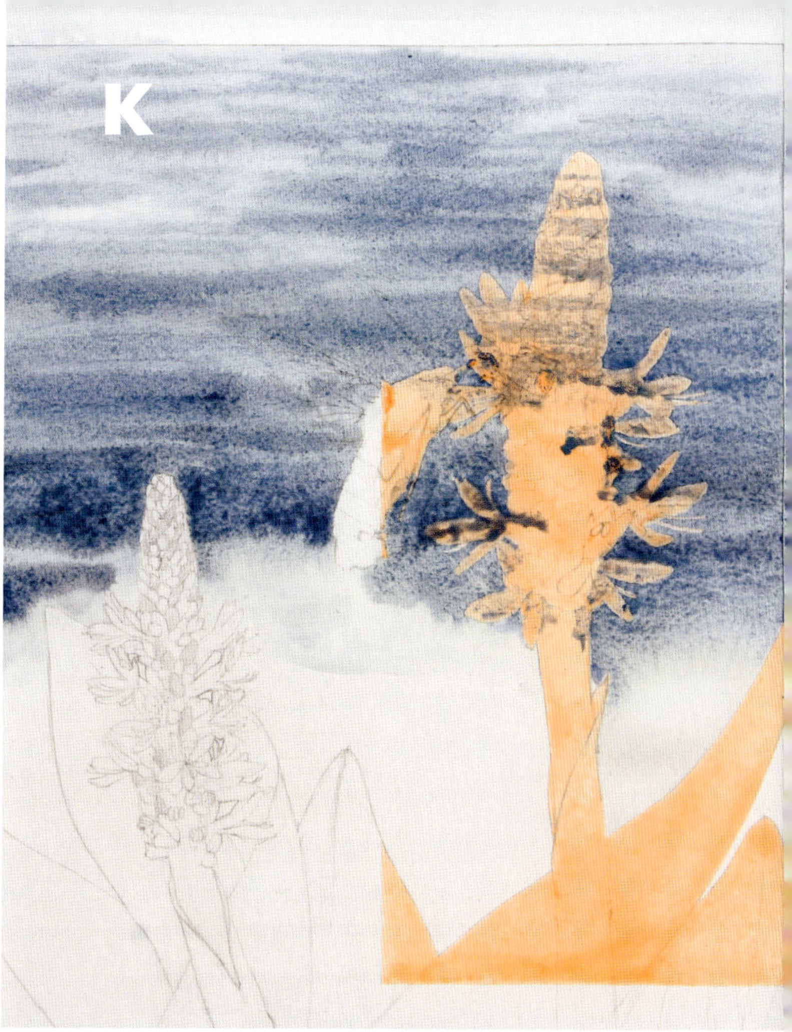

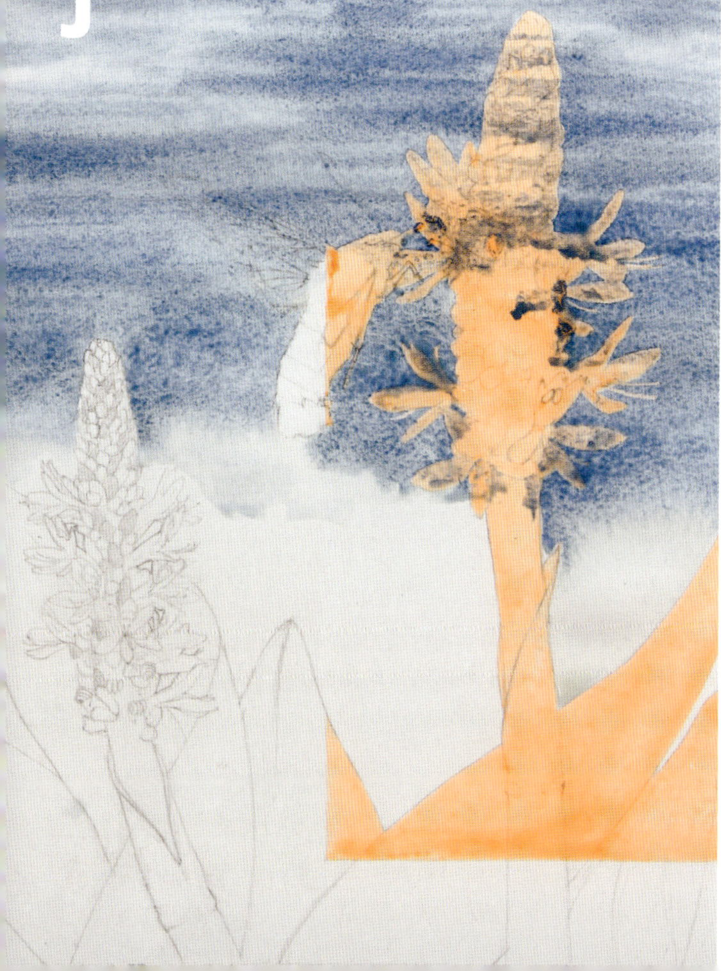

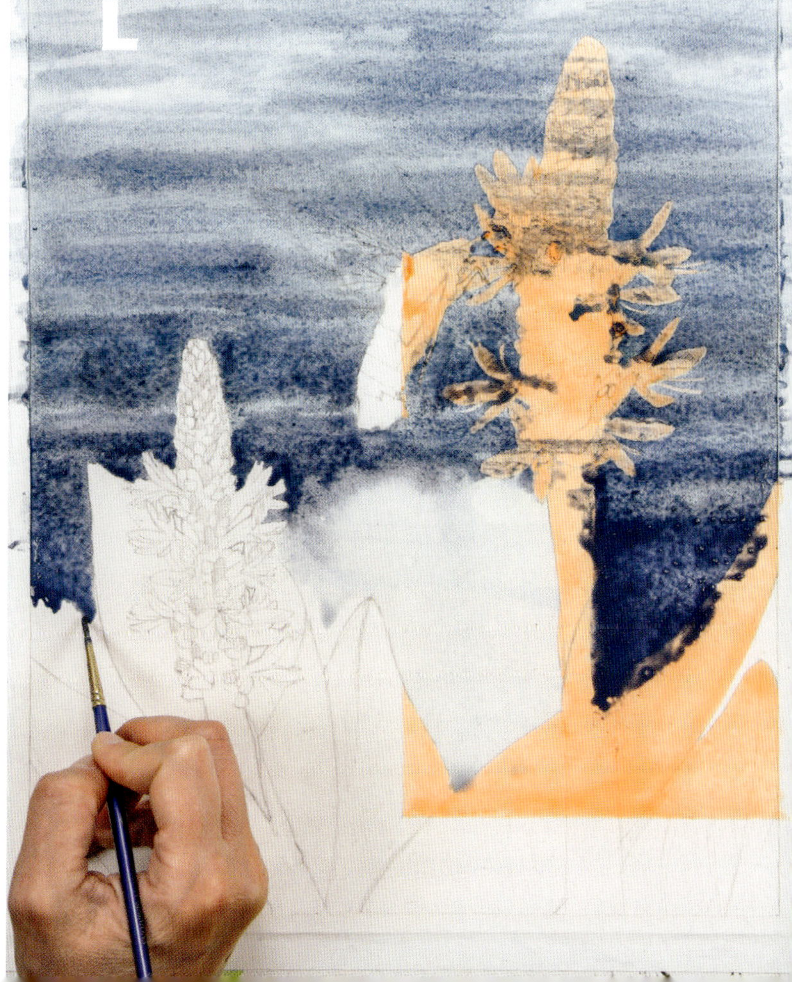

ADDING COLOR TO THE SUBJECTS FROM MULTIPLE REFERENCES

In this illustration, I selected the image with the moth to use as a primary reference. Because of the soft shadows and diffused highlights in the image, it seems likely that the photograph was taken on a bright yet overcast day. The other references, however, present an environment with either less light or direct sunshine. When you paint the elements from the secondary references onto your page, simply do your best to replicate the direction of the light source, amount of contrast, and coloration you see in the primary reference to create continuity throughout your illustration.

This advanced technique challenges you to implement the knowledge you have acquired by drawing from life about how subjects appear in the world regarding color, form, and value. Painting qualities that are beyond what is offered realistically within a reference image is great practice for the times when you need to work with a reference that is less than ideal or if you simply do not have a reference to work from.

CONSIDERING MULTIPLE TECHNIQUES ON THE MOTH

As with all of the other projects, I painted the botanical in this illustration before painting the focal point. However, I want to offer instructions for illustrating the moth first so that you can read the complex method used to create the flower spikes without interruption. As you work on your own illustration, simply refer to this section when you are ready to paint the moth.

Before coloring the wing on the right, I thought through both the pluses and minuses of using different media and techniques. Since I already decided to use colored pencil for the wing on the left, I recognized that having a similar appearance would likely create more balance even though it would take more time to apply. On the other hand, I could use paint to quickly create the soft blended edges shown in the reference image. A third option is to use a colorless blender pencil following the instructions described in the Tools and Materials chapter (page 19). When more than one direction could work well, I also weigh the potential level of enjoyment I would experience with each process.

Because I felt that it was worth it to replicate the reference image most accurately, I decided to use paint. If, after painting the wing, there was visual dissonance between one wing and the other, I knew that I could use a small amount of colored pencil to create more balance. In the end, I chose to enhance only the leading edge of the wing with a solid line, using the black colored pencil alongside a lighter line to make the structure a bit more pronounced than what you can see in the reference.

WORKING WITH A LIMITED COLOR PALETTE

Instead of waiting until you are missing a tool or run out of a color, you can intentionally choose to limit your palette. Then, when you need to find an alternative means, you already have practice creating high-quality creative work using a selection that is less than ideal. You could try removing a single colored pencil or limit your paint palette by using only the six base hues: cadmium yellow, cadmium red, cobalt blue, ultramarine blue, titanium white, and Mars black. Another option is to use all of your materials but try a very different technique than you would ordinarily have used. Just to offer one example, instead of creating the tiny hairs around the flower buds in your illustration, consider what would happen if you worked around a few so that the hairs became a negative space that revealed a lighter underlayer. While these options are not ideal, it develops the ability to solve problems savvily so that limitations in your studio do not have to limit your practice.

M To create the flower spikes in my illustration, I would ordinarily have used both violet and light green paint mixtures and the corresponding colored pencils. Instead, I created two different examples that compensate for a limited palette. As a result, the flower stalks are painted using one hue, while the other color is created entirely using colored pencil. My goal was to make both examples as close to the reference image as possible.

If you include colored pencils on your paint swatches, you can easily compare the hue and value range when you mix your paints. You can also test colored pencils on top of small dried areas of paint so you can see how the underpainting will influence each pencil color.

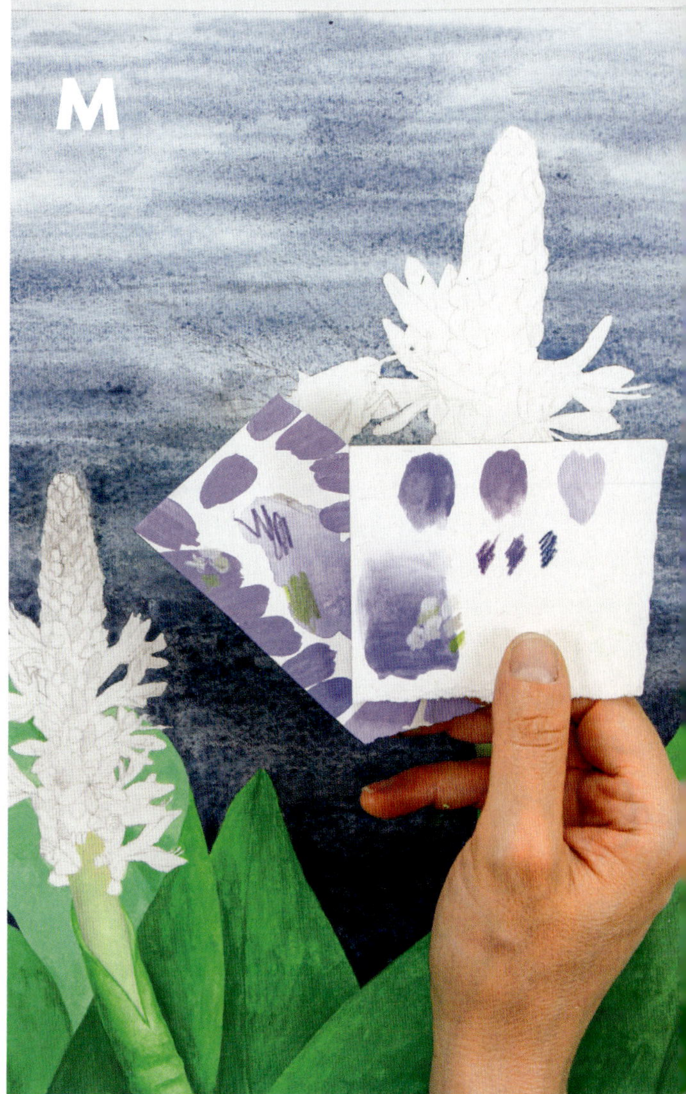

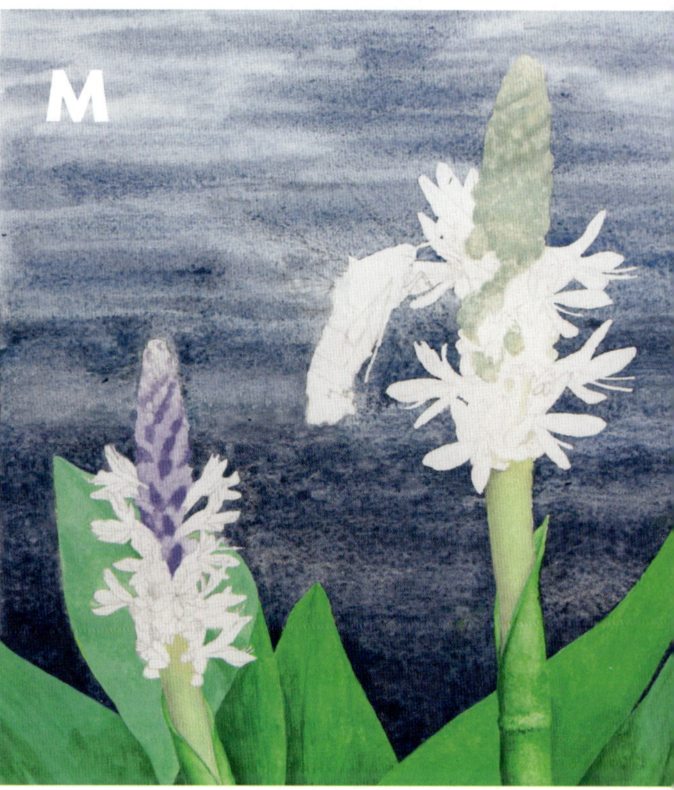

N On the green flower spike, I used violet, imperial violet, black raspberry, indigo blue, black, and French gray colored pencils. On the violet flower spike, I found that using only the lime peel layered on top of the lighter French gray pencil, and often with a little white, resembled the desired result.

I also gave myself the freedom to return to the previous paint mixtures to further darken shadows. Anytime that I paint in an area where colored pencil has already been added, I simply keep in mind that the paint will only absorb in between the waxy marks.

Since I only explored this challenge on the upper portion of the flower stalk, I filled in the lower half using an unlimited palette.

Learning to work with a limited palette without creating results that appear lacking takes a significant amount of time and effort. It forces problem solving, invites you to utilize the expanse of your skills, and can amp up your abilities as you explore options and resolve issues. It can also increase your ease and appreciation when you have a wider palette available. As you can see from these examples, your paint choices, the techniques you use, and the colored pencils you have at your disposal can often make up for what you do not have. While you might often need to wait to purchase a tool or product before continuing your work, do not let the limitation keep you from being creative.

ADDING NUANCED COLOR VARIATION

Another great way to deepen your creative practice is to look for subtle variations in the colors of any subject. Simply notice where there are slight changes in hue, texture, value, or intensity. For example, look at a violet petal and notice if the area you are viewing is more of a red-violet or blue-violet, or contains a hint of a different color. You also might consider whether it is slightly brighter or more vibrant than another petal or even compare different areas on the same petal. Maybe there is a gradual transition from this color to a neighboring section. If there is, look for the increments that define this change. When you observe shadows and highlights at this level, you can learn a significant amount about both the species and its environment, which you can incorporate into your artwork.

To create the flower petals, I worked with seven different mixtures. Some had a change in hue while others were merely a shift in value achieved by adjusting a single base color. Begin to think about how you can show realistic coloration, create continuity, and determine the number of paint mixtures that would be most advantageous to use.

O As I painted each leaf and selected colored pencils, I kept the surrounding colors in mind, so that it would not end up too light or too dark when I painted the neighboring leaves.

ADDING STEPS MID-PROCESS

Eventually, you will begin to recognize the steps that can wait to be addressed until a particular stage in the process. For example, in this project, you can lessen your preparation time by making the decision about how to create the right wing just before you work on the background. You could also pause again, just before you paint the moth, to consider what techniques to use to create the right wing. In future chapters, you will be instructed to consider combining your written steps with intentional in-the-moment microdecisions as a means to begin transitioning from a written process to a successful cerebral process.

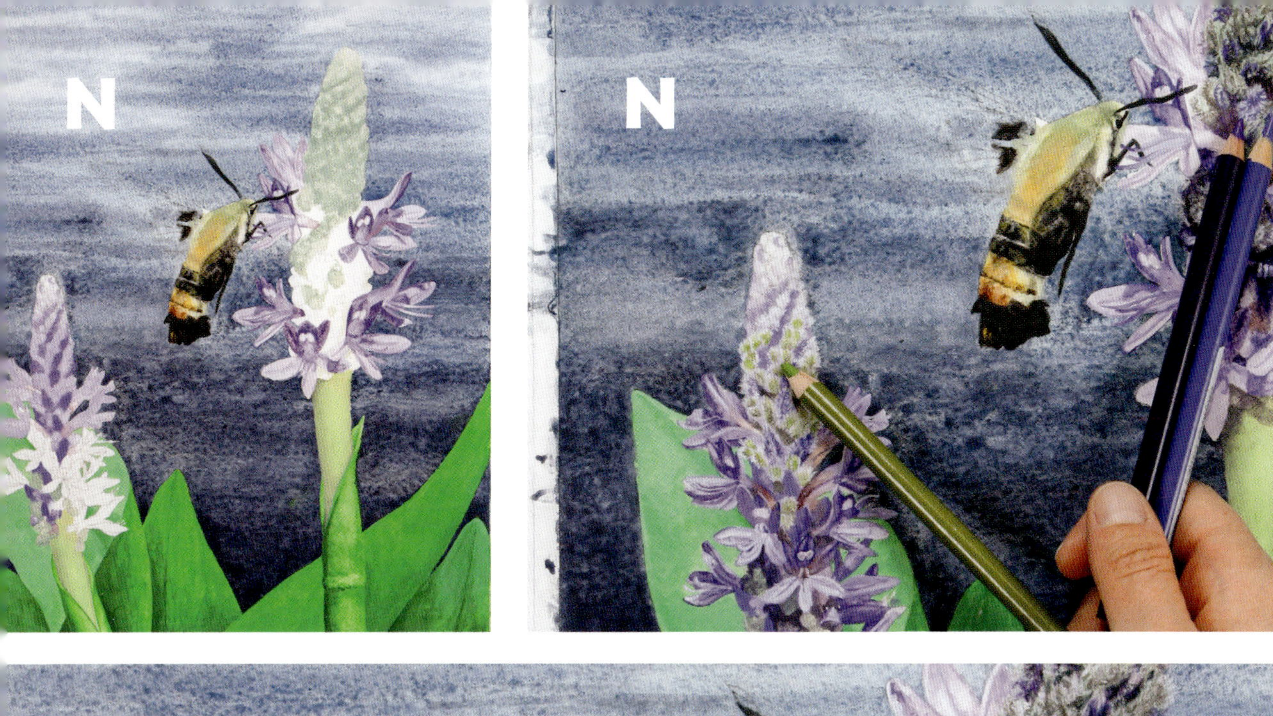
N
N 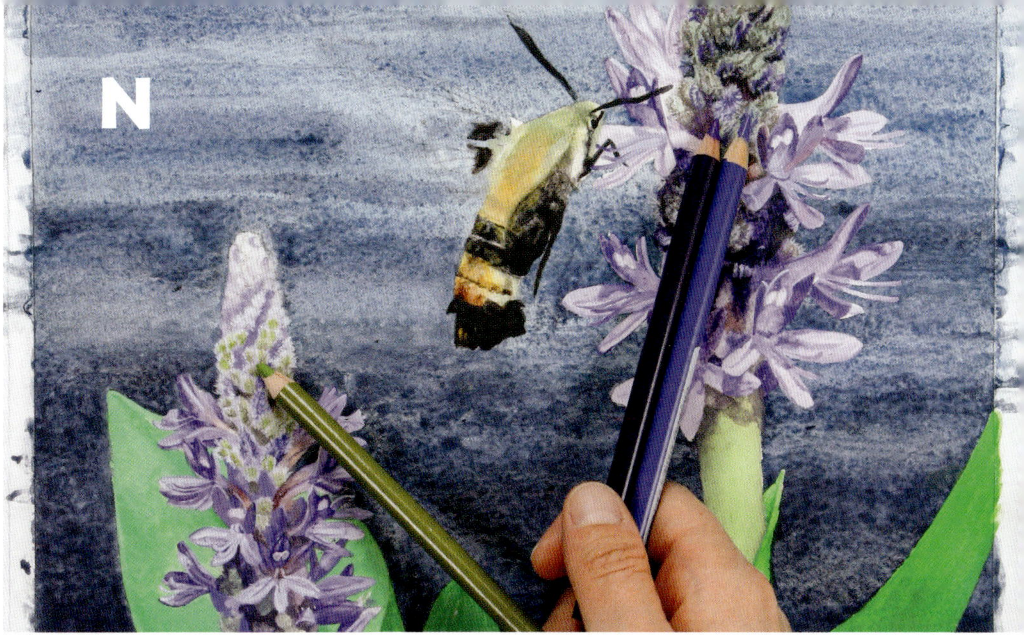
O

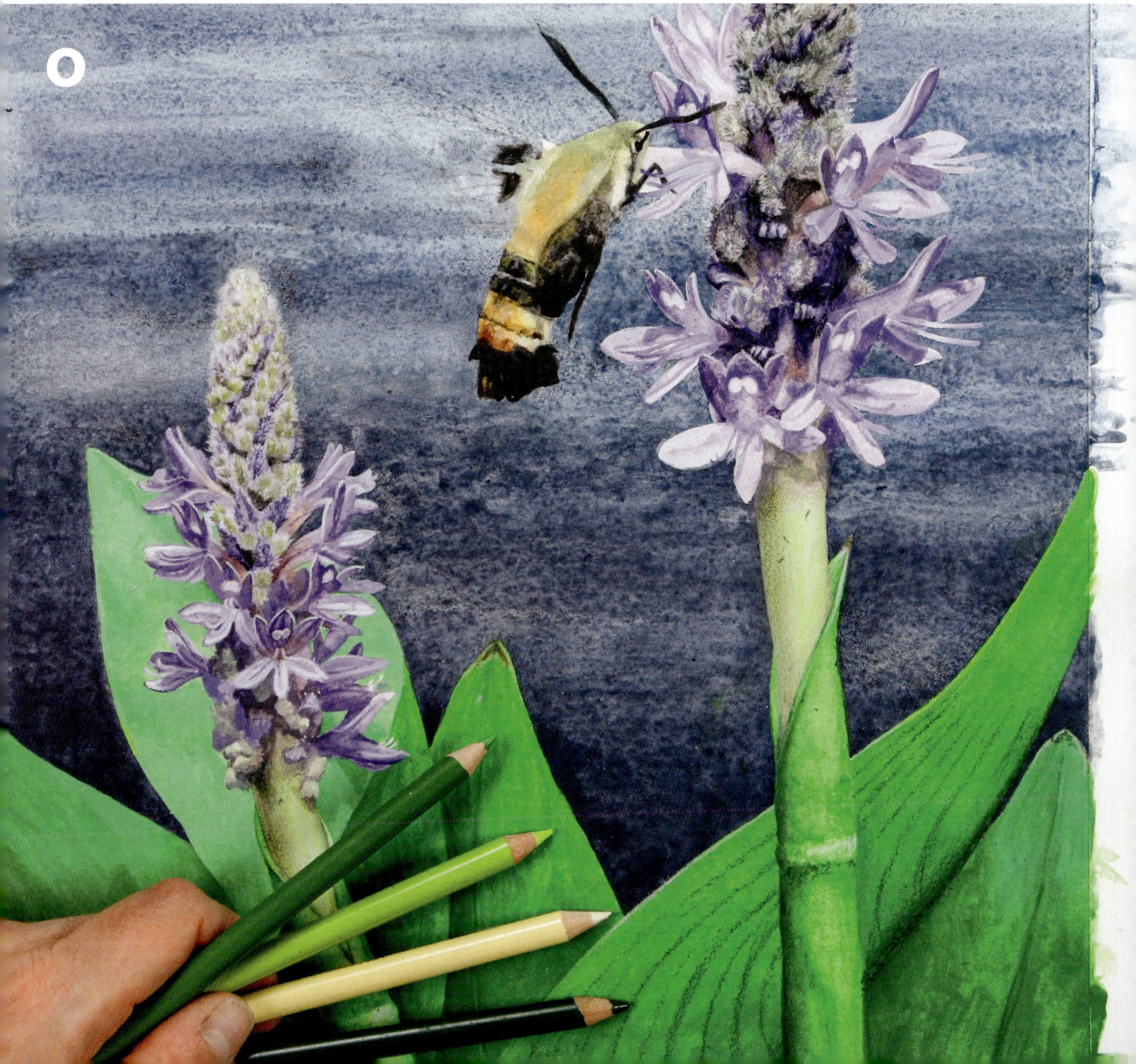

CREATING THE BLURRED WING OVER THE BACKGROUND USING COLORED PENCIL

P First, add the lines that are not blurred using colored pencil so that you can begin to create a visual structure to build upon. Next, following the reference image closely, work along the perimeter of the wing to create multiple edges that each blend slightly into the surroundings. When I added the darker sections, I often used light pressure with the sharp tip of my pencil in a very tight scrubbing motion. Rely on the tooth of the paper as well as the angle of your pencil to help you achieve this appearance. This is another great opportunity to explore using a colorless blender pencil.

Q You might find it helpful to add both shadows and highlights simultaneously so that you can focus on the entire quality of the blur in each area you are working on. Repeat forms and break up marks, especially highlights, into uneven dashes and dots. Allow the background to show through and let colors overlap and blend together. In the lower wing, you can also see that the highlights begin to make very small curves in the direction of the movement. You might even try creating a horizontal line using a series of very small vertical curved marks instead of using a solid line. When you want forms to reiterate speed and movement, it is still important to maintain an understanding of the anatomy, otherwise these sections can easily begin to appear jumbled or confusing to the viewer.

To differentiate the translucent sections of the wing from the background, you can add some muted highlights to these areas. This will help you communicate a clear substance as opposed to a hole through a surface. If any painted dots stand out, you can fill them in to reiterate the blending quality of the transparent film. You might also need to graze these areas very lightly with the indigo blue pencil to be sure that this section doesn't begin to appear only semi-clear or even an opaque white. Moving to the orange sections of the wings, I layered white with mineral orange.

If you begin to become confused about the form, pause to figure out what is different between your illustration and the reference image. You may periodically need to further darken or lighten some areas to maintain your own understanding of the structure.

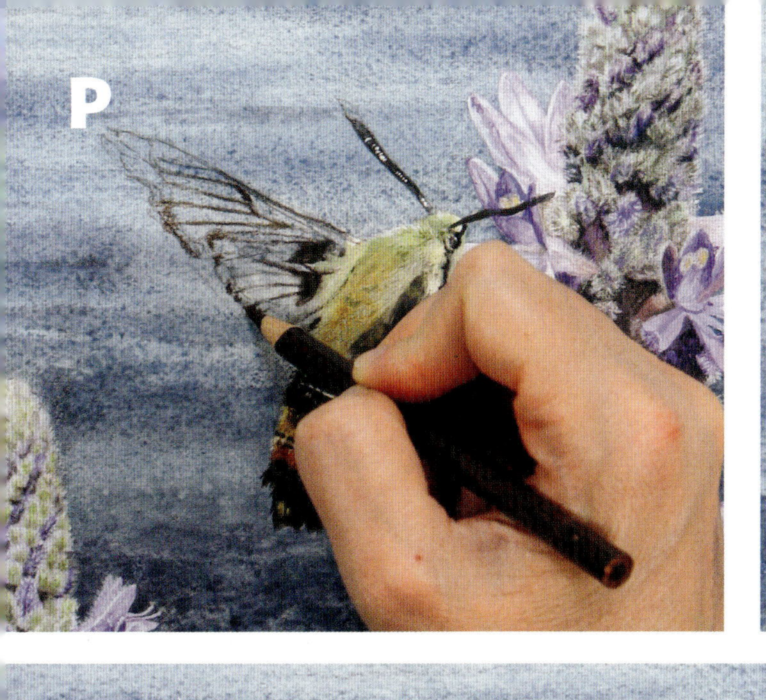
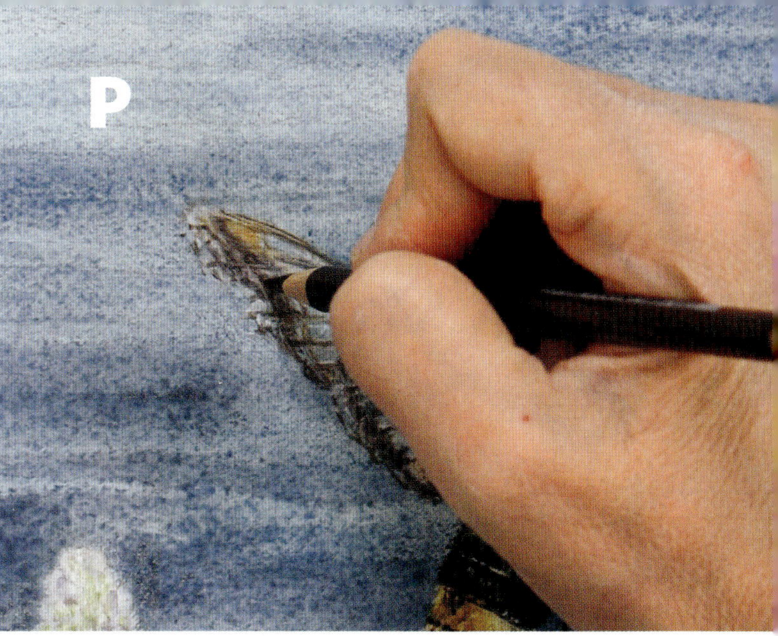

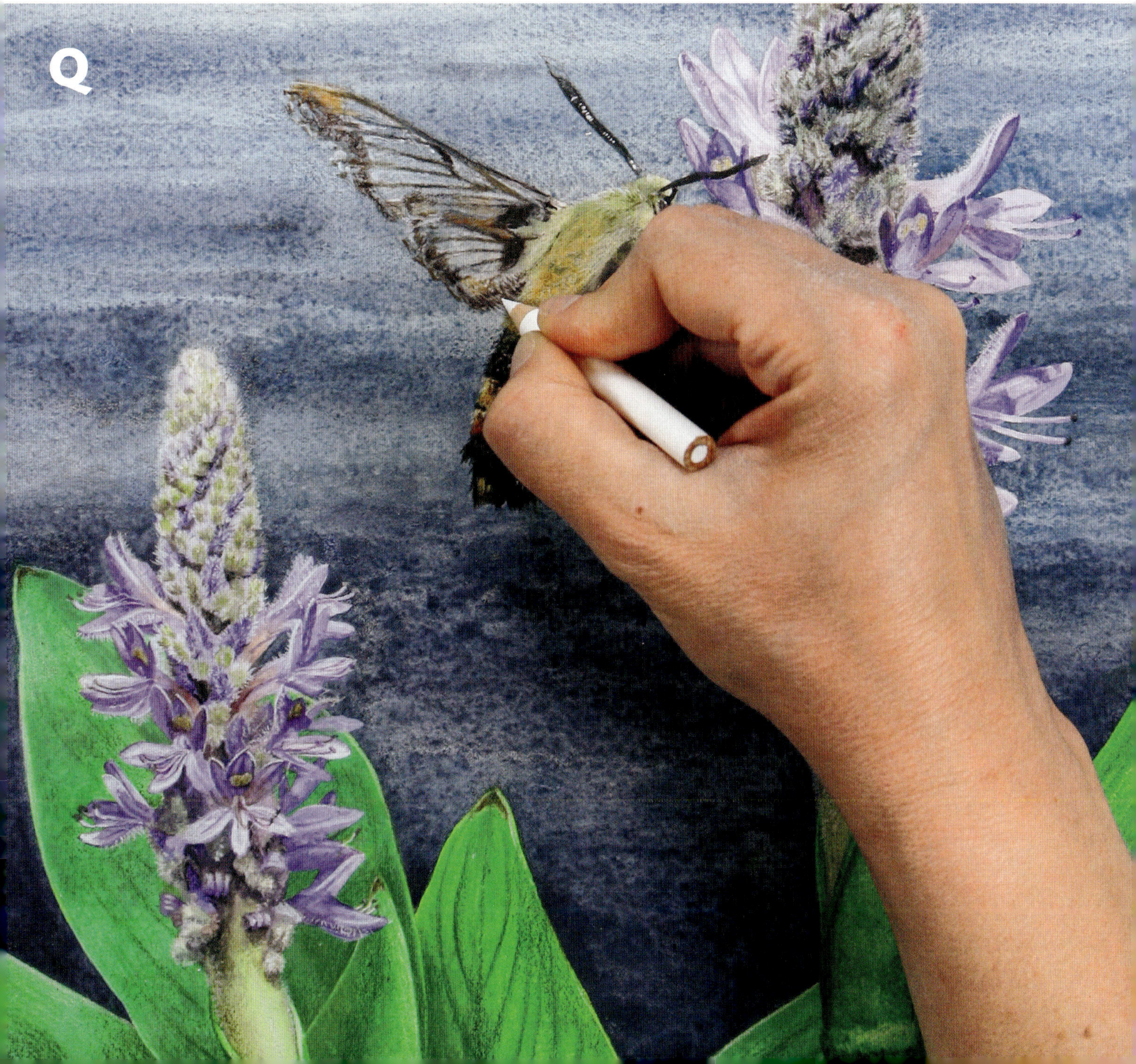

REVIEWING YOUR PREPARATION AND PROCESS

Just as you did in the previous chapter, review the steps you created before starting this illustration and compare them to the actual process needed to complete this work of art. Take a moment to notice if it would have been advantageous to add to, remove, change, or rearrange any of the steps. You might also want to recognize the steps you no longer need to write down beforehand because they are becoming part of your regular routine.

You are right in the middle of creating a process that is uniquely your own. Stick with it because you will soon have a streamlined process that works best for you. Now is the time to consider, assess, test, and make changes so that you can have a practice that greatly benefits you. Be sure to jot down any notes that can help you quickly refine this stage in the following chapters.

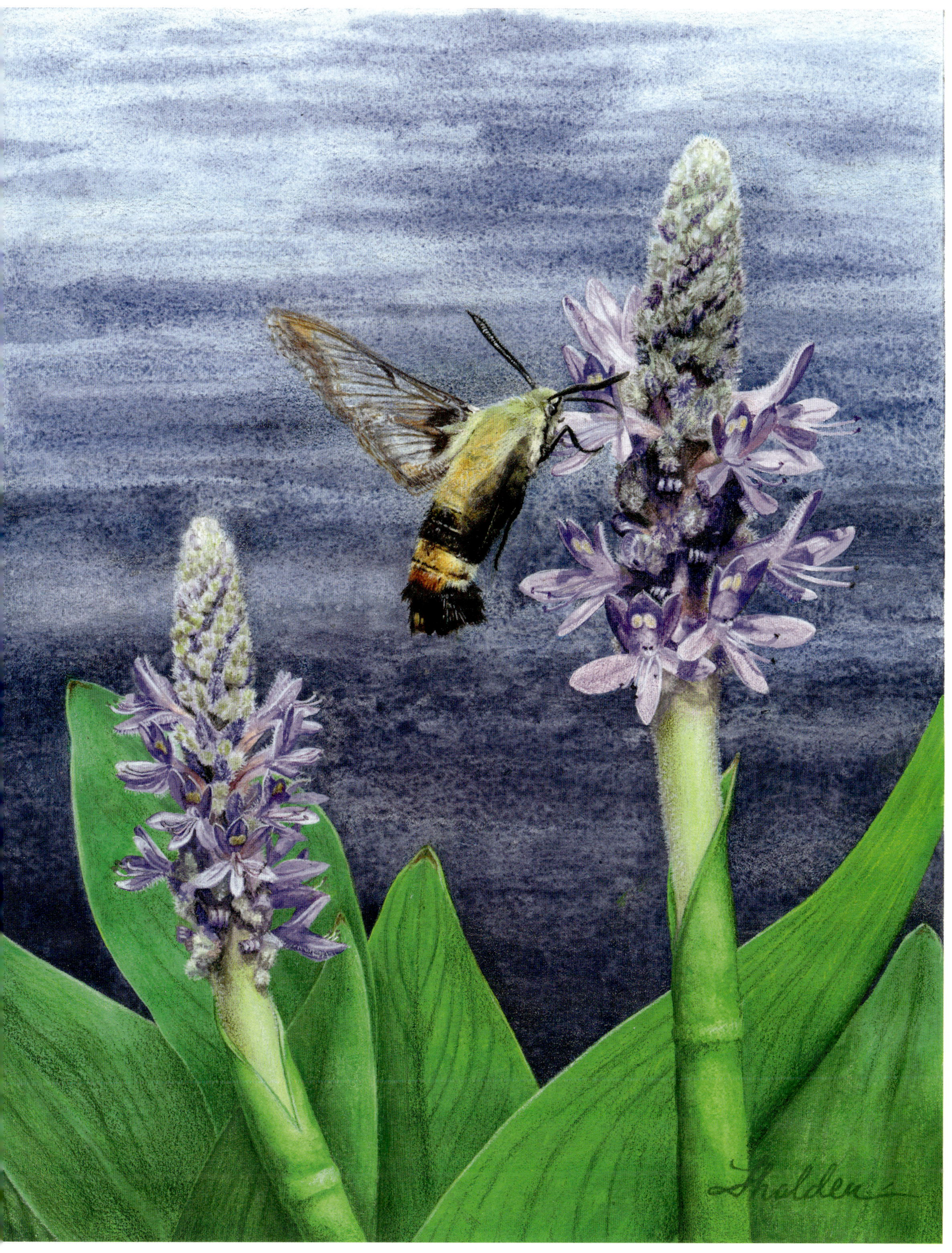

BEYOND THE SUBJECT

It's a delight to fill the background of a composition. This Nature Break is devoted to creating spatial backgrounds that maintain the hierarchy of the primary components. It's time to explore beyond the subject.

LOCATION: Select an area or subject that has simple repeating forms, such as a garden of flowers, the trunks of multiple trees, or leaves on a branch.

MATERIALS: Cropping tools, artist tape, watercolor paper, paint, and colored pencils.

OBSERVATIONS: Squint your eyes and notice the patterns created by color, size, shape, location, and orientation. Then focus your eyes on a single spot and observe the increasing level of blurring in your peripheral vision.

PRACTICE: Use artist tape to create multiple medium-size rectangles on a piece of watercolor paper. Use cropping tools to find a composition (page 158) that will fill one frame. Then paint the colors and patterns of the subjects in the distance, allowing them to be very blurry. When the wash is merely damp, add the middle ground and then foreground. Although your goal is to achieve varying levels of focus while a single wash dries on the page, in these experiments you can also let a layer dry and then reapply another wash.

As you play and experiment, consider either increasing or decreasing the level of blurring from front to back to change the perception of distance. After the paint has dried completely, use colored pencils to add details to either the focal point or the subjects closest to the front.

REFLECTION: Can you perceive an incremental change in depth from foreground to background? Are the subjects in the distance recognizable? What makes a composition look too busy? What choices helped you either increase or decrease the importance of an area? You might consider transforming these swatches into greeting cards.

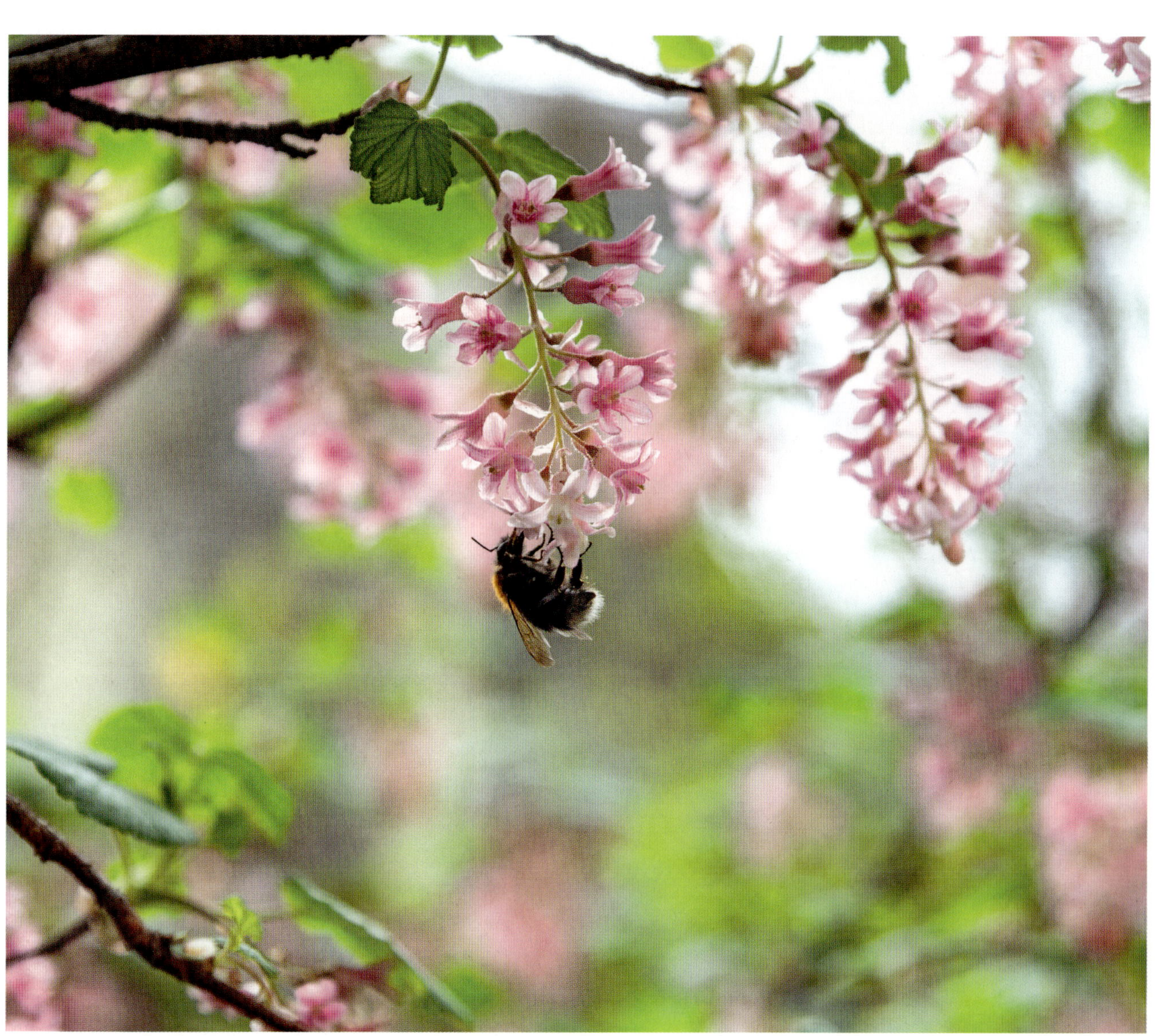

WESTERN HONEY BEE

APIS MELLIFERA

There are twenty thousand known species of bees worldwide, yet only a small number are considered honey bees. The colonies created by social bees are so highly organized in architecture, individual responsibilities, and communication that they are often considered a single biological unit. Bees can discern the ultraviolet colors on flower petals, which guide them to where the nectar and pollen are located. Western honey bees, like this worker bee, are not native to North America. They are often transported throughout the growing season for agricultural crop pollination. I was excited to offer this composition because the subject is surrounded by flowers. When you include an identifiable environment in your composition, you can create a wonderful sense of spatial distance. You need to be careful, however, that the complex patterns in the layout do not pull attention from the focal point. This composition provides you with the ability to address hierarchy from the foreground to the background.

SEE REFERENCE PHOTO ON PAGE 328

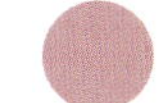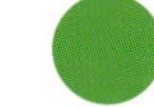

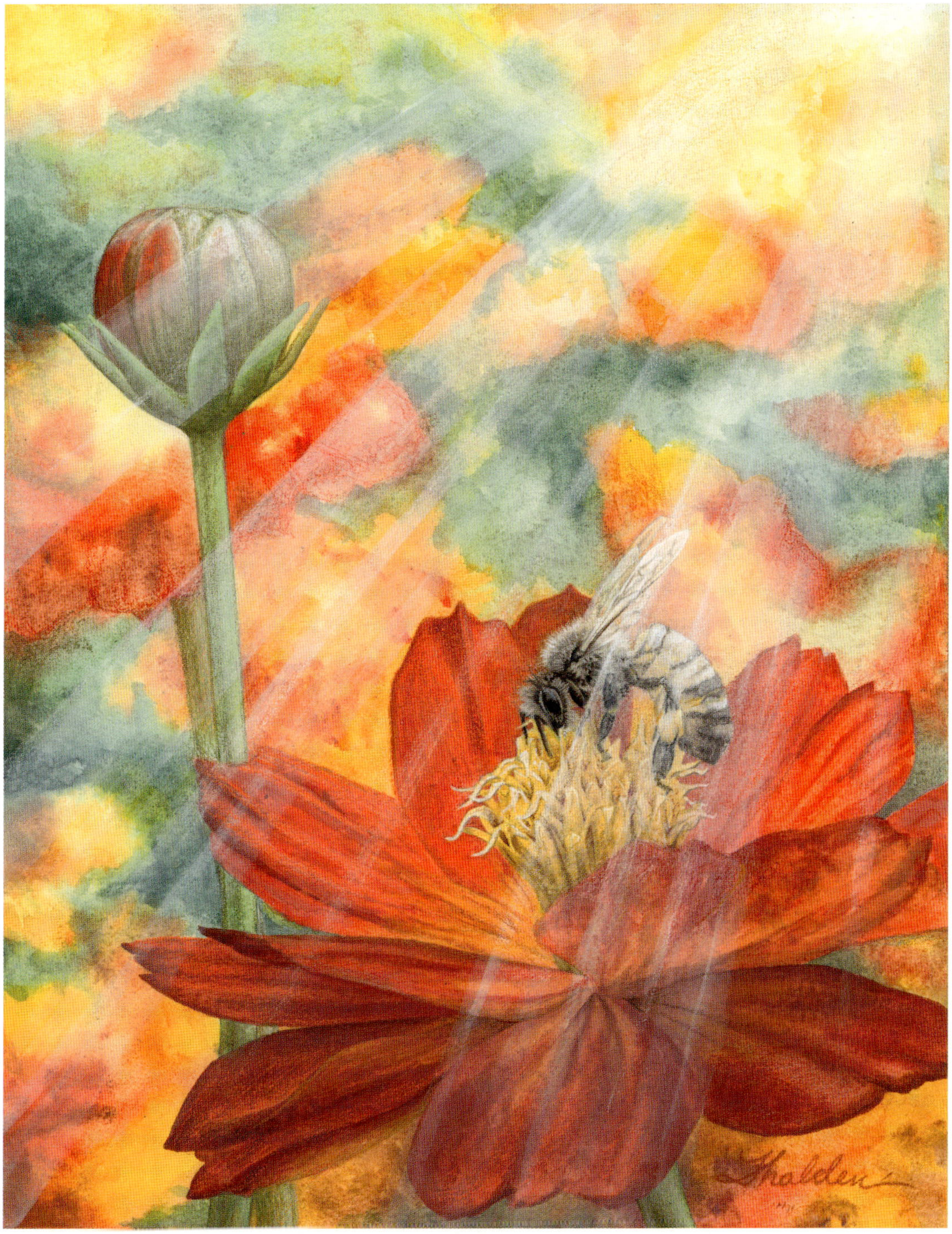

MATERIALS

- ☐ Fine-mist spray
  bottle (optional)

This composition requires minimal use of new techniques so that you could have the opportunity to strengthen both your creative process and the skills you have been acquiring through completing the projects in this book. Therefore, the overarching focus of this project is independent problem solving, creating an ideal sequence of steps, and replacing written preparations with a successful thought process.

As you work on this project, trust in your abilities and your knowledge base, take the time you need to think and work, and steadily follow the process that you have been developing. Also, offer yourself extra patience and understanding, knowing that you are honing the overall structure of your process to develop your future practice. If questions or challenges arise, let your past experiences and the information in previous projects support you.

DEVELOPING YOUR OWN PROCESS: PART 3

Since you will have minimal instruction, consider the sequence of your own steps carefully. At this point in your progress, skip any steps that have become inherent to your practice so that you can spend your time addressing areas that are either unfamiliar or potentially challenging. If you have the option of using more than one technique, you might list only the options instead of writing out each step, which will allow you to make decisions in mid-process.

Even with thoughtful preparation, there will likely be times when you arrive at a mid-process decision and realize that you have already completed a step that either locks you into a specific trajectory or creates a particular challenge.

Although these moments can be frustrating, know that both considering how to proceed and acknowledging what you would change in the future are inherent parts of an expanding practice. Anytime you remember to include a previously missed step or are able to solve a problem that had been difficult in the past, I highly recommend celebrating to a level that is equal to or slightly greater than the reaction you had to the original error.

GENERATING SUCCESSFUL DESIGNS

Whenever you ponder a new design, you might ask yourself these questions to help you generate ideas and create a successful composition: What colors, values, and shapes will help balance and unify the design? What forms, hues, or textures lead the eye in a circuit around the composition? Are any areas too dense or confusing? Are there holes or blank areas in the composition? How is the hierarchy emphasized? Does anything distract from the focal point? Finally, compare the foreground, middle ground, and background to determine how a sense of space is being achieved.

DRAWING LONG, SMOOTH CURVES

A If you include the flower bud in your composition, draw the long arc of the stem by holding your wrist steady and rotating from your elbow. It may help you to reread instructions for drawing curves located at the beginning of the drawing section in the forest pierrot project (page 214). When you are ready, practice the arc with your pencil hovering slightly above the page to check the location of both ends and the height of the curvature. You may need to make small adjustments to your position before you are ready to draw the line.

CREATING PAINTERLY BACKGROUNDS

As you prepare to paint, you can either use a pencil to indicate where each flower will be located in the background or leave the area blank and add the flowers one at a time while you are painting.

When you mix paints on your palette, you will need to create several colors that are similar to the pigments already in your paint tubes. Anytime this happens, carefully discern the difference between the reference image and the color on the scrap paper hovering over your page. When you do, look for a shift in both the hue and intensity, so that you can mix the nuanced color accurately.

B If you choose to add the botanicals during the painting stage, be sure that you pause to consider how the placement of each one will affect the overall visual circuit. You might also find it helpful to paint from a standing position. See if you can allow the process to be more playful than stressful.

To take this technique to the next level, apply these tips: First, refrain from getting lost in the pattern developing on your page. Instead, remain focused on envisioning flower forms so that the result can appear spatial. Second, you can create continuity and reiterate a sense of space by incrementally increasing the level of blur, from the botanicals located just behind the subjects to those in the distance. If you'd like, you could even blur the edges of both the bud and the farthest

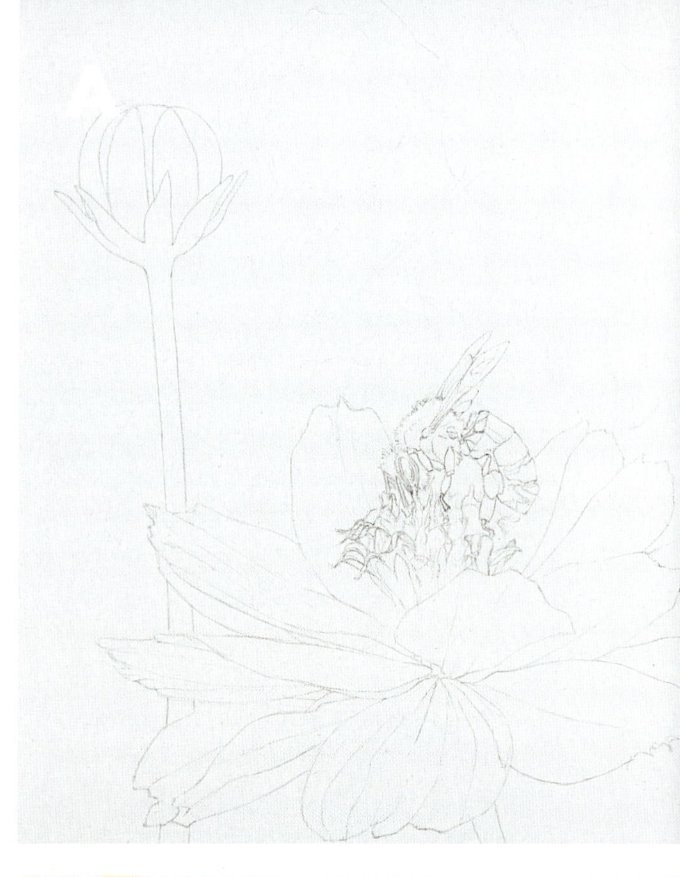

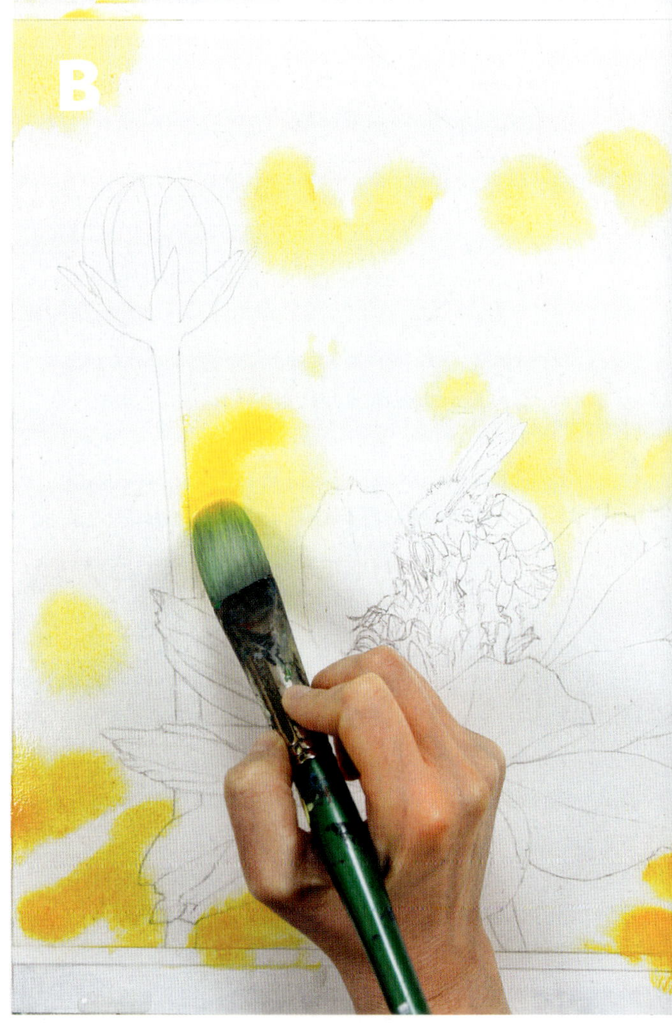

petals on the primary flower. Lastly, and possibly most significantly, be sure to scan the entire page periodically so that you can address any hard edges that develop before they dry and potentially flatten the appearance of depth.

In my illustration, I planned out the visual circuit ahead of time using loose pencil lines to merely suggest where essential flowers would be placed. Then, while adding a wash to the background, I switched to a smaller brush to carefully add water around the lighter sections of the bee. I painted the centers of all of the flowers, starting with the locations I had marked with pencil, then added as many flowers I felt were needed to complete the composition. Next, I added both orange and red paint mixtures until I could detect the flower forms I was creating. I then added just enough green to separate the flowers. Oscillating between the positive and negative background space allowed me to develop the entire background simultaneously and enhance one area based on the addition of the other.

As I did this, I allowed the pigments to bleed across the outline of the flower and bud, knowing that the value of the background would be overpowered by the colors of the subject. All the while, I kept a paper towel in hand to control the amount of color that spread into those areas. Admittedly, I wish I had noticed when some of the green paint had spread into the highlighted tip of the bud. Since it dried with a hard edge, I needed to spend time on this area later in the process to achieve the color and value I desired.

At this advanced stage of your practice, you may find it easier to identify other areas where you can save time and add ease without sacrificing the appearance of your artwork. Being selective about when and where you use precision is merely one example. This ability is another reason why it is helpful to think through the process and have an idea of what steps will follow.

KEEPING NEIGHBORING COMPLEMENTARY COLORS VIBRANT

C Similar to mixing complements on your palette, when you apply red and green paint next to each other on your page, they tend to both darken in value and lower in saturation. If you want a vibrant-looking garden in this composition, you can either let one color dry completely before adding the other or use these tips to apply both while your page is still wet.

First, when you are ready to change colors, refresh your rinse water so that there is no hidden pigment in your brush. Second, always have a paper towel or rag ready so that you can absorb excess paint and control the perimeter of the painted area. Third, if you need to rewet the page, instead of using a brush (which can blend colors together), you might consider using a small fine-mist spray bottle.

Using complements can work to your advantage. Since you have the ability to darken green using red, and yellow using violet, you can quickly create shadow paint mixtures. In my illustration, I relied on this hue-reducing technique on the flower bud and on the yellow disk florets in the center of the primary flower.

Also, keep in mind that you will be able to use vibrant colored pencils later in the process to create smooth transitions between these colors. In my illustration, I chose to use colored pencils to slightly define the flowers located directly behind the subject to create a distinctive middle ground.

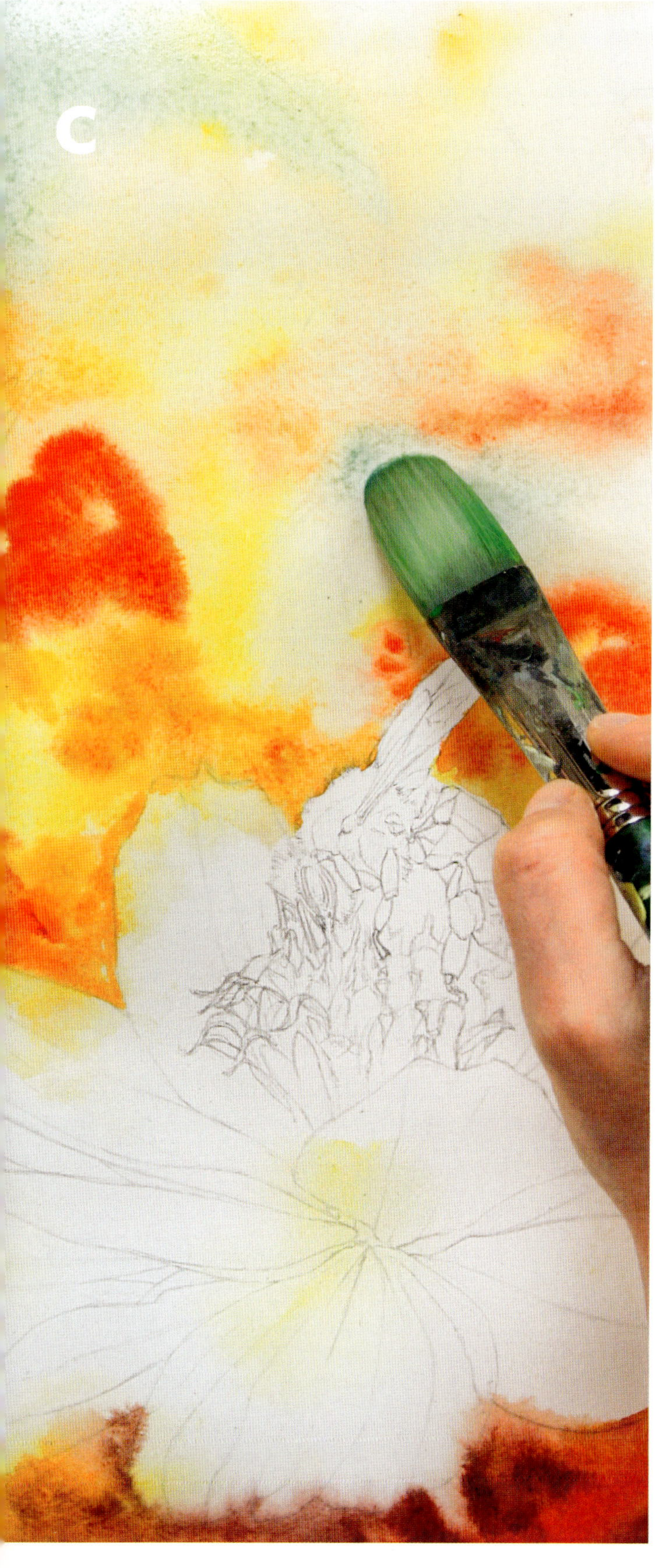

C

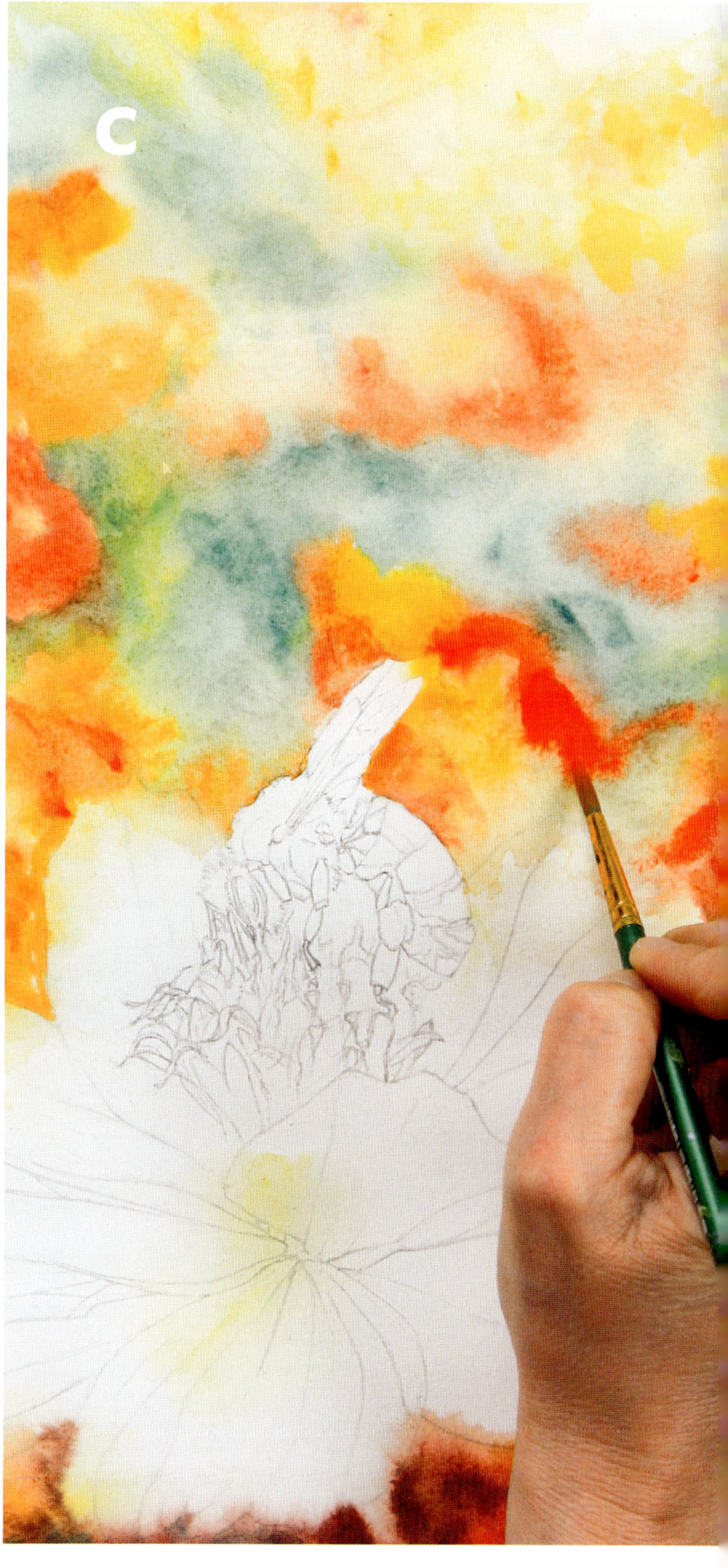

C

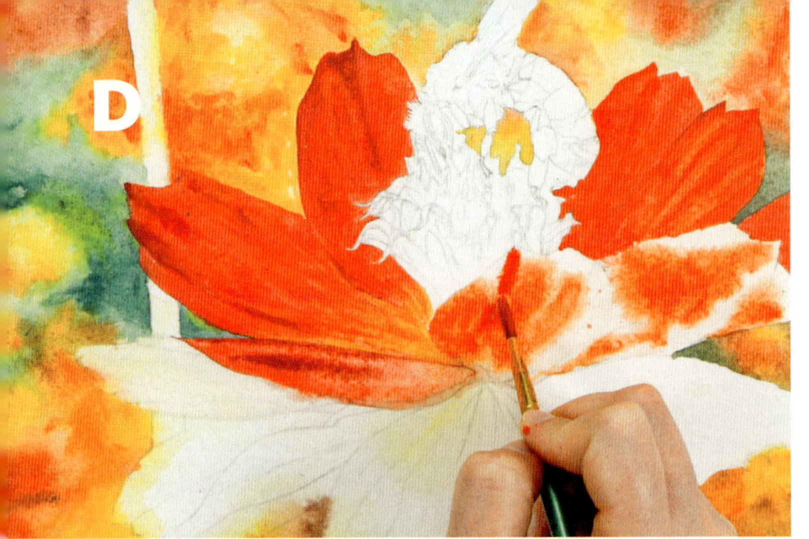

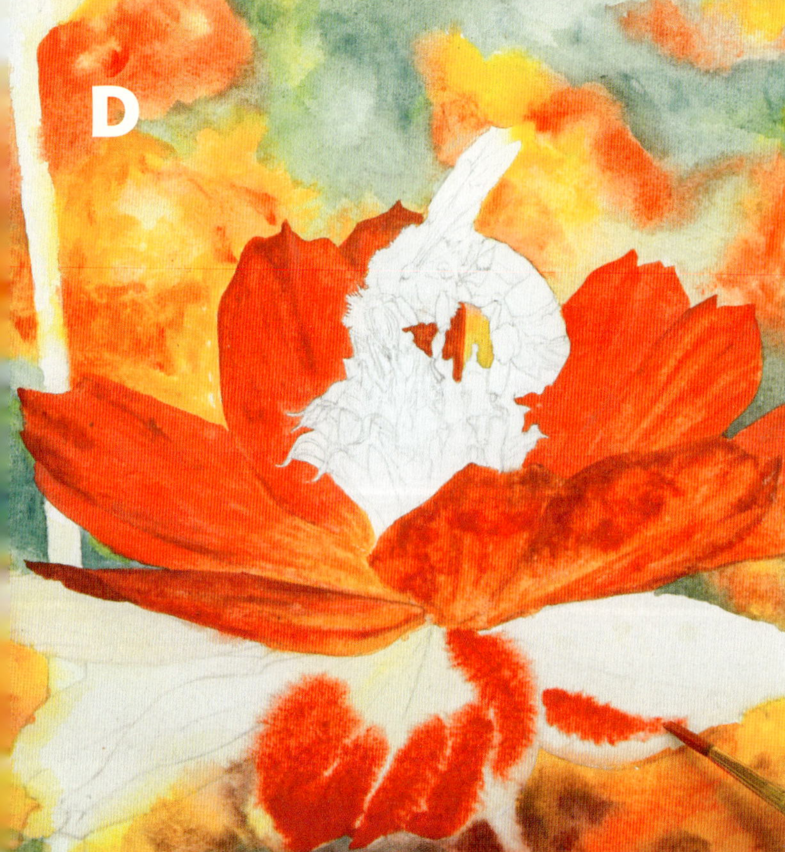

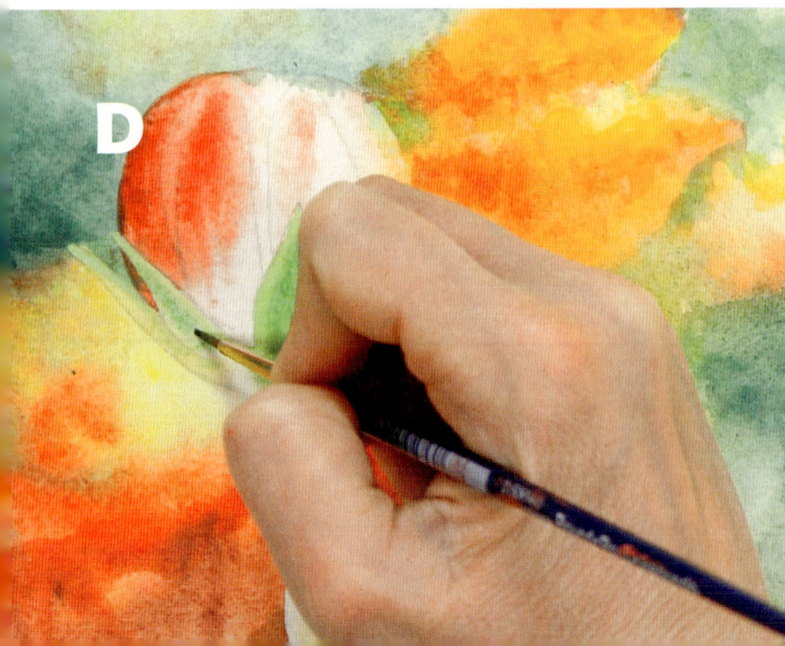

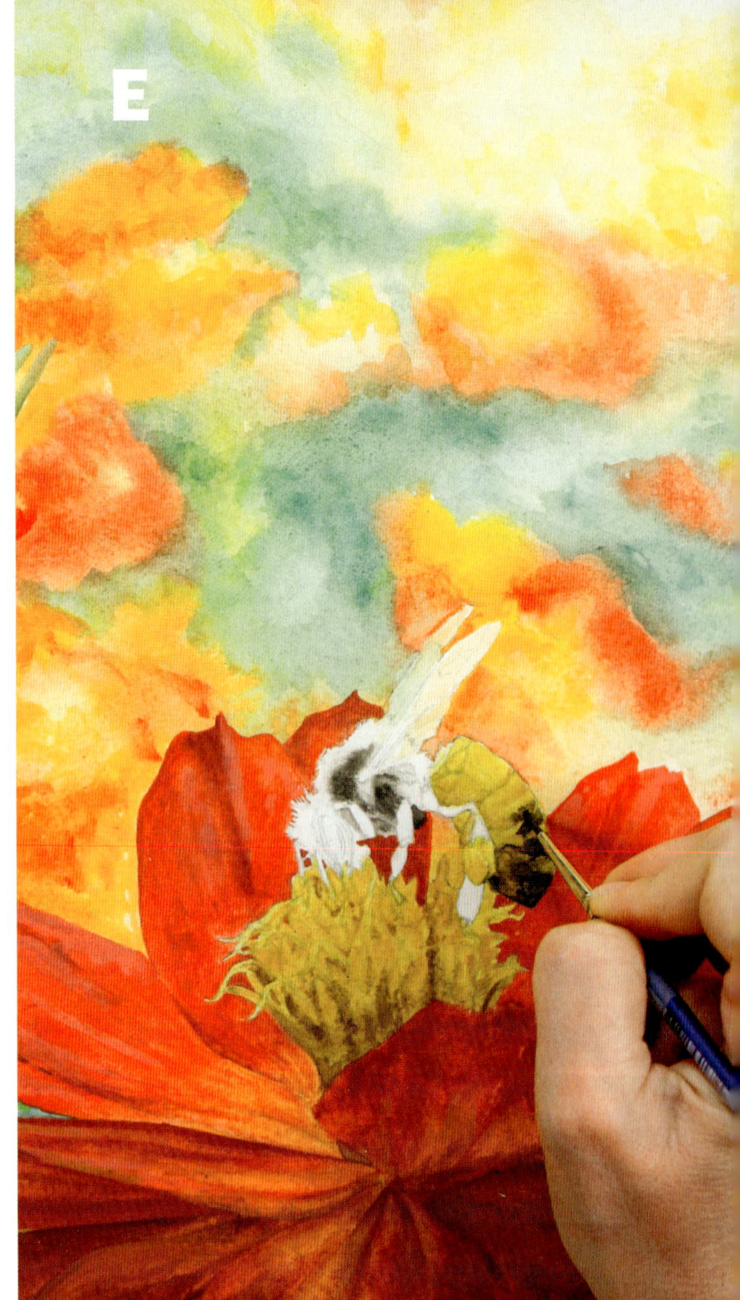

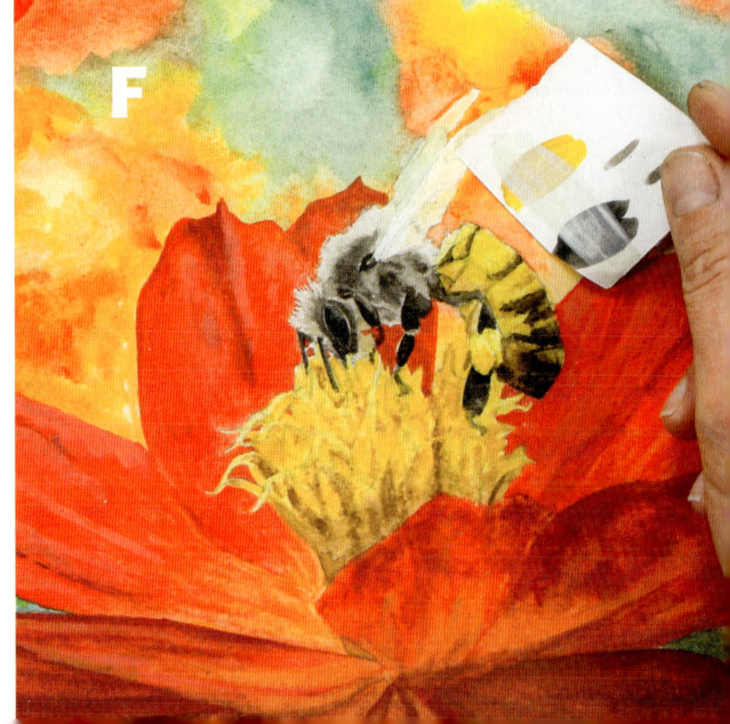

USING A PAINTERLY STYLE ON A SUBJECT

D Instead of painting each petal individually, you might apply one color mixture to multiple petals. As you add additional colors, be sure to monitor the level of the glisten on your page so that the colors can bleed into one another.

When you create paint mixtures, add the colored pencils you'll want to use later in the process to your scrap paper. To take this thinking to the next level, begin to imagine how you will use the colored pencils you have selected while you are painting. By doing this, you determine the level of refinement that will be necessary on the foreground subjects in the painting stage. Additionally, if you create some quick flower forms on a test sheet, you'll be able to practice painting sun rays later in the process.

MAKING MINOR ADJUSTMENTS TO COLOR MIXES TO ENHANCE REALISM

E When you need to paint sections of a subject that have similar colors, you could create mixtures with minor variations in hue or value instead of painting them with a single paint mixture. Even if the difference is subtle, it can further separate forms and enhance the lifelike appearance of your subject. When you paint the abdomen of the bee, you could separate a small portion of the paint mixture and adjust it to more accurately match

the intensity of the pollen packed onto the hindleg. Similarly, you might choose to discern the characteristics of the dark brown colors of the thorax, eye, and extremities.

USING A GLAZE TO CREATE HIGHLIGHTS

F Just before you transition to using colored pencil, adding a glaze can be a fun way to further enhance your compositions. You can make a glaze from any color and use it for numerous applications.

To create a glaze, you can mix a paint color or mixture with an acrylic medium. For this project, however, I simply recommend using water. Your goal is to use just enough water to make the paint appear translucent when you apply it on top of paint that has dried completely.

One way you can use a glaze is to create soft highlights on a subject. I find that the layers, as opposed to a single paint mixture that matches the reference image, can add a quality of aesthetic depth to a painting. If you would like to

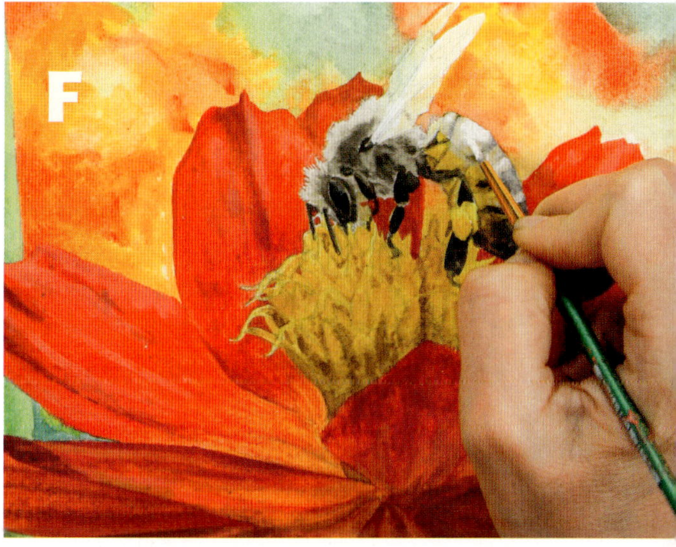

try this, you would first create a paint mixture that matches how you imagine the subject would appear without the highlight. Of course, the trick is to accurately guesstimate how saturated the color needs to be to create the desired results. Once you have created the glaze, apply it as you would any other paint. Since you are layering paints, be careful that you do not begin to build up thickness on your page. The paper should remain matte in appearance so that your colored pencils can continue to adhere to the surface. After applying the first layer of glaze in my illustration, I chose to create a slightly more saturated paint mixture to add brighter highlights.

CREATING RAYS OF LIGHT USING A GLAZE

G In reference images, light rays, streaks, and shapes can be created naturally by camera lens flare or can be computer generated. Regardless of how they are originally produced, they can be used as an artistic feature and contribute to both the aesthetic and the visual circuit of a composition.

To paint sun rays realistically, all of your lines need to be straight and must appear to originate from the same location. Since painting straight lines can be difficult, the following section is devoted entirely to tips that can help you succeed. In this endeavor, you might keep these considerations in mind: First, you can have complete freedom regarding the location, quantity, and level of transparency. In this regard, you might add each ray similar to the way that you added flowers to the background. You might also allow the rays to either intersect with the edge of the page, or begin and end within the composition. Second, you can make conscious choices regarding both the hierarchy and the visual circuit in your composition. In my illustration, I maintained the hierarchy by reducing the dynamic quality of the rays located farther from the subject while also leaving the head of the bee uncovered. You might compare the image prior to and just after adding the rays to see how they influence the design.

I want to forewarn you that when you add details later in the process, you will likely need to color match using various colored pencils if sun rays cover a portion of the subject. If you create paint tests on a scrap piece of paper prior, you can also use colored pencils to compare working on the areas that have a translucent layer to those that do not. This may help you determine both the location and number of rays you would like to have in your composition. In general, you may find that a minimal number of rays can be quite effective.

Always keep a damp rag or paper towel in your nondominant hand so that you can make any necessary corrections immediately. If you find that you need to re-create a line, be sure to pause, refocus, and begin again as if you were painting it for the first time.

Even with testing the technique ahead of time, choosing to paint across an entire composition is courageous. Offer yourself patience while you learn this technique. Just go for it, have fun, and see what happens. When you are finished, regardless of the result, commend yourself for creating the piece, honor your courage, and acknowledge your commitment to creative growth.

PAINTING STRAIGHT LINES

H First, the structure and position of your body can either help or hinder your ability to paint a straight line. When you create a long line, try using your shoulder like a hinge while leaning your upper body slightly in the direction in which you are painting. If you are standing, you might shift your weight from one foot to the other. All the while, keep in mind that wrists and elbows are ideal for creating arcs; therefore, you might want to keep them in a more fixed position. You may also want to start vertical lines from the top, diagonal lines from the bottom, and horizontal lines from the left (if you are right-handed).

Second, utilize the capability of your paintbrush to the fullest advantage. When you apply paint, lean the handle of your paintbrush slightly toward the destination, use a pulling motion, and keep your pinky finger lightly touching the page. To change the width of your lines slightly, you can either rotate a filbert paintbrush so that the bristles have a different thickness or adjust the pressure of a round paintbrush.

Last, just before your paintbrush touches the paper, visually connect the starting and ending point. To do this, simply glance at both locations so that when you begin, you know where your paintbrush is headed. While you are painting, instead of watching your brush, you might hold your gaze at the destination to see if that gives better results.

When this stage of the composition is complete, if you have created even a single straight line, I highly encourage you to celebrate.

ADDING COLORED PENCIL DETAILS WITH A GLAZE

I Before you begin any work, take a moment to simply notice the percentage of color shift created by the light rays. Then start to refine in an area devoid of light rays. Once you are familiar with the

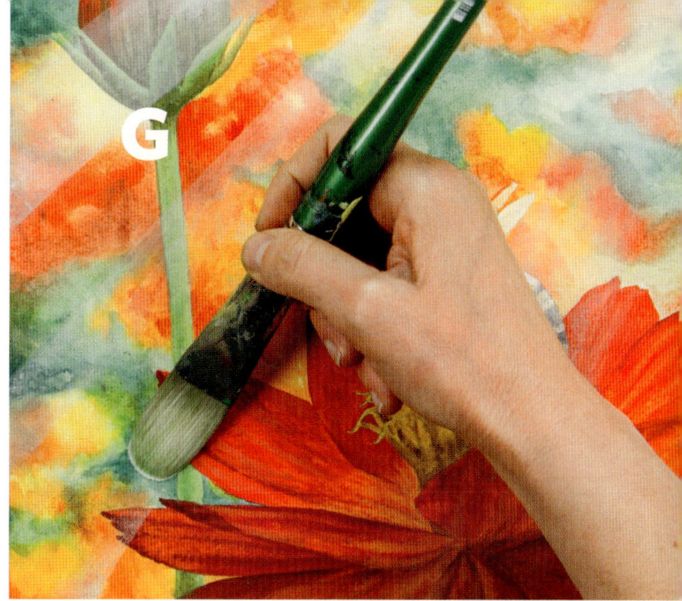

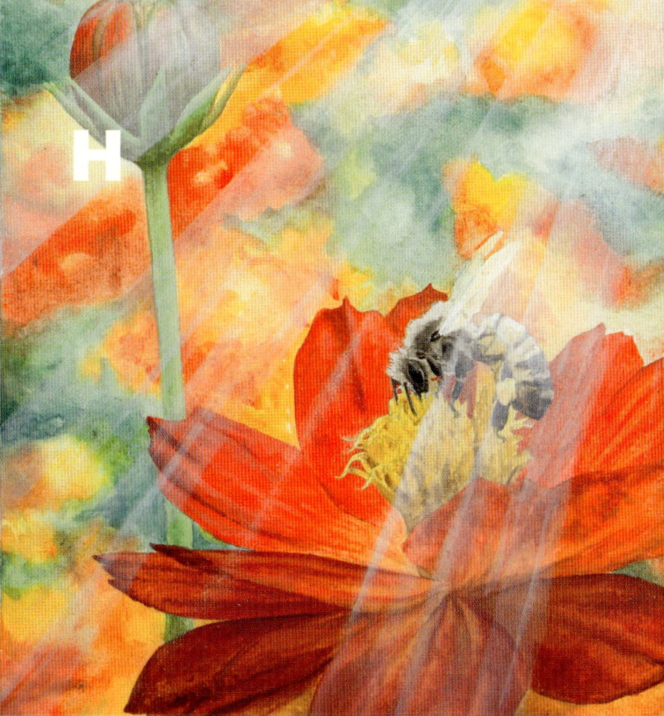

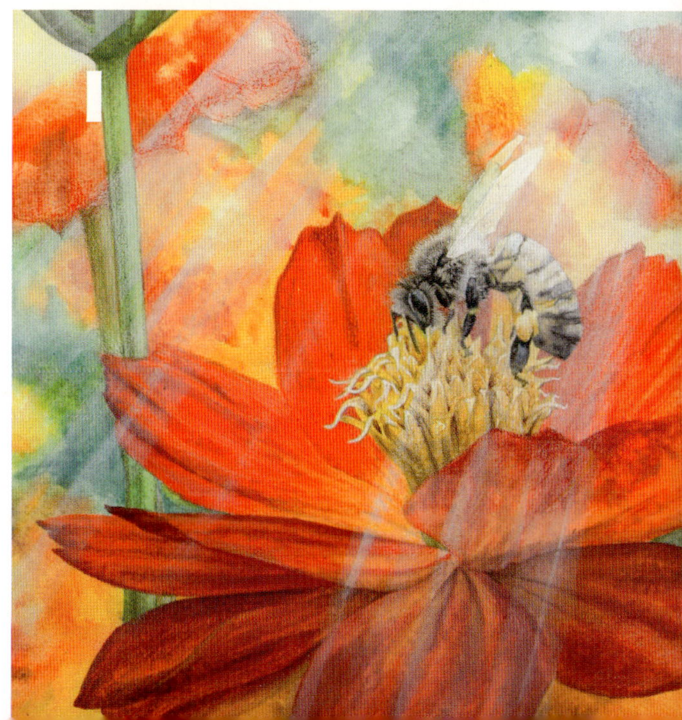

colors and details in that area, you can move to an adjacent section covered by a ray.

In regard to technique, there are several ways that you can approach this stage of the process. One option is to select two different colored pencils for the same anatomical form, one that matches the reference image and one with a lighter value that you can use in the areas covered by a ray of light. Of course, this is limited to the colored pencils that are available. Another possibility is to first use a colored pencil that matches the reference image on both sections. After the composition is complete, you can then erase lightly and apply a colored pencil on top that matches the ray. If you choose this second option, test the effect of layering *before* working on your piece to confirm that the pigment will appear appropriately muted. If you have used rich colored pencil colors such as dark red or violet in your composition, you might find it best to use only an eraser.

Either way, be aware of the direction of your pencil marks and eraser lines. Keep them aligned to either the subject underneath the ray or consistent with the lines of the ray so that they will blend into the composition. If you begin working at the edge of the ray and move inward, you can establish a boundary that can help you see the value of the remaining work more accurately.

REFINING AND PERSONALIZING YOUR STEPS

Continue to revisit and refine your preparation steps so that you begin future illustrations with a process that is most beneficial to your individual creative needs and practice.

Give extra attention to steps that include mid-process decision-making to be sure there was enough content included to guide you. Is there anything that could make your creative process go more smoothly, help you keep your focus, or support you in another way? You might want to write your discoveries and suggestions down in your sketchbook so that you have a guide to follow in the future.

While you develop this stage of your process, keep in mind that the act of adjustment and evolution is a courageous part of art making. It is not a time for regret, reprimand, or diminishing your effort. You deserve to have your hard-earned learning integrated into your practice, so that you can utilize all the tricks and techniques you have acquired and create artwork that expresses the artist you have become.

Congratulations on arriving at this stage in your practice. You are not only doing great; you are continuing to grow. Just think of how far you have come and what you have accomplished since the day you started your first illustration!

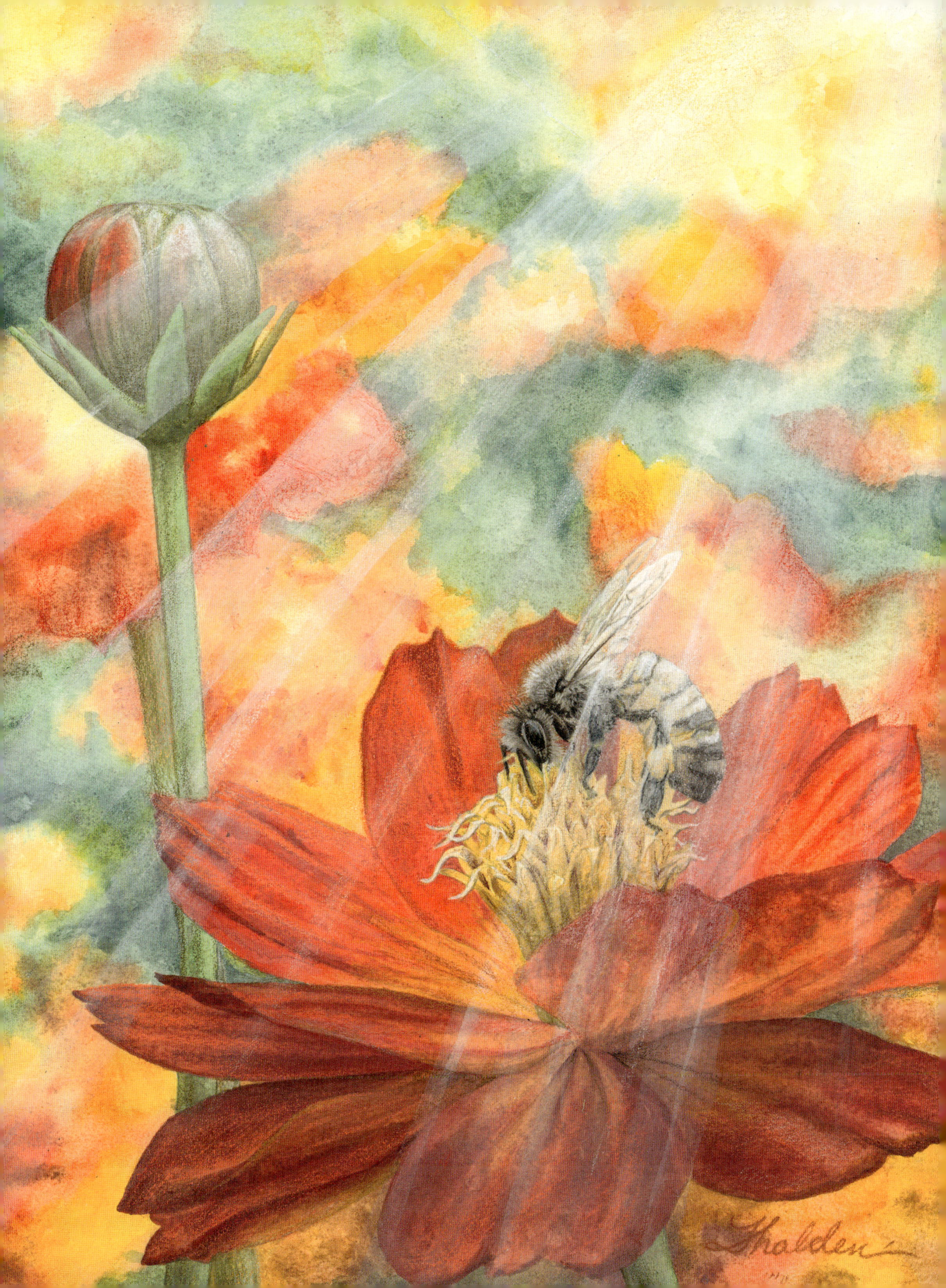

NATURE JOURNALING

Your artwork documents the world around you during a particular time span. When you include written thoughts or observations in your images, your drawings become illustrations of your story. This Nature Break combines image with the voice of the artist. It's time for nature journaling.

LOCATION: Various settings could work well, so you might choose one or several locations for this assignment. Perhaps you want to document an extended journey, a specific place, or particular subject.

MATERIALS: Pencil, pencil sharpener, and small sketchbook, possibly one solely devoted to this practice.

OBSERVATIONS: What is it about your surroundings or chosen subject that invites you to think, consider, or wonder about? What led you here or inspires you? What do you see, feel, hear, experience, or sense? What do you want to remember or help others understand about this experience?

PRACTICE: Create a composition that includes both visual components and blank space where you can write your observations or personal response to the environment or subject. Consider how your words may enhance the meaning of the image and vice versa.

You might choose to write first and then add drawings, or allow your words to fit in around your images. Either way, consider the shape, size, and placement of your text so that it becomes a creative element in the page layout. Allow the style, legibility, and alignment of each line of your handwriting to play a part in the overall aesthetics of the piece.

REFLECTION: After you have finished, take time to consider how text transforms your images. You might consider revisiting this journal entry at a later date as a reminder of this experience. Alternately, you could let it go entirely and gift it to someone who might enjoy receiving it.

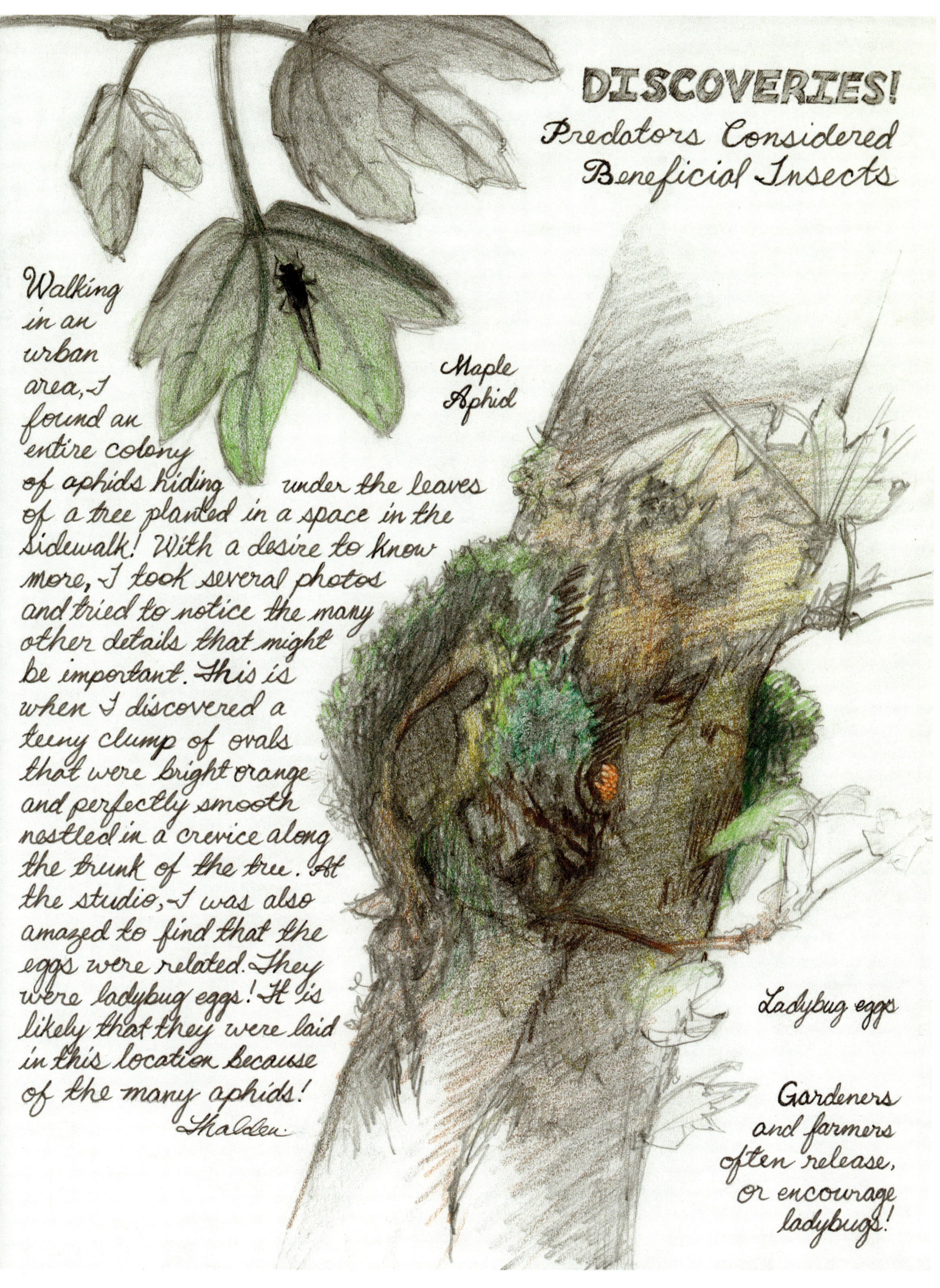

DISCOVERIES!
Predators Considered
Beneficial Insects

Maple
Aphid

Walking
in an
urban
area, I
found an
entire colony
of aphids hiding   under the leaves
of a tree planted in a space in the
sidewalk! With a desire to know
more, I took several photos
and tried to notice the many
other details that might
be important. This is
when I discovered a
teeny clump of ovals
that were bright orange
and perfectly smooth
nestled in a crevice along
the trunk of the tree. At
the studio, I was also
amazed to find that the
eggs were related. They
were ladybug eggs! It is
likely that they were laid
in this location because
of the many aphids!
        Malden

Ladybug eggs

Gardeners
and farmers
often release,
or encourage
ladybugs!

BLUE MORPHO BUTTERFLY

MORPHO PELEIDES

Morpho butterflies are among the largest butterflies in the world and live in the tropical forests of Latin America. Though not currently considered endangered, both decorative consumerism and increasing loss of forest habitat are causing a growing amount of concern. Their brilliant blue color is the result of an optical effect created by the interaction of light with the anatomical structure on the surface of their wings. I selected this subject to provide an opportunity for you to practice replicating a glistening surface by using primarily opaque pigments. In addition, you will have a chance to explore the color interaction between a subject that is both lighter and darker than the environment.

 SEE REFERENCE PHOTOS ON PAGE 329

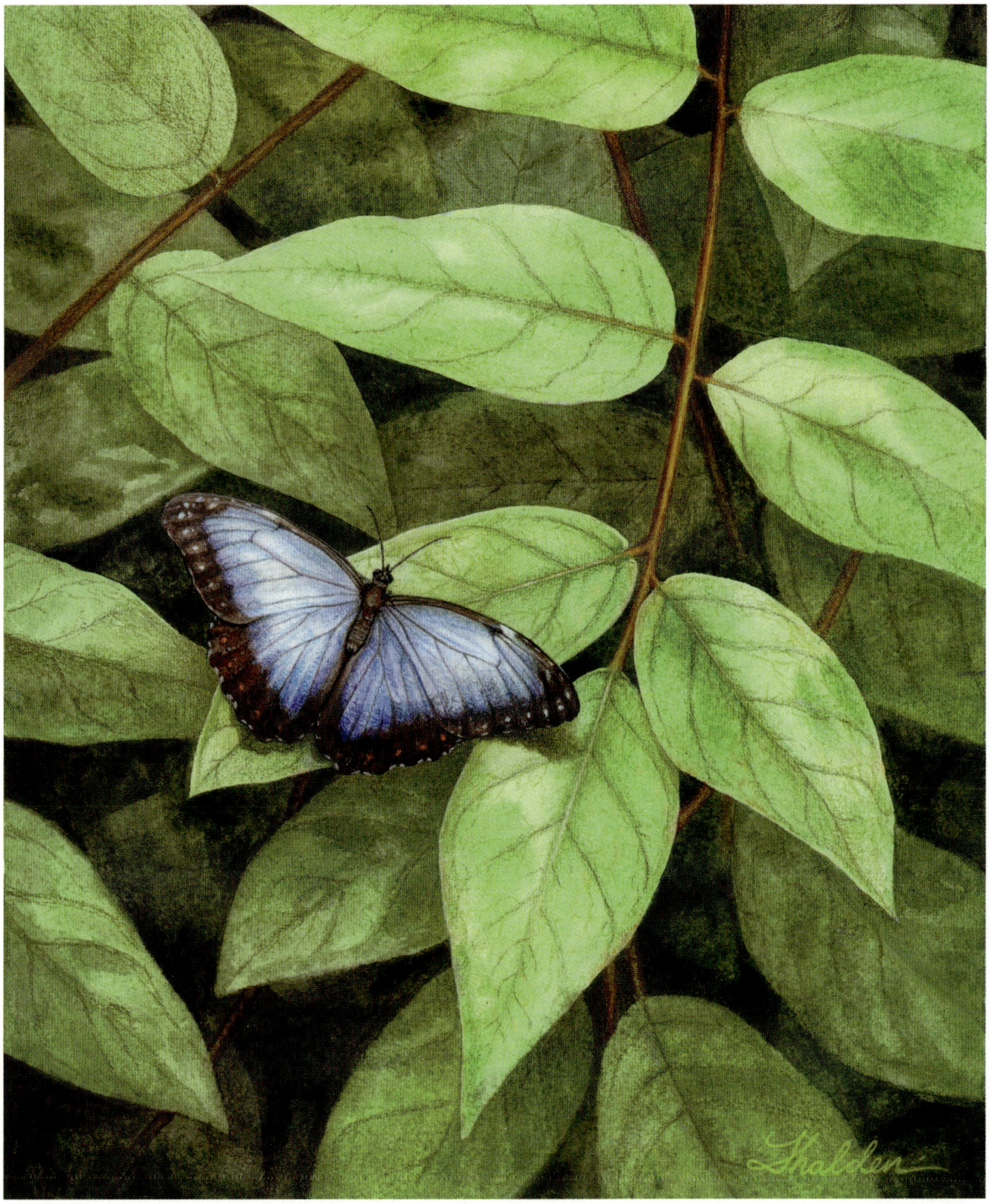

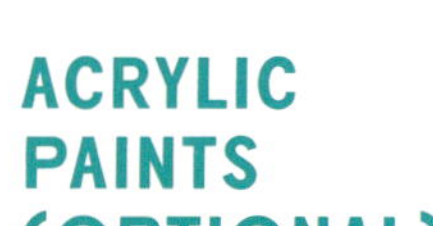

ACRYLIC
PAINTS
(OPTIONAL)
☐ cerulean blue
☐ cobalt teal
☐ interference blue
   (fine)

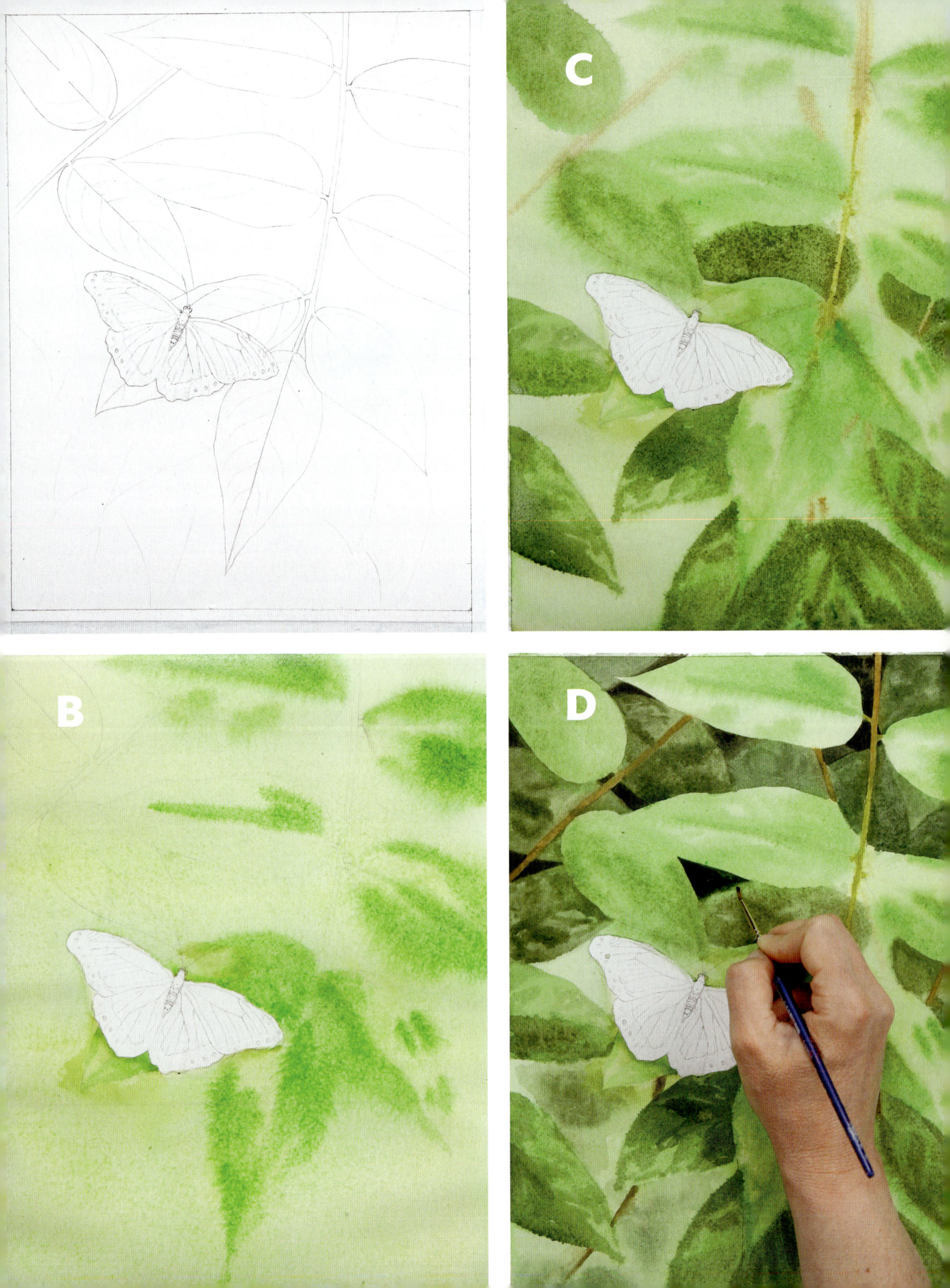

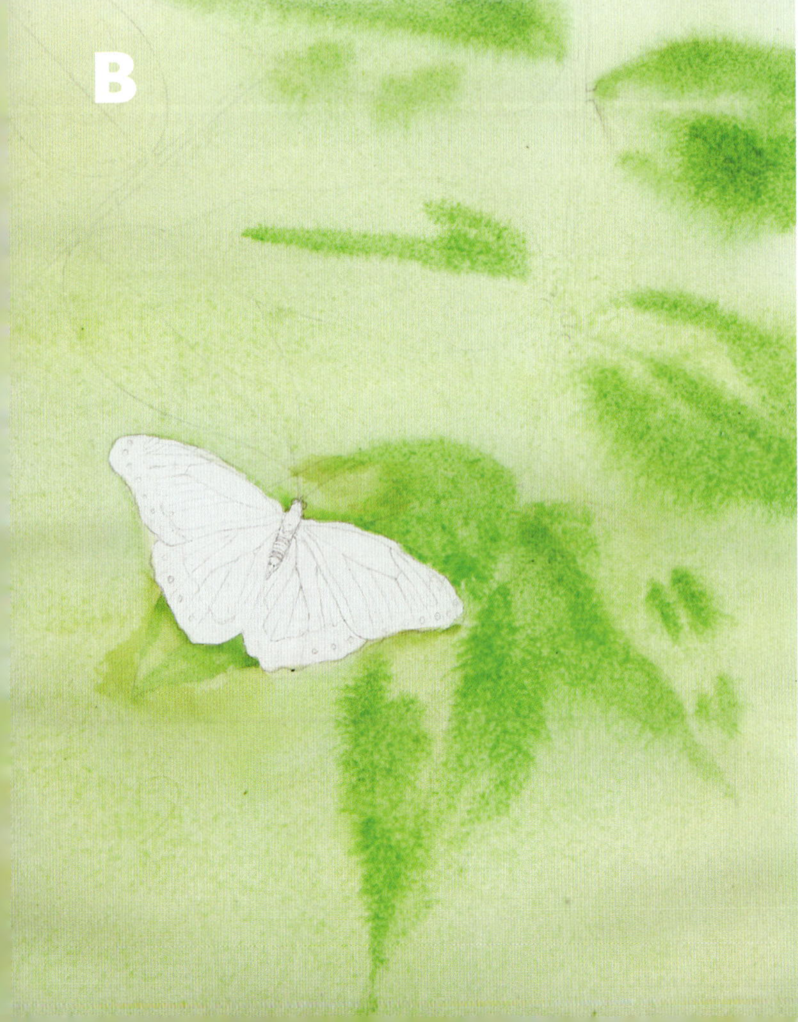
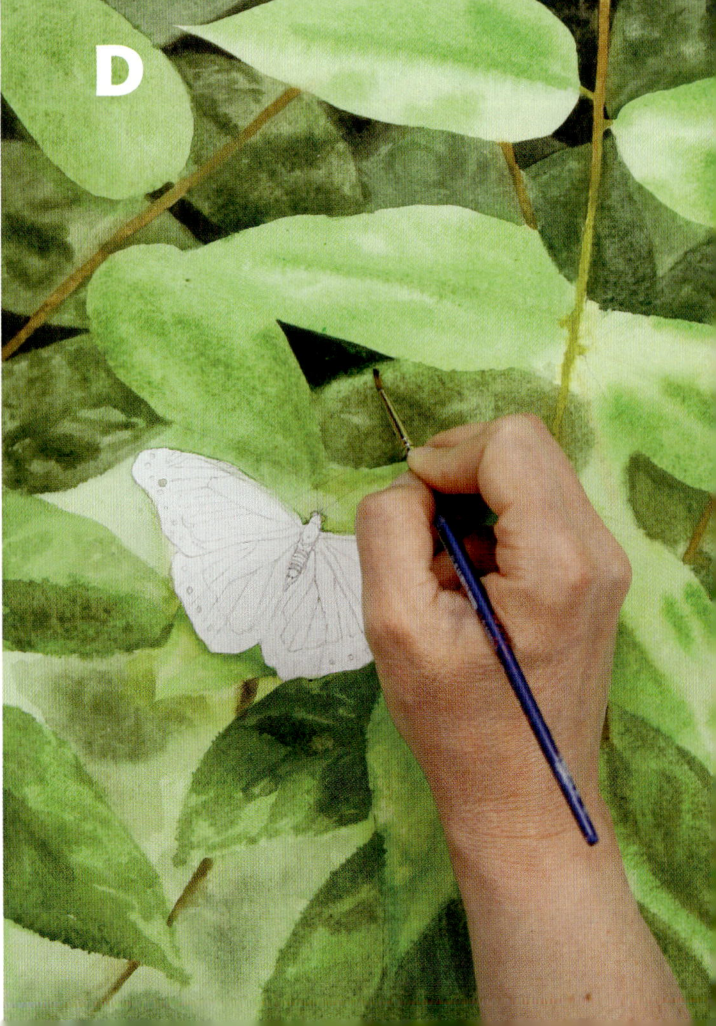

DEVELOPING YOUR OWN PROCESS: PART 4

When you create the steps for this project, you might reread your notes from the two previous projects so that your own recommendations guide you regarding how much information to write down or think through before beginning this project.

If you realize that you do not have enough information about a process after you begin working, always pause to address these unforeseen moments so that you can continue with intentionality.

DESIGNING COMPOSITIONS

A Use the knowledge you have gained to develop an original composition in your sketchbook. You might start by creating multiple thumbnail sketches with the focal point placed in drastically different locations. You can then determine how you could place the primary branch in each design to begin a visual circuit. In the background, you could repeat botanical forms to both suggest a dense forest environment and complete the visual circuit. It may help to think of branches as lines that link one area of the composition to another, and the shape, as well as the value of the pointy leaves, as suggesting movement toward or away from an area further in that direction. Since the reference image offers a limited amount of information, you can find additional photographs of foliage or create an entirely different background. This is a great time, however, to explore creating leaves using the information that is provided, coupled with the knowledge you have gained about the structure of plants. While the results may not describe a particular botanical scientifically, they can still look incredibly realistic.

PAINTING AROUND SHAPES TO CREATE LEAVES IN THE BACKGROUND

B Be sure to replicate the direction of the light source you see in the reference image so that the highlights and shadows in the background will be consistent with those on the butterfly. If you include foliage, you might even explore having bright highlights that look like stippled light shining through unseen foliage above. Next, you can add branches and leaves that are located in the middle ground.

C When the first layer of paint has dried completely, add all of the slightly darker leaves by carefully working around the outline of the primary branch. If you are able to rotate the page while you work, you can paint the arcs of the leaves more easily. After the second layer of paint has dried, apply a wash to the negative space, then use a dark-valued paint mixture to add more leaves. This makes the lighter leaves seem closer to the viewer, creates layers of depth, and alludes to the density of the foliage.

D To complete the background, add a very dark green paint mixture to all of the remaining negative space, which will distinguish the areas that are farthest away. As you add this layer, consider how much you want to blur the edges of the leaves.

When you review the overall composition, look for areas you can darken. For example, you might de-emphasize competing forms, reduce areas of contrast that could be distracting, and identify places where you would like the leaves to recede more incrementally. When you are finished, you might cover the paint on your palette so that you can easily darken a section without having to remix any colors while you are working.

UNDERSTANDING IRIDESCENCE

To understand iridescence as an artist, consider the fundamental components of color, both in the subject and in artist media. This can help you comprehend the appearance of the butterfly and explain why art materials can seem limiting when illustrating iridescence. If you would prefer to focus solely on technique, simply jump to the next section.

First, look at the dark brown areas of the butterfly that are not iridescent. These sections are covered in pigmented scales that will appear to be the same color from multiple angles and under magnification. On the other hand, while the scales in the iridescent areas appear blue, they are primarily transparent. Amazingly, they have complexly shaped ridges, and when light interacts and bounces off this highly dimensional surface, it creates wavelengths in the blue spectrum. Therefore, both the blue color and the shimmering quality that we see in the butterfly are the result of the microscopic structure of its wings.

Since artist paint colors are created using pigment, they are similar to pigmented colors in nature. For an artist setting out to replicate iridescence, this aspect of the material creates a fundamental challenge.

Interference paints rely on structural color to create different hues. Because of this, they are much closer to iridescence. Yet under the microscope, these paints are quite different from the iridescent portion of a butterfly's wing. They are made of microscopic plates of clear mica, which have been coated in metal oxide and suspended in a clear base. Similar to the effect of iridescence, when light interacts with these plates, they "flash" a particular wavelength of color, otherwise they appear transparent. They can be mixed into wet pigmented paints to add a little luster or applied on top of a dry layer to create a more dramatic effect. Unfortunately, when applied directly to the paper, they tend to highlight the surface where the color shift happens, therefore they can easily become overpowering and distracting or even reduce the dimensional quality of an illustration.

Though iridescent subjects appear complex and the science is baffling, you can utilize the same techniques you have been practicing to re-create them. In addition, you will be able to apply interference paint so that it adds a delightful and unexpected surprise to your illustration without taking away from the spacious aspects of the composition.

IDENTIFYING ATTRIBUTES OF COLOR BEYOND THE OPTICAL EFFECT OF IRIDESCENCE

Look closely at a single wing on the butterfly. To identify the appropriate paint mixtures you will need, try to see beyond the optical effect by focusing on the fundamental attributes of color: hue, value, and intensity. Pay close attention to the contour of the surface and changes in value. The shadows and highlights on iridescent surfaces tend to accentuate minute changes in angle and depth far more acutely than on pigmented surfaces. Locating the direction of the light source can help you see the peaks and valleys more clearly.

You might even take a moment to compare the quality of the colors on this butterfly to one or two of the noniridescent butterflies in earlier chapters. If you choose this visual investigation, try to identify specific qualities that visually communicate that a surface is either iridescent or matte. You might document both your findings and how you would re-create these characteristics using artist media in your sketchbook.

MIXING OPAQUE PAINT COLORS FOR CREATING IRIDESCENCE

To keep the painting process similar to previous projects, you might start by mixing a blue paint base that closely matches a mid-value section of the blue area. Then create a variation to paint shadows and another for bright highlights. To retain the color intensity in the highlighted areas, use white paint minimally. Instead, use diluted paint mixtures that allow the white color of the paper to lighten the value of your pigments. Another option is to create your mixtures with vibrant colors that are closer to the desired result, such as cobalt teal or cerulean blue paint. If you add a tiny amount of ultramarine blue when you create the dark cobalt blue paint mixture, you can produce the appearance of a color shift ever so slightly toward the violet side of the spectrum.

In my illustration, I wanted to offer an example without using additional colors. Through experimentation, I found that if I first painted and allowed the blue base color and variations to dry, I could paint on a highly diluted mixture of cobalt blue and cadmium yellow to create a slightly more blue-green appearance.

PAINTING IRIDESCENCE USING OPAQUE PAINT MIXTURES

E To begin painting, apply the lightest blue mixture over the entire blue area to unify the wings. Since the surface is complex, work on one side or even one wing at a time. Blend the blue back to the color of the paper just beyond the line where the color will turn to brownish black. While the paint is still wet, apply the middle values and then the shadows. While the paint is drying, add more and more details, focusing on one small section of the wing at a time. Also pay close attention to the degree which the hue, value, and intensity shifts so that you can more accurately replicate the color, contour, and sheen in your illustration. You might consider lightening the lower right wing more than what you see in the reference image to balance the overall appearance of the butterfly.

If you start to feel overwhelmed, you can always let an area dry, reapply a second or even a third wash, and continue painting until the blue section of the butterfly is complete. If you intend to use interference paint, you might want to take a moment to paint each blue mixture onto a scrap piece of paper so that you can practice later in the process.

PAINTING THE PERIMETER OF WINGS

F When you apply the brown paint mixtures around the blue sections, work from the edge of each wing inward. Be sure to overlap the blue section slightly to smoothly transition from one color to the other and to avoid developing a light ring between them.

APPLYING INTERFERENCE PAINT BEFORE COLORED PENCILS

If you'd like, you can apply interference blue paint to the butterfly. Just be aware that any colored pencil you add on top of the interference paint will dull the surface. For this reason, I often wait to apply the interference paint until after the colored pencil stage so that the entire surface will glisten a bit. If you do this as well, be aware that there is a chance that the waxy pencil marks could unexpectedly influence the water-based paint over time. Since this section only needed accents in colored pencil, I felt comfortable making this choice. If you prefer to work on this now, follow the instructions found at the end of this project.

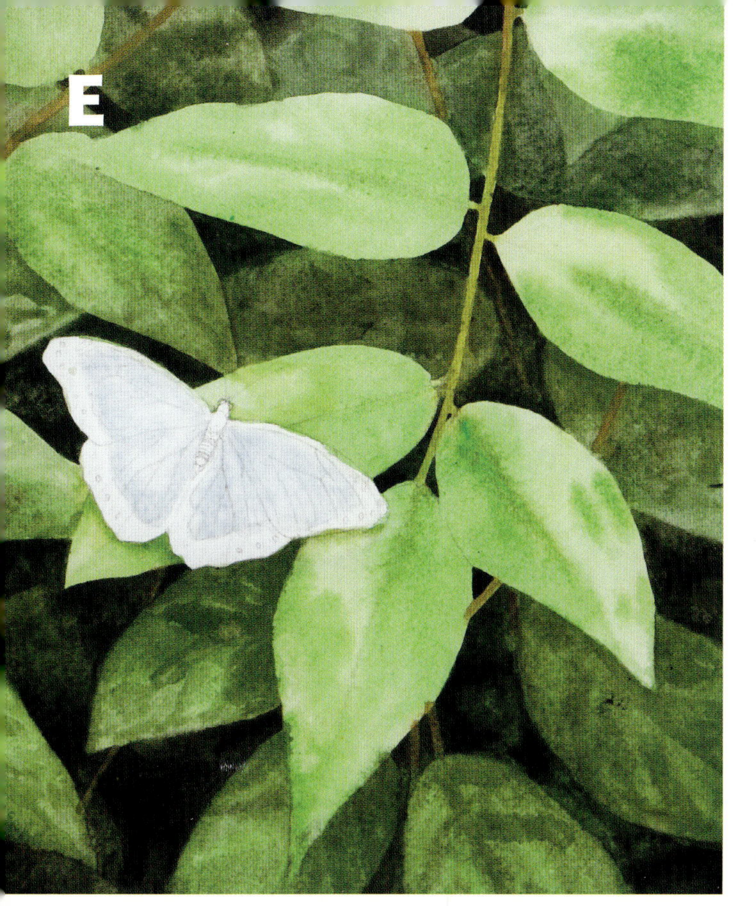
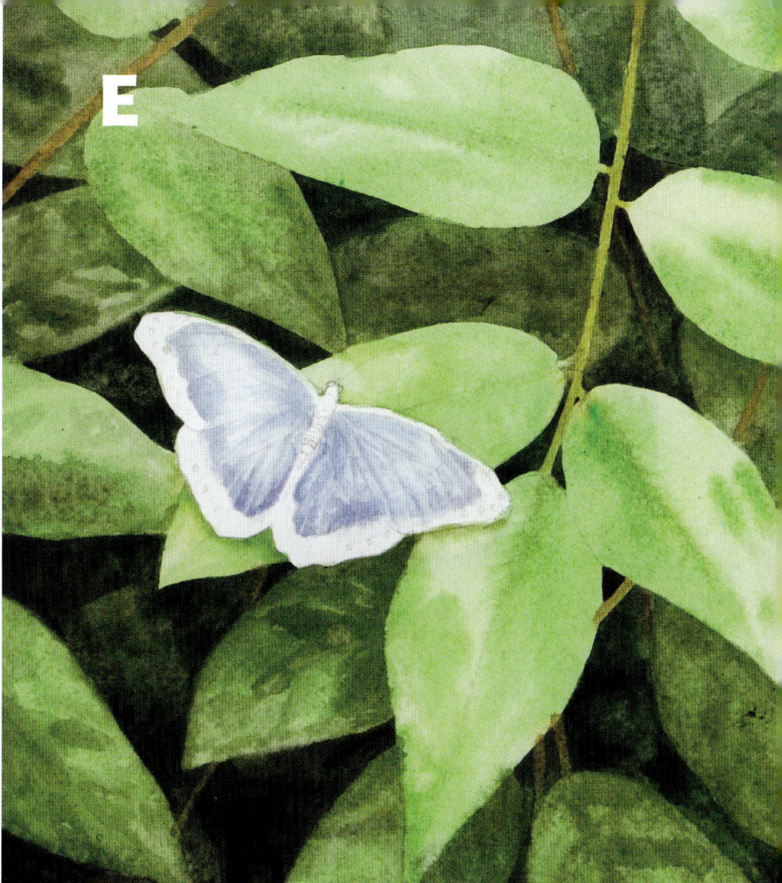

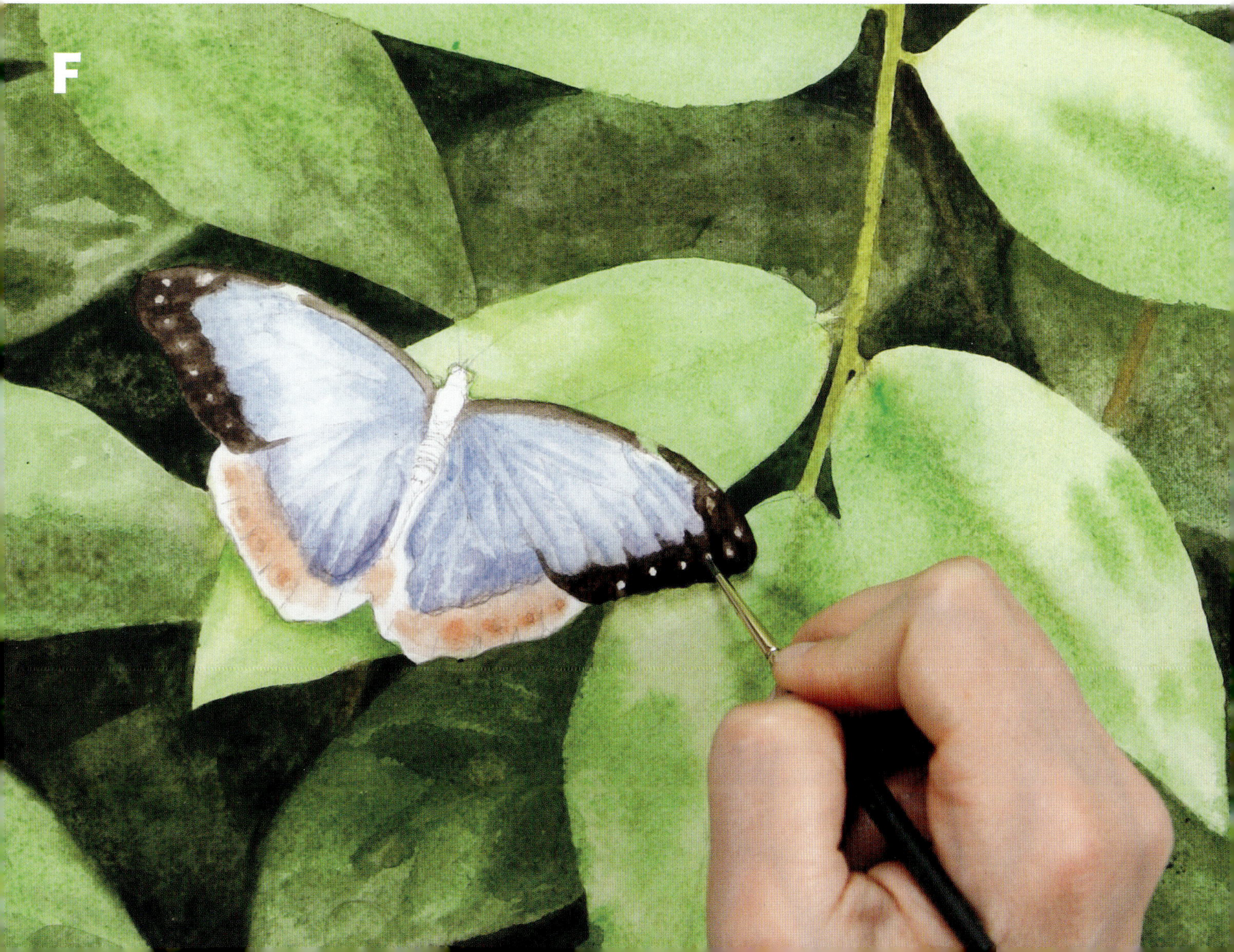

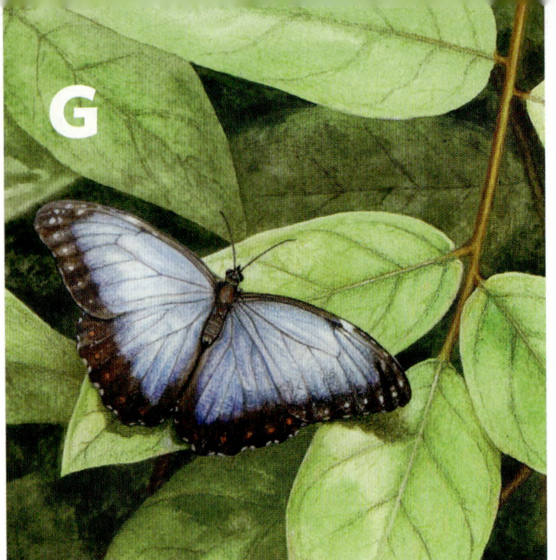

REFINING SUBJECTS AGAINST A DARK BACKGROUND

G Since the background is lighter than the subject in some areas and darker in others, you might use a colored pencil with a value that falls between these two extremes to define the edge of the wings. You can then select colored pencils to lighten or darken the value and to further differentiate the butterfly from its surroundings. If the edge is facing away from the light source, a very dark colored pencil with a very sharp tip can accentuate select sections along the edge to emphasize dimensionality.

If you included foliage, draw the veins carefully and lightly so that you are less likely to erase but can still make adjustments on top of the paint layer if needed. You might begin by working on the less important leaves in the composition and move toward the focal point so that you can refine your technique while you are working. If you add details to the leaves below the primary branch, be sure to replicate the appropriate amount of blur and minimize the amount of contrast between shadows and highlights.

While you are working on this illustration, pause periodically to celebrate your achievements.

ENVISIONING A REALISTIC SHADOW

Insects that are depicted in a natural environment often cast complex shadows onto uneven surfaces. If you are faced with the challenge of inventing a shadow, you might start by revisiting the Nature Break titled Shadows and Highlights (page 178), which explores the relationship between light and basic geometric shapes. Then return to the reference image and follow this two-part process: First, see if you can imagine how the angle of the light might cast a shadow of the butterfly onto a perfectly flat surface. Then consider how the contour of the actual surface would curve, elongate, blur, or darken the shape of the shadow. Another option is to look for references that replicate just the portion of the subject and shadow that you need. As a third option, you might even create a quick model to look at. To do this, simply cut both a wing and a leaf shape out of a piece of paper, alter them to emulate the general contour of the subjects, and position them similarly under a light source.

USING COLORED PENCIL TO ACCENTUATE IRIDESCENCE

This is a great time to graze paper with the side of the colored pencil lead to create the appearance of scales. As I suggested in the old world swallowtail project (page 56), be sure to rotate the pencil often as you work so that you can avoid creating a flat section on the lead. You might select one to three of the following colors to use in either the same or separate areas: white, sepia, violet, imperial violet, or a variation of blue. Apply the color sparingly and only in the area where it is most pronounced in the reference image. After these marks have been applied, avoid erasing so that you can keep both the vibrancy of the paint and the appearance of individual speckles.

ADDING INTERFERENCE PAINT AND OTHER FINAL TOUCHES

H In your experiments on scrap paper, use the interference blue paint first without any water and then dilute it until it is workable, but not quite liquid, so that you understand the difference in workability and results. Be aware that the paint needs to dry completely on the scrap paper before you see the lustrous effect. Depending on the angle of light hitting the page, the paint will either appear a slightly yellowed clear or flash a brilliant blue.

I When you're ready to apply the paint to your composition, add a very thin wash to the entire blue area on one side or even one wing of the butterfly. Then use a very small paintbrush to delicately apply a miniscule amount of the interference paint to the center of a highlighted area and fade it into the surroundings. This will help unify the iridescence with the opaque paint colors that make up the contour and color of the wings. You could have two paintbrushes to work with: one to apply the paint and another to fade the interference paint back into the color of the

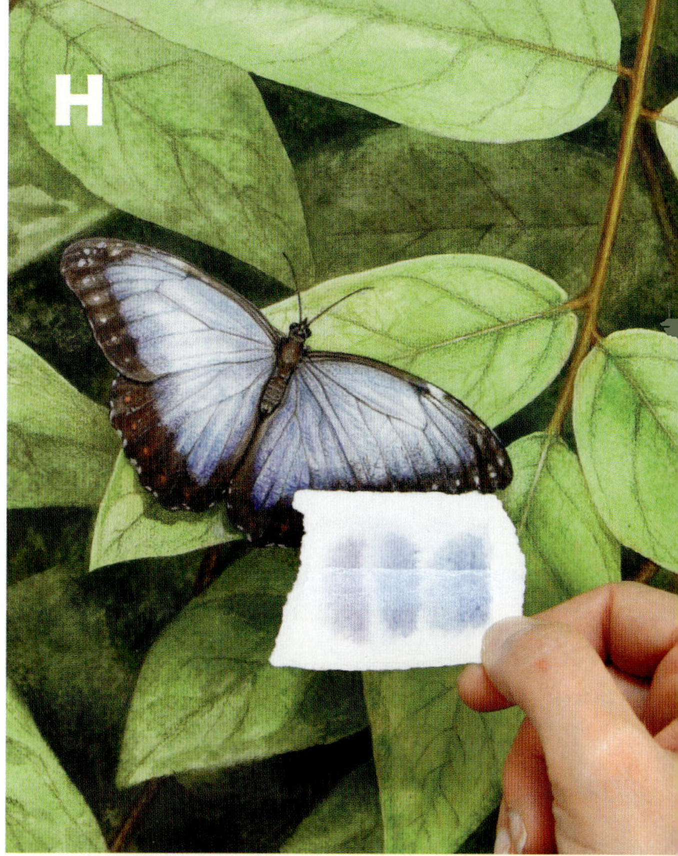

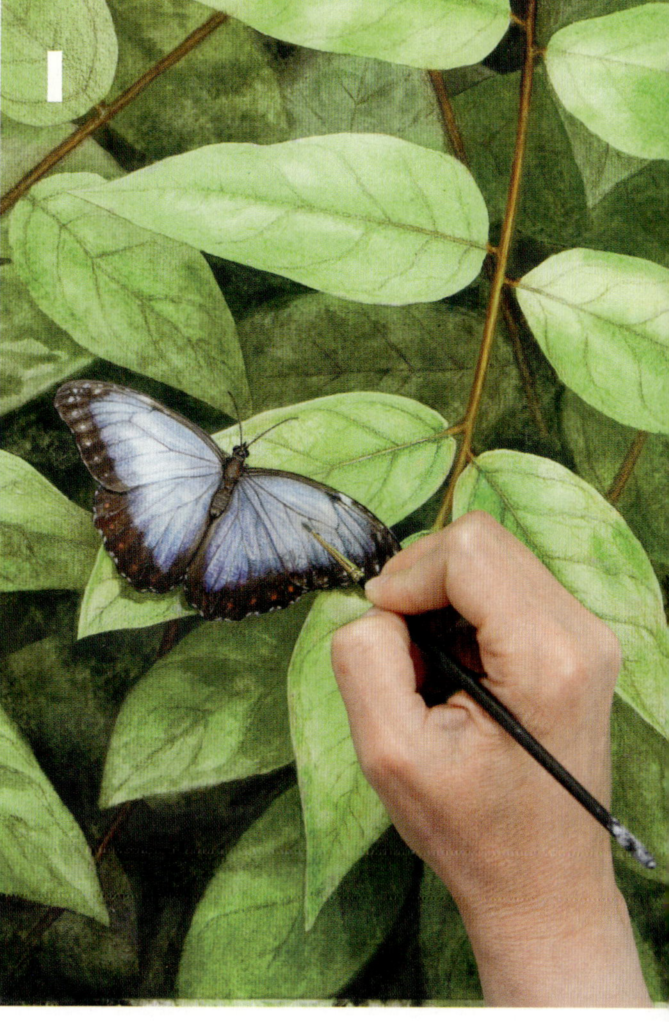

page. In the areas that have bright highlights, apply more paint by lightly dabbing the brush so that the application creates a stippled appearance. Individual strokes tend to draw attention to the surface of the paper, thereby making the image appear flat instead of dimensional. It can be helpful to angle your artwork toward the light in your studio so that it is easier to see where you are applying the paint.

J Remember that the interference is merely an embellishment on top of the iridescent appearance you have already created. The aim is to add a very subtle sparkle to the entire blue area, create a bit more intensity in the bright highlights, and let it all fade where the dark color begins around the perimeter.

Unlike replicating the anatomy of a subject, the goal here is to create a sense of surprise in your artwork similar to the experience of looking at an iridescent creature. You might glance at the reference image, but primarily allow the highlights in your artwork to guide you. In my illustration, I moved from one cell of the wing to the next while making a small amount of effort to avoid the veins.

As you paint, consider utilizing these tips: Unless you are painting along a vein line, avoid letting any hard edges dry on the wings. Because the sparkles are difficult to remove once the paint has been applied to the page, you should apply a reserved amount, let it dry completely, then add more if needed. If you did paint over any veins, you can lightly graze each line with either a colorless blender or a colored pencil with a very sharp tip to reestablish these noniridescent features.

Then rejoice in the miracle of structural color in both the natural world and in art supplies.

REVIEWING YOUR STEPS

Again, once your artwork is complete and you have celebrated thoroughly, revisit your preparation steps to compare the information to the actual experience of art making. Read the last section in the previous chapter again to help you steadily progress toward creating an ideal process.

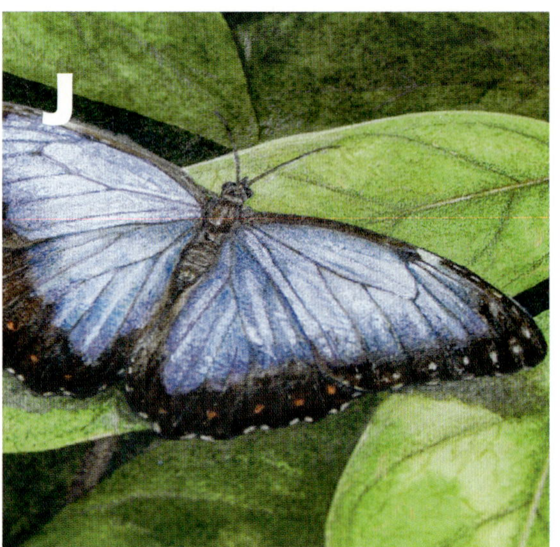

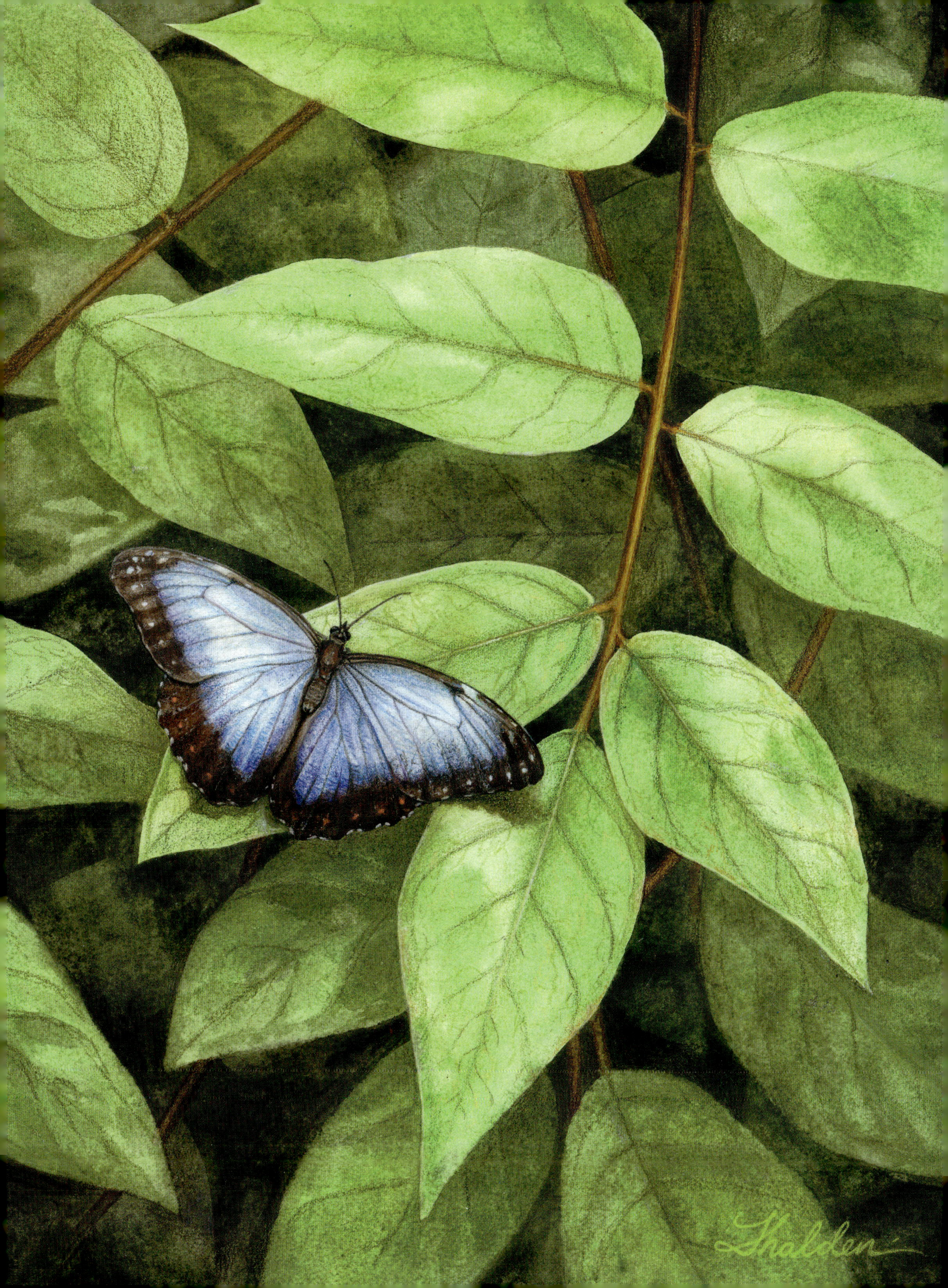

SPECIES IDENTIFICATION

Discovering facts and unique characteristics about your subject can enhance your knowledge and the realistic quality of your drawings. This Nature Break is devoted to learning about the subjects that most inspire you. It's time to embark on species identification.

LOCATION: Select a spot where the subject you choose is at rest and will hopefully remain still while you draw.

MATERIALS: Sketchbook, pencil, eraser, and a chair to sit on. You might want to bring a set of colored pencils as well as field guides, if you have them.

OBSERVATIONS: Before you draw, take a few moments to keenly observe the subject's physical attributes, position, and placement within the overall location.

PRACTICE: Design the layout of your composition. Make sure that both the size and location of each component contributes to a greater understanding of the subject. Leave enough room on your page for a title and your written notes.

As you draw, take time to adjust your lines and check proportions so that the features you are describing are easy to understand from the image. You can choose to keep a line drawing, add shading with pencil, or color the subject completely. You might want to include a portion of the environment to describe the subject more fully.

The text could provide information about unique physical characteristics, behavior, or the qualities of the environment where you found the subject. Field guides or online resources can help you identify the species and contribute more information. Be selective about the text you include and be sure to consider its placement on the page. Applying consistency in your lines and using legible handwriting will add both clarity and comprehension.

REFLECTION: How does scientific observation and research effect your perception, understanding, and drawing ability?

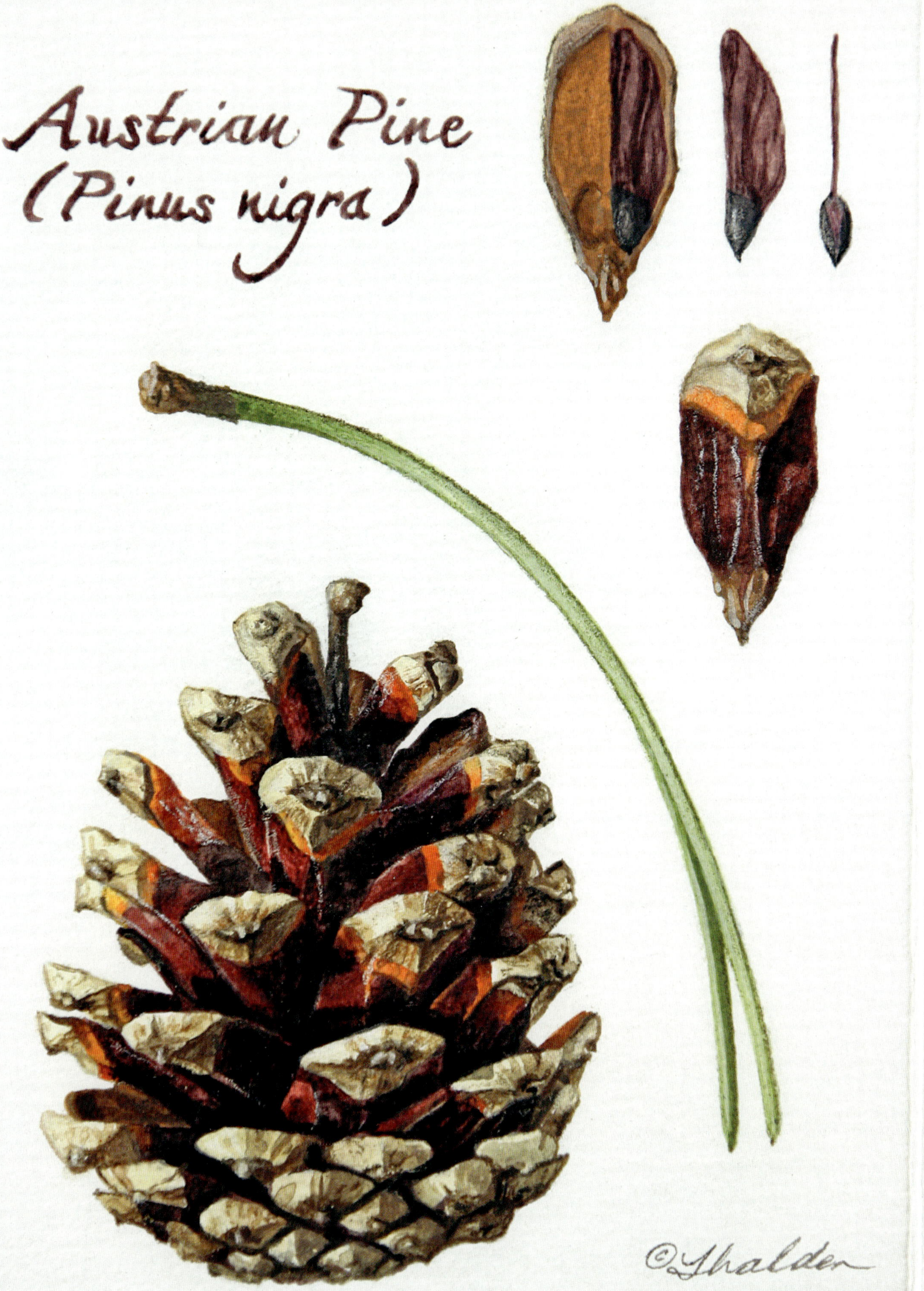

Austrian Pine
(Pinus nigra)

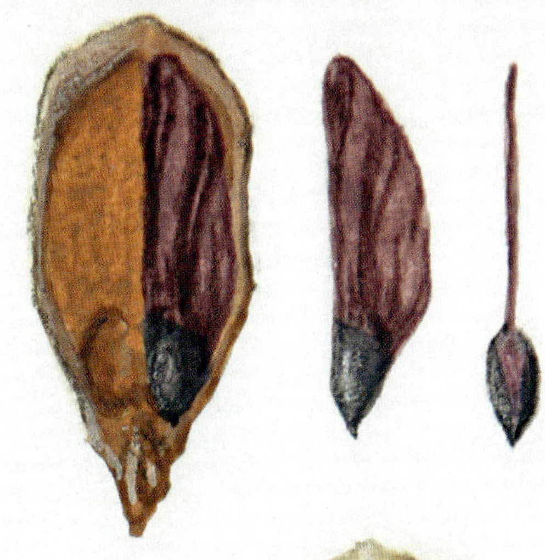

FINAL PROJECT

You have arrived at the final chapter of this book, which is an enormous accomplishment. This is a time to utilize your accumulated knowledge and put your skills to the test. This chapter offers an open project and gives you an opportunity to select your own composition. Consider the two options described on the following page, then decide on a reference to use for this project. I hope you find one that is both in line with the progression of this book and that you thoroughly enjoy working on.

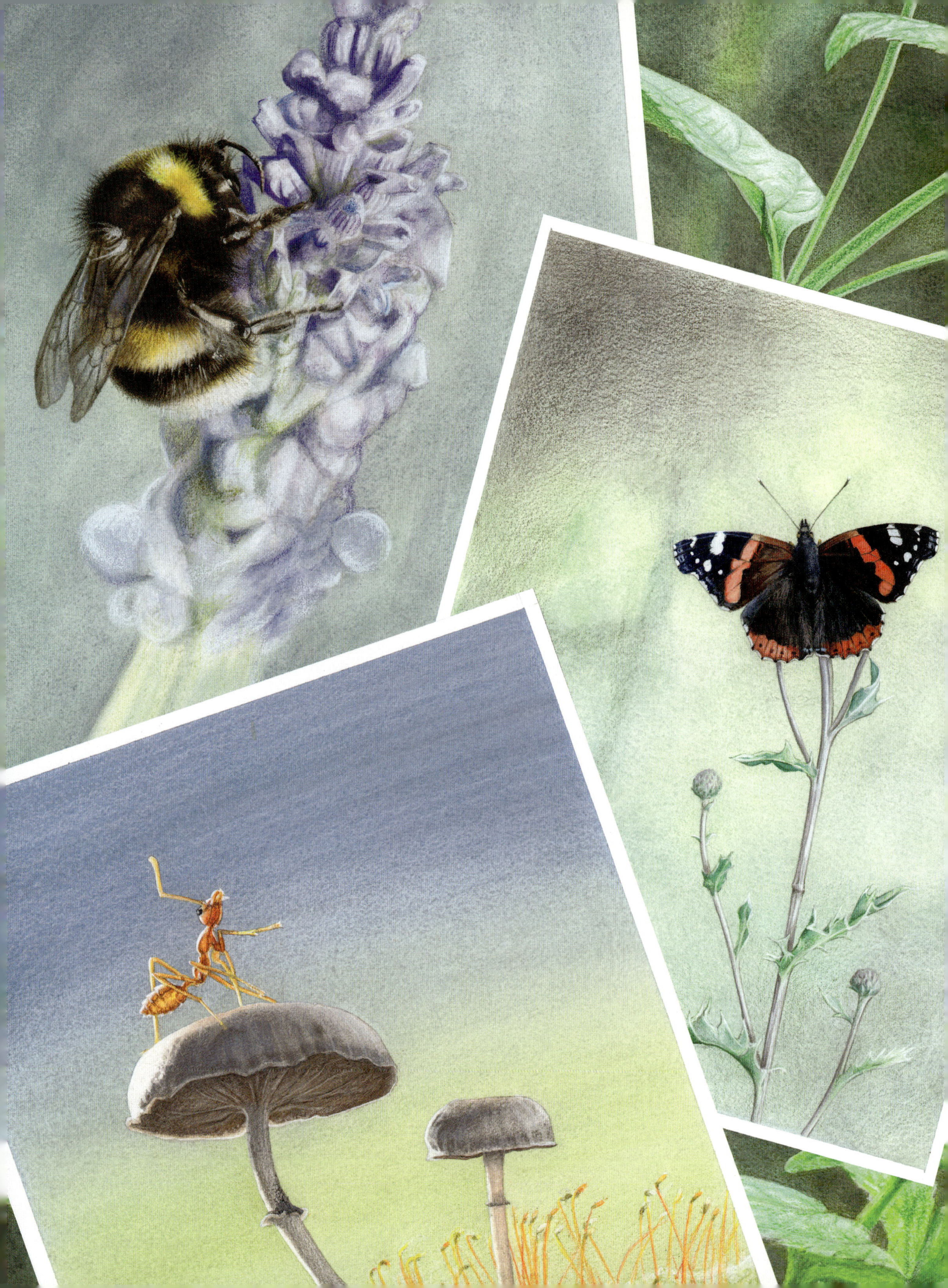

SELECTING A SUBJECT AND ESTABLISHING YOUR PROCESS

The first option, which I am a big fan of, is to select a project from earlier in the book and create a new illustration from your more experienced point of view. You might be surprised by what you notice while looking again at the reference image and going through the process of illustrating a new version. You could choose a project that went smoothly, one that you struggled with, or one that you avoided completely. Once you've made your selection, view the reference image to consider the design, process, and techniques you could use. Then, without rereading the pertinent chapter, rely on the skills you've learned from this book to provide both structure and guidance as you create the illustration. If you get stuck, take the time to problem solve to figure out ways to resolve the issue. (You can always refer to the instructions in the chapter if you need to.) But this is the time for you to rely on your acquired knowledge, integrate your abilities fully into your own practice, and allow everything you've gained up to this point to support you.

Alternatively, you might look for an entirely new reference. Use any insect as your subject, in any position and in an environment that appeals to you. You might select a photograph that you've taken, acquire an image from another photographer for this purpose, or use a three-dimensional reference. Ideally, pick a reference that offers achievable challenges so that you set yourself up for both continued learning and success.

Whichever direction you choose, take time to consider your processes in each stage of the illustration: preparation, design, drawing, painting, and layering with colored pencil. Depending on your decisions and experiences in the preparation stage of previous projects, you might consider reducing your written steps to only 25 percent to see if you can still make steady progress while you are working. You might also begin to envision how your own practice will look in the future. This project just might be an opportunity to make some adjustments so that you personalize your creative process and create an ideal studio practice to engage in far beyond the pages of this book.

REFERENCE PHOTOS

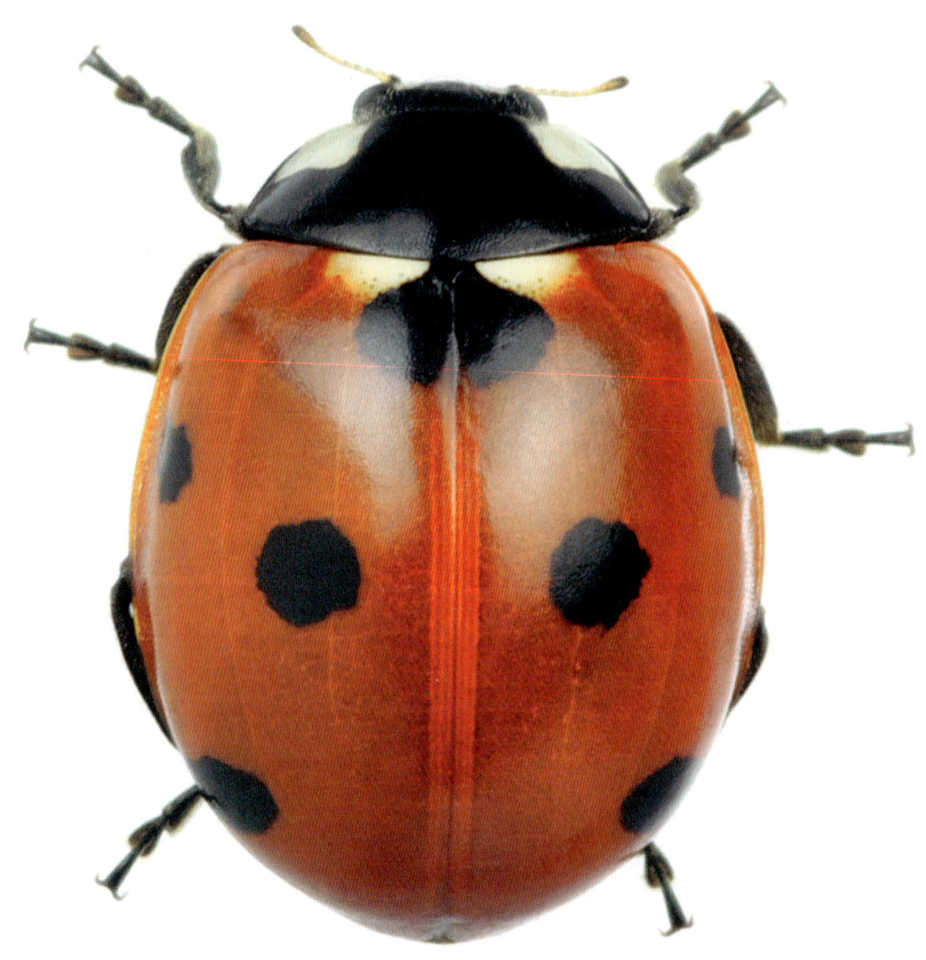

　SEVEN-SPOTTED LADYBUG BEETLE

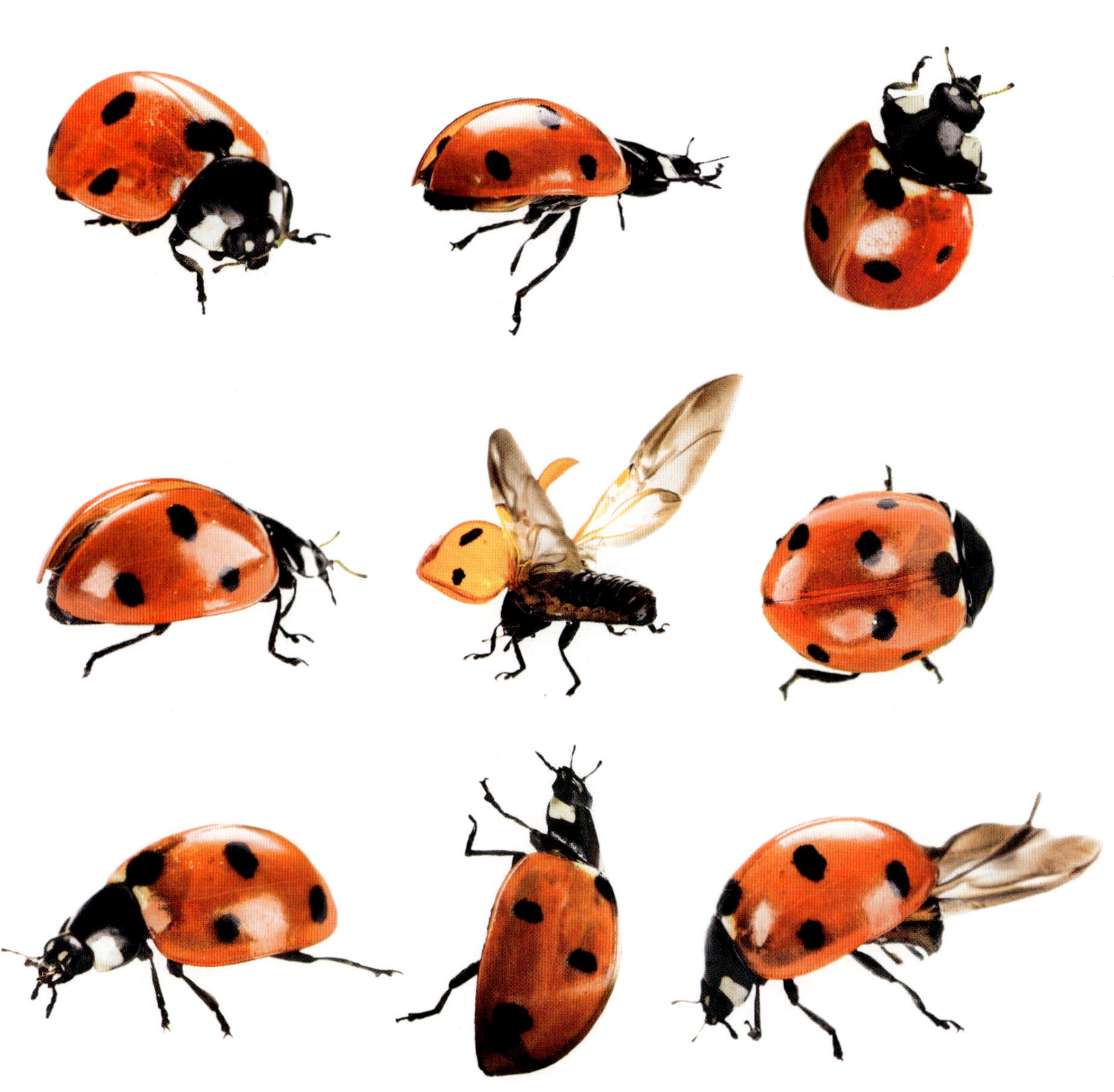

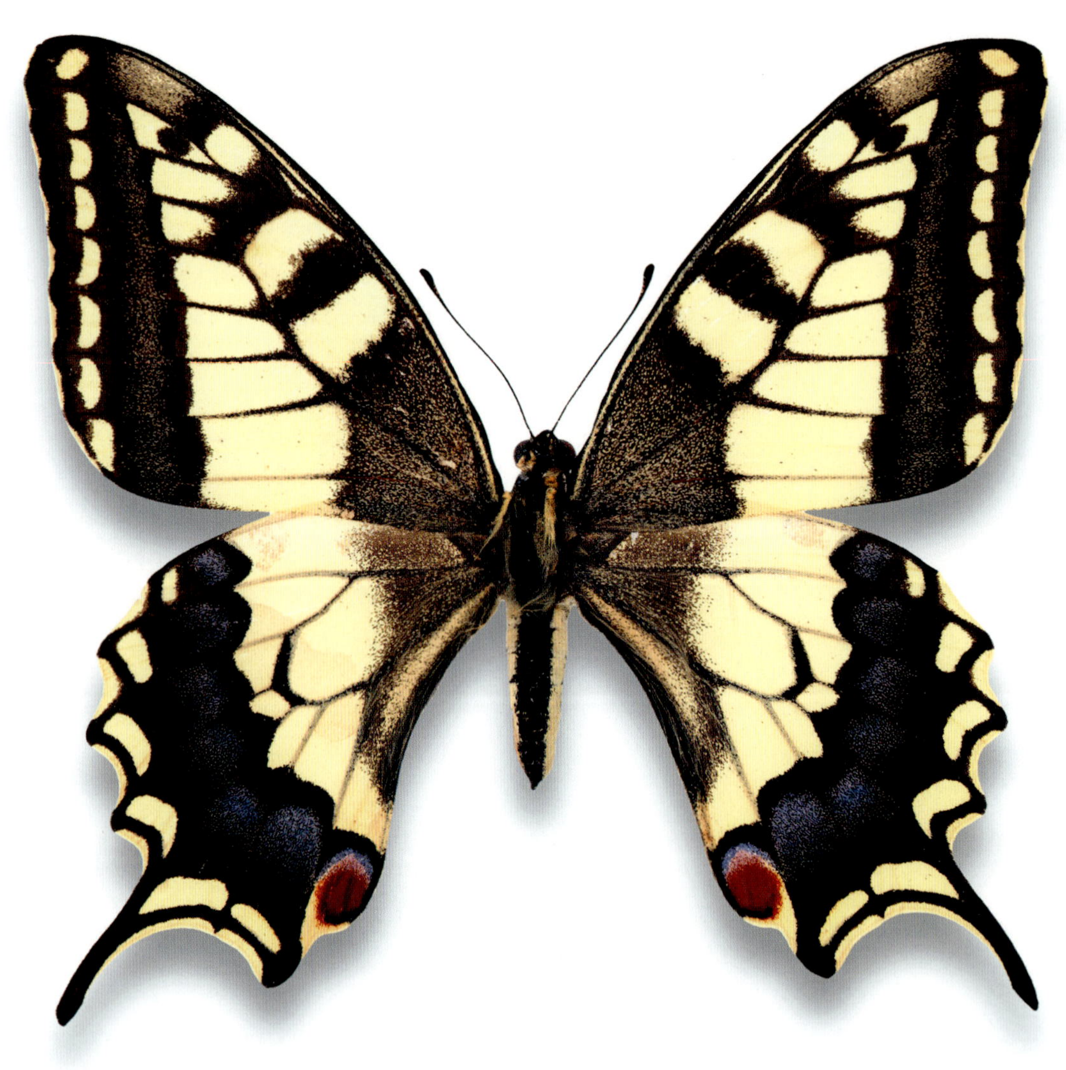

 OLD WORLD SWALLOWTAIL BUTTERFLY

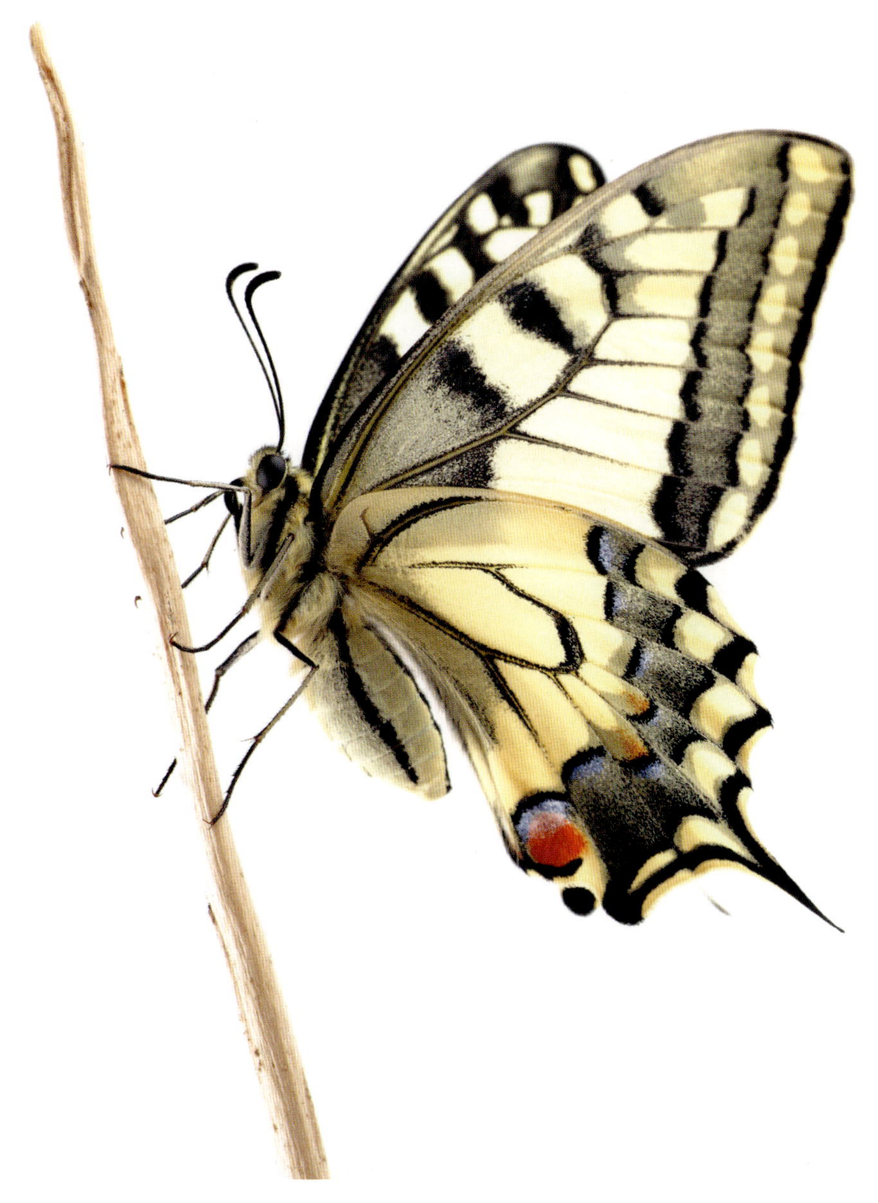

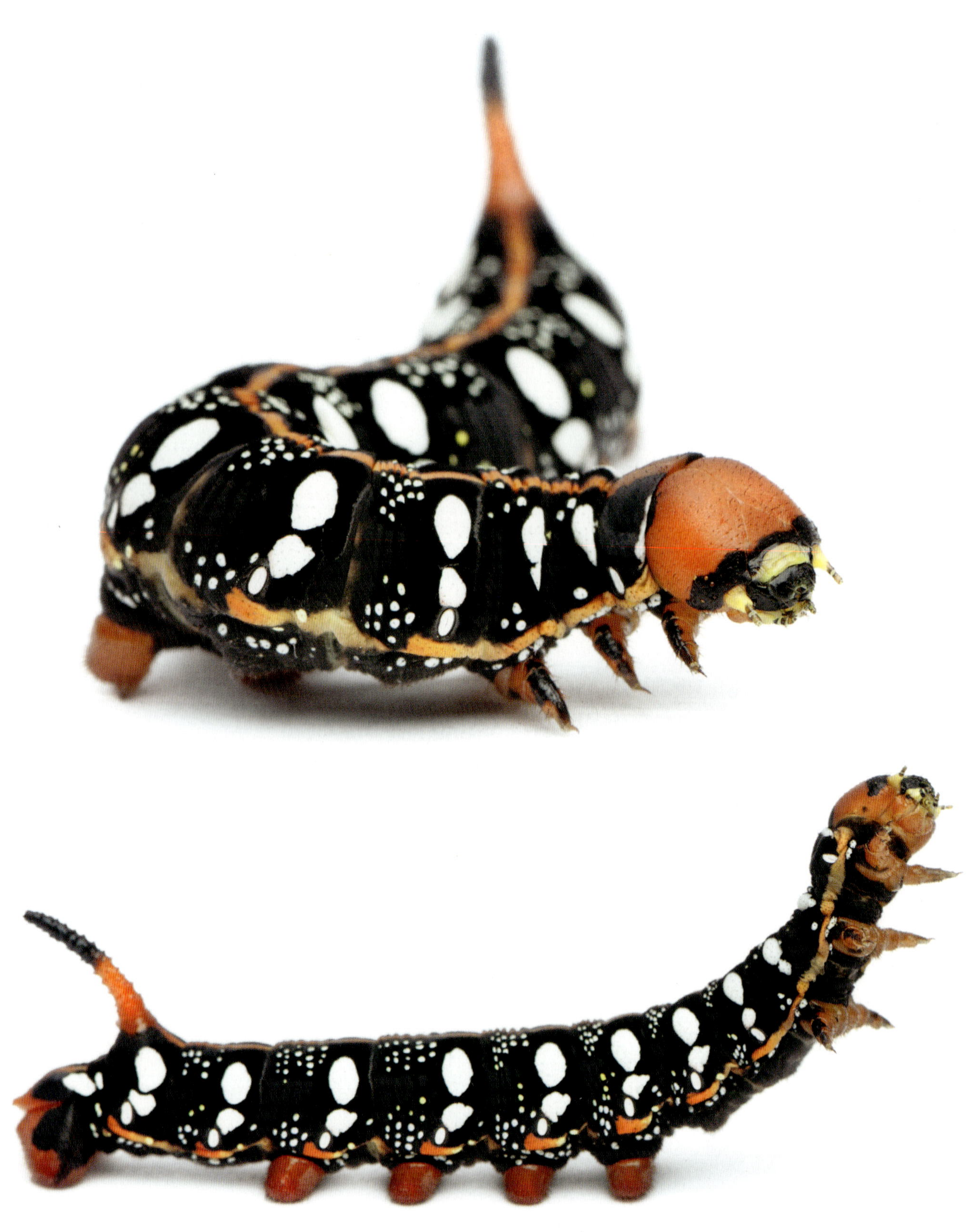

SPURGE HAWK MOTH CATERPILLAR

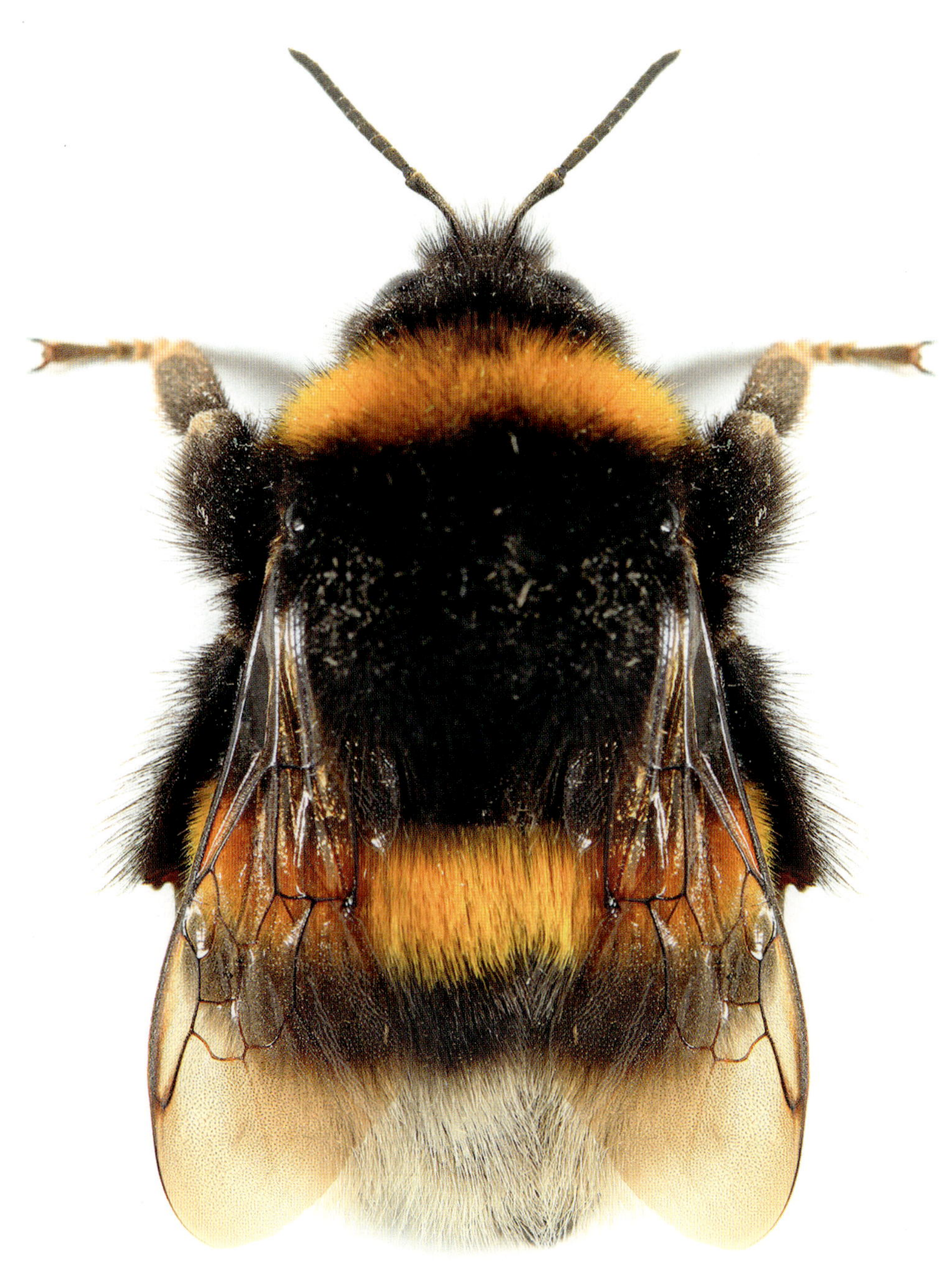

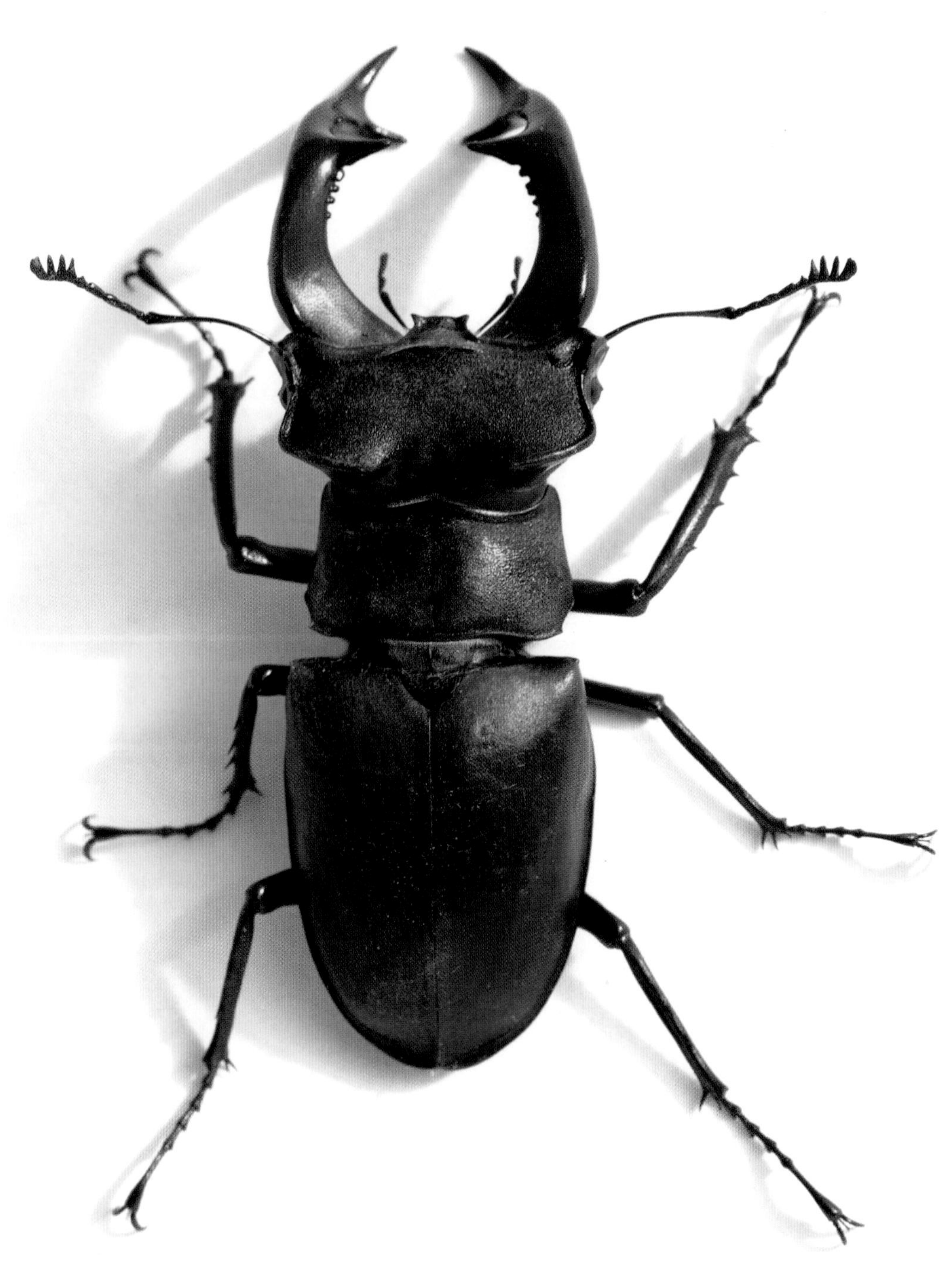

 EUROPEAN STAG BEETLE

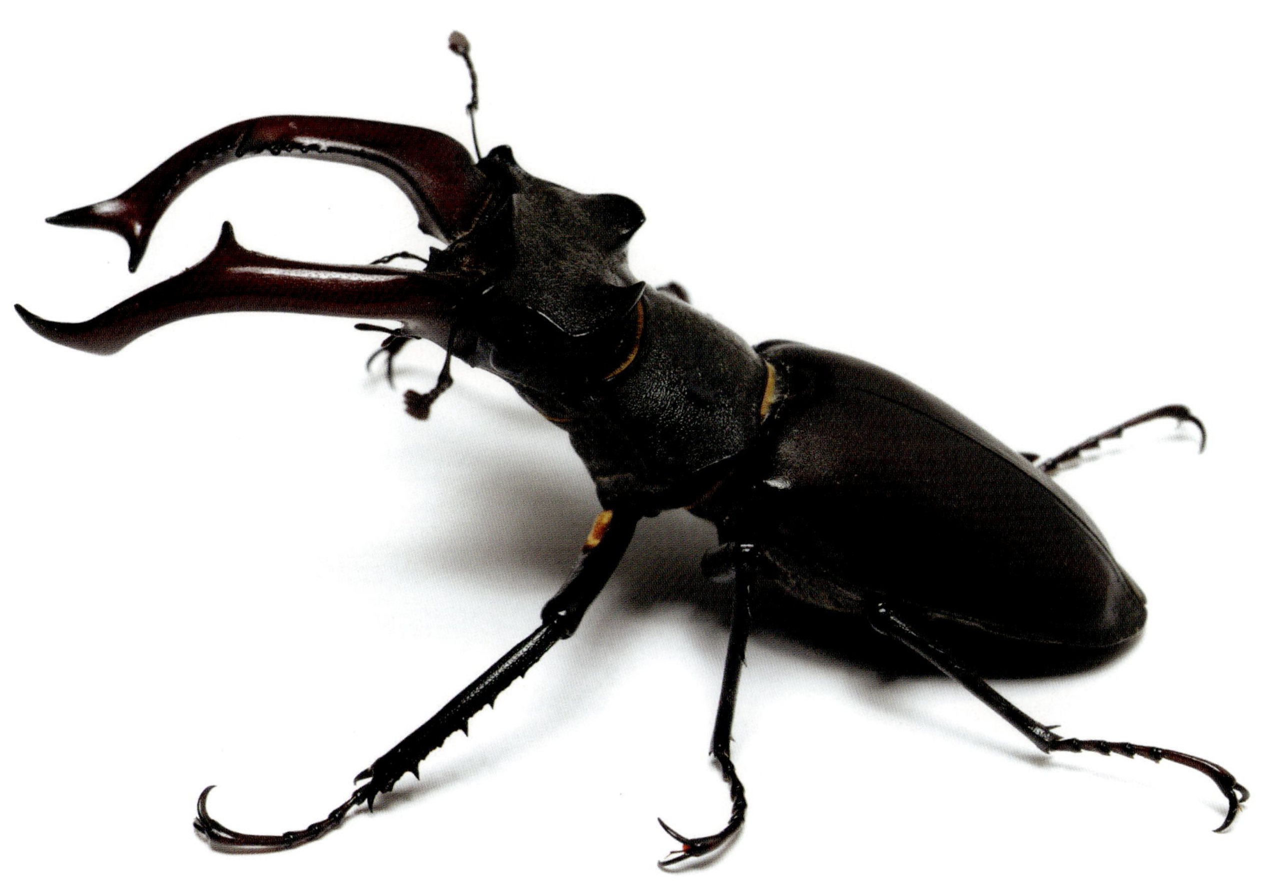

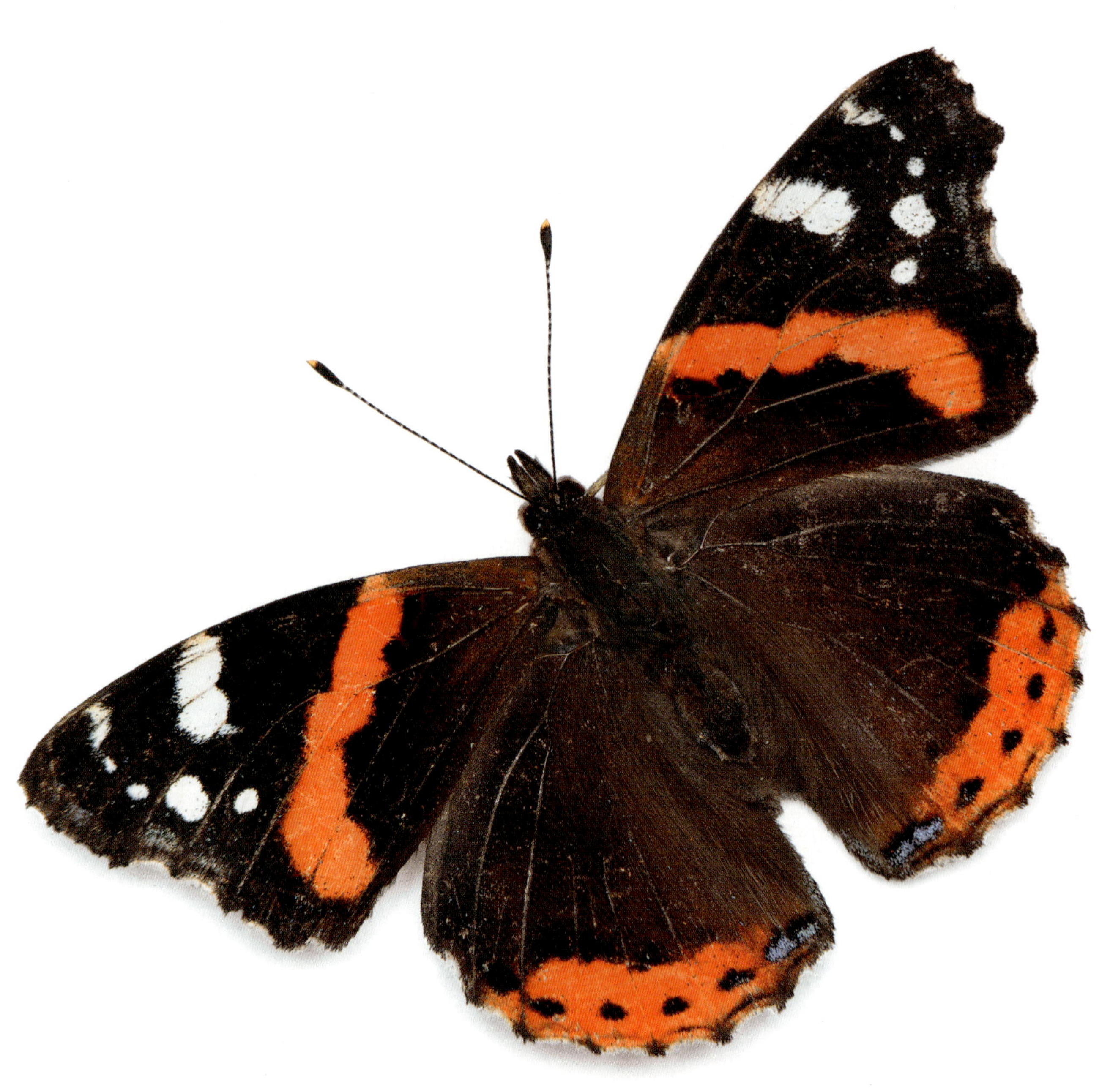

RED ADMIRAL BUTTERFLY

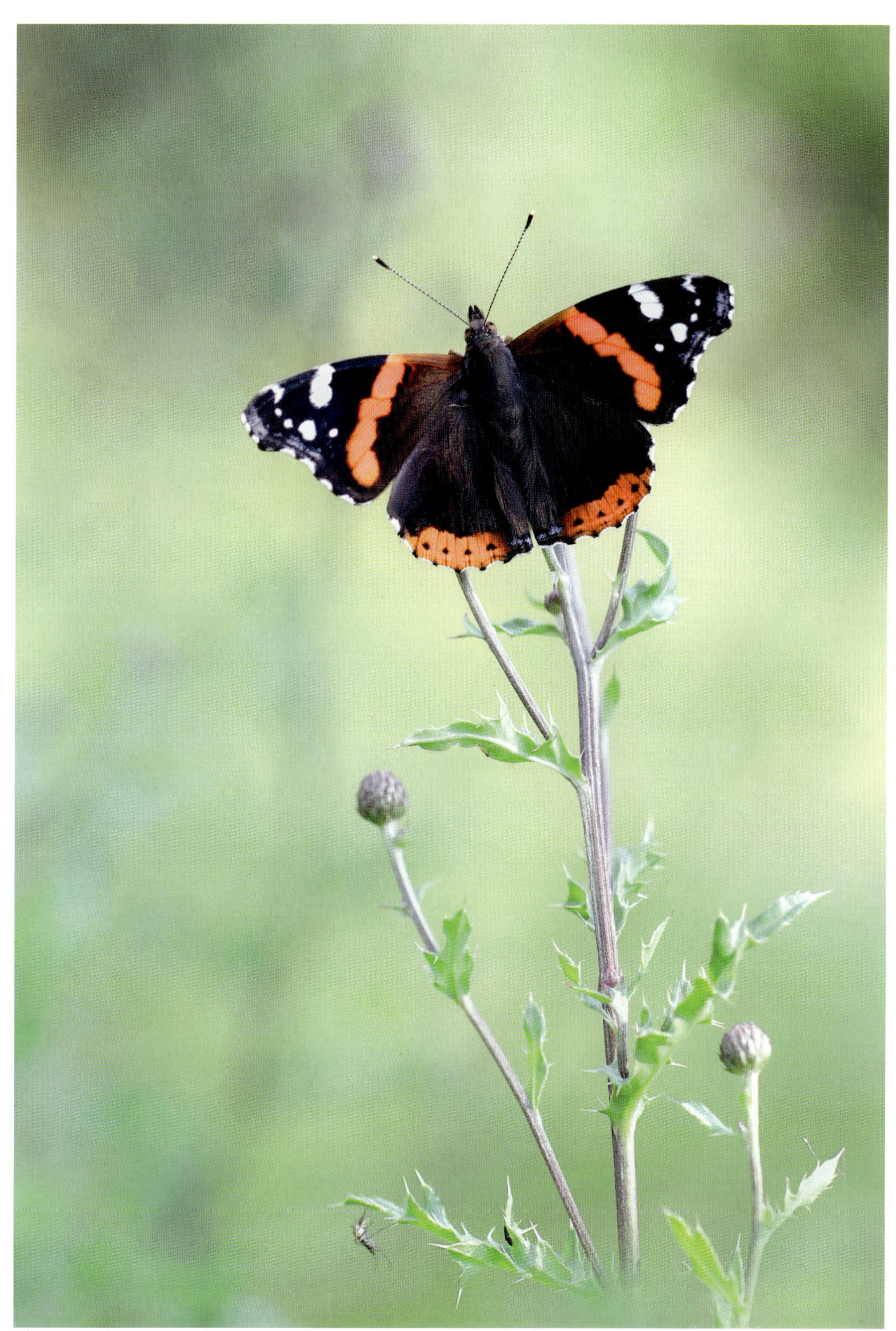

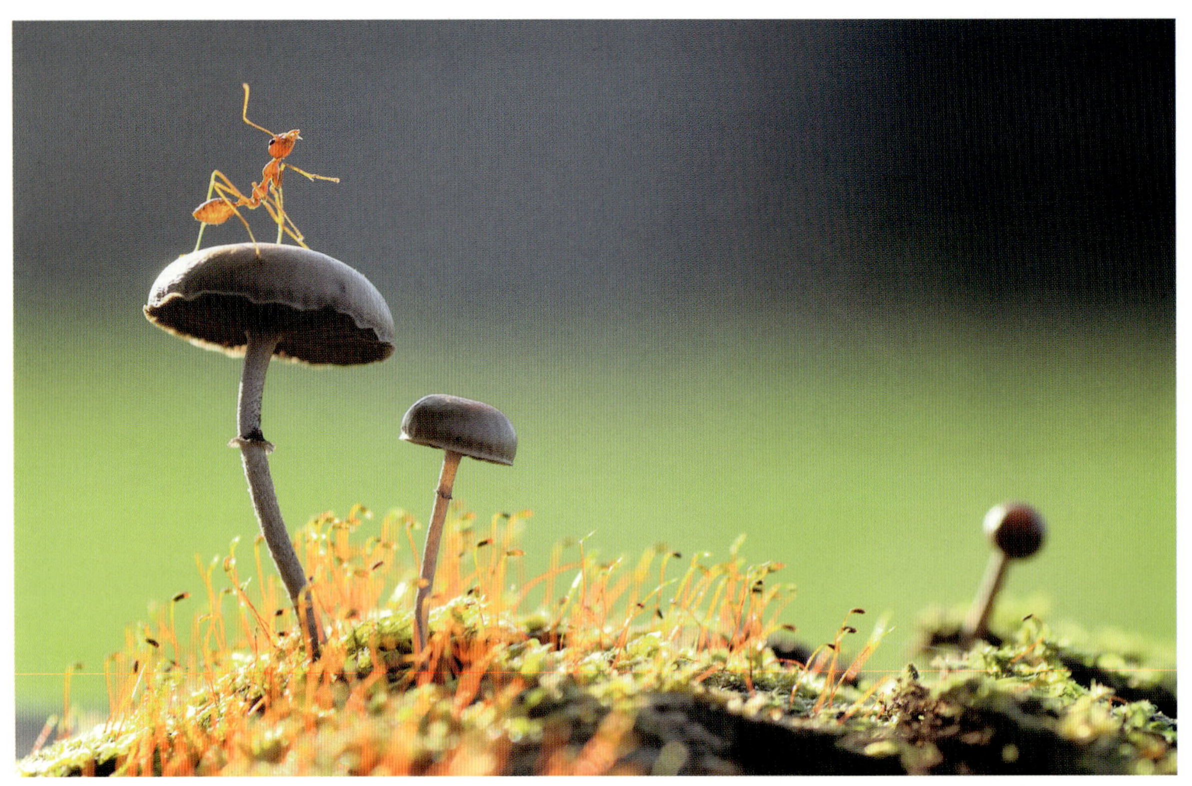

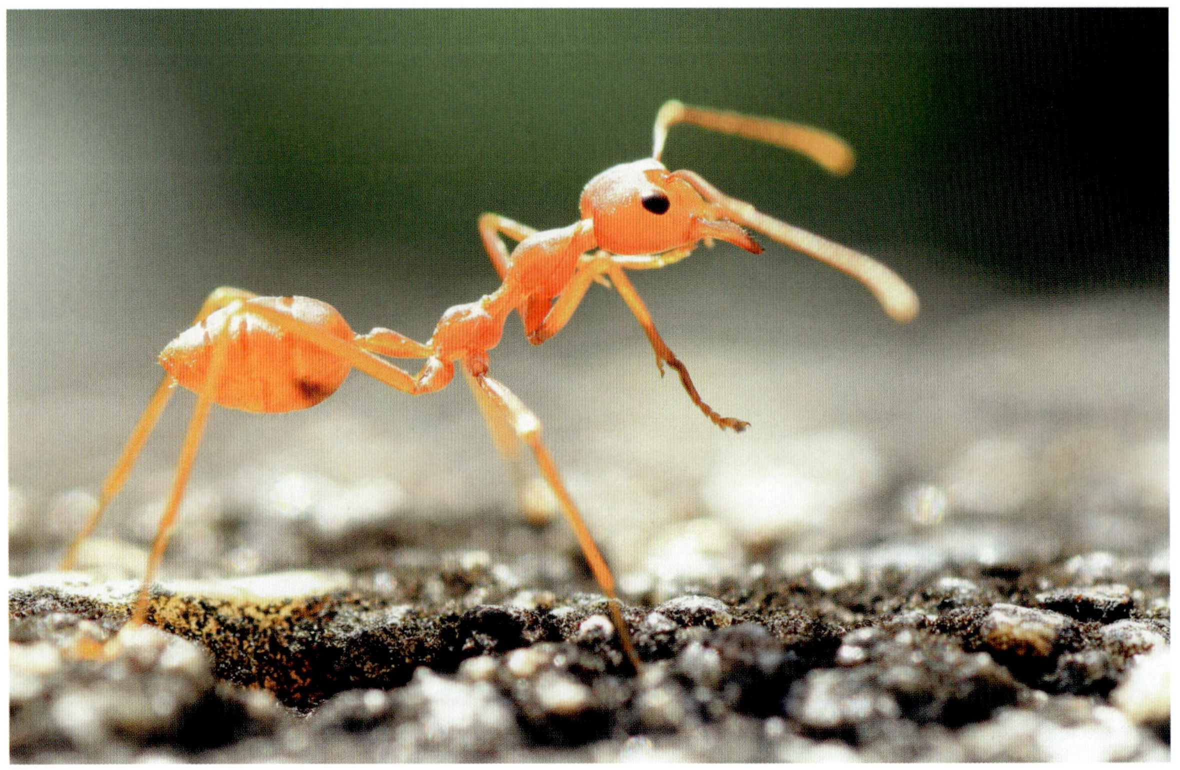

 WEAVER ANT

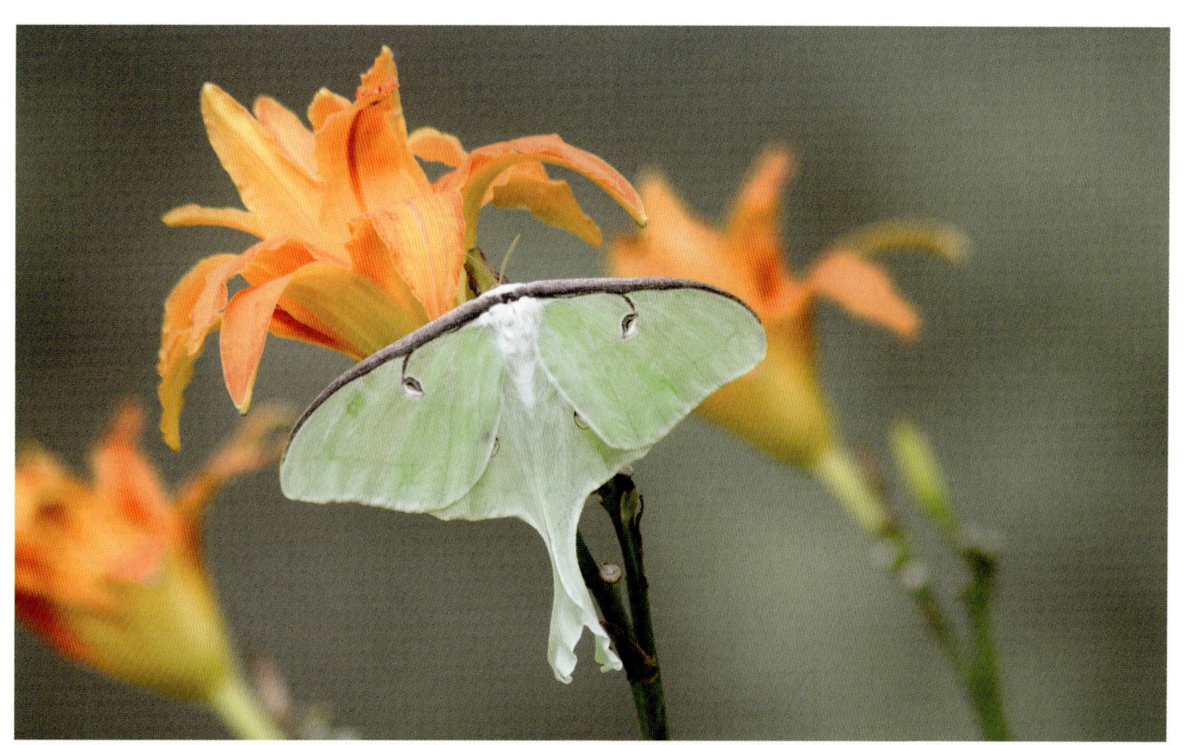

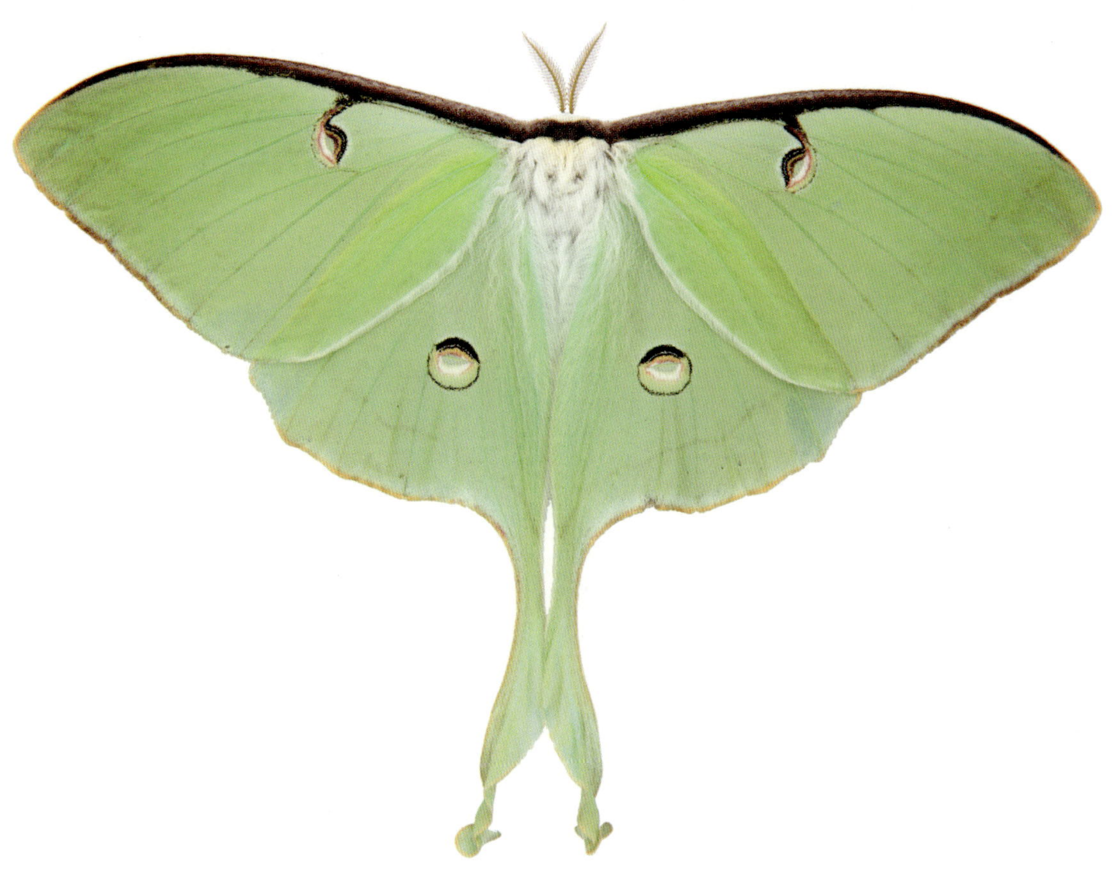

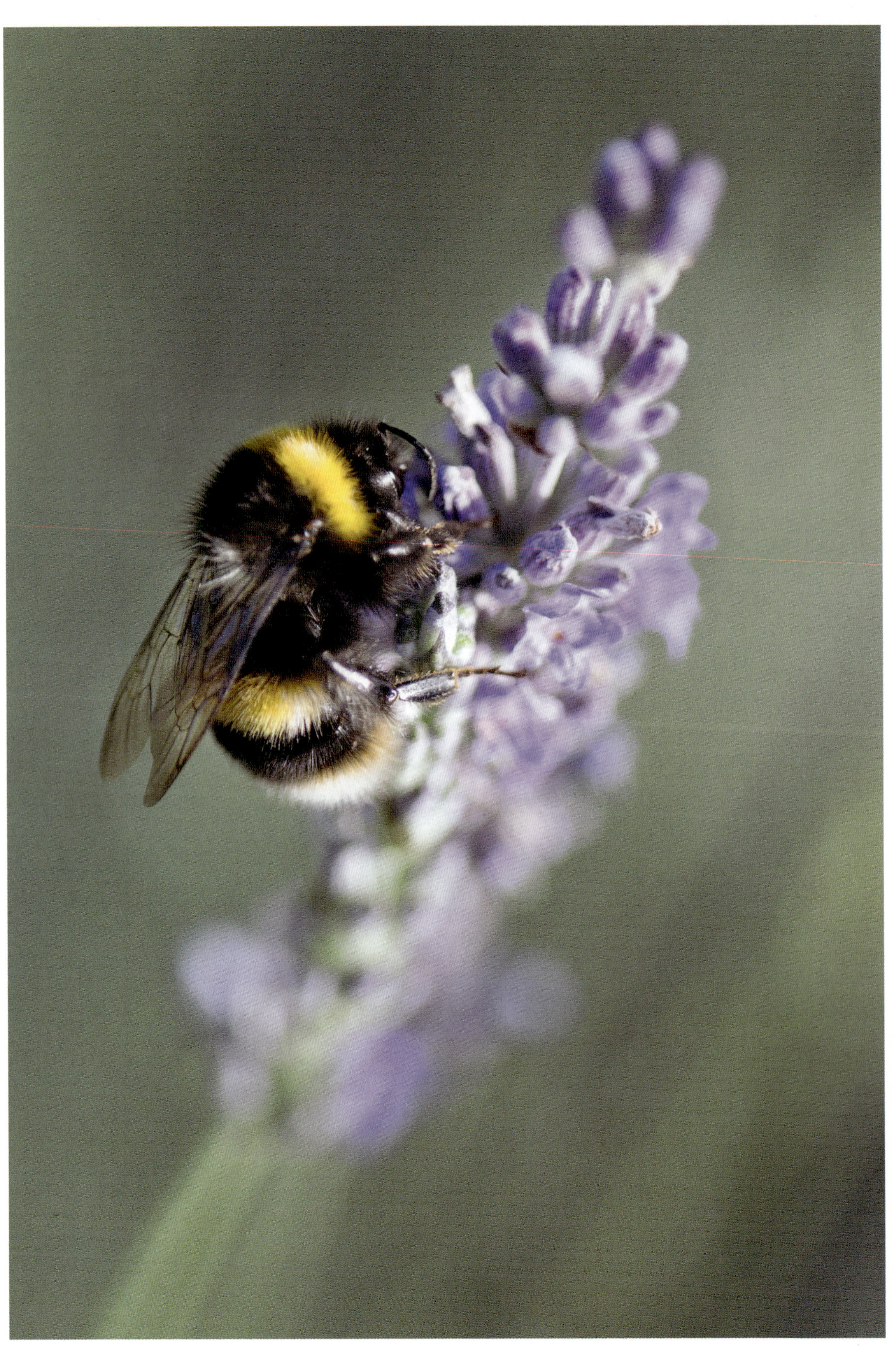

BUFF-TAILED BUMBLEBEE FORAGING

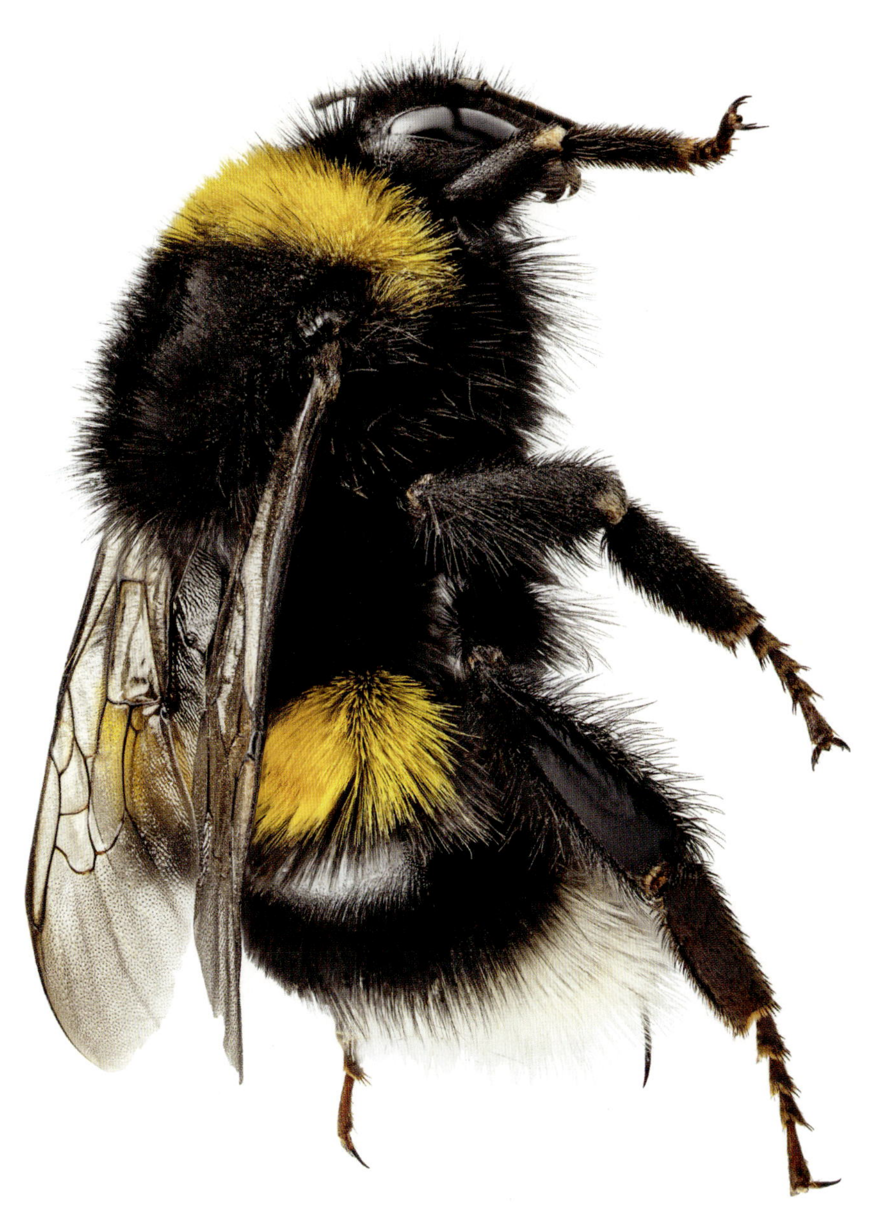

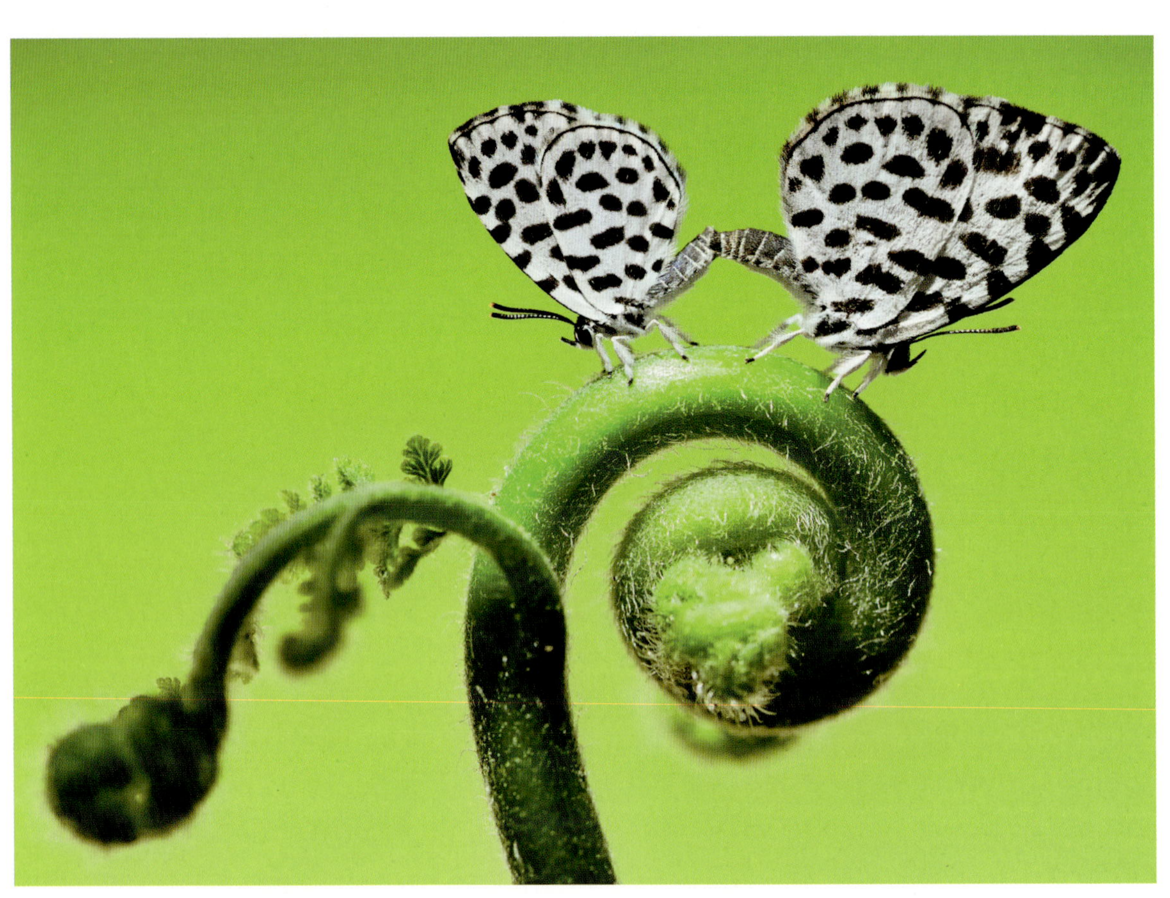

FOREST PIERROT BUTTERFLY

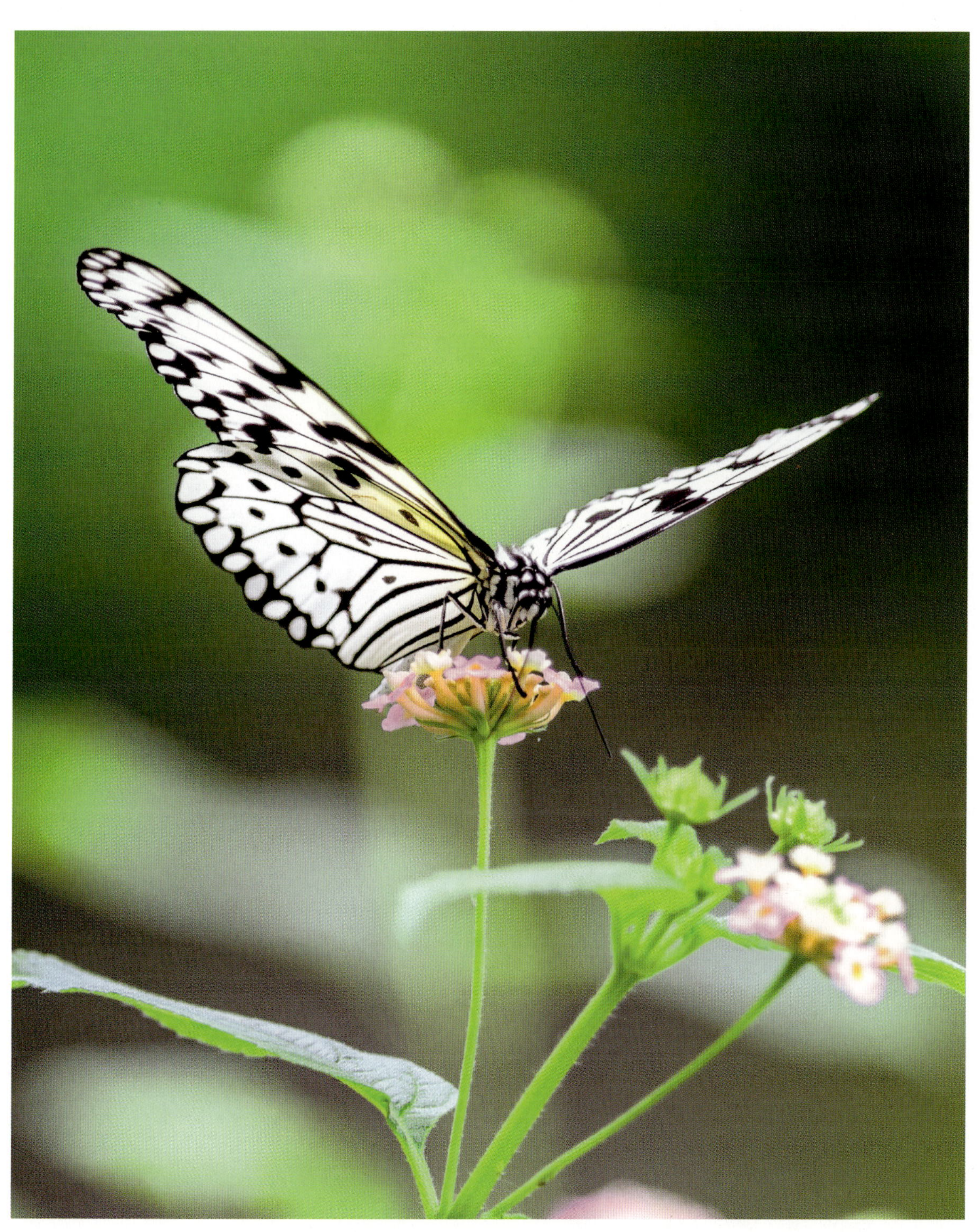

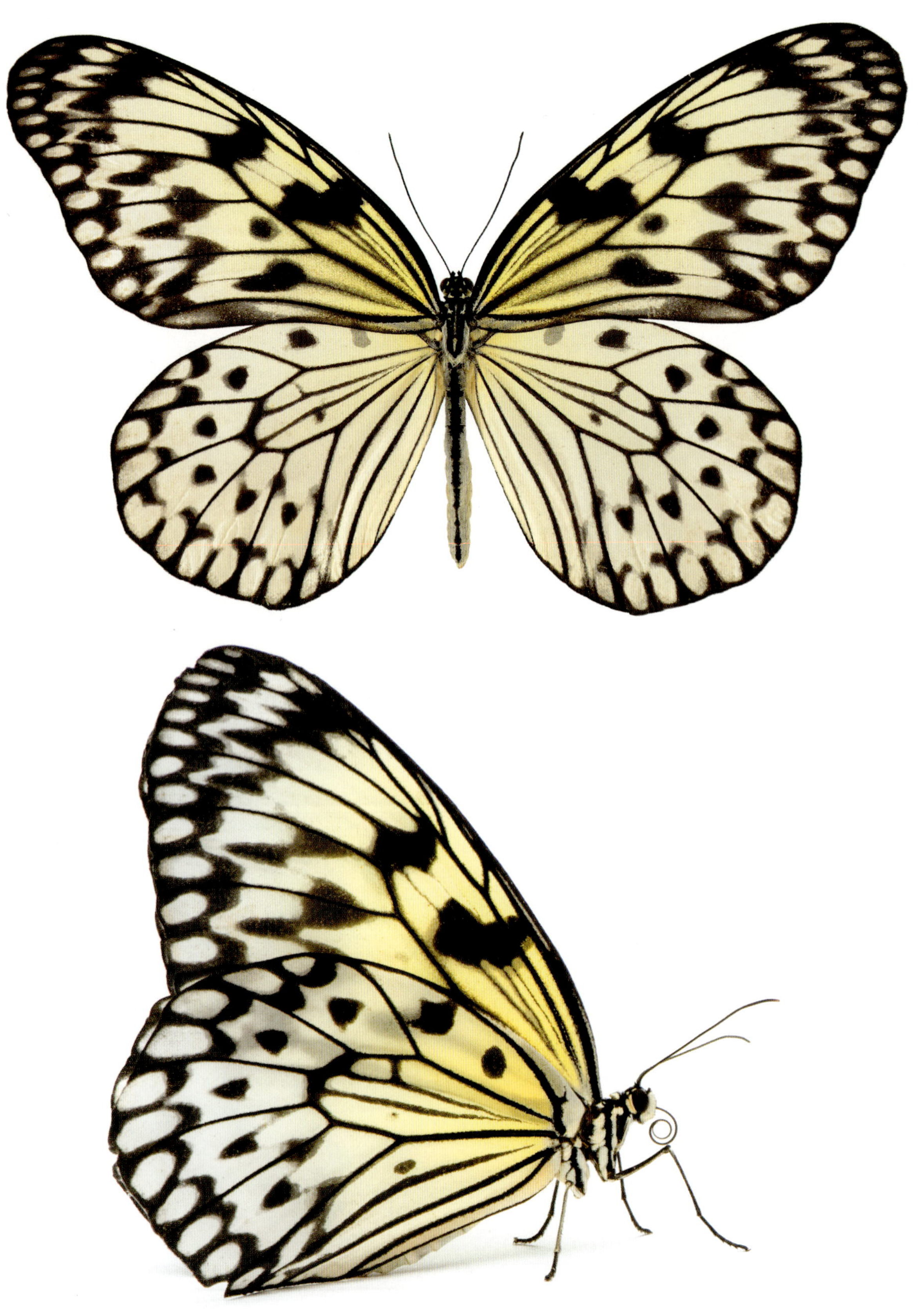

PAPER KITE BUTTERFLY

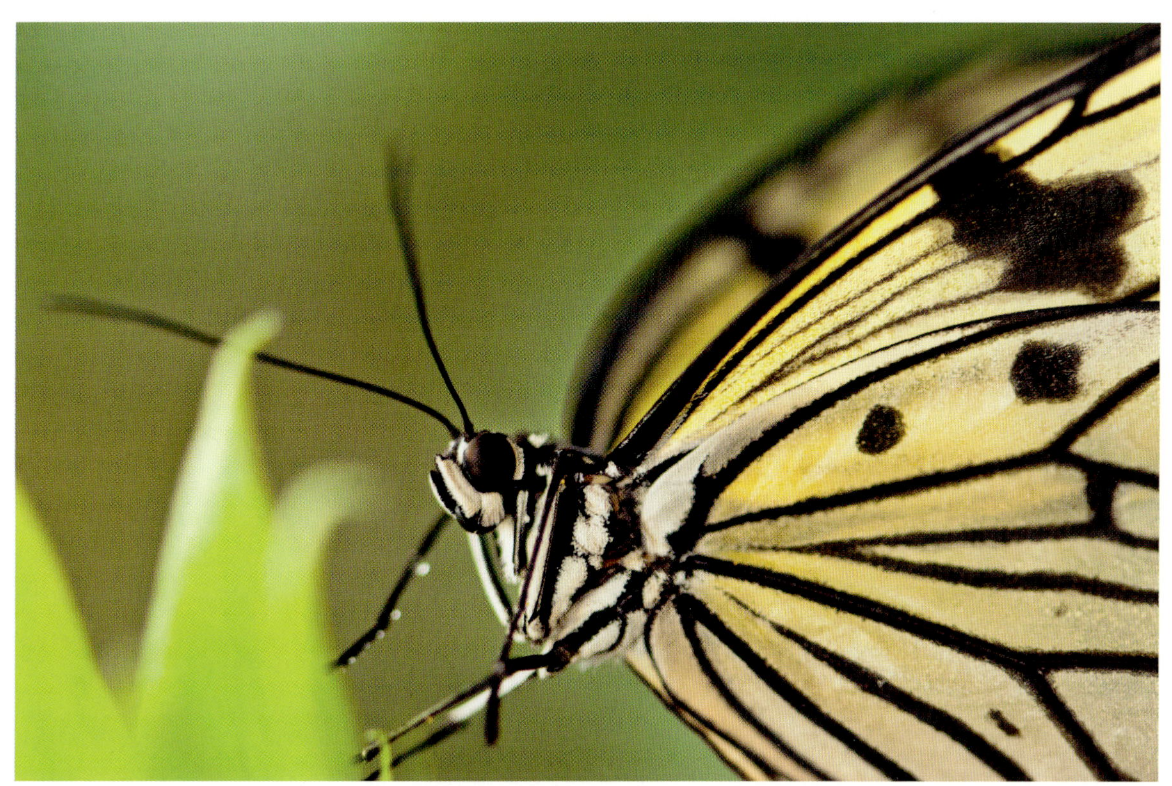

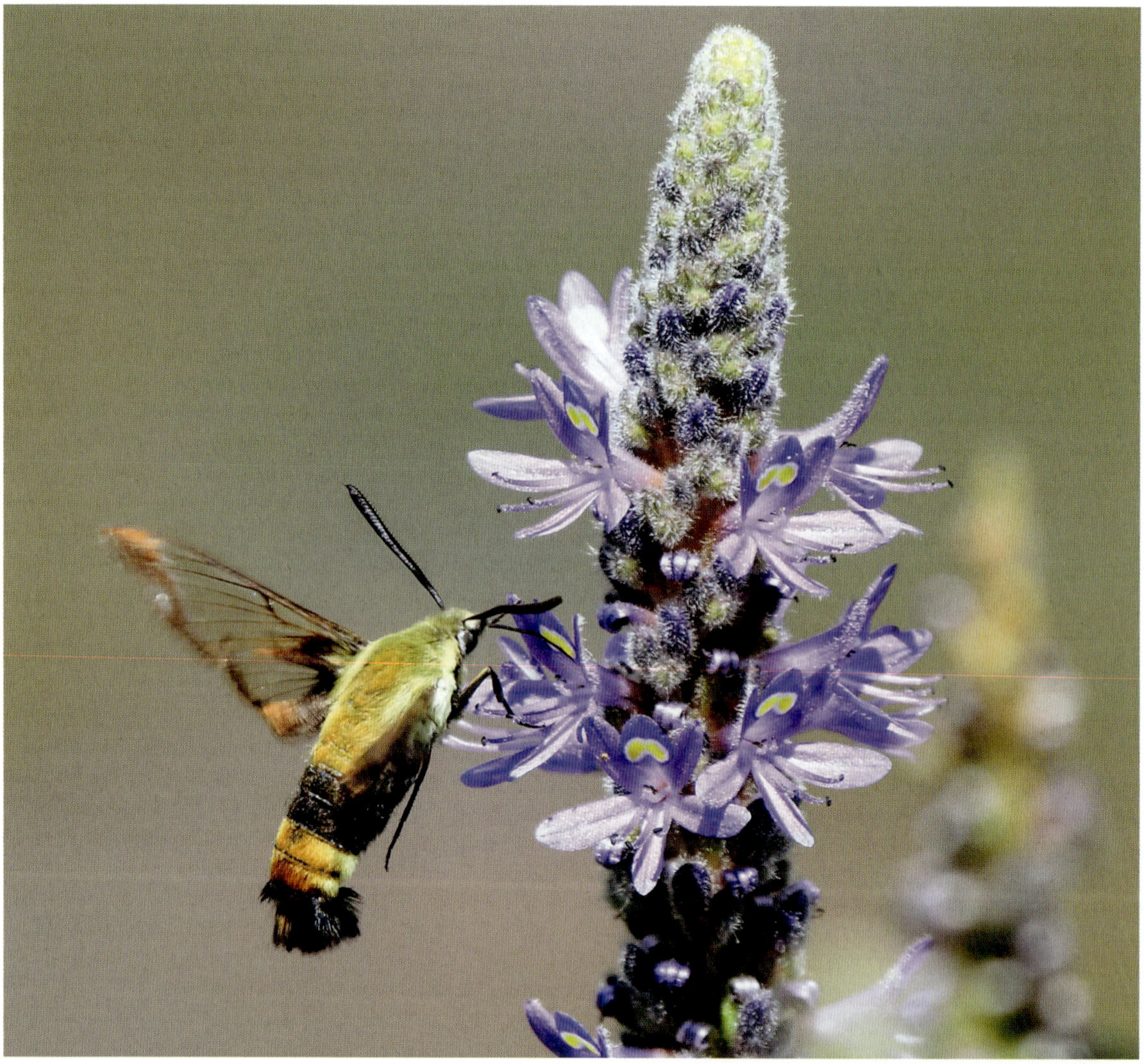

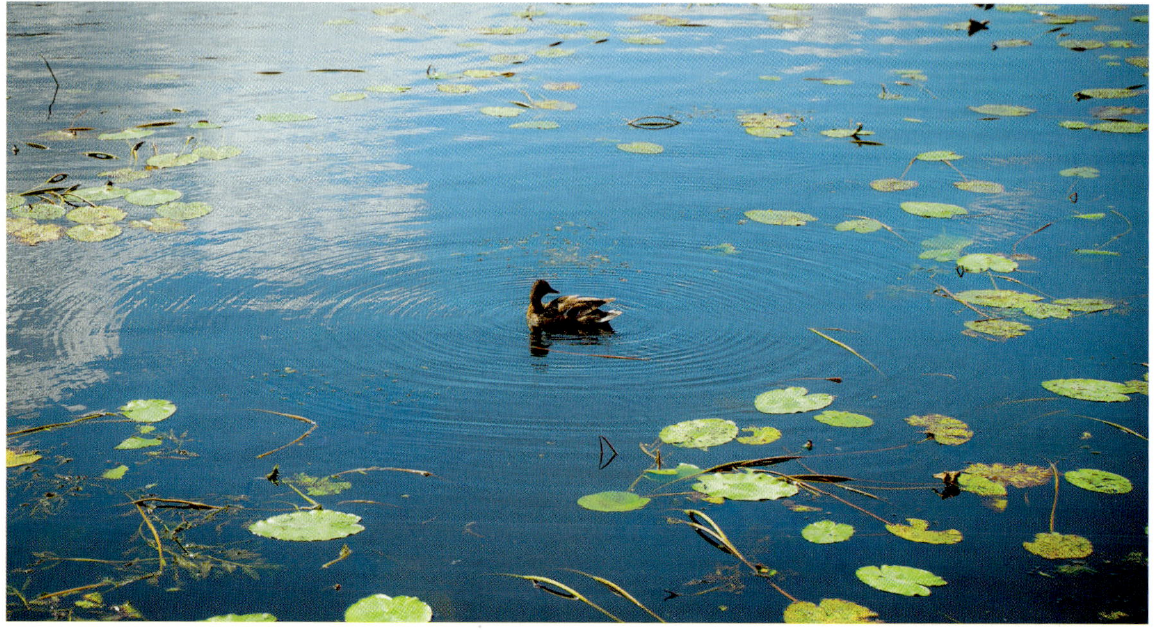

 SNOWBERRY CLEARWING MOTH

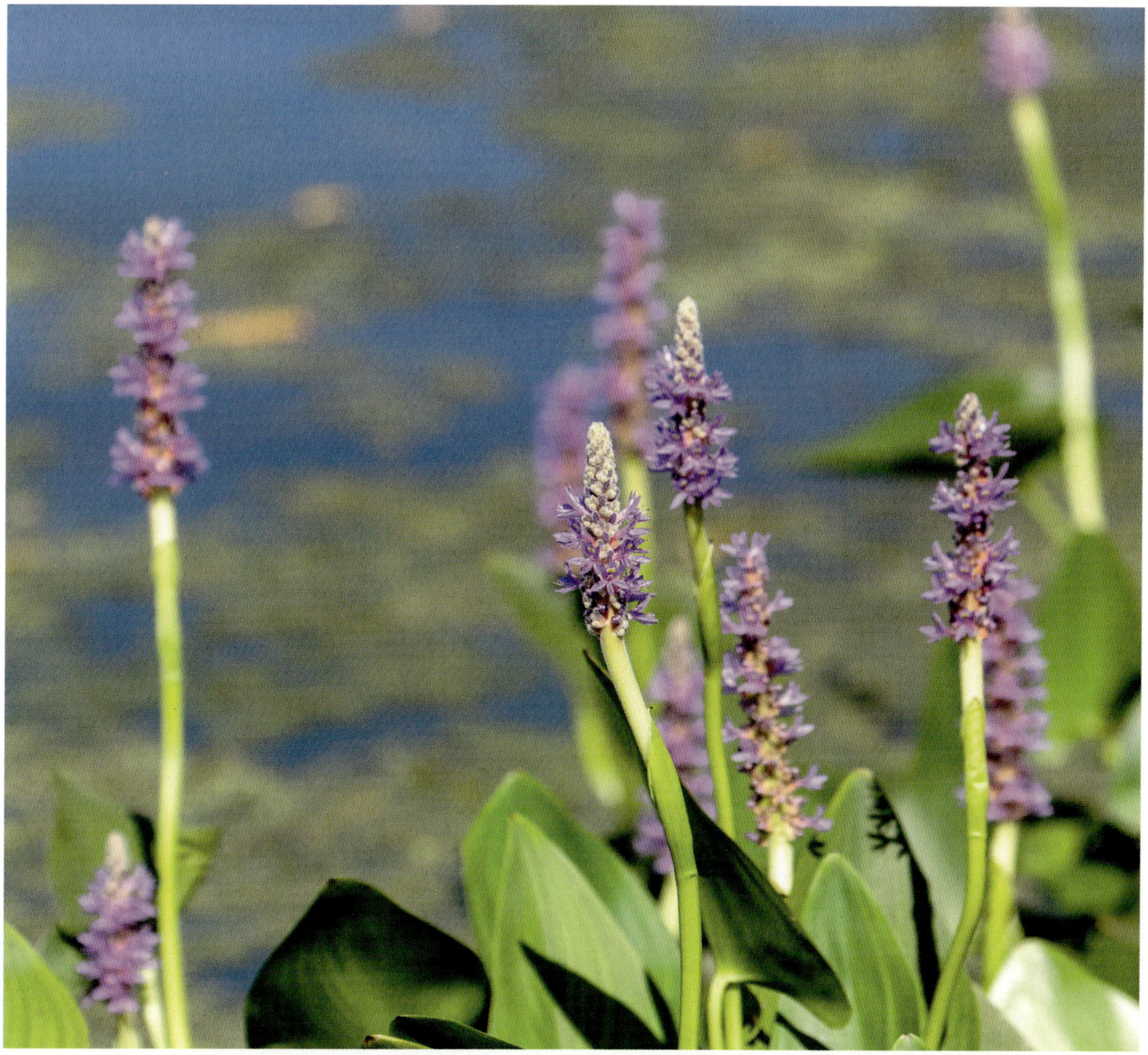

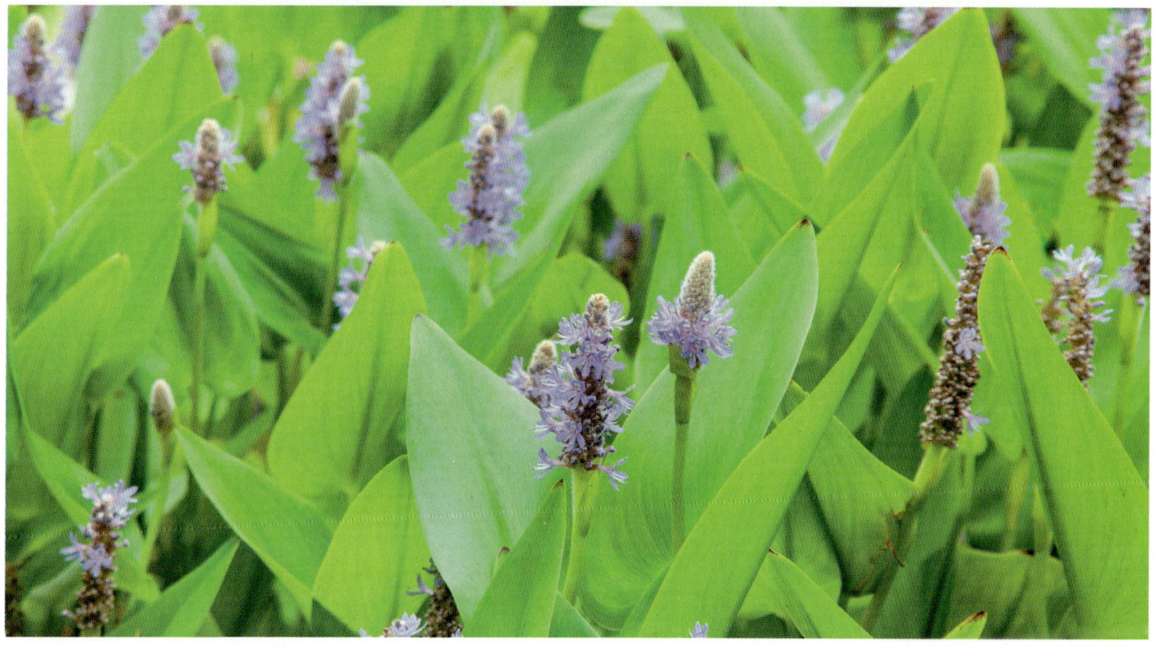

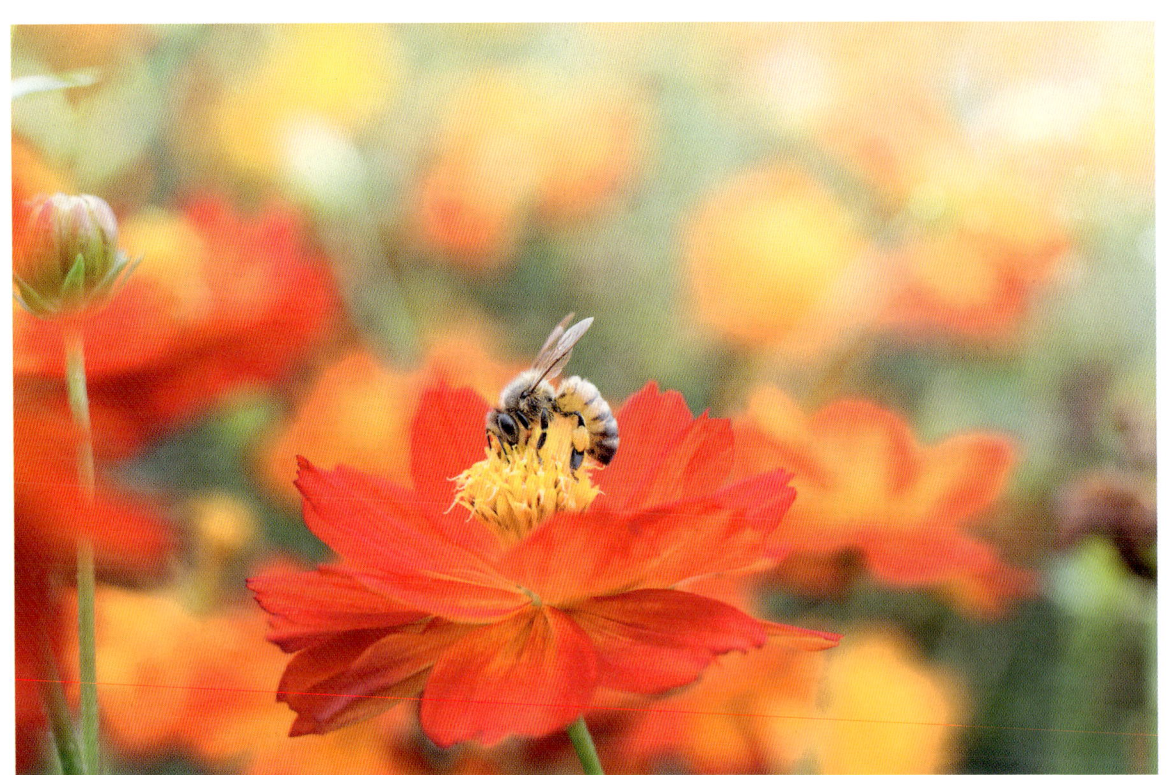

WESTERN HONEY BEE

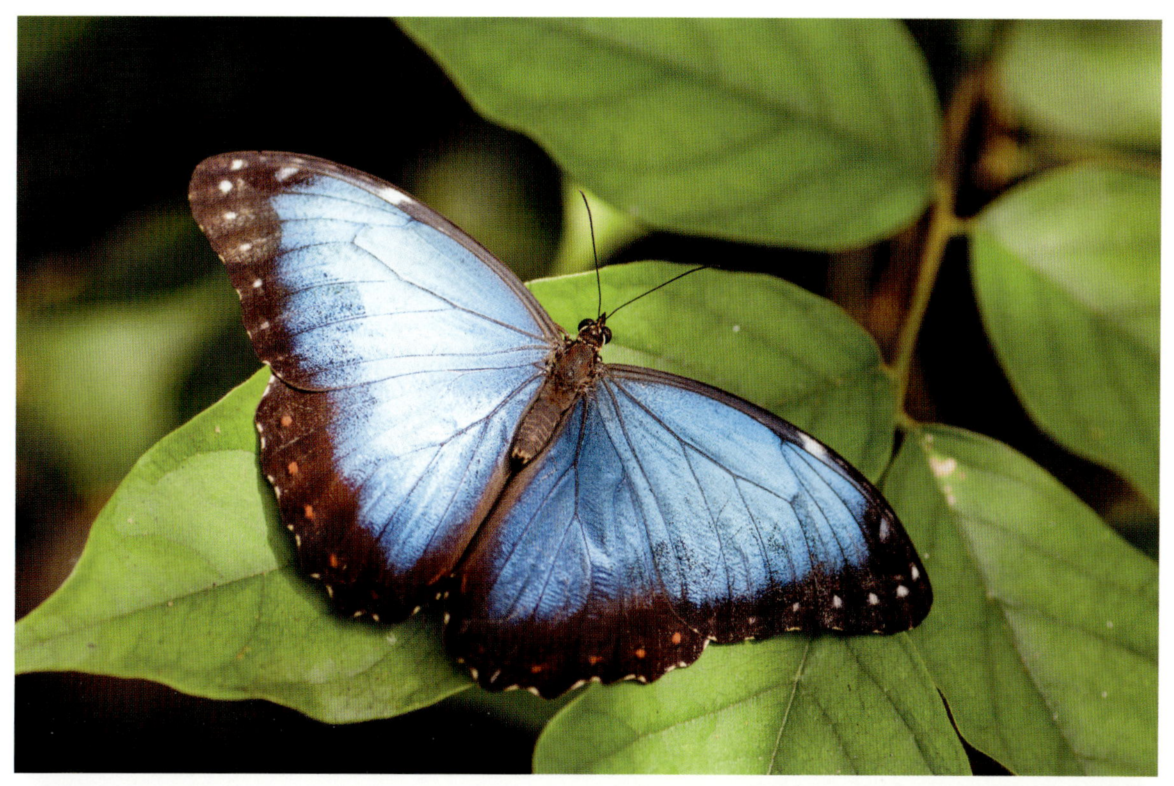

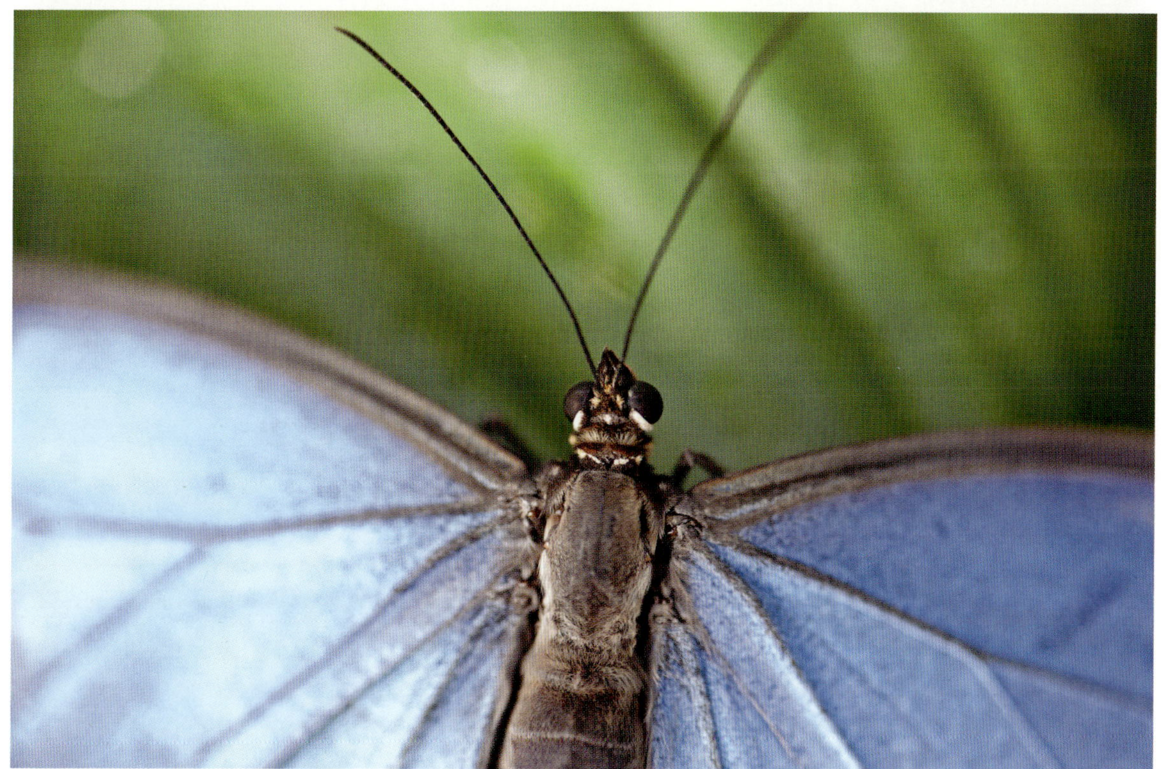

FINAL ARTWORK REVIEW

Congratulations on completing each piece in this body of artwork. It is time to honor your accomplishments, celebrate the artist that you get to be, revisit your goals, and recognize the time you have devoted to your practice. Before you begin the final review, it may be helpful to revisit the chapter The Courage to Be Creative, particularly the sections Critiquing Your Work and Supporting Your Practice. When you are ready, spread all your artwork in a large, clean area so you can see every project at once.

1. REJOICE IN YOUR ACHIEVEMENTS.

Look at each piece individually as well as part of a group. Focus for a moment only on your successes and offer yourself praise. Which pieces are you especially fond of and why? What do you see now that you did not notice as the work was accumulating? What skills or abilities have you acquired? Take a lot of time to do this portion of the critique. If a negative thought arises, simply tell yourself that you will address it later—because right now, it's time to celebrate.

2. HONOR YOUR CHALLENGES.

Now that you have some distance from the pieces you created or from experiences that were difficult, spend a moment to simply acknowledge your struggles. Then pick one or two of those struggles to focus on and explore further. Notice the thoughts and feelings that arise and whether your perception of the event or opinion of the artwork has changed over time. If you were faced with a similar situation now, what would you add, tweak, or avoid in regard to your workstation, artistic technique, personal choices, or emotional response? On the other hand, perhaps the challenge was simply a valley in the overall process or, alternately, it was a valuable process you benefited from addressing. Most important, recognize that you made it through to the other side and continued on your creative path.

3. ASSESS YOUR PRACTICE. Now return to the entire body of work and, with a more discerning eye, view it in consideration of your practice as a whole. What goals have you reached, are in the process of reaching, or have let go? What knowledge or techniques have been gained, stayed the same, or could be improved? What subject, mediums, or tools do you prefer to work with or want to try in the future? How has your artwork, practice, or experience of being an artist transformed? You might also consider your workspace, the condition of your media, your time commitment, and anything else that could influence your creative work. Keep this portion of the review succinct and to the point.

4. LOOK FORWARD. If you have specific goals that would add to your creative playground or expand your abilities, take this time to acknowledge what you would like to focus on in the future. This should feel motivational even if a bit daunting. If you have many goals, choose only the top few to focus on for the next stage of your creative life.

I want to work on ______________ .

I want to work on ______________ .

I want to work on ______________ .

5. DOCUMENT YOUR LESSONS AND GOALS. In your sketchbook, write down the key points and learning you gained from each portion of the review. List the goals you have chosen and a first step for each one that is easily accomplished. You might even provide a time frame. Then begin to work on this initial step and toward achieving your goals. You might date the page and refer to it in the future for encouragement, to remind yourself of your progress, and to witness your overall transformation through your artistic journey.

I wish you so much delight in your future practice and hope that it is nourishing, fulfilling, and rewarding. As you face challenges and gain more wisdom, may you enjoy the process and revel in the skills you have acquired. I also hope that you feel incredibly proud of the commitment you have to your craft, cherish the pieces you create, and deeply enjoy being a creative.

Rejoice, and keep making art.

GLOSSARY

BACKGROUND. The area of a composition around the focal point or primary subjects. If this area appears to recede in space, this term will either refer to the portion that is behind the subject or to the section that looks like it is the farthest from the viewer.

CELLS OF A WING. The anatomical sections of an insect wing located between visible structural veins. They can be transparent or opaque and have neutral to vivid coloration.

COMPOSITIONAL ELEMENT. Any subject or form that contributes to the layout of a composition.

CONTRAST. An art principle that measures the degree of change when comparing two adjoining areas of media. It may refer to the difference in value, intensity, detail, or texture.

COOL COLOR. Any color located on the half of the color wheel that has blue at the center of the arc.

FOCAL POINT. A component that represents the primary and most important subject or area in a composition.

FOREGROUND. The area of a composition that typically includes the primary subjects. If this area appears to recede in space, this term may refer to the portion in focus or closest to the viewer.

FORESHORTENING. An attribute of perspective when features appear smaller or overlapped as they recede in space. If you draw them as they appear, you can create a realistic sense of depth in your artwork.

FRAMING EDGE. A component of the composition where a line defines the perimeter of the layout.

HARD EDGE. A possible result associated with water-based paints when the perimeter of a painted line or section, in whole or in part, has dried with a well-defined boundary instead of one that blends into the surroundings.

HUE. A color in a pure and highly saturated form, typically presented around the perimeter of the color wheel.

IMAGE TRANSFER. A technique used to duplicate a drawing by placing a piece of tracing paper on top of a composition and using a pencil to replicate the outlines. When the paper is flipped over and the lines are retraced in another area of the layout, the original marks transfer to the page. (See image on page 102)

MIDDLE GROUND. The area in a spatial composition that is perceived as being located between the foreground and the background, usually directly behind the subject.

MIDLINE. The part of a measuring structure that uses a vertical line as an axis to obtain both horizontal and vertical measurements of a subject, on the reference as well as the page. It may bisect a symmetrical subject and can be used along with a horizontal axis line.

PAINT BLOOM. An effect caused when a heavily diluted paint mixture is applied to a wet surface and the water spreads or "blooms" on the page. If left to dry, the resulting form typically has an organic shape, a dark perimeter, and an interior that is much lighter than the surrounding environment.

PIGMENT. The ingredients that give paints, colored pencils, and other art supplies their particular coloration.

SATURATION. A property of color that describes the amount of intensity that a color has. Hues have the highest level of saturation and neutral colors have the lowest.

TOOTH. The inherent texture or smoothness of a prepared substrate, such as paper.

VALUE. A description of how light or dark a color is based on a spectrum. It can refer to the inherent attributes of a hue, the amount of white or black that has been added, or the level of translucency once applied to the page.

VEINS. The anatomical structural ridges that divide insect wings.

VISUAL DISCORD. A negative interaction between two or more components of a composition, which creates an uncomfortable tension that reduces the unity, harmony, and visual flow of the artwork. This term may refer to the design layout, color relationships, or techniques used. In this book, it refers to the amount of negative space between subjects or in relation to the framing edge.

WARM COLOR. Any color located on the half of the color wheel that has orange at the center of the arc.

METRIC CONVERSIONS

INCHES	CENTIMETERS
1/16	0.16
1/8	0.3
1/4	0.6
3/8	0.95
1/2	1.3
3/4	1.9
1	2.5
2	5.1
3	7.6
4	10
5	13
6	15
7	18
8	20
9	23
10	25

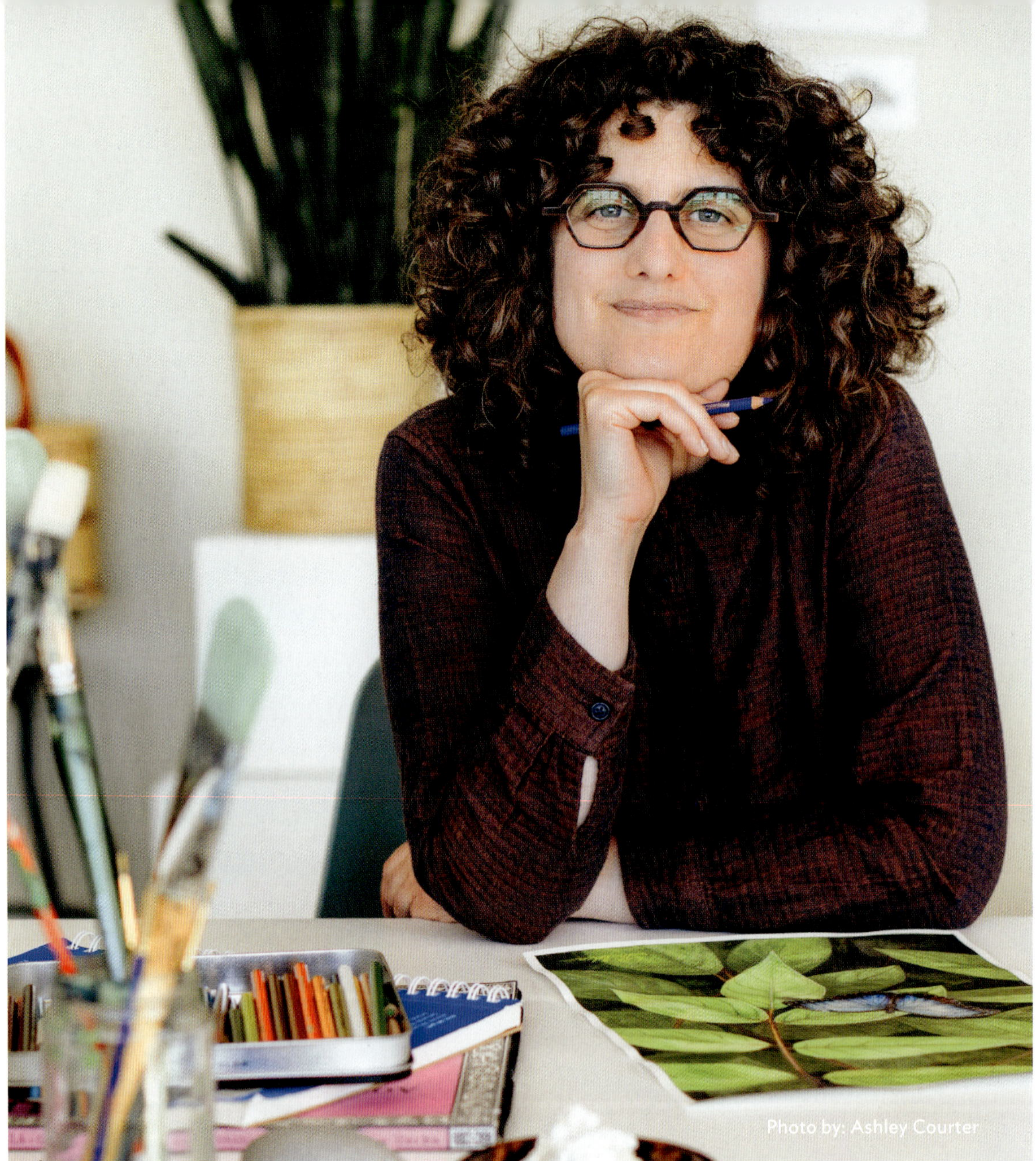

As an artist, educator, and author, **Zebith S. Thalden** honors an array of biological treasures. She shares her fascination of the numerous species on our planet: living, extinct, undiscovered, and those yet to evolve. Combining art and ecology, her work celebrates biological diversity and the interconnectivity between humans and other species.

Her teaching style is supportive, thoughtful, and tailored to individual artistic advancement. She encourages direct engagement with the natural world, courageous creativity, ecological stewardship, and connection through shared wonderment. She devotes her career to instruction, creative work, public speaking, and interdisciplinary collaborations.

She received a BFA from the Rhode Island School of Design and an MFA, focused on painting and entomology, from Goddard College. She has studied the Coleoptera Collection at the American Museum of Natural History in New York City as well as other state and university specimen collections. Her artwork has been featured in both solo and group exhibitions in galleries, cultural centers, and art museums throughout the United States and abroad. ZebithThalden.com